Historical and Conceptual Issues in Psychology

Visit the *Historical and Conceptual Issues in Psychology* Companion
Website at **www.pearsoned.co.uk/brysbaert** to find valuable **student**
learning material including:

- Summaries from the main book
- Details of key figures
- Annotated links to relevant sites on the web
- Questions to check your understanding
- An online glossary to explain key terms
- Comprehensive bibliography

We work with leading authors to develop the
strongest educational materials in psychology
bringing cutting-edge thinking and best
learning practice to a global market.

Under a range of well-known imprints, including
Prentice Hall, we craft high quality print and
electronic publications which help readers to understand
and apply their content, whether studying or at work.

To find out more about the complete range of our
publishing, please visit us on the World Wide Web at:
www.pearsoned.co.uk

Historical and Conceptual Issues in Psychology

Professor Marc Brysbaert Ghent University, Belgium

Professor Kathy Rastle Royal Holloway, University of London

PEARSON
Prentice
Hall

Harlow, England • London • New York • Boston • San Francisco • Toronto • Sydney • Singapore • Hong Kong
Tokyo • Seoul • Taipei • New Delhi • Cape Town • Madrid • Mexico City • Amsterdam • Munich • Paris • Milan

Pearson Education Limited
Edinburgh Gate
Harlow
Essex CM20 2JE
England

and Associated Companies throughout the world

Visit us on the World Wide Web at:
www.pearsoned.co.uk

First published 2009

ISBN: 978-0-273-71818-5

British Library Cataloguing-in-Publication Data
A catalogue record for this book is available from the British Library

Library of Congress Cataloging-in-Publication Data
Brysbaert, Marc.
 Historical and conceptual issues in psychology / Marc Brysbaert, Kathy Rastle.
   p. cm.
 Includes bibliographical references and index.
 ISBN 978-0-273-71818-5 (pbk.)
1. Psychology—History.   I. Rastle, Kathy.   II. Title.
BF81.B79 2009
150.9—dc22

                                                            2008052701

10 9 8 7 6 5 4 3 2
13 12 11 10

Typeset in 9.5/12 Sabon by 73
Printed by Ashford Colour Press Ltd., Gosport

Brief Contents

Contents

Chapter 3   The first attempts to establish psychology as an independent discipline

Chapter 4   Strengthening the scientific standing of psychology Behaviourism and cognitive psychology

Chapter 5   The input from brain research

Chapter 12 Psychology and society
The socio-political side

Supporting resources

Visit **www.pearsoned.co.uk/brysbaert** to find valuable online resources

Companion Website for students
- Summaries from the main book
- Details of key figures
- Annotated links to relevant sites on the web
- Questions to check your understanding
- An online glossary to explain key terms
- Comprehensive bibliography

For instructors
- Downloadable PowerPoint slides featuring figures from the book

Also: The Companion Website provides the following features:

- Search tool to help locate specific items of content
- E-mail results and profile tools to send results of quizzes to instructors
- Online help and support to assist with website usage and troubleshooting

For more information please contact your local Pearson Education sales representative or visit **www.pearsoned.co.uk/brysbaert**

Preface

From time to time it is good to pause and wonder how we got where we are now. For instance, why did you open this book? How did you become interested in psychology? But also: since when have we been able to study psychology? Why has this book been published? Why do all good degrees of psychology today include a course on historical and conceptual issues? What is the position of psychology in society? Is psychology really a science? What is a science? How is it possible that I am able to read this? Since when have people been able to read?

These are the questions addressed in this book (although you will not be surprised to hear that many of them cannot be fully answered on the basis of the present knowledge). They refer to the foundations of psychology, which consist of historical and conceptual issues.

Historical issues refer to the past of the discipline and can be approached in many different ways (see Chapter 9). One distinction is whether history is studied to find out what people at different points in time thought and knew, or whether history is studied to gain insight into how the present situation came about as the result of certain developments and choices in the past. The latter is the approach taken in this book, because it is of particular relevance to everyone wanting to become a psychologist.

Conceptual issues are more difficult to define. Basically, they refer to the big questions underlying a discipline. For psychology, these are questions like: 'What is the human mind?', 'Is it possible to know the mind of someone else?', 'Is it possible to know my own mind?', 'Is such information reliable and useful?' Importantly, these issues cannot readily be addressed in the way scientists love to do: by collecting data and testing new predictions made on the basis of the available knowledge (see Chapter 8). Conceptual issues relate to the convictions and opinions that underlie a particular discipline and that determine the meanings of the terms used (e.g. the meanings of 'consciousness', 'process' and 'personality'). Conceptual issues are shared by the researchers and practitioners of a discipline and are imposed on all newcomers. However, they usually remain tacit. They exert their influence by reliance on common understanding rather than by explicit teaching (if this sounds a bit woolly at the moment, come back to it after you have read the part on paradigms in Chapter 8). Indeed, even for us, the authors, writing this book has been eye-opening at times. Quite often we found ourselves saying 'Oh, that's where it comes from! That's what it means!'

Needless to say, historical and conceptual issues are closely intertwined. Historical developments depended on the conceptual issues at the time and, in turn, had an impact on the concepts and the convictions shared by the next generations. For instance, many psychologists today talk about 'cognitive processes', 'cognitive representations', 'personality traits' or 'intelligence'. They use these words based on a common understanding (every psychologist is taught them), but don't often realise the words are quite recent inventions. Where these terms came from, why at a certain point in time they were introduced, and why they subsequently conquered the whole discipline are questions that are left out of consideration in most teaching (for instance, you don't find them in introductory books on psychology or cognitive psychology). One reason for this is that you need a considerable amount of historical, philosophical and technical background before you can address them.

The main danger of a book on historical and conceptual issues is that it tries to cover too much. Just imagine: everything that ever happened and that was ever thought of is a possible topic for inclusion! Every chapter of this book could easily have been expanded into a 500-page book. Indeed, the most common complaint about courses of historical and conceptual issues is that lecturers try to cram too much into too short a period. To tackle this problem head-on, we decided not to try to write a 'complete book' (which is impossible anyway), but to start by asking what is feasible for a series of 12 two-hour lectures. Which are the main issues that must be covered? What is informative and interesting for psychology students (rather than what is known to historians and philosophers of science)? Therefore, do not expect to find everything in this book. Our purpose is simply to provide you with a basis. If this book entices you to want to know more, then we have achieved our goal. To help you with this, each chapter includes a few books we found interesting. There is also a lot of information freely available on the internet, links to which you can find on our website.

Although the writing of this book has been exceedingly fluent, we are aware that the current text is much better than the initial draft we had in mind. To a considerable degree this is due to the feedback we got from a group of dedicated and conscientious reviewers, who would not let anything substandard go unnoticed. Although it was impossible to respond to each and every individual comment, whenever there was convergence on a weakness we took it into account to improve the coverage. All in all, nearly half of the current text was rewritten, rearranged or added as a result of the comments we got.

We would also like to say a big thank-you to our commissioning editor, Janey Webb, who not only was one of the best reviewers, but also cheerfully guided us through the many dreadful details that have to be attended to in the conversion from an idea into a reader-friendly, printed book.

Finally, we thank our families for giving us the freedom and the time to write a book like this, even though the only compensation they got out of it was that they were able to freely choose what they wanted to watch on television.

Acknowledgements

We would like to thank the following reviewers:

Irina Anderson – University of East London
Adrian Brock – University College Dublin
Vivienne Brunsden – Nottingham Trent University
Maarten Derksen – University of Groningen, The Netherlands
Niels Engelsted – University of Copenhagen, Denmark
Paul Flowers – Glasgow Caledonian University
Paul Gardner – University of St. Andrews
Simon Hampton – University of East Anglia
Phil Higham – University of Southampton
Brian Hughes – National University of Ireland, Galway
Juhani Ihanus – University of Helsinki, Finland
Dai Jones – University of Gloucestershire
Daniel Nettle – Newcastle University
Rod Noble – University of Bolton
Katie Slocombe – University of York

We are grateful to the following for permission to reproduce the following material:

Figure 1.2 from Ifrah, G. (1988) *The Universal History of Numbers: From prehistory to the invention of the computer*, London: The Harvill Press. Reprinted by permission of The Random House Group Ltd; Figure 1.3 from Butterworth, B. (1999) *The Mathematical Brain*, London: Macmillan. Reprinted by kind permission of Professor Butterworth; Figure 2.2 from http://vikdhillon.staff.shef.ac.uk. Reproduced by permission of Vik Dhillon; Figure 2.8 from Diener, E., Suh, E.M., Lucas, R.E., and Smith, H.L. (1998) 'Subjective well-being: Three decades of progress', *Psychological Bulletin*, 125, 276–302, American Psychological Association. Reprinted with permission; Figure 3.2 (right) from Pomerantz, J.R. and Kubovy, M. (1986) 'Theoretical approaches to organization', in Boff, K.R. *et al.* (eds) *Handbook of perception and theoretical performance*, New York: Wiley. P. 31–36 and 36–42. Reprinted with permission of John Wiley & Sons, Inc; Table 3.3 from Edgell, B. (1947) 'Papers read at the British Psychological Society', *British Journal of Psychology*, 37. (Reprinted in 2001: *British Journal of Psychology*, 92 (1)). Reproduced by permission of the British Psychological Society © The British Psychological Society; Figure 4.2 from Thorndike, E.L. (1911) *Animal intelligence: Experimental studies*, Piscataway, NJ: Transaction Publishers; Figure 5.1 from Breasted, J.H. (1930) *The Edwin Smith Surgical Papyrus*, Vol. 2, Plates XVII and XVIIA, Chicago: Oriental Institute Publications. Reprinted courtesy of the Oriental Institute of the University of Chicago; Figure 5.3a from Reisch, G. (1503) *Margarita Philosophica*.

Cited in Gross, C.G. (1998) *Brain, vision, memory: Tales in the history of neuroscience*, Figure 1.7 on p. 33, The MIT Press; Figure 5.4 The withdrawal arc by Descartes. Stock Montage Inc. Reproduced with permission; Figure 5.5 from Thomson, J.A. (1922) *The outline of science: A plain story simply told,* copyright GP Putnam's & Sons. Reprinted with permission; Figure 5.7 from Geschwind, N. (1972) 'Language and the brain', *Scientific American*, 226, 4, 76–83, Scientific American Inc. With permission of the Estate of Bunji Tagawa; Figure 5.10 from Clarke, E. & Jacyna, L.S. (1987) *Nineteenth century origins of neuroscientific concepts*, Berkeley: University of California Press; Figure 5.11 and Figure 5.17 from Brysbaert, M. (2006) *Psychologie*, Belgium: Academia Press. Reproduced with permission; Figure 5.12 from Holmes, G.M. (1918) 'Disturbance of vision by cerebral lesions', *British Journal of Opthalmology*, 2, London: BMJ Publishing Group Ltd. Reproduced with permission of the BMJ Publishing Group; Figures 5.13 and 5.14 from Morton, J. and Patterson, K. (1980) 'A new attempt at an interpretation, or, an attempt at a new interpretation.' In M. Coltheart *et al.* (eds.), *Deep dyslexia*, London: Routledge & Kegan Paul; Figure 5.19 and Table 5.1 from Gross, Charles G. (1998), *Brain, vision, memory: Tales in the history of neuroscience*, Cambridge, MA: MIT Press. Figure on p. 54, table from p. 21, Copyright © 1998 Massachusetts Institute of Technology, by permission of The MIT Press; Figure 5.20 from Lieberman, M.D. (2007) 'Social cognitive neuroscience: A review of the core processes', *Annual Review of Psychology*, 58, Annual Reviews, 259–89; Figure 5.21 reprinted from Ellis, H.D. and Lewis, M.B. (2001) 'Capgras delusion: A window on face recognition', *Trends in Cognitive Science*, 5, 4, Figure 4. Copyright © 2001, with permission from Elsevier; Table 6.1 from Evans, J.S.B.T. (2002) 'Logic and human reasoning: An assessment of the deduction paradigm', *Psychological Bulletin*, 128, 978–96, American Psychological Association; Figure 6.1 from Kunst-Wilson, W.R., and Zajonc, R.B. (1980) 'Affective discrimination of stimuli that cannot be recognized', *Science*, 207, 557–8. Reprinted with permission from AAAS; Figure 6.2 from Marcel, A.J. (1983) 'Conscious and unconscious perception: experiments on visual masking and word recognition', *Cognitive psychology*, 15, (4). 197–237. Copyright © 1983, reprinted by permission from Elsevier; Figure 6.3 from Libet, B. (1985) 'Unconscious cerebral initiative and the role of conscious will in voluntary action', *Behavioural and Brain Sciences*, 8, Cambridge University Press; Figure 6.5 Pulvermuller, F. (2005) 'Brain mechanisms linking language and action', *Nature Reviews Neuroscience*, 6, 576–82. Copyright © 2005, reprinted by permission from Macmillan Publishers Ltd; Figure 6.6 from Dijksterhuis, A., Bos, M.W., Nordgren, L.F., & Van Baaren, R.B. (2006) 'On making the right choice: The deliberation-without-attention effect', *Science*, 311, 1005–7. Reprinted with permission from AAAS; Table 7.2 based on 'Multiple comparisons of mean performance on the science scale', *PISA 2006: Science Competencies for Tomorrow's World*, 1, 56, Figure 2.11b OECD 2007; Figure 7.2 reprinted from Rehman, S.U., et al. (2005) 'What to wear today? Effect of doctor's attire on the trust and confidence of patients', *The American Journal of Medicine*, 118, 11, 3, Figure 1B. Copyright © 2005, reprinted by permission from Elsevier; Table 7.3 Weisbord, M.R. (1985) 'Participative work design: A personal odyssey', *Organizational Dynamics*, 13, 4–20, Copyright © 1985, reproduced by permission from Elsevier, the original from Trist, E. (1981) *The evolution of socio-technical systems – A conceptual framework and an action research program*, Toronto, Canada: Ontario Ministry of Labour © 1981 Queens Printer for Ontario. Adapted and reproduced with permission; Figure 7.4 Allchin, D. (2004) 'Pseudohistory and pseudoscience', *Science & Education*, 13, 179–95. Reprinted with kind permission from Springer Science + Business Media; Figures 8.1 and 8.2 from

Edith Brysbaert; Figure 8.4a from Cambell, W.W. and Trumper, R. (1923) *Lick Observatory Bulletin*, 11, 41, © UC Regents/Lick Observatory; Figure 8.7 from Fischer, G.H. (1968) 'Ambiguity of form: Old and new', *Perception and Psychophysics*, 4, 189–92, Psychonomic Society, Inc.; Figures 8.8 and 8.9 from Isa Brysbaert, based on Fischer (1968); Table 9.1 from Bornstein, R.F. (2005) 'Reconnecting psychoanalysis to mainstream psychology: challenges and opportunities', *Psychoanalytic Psychology*, 22, American Psychological Association; Figure 9.1 from Boyack, K.W. (2005) 'Mapping the backbone of science', *Scientometrics*, 64, 351–74. Reprinted with kind permission from Springer Science + Business Media; Figure 9.2 from McDuffie Jr., T.E. (2001) 'Scientists – Geeks and nerds? Dispelling teachers' stereotypes of scientists', *Science and children,* 38. Copyright © 2001 National Science Teachers Association. Reproduced with permission of National Science Teachers Association in the format Other book via Copyright Clearance Center; Figure 9.4 adapted from Janda, L.H., England , K.J., Lovejoy, D., & Drury, K. (1998) 'Attitudes towards psychology relative to other disciplines', *Professional Psychology: Research and practice*, 29, American Psychological Association; Figure 10.1 from Doll, R., Peto, R., Boreham, J. et al. (2004) 'Mortality in relation to smoking: 50 years' observations on male British doctors', *British Medical Journal*, 328, 1519–28, BMJ Publishing Group. Reproduced with permission from the BMJ Publishing Group; Table 10.3 from Ward, N. (1998) 'Artificial intelligence and other approaches to speech understanding: reflections on methodology', *Journal of Experimental and Theoretical Artificial Intelligence*, (10), Taylor & Francis Ltd. Reprinted by permission of the publisher (Taylor & Francis Ltd, http://www.tandf.co.uk/ journals); Tables 10.4, 10.5 and 10.6 from Schraw, G., Wadkins, T. and Olafson, L. (2007) 'Doing the things we do: A grounded theory of academic procrastination', Journal of Educational Psychology', (99), 12–25, American Psychological Society, Copyright © 2007 American Psychological Association. Reprinted with permission. Table 10.7 from Starks, H. and Trinidad, S.B. (2007) *Qualitative Health Research*, 17, 1372–80. Copyright © 2007 Sage Publications Inc. Reprinted by Permission of SAGE Publications; Figure 11.1 adapted from Djordevic, J. et al. (2008) 'A rose by any other name would it smell as sweet?' *Journal of Neurophysiology*, 99, American Physiological Society. Adapted with permission of the author; Table 11.2 adapted from Hofstede, G. (2005) *Cultures and organizations: Software of the mind* (2nd edn.), McGraw Hill Professional; Figure 11.2a from DeRubeis, R.J., Gelfand, L.A., Tang, T.Z., and Simons, A.D. (2005) 'Cognitive therapy vs. medications in the treatment of moderate to severe depression', *Archives of General Psychiatry*, 62, American Medical Association. Copyright © 2005 American Medical Association. All rights reserved; Figure 11.2b from Hollon, S.D. et al. (2005) 'Prevention of relapse following cognitive therapy vs medications in moderate to severe depression', *Archives of General Psychiatry*, (62), American Medical Association. Copyright © 2005 American Medical Association. All rights reserved; Table 11.3 from Capron, C. and Duyme, M. (1989) 'Assessment of effects of socioeconomic status on IQ in full cross-fostering design', *Nature*, 340, 552–3. Copyright © 1989 reprinted by permission from Macmillan Publishers Ltd; (2001); unnumbered figure on page 174 from Goodglass, H. and Kaplan, E. (1983) *The assessment of aphasia and related disorders*, Philapdelphia: Lea and Feibiger. Reprinted with permission of Pro-Ed Inc; Table 12.2 from Redding (2001) 'Sociopolitical diversity in psychology: The case for pluralism', *American Psychologist,* 56, 205–15, American Psychological Association; Figure 12.1 from McKeown, T. (1979) The Role of Medicine: Dream, Mirage or Nemesis? © 1979 Blackwell Publishing Ltd. Reproduced with permission of Blackwell Publishing Ltd.

Pages 47–8, book review by Callow, S., August 4th 2007, 'Galileo Antichrist: A Biography', *The Guardian*, Copyright © 2007 Guardian News & Media Ltd; pages 83–5, excerpt from Nicolas, S.and Ferrand, L. (1999) 'Wundt's laboratory at Leipzig in 1891', *History of Psychology*, 2, 3, August, 194–203. Copyright © 1999 The American Psychological Association. Reproduced with permission, also with kind permission of Ludovic Ferrand. The use of APA information does not imply endorsement by APA; pages 86–7 excerpt from Cattell, J.M.(1888) 'The psychological laboratory at Leipsic', *Mind*, 13, 37–51 by permission of Oxford University Press; pages 92 and 93, excerpts from James, W. (1890) *The Principles of Psychology*, (1), New York: Henry Holt; pages 116 and 120–1, excerpts from Leahey, T.H. (2004), *A history of psychology: Main currents in psychological thought* (6th edn.), Upper Saddle River, NJ: Pearson Education Inc. Copyright © 2004, Pgs. 312, 330. Reprinted by permission of Pearson Education, Inc., Upper Saddle River, NJ; Pages 129–131, excerpts from Watson, J.B. (1913) 'Psychology as the behaviorist views it', *Psychological Review*, 20, 158–177, American Psychological Association. Reprinted with permission; pages 275–276 from Johnson, B., December 15th 2007, 'Twenty-eight people ask Hugh MacLeod to be their friend each day. What's so special about him?' *The Guardian*, Copyright © 2007 Guardian News & Media Ltd; page 287, excerpt from *The Times*, November 20th 2007. Copyright © NI Syndication Limited.

The publisher would like to thank the following for their kind permission to reproduce their photographs:

(**Key: b-bottom; c-centre; l-left; r-right; t-top**)

p. 43, Figure 2.1: The Royal Astronomical Society / Science Photo Library Ltd; p. 47, Figure 2.4: Chris Proctor; p. 49: Detlev Van Ravenswaay / Science Photo Library Ltd; p. 52: The Royal Astronomical Society / Science Photo Library Ltd; p. 53, Figure 2.5: Institute and Museum of the History of Science, Florence, Italy; p. 55: CCI Archives / Science Photo Library; p. 63: Getty Images / FPG; p. 90: US National Library of Medicine / Science Photo Library; p. 94: Science Photo Library Ltd; p. 98: Cornell University Library / Rare and Manuscript Collections; p. 100: Karl Pearson Science & Society Picture Library; p. 103: US National Library of Medicine / Science Photo Library Ltd; p. 108: National Library of Medicine / Science Photo Library; p. 125, Figure 4.1: Robert Mearns Yerkes Papers / Yale University Library / Manuscripts and Archives; p. 126: Humanities and Social Sciences Library / New York Public Library / Science Photo Library; p. 127: Ria Novosti / Science Photo Library; p. 131: Bettmann / Corbis; p. 161l: Heidi Cartwright / Wellcome Images; p. 161r: Daniel Templeton / Alamy Images; p. 164, Figure 5.3b: Rue de Archives / Mary Evans Picture Library; p. 171, Figure 5.6: BSIP, JACOPIN / Science Photo Library Ltd; p. 190: AJ Photo / Hop Americain / Science Photo Library Ltd; p. 191: Dr Jurgen Scriba / Science Photo Library Ltd; p. 193, Figure 5.18: © 2007 by the Massachusetts Institute of Technology; p. 192: Ralmund Koch / Photonica / Getty Images; p. 194: University of Durham / Simon Fraser / Science Photo Library Ltd; p. 250: Roger Ressmeyer / Corbis; p. 271: Popperfoto / Getty Images; p. 319t: Keystone / Getty Images; p. 319b: Bill Pierce / Time Life Pictures / Getty Images; p. 422: © David M. Buss, all rights reserved; p. 465: SIPA Press / Rex Features.

In some instances we have been unable to trace the owners of copyright material, and we would appreciate any information that would enable us to do so.

Guided tour

This chapter will cover
Gives a brief outline of the main points of each chapter, to help you understand what you will learn.

Introduction
Each chapter opens with a quote, extract or example to provide background on or to stimulate interest in the chapter topic.

Questions to consider
Each chapter opens with a range of thought-provoking questions to consider in relation to the historical and conceptual issues raised. These give an idea of topics considered in the chapter and encourage students to critically reflect on them.

What do you think? boxes

Offer a moment for students to pause and reflect on what they've learnt and consider their own stance on it.

Key figure box

Sums up the main facts about important figures in the field of psychology, and their contribution to our understanding of the subject.

Interim summary

Is a useful recap and revision tool interspersed throughout the chapters, helping the student get to grips with the main points.

Recommended literature

Offers some useful and manageable ideas for deeper study of the topics covered in each chapter. A handy feature for researching and writing essays.

01 The wider picture
Where did it all start?

This chapter will cover

Questions to consider

Historical issues addressed in this chapter

- How old is the Earth and when did the first human beings appear?
- When did the first civilisation start?
- When did the first writing systems appear?
- When did the first number systems appear and what did they look like? Why were the Ancient Greeks and Romans handicapped in their numerical cognition?
- Did the Ancient Greek civilisation end after it was conquered by the Romans?
- How did information from the Greek and Roman cultures survive the Dark Ages?
- How long did the Middle Ages last?
- Why did countries such as the UK, parts of Germany and the Netherlands at a certain point become more productive and scientifically minded than the other European countries?

Conceptual issues addressed in this chapter

- Why did *Homo sapiens* start to spread over the entire world some 50,000 years ago?
- How did the change from a nomadic hunter-gatherer society to farming and settlement affect human interactions?
- In what ways does the availability of written records change human thought?
- In what ways do current writing systems differ from the first ones? Is this an improvement?
- Can education change the way in which we read texts?
- How does arithmetic depend on the code that is used to represent numbers?
- Why were Christian schools after the fall of the Roman Empire unable to prevent a sharp decline in scientific knowledge?
- Is it possible to write a complete history of science?
- To what extent does our current scientific knowledge depend on the contribution of a small number of geniuses who achieved the major scientific breakthroughs?

Introduction

On Saturday 6 October 2007 the British newspaper the *Guardian* opened with an article claiming that the first artificial life had been created. A team of 20 top scientists led by a Nobel laureate had constructed a synthetic chromosome consisting of 381 genes. On page 4 of the newspaper it was announced that the British government wanted to create specialist integration teams to tackle tensions in communities sparked by changing patterns of migration. On page 5 McDonald's publicised the introduction of free high speed wireless internet access at most of its restaurants. On page 9 the case was described of a 72-year-old man who would become a sperm donor for his daughter-in-law after it had emerged that his son had fertility problems. Page 10 reported an analysis published in the journal *Sport Biomechanics* of Jonny Wilkinson's phenomenal kicking technique in rugby (England would play Australia in the world cup later that day). Page 11 warned the readers of identity theft on the internet. Page 19 featured the weekly column *Bad Science* (criticising the unscientific claims made by herbalists about the healing powers of herbs). Page 19 further announced a campaign launched by the British government to recruit more maths and physics teachers. Those were the main science-related stories published by one newspaper on a single day.

If you take a moment to look around, you can easily see how our society is pervaded by scientific products and scientifically based solutions to social problems. Because of this ubiquity we often forget that this situation is relatively recent, starting the moment our ancestors descended from their trees in Africa and ventured into the more dangerous savannah.

This book describes the growth of psychology as an independent branch of learning and tries to comprehend the essence of the discipline. Because it deals with fundamental questions, we will take a rather long run-up, addressing several issues about how our current Western civilisation came about. First, we consider the emergence of the physical world around us and how humankind developed. Next, we explore how the invention of writing and numerical systems allowed the accumulation of knowledge and understanding. We then present a short account of the ancient civilisations – the Greeks, the Romans, the Byzantine and Arab empires – and consider the role each played in the evolution of knowledge. We end with a brief description of the Renaissance. We focus on those events that shaped the emergence of the scientific approach as we now know it. Our review starts billions of years ago and ends on the eve of the scientific revolution in the seventeenth century.

1.1   The very beginning

The geological timeline

Era	Time (millions of years ago)	Important events
Cenozoic	0.0	present time
Cenozoic	less than 0.1	advent of modern humans
Cenozoic	2.4	ice age
Mesozoic	66.4	mass extinction
Mesozoic	141	first flowering plants
Mesozoic	195	birds evolve from reptiles
Mesozoic	230	first dinosaurs and mammals
Paleozoic	245	
Paleozoic	280	mass extinction
Paleozoic	340	reptiles appear
Paleozoic	360	first insects
Paleozoic	370	amphibians appear
Paleozoic	420	plants colonize land
Precambrian	540	Cambrian explosion
Precambrian	700	simple multicellular organisms evolve
Precambrian	2,100	oldest eukaryotic fossils
Precambrian	2,500	oxygen begins to accumulate in atmosphere
Precambrian	3,500	oldest prokaryotic fossils

Geological timeline.
Notice that the timeline in this picture is not linear. The space taken up by the more than four billion years before the Cambrian explosion (around 542 million years ago) is nearly the same as the space taken up by the last sixty-six million years.

How old is the Earth?

It is now generally accepted that the Earth is some 4.6 billion years old. This is much more than was thought for a long time and the age many people spontaneously think of. One of the first scientific attempts to establish the Earth's age resulted in an estimate of between 75,000 and 168,000 years. This estimate came from the French scholar Georges-Louis Leclerc and was based on the degree of heat lost by the Earth since its beginning. In the nineteenth century the estimate was first increased by the English scientist Lord Kelvin to some 100 million years (in 1862) but later 'corrected' to 24 million years (in 1897). Around the same time, his fellow-Englishman Charles Darwin thought the Earth had to be some 300 million years old for all the geological and evolutionary processes to have taken place. As it turned out, these were all wild underestimates. An analogy that is often used here is that of a day's duration. If 4.6 billion years stand for a full day, 168,000 years represent the last three seconds, 24 million years represent the last 8 minutes, and 300 million years equal the final 1.6 hours.

The different stages in the history of the Earth

The true age of the Earth was established within geology. This branch of science studies the surface of the Earth and, among other things, tries to understand its past by analysing the many layers of sediments that have been formed. A first big distinction that is made in the geological timeline is between the time period before 542 million years ago and the period after. Around this time a lot of macroscopic, hard-shelled animals started to appear, which left plenty of fossils in rocks. The sudden appearance of animals that resemble those in current life is called the Cambrian explosion, named after the place where the first fossils were found in the nineteenth century (Cambria = Wales). Because the Cambrian explosion is often presented as the beginning of 'real' life (e.g. with animals having a head, thorax and tail), this may explain why many people spontaneously think of the earth as being younger that it actually is. Notice that eight-ninths of the earth's history is actually situated before this pivot! Two important developments in those 4 billion years were the emergence of organic life forms (first simple cells, then complex cells and multicellular life) and the start of photosynthesis, the production of oxygen first by bacteria from water and then by plants from carbon dioxide.

Cambrian explosion

sudden presence of fossils in geological records starting some 542 million years ago; often presented as the beginning of 'real' life

The sudden onset of many new life forms in the Cambrian explosion (which in fact took several millions of years) creates some difficulty in understanding what exactly happened at this time. One idea is that the ancestors of the organisms went back much further in time (simple cell life probably started some 0.6 billion years after the origin of the Earth) but cannot be found in the fossils because they were too small or their composition did not lend itself to fossilisation. Another idea is that the Earth was hit by a major disaster (a meteor strike or a major volcanic eruption), killing many existing life forms and making room for new ones to develop. Still other proposals are that the oxygen level at this time started to become high enough to allow the creation of larger organisms or that changes in temperature first covered the entire Earth with snow and ice, followed by a thaw shortly before the Cambrian explosion.

The 540 million years since the Cambrian explosion are further divided into three eras: the Paleozoic era (540–250 million), the Mesozoic era (250–66 million) and the Cenozoic era (66 million to now). The names are less important than what happened at their transitions. In the first era the animals of the Cambrian explosion thrived and were accompanied by other life forms. This period saw the emergence of fish, land plants, insects, amphibians and reptiles respectively. Then, over a rather short period of time, some 95 per cent of marine species and 70 per cent of terrestrial species vanished. Again, it is not clear what calamity caused this sudden alternation: whether it was a climate change, the eruption of a volcano or the impact of a meteor. Whatever it was, it took millions of years for the Earth to recover.

The second era, the Mesozoic, is often called the Age of the Dinosaurs, after the most salient group of animals of that period. This period also saw the beginning of mammals, birds and flowers. Once again the era ended with a massive extinction, giving way to an expansion of the mammals which also grew larger, arguably because of the extinction of their predators. One species of mammals was the humans.

The timeline of mankind

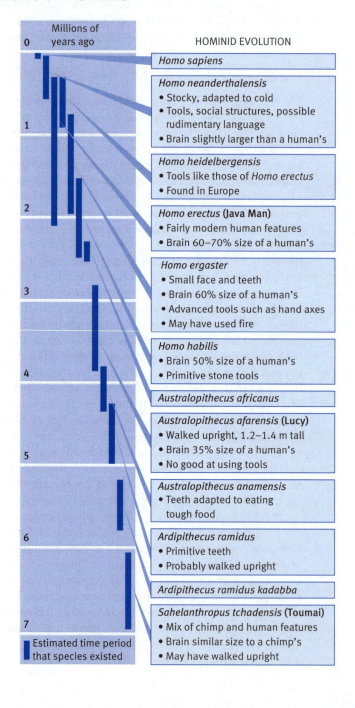

Millions of years ago

HOMINID EVOLUTION

Homo sapiens

Homo neanderthalensis
- Stocky, adapted to cold
- Tools, social structures, possible rudimentary language
- Brain slightly larger than a human's

Homo heidelbergensis
- Tools like those of *Homo erectus*
- Found in Europe

Homo erectus (Java Man)
- Fairly modern human features
- Brain 60–70% size of a human's

Homo ergaster
- Small face and teeth
- Brain 60% size of a human's
- Advanced tools such as hand axes
- May have used fire

Homo habilis
- Brain 50% size of a human's
- Primitive stone tools

Australopithecus africanus

Australopithecus afarensis (Lucy)
- Walked upright, 1.2–1.4 m tall
- Brain 35% size of a human's
- No good at using tools

Australopithecus anamensis
- Teeth adapted to eating tough food

Ardipithecus ramidus
- Primitive teeth
- Probably walked upright

Ardipithecus ramidus kadabba

Sahelanthropus tchadensis (Toumai)
- Mix of chimp and human features
- Brain similar size to a chimp's
- May have walked upright

Estimated time period that species existed

The emergence of humans

On the basis of scattered archaeological findings and genetic analyses, anthropologists and geneticists try to reconstruct the history of mankind. Although there are still many unknowns, there is evidence that some 6–7 million years ago a class of bipeds was forced out of the jungle into the savannah. According to one theory this was because around that time Africa became much drier as a result of North and South America being joined. This cut off the currents between the Pacific Ocean and the Atlantic Ocean, causing major changes in the climate. The bipeds leaving the jungle were ancestors of both the chimpanzees and modern humans. About 1–2 million years later the human line diverged from that of the chimpanzees (the separation from the gorilla ancestors had already taken place much earlier, some 10 million years ago).

Around 2 million years ago the bipeds resembled modern humans enough to be given the status of a new genus, *Homo*. They included *Homo habilis* and *Homo erectus*. The latter spread from Africa to Europe and Asia and are thought to be the first human beings to have used fire. The only species of this genus that survived was ***Homo sapiens***, the oldest fossils of which date back some 200,000 years and were also found in Africa, from where *Homo sapiens* started spreading over the globe. From genetic analysis, there is evidence of a major cataclysm that nearly eradicated the species some

Homo sapiens

species to which present humans belong; started in Africa some 200K years ago; nearly decimated some 100–50K years ago

Spread through Africa 150,000 years ago
Occupied Levant 180,000 to 80,000 years ago
Arrived in Australia and East Asia by 50,000 years ago
Arrived in Europe and Siberia by 40,000 years ago

The migration of *Homo sapiens* from 150,000 to 40,000 years ago.

100,000–50,000 years ago and reduced the human population to maybe as few as 1,000 breeding pairs. This would explain the small genetic variation in current humans. One hypothesis (the Toba catastrophe hypothesis) is that 75,000–70,000 years ago, an enormous volcanic eruption at Lake Toba blew a massive amount of dust into the air, seriously reducing the viability of life (including a nuclear winter and an ice age of some 1,000 years).

Expansion of Homo sapiens

Some 50,000 years ago, *Homo sapiens* began to spread to Europe and Asia, and from there to Australia. Several streams entered North America from Siberia around 30,000 BCE;[1] some 20,000 years later they reached the tip of South America. This massive expansion was accompanied by the production of more advanced tools. One hypothesis about the immense changes around this time is that humans had developed a language that was more than a mere collection of sound signals. Modern human language is characterised by productivity (the ability to combine sounds and words in new ways to convey new messages), semanticity (messages convey a rich semantic meaning that is shared between speaker and listener) and displacement (the ability to refer to things that are removed from the speaker in time and space).

The first civilisations

neolithic revolution

the transition from a nomadic hunter-gatherer society to farming and settlement around 10,000 BCE

Fertile Crescent

region in the Middle East with a high level of civilisation around 3,000 BCE; included the Ancient Mesopotamian and the Ancient Egyptian civilizations

A further major change was the transition from a nomadic hunter-gatherer society to farming and settlement. This is called the **neolithic revolution**. It happened on several locations in the different continents and was well established by 10,000 BCE. It is assumed that the greater complexity of the social interactions in settlements was a further impetus for thought and language development. Leakey and Lewin (1992) also claim that the accumulation of possessions in sedentary farming communities changed the human interactions from cooperation and sharing to the protection of goods and an increased level of conflict.

For Western culture in particular the developments in the so-called **Fertile Crescent** were important. This crescent included Ancient Mesopotamia and Ancient Egypt (figure 1.1). One of the many innovations coming from this region was the use of the wheel in the fifth millennium BCE. The crescent comprised the Sumerian (3,500–2,300 BCE), the Ancient Egyptian (3,200–340 BCE) and the Babylonian cultures (2,000–500 BCE).

The first evidence for modern civilisation in China dates back to 7,000 BCE (the Jiahu culture), with written records from 2,800 BCE. America had the Norte Chico (3,000–1,600 BCE) and the Olmec civilisations (1,200–450 BCE). The former was situated in current Peru, the latter in a region covering parts of Honduras, Costa Rica and Mexico. It was the forerunner of the Maya and the Aztec cultures.

[1] BCE stands for 'before the common era'; i.e. before the start of the Gregorian calendar used in the Western society (another notation in Christian cultures is BC [before Christ]); CE means 'the common era' and begins with the start of the Gregorian calendar (indicated in Christian cultures as AD [*Anno Domini*]).

Figure 1.1 The Fertile Crescent.

The preliterate culture

Because the civilisations of the Fertile Crescent left us with written testimonies, we know quite a lot about them. But how do we know what the life of people in prehistory would have been like, before writing was invented? Lindberg (1992) tried to discover the characteristics of such preliterate civilisations by studying existing illiterate cultures.

preliterate civilisation

civilisation before writing was invented

Three features of preliterate civilisations

A first characteristic Lindberg discerned was that, although illiterate cultures know how to make tools, start fires, obtain shelter, hunt, fish, and gather fruit and vegetables, their skills are not based on an understanding of how things work, but on practical rules of thumb of what to do when. Their knowledge is confined to 'know-how' without theoretical understanding of the underlying principles.

A second characteristic of a culture without written records is the fluidity of knowledge. Knowledge of the actual history of the tribe is limited to two generations and the function of the oral tradition mainly is the transmission of practical skills.

A third feature of an illiterate culture is the existence of a collection of myths and stories about the beginning of the universe, life and natural phenomena, in which human traits are projected onto objects and events (e.g. in the form of gods). The belief that objects and nature are inhabited by spirits with human-like characteristics, which cause events to happen, is called animism. The term was introduced by Sir Edward Burnett Tylor (1832–1917), one of the first anthropologists to draw a distinction between the thinking of 'primitive people' as opposed to the then growing 'scientific thinking' in the Western world. In Tylor's view, primitives (as they were called) looked at the world like children and endowed all things, even inanimate ones, with a nature analogous to their own (Bird-David, 1999).

Lindberg (1992) looked down upon the animistic thinking of preliterate civilisations less than Tylor did. For him the myths and stories reinforced the values and attitudes of the community and fulfilled the need humans have for explanatory principles capable of bringing order, unity and meaning to the events around them. In general, the myths are also related to the treatment of illnesses: the person with the greatest knowledge of the myths is the person to whom people turn when they have an ailment. At the same time Lindberg noticed that myths often contradict each other and contain inconsistencies, without any evidence that this hinders the preliterate people. Each story stands on its own. It is only when information is written down that patterns start to emerge and incompatibilities become visible. Therefore, Lindberg argued, scientific thinking cannot occur without written records.

animism

explanation of the workings of the world and the universe by means of spirits with human-like characteristics

Interim summary

- ■ Birth of the Earth = 4.6 billion years ago (much older than often assumed).

- ■ Stages in the geological timeline:
  - ■ Time before the Cambrian explosion (542 million years ago; start of 'real' life)
  - ■ Stage of the first fishes, land plants, insects, amphibians and reptiles
  - ■ Stage of the dinosaurs
  - ■ Stage of the mammals.

- ■ The timeline of humankind
  - ■ Around 2 million years ago beginning of genus *Homo* (*habilis*, *erectus*)
  - ■ Some 200K years ago beginning of *Homo sapiens* in Africa
  - ■ 50K years ago start of the expansion of the *Homo sapiens* (due to the development of language?)
  - ■ 10K BCE transition from a nomadic hunter-gather society to farming and settlement (neolithic revolution)
  - ■ For the Western culture in particular the Fertile Crescent was important.

Interim summary (continued)

- Features of the preliterate civilisation
  - Knowledge confined to 'know-how' without theoretical knowledge of the underlying principles
  - Fluidity of knowledge
  - Collection of myths and stories about the beginning of the universe (animism).

? What do you think?

Animistic reasoning is also prevalent among young children (objects and animals do things because they 'want to'). Can you think of such examples? Would it be possible for you to ask a 3-year-old why plants grow or why the moon waxes and wanes?

1.2 The invention of writing

Because science depends on the availability of written records and skills to count and measure things, it is interesting at this point to interrupt our chronological overview and look at when and where written words and numbers were invented. It is also interesting to consider what is so important about them.

The first writing systems

pictogram

an information-conveying sign that consists of a picture resembling the person, animal or object it represents

Written language appeared separately in at least four cultures: in China (around 6,000 BCE), Egypt (around 3,200 BCE), Sumer (also around 3,200 BCE) and America (Olmec and Mayan, 300 BCE). These four written languages were preceded by proto-writing, the use of symbols to represent entities without linguistic information linking them.

Characteristics of writing systems

phonogram

a sign that represents a sound or a syllable of spoken language; forms the basis of writing systems

Already from an early stage, writing systems were a combination of **pictograms** (pictures that resemble the persons, animals and objects they represent) and **phonograms** (signs to represent sounds of the spoken language). The Egyptian hieroglyphs, for instance, could only be deciphered when scientists realised that most hieroglyphs represented spoken syllables. The phonograms were gradually replaced by simpler signs symbolising meaningful sounds in the language (phonemes) or syllables. The former led to the alphabetic writing systems, starting with the Phoenician alphabet that formed the basis of the Arabic, Hebrew and Greek alphabets. The writing system that has remained closest to the pictograms is Chinese, where the physical correspondence between the signs and the words rapidly decreased, so that the writing system became logographic rather than pictographic (words are represented by written signs – characters – that no longer resemble the meanings they stand for). However, in this language as well, most written words consist of two characters that have a relationship to the word's meaning and that often include cues to the pronunciation.

Written documents form an external memory

Writing and the accumulation of knowledge

The importance of writing lies in the external memory written records provide about the knowledge available at a certain point in time. This is important for science because it allows an accumulation of knowledge. New scientists do not have to rediscover what has previously been found. They can simply read what their predecessors wrote. This does not mean that insights never get overlooked (certainly not when a lot is published and not always readily available), but it usually implies that the insights can be retrieved if one is motivated to look for them (the history of science is full of rediscoveries of seminal teachers who were only known to a small circle of ex-students).

A particularly revealing excerpt illustrating the importance of written documents is provided by a remark made by Socrates. Socrates (*c.* 470–399 BCE) was an important philosopher in Ancient Greece, who was not at all interested in keeping written records of his thoughts. In a dialogue with a young student (Phaedrus) Socrates recounted how the god Thoth of Egypt offered the king of Egypt all types of inventions, including dice, checkers, numbers, geometry, astronomy and writing. The god and the king discussed the merits and drawbacks of the various gifts and were in general agreement until they reached the gift of writing. Whereas the god stressed the advantage of being able to remember information, the king objected: 'If men learn this, it will implant forgetfulness in their souls; they will cease to exercise memory because they will rely on that which is written, calling things to remembrance no longer from within themselves, but by means of external marks.' From the remainder of the dialogue it is clear that Socrates wholeheartedly agreed with the king of Egypt and thought that the availability of books made students lazy and discouraged them from properly studying.

The irony of the dialogue is that we would never have heard of it, or indeed of any of Socrates' other memorable dialogues, if they had not been documented by Plato. An oral tradition would most certainly have changed the wording of the story and in all likelihood would never have survived the Middle Ages. In addition, the dialogue would not have been included in the present book, if it had not been present in Manguel's (1996) *A History of Reading* (p. 58), which we read in preparation of this chapter.

Written records provide the basis of the cumulative nature of science. Therefore, the first thing researchers do when they embark on a new question is to search in the literature for what is already known about the topic. They build on existing insights and are able to avoid the pitfalls that hindered their predecessors. Notice that this scientific approach is far from ubiquitous in society. How often is it that people venture advice and opinions without having looked at any evidence at all? Also notice that the use of texts depends on their availability. This is one of the reasons why the invention of communication tools (such as book printing and digital data sharing on the internet) has had a major influence on scientific progress.

> ## What do you think?
>
> Do you have the impression that your studies have convinced you of the necessity to collect the available evidence before you make a statement? Or do you experience this as a useless academic requirement that is of little help in daily life? When are literature reviews useful and when not?

The reader

Who can read?

Written records only have an impact if there is somebody to read them. For most of human history the number of people who could read was relatively small (it still is nowadays in some communities). For many centuries a large proportion of the population was excluded from acquiring reading skills. In addition, the early scripts lacked an important characteristic that makes alphabetic languages easier to read: spaces between the words. Even the ancient Greek and Latin texts were written in so-called *scriptio continua* (continuous script). Only in the eighth century did writers start to put spaces between the words. Saenger (1997) argues that this quality of texts made silent reading possible. Before, nearly all readers read aloud or at least had to mumble while reading (a practice that was still widespread in the nineteenth century). In 383 Aurelius Augustine (in the Catholic Church known as Saint Augustine) expressed his surprise when he met the bishop of Milan and saw that he could read silently. 'When he read,' said Augustine, 'his eyes scanned the page and his heart sought out the meaning, but his voice was silent and his tongue was still' (as cited in Manguel 1996: 42).

The influence of orthography

Reading nowadays still is a demanding skill, as is illustrated by the many efforts beginning readers have to invest to acquire it. Reading acquisition is easiest in languages with a transparent relationship between spelling and the sound, such as Spanish, Italian, Serbo-Croatian, German and Korean, where most children 'crack the code' in less than a year (although they need many more years of practice before the processes become automatic). In languages with a more opaque correspondence, such as English and Hebrew, children need up to four years in order to reach the same level of performance and are more likely to be confronted with reading difficulties (Hanley *et al.* 2004; Ziegler and Goswami 2005).

Reading without critical thinking

scholastic method

study method in which students unquestioningly memorise and recite texts that are thought to convey unchanging truths

Readers in the past differed on one more aspect from present-day scientific readers. In particular in the Middle Ages students were taught to read and understand texts exactly as they were. They were in no way encouraged (and often discouraged) to question the writings or to compare them with other writings. Books were the world's wisdom that had to be transmitted in its original form from generation to generation. As Manguel noted:

Essentially the **scholastic method** consisted in little more than training the students to consider a text according to certain pre-established, officially approved criteria which were painstakingly and painfully drilled into them. As far as the teaching of reading was concerned, the success of the method depended more on the students' perseverance than on their intelligence.

(Manguel 1996: 74)

The scholastic method was prevalent in universities well into the sixteenth century and according to the German sociologist Max Weber (1904/1905) its abandonment by the Protestant churches was one of the reasons why science took such a high flight in the countries that converted to this religion. Scholars started to look critically at the existing literature and tried to improve on it. We will return to this scientific revolution in Chapter 2.

Interim summary

- Written language appeared separately in a least four cultures; in each case it was preceded by proto-writing.

- Writing consists of a combination of pictograms and phonograms.

- Written records form an external memory, which allows an accumulation of knowledge.

- For a long time the number of readers was limited. In addition, they were not encouraged to think critically about what they were reading (scholastic method).

What do you think?

Is the current emphasis on 'critical thinking' exaggerated? Is it possible to think critically without first knowing the facts?

1.3   The discovery of numbers

Another development that has been crucial for the growth of science is the discovery of numbers. When we do a simple arithmetic operation, we rarely realise how much insight and knowledge are hidden behind the procedures we use. Interestingly enough, the history of numbers and numerical operations remained largely unexplored until the French maths teacher Georges Ifrah decided to take the issue in hand, a quest that took him over 10 years to finish (see Ifrah 1998).

The limits of visual perception and the special status of the number five

The ease of understanding the numbers one to three

The possession of goods required the ability to count them. The earliest archaeological evidence of counting dates back to 35,000–20,000 BCE. It consisted of lines or other markings carved in bones and stones. It is reasonable to assume that quite early in their evolution humans could make distinctions up to three, which were represented by one, two and three markings. Newborn babies and all kinds of animals can distinguish between one, two and three entities, a phenomenon that is known as *subitising*. Also a number of isolated tribes have been described with a number naming system that essentially consisted of three terms: one, two and many.

Larger numbers and the need for grouping the tallies

A problem with tallies to represent numbers is that they rapidly exceed the limits of perception. Whereas nobody has difficulties understanding the symbols I, II and III, the use of an analogue code (i.e. a code that represents numbers by a physical magnitude) rapidly starts to fall apart for larger quantities. Number representations like IIIIII and IIIIIIII are not very useful, even though they are still limited to quantities as small as six and eight. A first solution to this problem was a grouping of the tallies, as we still do when we write ~~IIII~~ I or ~~IIII~~ III. This method was used independently in several cultures. The most popular grouping had a base five (as in the example above). There are two reasons why this base appeared in many places. First, the number five is the first entity that really exceeds the perceptual limits (it is possible to grasp a grouping of four perceptually without counting the tallies, as in IIII). The number five also coincides with the number of fingers on a hand. Gradually, the base number five started to get a different symbol. For instance, the Etruscan civilisation used the following symbols for the numbers one to five in the sixth to the fourth centuries BCE: I, II, III, IIII, Λ (notice the similarity to the Roman numerals; the Etruscans lived in ancient Italy before they were conquered by the Romans).

Giving the numbers names and symbols

The names one to ten

An analysis of the origin of the number names gives some indication of the struggle humans had before they could come up with a handy numerical system. For instance, it is probably no coincidence that the number nine is related to the word 'new' in the Indo-European family of languages. At some point in time, this probably was a newly discovered number. The fact that all Indo-European languages share the same roots for the numbers one to ten further suggests that their names already existed before the original language began to split into its many branches around 2000 BCE. On the basis of the similarities of the number names in over 20 languages as divergent as Sanskrit, Russian and Spanish, Ifrah (1998, p. 32) postulates the following original number-set:

1. oino, oiko, oiwo

2. dwo, dwu, dwoi

3. tri

4. kwetwores, kwetesres, kwetwor

5. penkwe, kwenkwe

6. seks, sweks

7. septm

8. okto, oktu

9. newn

10. dekm

Notice how little these names have changed in the 4,000 or so years since.

The problem of naming the teens

Another feature of many of the Indo-European number names is the irregularity of the number names of the teens (i.e. the numbers 11–19). It is clear that some of these numbers were given their names before the base 10 of the number system was fully grasped. Due to the groupings of the tallies, at some point it was realised that large numbers were best represented as multiples of smaller numbers, so-called base numbers. The most frequently chosen base number was 10 (double five, not coincidentally the numbers of fingers on our two hands). However, the Sumerian number system had a base 60, the consequences of which we still experience in our time units (1 hr = 60 min = 60 × 60 s) and the French number names betray the fact that at some time a base 20 was used (97 = quatre-vingt dix-sept [four-twenty ten-seven]).

The names of the teens in the Indo-European languages illustrate the struggle humans had to integrate the base 10 system in their number names. So, instead of calling the number 11 'ten-one' (analogous to twenty-one), the English name turned out to be 'eleven'. This name is still related to the counting of the fingers (it comes from 'one left' [when the fingers of both hands have been counted]; the same is true for twelve), but the structure of the name betrays that it came into being before it was realised that the best way to represent numbers above ten was to treat them as combinations of tens and units. The irregular naming of the teens is not present in the Chinese number system, which according to some researchers may be one of the reasons why Chinese children have less of a problem understanding the base 10 system of numbers.

Representing numbers by symbols

Once the different numbers had their names, it was a small step to represent them by different symbols. From 600 BCE the Greeks developed a written system for the numbers 1–24 based on the 24 letters of their alphabet, going from alpha (1) to omega (24). This system is still in use in Hebrew for expressing the data by the Hebrew calendar, for chapters and verses of the Torah, and sometimes for the page numbers of books.

The fact that numbers in Ancient Greece could be represented by letters does not mean that such a notation was used for calculations. This would have created insurmountable difficulties as it would suggest a base system of 24. Instead, the Greeks

1 I	100 H	10,000 M
2 II	200 HH	20,000 MM
3 III	300 HHH	30,000 MMM
4 IIII	400 HHHH	40,000 MMMM
5 Γ	500 ſΉ	50,000 ᴘ
6 ΓI	600 ſΉH	60,000 ᴘ M
7 ΓII	700 ſΉHH	70,000 ᴘ MM
8 ΓIII	800 ſΉHHH	80,000 ᴘ MMM
9 ΓIIII	900 ſΉHHHH	90,000 ᴘ MMMM
10 Δ	1,000 X	
20 ΔΔ	2,000 XX	
30 ΔΔΔ	3,000 XXX	
40 ΔΔΔΔ	4,000 XXXX	
50 ſΔ	5,000 ſΧ	
60 ſΔΔ	6,000 ſΧ X	
70 ſΔΔΔ	7,000 ſΧXX	
80 ſΔΔΔΔ	8,000 ſΧXXX	
90 ſΔΔΔΔ	9,000 ſΧXXXX	

Figure 1.2 Number notation used by the Ancient Greeks (from 500 BCE onwards).
Apart from the vertical line for 1, all symbols are the first letter of the number names (Γ is the archaic form of pi, standing for Πεντε [Pente, five]; Δ stands for Δεκα [Deka, ten]; H for Ηεκατον [Hekaton, hundred], X for Χιλιοι [Khilioi, thousand]; M for Μυριοι [Murioi, ten thousand].

Source: Ifrah (1998, p. 182)

used a notation that was in line with a base 10 structure and that they adapted from previous cultures. This notation is shown in figure 1.2. Notice the similarity to Roman numerals.

The discovery of place coding

Although the Greek and the Roman number notation was a major achievement, it did not make arithmetic operations easy. Just try solving the following problems (using Roman numerals): IX × CXI and CMXCIX / IX (C = hundred, I = one, M = thousand, X = ten). The reason why these number notations are difficult to work with is that the base 10 is not clearly present in the symbols (compare the above Roman notations with 9 × 111 and 999 / 9).

A much better system was developed in India. There people started to work with nine different symbols to represent the numbers one to nine. In addition, they used the place of the symbols in the digit string to represent powers of 10. The first digit represented the units, the second digit the tens, the third digit the hundreds, and so on. So, 'thirty-two' no longer consisted of two vertical lines to represent the two units and three symbols of ten to represent the 30, but became a symbol of 2 in the units position and a symbol of 3 in the tens position. Such a **place coding system** only works properly if there is a symbol for the absence of a quantity at a certain slot. Otherwise, it is impossible to know whether the digit string 22 refers to the number 22 or to 202, 220, 2020, 2200, or to any other combination of two 2s and voids. In the beginning this problem was solved by inserting spaces between the symbols. Eventually, a symbol for 0 was invented. There is evidence that this system – with the symbol for 0 – was fully in use by 500 CE (see Ifrah (1998) for a review; see also Seife (2000) for a discussion of

place coding system

system in which the meaning of a sign not only depends on its form but also on its position in a string; is used for instance in Arabic numerals

Figure 1.3 The history of Hindu-Arabic numbers.
This figure shows how digits were written in various periods of time. Notice that the number 0 was not initially part of numbering systems.

Source: Butterworth (1999, p. 91).

the history of the number 0). The system was adopted and extended by the Arabs and subsequently taken up in Western Europe. The transition via the Arabs changed the order of the digits (i.e. the rightmost stood for the units, the second rightmost for the tens, etc.) and resulted in our current practice of calling them Arabic numerals.

It is widely believed that the Greek and the Roman number notation hindered the development of mathematics in these cultures. The power of the Indian/Arabic notation for arithmetic insights and mathematical operations must not be underestimated. Just try it: give the solution to the problem 'eight times seven' and then to the problem '9 × 6'. Research has shown that students need more than one second extra to solve simple mathematical questions in verbal form (also when the problems are spoken) than in Arabic form. In addition, the place-value system of the Arabic notation allows humans to represent large and complicated numbers is a compact form. So, seven hundred and thirty-four thousand, six hundred and forty-two becomes 734,642.

Interim summary

- Science largely depends on counting and measuring. The first written forms of counting consisted of lines in bones and stones.

- Because it is difficult to discern more than four lines in a glance, the tallies were grouped. The grouping usually occurred in fives (i.e. base 5 system).

Interim summary (continued)

■ Gradually a separate symbol was used for five and multiples of five.

■ Later number systems were based on multiples of 10 (i.e. base 10 system).

■ Number names indicate that the invention of numbers was a slow process; it took quite some time before a useful system was discovered.

■ The Greek and Roman number systems were deficient because their notation did not assign a meaning to the place of the digits. Such a place coding system was developed in India. This required the invention of a symbol for 0.

1.4   The classical world

The presence of written records marks the distinction between prehistory and history. As indicated above, the invention of writing happened independently in China, the Fertile Crescent, and America. Because only the developments in the Fertile Crescent are important within the history of psychology, we will limit our discussion to these civilisations and the ones that followed them.

The Fertile Crescent

The two most important civilisations in the Fertile Crescent for the origin of Western culture were Ancient Mesopotamia and Ancient Egypt. They both started keeping written records and developed a number system. Whether the inventions in both cultures occurred independently or whether there were some contacts, is still a matter of debate.

Ancient Egypt

Two other main contributions from the Egyptians were geometrical knowledge (e.g. calculating the area of a triangle and a circle or determining the volume of a pyramid) and the devising of a calendar consisting of 12 months of 30 days and an extra 5 days at the end of the year.

Ancient Mesopotamia

Mathematical knowledge was more sophisticated in Mesopotamia. In Babylonia, for instance, their number system was superior and they also mastered the basics of algebraic equations. One of the areas in which they applied their mathematical knowledge was astronomy, which they used for their calendar and to determine the times for planting and harvesting (in addition to astrology used to predict the king's fate). They kept maps of the heavens, which allowed them to gain insight into the motions of the 'wandering stars' – the Sun, the Moon, Mercury, Venus, Mars, Jupiter and Saturn. Some of their maps were used millennia later to search for recurring patterns in, for instance, eclipses and comets.

Conditions for growth in knowledge

Contemplating the conditions that made the growth of science possible in the cultures of the Fertile Crescent, Lindberg (1992) identified the following qualities: political stability, urbanisation, patronage and the availability of a writing system that was easy enough to be learned by enough people so that a critical mass could be reached. He claimed that the same factors explained why other cultures experienced similar spurts of knowledge.

What do you think?

Lindberg described several factors that were of importance for the growth of science. Can you order them? For instance, how important is political stability? As we will see in the next chapters, the scientific revolution started in the seventeenth century. Was this a less turbulent century in Europe than the sixteenth or the eighteenth century?

The Greeks

The start of philosophy

philosophy

critical reflection on the universe and human functioning; started in Ancient Greece

Without doubt the Greeks in the beginning borrowed heavily from Egypt and Mesopotamia. However, they soon added their own knowledge. They were probably the first culture that started to ask serious questions about the nature of the world they lived in. This was the beginning of **philosophy** around 600 BCE. One of the questions pondered was whether the foundations of life were constant or ever-changing. Heraclitus (535–475 BCE), for instance, argued that everything was constantly changing and that even if you did the same thing twice, it was different because the conditions were no longer exactly the same. Others argued that at the end of the explanatory road of the perceivable changing phenomena, there had to be something fixed and unchangeable. This culminated in Plato's (427–348 BCE) distinction between the realm of eternal, never-changing ideal forms and the realm of the ever changing material reality in which these forms or ideas are imperfectly realised. Because of this distinction, Plato came to assert that the true path to knowledge was the inward path of reasoning rather than the outward path of perception. People are born with innate knowledge of the ideal reality and, unlike animals, can uncover this knowledge by using their reason.

KEY FIGURE

Plato

- Greek philosopher (427–348 BCE).
- Founder of the Academy in Athens.
- Recorded the dialogues of Socrates.
- Made a distinction between the realm of eternal, never-changing ideal forms and the realm of the ever-changing material reality in which these forms or ideas are imperfectly realised (an analogy used here is that we are in a cave and only see the shadows of the real forms).
- Method of knowledge: rationalism (truth is based on thinking not on information from the senses; humans have innate knowledge that can be recovered through deductive reasoning).
- Plato's views appealed to the Christian churches and, therefore, his books were among the most widely available in the late Roman Empires and the Middle Ages.
- Also strongly influenced René Descartes (Chapter 2).

Achievements in scientific knowledge

The Greeks also had quite sophisticated models of the cosmos and the movements of the stars and the planets, culminating in the book *Almagest* by Claudius Ptolemy in Alexandria (Egypt) around 150 CE. They also made major strides in geometry (Euclid) and in medical treatment (Hippocrates, Galen).

The foundation of schools

Another quality of the Greeks was the (relatively) widespread use of reading and writing, with some very prolific authors. This had partly to do with the fact that this culture saw the emergence of a class of literate individuals who hired themselves out for teaching. In addition to these teachers, four different schools were established in Athens, which continued to educate pupils for centuries. The first was the Academy founded by Plato in 388 BCE. The second was the Lyceum established by Aristotle in 335 BCE. Previously, Aristotle had been a member of Plato's school for 20 years, but some years after Plato's death he established his own school, presumably because his opinions started to deviate too much from the Platonian view. Much more than Plato, Aristotle was an empirically guided scholar, who based his knowledge on careful observation of reality. For instance, he was one of the first to describe animals in great detail. His *History of Animals* mentioned more than 500 species of animals, often based on skilful dissection. He also wrote extensively on human physiology and psychology. Aristotle's work on human anatomy was later extended by Herophilus, Erasistramus (who were both involved in the first systematic dissection of the human body) and Galen (see Chapter 5).

Plato's and Aristotle's schools were later joined by the Stoa (312 BCE) and the Garden of Epicurus (307), which are both still famous for the lifestyle they promoted

KEY FIGURE

Aristotle

- Greek philosopher (384–322 BCE).

- Student of Plato.

- Founder of the Lyceum in Athens.

- Contributed to many subjects, such as:
  - Biology (careful descriptions of animals and plants)
  - Logic (defined the rules of logical thinking)
  - Metaphysics (model of the cosmos consisting of the earth surrounded by different spheres and made of five elements: aether, air, earth, fire, water; animistic elements)
  - Psychology (his book *De Anima* [On the Soul] would be central in teachings on psychology from the Renaissance until well into the eighteenth century)

- Knowledge less based on reason than with Plato; also room for observation.

- Would become the most popular author in the Renaissance; initially led to some tensions with the Roman Catholic Church.

(the Stoic approach based on self-control, fortitude and detachment from distracting emotions vs. the Epicurean approach based on a virtuous and temperate life with the enjoyment of simple pleasures obtained by knowledge and friendship).

Expansion of the Ancient Greek culture

After the Greek expansion under Alexander the Great (356–323 BCE) Greek culture was propagated over a much wider area expanding from Egypt to India, and including the whole Fertile Crescent. This created a completely new dynamic of interactions which became known as the Hellenistic culture. After Alexander the Great's death the empire fell apart into different states governed by his generals. One of the most successful (next to the Greek city-states) was Egypt, where Alexandria became a major cultural beacon with a massive library.

The Romans

Assimilation of Greek culture

By 200 BCE the Roman Empire had already expanded well outside the Italian peninsula and started to annex the Greek provinces. Because the Romans had much admiration for and interest in the Greek culture, this did not lead to its collapse. Rather the Greek methods and learning were transferred to Rome, where there was already quite a strong Greek presence and where many educated people mastered Ancient Greek and visited the Greek schools as part of their education. According to the Roman writer Horace, Rome might have captured Greece militarily and politically, but the artistic and intellectual conquest belonged to the Greeks (as cited in Lindberg (1992, p. 134).

The Hellenistic World, cities and empires in 240 BCE.

The Roman Empire at its largest (around 100 CE).

Emphasis on practical knowledge

One major difference between the Romans and the Greeks was that the Romans were much more interested in practical questions than the philosophical debates that pre-occupied the Greeks. Therefore, the transfer of Greek knowledge did not so much involve the subtleties of metaphysics or the advanced levels of Greek mathematics, astronomy, and anatomy, but subjects of practical value and intrinsic appeal. For the same reason, the Roman legacy is much more dominated by technological inventions and improvements (e.g. their road-building and invention of road maps) than by their profound philosophical writings.

Interim summary

- Civilisations in the Fertile Crescent:
  - Ancient Mesopotamia: mathematics (algebra, astronomy, calendar)
  - Ancient Egypt: geometrical knowledge, calendar, hieroglyphs.
- Ancient Greeks
  - Birthplace of philosophy (Heraclitus, Socrates, Plato, Aristotle)
  - Astronomy (Ptolemy)
  - Geometry (Euclid) and medical treatment (Hippocrates, Galen)
  - Four schools of Athens:
    - Academy (Plato)
    - Lyceum (Aristotle)
    - Stoa (self control)
    - Garden of Epicurus (enjoyment of simple pleasures)
  - Under Alexander the Great big expansion and interactions with other cultures leading to what is called the Hellenistic culture.
- Ancient Romans
  - Assimilated the Greek methods and knowledge
  - Were more interested in technological advances than in philosophy.

1.5   The late Roman empires, the Arab Empire and the Middle Ages

Towards the end of the second century CE the time of political stability and patronage in the Roman Empire began to fade away. Civil wars gave rise to the division in the East and the West Empires around 300.

The Byzantine Empire

Whereas Rome was situated in the West Empire, the east civilisation or the Byzantine Empire, to which Greece belonged, was much stronger and more science-friendly. Its capital was Constantinople (currently Istanbul in Turkey). During much of its history it was also known as the Empire of the Greeks because of the dominance of the Greek language and culture. It lasted till 1453 when Constantinople fell to the Ottoman Turks (although there had been a few upheavals in the thirteenth century when Constantinople was attacked and the crusaders established the Roman Empire between 1204 and 1261).

The Byzantine Empire around 500 CE.

Preservation of the Ancient Greek legacy

Intriguingly, despite nearly 1,000 years of relative prosperity and political stability, Byzantine science never reached the same level as that of the Ancient Greeks. The main contribution of Byzantium to the history of science seems to have been the preservation of the legacy of the Ancient Greeks.

Role of religion

The main factor that is quoted for the decline of scientific advancement (also in Western Europe) is the emergence and eventual dominance of the Christian religion (see e.g. Lindberg 1992). Although it has often been claimed that the halting of science was the result of active opposition by the Christian religion, this does not seem to be completely true (although there are examples of unpleasant standoffs as we will see further on). For centuries, religious orders and schools were the main conservators and proponents of the intellectual achievements. A more likely explanation is that they simply were not interested in natural science and considered it as inferior knowledge (on par with manual skills). Their attention was much more directed towards religion-related and cultural topics. Not only did the Christian religion have to defend its position against rival contenders, there were also internal divisions, which eventually led to the schism between Roman Catholicism and Eastern Orthodoxy in the eleventh century. As a consequence of the change of focus the brightest pupils were directed away from scientific issues and science was often associated with paganism.

What do you think?

How has science been presented in your primary and secondary education? Was it seen as less interesting and creative than literature, art and rational thinking?

The Arab Empire

Expansion of the Arab Empire

The Arabian peninsula had been untouched by Alexander's military campaigns. As a result, it was not very much affected by Byzantine culture either. In one of the cities of the peninsula, Mecca, Mohammed was born late in the sixth century. He preached a new religion, Islam, on the basis of a series of revelations, which were preserved in the Koran, one of the first books in written Arabic.

By the time of Mohammed's death in 632 his followers had taken over the Arabian peninsula and were pushing northwards. By 661 they had occupied the Fertile Crescent and Persia. By 750 they controlled the north of Africa and nearly all of Spain, where Cordoba and Toledo became important intellectual centres.

The Arab Empire around 750 CE.

Scientific achievements

Interest in science got a strong impetus when in 749 the dynasty of the Abbasid family came to power and started a period of stronger political stability and patronage. Around this time the translation of Greek works into Arabic started. Agents were sent to Byzantium in search of manuscripts and a research institute was founded in Baghdad: the House of Wisdom (ninth century). At the same time, Islamic scholars advanced Greek knowledge in medicine, astronomy, mathematics and optics. For instance, Ibn al-Haytham's book *Optics*, written in the eleventh century, far surpassed its predecessors. As we have seen in a previous section, they also adopted the Indian number system and turned it into a much more efficient mathematical system than what the Greeks and the Romans had achieved. In particular, al-Khwarizmi's book *Algebra* (around 820) was a milestone.

The remains of the Western Roman Empire

Science arguably received its biggest blow in the Western part of the Roman Empire, including Rome itself. Already before the Roman Empire fell to the German tribes there was a sharp decline in scientific endeavour because of the political upheaval and economic downfall.

Decreased access to Greek knowledge

One factor that contributed to this decline was the diminishing knowledge of the Greek language. As argued by Myers-Scotton (2006), the motivation to learn a second language decreases as a function of economic dominance. In particular, members of non-dominant groups are eager to learn a language in addition to their mother tongue, in order to improve their life circumstances and (in the case of scientists) to enlarge their audience. As a consequence, Myers-Scotton argues, the 'universal language' (lingua franca) of science has always closely followed the shifts in economic dominance (and is likely to continue to do so in the future). Because the Romans dominated the other nations, it became increasingly unnecessary to study languages other than Latin, whereas more and more individuals became inclined to learn Latin as a second language, rather than Greek. As a result, a language barrier emerged between the Romans and Greek science. This was partly alleviated by an increased availability of Latin translations, but translations did not conserve the full richness of the Greek legacy. Only the works that were thought of interest to the Romans made it into Latin and were preserved. For instance, when Christianity became the dominant religion in the third century, there was much more interest in Plato's writings than in those of the other philosophers, because Plato's views of a higher, ideal world of which we only see the shadows, coincided with the Church's view. As a consequence, Plato's works were among the most widely available.

The contribution of the Catholic Church

Dark Ages

name given in the Renaissance to the Middle Ages, to refer to the lack of independent and scientific thinking in that age

After the fall of Rome in 476 and the take over by Germanic tribes, the Catholic Church became the patron of learning through the creation and support of schools. As in the Byzantine Empire, however, science was not at the forefront of the education (to put it mildly), which was centred on theological, ecclesiastical and literary knowledge. In addition, Catholic education was not the sort to foster critical thinking in students (see the scholastic method on pages 13–14). As a result, scientific knowledge not only stalled but fell back from the level it had reached at the height of the Roman Empire. For this reason, scholars in the fourteenth and the fifteenth centuries tended to refer to the Middle Ages in Western Europe as the 'Dark Ages'.

Interim summary

The post-Roman developments

- Byzantine Empire
  - Eastern part of the Roman Empire; capital Constantinople; lasted till 1453.
  - Preservation of the legacy of the Ancient Greeks.

- Arab Empire
  - Founded on Islam; contained the Fertile Crescent.
  - Translation and extension of the Greek works.
  - Particularly strong on medicine, astronomy, mathematics (algebra) and optics.
  - Occupied most of Spain.

- Western Roman Empire
  - Largest decline in scientific knowledge.
  - Catholic Church main preserver; not very science-oriented.
  - In the Renaissance referred to as the 'Dark Ages'.

1.6   Turning the tide in the West

The foundation of schools and universities

The revival of learning in the West has a long history. Lindberg (1992) identifies a whole series of small steps. First, there were the efforts of Charles the Great around 800 to improve the education in his Carolingian Empire, in particular in the capital, Aachen. Second, as a result of better agricultural techniques (which included the invention and use of the plough) there was a population explosion between 1000 and 1200. This resulted in renewed urbanisation and the foundation of larger cathedral schools with broader educational aims. These schools in turn increased the appetite for knowledge in the intellectually able, which created a market for independent teachers, called masters. To improve their living conditions, the teachers organised themselves in guilds, which they called 'universities'. Bit by bit the guilds acquired wealth and started to lobby for tax exemptions and patronage. The first charters leading to independent university status were awarded in Bologna (1150), Paris (1200) and Oxford (1220).

Students who finished the master's programme at the universities had the right to teach everywhere (*ius ubique docendi*), which led to increased mobility of the masters and a harmonisation of the curricula. At the same time, scholars became aware of the much richer cultures on the outskirts of Western Europe and the translation of Arabic and Greek texts into Latin reached a high point. The former mainly happened in Spain, the latter in Italy.

Inclusion of Greek and Arabic texts in the curricula

Many of the Greek and Arabic books were integrated within the curriculum without problems, as they were clearly superior to what was available and often filled a void. This was, for instance, the case for Euclid's *Elements*, Ptolemy's *Almagest*, al-Khwarizmi's *Algebra*, Ibn al-Haytham's *Optics*, the Greek and Arabic works on medicine and the *Canon of Medicine* written by the Arab scholar Avicenna. There were more difficulties with Aristotle's works. For many scientifically minded scholars, his views and methodology were more inspiring than those of Plato and the Christian theology that had been built on it. This led to some skirmishes at the University of Paris (but not at other universities), where the teaching of Aristotle was forbidden first by the Catholic bishop in 1210 and later by the papal legate. However, in practice this did not prevent the works from being widely available and by 1255 the University of Paris followed the other universities and put Aristotle at the centre of the teaching in philosophy.

One of the problems with Aristotle was that he claimed that the universe, including the Earth, was eternal, without beginning and end, whereas the Bible clearly indicated the beginning (Genesis) and the end (the Last Judgement) of life. This aspect of Aristotle's view called into question the dependence of life on God, the creator, and his power to intervene in worldly matters. Another problem was that Aristotle saw the soul as the actualisation of the potentialities of the body, which meant that the soul could not exist without a body and ended together with the body. Needless to say, such a view was incompatible with the Christian doctrine of an independent and immortal soul.

Most universities sailed around these contentious issues by not including them in the parts of Aristotle they were teaching. However, the issues were more than isolated differences of view. They arose because Aristotle had come to his conclusions on the basis of rational activity (logic) and naturalistic observations rather than biblical revelation and church tradition. As these were the elements in Aristotle's philosophy that attracted the scholars, other disagreements were soon to follow. By 1277 the Catholic bishop of Paris, Etienne Tempier, already had a list of 219 propositions related to Aristotelian philosophy that he forbad to be taught at the University of Paris.

A cultural movement based on imitation of the Greek and Roman civilisations

Renaissance

cultural movement from the fourteenth to the seventeenth century based on a rediscovery and imitation of the classical Greek and Roman civilisations

The availability of the ancient texts not only influenced scientists but also society as a whole. Slowly but surely the Middle Ages gave way to the Renaissance, a cultural movement based on an imitation of the classical Greek and Roman civilisations. This started in Italy in the fourteenth century and lasted until well into the seventeenth century. Its presence was most visible in architecture and painting (where perspective was discovered) and it produced artists such as Leonardo da Vinci, Jan van Eyck, Michelangelo and Raphael.

This period also saw the return of scientists in Western Europe of a stature high enough to be remembered today. One of them was Nicolaus Copernicus (1473–1543), who started to question Plato's and Ptolemy's conviction that the Earth was the centre of the universe and who we will meet again in Chapter 2. Other noteworthy names were Andreas Vesalius (1514–1564), who restarted and dramatically extended the Greek studies on human anatomy (including dissection), and Gerardus

Mercator (1512–1594) who developed a new technique to make more accurate maps of the world.

The Protestant Reformation

Protestant Reformation

movement against the Roman Catholic Church, which was important for the development of science, because it emphasised the need for education, critical thinking, hard work and worldly success

The Renaissance also saw the birth of Martin Luther who revolted against the perceived greed and corruption of the Papacy. Eventually, this led to the Protestant Reformation starting in 1516, which resulted in large parts of Europe no longer being under the control of the Roman Catholic Church (most of present-day Germany, the Netherlands, Scandinavia and Switzerland). In the middle of the upheaval, Henry VIII of England founded the Church of England and joined the Reformed movement, although the Church of England always kept its independence from the other Protestant movements. The Reformed Churches stressed much more than the Roman Catholic Church the need for education and critical thinking (in order to be able to read and understand the Bible) and the importance of hard work and worldly success. As indicated above, according to the sociologist Max Weber, this is one of the reasons why the Protestant countries started to outperform the Catholic countries scientifically and economically. Much later David McClelland (1961) would indeed show that achievement motivation was higher in children of the reformed countries than in

The religious map of Europe c. 1600.

children of Catholic countries, and Bradburn and Berlew (1961) were able to correlate the increase in references to achievement in British children's books with industrial growth one generation later.

Book printing

Interwoven with all these developments (both at the origin of them and heavily relied on by them) was the invention of book printing in Europe. First (by 1300), letters were carved in a woodblock and printed on cloth, which allowed mass production of a small number of pages. Later (around 1450) movable printing was invented by Johannes Gutenberg, a technique in which individual metal letters were placed in a matrix and could be recycled for other texts. This allowed cheap production of all types of texts, leading to a rapid and massive availability of information to everyone who was interested, not only in Latin but increasingly in the native languages as well.

Colonisation of the world

Finally, the European powers had started their exploration and colonisation of the world, beginning with the occupation of shores in Africa and Asia, and the discovery of America in 1492. This would rapidly turn into a race between the different nations to conquer as much as possible of the newly discovered territories, increasing the demand for technical and scientific inventions that could be of use. It also firmly established that the Earth was round and not flat as widely believed before.

Interim summary

Post-medieval developments in Western Europe

- The establishment of (cathedral) schools and universities
  - Increased mobility of the scholars
  - Discovery of the Ancient Greek and Arabic texts
  - Growing impact of Aristotle's works
- A cultural movement
  - Increased interest in and imitation of the Ancient Greek and Roman cultures (Renaissance)
  - Increasing status of science and scientists
- The Protestant Reformation
  - Rebellion against the dominance of the Catholic Church
  - More importance to education, critical thinking, hard work and worldly success
- Book printing
  - Rapid and massive availability of information
- Colonisation of the world
  - Need for technological and scientific innovations.

1.7   Focus on: The limits of history writing

In the preceding sections we have depicted the broad lines of the history of science up to the seventeenth century, as it can be found in current history books. However, we do not want to conclude this chapter without giving consideration to the limits of history writing that have become clear in the past decades and which have questioned history writing as the unearthing of *the* truth. First, we discuss some biases that are – often implicitly – present in nearly all historical accounts. Then we discuss the implications for this particular chapter and the historical chapters that are still to follow.

What do you think?

Which type of history writing do you prefer? One focusing on individuals and their struggles to get their ideas accepted, or one focusing on the ideas themselves and the impact they had? List the pros and cons of each approach and keep them close to hand as we progress through the book.

Biases in history writing

Looking at historical writings, it is not difficult to discern a number of biases in them. Here we discuss just a few of the most important.

Too much centred on persons

A typical characteristic of historical writings is that they tend to focus on individuals. As a result, the history of science is presented as a succession of discoveries and insights made by geniuses that far exceeded the intellectual level around them. For instance, in Chapter 2 we will discuss the ground-breaking contributions of Galilei and Newton. After reading them you might wonder what would have happened to science if they had never lived. The answer, however, in all likelihood is that it would not have mattered much. As Gratzer (2002) reflects in the introduction of his book *Eurekas and euphorias: The Oxford book of scientific anecdotes*:

> Science differs from other realms of human endeavour in that its substance does not derive from the activity of those who practise it; the nature of the atom or the structure of DNA would have been discovered if Bohr and Rutherford, and Watson and Crick had not lived. It would merely have taken longer. Science is above all a collective activity. *L'art c'est moi, la science c'est nous*, was how Claude Bernard, the father of modern physiology, put it. In this sense individuals are of minor importance.

Centring histories of writing on individual scientists makes the reading more interesting, as magisterially demonstrated by Bill Bryson (2003) in his science history directed to a wide audience, but is essentially wrong. It has been shown over and over again

zeitgeist

word used in the history of science to indicate that the time was right for a certain discovery; the discovery did not originate from a single genius, but from a much wider development leading to the discovery

that discoveries have been prepared over a long time (and often have happened independently at several places) and that the time simply was right for them. Of course, there was the genius of the individual who brought everything together and made the decisive move, but in all likelihood other individuals would have come to the same conclusion around the same time or shortly after (as ironically again illustrated in Bryson's book, when he amusingly tells how virtually no discovery is entirely due to the person history remembers for it). In this respect, historians talk about the importance of the zeitgeist, a German word that refers to the spirit of the age, the intellectual climate of the period.

The Matthew effect

Matthew effect

the tendency to give more credit to well-known scientists than they deserve; increases the perceived impact of these scientists

One of the reasons why histories of science are centred on individuals is that more credit is given to eminent scientists than they actually deserve. Contributions from less well-known colleagues and contemporaries are ascribed to the most famous person of the era, a tendency known as the Matthew effect (the effect got its name from a line of the Matthew Gospel in the Bible: 'For unto every one that hath shall be given, and he shall have abundance: but from him that hath not shall be taken away even that which he hath'). As a result of the Matthew effect, individuals become the condensation of the intellectual climate that was shared by a larger group.

Hindsight bias

Another reason why individual scholars get more prominence in history books than they usually deserve is that we have a tendency to assume that they knew more than they actually did. On the basis of what we now know, we assume that the same knowledge was shared by the person who first described the phenomenon. We also have a tendency to believe that the evidence presented by that individual was much more convincing than it actually was. After all, classical discoveries must be clear-cut discoveries, not a slow and messy unearthing of evidence that took decennia to sort out.

Ethnocentrism

Another feature of history writing is that authors have a tendency to attach excessive weight to the contribution of their own group and the group of their readers. So, Anglo-Saxon reviews of the history of science are too much centred on the contribution of the Ancient Greek, Latin, British and American scholars. The Matthew effect and the hindsight bias are applied to increase the dominance of one's own research group over that of other groups. In addition, writings about their contributions are much more easily available. This results in a tendency to give too much credit to the input of economically dominant groups. For instance, at several places in this book we were struck by how much easier it is to find information about the American situation than about the developments in other countries, which to some extent biased our coverage of topics.

What do you think?

Would you object having to study a textbook that describes the history of psychology as it happened in Lithuania, Switzerland, Turkey or South Korea?

History reviews are summaries of summaries

The above biases are particularly strong because very few general history books (including the present chapter!) are based on a full analysis of the original sources. Rather they build on other books that summarise part of the history to be described and try to maximise the clarity and the persuasiveness of the message. As a result, an error in one book can be exaggerated and pervade the knowledge of a complete community. This is particularly the case if the information is 'too good not to be true' (see Chapter 7).

History writing: Rewriting or streamlining the past?

History writing and reshaping the past

The big question of course is whether the above biases result in such a distorted account of the past that history writing becomes a reinterpretation of what happened. Such a position has been defended by Thomas Kuhn, one of the main philosophers of science, who we will encounter again in Chapters 4 and 8, when we talk about what makes science. In Kuhn's view, science does not progress via a linear accumulation of new knowledge, and science as we know it now is only one of the possible interpretations of reality. As a result, the present review of the history of science is the view of twenty-first-century scientific psychologists writing for an Anglo-Saxon audience. It gives the illusion of an objective and straightforward account of the progress in science in the past 10,000 years, but may have no overlap at all with the history of science as it will be written within 400 years by an Indian physicist. This is because both histories are just that: interpretations of what may have happened directed by the current set of convictions that are shared within a particular research community.

History writing and simplifying the past

The alternative position is that all the biases mentioned above indeed happen, but are motivated by the need to make the knowledge digestible given the constraints under which it has to be transmitted. According to this position, the present chapter is a simplification of what has happened because it has to be summarised in a chapter of 15,000 words. Although it may contain elements that do not stand up to further scrutiny, these inaccuracies are not meant to reinterpret the past and do not detract from the basic message. They are the result of a streamlining of the rich and often conflicting raw materials that are just too much for us to grasp. For instance, it could rightly be objected that Aristotle's writings are much more contradictory and contain many more ambiguous passages than has been suggested here. Indeed, large numbers of scholars have debated for over 2,000 years about what exactly Aristotle may have meant in some of his passages and to what extent his method of knowledge resembles and differs from the scientific method as we know it now. However, we do not think that any of these nuances would add much to our basic messages that Aristotle has had a large impact on the way scientific thinking emerged and that scholars at a certain point in time struggled to overcome its limitations.

A nice illustration of the limits and the strengths of history writing has been documented by Endersby (2007) in his book *A Guinea Pig's History of Biology: The plants and animals who taught us the facts of life* (although we hasten to say that similar accounts can be found elsewhere). When he discusses Mendel's contribution to genetics in the second half of the nineteenth century, he first mentions the story you can find in many (popular) books:

> [Gregor] Mendel was obscure in his lifetime, but today most people are aware that he was a simple, uneducated Austrian monk who, while playing around with pea plants in his garden, discovered the basic laws of modern genetics. Yet this break-through was ignored, partly because he was cut off from the scientific world of his day, but also because the one famous scientist he contacted, the botanist Carl von Nägeli, sent Mendel off on a wild goose chase to investigate the genetics of hawk-weeds. Nägeli may even have done this deliberately: jealous of his younger rival's brilliance, he set poor, innocent Mendel to work on a famously intractable group of plants, confident that the monk would never be able to sort them out. Frustrated by his failure, Mendel died in heartbroken obscurity. One final ironic twist to the story is added by the fact that Mendel . . . sent a copy of his paper on peas to Charles Darwin, who never read it. (Endersby 2007, p. 103–4)

This is the type of heartbreaking story that makes history books worthwhile reading! Unfortunately, Endersby goes on to show that nearly every detail is wrong. Here are just a few facts:

- Mendel was not Austrian.
- Mendel had studied both biology and mathematical physics at the University of Vienna, where he had been taught by some of the best-known scientists of the day.
- Mendel did not discover anything by accident; he performed carefully planned and well-designed experiments, for which he could rely on several helpers.
- The scientific society he belonged to had many distinguished members and its journal was widely read; as a consequence, Mendel's work was mentioned in the *Encyclopaedia Britannica*.
- Mendel never sent a copy to Darwin (or at least there is no evidence that he ever did so).
- One of the reasons why Mendel did not pursue his work was that he became the abbot of the abbey.
- Mendel was interested in hawkweeds, because he believed that the big variety in this species would give him more insight.
- The main reason why Mendel did not have the impact he may have wanted, is that he did not understand what was going on. He carefully noted and published the results of his experiments, but was at a loss to explain the underlying mechanisms. The explanation of alleles on chromosomes coming from the father and the mother and leading to dominant or recessive inheritance we are now familiar with and which we attribute to Mendel, only became clear many decades later (involving a whole series of scientists never mentioned except in specialised books). Only then did researchers realise the full importance of Mendel's findings and was he crowned as the father of genetics (the reasons why hawkweeds behave so differently from other plants took nearly one century to be understood).

The story of Mendel nicely illustrates the biases we have mentioned (try to find them!). At the same time, it illustrates that although nearly all the details are wrong, the summary still conveys the basic message that at some point in time (zeitgeist) science was advanced enough to begin to question the mechanisms of inheritance and to look for answers. It is sensationalising and dramatising the history of Mendel to a point that is no longer acceptable in scientific terms (though see Chapter 8), but is still not reinterpreting the past.

Similarly, we are confident that our summary in its broad brushstrokes will stand up to time, despite its unavoidable selectiveness and biases (although we hope to have done better than the Mendel example!). However, nothing prevents you from reading much more about the history of science and filling in the many omissions that give the present chapter a much smoother appearance than is warranted by history.

Interim summary

- History writing always involves simplification and streamlining.
- Therefore, biases easily slip in:
  - Centred on persons rather than on zeitgeist
  - Too much credit is given to a small number of people (Matthew effect)
  - Facts are interpreted on the basis of what happened afterwards (hindsight bias)
  - Too much attention is given to the contribution of the authors' own group (ethnocentrism)
  - History writers often rely on summaries and interpretations made by other writers.

Recommended literature

History is one of the topics well covered in encyclopaedias. For instance, a lot of additional information can be found on www.wikipedia.org, of which we have made use as well. If you prefer books, here are some recommendations:

Prehistory
An easy to read and reasonably accurate review can be found in Bryson, B. (2003) *A short history of nearly everything* (London: Doubleday). The book contains further references to the main sources.

Writing
As you could read, we relied on Manguel, A. (1996) *A history of reading* (London: HarperCollins). If you want to read more about psychological research on reading and writing, see Harley, T.A. (2007) *The psychology of language: From data to theory* (3rd edition) (Hove: Psychology Press).

Numbers
The best book for the history of numerical systems is Ifrah, G. (1998) *The universal history of numbers: From prehistory to the invention of the computer* (London: The Harvill Press). Easy to read introductions to the psychology of number processing can be found in Dehaene, S. (2000) *The number sense: How the mind creates mathematics* (Oxford: Oxford University Press), and Butterworth, B. (1999) *The mathematical brain* (Basingstoke: Macmillan).

History of science
The book we found most useful, in addition to the ones mentioned in Chapter 2, was Lindberg, D.C. (1992) *The beginnings of Western science: The European scientific tradition in philosophical, religious, and institutional context, 600 B.C. to A.D. 1450* (Chicago: The University of Chicago Press).

References

Bird-David, N. (1999) '"Animism" revisited: Personhood, environment, and relational epistemology', *Current Anthropology*, **40**: S67–S91.

Bradburn, N.M. and Berlew, D.G. (1961) 'Need for achievement and English economic growth', *Economic Development and Cultural Change*, **10**: 8–20.

Bryson, B. (2003) *A short history of nearly everything*. London: Doubleday.

Butterworth, B. (1999) *The mathematical brain*. London: Macmillan.

Endersby, J. (2007) *A guinea pig's history of biology: The plants and animals who taught us the facts of life*. London: William Heinemann.

Gratzer, W. (2002) *Eurekas and euphorias: The Oxford book of scientific anecdotes*. Oxford: Oxford University Press.

Hanley, J.R., Masterson, J., Spencer, L.H. and Evans, D. (2004) 'How long do the advantages of learning to read a transparent orthography last? An investigation of the reading skills and reading impairment of Welsh children at 10 years of age', *Quarterly Journal of Experimental Psychology*, **57A**: 1393–410.

Ifrah, G. (1998) *The universal history of numbers: From prehistory to the invention of the computer*. London: The Harvill Press. (Translation of the French original (1994): *Histoire Universelle des chiffres*. Paris: Editions Robert Laffont.)

Leakey, R. and Lewin, R. (1992) *Origins reconsidered: In search of what makes us human*. London: Doubleday.

Lindberg, D.C. (1992) *The beginnings of Western science: The European scientific tradition in philosophical, religious, and institutional context, 600 B.C. to A.D. 1450*. Chicago: The University of Chicago Press.

Manguel, A. (1996) *A history of reading*. London: HarperCollins.

McClelland, D.C. (1961) *The achieving society*. Princeton, NJ: Van Nostrand.

Myers-Scotton, C. (2006) *Multiple voices: An introduction to bilingualism*. Malden, MA: Blackwell Publishing.

Saenger, P. (1997) *Space between words: The origins of silent reading*. Stanford, CA: Stanford University Press.

Seife, C. (2000) *Zero: The biography of a dangerous idea*. London: Souvenir Press.

Weber, M. (1904/1905) 'Die protestantische Ethik und der Geist des Kapitalismus' [Translated in 1905 as The protestant ethic and the spirit of capitalism]. *Archiv für Sozialwissenschaft und Sozialpolitik*, **20**: 1–54; **21**: 1–110.

Ziegler, J.C. and Goswami, U. (2005) 'Reading acquisition, developmental dyslexia, and skilled reading across languages: A psycholinguistic grain size theory', *Psychological Bulletin* **131**: 3–29.

02 The scientific revolution of the seventeenth century

This chapter will cover

Questions to consider

Historical issues addressed in this chapter

- When did the scientific revolution take place?
- Which three developments formed the core of this revolution?
- How did science increase its status and power in the eighteenth and the nineteenth centuries?
- Which four developments helped the establishment of psychology as an independent branch of learning?

Conceptual issues addressed in this chapter

- What impact did the transition from the geocentric to the heliocentric model of the universe have on the Western European society?
- To what extent does our knowledge of the world and the universe depend on the equipment we have?
- How did the changes introduced by Descartes to Aristotle's world view advance the development of science?
- To what extent is it a coincidence that the laws of physics were discovered in the UK?
- What method should a natural philosopher use (i.e. which ideas did eighteenth- and nineteenth-century scholars have about the scientific method)?
- To what extent can present-day humans be considered as the end product of evolution?
- Do scientific discoveries have an impact on people's well-being?

Introduction

Is it not evident, in these last hundred years . . . that almost a new Nature has been re-veal'd to us? that more errours of the School have been detected, more useful Experiments in Philosophy have been made, more Noble Secrets in Opticks, Medicine, Anatomy, Astronomy, discover'd, than in all those credulous and doting Ages from Aristotle to us? so true it is that nothing spreads more fast than Science, when rightly and generally cultivated.

(John Dryden: Essay of Dramatick Poesie, *1668; as cited in Cohen (1994, p. 1))*

In this chapter we continue our quest for the origins of psychology. The word *psychology* did not appear in the literature before 1500 and was not used in the title of an influential book until the 1730s. What happened between the Renaissance and the eighteenth century that made authors use this particular word?

Our discussion falls in two main parts. First we deal with the increasing impact and status of scientific research in Europe. In Chapter 1 we talked about the beginnings of this movement in the Renaissance. In the present chapter we see how this trend gained extra momentum in the seventeenth century as a result of three key developments:

1. The realisation that the Earth did not form the centre of the universe.

2. The realisation that many things on Earth (including the human body) could be understood as (complicated) machines.

3. The actual demonstration that many movements on Earth and in the universe could be described with a handful of relatively simple mathematical equations, which became known as the laws of physics.

scientific revolution

name given to a series of discoveries in the seventeenth century, involving Galilei, Descartes and Newton, that enhanced the status of science in society

Together these three developments and the subsequent enhanced status of scientific research are summarised in history writings as the scientific revolution. Interestingly, this name only became used after the 1930s (Cohen 1994). Before, historians and scientists saw the changes of the seventeenth century more as a continuation of previous developments than as a radical discontinuity with prior thought.

? What do you think?

Cohen (1994) argued that by calling the developments of the seventeenth century a revolution, we changed our perception of what happened. Can you think of other instances in which the name given to a phenomenon biases its interpretation?

The second part of our discussion deals with those developments in scientific research and the society at large in the eighteenth and nineteenth centuries that specifically led to the development of psychology as the scientific study of the human mind and human behaviour. They are:

1. The impact of Darwin's evolutionary theory.

2. Increased attention to the functioning of humans.

3. Medical studies dealing with the nervous system and human responses to physical stimuli.

4. The development of statistics, which allowed researchers to find systematic patterns in samples of data, which individually were not predictable.

We start with the three events that marked the onset of the scientific revolution. Because of the biases described in the previous chapter, these events are mostly associated with individual scholars in history books (respectively Copernicus and Galilei; Descartes; and Newton). However, it is important to keep in mind that they were broad events, involving hundreds and possibly thousands of the most influential thinkers.

2.1   From a geocentric to a heliocentric model of the universe

In the sixteenth century there was extra interest in astronomy because the Julian calendar, used since the days of Julius Caesar, was getting out of phase with reality. Because a year comprises 365.2425 days, the Julian calendar (based on three years of 365 days and one leap year of 366 days) underestimated the length of a year by 11 minutes, meaning that one day was 'missed' every 134 years. As a consequence, by the sixteenth century the calendar was already 11 days short of target. Eventually, this was corrected when in 1582 the Julian calendar was replaced by the Gregorian calendar (which is still in use today) and Thursday 4 October was followed by Friday 15 October. However, in order to get the new calendar right, a lot of fine-grained astronomic observations and calculations were needed. One of the people who got involved in this effort was the Polish astronomer Nicolaus Copernicus (1473–1543).

The geocentric model of the universe in the sixteenth century

The Earth as the centre of the universe

The length of a year depends on the movements of the Sun and the Earth relative to each other. These two celestial objects were the main players in the then known universe, which in addition comprised six wandering stars (the Moon, Venus, Mercury, Mars, Jupiter and Saturn) and the fixed stars that could be seen with the naked eye.

geocentric model

model of the universe in which the Earth is at the centre; was dominant until the seventeenth century

The model of the universe that was used in the sixteenth century was originally the model proposed by Aristotle (who built on others) and Ptolemy. The universe of Aristotle was a finite universe with the Earth at its centre; that is, it was a geocentric model (figure 2.1). Around the Earth circled the wandering stars, starting with the Moon, followed by Mercury, Venus, the Sun, Mars, Jupiter and Saturn. Beyond Saturn there was the turning sphere of the fixed stars, the stars that stayed stationary relative to one another.

Two distinct regions were discerned in the universe: one from the Earth up to the Moon (the sub-lunar region) and one from the Moon to the end of the universe (the super-lunar region). It was believed that nothing existed outside the universe, not even space.

The five elements of the Aristotelian universe

Everything in the super-lunar region was made of an incorruptible element called aether. As a consequence, all stars were viewed as faultless objects moving in perfect harmony. The sub-lunar region was less orderly. Everything there was a mixture of four elements – air, earth, fire and water – and showed growth and decay, generation and corruption. Each of the four elements had a natural place: for earth and water this was near the centre of the Earth (which is why soil, water and solid objects fall to the Earth); for air and fire this was near the Moon's orbit (which is why air and flames go up). Aristotle assumed that all objects had a propensity to go in a straight line to

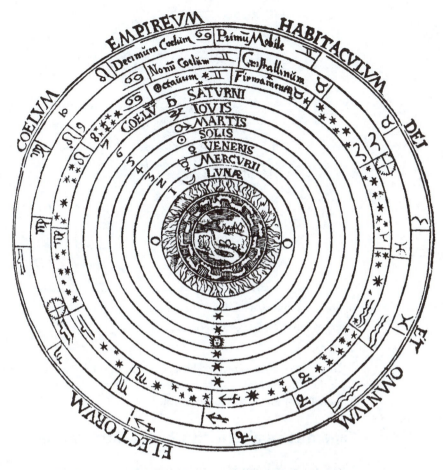

Figure 2.1 Depiction of the Aristotelian universe in the Renaissance.

Source: Royal Astronomical Society / Science Photo Library Ltd.

their natural place (either upward or downward). No other motions were possible, unless they had an external cause (e.g. chariots that were drawn by horses).

The addition of epicycles

Ptolemy noticed a problem with the Aristotelian universe. If he looked on successive nights at the wandering stars (always at the same time), he saw that in general they moved a bit to the east relative to the previous night. However, the displacements were not fixed, as would be expected if the wandering stars were circling around the Earth. Occasionally the displacement seemed to slow down, to stop, to turn into a displacement in the opposite direction, then again to stop and resume its usual eastward movement. (Incidentally, you can observe these movements yourself if you have enough spare nights, and compare them to Ptolemy's observations.) To capture this aspect of the movements, Ptolemy introduced the term 'epicycles'. These are small cycles the wandering stars make in addition to their main orbit around the Earth (figure 2.2). The introduction of epicycles allowed Ptolemy to develop a model with a better fit to the reality he observed, but it did not take away all the oddities. Therefore Ptolemy had to introduce higher order epicycles for some wandering stars.

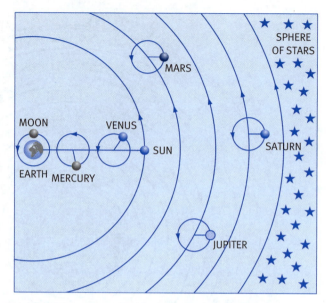

Figure 2.2 Ptolemy's model of the universe with simplified epicycles.

Source: Vik Dhillon. Reproduced with permission.

In the sixteenth century, the geocentric model was still in use. By this time, the Catholic Church had adopted it, because it fitted in well with their teaching that God had created a universe around Man.

Copernicus's alternative heliocentric model

The Sun as the centre of the universe

Aristotle's model was not the only one that had been proposed in the ancient cultures. Several authors had suggested the possibility of the Earth orbiting the Sun rather than the reverse, but their views had never been taken seriously. Copernicus became interested in this model and saw it as a valid alternative (figure 2.3). In Copernicus's **heliocentric model,** there was first the Sun, then Mercury, Venus, the Earth (orbited by the Moon), followed by Mars, Jupiter, Saturn and the sphere of immobile stars. Other features of the model were that one turn of the Earth around the Sun took one year (instead of the daily orbit of the Sun around the Earth) and that the Earth spun around its axis in one day, causing the alternation of day and night and the movements of the fixed stars. Later, Copernicus also had to add epicycles to his model, in order to predict the movements of the wandering stars more precisely. (The problem of the epicycles would only be solved much later when Kepler realised that the orbits were not circular but elliptical.)

Why Copernicus waited to publish his model

Copernicus wrote a short commentary on his heliocentric model in 1514 and made it available to a few friends, who had approached him with respect to the calendar problems. Although the model was widely discussed, Copernicus was not interested

heliocentric model

model of the universe in which the Sun is at the centre; started to dominate after Galilei's seventeenth-century book

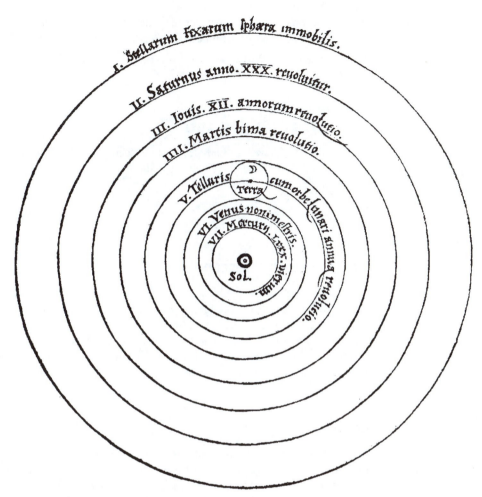

Figure 2.3 Copernicus's model of the universe.
This picture does not include the epicycles Copernicus had to add in order to fit the movements of the wandering stars.

in publishing it (yet). Only shortly before his death (in 1543) could he be convinced to have the book printed. The popular story is that Copernicus was afraid of the response he would get from the Roman Catholic Church (which was his employer). Another reason may have been that Copernicus did not feel the evidence for his model was strong enough to justify publication. Chalmers (1999) reports the following objections Copernicus would have been able to foresee from his colleagues:

- What is the practical utility of the model relative to Ptolemy's? (In the end, both were nearly of the same complexity, because of the need for epicycles.)

- If the Earth moves, why is it that if you throw a stone from a high tower, it ends exactly at the bottom of the tower (and not a few metres away from the tower, as you would expect if the Earth moved so rapidly)?

- If the Earth spins around its axis, why is it that people and objects are not flung from the surface (as would happen if they stood on a spinning wheel)?

- Would this model not predict that the stars should increase and decrease in magnitude as a function of where the Earth is (nearby or far away)?

- Why does the Moon keep following the Earth? Why is it not orbiting the Sun as well?

What do you think?

Do you know the answers to the objections against Copernicus's heliocentric model? For instance, why does a stone thrown from a tower land at the bottom? If you are in a fast moving train and you drop something, does it fall straight down? Why?

Galilei uses a telescope

Because of the many problems with Copernicus's model, it failed to have much impact and it was Ptolemy's model that was used to calculate the Gregorian calendar. If Copernicus's model was taught, it was mentioned as an example of a faulty model, until the time of Galileo Galilei (1564–1642). In 1609 Galilei heard of Dutch inventors who had made a 'telescope' by using a combination of a convex and a concave lens. Apparently this telescope made it possible to have distant objects look nearer and larger.

Galilei's observations

Galilei was not only one of the finest scholars of his time; he was also a handy craftsman. In less than a week he built his own telescope. Although he immediately saw the military use of the instrument (and seized the opportunity to get a permanent position at the University of Padua with a big salary increase), he turned his eyes to the sky. Even though the telescope only magnified ninefold, he saw some amazing things:

1. There were many more stars than were visible to the naked eye.

2. The surface of the Moon was not smooth as claimed by Aristotle, but comprised mountains and craters (Galilei could discern the mountains because some surfaces in the dark half were lit when he looked at a half moon).

3. Jupiter had four moons.

4. The sizes of Mars and Venus changed. In addition, Venus had phases just like the Moon (figure 2.4).

Response of the Roman Catholic Church

On the basis of this evidence Galilei argued that Copernicus's heliocentric model was much more likely than Ptolemy's geocentric model. Unfortunately for Galilei, this time the Roman Catholic Church decided to take action against him for questioning their doctrine. Galilei was summoned to Rome and put under house arrest for the final years of his life.

Figure 2.4 Changes in the magnitude and phases of Venus showing that Venus orbits the Sun with a diameter smaller than that of the Earth.

Source: Photographed at the TBGS observatory by Chris Proctor. Reproduced with permission.

The popular account of this episode is that of a religion fanatically (and desperately) defending its position against the growing influence of science, as illustrated by the following excerpt:

In June 1632, Galileo Galilei, unquestionably the greatest scientist of his age, was formally humiliated by the Roman Catholic church for promulgating the heretical doctrine that the Earth revolved around the Sun. He was not burned at the stake, nor was he imprisoned, but he was officially muzzled and confined under house arrest for the rest of his life. This action threw the intellectual community in Catholic lands into a state of fear and circumspection, just as it had been intended to. Elsewhere, however, the church's grand symbolic gesture was greeted with a mixture of ridicule and outrage, galvanising the movement towards the secularisation of science that would reach its final destination in the 19th century . . .

A treasurable typographical error in the book refers to a 'Professor of Scared Scripture', and that of course is what the authorities were. They understood that to challenge any orthodoxy threatened, like pulling a stray thread of wool in a cardigan, to unravel the whole false fabric of theology. It is impossible not to read the transcript of the trial without wanting to shout out in rage: Italy produced no physical scientist of the slightest importance for two centuries after Galileo.

(S. Callow, The Guardian, *4 August 2007; book review of* Galileo Antichrist: A biography, *by Michael White. Copyright Guardian News & Media 2007.)*

As is often the case, a closer look at the historical evidence seems to point to a slightly more moderate picture. These were some mitigating circumstances:

■ The Roman Catholic Church had been confronted by the Reformation and did not want to be seen as weak. In addition, the pope was involved in wars to defend and extend his territories. (Italy in those days did not exist, but was divided in to several city-states.)

■ Galilei ridiculed the Catholic Church in his book by putting the views of the Church in the mouth of an individual called Simplicius.

■ Before, during and *after* his trial, Galilei was helped by cardinals who did not approve of what had happened.

■ Disagreements between scientists and the establishment take place in all periods (as exemplified by the current ethical issues surrounding embryonic research) and power struggles have not been limited to the Roman Catholic Church. For instance, in England admission to the Universities of Oxford and Cambridge was limited to members of the Church of England until well into the 1850s (Twaddle 1966).

? What do you think?

The criticism of the role of the Roman Catholic Church in the development of science has been most scathing in Anglo-Saxon literature. To what extent could this be because the English-speaking countries dissociated themselves from the influence of the Roman Catholic Church?

Independent of the reasonableness of what happened, the main outcome of Galilei's research was that the evidence he presented (and which could easily be verified by others once they had a telescope) was so convincing that the heliocentric view rapidly came to dominate astronomy (although it was not until 1822 that Pope Pius VII would allow the printing of works based on the heliocentric theory in Rome). As such, the episode was an important triumph for natural philosophy. In a subtle way it also pushed humans out of the centre of the universe. After all, the universe had not been created around man.

Interim summary

■ The need for an improved calendar renewed interest in the motions of the Earth, the Moon and the Sun relative to one another.

■ The model of the universe that was used was the geocentric model of Aristotle and Ptolemy. This model has the Earth at the centre of the universe.

■ Copernicus got interested in an alternative heliocentric model with the Sun at the centre. He did not publish this model until the year of his death, partly because he thought the evidence was not convincing enough and partly because he did not want to upset the Roman Catholic Church.

■ Nearly a century later Galileo Galilei used a telescope to look at the night sky and observed several phenomena that were easier to explain on the basis of a heliocentric model than on the basis of a geocentric model. In doing so, he upset the Catholic Church.

■ Because the evidence was so convincing and could be verified by others, the heliocentric model rapidly came to dominate astronomy despite the Catholic Church's resistance.

KEY FIGURE

Galileo Galilei

Source: Detlev van Ravenswaay / Science Photo Library Ltd

■ Italian scholar (1564–1642).

■ Famous for his contributions to:
  ■ Astronomy: heliocentric model, discovery of Jupiter's largest moons.
  ■ Physics: experiments on and mathematical descriptions of motions of bodies (e.g. falling objects and the trajectories traversed by cannonballs).
  ■ Technology: improved several pieces of equipment (e.g. the telescope).

■ Controversy with the Roman Catholic Church
  ■ First tried to convince the Church authorities of the heliocentric model in 1616. Was not successful but could continue to mention his model hypothetically.
  ■ Published a book on heliocentrism in 1632 after the election of his friend Cardinal Barberini as Pope Urban VIII. However, he offended the Pope and was confronted with a Church that saw a need to defend its stance.
  ■ Ordered to stand trial on suspicion of heresy in 1633. Had to recant his ideas, put under house arrest, and saw his book banned.

■ Importance for the advancement of science
  ■ New view of the organisation of the universe.
  ■ The fact that the heliocentric model prevailed despite the resistance of the Church authorities is generally considered as the turning point in the advancement of science.

■ Two main works
  ■ *Dialogue Concerning the Two Chief World Systems* (1632), book in which he put forward a heliocentric view of the universe.
  ■ *Discourses and Mathematical Demonstrations Relating to Two New Sciences* (1638), particularly known for its law of falling bodies (Chapter 8).

2.2   Mechanisation of the world view

Descartes' philosophy of man

One of the first people to be affected by the Roman Catholic Church's harsh treatment of Galilei was René Descartes (1596–1650), a French scholar and philosopher who lived in the Netherlands. He was about to publish a book of his world view, *Le Monde*, which also included a heliocentric model of the universe. Although he was quite safe in the Netherlands, which were dominated by the Protestants, he decided to shelve the study. (It was only published more than 10 years after his death.) However, the result of Descartes' decision was not that he stopped thinking about natural philosophy, as arguably the Roman Catholic Church had hoped, but that he started to look at how he could build a new philosophy, which would reconcile the Church with natural philosophy. In the end, this turned out to be equally devastating for the status of the religious world view.

Dualism

dualism

view of the mind–body relation according to which the mind is immaterial and completely independent of the body; central within religions and also in Descartes' philosophy

Descartes identified the soul as being divine and independent of everything else. His first move, therefore, was to clearly separate the human soul from the rest of the universe, as had been done before by Plato and the Catholic Church. Because the human soul was divine, human thoughts and feelings could not be studied by the natural sciences and fell under the remit of philosophy and religion. In line with Plato, Descartes was convinced that the soul had innate knowledge, which could be recovered on the basis of reasoning (see rationalism below). The assumption of a sharp distinction between the immaterial mind and the material body is known as dualism. We will return to the relationship between mind and body in Chapter 6.

Mechanistic view of the universe, including the human body

mechanistic view

world view according to which everything in the material universe can be understood as a complicated machine; discards the notion that things have goals and intentions as assumed by the animistic view; started with Descartes

The second move of Descartes was to view the universe and all the matter in it (including the human body) as one big, sophisticated machine that could be studied by humans. Descartes believed that God had created a self-perpetuating machine, so that He did not have to continuously look after His creation. Humans were endowed with reason so that they could grasp the workings of the machinery. In this respect, Descartes was strongly influenced by the views of Dutch Protestant philosophers, in particular Isaac Beeckman.

To understand why the mechanistic view was important for the development of science, we must have a look at the Aristotelian model it replaced. Although Aristotle's writings were much more appealing to scholars than those of Plato and the Catholic Church, they did not coincide with modern science. For instance, for Aristotle matter was continuous and made up of a combination of the five elements (earth, water, air, fire and aether). Also Aristotle's thinking centred around causes. He discerned four of them, to be discovered for each phenomenon under investigation by observation and logic:

1. the material cause (what parts is a phenomenon made of)

2. the formal cause (what is the plan of a phenomenon)

3. the efficient cause (which processes make a phenomenon work)

4. the final cause (what is the purpose of the phenomenon).

Because of the final cause, Aristotelian explanations of nature often referred to the perceived goals and aims of an object (e.g. the final cause of rain was to let the plants grow). This aspect of Aristotle's teaching was retained by scientists in the Renaissance: things had a soul that made them function in order to achieve the goals they were made for. As we saw in Chapter 1, such a view is described as animistic. Descartes rejected all goals, emotions and intelligence in nature and claimed that everything in the universe (except for the human soul) was a perfectly designed mechanism, made to function independently, so that God did not have to attend to it any more. Natural philosophers could study these mechanisms.

Implications for the advancement of science

Although Descartes meant to make a sharp division between religion and science, thereby protecting one from the other, his views primarily benefited science. Not only did the mechanistic view of the world invite further scrutiny of its workings (as was intended); very soon questions were asked about how the soul could steer the mechanism of the human body if it was separated from it. Descartes conjectured that the soul could influence the body via the pineal gland (a small gland in the middle of the brain), but rapidly this view was found unconvincing. As a consequence, the 'soul' got dragged into the mechanical part of the universe and became the subject of natural investigations as well, as we will see in the next chapter.

Interim summary

- The response of the Roman Catholic Church against Galilei encouraged René Descartes to build a new philosophy of man.

- In this philosophy a clear distinction was made between the soul, which was divine and could not be studied with scientific methods, and the rest of the universe (including the body), which was a complex machine that could be studied scientifically. This became known as (Cartesian) dualism.

- The mechanistic view of the world came to replace Aristotle's view, which still contained animistic elements.

KEY FIGURE

René Descartes

Source: Royal
Astronomical Society /
Science Photo Library
Ltd

- ■ French scholar living in the Netherlands (1596–1650).
- ■ Famous for his contributions to:
  - ■ Mathematics: Cartesian geometry, exponential notations.
  - ■ Philosophy: rationalism, dualism, the undeniable existence of thought ('I think, therefore I am' [*cogito, ergo sum*]).
- ■ Impact for the advancement of science
  - ■ Mechanistic world view.
  - ■ Body can be studied scientifically.
  - ■ Idea of innate knowledge and the importance of deductive reasoning (rationalism).

2.3   The formulation of the first laws of physics

Why is the Earth orbiting the Sun?

One of the big mysteries of the heliocentric universe was why the planets orbited the Sun and why some planets were orbited by one or more moons. Remember that in the Aristotelian universe there were only two 'natural' movements: one downwards to the centre of the Earth (applicable to earth and water) and one upwards to the edge of the sub-lunar region (fire and air). All other movements needed a continuous, external cause. According to some medieval views this meant that that the Sun and the stars were constantly being pushed by angels. However, what was pushing the Earth around the Sun?

Movements are the result of forces

It would take the genius of the British scientist Isaac Newton (1643–1727) to bring all the available evidence together and formulate an account that in hindsight was so elegant and simple that it is hard to believe no-one else had come to the insight before. (It is thought by some that Descartes came close when he aborted his studies of physics and turned to his philosophical treatise about the nature of the universe and the place of man in it.) Newton's starting point consisted of studies by Galilei (yes, him) on the trajectory of cannonballs. Galilei noticed that the path of a cannonball was a parabola, the curvature of which depended on the force with which the ball had been propelled: The stronger the force, the further the ball went (figure 2.5). This relationship could be described mathematically.

Newton's clever insight was that if you placed the cannon on a mountain and shot the ball with enough force, then it would not fall fast enough to touch the Earth but would circle around it (figure 2.6). In addition, if you took away the friction of the

Figure 2.5 Drawing by Galilei of the parabolic trajectories of cannonballs as a function of the propelling force.

Source: Institute and Museum of the History of Science.

Figure 2.6 Newton's insight that a cannonball will orbit the Earth if it is fired with the right force.

air, the motion would continue *ad infinitum*. Could this be the reason why the Moon orbited the Earth?

But why were the cannonball and the Moon attracted to the Earth? Why is the trajectory of the cannonball not a straight path out of the mouth of the cannon? These questions brought Newton to another important insight: objects were attracting each other. The Earth attracted the cannonball and the cannonball attracted the Earth. Because of the big difference in mass, however, the pulling force (called the gravitational force) of the Earth on the cannonball was immensely larger than the other way around.

The Principia Mathematica

All that was left for Newton to do was to calculate the exact magnitudes of the different forces. The end result was a book, *Philosophiae Naturalis Principia Mathematica*, published in 1687, in which all known movements in the Copernican universe were adequately described on the basis of three laws and the postulation of a gravitational force. Each of the components was described in mathematical terms, allowing precise calculations of the orbits.

Principia Mathematica

book in which Newton presented his laws of physics (1687); considered to be the primary reason for the increased status of science

The magnitude of the impact of the *Principia Mathematica* (as it is usually abbreviated) can hardly be described. For nearly a century scholars had argued that the universe could be thought of as a perfect machine, the workings of which could be studied and understood by natural philosophy. Suddenly they had their wildest dreams fulfilled: here was a book that described all motions (both on Earth and in the universe) on the basis of a handful of equations that could be understood by everyone with a bit of mathematical sophistication! The mechanisms of the universe were laid bare to the human eye. It was only a matter of time before similar equations would be discovered for the other parts of the machine.

The boost science got from Newton's *tour de force* persists today. Scientists after Newton felt much less need to keep abreast of philosophical issues than before. In contrast, philosophers without scientific knowledge saw their status sharply decreased. (Although for the sake of completeness it must be added that Newton's theory has since been upgraded by Einstein's relativity theory and that physicists still do not know how celestial bodies can attract each other over large distances without any apparent matter between them.)

Interim summary

■ Newton solved the problem of why planets orbit the Sun and moons orbit planets.

■ In doing so, he not only defined the relevant forces, but described them in such detail that they could be calculated precisely.

■ The resulting mathematical equations were the first laws of physics, published in the *Principia Mathematica*, convincing scientists that science could uncover the mechanisms underlying the universe.

KEY FIGURE

Isaac Newton

Source: CCI Archives / Science Photo Library Ltd

- British physicist and mathematician (1643–1727).
- Famous for his contributions to:
  - Mathematics: development of calculus.
  - Optics: showed that white light is the sum of all the colours of the rainbow.
  - Physics: described gravitation and three laws of motion that would form the basis of mechanics and the scientific understanding of the universe for the next two centuries.
- Impact for the advancement of science
  - Showed that science could uncover the mechanisms underlying reality.
  - Seemed to suggest that all scientific knowledge could be summarised in mathematical laws.

2.4   The expansion of science

Science and nations in search of power and prosperity

Newton's physics gave the natural philosophers extra vigour. They found fertile ground in Britain, where already by the beginning of the seventeenth century members of the ruling powers were beginning to invest in natural philosophy to strengthen the power of the state (this was the time the British Empire took off). A particularly forthright person in this respect was the politician Francis Bacon (1561–1626). He argued that the government could be made more efficient and gather extra wealth by learning more about nature. He also stressed that technological advances should be integrated into natural philosophy (remember that the 'educated circles' tended to look down upon this type of practical skill). Bacon realised the importance of the recent advances in shipbuilding, navigation, ballistics, printing and water engineering. A similarly pragmatic alliance between natural philosophy and mechanics occurred in the Netherlands, which not only made the most of its recently acquired independence of the Spanish Empire (in 1568) but also profited from the 'brain gain' as a result of the Spanish prosecution of people who had converted to the Protestant religion (see Chapter 1). It was not really a coincidence that the first laws of physics were discovered by a British scholar: the country had nourished natural philosophers and was, so to say, primed for the discovery.

The method of the natural philosopher

As part of the scientific revolution, scholars also started to wonder how scientific progress was best achieved (although the term 'science' was not yet used; this would only happen in the 1800s). Again, Britain was at the forefront of the movement.

What do you think?

The question of what exactly science is will be a theme throughout this book. It may be a good idea at this moment to write down your opinions. What do scientists do? What methods do they use? In what ways does scientific knowledge differ from other types of knowledge? Keep your answers at hand and compare them with the text below and the following chapters (in particular Chapter 8).

Precise observation instead of deductive reasoning

rationalism

view according to which knowledge is obtained by means of reasoning; usually through deductive reasoning on the basis of innate knowledge

As we saw in Chapter 1, Plato thought the way to understanding was inward. By focusing on their own thoughts and reason, humans could get in touch with the realm of the never-changing Forms. This view is known as rationalism, the conviction that reason is the source of knowledge and that truth is established on the basis of logic and not on the basis of perception. The main investigation method in rationalism is deduction, a way of reasoning in which one starts from a number of indisputable premises from which new conclusions are drawn. The conclusions are guaranteed to be true if the correct logical rules have been followed (see also Chapter 8). Rationalism was embraced by the Catholic Church and dominated the Middle Ages. As we saw above, it also formed the core of Descartes' philosophy: the divine soul had innate knowledge which could be made explicit by thinking. Descartes did not deny the existence of sensory experiences, but he minimised their significance:

deduction

form of reasoning in which one starts from a number of indisputable premises, from which new, true conclusions can be drawn if the rules of logic are followed

> I cannot doubt that there is in me a certain passive faculty of perceiving, that is, of receiving and recognizing the ideas of sensible objects; but it would be valueless to me and I could in no way use it if there were not also in me or in something else, another active faculty capable of forming and producing these ideas.
>
> *(as cited in Gardner (1987, p. 52))*

Aristotle attached more importance to precise observations as the start of knowledge, but he too gave predominance to insight and reason as the basis of understanding (Aristotle was the founder of logic, the formulation of rules that made it possible to draw valid conclusions from premises). If there was a divergence between observation and logic, it was not unusual for Aristotle to treat the observation as a mere exception to the 'logical' conclusion. Such exceptions were possible and said nothing about the 'natural' flow of reality; they were just exceptions to the general rule.

empiricism

view according to which knowledge is obtained by means of perceptual experiences; usually involves idea of associations between ideas to combine the individual perceptions; also emphasis on inductive reasoning

A completely different view was defended by the empiricists in Britain who argued that all human knowledge was derived from perceptual experiences. Although as usual many forerunners can by found, the first explicit formulation of empiricism as a doctrine was presented in *An Essay Concerning Human Understanding*, published in 1689 by a Scot, John Locke (1632–1704). In this book Locke defended the view that the human mind at birth was a blank page (or *tabula rasa*) on which experiences left their marks and made associations with the marks already present. As a consequence, all human experience was based upon experience, and meticulous observation should be the basis of the scientific method: if you want to understand a phenomenon, you must not start by forming an opinion about it on the basis of your

induction

form of reasoning in which one starts from observations and tries to reach general conclusions; is needed in science to turn observed phenomena into scientific laws

intuitions and reason, but with careful observation of the phenomenon (in modern terms, knowledge should be evidence-based and not principle-driven). The main type of reasoning in empiricism is induction, which tries to reach general conclusions on the basis of the specific observations that have been made (Chapter 8).

It was not a coincidence that Locke's book appeared a few years after the *Principia Mathematica*. Locke was heavily influenced by the success of Newton's physics. (They knew each other well, though Locke, just like Descartes, wrote the majority of his essay while he was in exile in the Netherlands, after a botched plot against King James II with which he was associated.) Empiricism suited the natural philosophers very well, because they rapidly became convinced that knowledge had to start from meticulous observation.

Interim summary

Rationalism

- existence of innate knowledge

- reason is the source of knowledge

- main research method: deductive reasoning

- main applications: logic, mathematics

- main proponents: Plato, Descartes, Wolff, Kant

Empiricism

- no innate knowledge (blank slate)

- perception is the source of knowledge

- main research methods: observation, experimentation, inductive reasoning

- main applications: natural sciences

- main proponents: Locke, Berkeley, Hume, scientists

experimentation

method of investigating a phenomenon by means of experiments; in these experiments aspects of the phenomenon are systematically manipulated to observe their consequences; usually done to test predictions that have been derived from the existing understanding by means of deductive reasoning

The importance of experimentation and precise measurements

At the same time, however, the events of the astronomers also warned against a blind reliance on human observations. After all, didn't the perception of a fixed world give humans the false impression of a geocentric universe? And were the failures to see differences in the brightness of Venus and to detect the moons around Jupiter not the reasons why Copernicus's heliocentric theory was disregarded for almost a century? It was only after Galilei used a telescope to look at the stars, that the true evidence became available. So, human perception was both fallible and limited.

Two remedies were proposed to circumvent the limits of observation. The first was to formulate predictions on the basis of existing knowledge and deductive reasoning. These predictions were subsequently tested by means of experimentation. If a phenomenon is really understood, then it must be possible to formulate a new prediction on the basis of what is known and to check empirically whether this prediction is confirmed by introducing experimental manipulations. In this approach, findings that deviated from expectations were no longer exceptions to the rule but became the centre of interest. Although in Chapter 8 we will see that hypothesis testing does not really circumvent the limitations of perception (just as the conclusions reached through inductive reasoning are not guaranteed to be correct), it suited the scientists well enough. They took a very pragmatic approach: only theories that led to practically useful knowledge were considered of interest and pursued.

The second remedy for the unreliability of human observations was to devise more and better instruments to help with the observations. Just as the telescope made a breakthrough possible in astronomy, so would other equipment allow scientists to observe things that were not perceptible to the naked senses. An example that immediately springs to mind in this respect was the invention of the microscope (with a decisive contribution of the Dutch scholar van Leeuwenhoek).

scientific method

until halfway through the twentieth century seen as a method of accumulating information by means of learning the existing knowledge and adding new knowledge on the basis of objective, value-free observation, careful measurement and experimentation; the definition became more complicated in the second half of the twentieth century (Chapter 8)

More than anything else, the adoption of the scientific method was the reason why science took such a high flight from the seventeenth century on. One of the first research areas to profit from the application of the scientific method after physics was chemistry. Whereas before it was a widely erratic business, known as alchemy (to which Newton devoted more time than to physics!), the introduction of scientific rigour in a few decades turned it into a respectable science, with the rapid discovery of chemical elements and the laws that governed their behaviour. A central figure in this transition was the British scholar Robert Boyle (1627–1691), who in 1662 published a law of the behaviour of gas, and, who is seen by many (especially chemists) as another central figure in the scientific revolution.

Strengthening the scientific structures

Learned societies

Together with the increased status of science, structures were established to solidify and advance its progress. Next to the universities, which were also growing in strength and number, learned societies were founded, such as the Italian Accademia dei Lincei (1603), the Académie Française (1635) and the Royal Society of London (1660). These societies offered a place for scientists to meet and share ideas. They also published proceedings that allowed researchers to disseminate their ideas. Maybe as a result of their culture of gentlemen's clubs, most research groups in Britain founded a society as soon as they had enough members. So, in addition to the Royal Society of London, we got the Royal Society of Edinburgh (1783), the Linnean Society of London (1788, devoted to the description of biological species), the Geological Society of London (1807), the Royal Astronomical Society (1820), the Royal Statistical Society (1834), the British Archaeological Association (1843), the Ethnological Society of London (1843) and many, many more.

Specialisation

The proliferation of learned societies was testimony to a development that gained pace after the seventeenth century. Soon there was a vast amount of specialised knowledge, which was so demanding that it was impossible to be at the cutting edge of everything. Scientists began to specialise and clustered in groups devoted to ever narrower topics. The same happened to scientific journals, a development that was further enhanced by the creation of associations that no longer had a permanent address (i.e. an academy building), but assembled around a journal or a series of conferences.

What do you think?

To many non-scientists the far-reaching specialisation of science is seen as a weakness (scientists have but a very small area of expertise). What do you think? Should scientists aim for breadth or for depth?

Age of Enlightenment

name given to the Western philosophy and cultural life of the eighteenth century, in which autonomous thinking and observation became advocated as the primary sources of knowledge, rather than reliance on authority

positivism

view that authentic knowledge can only be obtained by means of the scientific method; saw religion and philosophy as inferior forms of explanation

industrial revolution

name to refer to the socio-economic and cultural changes in the nineteenth century caused by the invention of machines; involved, among other things the replacement of the labour of peasants and craftsmen by mass production in factories and the resulting massive relocation from the countryside to the towns

Explicit claims of the superiority of scientific knowledge

By the beginning of the eighteenth century the scientific approach became so prevalent in intellectual circles that this century is referred to as the **Age of Enlightenment**. Another testimony to the status of science came from the French philosopher Auguste Comte who at the beginning of the nineteenth century formulated his law of the three stages in which knowledge was acquired:

> This law is . . . that each branch of our knowledge passes successively through three different theoretical conditions: The Theological or fictitious, the Metaphysical or abstract, and the Scientific or positive. In other words, the human mind, by its nature, employs in its progress three methods of philosophizing, the character of which is essentially different and even radically opposed.
>
> *(Comte (1855) as cited in Jahoda (2007) p. 75)*

In other words, for Comte the scientific approach was the method of educated people. Religious and philosophical accounts were associated with primitive and ignorant groups. Notice the contrast with Galilei's time: rather than religion being the golden standard against which scientific insight was compared, for Comte religion was a form of 'inferior knowledge'. The view that considers scientifically obtained knowledge as the only authentic knowledge is known as **positivism** (Comte himself called his approach 'positive psychology').

What do you think?

Do you agree with Comte's assessment that scientific explanations are more educated than religious or philosophical explanations? Is this true for all types of questions?

Social impact of the technological advances

The nineteenth century was also the century of the **industrial revolution**. Due to the invention of machines (in particular, the steam engine), the manual labour of peasants and craftsmen was replaced by mass production in factories. This resulted in a massive relocation of the population towards cities and an increase in wealth (though not for everyone). At the same time, due to the increased use of experimentation and advanced equipment, natural philosophers distanced themselves from philosophy and started to call themselves 'men of science', studying the natural sciences. The word *scientist* would be coined in 1833.

Interim summary

■ Some nations invested heavily in natural philosophy because they saw it as a means to achieve power and prosperity.

■ The success of natural philosophy made philosophers rethink the way in which knowledge is achieved. Rather than stressing the importance of innate knowledge derived on the basis of deductive reasoning (rationalism), they pointed to the importance of careful observation, experimentation, precise measurement and inductive reasoning (empiricism).

■ The initial successes were solidified within the wider society:
  ■ Foundation of learned societies.
  ■ Explicit claims of the superiority of scientific knowledge (e.g. positivism).
  ■ New names: 'natural sciences' instead of natural philosophy and 'scientist' instead of natural philosopher.

2.5   Developments in the eighteenth and nineteenth centuries that led to the emergence of psychology as an independent branch of learning

Because of the expansion of the sciences in the eighteenth and nineteenth centuries it is no longer possible to keep track of all its developments. Therefore, in the remainder of this chapter we will limit ourselves to those developments that had a direct impact on the emergence of psychology as an independent branch of science.

Darwin and the evolutionary theory

Many scientists consider Darwin's (1809–1882) insights about the evolution of organisms as the second largest discovery in science (or even the largest). Whereas Newton (and since him, the physicists) discovered the way the universe functions, Darwin (and with him the biologists) unravelled the way life in the universe came about, constantly changes, and adapts itself to changing circumstances.

The right zeitgeist

In hindsight, the Darwin's theory about the evolution of species was bound to be discovered around the mid-nineteenth century, most likely in the UK. Ever since the Swedish physician Carolus Linnaeus had started his work on the classification of plants and animals in the eighteenth century and published his *Systema Naturae* (1st edition in 1735, 11 pages; 13th edition in 1770, 3,000 pages), botanists from many countries had contributed to the enterprise, none more enthusiastically than the British (who, as we have seen, established the Linnean Society of London in 1788). The taxonomy of biological species not only confronted the scholars with thorny issues about how to define distinctions and similarities; it also made them wonder how the diversity had originated. Linnaeus himself, for instance, came to the conclusion that he had no other option than to classify humans in the same grouping as primates.

Around the same time, the first writings about fossils started to appear. In 1787 a huge thigh bone was found in New Jersey that did not seem to match any existing animal. It turned out to be from a dinosaur, although it took quite some time (and many more finds) before this was realised. In the UK geologists began to look for fossils of small animals and plants to estimate the age of rocks. These findings raised more questions about how all these layers of fossils (some of them unlike existing animals) had come about and disappeared.

In the 1840s the British Prime Minister, Sir Robert Peel, replaced the tax on glass (and other visible signs of wealth) by an income tax. One of the consequences of this abolishment was a vast proliferation of greenhouses in which exquisite, exotic and continuously evolving plants were cultivated. Charles Darwin had several of these greenhouses. As a young man he had spent five years collecting and documenting specimens of unknown plants and animals, as part of a voyage on the *Beagle* to new territories. Darwin had been invited along because the captain, who was weary of the loneliness of a long expedition, had required a gentleman companion. After the expedition with the *Beagle* Darwin never again left Britain and he became a recluse in his home from where he conducted a rich correspondence with friends, family members and scientific colleagues. While pondering his recollections from the voyage and cultivating his exotic plants, Darwin inevitably started to wonder about the origin of the variety he observed.

natural selection

process in Darwin's evolutionary theory by which the environment results in the continuation and multiplication of organisms with certain genetic features and hinders the reproduction of organisms with other genetic features; the first type of features are called favourable (within the prevailing environment), the second type unfavourable

Cross-fertilisation and natural selection

A first observation that struck him was that, although many plants were capable of self-fertilisation, they seemed to avoid it. Furthermore, if it happened, the offspring were on average less healthy. Cross-fertilisation produced variation in the offspring that was more vital and sometimes even resulted in the creation of a new type of flower. (This finding was also of non-academic interest to Darwin, because he had married one of his cousins, as quite often happened in the upper-class families of those times. Later he would become a supporter of measures to dissuade this type of marriage.)

Darwin was at a loss to understand how the new offspring could start to dominate and eventually replace the old variety. The breakthrough came when he read a book by the economist Thomas Malthus, who defended the position that if humans did not obey 'moral constraint' their growth would outstrip food production, which would inevitably result in either famine or war. Darwin now realised that the struggle for existence in a world of limited resources was the reason why some variants had an advantage and started to outgrow the variants without that advantage. Later this insight became was encapsulated in the phrase natural selection or (more popular, but less correct) survival of the fittest (a term introduced by Herbert Spencer; see Chapter 4).

survival of the fittest

term introduced by Herbert Spencer to describe the outcome of natural selection: only organisms that fit within the environment and can produce viable offspring survive

The Origin of Species

Darwin was reluctant to publish his insights and only did so at the age of 50, when he was warned that one of his correspondents, Alfred Russel Wallace, was about to publish a very similar thesis. The first edition of the book *On the Origin of Species by*

The Origin of Species

book by Charles Darwin (1859) in which he presented the evolutionary theory

Means of Natural Selection, or The Preservation of Favoured Races in the Struggle for Life (usually abbreviated to *The Origin of Species* or the *Origin*) appeared in 1859.

The dilution problem

Although the book was an instant success and led to lively debates (which Darwin refused to attend), its initial impact was less impressive than we nowadays spontaneously think. One element that Darwin failed to explain and that would haunt him until his death (and evolutionary theory for nearly half a century longer) was how a single new plant or animal could come to dominate the rest. This criticism was best formulated by the Scottish engineer Fleeming Jenkin. According to Jenkin, when an organism with a new feature is placed amid a group of other organisms, this new feature will not expand but dilute in the pool of existing features until in the end virtually nothing remains. He gave the example of a white man shipwrecked on an island inhabited by black people. If this man becomes part of the community and has children, his whiteness will never become dominant, not even if the trait is better suited to the environment. After a few generations the whiteness of the forefather will have all but vanished because it is overruled by the more prevalent blackness.

Darwin never found a proper answer to Jenkin's dilution argument. In the fifth edition of the *Origin* (1869), he agreed that a single new random variant could not alter the nature of a species and that evolution was only possible when a change in the environment favoured a *whole group of individuals* at the same time, for instance when a drought favoured birds with strong beaks. Because of the blending problem, the impact of the evolutionary theory on other biological scientists was almost nil around 1900. Only a few decades later, when biologists started to unravel the nature of inheritance and understood that genes are not blended in the process of conception, did the real impact of the evolutionary theory become clear, as we will see in later chapters.

Common misunderstandings of the evolutionary theory

Although the evolutionary theory is quite straightforward, it is often misunderstood. One of the misinterpretations is that the genes *induce* a change in a plant or animal so that it becomes more adapted to the environment. This is wrong because the genetic material has no knowledge of the environment and so cannot change in a desirable direction. All that happens is that the material now and then has a random alteration. Most of these changes result in offspring that do not differ in an observable way from the parents. Sometimes, a change results in a descendant that is barely viable or that does not result in further offspring. Such a mutation is not passed on to further generations. Occasionally, however, an alteration results in a characteristic that is particularly well adapted to the prevailing environment and that increases the chances of the organism to survive and have descendants. This new variant gradually increases in number at the expense of the variants without the characteristic.

A second misunderstanding about evolution is that each genetic mutation that survives results in a better, stronger and more complex organism. (How else could humans have evolved from primates? Or how else can we explain that each new generation of humans becomes smarter?) Jones (1999) gave a particularly forceful example of how adaptations need not be for the better. First, he described how predators such as wolves and mammoths dramatically declined (often to extinction) as soon as humans invaded their territory. At the same time, a few species sharply increased in number. These were the species humans kept as pets or for food, such as dogs and pigs. In general, Jones argued, these species are dumber and meeker than the ancestors from which they were bred, because the humans did not want dogs with their own initiative or pigs that were smart. They wanted helpless animals that were lost without the human presence and that constantly showed their affection and dependence. The same would happen if the Earth were suddenly invaded by a new species that kept humans as pets. Those humans who opposed the occupation (because they were too proud, intelligent or aggressive) would be killed and would no longer be able to pass on their genes. In contrast, mentally feeble humans that depended on their masters for survival would be bred and rapidly increase in number.

KEY FIGURE

Charles Darwin

Source: FPG / Getty Images

- British biologist (1809–1882).
- Famous for his contributions to:
  - Biology: description of new species, importance of cross-fertilisation, development of the evolutionary theory.
- Impact for the advancement of science
  - Focused on the similarities among animals and humans.
  - Pointed to the importance of heredity.
  - Developed a theory of how life adapts to changing situations.

An increased interest in human psychological functioning

Philosophy turns to questions about man and his place in the universe

The eighteenth and the nineteenth centuries were also characterised by a growing interest in human functioning. Philosophers turned their interests from metaphysical questions (questions about the universe) to questions about man and his place in the universe. We have already seen how they addressed the issue of how knowledge originates, resulting in the discussion between rationalists and empiricists. Another important name in this debate was Immanuel Kant (1724–1804). Kant is particularly known for his attempts to synthesise empiricism with rationalism by stating that the mind, through innate categories (such as space, time and causality), constructs the sensory experiences along certain lines (Chapter 11). However, in 1798 as an aside he also published a book on anthropology, *Anthropologie in pragmatischer Hinsicht*, based on his lecture notes. In this book he addressed topics such as self-consciousness, self-observation, unconscious ideas and mental processes, the distinction between sensation and thinking, the role of pleasure and pain in human life, how to define and control emotions and passions, how to derive the character of persons from their comportment and physiognomy, and what the differences were between the characters of the French, British, Spanish, Italians, Germans, Greeks and Armenians.

Kant was by no means the first to teach about human functioning in his courses of philosophy. By the end of the 1700s such lectures were an established part of the curricula of the French and German-speaking colleges and universities (Hatfield 1998). In addition, philosophers increasingly began to use the word 'psychology' to refer to this subject. The first book with psychology in its title was published by a British chaplain, John Broughton, in 1703. (The first documented record of the term psychology is by the Croatian scholar Marko Marulić around 1500.) The title of Broughton's book was 'Psychologia: or, an Account of the Nature of the Rational Soul.' It failed to make an impact and was described by a correspondent to John Locke as 'a Discourse upon nothing' (Letter of Anthony Collins to Locke on 30 June 1703).

The word psychology gained momentum after it was used by the German philosopher Christian Wolff in the 1730s in two successive books: *Psychologia Empirica* and *Psychologia Rationalis*. These books were translated in French and picked up by Diderot in his famous *Encyclopédie*. In 1755 the French author Bonnett published a further book entitled *Essai de Psychologie*, in which he surprisingly felt the need to issue an apology for contributing to a field in which 'so many books have been written' (as cited in Hatfield 1998). From 1758 on we see the word appear in French and English dictionaries (e.g. *Dictionnaire universel des arts et des sciences, françois, latin et anglois*). The new word clearly met a need to refer to the growing philosophical interest in the human mind.

Can psychology be studied with the scientific method?

An important point of dispute in the early writings on psychology was whether the human psyche could be studied in the same way as in natural philosophy, using the scientific method. Kant and Comte thought not, but others disagreed. One source of inspiration was Newton's *Principia Mathematica*. If Newton could summarise the functioning of the universe in a handful of laws, then surely it had to be possible to capture the essence of human functioning with a few psychological laws as well? In 1725 the Glasgow professor Francis Hutchinson published a treatise in which he introduced 'mathematical calculations in subjects of morality' (Jahoda 2007: 28). He produced a quasi-algebraic set of formulae designed to compute the morality of actions. For instance, the Moral Importance (M) of agents was a function of their Benevolence (B) multiplied by their Abilities (A), or $M = B \times A$. The German scholar Johann Freidrich Herbart made a similar attempt in 1816 when he published a *Lehrbuch zur Psychologie* in which he presented his main ideas in mathematical terms.

Observations of human behaviours

Others took the scientific method as their point of departure. If psychology wanted to be part of natural philosophy, it had to start from careful observation. The first big initiative to bring together people interested in the empirical study of humans in society was taken in France by Louis-François Jauffret, who in 1799 founded the *Société des Observateurs de l'Homme* (The Society of the Observers of Man: see Jahoda 2007, p. 18–25). This society attracted some 60 members interested in 'the physical, moral, and intellectual aspects of the science of man'. One of the first deeds of the Society was to study the 'wild boy of Aveyron'. In 1799 a naked and mute boy of some 10–11 years had been captured in Aveyron; apparently he had been left behind in the forests as a baby and had been nourished by wolves and other wild animals.

The availability of a wild boy who never had been in contact with civilisation presented a unique opportunity for the Society to observe the transition from the raw human material to a civilised person. It was decided that one of the members, Jean-Marie Itard, would educate and civilise Victor (as the boy came to be called), carefully observing and recording the stages of progress. Unfortunately for the Society, Victor did not make much progress. He remained more or less as he had been found. In addition, it became hotly debated whether the small progress Victor made could be considered as evidence for the claim that humanity was impossible without the constant availability of a civilisation for the developing infant to imitate. The final blow to the study came when the Society asked the famous physician Philippe Pinel to examine Victor. On the basis of his studies, Pinel concluded that Victor displayed characteristics of someone who was profoundly mentally handicapped. For instance, Victor never learned to open a door with a key, although he observed this action over and over again. According to Pinel, Victor was not a prototypical 'natural man', but a mental defective who had been abandoned by his parents and spent some time roaming in the wild before being found. It is not clear whether the impact of the Society would have been any higher if the first 'experiment' had been more successful (Jahoda (2007, p. 22–24) describes another messed up attempt by the Society to scientifically study 'savages'), but the mere existence of the Society illustrates the awakening interest among scholars in looking at the human psyche with the methods of the natural philosophers.

Increased interest in psychological functioning in the general literature

Not only did philosophers and natural philosophers focus their attention on psychological matters. The period 1700–1900 also saw the birth of the novel, in which characters are depicted with some depth, ruminating about their existence and their relations to others. Before, adventures were the centre of the stories and the protagonists were not much more than stylised figures responding in uniform and predictable ways. Novels from this period that have stood the test of time are Daniel Defoe's *Robinson Crusoe* (1719), Johann Wolfgang von Goethe's *Die Leiden des jungen Werther* (1774), Jane Austen's *Pride and Prejudice* (1813), Honoré de Balzac's *Comédie Humaine* (1842), Emily Brontë's *Wuthering Heights* (1847) and Gustave Flaubert's *Madame Bovary* (1856).

Studying physiological functions

A third development that primed the world for the establishment of psychology as an independent branch of research came from the medical sciences. Like all the other branches, medicine made important progress in the seventeenth–nineteenth centuries, although its advance was slower than in physics or chemistry. Much of the progress was limited to understanding the body and the factors that had an impact on it. For instance, in 1847 the Austrian-Hungarian physician Ignaz Semmelweis dramatically reduced the death rate of new mothers from childbed fever by requiring physicians to clean their hands before attending to women in childbirth.

Of particular interest for the emergence of psychology was the research on vision and on the speed of signals in nerves. This research was done by physiologists, physicians who tried to understand the bodily functions of living animals and humans.

Optics and vision

Optics (the study of the transmission of light) was one of the topics that had been studied since ancient times and that had achieved a fair degree of sophistication. It had also led to practical applications (such as telescopes, microscopes and glasses). However, much less was known about how the stimulus of physical light was translated by the eyes and the brain into visual sensations.

One of the first discoveries was made in 1802 by the British physician Thomas Young. Some 150 years before, Isaac Newton had demonstrated that white light consisted of the sum of all the colours of the rainbow. When white light was dispersed with the use of a prism, the resulting image was a rainbow going from red, to orange, yellow, green, blue, indigo and violet. When subsequently the dispersed rays were converged by a new prism, the resulting light was white again. This was not the case when Newton blocked one of the colours of the rainbow. This proved to Newton that white light was the sum of all the rainbow colours. The new element Young added was to produce all the colours in a human observer by superimposing just three lights in different intensities: red, green, and blue. On the basis of this finding, Young conjectured that the perception of colour in humans was the sum of three primary colours (red, green and blue), a conclusion that some 50 years later would be reached by Hermann von Helmholtz as well.

In 1860 the German professor Gustav Fechner published *Elemente der Psychophysik* (Elements of Psychophysics), in which he tried to find the mathematical relation between the magnitude of an input stimulus and the magnitude of the resulting sensation. For instance, how does the brightness perception of a white light change as a function of the intensity of the light? This required both the stimulus and the perception to be expressed in numbers. Because the stimulus intensity could already be expressed as a number of physical units, Fechner's challenge was to find a way to express the brightness sensations in numbers. It would take us too long to explain how Fechner did so, but the end result was that he had a strong case to claim that the perception coincided with the logarithm of the stimulus intensity. This was the birth of psychophysics, a branch of research that deals with the relationship between physical stimuli and their subjective correlates. Fechner's work was the first to show that some aspects of human psychological functioning could be expressed as scientific laws, namely: Sensation (S) is a function of the logarithm of the stimulus intensity (I), or $S = k * \log(I)$ (figure 2.7), where S = magnitude of the sensation, k = a constant, I = intensity of the stimulus.

psychophysics

part of psychological research dealing with the relationship between physical stimuli and the corresponding sensation

Measuring the speed of signal transmission and response times

Around the time Fechner was elaborating the psychophysical law in Leipzig, his colleague Hermann von Helmholtz in Königsberg started a series of studies to measure the speed of nerve impulses. For a long time, it had been assumed that information transfer in the brain and the nerves was so fast that it was practically immeasurable. Von Helmholtz tested this hypothesis in the frog by using the motor nerve that runs the length of the leg. By stimulating the nerve at a certain place and measuring the passage of the signal at several distances, he could estimate the transmission speed of the nerve. With this technique von Helmholtz was able to show that the speed was actually rather slow: only 30 metres per second in a frog (i.e. slightly more than 100 km/h).

Figure 2.7 Graph illustrating Fechner's psychophysical law.
First Fechner defined S1 as the first stimulus a person could detect. Then he defined S2 as the first sensation that could be distinguished from S1, S3 as the first sensation that could be distinguished from S2, and so on. Previous research by Ernst Heinrich Weber had shown that the just noticeable difference between two stimuli corresponded to a difference in intensity (ΔI) equal to a percentage of the first stimulus (e.g. to be perceivable the magnitude of the second stimulus had to be 50% more than that of the first stimulus – this is for illustration purposes: in reality the percentages are much smaller). On the basis of this finding, Fechner argued that the psychophysical function was a logarithmic function.

mental chronometry

using reaction times to measure the time needed for various mental tasks; on the basis of a comparison of different tasks, models of the mental processes involved in the tasks are postulated

In the Netherlands, the ophthalmologist Franciscus Cornelis Donders (1868) wondered whether he could use von Helmholtz's technique to measure the speed with which humans could perform mental tasks. He first used a very simple task. A single stimulus was presented (e.g. the auditory stimulus 'ki') and the participant had to repeat it as fast as possible. Donders measured the time between the presentation of the stimulus and the start of the response up to a millisecond (i.e. one-thousandth of a second) accuracy. He found that the mean response time for this simple type of reaction was 197 milliseconds. Then he made the task slightly more difficult. He presented five possible stimuli ('ka, ke, ki, ko and ku') and the participant had to repeat the stimulus as soon as he heard 'ki'. In this condition, there was uncertainty about the stimulus that would be presented but not about the response that had to be made. The mean response time now was 243 milliseconds. By comparing the response times in the two conditions, Donders concluded that the time needed to perceive the identity of the stimulus, was 243 − 197 = 46 milliseconds. Finally, Donders presented a condition in which the participants got the same five stimuli and had to repeat each of them. Now there was uncertainty both with respect to the stimulus that would be presented and the response that had to be given. The response time now was 285 milliseconds, making Donders conclude that the time needed to choose the correct response out of five alternatives was 285 − 243 = 42 milliseconds. Donders' technique has been the basis of the mental chronometry, the use of reaction times to measure the time that is needed to perform mental tasks or task components. This technique is still in use in psychological research today.

Fechner's and Donders' techniques could be implemented without further ado in any laboratory to measure human functioning with the scientific method, which is exactly what happened, as we will see in the next chapter. Fechner and Donders themselves were not interested in this type of research, because they had other priorities.

The use of statistics

Psychological research requires the analysis of many observations to detect the underlying patterns

The development of statistics was another innovation of capital importance for the viability of psychological research. A crucial difference between physics and psychology is that processes in the former usually yield very much the same outcome each time they are repeated. In contrast, psychological outcomes usually differ between individuals and they also differ when an individual does the same task twice. The latter can easily be shown. When participants are asked to press a response key as quickly as possible when they hear a stimulus (cf. Donders' first task), their responses are not always exactly 197 ms. In some trials their reaction time can be as fast as 150 ms, in others it can be as slow as 300 ms, even when the participants are highly motivated to respond as fast as possible on each trial. This is because psychological measures are embedded in a lot of noise, which can be random (e.g. in some trials the participant was blinking at the moment the stimulus was presented), or due to the influence of some other systematic variable (e.g. the position of the hand relative to the response key).

Because of the intrinsic variability in psychological measures, it is not possible to get rid of the noise simply by trying to improve the accuracy of the measurement, as in physics. Discrepancies will always remain between successive observations. This means that the same measurement techniques cannot be used in psychology as in physics (the exception being some aspects of psychophysical research, where methods similar to those in physics can be applied). In physics, good research requires *extremely accurate measurements* of a few observations; in psychology good research usually consists of *a sufficiently large number* of observations, so that the inherent noise in the data can be partialled out.

Quetelet's contribution

The importance of statistical analyses for behavioural data was first realised by Adolphe Quetelet (1796–1874), a Belgian astronomer and professor of mathematics. He was analysing crime statistics from several countries. A problem with criminal activities is that it is nearly impossible to predict when and where they will happen (because they are the result of many random factors). However, what struck Quetelet was that, despite this inherent noise in the individual data points, the sums of the crimes looked very similar year upon year. Or as he wrote:

> Thus, as I have occasion to repeat already several times, one moves from one year to another with the sad perspective of seeing the same crimes reproduced in the same order, and attracting the same punishments in the same proportions . . . The greater the number of individuals, the more the single individual will becomes

obliterated and allows general facts to predominate, facts which depend on causes, facts according to which society exists and preserves itself.

(Quetelet (1835) as cited in Jahoda (2007) p. 82)

Whereas Quetelet was not able to predict a single crime, he was able to predict how many crimes there would be in the next year and which variables affected this number (e.g. differences between men and women, between countries, between seasons and so on). A similar observation was made by the American mathematician, Elizur Wright (1804–1885), who specialised in life insurance. He wrote: 'While nothing is more uncertain than the duration of a single life, nothing is more certain than the average duration of a thousand lives' (Gerteis 1991). The calculation of totals based on reasonably large samples was but the first step in which statistics helped to analyse behavioural data. Soon, this step was augmented by other, more sophisticated statistical measures and techniques.

Statistics help to design a proper study

Statistics not only allowed researchers to analyse their data, they also provided them with information of how to design a study so that valid conclusions could be drawn. This became painfully clear when the great British statistician Ronald Fisher (1890–1962) was called upon by the agricultural research institute at Rothamsted to sort out the data mess they had got themselves into (as recounted by Salsburg 2001). The purpose of the station was to find ways to improve crop cultivation. This was done by trying out different types of fertilisers on different fields. Each year the harvest was carefully registered and compared with the other fields and the produce of the previous years. Unfortunately, the resulting pattern became increasingly complex and chaotic, so that it was impossible to decide which fertilisers worked and which didn't. Hence, the call for help to Fisher.

In the end, Fisher was able to sort things out to some degree (in the process inventing or massively improving statistical techniques such as time series analysis and multiple regression analysis), but soon he started to explain to the users why the analysis had become so complicated and what could be done to simplify it. All that was needed was that the researchers at Rothamsted split up their fields into many small patches, some of which got the experimental fertiliser and others not. Then, simply by comparing the average harvest of both types of patches, the scientists would know whether the fertiliser had any effect, because all the other – confounding – variables (weather, soil, weeding practice, compatibility with the crops grown in the previous years, etc.) would be averaged out.

The choice of our example may have surprised you (you probably didn't expect to read about fertilisers in a book on historical and conceptual issues in psychology). However, the example can easily be extended to psychological studies (think of children in different classes, participants in different situations). The issues faced by psychological researchers turned out to be exactly the same as those encountered by agricultural researchers and they require very much the same type of experimental designs and statistical analyses.

Students of psychology are often surprised when they hear that a considerable part of their education consists of statistics and research methods, but a look at the many mistakes that were made before these techniques became widely available convinces each historian of their enormous value. Otherwise, students of psychology would simply repeat the errors made by the Society of the Observers of Man and the Rothamsted station, who did not know any better.

Interim summary

Four developments contributed heavily to the foundation of psychology as an independent branch of science:

- Darwin's evolutionary theory showed that living creatures evolve because of natural selection, and pointed to the importance of adaptation and the fact that humans may have evolved from animals.

- Philosophy and the society as a whole became more interested in the human mind; led to the use of the word 'psychology' and to discussions about how human functioning was best investigated.

- Advances in physiological studies; led to a theory of colour perception, psychophysics and the measurement of information transmission in the nervous system.

- The development of statistics; made it possible to analyse 'messy' data and pointed to the need of good research designs to draw valid conclusions.

KEY FIGURES

Scholars who paved the way to psychological research

- Thomas Young: British physician (1773–1829) who proposed that colour vision in humans was based on the perception of three primary colours (red, green and blue).

- Gustav Fechner: German university professor (1801–1887) who argued that the magnitude of a sensation corresponded to the logarithm of the stimulus intensity; founder of psychophysics.

- Hermann von Helmholtz: German physician (1821–1894) who proposed several theories of vision and is well known for the first studies on the speed of information transmission in nerves.

- Franciscus Cornelis Donders: Dutch ophthalmologist (1818–1889) who used differences in human reaction times to estimate the time taken by psychological processes; founder of mental chronometry.

- Adolphe Quetelet: Belgian astronomer and mathematician (1796–1874) who argued that averages of unpredictable phenomena were predictable; founder of the use of statistics in social research.

- Ronald Fisher: British mathematician (1891–1962) who was crucial in the development of analysis of variance, and who taught scientists how to do research, so that the data could easily be analysed statistically.

2.6 Focus on: Science does not attract everyone and does not seem to make society happier

In the previous and the present chapter we have depicted a largely positive picture of science. It should be acknowledged, however, that not everyone has been impressed or pleased with the increasing role of science in society. We discussed the ambivalent and at times hostile response of the Catholic Church (which also had to take into account an erosion of its power due to the increased respect given to 'scientific ways of thinking'). However, this was not the only negative reaction. Individuals also opposed what they perceived as a danger to the quality of their life. According to Dawkins (1998), the poet Keats criticised Newton for 'unweaving the rainbow'. Keats contended that by reducing the rainbow to a series of prismatic colours, Newton took away all the poetry and amazement evoked by the phenomenon.

Reactions against science

Leahey (2004) mentioned two types of reactions in individuals who did not feel at ease with the prominent place of science in their life. The first was a turn to Romanticism; the second was a turn to religion.

A turn to Romanticism

Romanticism is associated with a movement in eighteenth-century Western Europe that revolted against the changes due to the scientific and industrial revolutions. It was a revolt against the scientific rationalisation of life and the depiction of the world as a soulless machine. Romanticists stressed strong feelings and unconscious, non-rational intuitions as the bases of knowledge. They believed in a reality beyond the universe of atoms. They rejected the idea that human society could be based on rational grounds and scientifically controlled by man. For them, society was a living organism that spontaneously grew into a rich set of customs, norms and beliefs. People were wild beasts with a free will, not robots adhering to the rules set out by dreary scientists.

Although Romanticism as an artistic and intellectual revolt was rather short-lived, its legacy remains strong among people who are not impressed by the mantra that the scientific method is something we have developed over the past 200 years which lets us decide on the basis of a proven method what works and what does not. They do not see their private experiences as a liability and happily use them as the basis of actions and decisions. According to Eicher (1982), Romanticism also saved the arts: because science searches for universal laws, adherence to scientifically based aesthetics would have resulted in endless imitation and repetition of proven procedures.

A turn to religion

The second response against science Leahey (2004) discerned is a turn towards religion, mainly organised religion, such as evangelical Christianity or Islam, which provides alternative world views and belief systems. However, religion can also be a pagan or mystical movement without clear rules of conduct, in which case there often is a fuzzy boundary with the turn towards Romanticism. According to Leahey, the turn to religion as a reaction against the dominance of science in society has been more prominent in America than in Europe.

Folk science

Arguably the most common response people have to scientific findings is not so much a reaction *against*, but a more laid-back approach in which scientific insights are considered as just another source of information, on a par with their own intuitions and the information obtained from friends, relatives, popular books, magazines, television, the internet and so on. Scientific findings that strike a chord with their own thinking are incorporated, the rest is ignored. The Dutch forensic psychologist Eric Rassin (2008) recounted how in his experience judges rarely take into account empirical findings that do not agree with their own judgement. When it comes to reason versus lab results, judges side with Plato. They assume that their own reasoning is the golden standard and that empirical findings are the underdog, which have to prove their worth. Similarly, for most people anecdotes and their own speculations have the same (or even more) weight as scientifically gathered data.

folk science

intuitive theories people have about the workings of the world, based on a combination of scientifically gathered and non-scientifically gathered information

The combination of scientifically gathered and non-scientifically gathered information to build intuitive theories about the workings of the world is called folk science. Keil (2003) argued that people's folk science in general is far less detailed than they themselves believe. Humans' intuitive theories are rarely more than vague sketches of what is going on. Keil called this the 'illusion of knowledge depth'. For instance, when people are asked how a helicopter functions, their understanding usually goes no further than the knowledge that the turning blades lift the machine. In particular, people have a tendency to overestimate their explanatory understanding (i.e. knowing what is the origin of what). They are less biased in assessing their knowledge of specific facts or procedures (e.g. what exactly makes the blades turn, or from what materials they are made).

According to Keil, intuitive theories are framework theories without details. They provide conceptual umbrellas that give a feeling of coherence and sense, but that break down as soon as a practical intervention is required in a new situation. Then, people have to elaborate explanations on the fly on the basis of their conceptual frameworks and the knowledge they have. In addition, they can make use of distributed cognition. That is, they can search for an individual who knows more. The existence of such mutually supporting roles makes it possible for a group of individuals to achieve more than each person individually.

? What do you think?

What is your stance towards science and products of science? Do you believe the scientific method should be applied to find answers to all types of questions? Do you think science impoverishes life? Or are you a happy consumer of scientific insights and scientific products that interest you, without this having much impact on the rest of your life?

Scientific advances and human well-being

Another question one can ask is whether the recent scientific advances have made people more or less happy.

What do you think?

Do scientific discoveries make people more or less happy?

Changes in well-being

The scientific advances of the past century have provided us with more easily obtainable food, a much longer life expectancy, more comfortable housing and better medical treatment. They also gave us gadgets such as radios, televisions, computers connected to the internet, telephones, cars, planes and so on. At the same time, they have resulted in an ever increasing number of people living in overcrowded cities, increased pollution, an increased complexity of human interactions, a higher information load, higher performance pressure, etc.

A way to gauge the consequences of all these changes for the well-being of people is to ask them. This can be done, for instance, by asking them to rate their degree of agreement with statements such as 'In most ways my life is close to my ideal', 'I am satisfied with my life' and 'If I could live my life over, I would change almost nothing' (e.g. Pavot *et al.* 1991). Figure 2.8 shows the results of a 45-year-long study in the USA based on this type of question. Even though incomes over this period more than doubled, people did not rate themselves as happier at the end than at the beginning; they did not rate themselves as unhappier either. This agrees with many other studies,

Figure 2.8 United States income and subjective well-being (SWB).

Source: Diener *et al.* (1998).

suggesting that the degree of well-being does not differ much as a function of life conditions, as long as there is no famine.

So there is some truth to the allegation that recent scientific advances have not made humankind any happier. People seem to have a basic level of (un)happiness that is relatively unaffected by their personal circumstances (bar short-term fluctuations due to positive or negative events and some long-term consequences of seriously life-interfering events such as a major disability; Lucas 2007). On the basis of figure 2.8 it can safely be concluded that the current level of well-being in society would not have been lower if none of the scientific inventions of the last 50 years had happened. On the other hand, figure 2.8 also shows that people are wrong when they assume that science has made life miserable. What seems to happen is that some people consistently report a rather low level of subjective well-being largely independently of what happens to them, whereas other people consistently report a higher level (Diener *et al.* 1998). Scientific advances do not seem to alter that.

Interim summary

- Not everyone has been impressed with the increasing role of science in life. Three common types of reactions in these people have been:
  - a turn to Romanticism,
  - a turn to religion,
  - the inclusion of scientific findings along with other experiences and opinions, giving rise to folk science.

- Despite the scientific and technological advances of the last 50 years, people do not seem to have become happier. On average they have not become less happy either.

Recommended literature

As in Chapter 1, a lot of extra information on the historical events can readily be found in encyclopedias (e.g. www.wikipedia.org). The full texts of many of the books described here also are available on the internet (e.g. through google books). These were the other texts we used to write the present chapter.

The Copernican revolution
The impact of Copernicus and Galilei for the development of science is well described in Chalmers, A.F. (1999) *What is this thing called science?*

(3rd edition). Maidenhead: Open University Press. Very readable introductions about the lives, works, and times of Galilei, Descartes and Newton are respectively: Sobel, D. (1999) *Galileo's daughter* (London: Fourth Estate); Grayling, A.C. (2005) *Descartes: The life of René Descartes and its place in his times* (London: Pocket Books); Gleick, J. (2003) *Isaac Newton* (London: Harper Perennial).

Darwin and evolutionary theory
The original *Origin of Species* is in print and remains a worthwhile read. Jones, S. (1999)

Almost like a whale: The origin of species updated (London: Doubleday) is an equally readable introduction to the evolutionary theory. Particularly worthwhile reading is Endersby, J. (2007) *A guinea pig's history of biology* (London: William Heinemann), which describes the various plants and animals that have played a central role in working out the mechanisms of the evolutionary theory.

Developments that led to the emergence of psychology

The book we found most informative to understand how psychology came about was Leahey, T.H. (2004) *A history of psychology* (Upper Saddle River, NJ: Pearson Prentice Hall). Another book that contains many interesting insights is Jahoda, G. (2007) *A history of social psychology* (Cambridge: Cambridge University Press).

References

Chalmers, A.F. (1999) *What is this thing called science?* (3rd edn). Maidenhead: Open University Press.

Cohen, H.F. (1994) *The scientific revolution: A historiographical inquiry.* Chicago: University of Chicago Press.

Dawkins, R. (1998) *Unweaving the rainbow: Science, delusion, and the appetite for wonder.* Boston: Houghton Mifflin.

Diener, E., Suh, E.M., Lucas, R.E. and Smith, H.L. (1998) 'Subjective well-being: Three decades of progress', *Psychological Bulletin,* 125: 276–302.

Eicher, H. (1982) 'The rise of modern science and the genesis of romanticism', *Publications of the Modern Language Association of America,* 97: 8–30.

Gerteis, L.S. (1991) Book review of 'Abolitionist, actuary, atheist: Elizur Wright and the reform impulse, by Lawrence B. Goodheart', *The Journal of American History* 77: 1360–1.

Hatfield, G. (1998) 'Kant and empirical psychology in the 18th century', *Psychological Science,* 9: 423–8.

Jahoda, G. (2007) *A history of social psychology.* Cambridge: Cambridge University Press.

Jones, S. (1999) *Almost like a whale: The origin of species updated.* London: Doubleday.

Keil, F. C. (2003) 'Folkscience: Coarse interpretations of a complex reality', *Trends in Cognitive Sciences,* 7: 368–73.

Leahey, T.H. (2004) *A history of psychology.* Upper Saddle River, NJ: Pearson/Prentice Hall.

Lucas, R.E. (2007) 'Adaptation and the set-point model of subjective well-being: Does happiness change after major life events?', *Current Directions in Psychological Science,* 16: 75–9.

Pavot, W., Diener, E., Colvin, C.R. and Sandvik, E. (1991) 'Further validation of the satisfaction with life scale: Evidence for the cross-method convergence of well-being measures', *Journal of Personality Assessment,* 57: 149–61.

Rassin, E. (2008) *De hand in eigen boezem [Searching our own heart].* Inaugural lecture on the acceptance of the post of professor at the Erasmus University Rotterdam.

Salsburg, D. (2001) *The lady tasting tea: How statistics revolutionized science in the twentieth century.* New York: Freeman.

Twaddle, M. (1966) 'The Oxford and Cambridge admissions controversy of 1834', *British Journal of Educational Studies,* 14: 45–58.

03 The first attempts to establish psychology as an independent discipline

This chapter will cover

Questions to consider

Historical issues addressed in this chapter

- When did psychology start?
- Which types of textbooks influenced the emergence of psychology as an independent academic discipline?
- When and how did the first psychological laboratory come about?
- Which research methods did Wundt use?
- Who were the founders of psychology in the USA?
- When did psychologists start to measure intelligence?
- How did the treatment of mental health problems evolve up to the twentieth century?
- Which new elements did Freud introduce?

Conceptual issues addressed in this chapter

- Can a complex discipline, such as psychology have a single birthday?
- To what extent do degrees at universities depend on socio-political choices in the wider society?
- Does Wundt's fame as the founder of psychology also mean that he has a lasting scientific legacy?
- To what extent has the history of early psychology been misrepresented in the writings of Boring?

Introduction

Psychology stands in a peculiar relation to the sciences of life and to the physical sciences, for it is one of the youngest of Philosophy's children and, on that account, has fallen heir, as do the successive members of any growing family, to a number of family treasures, some good, some bad, and some indifferent. Among other things, it has inherited from the physical sciences a well-rounded methodology and a refined laboratory technique; and from the sciences of life, a 'genetic' way of regarding mind in its relation to life. Moreover, in the near future, some one will write a history of the development of scientific concepts and it will then be discovered that psychology has fallen heir, also, to scientific ways of regarding the world at large, ways that became established a hundred years or so before mind was brought into the laboratory.

(Griffith 1921, p. 17)

In the previous chapter we saw how changes in society and progress in knowledge primed the Western world for the scientific study of the human mind. In the present chapter we discuss the first attempts to establish psychology as an independent academic discipline. First, we look at the role of textbooks as precursors of the movement. Next we talk about the establishment of the first psychology laboratory in Germany and how psychology in only a few years came to flourish in the USA (which would soon dominate the field). Then we point out how psychology became applied to pressing social issues, such as helping children with educational needs and patients with mental problems. As in Chapter 1, we end with a section on how history writing not only describes the past but also to some extent shapes it.

3.1   Psychology textbooks as precursors of the new movement

We saw in Chapter 2 that by the mid-1800s there was no shortage of writings and books on psychology (see also Hatfield 1998; Teo 2007). The reason for this was that long before psychology became institutionalised (i.e. recognised as an independent academic discipline), it was a topic of philosophical reflection and, hence, part of the philosophical curriculum. The teaching of psychology further intensified when it became a compulsory course in several curricula (e.g. in the education of teachers in Germany from the early nineteenth century on; Gundlach 2004). This created a market for textbooks giving a systematic presentation of the subject. Some of these textbooks not only contained the (then) state of the art, but in addition had a strong impact on how the subject was perceived and, hence, on its further developments.

Textbooks inspired by philosophy

The earliest books remained close to philosophy and were centred on questions such as 'Does advancement of knowledge in psychology depend on rational or on empirical methods?', 'What does human consciousness exist of?' and 'How many faculties does the human mind have?' Some of the most important books are given below.

Rational vs. empirical psychology

In the 1730s the German philosopher Christian Wolff published two books, in which he proposed a distinction between *rational psychology* and *empirical psychology* (Chapter 2). Rational psychology was conceptualised as the science of the nature of the human soul. It was based on deduction and addressed issues such as the soul's substantiality, simplicity, immateriality and immortality, as well as the mind–body problem. Empirical psychology dealt with what actually happened in the human soul (such as the ability to know and to desire) and was based on the experiences people had. This distinction would heavily influence the later textbooks of the eighteenth and the nineteenth centuries.

Associationism

associationism

speculation that the mind learns by associating the elements obtained through perception; two main principles of association are similarity (similar elements get associated) and contiguity in time and space (elements that co-occur get associated)

Around 1855 the Scottish scholar Alexander Bain published two highly influential books, *The Senses and the Intellect* and *The Emotions and the Will*, in which he tried to explain a broad series of psychological phenomena on the basis of associationism and physiology. Associationism refers to the assumption that all human knowledge consists of associations between simple elements obtained through perception. This view goes back to Plato and Aristotle but is particularly linked to the British empiricist school, starting with John Locke (Chapter 2). Two principles were claimed to underlie the formation of associations between elementary sensations: similarity and contiguity in time and space. Sensations that resembled one another became associated, so that humans could generalise from individual perceptions to permanent concepts. Experiences that followed each other closely in time or space also got associated and formed the basis of the human knowledge about causes and consequences.

As we will see in this and the next chapter, associationism would form the cornerstone of nearly all psychological theories of human knowledge until well into the second half of the twentieth century.

Textbooks inspired by physiology

Philosophy was not the only source of inspiration for textbooks of psychology. Another string of books was guided by the research done on the bodily functions of living organisms (i.e. physiology). Below we list two examples.

Case studies of brain damage

In 1770 the German physician Johann Gesner published his *Sammlung von Beobachtungen aus der Arzneygelahrtheit und Naturkunde* (Collection of Observations from the Medical Scholarship), in which he collected numerous observations on brain-damaged patients as natural experiments in psychology. It included a 75-page chapter on language difficulties after brain injuries.

Research methods used by the physiologists

In 1873 the German scientist Wilhelm Wundt published the textbook *Grundzüge der physiologischen Psychologie* (Principles of Physiological Psychology), in which psychology was defined as the study of the way in which persons look upon themselves, on the basis of internal physiological changes that inform them about the phenomena perceived by the external senses. Or as Wundt formulated it, the aim of 'physiological psychology' was:

> first, to investigate those life processes that, standing midway between external and internal experience, require the simultaneous application of both methods of observation, the external and the internal; . . . [This new science] begins with physiological processes and seeks to demonstrate how these influence the domain of internal observation. . . . The name physiological psychology . . . points to psychology as the real subject of our science. If one wishes to place emphasis on methodological characteristics, our science might be called experimental psychology in distinction from the usual science of mind based purely on introspection.
>
> *(Wundt (1873) p. 157; as cited in Leahey (2004) p. 234)*

Wundt called this psychology 'physiological psychology' not only because he thought physiology should form the basis of psychology, but also because he was convinced that psychology should use the experimental methods that had been pioneered by the physiologists, in particular the registration of response times (Chapter 2). A few years after the publication of his book Wundt would effectively start to study the new physiological psychology, rather than simply writing about the viability of such investigations, as all textbook writers had done before him.

What do you think?

For most people a textbook is the first contact with a particular topic. Do you have memories of how a textbook affected your perception of a particular subject? Did you come to dislike a subject because of the way it was presented? And conversely, did you unexpectedly become interested in a topic because of the textbook used?

Interim summary

Before psychology existed as an independent discipline, important ideas were published in textbooks by authors who themselves did not do psychological research. These ideas came from:

- philosophy:
  - some psychology questions can be investigated empirically, others require rational analysis
  - knowledge consists of associations between elementary sensations
- physiology:
  - knowledge can be gathered from case studies of people with brain damage
  - the methods used by the physiologists (e.g. response time measurement) can be used to address psychological questions.

3.2   The foundation of the first laboratory of experimental psychology by Wundt

Although by 1850 there was a considerable range of psychology textbooks, which were used for psychology courses in colleges and universities, it is hard to consider them as exponents of a truly independent academic discipline. What was lacking was a group of scholars who called themselves psychologists and who studied psychology in the same way as other scientists investigated their subjects. As such, despite the availability of textbooks and the fact that psychology was taught in several curricula, psychology as a distinct *field of study* or a distinct *discipline* did not yet exist. This would only happen when Wilhelm Wundt got appointed as professor at the University of Leipzig and started his laboratory of experimental psychology.

What do you think?

If you are studying at a university with a centuries-old history, it may be interesting to try to find out (1) when at your university the first course of psychology was taught, (2) when the first chair (professorship) in psychology was established, and (3) when the first psychology degree was awarded. Usually, these three markers of the establishment of a discipline do not coincide. Sometimes there are several decades in between!

Wundt's background

Education

Wilhelm Wundt (1832–1920) was born to an intellectual family (his father was a minister, and on both sides of the family were professors and physicians). Wundt was an unmotivated and rather poor student in secondary school, but pulled himself together when he studied medicine and started to excel. After his PhD (or at least the equivalent of it), he obtained an assistantship with Hermann von Helmholtz, the man who had started to measure the speed of signal transmission in nerves (Chapter 2). Here Wundt began to identify himself as a scientific psychologist. In 1862 he gave his first course in 'Psychology as a Natural Science' and in 1874 he published his book on physiological psychology, referred to above.

German universities as centres of independent research

The nineteenth century was an interesting time for German academics. Before, Germany existed as a nation under the name of the *Holy Roman Empire* (including at its height present-day Germany, Austria, Hungary, Belgium, the Netherlands, Luxembourg, the Czech Republic and Slovenia), but in reality it was a confederation of tens of smaller kingdoms, principalities, duchies and free cities, which acted more or less as sovereign states and occasionally had battles over land disputes. The empire broke down in two parts in 1805–1806, when Napoleon first defeated a coalition around the Austrians in the south (this part would continue as the *Austrian Empire* and later as the *Austro-Hungarian Empire*) and then a coalition around the Prussians in the north (which would later unify into the forerunner of the present-day *Federal Republic of Germany*, consisting of a federation of 16 states).

The defeat by the French particularly upset the Prussians, who decided it was high time to modernise their country. The school system was reorganised and a new model of university was installed. Previously, the universities had been places of education, mainly aimed at the training of physicians, lawyers and clergy. Science was secondary and, therefore, not financed. It was left as a pastime to prodigies of wealthy families or to scholars who were supported by wealthy patrons. In Berlin, the capital of Prussia, a new type of university was inaugurated based on two goals that were both financed: *Wissenschaft* (scholarship and scientific research) and *Bildung* (the making of good citizens). The power of the university was in the hands of a small number of professors who were given quite generous resources for their research and who had a number of assistants and lecturers under their command. This type of university rapidly expanded over the entire German federation. The emphasis on scientific research made the German universities open to the creation of new areas for scientific investigation and by the end of the nineteenth century Germany was one of the front-runners in the industrial revolution.

In 1875 Wundt was appointed Professor of Philosophy in Leipzig (after a short stay in Zurich), the university where Fechner had published his *Elements of Psychophysics* (Chapter 2). It was at this university that Wundt in 1879 created the first laboratory of experimental psychology. This is universally accepted as the birth of psychology.

What do you think?

We will return in Chapter 9 to the question of why the establishment of Wundt's laboratory is defined as the beginning of psychology and not the publication of a major book with psychology in its title or the award of the first degree in psychology. Can you think of reasons why psychologists saw the opening of a laboratory of scientific research as an especially promising sign for the start of psychology as an independent discipline?

Research in Wundt's laboratory

Teaching psychological research

One of the reasons why Wundt's laboratory had a strong impact on the creation of psychology is that Wundt used it to actively promote psychological research. He not only created a journal (which he surprisingly called *Philosophische Studien* [Philosophical Studies]), but he also set up a 6-month introductory course, to which he invited students and colleagues from all over the world. We know quite a lot about the workings of the laboratory, because a few participants published a short account of what happened. The most interesting of them was written by a Belgian professor, Jules-Jean Van Biervliet, who had managed to get his own psychology laboratory at Ghent University and as part of his preparation went for training to Wundt's laboratory. In 1892 he wrote an account of his experiences in French, which was recently translated into English (Nicolas and Ferrand 1999). Because the report itself is so lively, we quote extensively from it.

> Thanks to the generosity of the Saxon government, Mr. Wundt was able to fit out premises, buy essential measuring apparatus, and give the first practical training in psychology. The Leipzig institute, founded about 10 years ago, includes at the moment a relatively large number of workers. During the last summer semester, 24 young persons, among them 8 foreigners, did original research under the close supervision of Mr. Wundt. Several former students of the master have founded

laboratories similar to the one at Leipzig at universities such as Göttingen, Freiburg, and Bonn. A very modest laboratory is directed by Professor Ebbinghaus at Berlin. The Americans, always numerous at Wundt's institute (there were five of them last summer), founded about 20 institutes of psychology in their own country. However, Leipzig remains the center in which the most numerous and important works are done . . .

The distinguished professor, as well as his assistants, Messrs. Külpe and Kirschmann, introduced us with the greatest kindness to the smallest details of their scientific installations . . .

The young people who intend to tackle issues of experimental psychology come to the institute with very different backgrounds of theoretical preparation and practical training. In addition to medical students and candidates for a PhD in science, there are philosophy students, lawyers, and even teachers of primary education.

The goal of the introductory course is to introduce this heterogeneous group to the specific aspects of experimental work, to familiarize the newcomer with the main equipment used in the laboratory, and to discuss and criticize the various methods used until now in the collection of data. This course, limited in time – it contains only 15 sessions – is repeated every 6 months. Thus, every semester new students attend the seminar in psychology.

Dr. Külpe is in charge of this preliminary course. The course, intended for a necessarily restricted audience, is conducted in an informal manner. The professor has in front of him the apparatus, of which he explains the use and the function. A blackboard nearby allows the professor to draw curves, to do arithmetic. The audience is often questioned on the way it would run an experiment, to avoid misinterpretations. The professor discusses the answer, shows the weak points, then himself gives the right answer. The audience is allowed to interrupt the professor, to raise objections, to ask for clarifications. The end of the course is often devoted to running a series of experiments with the equipment previously described, applying the methods just discussed.

When the introductory course is nearing its end, Mr. Külpe proposes to his audience two or three subjects of original research. The students have 8 days to develop a design, to determine the technical arrangement, to choose the methods that, according to them, will give the best solution to the problem.

The last two sessions are devoted to a detailed examination of the different proposals given during the course. This sort of examination allows the professor to estimate the benefit the students have gained from the introductory course . . .

To provide for the numerous needs of the laboratory, Mr. Wundt has an annual sum of money of only 1,500 Deutschmarks at his disposal; it is really insufficient to equip a laboratory consisting each year of more than 20 people. So it would be wrong to expect luxurious installations at Leipzig. Some Americans told us that laboratories of psychology in the United States are far better equipped . . .

Invariably every day, Mr. Wundt spends his afternoon in the laboratory. From time to time he visits the groups of workers; always unassuming and affable, he listens to the remarks, examines the installations, criticizes a detail, suggests an improvement . . .

Indeed, workers are organized in groups. . . . For each project, we name a chief experimenter, some assistants if necessary, and one or several subjects. The experimenter, head of the group, is generally an experienced person; having worked in the laboratory for several semesters, he is familiar with psychophysiological techniques. The apparatuses are familiar to him, the electricity has no more secrets for him. If the reader remembers how workers are recruited, he will understand the necessity of this organization. Besides the physicists and the physiologists, always relatively rare, we find a large number of students in philosophy and law. These students are able to supervise researchers only after a long initiation, after devoting two or three semesters, either as a subject or as an assistant experimenter, to become familiar with the specialized equipment used at the institute.

The head of a group is an important person; the success of the project depends largely upon him, . . . The subject or the subjects also have an important role in this success; the fundamental quality required from them is absolute sincerity. A subject must above all be conscientious; he must react naturally without bias, especially without preconceived ideas. . . . The subject is not always the same. To test a law, it is very often necessary to use a series of subjects. So the assistants, the fellow students of the workers, even the foreigners often serve as subjects of the ongoing experiments . . .

The necessary complement of experimental installations is a good library, . . . Among the books in the collection, next to purely philosophical works of Leibnitz, Kant, Herbart, Schopenhauer, we find the works of Fechner, Stumpf, Ribot, Preyer, Taine, Bain, Spencer, Delboeuf, Bucola. The treatises of physiology by Hermann and Wundt, the medical physic of the same author, the works of Helmholtz, Pflüger's archives of physiology, and so forth . . .

(Van Biervliet (1892) as cited in Nicolas and Ferrand (1999) p. 196–201).

The methods used by Wundt

Van Biervliet's account is in line with what is currently known about Wundt's methodology (as we will see below, Wundt's work for a long time has been misrepresented in history books and introductory books). Wundt used three groups of methods for three different types of problems.

Experimental methods

First, Wundt and his students used experimental methods. These methods included:

1. psychophysical methods to study the connection between physical stimuli and their conscious states,

2. the measurement of the duration of simple mental processes,

3. the accuracy of reproduction in memory tasks.

Wundt was very familiar with Fechner's work on psychophysics (Chapter 2). So, quite a lot of energy was devoted to the psychophysical measurement of barely noticeable differences, i.e. the minimum perceivable difference between two stimuli. The following account by James McKeen Cattell (1888), one of Wundt's best-known American students, gives a flavour of what was investigated and found:

> Ever since Helmholtz published, in 1862, his classical researches on sound, much attention has been given to the perception of musical notes, investigations having been undertaken by Mach, Preyer, Hensen, Stumpf and others. Careful experiments, not yet published, have also been carried on for several years past in the Leipsic [sic] laboratory. Luft with tuning-forks and Lorenz with an apparatus on the principle of the harmonium have been investigating the least noticeable difference in pitch in the same manner as the loudness of sound has been studied. We have seen that the ear does not readily distinguish differences in loudness; in pitch, on the contrary, small changes can be noticed with marvellous accuracy, and this whether the observer be 'musical' or not. In the range most easily covered by the human voice (from about c' to c''', 256 to 1024 vibrations per second) successive notes can be distinguished when the difference between the physical stimuli is 1/4 to 1/5 of a vibration per sec. Where the pianoforte machine gives 24 notes the ear can distinguish over 3000.
>
> (Cattell, J.M. (1888) 'The psychological laboratory at Leipsic', Mind, *13*, p. 37–51. Reproduced by permission of Oxford University Press.)

Reaction times were measured to get insight in the mental processes that were required to perform a task. Here again a description by James McKeen Cattell:

> The term *psychometry* can . . . be confined to . . . the subject which we are about to take up, the measurement of the duration of mental processes. Psychometry has received abundant attention from astronomers, physicists, physiologists and psychologists; nearly half the researches undertaken in the Leipsic laboratory are concerned with this subject. We are naturally glad to find it possible to apply methods of measurement directly to consciousness; there is no doubt but that mental processes take up time, and that this time can be determined. The measurements thus obtained are not psycho-physical as those which we have been recently considering, but purely psychological. It may be true that we are in some sort measuring the 'outside' of the mind, but the facts obtained, when we learn how long it takes to perceive, to will, to remember, etc., are in themselves of the same interest to the psychologist, as the distances of the stars to the astronomer or atomic weights to the chemist. But, besides the general interest of psychometrical facts as a part of a complete description of the mind, these times are of further and great use to the psychologist, as they help him in analysing complex mental phenomena, and in studying the nature of attention, volition, etc. It should also be noticed that psychometrical experiment has brought, perhaps, the strongest testimony we have to the complete parallelism of physical and mental phenomena; there is scarcely any doubt but that our determinations measure at once the rate of change in the brain and of change in consciousness. . . .
>
> It will not be necessary to describe at length the psychometrical researches undertaken at Leipsic, as the most recent of these have been printed in [the journal] *MIND*. Most of the earlier work on this subject was then reviewed; attention should, however, be called to researches by Kraepelin and by Berger. Kraepelin studied the effects of certain drugs on the duration of a reaction and of simple

mental processes. These times seem to be at first lengthened and then shortened by ether and chloroform, and at first shortened and then lengthened by alcohol, a difference of action which, perhaps, has less to do with different effects of the drugs on the nervous system than with the method of taking them, ether and chloroform being inhaled and alcohol drunk. Berger, in experimenting with light, sound and electric shock, found the reaction-time to become shorter as the stimulus was taken stronger. According to these experiments, the reaction-time for the several colours is the same.

(Cattell, J.M. (1888) 'The psychological Laboratory at Leipsic', Mind, 13, p. 37–51. Reproduced by permission of Oxford University Press.)

These excerpts also show that Wundt's lab did not form an island, but was part of a network of laboratories that did very similar research and communicated intensively with each other. Finally the fragments (and the larger texts they come from) show how the early psychological researchers tried to apply the methods of physics to their topics. The texts describe extensively the efforts made to reduce the variability in the measurements, both by more accurate measurements and by making use of a small number (sometimes only 1!) of trained participants. What was not yet known at that time was that variability is an inherent characteristic of biological processes and that demand characteristics have a strong influence on psychological findings, even when people try to be conscientious and react naturally without bias and without preconceived ideas. Demand characteristics refer to the fact that participants change their behaviour (often without awareness) when they have information about the experiment's purpose.

Introspection

introspection

one of the three research methods introduced by Wundt; consists of a person looking inside and reporting what he/she senses, thinks or feels

The experimental methods were particularly important in Wundt's early years when he defined physiological psychology and established the laboratory of experimental psychology. However, Wundt also strongly believed in a second method: introspection. This is a process by which a person looks inside and reports what he/she is sensing, thinking or feeling. It is based on the belief that people have conscious access to (parts of) their own mental processes and can report them. Wundt's affection for introspection became painfully clear when his assistant, Oswald Külpe, published his own textbook of experimental psychology, *Grundriss der Psychologie* (Outlines of Psychology, 1893). In this book Külpe defended the thesis that psychology should be a natural science, exclusively based on the experimental method. Psychology should be limited to those psychological processes that are amenable to experimental methods (nearly three quarters of the book was devoted to sensation).

Three years after the publication of Külpe's book Wundt (by that time already well over 60) published his own book with the same title, in which he refuted Külpe. First, he emphasised that there was a big difference between the natural sciences and psychology. Whereas the former were concerned with objects, independently of the perception of the subject, the latter dealt with perception itself and the way it was influenced by the person. The research method of preference here was introspection, looking at the contents of the mind from inside. For Wundt this was the way to study the nature of human consciousness, even though he was well aware of the criticisms that had been raised against the method. For many scientists introspection was not a valid, objective observation method and did not differ from what philosophers had been doing since ancient times. Auguste Comte, for instance, was very clear in this respect. For him psychology could never be a science because of its reliance on introspection, as can be seen in the following excerpt:

> I limit myself to pointing out the principal consideration which proves clearly that this pretended direct contemplation of the mind by itself is a pure illusion. . . . It is in fact evident that, by an invincible necessity, the human mind can observe directly all phenomena except its own proper states. For by whom shall the observation of these be made? It is conceivable that a man might observe himself with respect to the passions that animate him, for the anatomical organs of passion are distinct from those whose function is observation. Though we have all made such observations on ourselves, they can never have much scientific value, and the best mode of knowing the passions will always be that of observing them from without; . . . The thinker cannot divide himself into two, of whom one reasons whilst the other observes him reason. The organ observed and the organ observing being, in this case, identical, how could observation take place? This pretended psychological method is then radically null and void. On the one hand, they advise you to isolate yourself, as far as possible, from every external sensation, especially every intellectual work, – for if you were to busy yourself even with the simplest calculation, what would become of internal observation? – on the other hand, after having with the utmost care attained this state of intellectual slumber, you must begin to contemplate the operations going on in your mind, when nothing there takes place! Our descendants will doubtless see such pretensions some day ridiculed upon the stage. The results of so strange a procedure harmonize entirely with its principle. For all the two thousand years during which metaphysicians have thus cultivated psychology, they are not agreed about one intelligible and established proposition. 'Internal observation' gives almost as many divergent results as there are individuals who think they practice it.
>
> *(Comte (1830–1842) as cited in James (1890) Vol. 1, p. 188).*

Wundt thought he could get away with the limitations of introspection by introducing more control into the experimental situation. He made a distinction between *Innere Wahrnehmung* (internal perception) and *Experimentelle Selbstbeobachtung* (experimental self-observation). The former referred to armchair introspection as practised by philosophers; the latter pointed to self-observation in highly controlled circumstances, where a stimulus was presented repeatedly and the participants reported their experiences to the stimulus. Wundt claimed that experimental self-observation was a valid scientific method to get information about the contents of consciousness, whereas internal perception was not.

historical method

one of the three research methods introduced by Wundt; consists of studying the human mind by investigating the products of human cultures; according to Wundt particularly well suited to investigate the 'higher' functions of the mind

? What do you think?

The limits of introspection are usually well explained in introductory textbooks. Do you think this method is still used today? If so, why? If not, what has changed since Wundt's time?

The historical method

Finally, Wundt's third method consisted of a study of the products of the human mind. In particular, towards the end of his life he became a firm believer in the historical method, the study of mental differences as revealed by differences between cultures (both in time and in space). This method was particularly well suited to studying 'higher' psychological functions, such as the social aspects of human thought and behaviour, for which the experimental methods could not be used. Wundt believed that the development of an individual recapitulated the evolution of mankind. So, a person's development could be studied by examining the historical development of the human race. Wundt called this type of psychology *Völkerpsychologie* (Psychology of the Peoples or Folk Psychology), to which he devoted the last two decades of his life (and 10 book volumes). Because of this work, Wundt is also sometimes considered as the founder of anthropology, the study of cultures and societies.

Wundt's legacy

Despite the fact that Wundt had a career of 65 years, was head of the best laboratory in the world, and was a prolific writer (he published more than 50,000 pages, in a time when texts were still written by hand), his scientific legacy is not very much more than that of being 'the father of experimental psychology'. The main reason for this is that Wundt did not produce a useful theory like Newton or Darwin, or make an empirical discovery that had a wide-ranging, lasting impact (such as Lavoisier's discovery that oxygen was needed for the burning of a substance). Furthermore, although Wundt was considered to be a good teacher, his writings were far from clear and easy to read. Below you find two examples. The first is from one of his 'easiest' books (*Grundriss der Psychologie*, 1896), the other is from the *Völkerpsychologie*.

> If we apply these considerations to psychology, it is obvious at once, from the very nature of its subject-matter, that exact observation is here possible only in the form of *experimental* observation; and that psychology can never be a *pure* science of observation. The contents of this science are exclusively *processes,* not permanent objects. In order to investigate with exactness the rise and progress of these processes, their composition out of various components, and the interrelations of these components, we must be able first of all to bring about their beginning at will, and purposely to vary the conditions of the same. This is possible here, as in all cases, only through experiment, not through pure introspection. Besides this general reason there is another, peculiar to psychology, that does not apply at all to natural phenomena. In the latter case we purposely abstract from the perceiving subject, and under circumstances, especially when favored by the regularity of the phenomena, as in astronomy, mere observation may succeed in determining with adequate certainty the objective components of the processes.
>
> *(Wundt 1896/1897, p. 20–1)*

> In so far as Völkerpsychologie can find any psychological laws of independent content, these will always be *applications* of principles valid for individual psychology. But one can also assume that the conditions of mutual mental interaction will bring out new and special manifestations of the general psychic forces that could not be predicted from the mere knowledge of the properties of individual consciousness; these again will augment our insight into the functioning of individual mental life.
> *(Wundt (1908) as cited and translated in Jahoda (2007) p. 127)*

Finally, there were several contradictions in Wundt's writings over the period of more than 60 years (e.g. in the higher importance he attached to experimental methods in his early writings than in his late writings). The American psychologist William James saw an inverse ratio between Wundt's productivity and his wisdom and let the following (for him uncharacteristically derisory) quote slip:

> He aims at being a Napoleon of the intellectual world. Unfortunately he will never have a Waterloo, for he is Napoleon without genius and with no central idea . . . Whilst they make mincemeat of some of his views by their criticisms, he is meanwhile writing a book on an entirely different subject. Cut him up like a worm, and each fragment crawls; there is no *noeud vital* in his mental medulla oblongata, so that you can't kill him all at once.
>
> *(as cited in Boring (1950) p. 346)*

KEY FIGURE

Wilhelm Wundt

Source: US National Library of Medicine / Science Photo Library Ltd

- Germany, 1832–1920.

- Studied with von Helmholtz (measurement of reaction times).

- Wrote a book on *Physiological Psychology* in 1873.

- Once he became professor, he founded the first laboratory of experimental psychology at the University of Leipzig in 1879.

- Offered a course in psychological research which would attract many beginning psychologists from all over the world.

- At first mainly promoted experimental methods (reaction time measurement, psychophysics, memory performance). Later stressed the importance of introspection for the study of higher mental processes. Towards the end of his life invested heavily in the historical method.

- His writings were not easy to read, sometimes contradicted each other, and did not contain lasting insights. As a result, his scientific legacy is very limited.

Interim summary

- Wundt was a German physician who became interested in applying the physiological methods to psychological phenomena.

- He made use of the possibility offered by German universities to establish a new laboratory in Leipzig in 1879. This event is considered to be the birth of psychology.

- Wundt not only used the experimental methods from physiology, but also thought that introspection was a valid research method and that information about the psychology of individuals could be obtained by looking at cultures. The impact of the latter two methods increased as he grew older.

- Many psychologists got their initial training in Wundt's laboratory.

3.3   Starting psychology in America: James and Titchener

James's *Principles of Psychology*

Introductory psychology courses in the American curricula

In 1875, William James (1842–1910) started to teach a course of psychology at Harvard University. The curricula of many colleges and universities in the USA included such a course as the introduction to the study of philosophy (just as a course of psychology was taught in Germany and France). The fact that James taught this course was testament to the breadth of his interests, and also demonstrated that psychology was not yet considered as an independent discipline. James had started to study chemistry and finally settled on medicine. He already taught a course on physiology. At other universities, the introductory psychology course was given by lecturers who primarily taught courses in philosophy or education. For example, at one university it was taught by a member of staff of the Department of English and History, and at another it was delivered by a lecturer with the title 'Professor of anatomy, physiology, and geology' (Fuchs 2000).

The impact of the Principles

James turned out to be a great success in the classroom. Gradually he planned to write his own textbook and in 1878 signed up to a publisher. What followed was a 12-year struggle to finish his two-volume book, *The Principles of Psychology* (1890), which may be one of the reasons for the scornful comment on Wundt mentioned above (Wundt published about one volume a year). However, James's book turned out to be what Wundt's writings never were: an accessible and clear account of what was known and conjectured about psychology at the end of the nineteenth century. Within a few years the *Principles* (or rather its shorter version that was published in 1892 and known as '*the Jimmy*') would become the textbook of choice at many colleges and universities in the English-speaking world. Because of his textbook James has been one of most influential people in the early history of psychology, even though a few years after the book's publication he decided that psychology was not interesting enough and turned towards philosophical issues. As such, James fits more into the tradition of the textbook writers mentioned at the beginning of this chapter than into the tradition of the psychology researchers. However, because James wrote extensively about ongoing research in the psychological laboratories and because he was instrumental in the development of psychology as a discipline, he is generally considered as one of the first psychologists.

James and research methods

For James, introspection was the best available method, despite its limitations:

> Introspective observation is what we have to rely on first and foremost and always. The word introspection need hardly be defined – it means, of course, the looking

into our own minds and reporting what we there discover . . . The inaccuracy of introspective observation has been made a subject of debate . . . Some authors take high ground here and claim for it a sort of infallibility . . . Others have gone to the opposite extreme, and maintained that we can have no introspective cognition of our own minds at all. A deliverance of Auguste Comte to this effect has been so often quoted as to be almost classical . . . Our general conclusion [is] that introspection is difficult and fallible; and that the difficulty is simply that of all observation of whatever kind. Something is before us; we do our best to tell what it is, but in spite of our good will we may go astray, and give a description more applicable to some other sort of thing. The only safeguard is in the final consensus of our farther knowledge about the thing in question, later views correcting earlier ones, until at last the harmony of a consistent system is reached. Such a system, gradually worked out, is the best guarantee the psychologist can give for the soundness of any particular psychologic observation which he may report. Such a system we ourselves must strive, as far as may be, to attain.

(James 1890, Vol. 1, p. 185–6, 191–2)

James was not fond of the experimental methods, as the following quote shows (which incidentally also is an example of the humour and the light touch that made the book so digestible):

But psychology is passing into a less simple phase. Within a few years what one may call a microscopic psychology has arisen in Germany, carried on by experimental methods, asking of course every moment for introspective data, but eliminating their uncertainty by operating on a large scale and taking statistical means. This method taxes patience to the utmost, and could hardly have arisen in a country whose natives could be bored. Such Germans as Weber, Fechner, Vierordt, and Wundt obviously cannot; and their success has brought into the field an array of younger experimental psychologists.

(James 1890, Vol. 1, p. 192)

In the rest of the *Principles* James elaborates on subjects such as:

- the stream of thought,
- consciousness of the self,
- attention,
- discrimination and comparison,
- association,
- perception of time,
- memory,
- sensation,
- imagination,
- perceptions of 'things' and space,
- perception of reality,

- instinct,
- emotions,
- the will,
- hypnotism.

The impact of the evolutionary theory

James was very familiar with Darwin's evolutionary theory, which had a large following in the USA (Chapters 2 and 4), and saw the Darwinian ideas as an interesting framework. For James, the human mind had emerged as an adaptation, to increase the chances of survival, as can be seen in the following excerpt:

> We talk, it is true, when we are darwinizing, as if the mere body that owns the brain had interests; we speak about the utilities of its various organs and how they help or hinder the body's survival . . . We forget that in the absence of some such superadded commenting intelligence (whether it be that of the animal itself, or only ours or Mr. Darwin's), the reactions cannot be properly talked of as 'useful' or 'hurtful' at all . . . the moment you bring a consciousness into the midst, survival ceases to be a mere hypothesis . . . Real ends appear for the first time now upon the world's stage . . . Every actually existing consciousness seems to itself at any rate to be a fighter for ends, of which many, but for its presence, would not be ends at all. Its powers of cognition are mainly subservient to these ends, discerning which facts further them and which do not.
>
> *(James 1890, Vol. 1, p. 140–1)*

functionalism

name given to an approach in early American psychology research, that examined the practical functions of the human mind inspired by the evolutionary theory

For James the precise contents of the mind were less important than what consciousness did, what functions it served for man and animal (in particular with respect to survival). This view struck a chord with many psychologists in the USA, who became known as the functionalists, because they were primarily interested in the practical functions of the mind, not what the mind comprised, what structure it had.

James's stress on the adaptive role of the human mind also opened the way to *comparative psychology*, the comparison of the abilities in various animal species. For instance, the undergraduate Edward Lee Thorndike (1874–1949) became interested in psychology after reading the *Principles* and decided to go to Harvard to study with James. He was interested in children and pedagogy but because of difficulties getting child subjects, he turned to learning in chicks and cats. This research would be the start of his very influential work on instrumental learning, as we will see in Chapter 4.

Titchener's structuralism

Titchener

Another student of Wundt was the Englishman Edward Bradford Titchener (1867–1927). After studies at Oxford (during which he translated the 3rd edition of Wundt's *Grundzüge der physiologischen Psychologie* into English) he went to study with the Master himself and obtained a doctorate in 1892. Upon his return to England, he found this country unreceptive to psychologists, crowded as it was with biologists and philosophers. After a short stint as a biology lecturer, Titchener left for the USA to

KEY FIGURE

William James

Source: Science Photo
Library Ltd

- United States, 1842–1910.

- Wrote a textbook of psychology (*The Principles of Psychology*, 1890) as part of his teachings. This book included much research done in the previous 10 years and conjectures that inspired further researchers.

- Was also very influential in the foundation and expansion of psychology as a science in the USA.

- Defended introspection as the best available research method.

- Was strongly influenced by the evolutionary theory. Sought to outline the functions of the human mind for survival. As such, he was one of the fathers of functionalism.

- Saw a continuity between animal behaviour and human behaviour and, therefore, was receptive to comparative psychology (e.g. helped Thorndike).

---

structuralism

name given by
Titchener to his
approach to psychology, consisting
of trying to discover
the structure of
the human mind
by means of
introspection

Würzburg school

group of psychologists at the University of Würzburg
who used introspection as the research
method, but came
to different
conclusions from
those of Wundt and
Titchener; in particular they claimed
that many thought
processes were not
available to introspection (imageless
thoughts)

teach at Cornell. As shown in table 3.1, the first laboratory of psychology in Great Britain would only be founded in 1897.

Structuralism

Titchener turned Cornell into the centre of structuralism. This was an approach that via introspection tried to discover the structure of the human mind. Inspired by the British philosophical tradition of empiricism and associationism, Titchener tried to discern which sensation elements formed the basics of knowledge and how they were associated with one another.

Structuralism did not inspire many psychologists (even though Titchener was a successful textbook writer). There were three main reasons for this. The first was that introspection did not intuitively give rise to the experience of elementary sensations. This was first made explicit by the Würzburg school, a group of psychologists at the University of Würzburg of whom Külpe for some time was Professor (although the theorising was mainly done by others). While studying the associationist theory they noticed that the participants (as usual including themselves) often made associations to stimuli without any intervening conscious process at all. Participants did not seem able to describe these processes; all they could say was that they had had them. This was even true when the processes dealt with decision making. The researchers found that the participants often came to a conclusion without having a clue of the processes that underlay it. These unconscious processes became known as *imageless thoughts*, thoughts without a conscious trace. The French psychologist Binet (see below) independently came to the same conclusion as the Würzburg school: clear images such as those found in daydreaming were incompatible with the rapid processes of thought; thought was an unconscious act that needed words and images to become conscious (as cited in Mandler (2007) p. 79). Titchener objected to this criticism that imageless thoughts might be true for naïve individuals, but that

Table 3.1 The establishment of psychology laboratories throughout the world. For each country we list the first few universities

Country	Year	University
Germany	1879	University of Leipzig (W. Wundt)
	1881	University of Göttingen (G.E. Müller)
	1886	University of Berlin (H. Ebbinghaus)
USA	1883	Johns Hopkins University (G.S. Hall)
	1887	Indiana University (W. L. Bryan)
	1887	University of Pennsylvania (J.M. Cattell)
Denmark	1886	University of Copenhagen (A. Lehmann)
Russia	1886	Kazan University (V. Bechterev)
	1895	University of St. Petersburg (V. Bechterev)
Japan	1888	University of Tokyo (Y. Motora)
	1906	University of Kyoto (M. Matsumoto)
	1922	Kwansei Gakuin University, Kobe (M. Imada)
Canada	1889	University of Toronto (J.M. Baldwin)
	1910	McGill University (W. Dunlop)
France	1889	Sorbonne (M. Liard and H. Beaunis)
	1896	University of Rennes (B. Bourdon)
	1906	University of Montpellier (M. Foucault)
Italy	1889	University of Rome (G. Sergi)
	1896	Reggio Emilia Hospital (G.C. Ferrari and A. Tamburini)
Belgium	1891	Ghent University (J.J. Van Biervliet)
	1892	University of Louvain/Leuven (A. Thiéry)
	1897	University of Brussels (G. Dwelshauvers)
Netherlands	1892	University of Groningen (G. Heymans)
	1907	University of Amsterdam (T. De Boer)
	1915	University of Utrecht (F. Roels)
Switzerland	1892	University of Geneva (T. Flournoy)
Austria	1894	University of Graz (A. Meinong)
Poland	1897	University of Cracow (Heinrich)
UK	1897	University of Cambridge (W.H. Rivers)
	1898	University College London (J. Sully)
	1900	King's College (W.G. Smith)
Argentina	1898	University of Buenos Aires (H. Pinero)
Brazil	1899	University of Rio de Janeiro (M. de Madeiros)
Spain	1902	University of Madrid (L. Simarro)
	1928	University of Madrid (G. Rodriguez Lafora)
	1928	University of Barcelona (E. Mira-López)
Hungary	1905	University of Budapest (P. Ranschburg)
Chile	1908	University of Chile (G. Mann)

▶

Table 3.1 *(continued)*

Country	Year	University
New Zealand	1908	Victoria College (T. Hunter)
Mexico	1916	Mexico National University (E. Aragon)
China	1917	University of Peking (C. Daqi and C. Yuanpei)
Finland	1922	University of Turku (E. Kaila)
Australia	1929	University of Sydney (H.T. Lovell)
Sweden	1948	University of Uppsala (R. Anderberg)

participants could be trained to become perceptive of their sensations. As we will see in Chapter 4, this training element further weakened the status of introspection as a valid scientific research method.

The second reason why structuralism never became a big movement in psychology was that it did not address the issues most American psychologists saw as important. Influenced by James and Darwin, they were much more interested in pragmatic issues such as, how could psychology advance the conditions of individuals and of American society? The question of what consciousness was made of might very well be interesting to philosophers but did not help anybody forward. Therefore, many more psychologists found themselves interested in functionalism than in structuralism, certainly when Titchener came to the conclusion that there were no fewer than 30,500 basic visual elements.

Finally, Titchener's structuralism even failed to convince the researchers who remained interested in the contents of consciousness. Very rapidly the objection was made that you cannot discover the nature of the human mind by trying to break it down into its 'atoms'. It would be like trying to understand the perception of a musical chord by breaking it down into its individual tones or trying to understand a text by focusing on the letters it was made of. Human perception was more than the sum of the individual sensations the stimulus elicited. This countermovement became known as Gestalt psychology. According to the Gestalt psychologists the brain had self-organising principles and people experienced the world in terms of gestalts (from the German word *Gestalt*, which translates as 'pattern', 'whole', 'organisation'). One of the illustrations the Gestalt psychologists used to make their point was the existence of visual illusions as shown in figure 3.1. In these illusions we see something different than what is physically presented. We see bendy vertical lines whereas in reality the lines are straight, or we see figures of different sizes that in reality have the same size.

The main proponents of Gestalt psychology were Max Wertheimer (1880–1943), Kurt Koffka (1886–1941) and Wolfgang Köhler (1887–1967). The first two had studied at Würzburg. Gestalt psychology also attracted attention in Scandinavia, with the best known researchers being the Danish psychologist Edgar Rubin (1886–1951), who provided compelling examples of the fact that perception entails a distinction between figure and background (figure 3.2), and the Swede Gunnar Johansson (born in 1911), who discovered that motion is a strong organising principle in perception. When all you can see of people is a few lights attached to their joints, you still immediately recognise what is going on when they start to perform familiar actions (e.g. walking), despite the fact that the stimulus is extremely poor.

Gestalt psychology

group of psychologists who argued that the human mind could not be understood by breaking down the experiences into their constituting elements; perception is more than the sensation of stimuli, it involves organisation

(a) Hering illusion   (b) Zolner illusion

(c) Fick illusion   (d) Poggendorf illusion   (e) Ebbinghaus illusion

Figure 3.1 Illusions used by the Gestalt psychologists as evidence against structuralism.
The Gestalt psychologists argued that humans cannot be understood as simply the sum of
the constituting elements. They defended this thesis by pointing to the fact that what we
perceive often deviates from the elements that are presented in the stimulus. The vertical
lines in the Hering and Zolner illusions are straight (test it with a ruler). The vertical line of
the Fick illusion has the same length as the horizontal line. The two oblique line segments
in the Poggendorf illusion are in line with each other, and the two inner circles of the
Ebbinghaus illusion have the same diameter.

**Figure 3.2 Figures made by Edgar Rubin showing that perception involves the separation
of figure and background.**
Both figures are reversible: either the white part can be the figure or the blue part. In
particular the right figure shows that the figure – background assignment can affect the
interpretation (a vase vs. two facing faces) despite the fact that the stimulus and the
associated sensations remain the same. This illustrates the point the Gestalt psychologists
wanted to make, that the interpretation of a stimulus (the perception) is more than a
simple sum of the sensations elicited by the stimulus.

Source: (right) Pomerantz, J.R. and Kubovy, M. (1986). Reproduced with permission of John Wiley & Sons, Inc.

Edward Titchener

Source: Cornell University Library / Rare and Manuscript Collections

- Englishman in the USA, 1867–1927.

- Studied with Wundt.

- Promoted structuralism, an approach that tried to discover the structure of the human mind with the use of introspection.

- Was not very influential because of criticism from three sides:
  - Würzburg school and Binet: humans are not aware of many thought processes and cannot report them, let alone dissect them.
  - Functionalists: not enough practical advantages in knowing the precise structure of the mind.
  - Gestalt psychology: humans are more than the sum of their individual sensations (e.g. in perception interpretation is added to the stimulus).

- Defended introspection as the main research method; thought participants had to be trained to do this properly.

- Was strongly influenced by empiricism and associationism.

Interim summary

- James was an American physician who became interested in psychology through his teachings. Arguably wrote the most influential textbook of early psychology.

- James was influenced by Darwin's evolutionary theory. This resulted in interest in the survival functions of the human mind and in comparative research of animals and humans.

- Titchener promoted structuralism on the basis of introspection in the USA.

- Had a limited impact because of criticisms against the method (introspection), the limited usefulness of the knowledge (functionalism), and the objection that humans are more than the sum of the individual sensations (Gestalt psychology).

? What do you think?

Can you think of a situation in which the analytic dissection advocated by Titchener is useful? Could it be used to break down a complex process into its constituents?

3.4   Psychology in France: Binet and the IQ-test

Clinical psychology in France

As we saw in Chapter 2, psychology was in the forefront of French thinking as well. So it was to be expected that the developments in Germany and the USA would have consequences in this country. In France, however, psychology was much more related to medicine than in the other countries, as can be seen in the following quote:

> With relatively few exceptions, the psychologists of my country have left the inves-tigations of psychophysics to the Germans, and the study of comparative psychol-ogy to the English. They have devoted themselves almost entirely to the study of pathological psychology, that is to say psychology affected by disease.
>
> *(Binet (1890/1915) as cited in Leahey (2004) p. 219)*

Unfortunately for France, its fame in early psychopathology has been eclipsed by that of Vienna (see below). In many histories of pyschology France is only mentioned as the place Freud visited in his early days to learn about hypnosis and hysterical paralysis from Charcot (hysterical paralysis is a psychogenic paralysis that is only present when the patients are conscious, not when they are hypnotised).

The first valid intelligence test

IQ-test

test developed by psychologists to measure the intelli-gence of a person; first useful test published by Binet and Simon in 1907

France achieved its place in the history of psychology, however, for its contribution to the development of the IQ-test, one of the main achievements of applied psychology (see Chapter 7). The history of this test starts in England, where Francis Galton (1822–1911) tried to find evidence for Darwin's evolutionary theory by showing that features were inherited. First, he tried unsuccessfully to demonstrate this in rabbits (by transfusing blood from black and white rabbits into silver-grey rabbits and looking at their offspring), then he had some mixed results with sweet peas, but his ultimate goal was to show the heredity of human traits, in particular intelligence. In 1869 he pub-lished *Hereditary Genius*, in which he claimed that mental qualities were inherited. He did so by pointing to the many family ties that existed between the intellectuals of England (for instance, Galton had a grandfather in common with Darwin). Galton's contemporaries were not impressed, however, because it was generally believed that mental capacities were divine. These capacities set humans apart from animals and were influenced by the health and the habits of the parents. Alcoholism, for instance, was considered a degenerative disease, whose effects were inherited but this was thought to be caused by the fact that drunken parents weakened their minds and bod-ies and then passed these weaknesses on to their children.

?   What do you think?

Is heredity the only possible reason why there were many family ties between the intellectuals of nineteenth-century England?

Because of the resistance Galton encountered, he set out to *measure* human intelligence. His most ambitious attempt took place in 1884 during the International Health Exhibition in London, attended by over 4 million people. Here he installed an Anthropometric Laboratory, where various aspects of men were measured: their principal physical dimensions, their hearing power, the accuracy of their eyesight, and various measures of physical speed and strength. Galton was convinced that individual differences in mental ability were due to inherited differences in the quality of the senses and he set out to prove this. During the six months of the exhibition, 17 different measures were made of over 9,000 visitors. Afterwards Galton obtained a room in the Science Galleries of the South Kensington Museum, in which the laboratory continued for another six years, gathering data on over 4,000 more individuals. Unfortunately for Galton, his measures again turned out to be far from convincing (as a matter of fact, he never published them; his claims remained based on impressions and anecdotes; Deary 1994).

In 1884 Sir Francis Galton opened an anthropometric laboratory at the South Kensington Museum, in which he gathered sensory and physical data from over 4,000 individuals. Before, he had collected measures of over 9,000 visitors at the International Health Exhibition in London. Unfortunately, none of the measures correlated highly with the intelligence of the people, as Galton had hoped.

Source: Photograph plate taken from 'The Life, Letters and Labours of Francis Galton' (Volume 2, 1924) by Karl Pearson. Science and Society Picture Library. Reproduced with permission.

Galton's initiative inspired other researchers to correlate empirical measures from the new psychological laboratories (in particular just-noticeable differences and reaction times) with mental ability, all with less than impressive results (in addition, there were serious problems in the designs used, which would prevent those studies from being published nowadays; Deary 1994). A different approach, however, was taken in Paris by the psychologist Alfred Binet (1857–1911), who had joined the psychology laboratory of Beaunis (table 3.1). After having published several articles on psychophysical measurements and craniometry (measurement of the skull), he suddenly decided to change direction and presented children with poems they had to memorise. After a fixed study period, followed by a distraction period, the children had to write down as much as they remembered of the poem.

In 1904, Binet published his first findings, showing how much bigger the difference on this measure was between good and poor pupils than a similar attempt by his Belgian colleague Van Biervliet based on the sharpness of vision (Binet 1904). In the same journal issue, Binet and his collaborator Théodore Simon published an article about other tasks they had tried out with children, to see which correlated with mental retardation. Three years later, they presented the first validated intelligence test (Binet and Simon 1907).

The Binet–Simon test was based on the assumption that developing children can solve problems of increasing difficulty. A sequence of tasks was assembled that allowed the researchers to assess the mental age of a child. By comparing the mental age with the chronological age of a child it was possible to see whether the child was performing as expected, better or worse. Binet and Simon explicitly aimed for tasks that were fairly independent of what was taught in schools, so that a child's results were little influenced by the quality of the education received. Table 3.2 lists the tasks that were used. Notice how similar they are to contemporary intelligence tasks!

Table 3.2 Tasks used by Binet and Simon (1907) in their intelligence test (a few tasks that would require too much explanation have been omitted)

Age (years)	Action
3 years	Touch nose, eyes, mouth Repeat 2 digits Repeat a sentence of 6 syllables Give family name
4 years	Give gender Give the name of a key, a knife and a coin Repeat 3 digits Compare the length of 2 lines
5 years	Compare 2 weights Copy a square Repeat a sentence of 10 syllables Count 4 coins
6 years	Repeat a sentence of 16 words Compare 2 pictures on aesthetic grounds Define familiar objects Give your age Make a distinction between morning and evening

▶

Table 3.2 *(continued)*

Age (years)	Action
7 years	Indicate missing parts in pictures How many fingers on left hand, right, total? Copy a written sentence Copy a triangle and a diamond Repeat 5 digits Count 13 coins
8 years	Read a short story and remember 2 elements Count money (3 coins of 1 cent and 3 coins of 2 cents). Name 4 colours Count backwards from 20 to 0 Write to dictation
9 years	Give the full date (day, month, year) Name the days of the week Read a story and remember 6 elements Return money when an object of 16 cents is paid with a coin of 20 cents Rank 5 weights
10 years	Name the months Give the value of the 9 familiar coins that are shown Use 3 words in 2 sentences Answer 2 lists of comprehension questions
11 years	Indicate absurdities in sentences Use 3 words in a single sentence Find more than 60 words in 3 minutes Give abstract definitions Put words in the right order
12 years	Repeat 7 digits Give 3 words that rhyme with a given word Repeat a sentence of 26 syllables Answer questions (e.g. 'Recently my neighbour had many visitors: First a doctor, then a lawyer and a priest. What may be going on?')

Source: Binet and Simon (1907)

Within a few years, Binet and Simon's intelligence test was known all over the world. Stern developed a German version in 1912, Terman published an American version in 1916 (known as the Stanford–Binet test), and Kubo standardised a Japanese version in 1918.

Binet and Simon also had a strong impact on the emergence of developmental psychology. Jean Piaget (1896–1980), a Swiss psychologist who came to study in Paris, started to wonder why children of 11 years had no problem seeing the absurdity in a sentence such as 'If I wanted to kill myself, I would never do that on a Friday, because that brings bad luck', whereas otherwise intelligent children of 8 years could not do that. This would be the origin of Piaget's theory of cognitive development in children in different stages (see any book on developmental psychology for an account of this theory).

KEY FIGURE

Alfred Binet

- France, 1857–1911.

- Best known for the development of the first valid intelligence test.

- First tried to measure intelligence on the basis of psychophysical measures and craniometry.

- Then changed track and used meaningful questions. Made sure, however, that the solutions to the questions did not rely too much on information learned in school.

- Test comprised tasks of increasing difficulties, suited for children of different ages.

Source: US National Library of Medicine / Science Photo Library Ltd

Interim summary

- At the end of the nineteenth century there was a lot of interest in psychopathology in France.

- French psychology of this time is mostly known for the development of the first valid intelligence test by Binet and Simon.

- Before, Galton and others had tried in vain to measure intelligence on the basis of psychophysical measures and other measures from the psychological laboratories.

? What do you think?

It may be worthwhile at this point to make a list of the pros and cons of IQ-tests. Use this list when we continue the discussion of IQ-tests in Chapters 7 and 12.

3.5   Freud and psychoanalysis

Whereas the previous developments occurred at universities, the last movement of the nineteenth century with a long-term effect on psychology started within the practice of a neurologist in Vienna, at that time the capital of the Austro-Hungarian Empire. We first discuss the different views of insanity and its treatment in the history of the Western world. Then we cover Freud's place within this evolution; and we end by commenting on Freud's research method.

Changes in the treatment of mental disorders

Informal support

Very little is known about the conditions of people with mental problems in early times. Historical writings are mainly confined to strong people (the conquerors) and the few writings we have about the weak mainly consist of sensational events, such as the burning of witches or fathers who killed their disabled babies. However, there are reasonable grounds to assume that people with mental difficulties have mostly been treated with a combination of compassion and contempt (sometimes hostility). The compassion came from the parents and other members of the (extended) family; the contempt from the society outside the family. As long as the symptoms were not too bad or dangerous, these people stayed in the village and died young, as did the majority of humans in those days. If the family or the relatives could no longer take care of them, they became homeless and part of the larger group of outcasts, who survived on the basis of begging and petty crime. Because there was a widespread belief that insanity was due to the devil or a bad ghost, they also risked being seen as a source of disaster.

Asylums

From the sixteenth century onwards, changes in society led to an increased role for the authorities in the treatment of people with a deviation. There was a massive move from the countryside (where people had been serfs for centuries) to the cities where life became more complex. Labour differentiated. People were required to take up more individual responsibility and they had to interact with an increasing number of other individuals. This required better manners with more emphasis on self-discipline. The tolerance for deviant behaviour dwindled. As a consequence, the authorities were forced to take action against the outcasts, who were not economically useful and became seen as a disturbance to the established order. Institutions were founded to confine them. In these **asylums** they were treated as prisoners, with a regime of forced labour and religious exercises to re-educate them as good members of society.

asylum

name given to the institutions for the insane established from the eighteenth century on; first modelled after prisons, later after hospitals for chronic patients

From prisoners to patients

Gradually in the eighteenth century, under the influence of the Enlightenment, the conviction grew that the inhabitants of asylums were not real criminals but ailing patients. Important names in this evolution were William Battie in England, who published the first book on psychiatry *Treatise on Madness* (1758), and Philippe Pinel in France, who liberated the insane of Bicêtre from their chains after the French revolution. A remaining problem, however, was how to treat the disorders of these patients. Some attempted common-sense 'medical' practices to bring the patients back to their senses, such as cold showers, fast spinning around or cures with leeches. Others turned to educational measures to re-instil morality in the mental life. This so-called 'moral treatment' consisted of trying to persuade and influence the patient to behave normally, under the influence of the moral authority of the doctor. In cases of non-adherence, retaliation was swift with straitjackets, padded cells or other types of confinement. A further problem was the financing of the institutes. Except for patients of wealthy families, who could afford a cure on the basis of rest and tranquillity, living conditions were appalling.

Neurologists

Because the educational approach seemed to lead to (slightly) better results than the medical cures, it was the dominant therapy in the first half of the nineteenth century (Abma 2004). Psychiatrists had a low status. Gradually, however, the biological view of mental illness regained impetus. An important element in this evolution was the discovery of the microbe that caused syphilis, which in those times was a major cause of insanity. Towards the end of the nineteenth century a new group of physicians entered the scene. They called themselves neurologists and were particularly interested in the milder forms of mental disturbances, which they called 'nervous disorders' or 'neurasthenia' (weakness of the nerves). They rejected the asylum system (which they limited to the handling of the worst cases of madness) and advocated treatment in private settings including methods such as hypnosis and suggestion. One of the main figures of the movement was Jean-Martin Charcot (1825–1893), who gave lectures and demonstrations to scholars from all over Europe and America. One of them was Sigmund Freud.

Freud and psychoanalysis

Sigmund Freud (1856–1939) was born in the Austro-Hungarian Empire. He trained as a physician and then did research on topics such as aphasia and poliomyelitis under the supervision of Ernst Wilhelm von Brücke, a neuro-anatomist. Von Brücke was a strong believer in *psychodynamics*, a view that considered living organisms as energy systems governed by the principles of physics and chemistry. This view would have a strong impact on Freud's own stand.

Freud's psychological treatment

Because a university position as Professor (more or less with the same status as in the Prussian system) was unlikely, Freud started a private medical practice in 1886, after a stay in Paris. He specialised in the new discipline of neurology. Here, together with his colleague Josef Breuer, he started a new type of treatment based on conversations with patients (remember that previously treatments were either medical or educational). On the basis of this psychological treatment (or talking cure, as it was sometimes called), Freud became convinced that hysterical symptoms (vague pain, insomnia, hysterical paralysis, numbness, lack of appetite or sexual desire) were due to repressed sexual childhood experiences (later childhood fantasies). These symptoms could be alleviated by the painful process of bringing the unconscious memories into the patient's consciousness and by freeing them from their emotional energy.

Freud was not the first to talk about unconscious mental processes, but nobody before him had given these processes such an explosive emotional power or made them the real drive of human behaviour. Freud himself considered the insight that human reason was not the real master of a person's action to be a revolution on the same scale as Copernicus's insight that the Earth orbited the Sun and Darwin's insight that man had evolved from animals (as cited in Leahey (2004) p. 264).

Psychoanalysis, as Freud's theory and therapy became called, provided the first coherent framework for the treatment of nervous disorders and, therefore, received a warm welcome among the neurologists, the more so because Freud's views were quite compatible with those of Charcot (another of whose students, Pierre Janet, came independently to very similar conclusions). The neurologists with their new, forceful theory replaced the ill-reputed psychiatrists in the asylums (although they took up the

neurologist

name used at the end of the nineteenth century by physicians who were interested in the treatment of milder forms of mental problems outside the asylum; the term was later used to refer to specialists of the nervous system, when the original neurologists merged with the psychiatrists and took up the latter's name

psychological treatment

treatment of mental health problems consisting of conversations between the patient and the therapist; initiated by Freud as an alternative to the prevailing medical and educational treatments

psychoanalysis

name given to Freud's theory and therapy

latter's title when neurology moved on to become confined to the examination and treatment of the nervous system itself).

Freud's research method

Medical case studies

case study

within medicine and clinical psychology, the intensive study of an individual patient within the context of his/her own world and relations, to understand and help the individual patient

Freud's psychoanalytical method was inspired by medical practice and involved case studies, the intensive study of individuals within the context of their own world and their relationships (past and present). The aim of each study was to understand and help the individual patient. The validity of the ideas generated depended on good thinking and on cross-checking with the clinical evidence.

Introspection and interpretation by the therapist

Freud's method was also based on introspection: patients talked about their thoughts, dreams and feelings. However, contrary to Wundt's and James's introspection, the literal meaning of what the patients said was of little value, because, according to Freud, the patients did not have access to their own unconscious drives. Freud considered that it was the therapist's task to be attentive for occasional slips during which the unconscious forces revealed themselves, and to reinterpret the contents of the introspection according to the psychoanalytic theory. The clearest example of this reinterpretation was the distinction Freud drew between the manifest message and the latent message in dream analysis (i.e. what the patients said vs. what they actually meant), as is shown in the following excerpt:

> Another guileless dream of the same patient, which in some respects is a pendant to the above. Her husband asks her: 'Oughtn't we to have the piano tuned?' She replies: 'It's not worth while, the hammers would have to be rebuffed as well.' Again we have the reproduction of an actual event of the preceding day. Her husband had asked her such a question, and she had answered it in such words. But what is the meaning of her dreaming it? She says of the piano that it is a disgusting old box which has a bad tone; it belonged to her husband before they were married, etc., but the key to the true solution lies in the phrase: It isn't worth while. This has its origin in a call paid yesterday to a woman friend. She was asked to take off her coat, but declined, saying: 'Thanks, it isn't worth while, I must go in a moment.' At this point I recall that yesterday, during the analysis, she suddenly took hold of her coat, of which a button had come undone. It was as though she meant to say: 'Please don't look in, it isn't worth while.' Thus box becomes chest, and the interpretation of the dream leads to the years when she was growing out of her childhood, when she began to be dissatisfied with her figure. It leads us back, indeed, to earlier periods, if we take into consideration the disgusting and the bad tone, and remember how often in allusions and in dreams the two small hemispheres of the female body take the place – as a substitute and an antithesis – of the large ones.
>
> *(Freud (1900) translated by Brill)*

Finally, Freud's research method was characterised by a surprisingly large input from himself. On the basis of rather little data, a rich and all-embracing theory of human functioning was built. On a continuum from evidence-based to principle-driven research (Chapter 1), psychoanalysis clearly was biased towards the latter pole. This was not necessarily bad, as long as the new ideas and insights were helpful. Otherwise, the small empirical base was likely in the end to turn against the theory.

The impact of psychoanalysis on early psychology

Psychoanalysis not only took the neurologists by storm, it also exerted a strong attraction on the developing field of psychology, because it was the first complete theory of human psychological functioning, starkly deviating from the piecemeal approach found in the university laboratories.

Many indications can be listed of the rapidly growing impact of psychoanalysis on psychology. In 1908, G. Stanley Hall, the founder of the first psychology laboratory in the United States (table 3.1), began to give courses on psychoanalysis, and in 1909 he invited Freud to Clark University (together with Jung and Ferenczi). The impact of Freud in Britain can be derived from the papers that were read at the British Psychological Society (table 3.3). This society was founded in 1901, shortly after the installation of the first psychological laboratories in the UK. In 1910 we see the first paper on psychoanalysis,

Table 3.3 A selection of papers read at the British Psychological Society. From 1910 the first papers on Freud and psychoanalysis started to appear

Year	A selection of paper read at the BPS
1902	'The Evolution of Laughter' 'Fechner's Paradoxical Experiment' 'Pathological Changes in Immediate Memory and Association' 'Psychophysical Parallelism'
1903	'Bilateral Cortical Lesion, causing Deafness and Aphasia' 'Various Types of Insanity' 'The Functions of the Frontal Lobes'
1904	'Subconsciousness' 'Bearing of Modern Experimental Work on the Problem of the Unity of the Mind' 'Theories of Consonance and Dissonance'
1905	'The Brain of the Chimpanzee Sally' 'Relation of Intelligence to Instinct and to Rational Thought' 'The Rhythmical Sense of Primitive People'
1906	'The Fundamental Forms of Mental Interaction'
1907	'A Suggested Physiological Basis for the Distinction between Sensation and Revived Image' 'Some Points of Psychosocial Interest Suggested by a Case of Experimental Nerve Division'
1909	'On the Grouping of Afferent Impulses in the Spinal Chord' 'The Influence of Alcohol on Muscular and Mental Efficiency' 'Visual Acuity in Different Races of Man' 'The Illusion of Horizontal and Vertical Lines with Momentary and Prolonged Exposure' 'Observations on Contrast with Smoothly Graded Disks' 'Character' 'An Objective Study of Mathematical Intelligence'

▶

Table 3.3 *(continued)*

Year	Paper read at the BPS
1910	'Instinct and Intelligence' 'The Nature and Development of Attention' 'The Aesthetic Appreciation of Simple Colour Combinations' **'The Psychology of Freud and his School'** 'A Possible Factor in the Monocular Appreciation of Spatial Depth' 'Statistical Methods' 'The Calculation of Correlations'
1913	'Are Intensity Differences of Sensation Quantitative?' 'Can there be Anything Obscure or Implicit in a Mental State?' **'An Analysis of some Personal Dreams, with Special Reference to Freud's Interpretation'** **'The Psychological System of Sigmund Freud, as set forth in Chapter VII of *Traumdeutung*'** 'Wonder, Fascination and Curiosity'

Source: Edgell (1947)

followed by a rapid increase in the succeeding years, or as the historian of the society described it:

> [In the 1910s and 1920s] papers of the experimental type were less conspicuous than in the previous period. During the first enthusiasm for psychoanalysis with its startling revelations, the results obtained by the often laborious method of experiment seemed dull and even insignificant.
>
> *(Edgell 1947, p. 16)*

In later chapters we will have more to say about the relationship between psychoanalysis and the other approaches.

KEY FIGURE

Sigmund Freud

Source: National Library of Medicine / Science Photo Library Ltd

- Austria, 1856–1939.

- Neurologist who started psychological treatment of his patients (talking cure).

- Built a theory and a therapy on the idea that people's actions are controlled by their unconscious (psychoanalysis).

- Used medical case studies as research method. Evidence derived from introspections by the patients that had to be interpreted by the therapist.

Interim summary

- Freud was one of the first neurologists. These were a new group of therapists, replacing the disgraced psychiatrists, who worked in the asylums. Before, people with mental disorders had been taken care of first on an informal basis and then – increasingly – in institutions where they were treated as prisoners or patients. Basic treatment consisted of attempts to re-educate the patients.

- Freud was the first to actually talk to his patients (psychological treatment). On the basis of these talks he constructed the psychoanalytical theory, which argues that the unconscious mind plays a strong role in the control of people's actions.

- Psychoanalysis had a massive impact, both on neurologists and on psychologists, because it provided a coherent and attractive theory of psychopathology.

3.6   Focus on: Edwin Boring and the creation of five schools in early psychology

Maybe you took an introductory psychology course before you started reading this book? In that case, you may have wondered why in the present chapter we did not use the classical division of early psychology into five schools: structuralism, functionalism, Gestalt psychology, behaviourism and psychoanalysis. After all, isn't it received wisdom that psychology started with structuralism in Wundt's laboratory, which was brought to America by Titchener, where it had to fight first against functionalism and later against behaviourism, while it remained unchallenged in Europe until the rise of the Gestalt psychology? Meanwhile, psychoanalysis steadily grew as a kind of a non-scientific 'outsider'.

To be honest, this was very much the organisation we had in mind before we started to research the present chapter. Gradually, however, we realised that if you look at the original materials, such as the articles published in journals or the papers read at meetings (e.g. table 3.3), there are surprisingly few traces of the supposedly heroic fights between the schools. Most of the time, the articles and the talks dealt with concrete topics that were tackled with a variety of research methods.

Further research reveals that the origin of the five big, quarrelling schools comes from Edwin Boring (1886–1968). This man with the rather unfortunate family name was the first great historian of psychology. He published an extremely popular book *A History of Experimental Psychology* (1st edition 1929; 2nd, revised edition 1950), in which he introduced the five schools as the core of early psychology, an idea that ever since has pervaded psychology textbooks.

In recent decades, historians have become aware of the fact that Boring's attempts to describe the early history of psychology were subject to a number of biases (Cerullo 1988), the most important of which are:

1. Boring overestimated the importance of structuralism. He was a student of Titchener, who time and again incorrectly claimed that he was the true successor of Wundt's ideas. Boring followed his supervisor, with the result that the following types of quotation were common in psychology books until quite recently: 'Edward Bradford Titchener worked so vigorously and so consciously in the Wundtian tradition that he became the recognized representative in America of that point of view' or 'It was never necessary for Wundt to go to the United States to promote his psychology, for Titchener in a very real way epitomized Wundtian psychology in America' (as cited in Zehr (2000) p. 123).

2. Boring loved an approach to history that was introduced by the philosopher Georg Hegel (1770–1831). According to this approach you first have a thesis (a proposition), then an antithesis (a reaction against the proposition), followed by a synthesis (a compromise between the thesis and the antithesis). Boring believed in controversy as the driving force of science and, therefore, he magnified existing discussions to true fights between schools involving a string of theses and antitheses (structure vs. function, elements vs. gestalts, introspection vs. behaviourist experimentation, consciousness vs. unconscious drives). This approach had the advantage that Boring (and many history teachers after him) could position himself as the great conciliator, the synthesis-maker.

3. Boring looked down upon applied psychology. Therefore, Binet's research did not figure prominently in his history, nor did any other practical applications of psychology. Even today, applied psychology remains heavily underrepresented in many history books of psychology (see Jansz and van Drunen (2004) for an exception).

Because of these biases Boring enormously simplified the research of the early psychologists and also made psychology look more quarrelsome and fragmented than it actually was. This is nicely summarised by the American psychologist Robert S. Woodworth at the end of his textbook on the different schools (1st edition 1931; 8th, revised edition 1948, Chapter 8):

In view of all the divergent movements that we have surveyed, all these 'warring schools' of contemporary psychology, the reader may easily carry away the impression that we psychologists are anything but a harmonious body of scientific workers. Looked at from outside, our fraternity has seemed to be a house divided against itself . . . You would get a very different impression from attending one of the International Congresses of Psychology or a meeting of one of the national societies such as the American Psychological Association. You would hear papers read on various psychological topics, with very little mention of any of the schools and with discussions of the usual scientific type, free from acrimony though not of course from the give and take of doubt and criticism . . .

Another reason for the continued unity of psychology is found in the fact that only a minority of psychologists have become active adherents of any of the schools. Some may lean toward one school and some toward another, but on the whole the psychologists of the present time are proceeding on their way in the middle of the road.

Costall (2006) argues that Boring's approach keeps being mentioned in textbooks because it contains another, nearly irresistible Hegelian sequence to summarise the 'history' of psychology:

1. Thesis: Psychology, as instituted in the universities, began as the study of mind, based, almost exclusively, on the unreliable method of introspection (structuralism, functionalism, Gestalt psychology).

2. Antithesis: In reaction to the blatant unreliability of the introspective method, behaviourism then redefined psychology as the study of behaviour, based, primarily, on the objective method of experimentation (see Chapter 4).

3. Synthesis: In reaction to the limited research agenda and the theoretical bankruptcy of behaviourism, the 'cognitive revolution', in turn, restored the mind as the proper subject of psychology (but now with the benefit of the rigorous experimental methods developed within behaviourism).

The present chapter shows that the thesis is wrong (or at least much exaggerated), because from the onset experimental methods were a vital part of psychological research. In the chapters to come we will see that the antithesis and the synthesis are exaggerated as well.

For the above reasons we have not presented early psychology in the way Boring did. This does not mean, of course, that psychology did not have a hard time finding its way (as a matter of fact, it is still struggling, as we will see in later chapters). However, the problems psychology struggled with were not so much the ones Boring stressed, but the difficulty of finding good ways to study the subject. Two main problems stood out:

1. **Which research methods provide valid information to build psychological theories on?** For instance, a major mistake the early psychologists made was that they, in line with previous philosophers, turned inwards to search for information (introspection, experimentation on colleagues who were in the know) rather than looking outwards (i.e. observing people who were naïve with respect to the research question).

2. **To what extent is scientifically obtained evidence necessary as the basis of psychological theories?** As will be discussed in the coming chapters, not everyone is convinced that psychology ought to be based on the same methods as the natural sciences. The first clear evidence of this was the methodological divide between psychoanalysis and the other research paradigms we discussed.

Interim summary

- The historian Boring distinguished between five schools of psychology (structuralism, functionalism, Gestalt psychology, behaviourism and psychoanalysis) as characterising the beginnings of psychological research.

- Over the years this distinction has become ever more prominent, so that it looks as if all research was centred on the 'divisions' between these schools.

Recommended literature

Many of the early writings that have been described in this chapter are freely available on the internet (use a search engine!). The best site to start with is http://psychclassics.yorku.ca, from which we quoted extensively.

If you speak German, *Projekt Gutenberg – DE* is another good place (http://gutenberg.spiegel.de/).

Finally, if you speak French, you certainly must have a look at the first issues of *L'Année Psychologique,* the journal Binet founded and in which he published his first intelligence test with Simon (http://www.persee.fr/).

An increasing number of early books have also become fully available on Google Book search (www.books.google.com).

As for books, there are many good books on the history of psychology, which are much more detailed than what is covered here. We relied heavily on Leahey, T.H. (2004) *A history of psychology* (6th edition) (Upper Saddle River, NJ: Pearson Prentice Hall). Other books we used were Benjafield, J.G. (2005) *A history of psychology* (2nd edition). (Oxford University Press); Hergenhahn, B.R. (2004) *An introduction to the history of psychology* (Belmont, CA: Wadsworth); and Mandler, G. (2007) *A history of modern experimental psychology* (Cambridge, MA: The MIT Press). Two books that approach history from a critical point of view (Chapter 9), are Richards, G. (2002) *Putting psychology in its place: A critical historical overview* (2nd edition) (London: Routledge); and Jones, D. and Elcock, J. (2001) *History and theories of psychology: A critical perspective* (London: Arnold).

References

Abma, R. (2004) 'Madness and mental health.' In J. Jansz and P. van Drunen (eds.), *A social history of psychology.* Oxford: Blackwell, p. 93–128.

Binet, A. (1904) 'A propos de la mesure de l'intelligence', *L'Année Psychologique,* **11:** 69–82 (available on http://www.persee.fr/web/revues/home/prescript/revue/psy).

Binet, A. and Simon, T. (1907) 'Le développement de l'intelligence chez les enfants', *L'Année Psychologique,* **14:** 1–94 (available on http://www.persee.fr/web/revues/home/prescript/revue/psy).

Boring, E.G. (1950) *A history of experimental psychology* (2nd edn). New York: Appleton-Century-Crofts.

Cattell, J.M. (1888) 'The psychological laboratory at Leipsic', *Mind,* **13:** 37–51 (available on http://psychclassics.yorku.ca).

Cerullo, J.J. (1988) 'E.G. Boring: Reflections on a discipline builder', *The American Journal of Psychology,* **101:** 561–75.

Costall, A. (2006) '"Introspectionism" and the mythical origins of scientific psychology', *Consciousness and Cognition,* **15:** 634–54.

Deary, I.J. (1994) 'Sensory discrimination and intelligence: Postmortem or resurrection?' *The American Journal of Psychology,* **107:** 95–115.

Edgell, B. (1947) 'The British Psychological Society', *British Journal of Psychology,* **37:** 113–32. (Reprinted in 2001: *British Journal of Psychology,* **92:** 3–22.)

Freud, S. (1900/1913) *The interpretation of dreams* (English translation by A.A. Brill). New York: Macmillan (available on http://psychclassics.yorku.ca).

Fuchs, A.H. (2000) 'Teaching the introductory course in psychology circa 1900', *American Psychologist,* **55:** 492–5.

Griffith, C.R. (1921) 'Some neglected aspects of a history of psychology', *Psychological Monographs,* **30:** 17–29 (available on http://psychclassics.yorku.ca).

Gundlach, H. (2004) 'Reine Psychologie, angewandte Psychologie und die Institutionalisierung der Psychologie [Fundamental psychology, applied psychology, and the institutionalization of psychology]', *Zeitschrift für Psychologie*, **212**: 183–99.

Hatfield, G. (1998) 'Kant and empirical psychology in the 18th century', *Psychological Science*, **9**: 423–8.

Jahoda, G. (2007) *A history of social psychology.* Cambridge: Cambridge University Press.

James, W. (1890) *The principles of psychology* (2 vols.) New York: Henry Holt (available on http://psychclassics.yorku.ca).

Jansz, J. and Van Drunen, P. (eds.) (2004) *A social history of psychology.* Oxford: Blackwell.

Leahey, T.H. (2004) *A history of psychology* (6th edn). Upper Saddle River, NJ: Pearson Prentice Hall.

Mandler, G. (2007) *A history of modern experimental psychology.* Cambridge, MA: The MIT Press.

Nicolas, S. and Ferrand, L. (1999). 'Wundt's laboratory at Leipzig in 1891', *History of Psychology*, **2**: 194–203.

Pomerantz, J.R. and Kubovy, M. (1986) 'Theoretical approaches in organization', in Boff, J.P. Kaufman and Thomas, J.P. (eds) *Handbook of perception and human performance.* New York, NY: Wiley.

Teo, T. (2007) 'Local institutionalization, discontinuity, and German textbooks of psychology, 1816–1854', *Journal of the History of the Behavioral Sciences,* **43**: 135–157.

Woodworth, R.S. (1931) *Contemporary schools of psychology.* New York: Ronald Press.

Wundt, W.M. (1896/1897) *Outlines of psychology* (English translation by C.H. Judd). Leipzig: Wilhelm Engelmann (available on http://psychclassics.yorku.ca).

Zehr, D. (2000) 'Portrayals of Wundt and Titchener in introductory psychology texts: A content analysis', *Teaching of Psychology,* **27**: 122–5.

04 Strengthening the scientific standing of psychology
Behaviourism and cognitive psychology

This chapter will cover

Questions to consider

Historical issues addressed in this chapter

- When did psychology as an independent discipline start in the USA?
- What did people expect from psychology around that time?
- When did behaviourism start?
- Why was Watson's influence limited in time? Who succeeded him?
- When did cognitive psychology start? What were key events in its initial development?

Conceptual issues addressed in this chapter

- Why did the centre of gravity in psychological research shift from Europe to the USA?
- In what ways is psychological research influenced by the wider society in which it occurs?
- To what extent was original psychological research inspired by eugenics?
- To what extent was the 'new psychology' a break with the past?
- How did animal research inspire psychologists?
- What did behaviourists see as the essential elements of scientific research?
- What inspired psychologists to include cognitions in their research?
- In what ways has the history of psychology been influenced by the invention of the computer?
- What were the specific features of cognitive psychology?
- Have present-day scientists and history writers a tendency to over-use the word 'revolution'?

Introduction

It is appropriate to begin the history of modern psychology in 1892 because in that year the American Psychological Association (APA) was founded. Our attention from now on will be fixed on American psychology, for although Germany granted the earliest degrees in psychology, it was in America that psychology became a profession . . . For better or worse, modern psychology is primarily American psychology. American movements and theories have been adopted overseas – so much so that a 1980 German text in social psychology was filled with American references and made no mention of Wundt or Völkerpsychologie.

(Leahey, T. H. (2004) A history of psychology: Main currents in psychological enquiry (6th edn), p. 330.
Copyright © 2004. Reprinted by permission of Pearson Education, Inc., Upper Saddle River, NJ)

In this chapter we discuss the efforts made by the academic psychological laboratories to become recognised as *scientific* laboratories, with the same status as other science laboratories. Because this struggle was particularly outspoken in the USA and because the USA began to rule the discipline in the twentieth century, we limit our discussion to this nation. While Europe was crippled by two devastating wars, the USA became an economic superpower that in addition invested heavily in all types of science. This does not mean that nothing relevant to psychology happened in other parts of the world, but for the present chapter these developments were rather marginal.

US dominance was not only due to the sheer amount of research done, but also to the high quality of the textbooks produced. In Chapter 3 we saw how James's *Principles* eclipsed Wundt's psychology books (available in English through Titchener's translations) because of its clarity and accessibility. Very much the same was true of the later textbooks. One particularly successful author in the early years was Robert S. Woodworth, who sold over 400,000 copies of his introductory text *Psychology* between 1922 and 1939 and who in 1938 published a most authoritative book, *Experimental Psychology*, reviewing the complete literature of laboratory research on topics ranging from psychophysics to the psychology of thinking (Benjafield 2005). Increasingly lecturers throughout the world either used these books in their courses or relied on them to write their own syllabuses. Therefore, in the twentieth century the history of psychology very much became the American history of psychology.

? What do you think?

Because of the dominance of the English language in the textbook market, it may be argued that the European history of psychology is largely the history as seen from the Anglo-Saxon part of the world. Do you agree? Which other sources do you have at your disposal to learn about the history of psychology (or the history of science for that matter)?

As will become clear, however, not all was benevolent for the psychology researchers in the USA. In the first part of this chapter we discuss the developments that culminated in behaviourism; in the second part we look at the changes that resulted in the rise of cognitive psychology.

4.1 Making a science of behaviour

The perception of psychology in the USA at the beginning of the twentieth century

The expansion of psychology around the turn of the century

In Chapter 3 we talked about the creation of psychology laboratories and what a success story this was in the USA. By 1900 there were already 41 of them. This can be contrasted to the situation in the UK. Chapter 3 explained how Titchener found it impossible to be appointed as a psychologist and emigrated to the USA. A similar story can be told about William McDougall (1871–1938; see also Chapter 11). He finished medical studies in Cambridge and London, but after reading James's *Principles*, decided to turn to psychology. In 1897 he obtained a fellowship at the University of Cambridge to collaborate with Rivers in the first psychological laboratory in the UK (Chapter 3). Four years later he was appointed Reader in Mental Philosophy at Oxford, on the explicit condition that he would forsake building his own experimental laboratory. This probably was one of the reasons why in 1920 he accepted an offer to go to Harvard. There he remained for seven years before going to Duke University, where he would end his career.

According to Benjamin (2000), the psychology laboratories were part of the 100-year American love affair with science and technology, starting around the mid-1800s. In that period the USA turned from a land of isolated groups of rural settlers into a nation-state dominated by large cities with extensive communications and exchanges (in 1880 only 25 per cent of the population lived in cities; by 1900, 40 per cent did so). Psychology profited from these developments.

As well as the laboratories, in 1892 the American Psychological Association was founded, giving psychology researchers a forum to meet and discuss their findings, and two journals were established that would dominate the field and that still exist today. In 1887, G. Stanley Hall founded the *American Journal of Psychology*; and in 1894, J.M. Baldwin and J. McKeen Cattell started the *Psychological Review*.

The first American psychology: functionalism

As psychology in the USA expanded, it got moulded by the expectations and preoccupations of American society. One of these inputs was a strong interest in Darwin's evolutionary theory. This interest was partly inherited from the UK, but also appealed directly to the American citizens because of their struggle to establish a new nation. 'Survival of the fittest' had a very personal touch for many immigrants.

Natural selection involved two elements: inheritance and adaptation to the environment. As for the inheritance part, the USA was one of the first countries where eugenics had a strong impact. Eugenics is a social philosophy claiming that the fate of a nation can be improved by selective breeding of its inhabitants. It started with Galton who saw this as a logical consequence of Darwin's evolutionary theory. However, whereas Galton predominantly preached positive eugenics (improve society by encouraging people with desirable features to have more children), others after him diverged towards negative eugenics (improve society by preventing people with undesirable features from entering the country and/or having children). Several US states adopted legislation aimed at preventing marriage or at compulsory sterilisation of certain individuals (e.g. mentally retarded people). For instance, in 1913, Iowa supported the establishment of sterilisation laws aimed at 'the prevention of the procreation of criminals, rapists, idiots, feeble minded, imbeciles, lunatics, drunkards, drug fiends, epileptics, syphilitics, moral and sexual perverts, and diseased and degenerate persons' (as cited in Jansz and Van Drunen (2004) p. 28).

At the same time, however, the Americans believed in the importance of the environment. Being a country of immigrants, they were convinced that human characteristics and achievements were not solely due to inheritance but depended on the environment as well. Among other things, this meant that one could change and

eugenics

social philosophy claiming that the fate of a nation can be improved by selective breeding of the inhabitants control human actions for the better, a conviction that was shared by the dominant Protestant religion.

Finally, there was mistrust of intellectualism, knowledge for the sake of knowledge. America was a nation of common-sense businessmen, not interested in abstract science (which was left to Europe), but in practical accomplishments that at the same time made money, revealed God's glory, and advanced the American dream. Or as Richards (1996, p. 27) phrased it:

> Psychological expertise would enable [the Americans] to educate the young efficiently, diagnose and deal with harmful deviancy and pathology, inform their policies towards, and treatment of, various social groups and subject populations, and enable them to direct those they governed into the most fitting walks of life, as well as improving industrial efficiency by a better understanding of phenomena such as fatigue and attention.

If psychology was to prosper, it had to subscribe to American values, which it readily did (except for Titchener). In Chapter 3 we saw how an increasing number of American psychologists started to call themselves functionalists and to take distance from the European tradition, which they identified with the introspective study of consciousness and structuralism.

Psychology and its position within universities

The above description about the establishment of psychological laboratories and the turn to functionalism is the story you find in the history books of psychology up to the 1980s. It is part of the celebratory narrative, the tale of how scientific psychology conquered the world. At the same time, however, it is very self-centred, the view seen from within psychology. From the outside, psychology's fate looked less glamorous, certainly in the early decades.

For a start, most psychology laboratories were set up within philosophical and theological institutes. Saying that the other members of staff always greeted the newcomers with enthusiasm and generosity would be stretching the truth, as has been described endearingly by Benjamin (2000). He recounted the experiences of Harry Kirke Wolfe who tried to establish his own laboratory at the University of Nebraska. Wolfe received a doctorate with Wundt in 1886 and started his laboratory at Nebraska in 1889 with very minimal equipment that he built himself, borrowed from other departments, or purchased using funds from his library book budget. The next year he applied for $500 to further equip the laboratory. In the application he used phrases like: 'I cannot emphasize too strongly the necessity of providing some facilities for experimental work . . . It is possible to build up an experimental dept. in Psychology with little outlay . . . No field of scientific research offers such excellent opportunities for original work; chiefly because the soil is new' (as cited in Benjamin (2000) p. 320–1).

Unfortunately, Wolfe did not get his money, so he had to spend even more of his book budget. The year after, Wolfe applied again using stronger appeals and drawing links between psychology and agricultural sciences (a stronghold at Nebraska), alas to no avail. All he got was a written warning about spending book money for other purposes! (This reception did not stop Nebraska, however, from being listed as the fifth university in the USA to found its own laboratory of experimental psychology.)

On other occasions experimental psychologists were told not to stray too far away from the good old psychology as developed in philosophical writings. In 1894, the president of Princeton University urged psychologists attending a meeting of the American Psychological Association (APA) to retain the close ties that psychology had with philosophy and to not let psychology fall 'to the level of a mere science' (as cited in Fuchs (2000) p. 492). Similarly, George Trumbull Ladd, the second president of the APA, reviewed William James's *Principles of Psychology* (1890) and criticised it for reducing psychology to an unattainable 'cerebral psychology', because James excessively related mental phenomena to activities of the brain (Fuchs 2000, p. 493).

A very similar story could be told about the reactions of the 'hard' scientists at the universities. For reasons that will be outlined in later chapters, many of them have never been able to see psychology and the other behavioural and social sciences as full members of the club. For them, psychology always had the flavour of a 'wannabe science'.

? What do you think?

What do you think of the assessment of psychology as a 'wannabe science'? And what do you think of the advice 'not to let psychology fall to the level of a mere science'? What do you think these two opinions tell you about the world views of their authors? Can you relate this to Comte's hierarchy of explanations discussed in Chapter 3?

Trying to win over the public

If psychologists had a hard time convincing the hugely expanding and specialising universities of their importance, these efforts were dwarfed by the uphill struggle they faced to convince the public at large. Around 1900, lay society associated psychology with phrenology, spiritualism and other occult subjects.

phrenology

view that mental functions are localised in the brain and that the capacity of a function corresponds to the size of the brain part devoted to it; gave rise to personality assessment by means of analysing bumps on the skull; initiated by Gall and Spurzheim at the beginning of the nineteenth century

Phrenology started with the work of the German physician Franz Joseph Gall (1758–1828; see also Chapter 5). Gall was one of the first to hypothesise that different functions were controlled by different parts of the brain. In addition, he conjectured that well-developed functions were supported by parts of the brain with a larger volume. By measuring the skull, it was thus possible to predict the strengths and weaknesses of a person. Gall called this technique 'cranioscopy', a term that was later changed by his associate, Johann Caspar Spurzheim, into 'phrenology', and applied specifically to the prediction of character, personality and propensity to crime.

Spurzheim exported phrenology to Britain (where Queen Victoria and the young Galton made use of it) and to the USA, where it found particularly fertile soil in the hands of the Fowler brothers. This is how Leahey (2004, p. 312) describes their impact:

They minimized the scientific content of phrenology, maximized the practical applications, and set up an office in New York where clients could have their characters read for a fee. They wrote endlessly of the benefits of phrenology and published a phrenological journal that endured from the 1840s to 1911. They traveled around the country, especially the frontier areas, giving lectures and challenging skeptics. Like the great magician Houdini, they accepted any kind of test of their abilities, including blindfolded examinations of volunteers' skulls. What made the Fowlers' phrenology so popular was its appeal to the American character. It eschewed meta-physics for practical application. It pretended to tell employers what people to hire and to advise men which wives to take.

(Leahey, T. H. (2004) A history of psychology: Main currents in psychological enquiry (6th edn), p. 312. Copyright © 2004. Reprinted by permission of Pearson Education, Inc., Upper Saddle River, NJ)

spiritualism

belief that the spirits of the dead can be contacted by mediums; flourished in English-speaking countries at the end of the nineteenth and the beginning of the twentieth century

Another movement that preoccupied the Americans was spiritualism, the belief that the spirits of the dead could be contacted by mediums. It started in 1848 when two young adolescent girls began to hear rapping sounds which they believed to be messages of a deceased. Their case was investigated by the Quaker abolitionists, who decided it was genuine. The girls were taken to lecture halls and private meetings, and from there the enthusiasm spread rapidly, the more so because the raging Civil War claimed many lives. One of the people who caught an interest was William James, to the despair of most of his psychology colleagues (Coon 1992). James's successor at Harvard's laboratory of psychology, Hugo Münsterberg (1863–1916), described in one of his writings how he was asked weekly to explore or comment on some mystical or spiritualistic phenomenon. He generally (but not always) refused, because it was 'not . . . part of scientific psychology to examine the so-called mystical occur-rences' (Münsterberg (1910) as cited in Coon (1992) p. 145).

In a desperate effort to turn the tide, the 'new psychologists' (as they called them-selves) published hundreds of articles about the new, scientific psychology in popular magazines. Benjamin (2000) described one attempt in *McClure's Magazine*, in which an assistant of Münsterberg announced that a psychology laboratory resembled any other science laboratory with a lot of equipment for precise measurement. The psy-chologists also held thousands of popular speeches, 'reaching out to the public'. Unfortunately, their impact was limited, because the topics they talked about failed to capture the public's imagination to the same degree as phrenology and spiritualism. The lay audience arguably felt as convinced about the burning necessity of scientific psychology as the parents of James McKeen Cattell after reading the following letter from their 24-year-old son at Wundt's laboratory:

I spend four mornings and two afternoon's [sic] working in Wundt's laboratory . . . . Our work is interesting. If I should explain it to you you might not find it of vast importance, but we discover new facts and must ourselves invent the methods we use. We work in a new field, where others will follow us, who must use or correct our results. We are trying to measure the time it takes to perform the simplest mental acts – as for example to distinguish whether a color is blue or red. As this time seems to be not more than one hundredth of a second, you can imagine this is no easy task.

(Cattell (1886) as cited in Benjamin (2000) p. 320)

? What do you think?

Is the perception of psychology among the public nowadays different from the perception in the USA at the turn of the twentieth century? If yes, what has changed? If no, why haven't psychologists been able to change it?

This then was the environment the fledgling psychology research faculty found itself in. It can be argued that within the wider American society the first laboratories were not the glowing beacons of psychology's victory march towards the guild of sciences, as psychology historians liked to describe them, but rather a few speckles of penicillin in a colony of bacteria. According to some psychologists, the precarious position of scientific psychology was due not only to the public's perception but also to the fact that psychology's scientific message lacked strength, as can be read in the following excerpt:

> [They] decided either to give up psychology or else to make it a natural science. They saw their brother-scientists making progress in medicine, in chemistry, in physics. Every new discovery in those fields was of prime importance; every new element isolated in one laboratory could be isolated in some other laboratory; each new element was immediately taken up in the warp and woof of science as a whole. One need only mention wireless, radium, insulin, thyroxin, to verify this. Elements so isolated and methods so formulated immediately began to function in human achievement.
>
> *(Watson (1924) as cited in Mackenzie (1977) p. 14)*

The dissenters took their inspiration from research on the behaviour of animals, as we will see below.

More continuity than acknowledged by the pioneers

Although the functionalists established a new academic discipline, Richards (1996, p. 40–41) argued that there was much more continuity with what had been going on before at the American universities than was suggested by the repeated claims of a revolutionary break with the past. Just as in Europe, psychology had already been taught as a course in many degrees for a long time (you may have noticed in Chapter 3 that James started to teach psychology four years *before* Wundt established the first psychology laboratory and the history of psychology supposedly took off). In particular, most universities, which had very strong religious affiliations, contained a compulsory course of Mental and Moral Philosophy, in which the relationships between religion, philosophy and logic were discussed. An analysis of the contents of these courses indicated that already in the 1860s they contained contemporary subjects such as evolutionary theory and the scientific attempts to study human functioning. Indeed, several of Wundt's American students had been encouraged by their lecturers of the Mental and Moral Philosophy course to go to Germany.

As a result, there was a great deal of overlap between the new psychology textbooks (including James's *Principles*) and the textbooks used in the Mental and Moral Philosophy courses. The new books were just more secular (i.e. non-religious) and scientific in tone. For that reason Richards (1996) considered the rhetoric of a revolutionary change in psychology more an expression of aspiration than achievement.

? **What do you think?**

What are the advantages of presenting new subject matter as revolutionary (i.e. as a break with the past)? Also, there is evidence that scientists tend to sell their findings to the public as innovative and breaking new ground, even though they are already well known to peer researchers. Why would they do that?

Interim summary

■ Scientific psychology expanded rapidly in the USA: many laboratories were established at universities, the APA was founded, and two important journals were initiated.

■ Meanwhile psychology changed to address concerns prevalent in American society (adaptation to the environment, practical usefulness). This led to functionalism.

■ At the same time, the position of the psychology laboratories was precarious. They were mostly part of philosophical institutes (rather than science faculties), and the public at large did not associate psychology with science but with phrenology and spiritualism. This created pressure to further enhance the scientific status of psychology.

■ There is also evidence for a much larger overlap between the new psychology textbooks and the philosophical textbooks they replaced than was acknowledged by the first psychologists.

Inspiration from animal research

Researching the preservation of races in the struggle for life

In Chapter 3 we saw how Galton endorsed Darwin's evolutionary ideas and tried to test them by examining the heredity of human intelligence. Another central person in the dissemination of the evolutionary theory was Herbert Spencer (1820–1903), who in 1864 coined the phrase 'survival of the fittest'. Spencer wrote an essay on evolution two years before Darwin published his *Origin of Species*. In this text he defended the view that life started from very simple, homogeneous organisms and constantly became more complex and better integrated. After the publication of the *Origins* he integrated Darwin's ideas into his own, claiming that evolution had a direction and an equilibrium endpoint (which more or less coincided with the English upper class). He also adopted an idea initially proposed by Jean-Baptiste Lamarck (1744–1829) that organisms could pass on newly learned skills to their offspring (remember from Chapter 1 that nothing was known of the genetic inheritance mechanisms at that time; in Chapter 3 we saw how Galton thought that the skin colour of rabbits could be passed on through blood).

As a result of Darwin's and Spencer's writings, many learned individuals got interested in animal behaviour and started to interpret it in terms of the struggle for life. They looked for similarities between human and animal behaviour to place the different species on the evolution scale, and they searched for evidence of intelligent behaviour that had been passed on from generation to generation.

Early research: Trying to understand the animal's mind

In the beginning much of the evidence gathered was anecdotal and based on the interpretation of the underlying reasoning by the animal. An important name in this enterprise was the Briton George Romanes (1848–1894). According to him, the approach combined observations of behaviour with inference of the animal's adaptive capacities. These capacities were considered to be the result of a mind that resembled that of humans. In other words, the mental processes in animals were thought to be of the same sort as you would expect to find after introspection of your own consciousness. Or as Romanes described the method:

> [I]f I contemplate my own mind, I have an immediate cognizance of a certain row of thoughts and feelings, which are the most ultimate things – and, indeed, the only things – of which I am cognizant. But if I contemplate Mind in other persons or organisms, I can have no such immediate cognizance of their thoughts and feelings; I can only *infer* the existence of such thoughts and feelings from the activities of the persons or organisms which appear to manifest them . . . That is to say, starting from what I know subjectively of the operations of my own individual mind, and of the activities which in my own organism these operations seem to prompt, I proceed by analogy to infer from the observable activities displayed by other organisms, the fact that certain mental operations underlie or accompany these activities.
>
> *(Romanes (1884) as cited by Mackenzie (1977) p. 56–7)*

An example of the approach is provided by Mr. Bidie's observation published in the scientific journal *Nature*. Mr. Bidie had a heavily pregnant cat that he had to leave behind when he went on a journey. During his absence two youngsters trespassed his quarters and repeatedly teased the cat. Upon his return Mr. Bidie chased the youngsters and shortly afterwards the cat moved her kittens from a concealed nest to his dressing room. According to Mr Bidie, '[the cat's] train of reasoning seems to have been the following "now that my master has returned, there is no risk of the kittens being injured . . . so I will take them out for my protector to see and admire" ' (Bidie (1879) as cited in Galef 1998).

The above example is typical of most of the research done on animal behaviour in the second half of the nineteenth century. On the basis of anecdotal evidence authors claimed that animals had reasoning capacities similar to those of humans. This is a typical instance of anthropomorphic interpretation, the attribution of human motives and human-like intelligence to other living creatures.

anthropomorphic interpretation

interpreting behaviour of non-human living creatures by attributing human motives and human-like intelligence to them

Thorndike's puzzle box

A different approach was taken by Edward Lee Thorndike (1874–1949). As mentioned in Chapter 3, Thorndike was attracted to psychology after reading James's *Principles*. He went to study with James, who advised him to investigate learning in children (as part of the aim to increase the functionality of scientific psychology). Unfortunately for James and Thorndike, they ran into difficulties when they tried to recruit participants. Eventually Thorndike proposed to study instinctive and intelligent behaviour in chickens. The proposal was accepted by the Harvard authorities, as long as Thorndike kept the animals in his apartment. James could not convince the authorities to make space for them at the university, and when Thorndike ran into difficulties with his landlady, James had no other option than to house the chickens in the basement of his own house (Benjafield 2005, p. 139–40). Thorndike eventually left Harvard when he was invited to Columbia by James McKeen Cattell and there he finished his famous research with the puzzle box.

A first change Thorndike introduced was that he did not rely on anecdotal evidence, but on careful observation of animals put in controlled environments. The

Figure 4.1 One of the puzzle boxes made by Thorndike.

Source: Robert Mearns Yerkes Papers/Yale University Library/Manuscripts and Archives

second change was that he based his conclusions on the animals' behaviour, not on what supposedly went on in their minds. He put hungry animals (chickens, rats, dogs and in particular cats) in puzzle boxes he constructed himself (even though he was not the most skilled carpenter, as can be seen in figure 4.1). Outside the box, food was presented which the animal could reach if it managed to solve the puzzle and open the door (e.g. by moving a lever, pulley or treadle).

Thorndike noted how long it took the animal to get out of the box. He observed that the time rapidly decreased on successive trials (figure 4.2), because the animal did

Figure 4.2 Time needed by a cat to escape from one of Thorndike's puzzle boxes in successive trials.

Source: Thorndike (1911)

law of effect

behavioural law introduced by Thorndike to refer to the fact that behaviours followed by positive consequences are strengthened and more likely to be repeated

not repeat the behaviours that had failed before but focused on the behaviours that had been successful. Thorndike called this the law of effect. Behaviours that are followed by positive consequences are strengthened and repeated; behaviours that are not followed by such consequences are not repeated.

Thorndike further wanted to see whether the animal had any 'knowledge' of the contingency involved. To this end, he had cats observe other cats solve the puzzle. Afterwards he put these 'expert' cats in the box and examined whether they solved the puzzle faster than naïve cats that had not observed the required behaviour. Given that this was not the case, Thorndike concluded that the learning consisted of making an association between the situation of being in the box and performing the appropriate act. The learning did not involve the animal solving the problem by associating ideas of actions and rewards. The cat did not have insight into the contingencies. Thorndike called this type of learning instrumental conditioning.

instrumental conditioning

name introduced by Thorndike to refer to learning on the basis of the law of effect; called operant conditioning by Skinner

This is how Thorndike summarised his findings:

> The cat does not look over the situation, much less *think* it over, and then decide what to do. It bursts out at once into the activities which instinct and experience have settled on as suitable reactions to the situation 'confinement when hungry with food outside.' The one impulse, out of many accidental ones, which leads to pleasure, becomes strengthened and stamped in thereby, and more and more firmly associated with the sense-impression of that box's interior.
>
> *(Thorndike (1898) as cited in Benjafield (2005) p. 140)*

comparative psychology

study of behaviour of animals, usually with the intention to shed light on human functioning within the framework of the evolutionary theory

It must be noted that Thorndike's claim against social learning in animals has since been proven wrong; imitative learning happens in all kinds of species, as we will see in Chapter 11.

Thorndike's work had an enormous impact on animal research, because his approach was much more in line with the research methods in the natural sciences than the previous anecdotal and anthropomorphic attempts. For this reason, 1898, the year in which Thorndike published his PhD thesis on animal learning, is celebrated as the birthday of comparative psychology, even though Thorndike after his PhD returned to his first love, educational psychology.

KEY FIGURE

Edward Thorndike

Source: Humanities and Social Services Library/New York Public Library/Science Photo Library Ltd

- American psychologist (1874–1949).

- Is seen as the father of comparative psychology because he was the first to study animal psychology in an objective way (as part of his PhD). He did so by placing an animal in a controlled environment and drawing conclusions on the basis of the animal's behaviour.

- Introduced the terms 'instrumental conditioning' and 'the law of effect'.

- After his PhD, turned to educational issues and, therefore, is also celebrated as the father of educational psychology.

Pavlov's research on classical conditioning

Thorndike's lead of studying the behaviour of animals without trying to explain it in terms of conscious thoughts and feelings got a further impetus when researchers became informed of Pavlov's work in Russia (an English account of which was published in 1909 in the journal *Psychological Bulletin*).

classical conditioning

form of learning discovered by Pavlov in which an association is made between two events in the environment; usually studied with a stimulus that elicits a reflex-like response (e.g. food in mouth → salivation) to which a second, initially neutral stimulus is coupled

Ivan Pavlov (1849–1936) was a physiologist who studied the digestive system of animals (mainly dogs). He devised a procedure that allowed him to continuously measure the secretion of fluids by the digestive organs. This gave him a much more detailed picture of what was going on than the previous attempts based on vivisections at different times after the meal. In his research Pavlov was inspired by the Russian physiologist I.M. Sechenov, who argued that mental life could be understood in terms of physiological reflexes. Pavlov observed that many digestive processes indeed consisted of reflexes. When food was placed on the animal's tongue, the salivary glands automatically started to emit drivel and the stomach started to excrete gastric juices.

Shortly after 1900 (when he was already more than 50 years old and about to get his Nobel Prize for Medicine) Pavlov started to become interested in a curious phenomenon: after a few experiences of food delivery, the animal started to secrete digestive fluids *before* the food arrived in the mouth, namely as soon as the animal saw the preparations of the experiment taking place. Pavlov decided to investigate this 'psychic reflex' methodically under strictly controlled circumstances. That was the beginning of the research on classical conditioning, which showed that a neutral stimulus (e.g. a tone) which is presented shortly before a stimulus (food) that automatically elicits a reflex response (salivation) after a few pairings starts to elicit the response as well.

KEY FIGURE

Ivan Petrovich Pavlov

Source: Ria Novosti Science Photo Library Ltd

- Russian physiologist (1849–1936).
- Studied digestive system in animals (Nobel Prize in 1904). Introduced techniques that allowed him to continuously measure the secretion of fluids by the organs.
- After 1900 became interested in the question why organs started to secrete fluids *before* the food was presented. This would be the start of research on classical conditioning.
- Was part of a Russian school which held that psychology could be reduced to physiology: thinking consisted of reflexes.
- Had a big impact on the development of behaviourism.

Pavlov's research, just like Thorndike's, brought research on animal behaviour into the realm of the natural sciences (the story goes that Pavlov resented people calling him a psychologist). The potential of this change in research method was summarised as follows by a young researcher in a popular magazine:

The possibility of learning more about the mental life of animals becomes a probability when we consider that our knowledge of the mental processes of infants, children and defective individuals is obtained almost entirely without the aid of language. The moment we take this broader point of view, that the behavior of man expresses his psychology, and are willing to admit that we can scientifically study his behavior, it follows at once that we can build up an animal psychology, because we can study the behavior of animals just as scientifically as we can study the behavior of man.

The study of behavior thus becomes a broad science; normal adult human psychology forms only a part of its subject matter. The psychology of infants, of children, of the feeble-minded, of primitive peoples, of animals, all form a part of the world to be observed by the psychologist.

(Watson 1907, p. 421–2)

A few years later this young man, John B. Watson (1878–1958), would publish a pamphlet that would become a decisive moment in the history of psychology.

Interim summary

- The evolutionary theory led to an increased interest in animal behaviour.

- Initially animal behaviour was studied by focusing on anecdotes of intelligent behaviour. These were explained by assuming the same reasoning processes in animals as in humans (anthropomorphic interpretation).

- Thorndike introduced a different approach. Animals were put into a controlled environment (a puzzle box) and conclusions were drawn on the basis of the animals' behaviour (instrumental conditioning resulting in the law of effect).

- The focus on the animal's behaviour (rather than its mind) was further strengthened by Pavlov's work on classical conditioning.

- Together the changes resulted in a research method that much more resembled the methods used in the natural sciences. Watson started to make the claim that the method would also be good for the study of human functioning.

The 1913 behaviourist manifesto

In 1907, Watson was poached by Baldwin, a famous developmental psychologist and one of the founders of *Psychological Review* (see above), to become professor at the Johns Hopkins University. Within weeks after Watson's arrival, however, Baldwin was forced from his chair because of a scandal involving a brothel, which left Watson in charge of both the department and the journal. (Baldwin would go to the University of Toronto and there found the first psychology laboratory of Canada and, at that time, the British Empire.)

Watson used his position as editor of *Psychological Review* to promote the case for animal research. In 1913, he published a scathing article against the lack of scientific

behaviourism

movement in psychology arguing that observable behaviours are the most important aspect of human functioning to be understood; denies to various extents the relevance of information processing going on in the mind; particularly strong in the USA in the first half of the twentieth century

rigour in the ongoing investigations in most of the psychological laboratories. This article would become the beginning of behaviourism. Because of its importance, both in terms of the impact on the history of psychology and in terms of how psychology came to define its subject and its research methods, we will discuss the article in some detail. (Incidentally, the article is well worth reading in its entirety. It is meant to convince people, so it is very accessible.)

The article (available on http://psychclassics.yorku.ca) begins with the following statement:

> Psychology as the behaviorist views it is a purely objective experimental branch of natural science. Its theoretical goal is the prediction and control of behavior. Introspection forms no essential part of its methods, nor is the scientific value of its data dependent upon the readiness with which they lend themselves to interpretation in terms of consciousness. The behaviorist, in his efforts to get a unitary scheme of animal response, recognizes no dividing line between man and brute.

In this statement we clearly see the transition from *introspection* into one's own mind to the *observation* of others' behaviour. As we indicated at the end of Chapter 3, this was a defining insight in the growth of psychological research. Even though Wundt and the other early psychologists made use of experimental methods, they still ran the studies on themselves as participants.

An element that played a role in the shift from introspection to observation was the impact of the evolutionary theory on American psychology. Survival in a context of natural selection primarily depends on how the animal acts, not on what it 'thinks'. Thoughts were the playground of philosophers; biologists had to predict behaviours. Another element that contributed to the shift was that introspection, as described by Titchener in his handbooks, turned out to be a very counterintuitive and difficult procedure for students to use in their practicals. They found it much easier simply to observe what others were doing.

Watson's manifesto continued as follows:

> It has been maintained by its followers generally that psychology is a study of the science of the phenomena of consciousness. It has taken as its problem, on the one hand, the analysis of complex mental states (or processes) into simple elementary constituents, and on the other the construction of complex states when the elementary constituents are given . . . It is agreed that introspection is the method par excellence by means of which mental states may be manipulated for purposes of psychology. On this assumption, behavior data (including under this term everything which goes under the name of comparative psychology) have no value per se. They possess significance only in so far as they may throw light upon conscious states.

Here we see Watson turning his bile on Titchener's structuralism, which as we have seen in Chapter 3 was easiest to attack, given its isolated position. This attack continued for several more paragraphs, including sentences such as:

> I do not wish unduly to criticize psychology. It has failed significantly, I believe, during the fifty-odd years of its existence as an experimental discipline to make its place in the world as an undisputed natural science. Psychology, as it is generally thought of, has something esoteric in its methods. If you fail to reproduce my findings, it is

not due to some fault in your apparatus or in the control of your stimulus, but it is due to the fact that your introspection is untrained . . .

The time seems to have come when psychology must discard all reference to consciousness; when it need no longer delude itself into thinking that it is making mental states the object of observation.

What do you think?

Can you see how Watson's text influenced the views writers of introductory books in the twentieth century had about psychology before behaviourism? Rather than consulting the original materials, authors simply took over Watson's criticisms of structuralism and introspection.

Next, Watson turned his stare to functionalism and wrote:

My psychological quarrel is not with the systematic and structural psychologist alone. The last fifteen years have seen the growth of what is called functional psychology. This type of psychology decries the use of elements in the static sense of the structuralists. It throws emphasis upon the biological significance of conscious processes instead of upon the analysis of conscious states into introspectively isolable elements. I have done my best to understand the difference between functional psychology and structural psychology. Instead of clarity, confusion grows upon me.

Then, Watson formulated the alternative:

This leads me to the point where I should like to make the argument constructive. I believe we can write a psychology [as just described] . . . and never go back upon our definition: never use the terms consciousness, mental states, mind, content, introspectively verifiable, imagery, and the like. I believe that we can do it in a few years . . . It can be done in terms of stimulus and response, in terms of habit formation, habit integration and the like. Furthermore, I believe that it is really worth while to make this attempt now.

In order to become a real science, psychology had to focus on observable behaviour (just like Thorndike had done) and ignore everything that referred to consciousness, thinking, feelings, motives, plans, purposes, images, knowledge or the self. This meant that some topics could not be addressed with the behaviourist method:

The situation is somewhat different when we come to a study of the more complex forms of behavior, such as imagination, judgment, reasoning, and conception. At present the only statements we have of them are in content terms. Our minds have been so warped by the fifty-odd years which have been devoted to the study of states of consciousness that we can envisage these problems only in one way. We should meet the situation squarely and say that we are not able to carry forward investigations along all of these lines by the behavior methods which are in use at the present time . . . As our methods become better developed it will be possible to undertake investigations of more and more complex forms of behavior. Problems which are now laid aside will again become imperative, but they can be viewed as they arise from a new angle and in more concrete settings.

Although Watson in his manifesto left an opening for later research on information processing in the mind, in subsequent writings he hardened his stance and came to deny the importance/existence of any process that was not observable.

Interim summary

- In 1913 Watson used his position as editor of *Psychological Review* to launch the behaviourist manifesto.

- Psychology was defined as a purely objective experimental branch of natural science, based on the prediction and control of behaviour.

- In the manifesto Watson argued that previous research with introspection into consciousness had failed significantly.

- In the manifesto Watson left an opening for later study of more complex behaviour (such as imagination and reasoning). In his later writings he came to deny the importance of such behaviour.

KEY FIGURE

John B. Watson

Source: Bettmann / Corbis

- American psychologist (1878–1958).

- Did a PhD in 1903 on animal psychology. Was influenced by Thorndike's approach and saw this as the approach that would bring all of psychology into the realm of the natural sciences.

- Moved to Johns Hopkins University in 1907 and became editor of the prestigious journal *Psychological Review*.

- Used his position as editor in 1913 to publish the behaviourist manifesto.

- Became the main promoter of behaviourism through the publications of books and articles. Tried to show, together with Rosalie Rayner, that phobias originated on the basis of classical conditioning. Demonstrated this by making a toddler – Little Albert – afraid of a white rat by associating the presence of the rat with a horrendous noise (Watson and Rayner 1920).

- Had an extramarital affair with Rosalie Rayner, which forced him to leave the university in 1920. Kept on publishing about behaviourism until 1930.

- Behaviourist work was continued primarily by Hull, Skinner and Tolman, who agreed on the method, but came up with different views about the relationship between stimuli and responses.

positivism

philosophy stating
that only empirically
obtained and verifi-
able information is
authentic informa-
tion; started by
Comte in the eigh-
teenth century; also
often used to refer
to an opinion
according to which
science and scien-
tifically obtained
information are the
motors of progress

The influence of the philosophy of science

Positivism and the search of what makes a real science

Watson's attempt to increase the scientific standing of psychology was embedded within a wider movement to make science the cornerstone of human progress. Impressed by the success of technology, physics and chemistry, scientific inventions were seen as the way forward. Indeed, the nations that invested heavily in them (UK, USA, Prussia, the Netherlands) saw their power and status grow much more than the countries that did not do so. This movement, which saw science as the motor of progress, was known as positivism, a name introduced by Auguste Comte (Chapter 2).

Given the positivist tenet that the natural sciences were the most successful development in human reasoning, philosophers and scientists started to examine what exactly was the core of the scientific approach, so that other knowledge areas could adopt this method as well. Their subject matter became known as the philosophy of science (Chapter 8).

philosophy of
science

branch of philoso-
phy that studies the
foundations of sci-
entific research, to
better understand
the position of sci-
entific research rel-
ative to other forms
of information
acquisition and
generation

One principle that had caught everyone's attention since Newton's *Principia Mathematica* was the importance of mathematical laws to describe reality. However, this turned out not to be enough. As we saw in Chapter 2, several natural philosophers in vain tried to build a Newtonian theory of psychology on the basis of mathematical equations (e.g. Hutchinson in the UK and Herbart in Germany). What exactly was missing?

The requirement of operational definitions

From the writings about the philosophy of science, psychologists distilled three new ideas that were important for the further development of behaviourism and scientific psychology in general. The first was that you had to be able to represent the elements of a mathematical law as numbers. There was no point in trying to establish a mathematical relationship between two variables, if you could not express them numerically. The best way to do so was to represent the variables in terms of the way they had been measured (e.g. weight expressed in kilograms). Such a definition became known as an operational definition. It was first formulated by the Harvard physicist and Nobel laureate Percy Williams Bridgman in 1927 and introduced to psychologists by his university colleague Stanley Smith Stevens in 1935.

operational
definition

definition of a vari-
able in terms of
how the variable
has been measured;
allows description
of the variable in
quantitative form

The importance of operational definitions can easily be demonstrated with Newton's law. One of these laws states that $F = ma$ (the force on an object is equal to its mass multiplied by its acceleration). Such a law only becomes useful if you are able to measure the force, the mass and the acceleration, and express them in units. Similarly, it is not enough to say that the Moral Importance (M) of people is a function of their Benevolence (B) multiplied by their Abilities (A) to have a scientific theory, as Hutchinson claimed (Chapter 2). You must be able to express the variables in numbers, by referring to the way in which you measured them.

The need for operational definitions explained to psychologists why psychophysics had been so successful (Chapter 3). Here they were able to describe both the stimulus intensity and the resulting sensation in numerical form, so that it was possible to search for the best fitting mathematical equation between them. The immediate challenge for the behaviourists, therefore, was to achieve something similar for their learning theories. The person who took this approach the furthest was Clark L. Hull (1884–1952), who sought to explain all learning and motivation by the use of mathematical equations with variables that were operationally defined. For instance, an equation from his book *Principles of Behavior* (1943) was:

$$_sE_R = {}_sH_R * D * V * K,$$

in which

$_sE_R$ = the excitatory potential of the stimulus to elicit the response,

$_sH_R$ = the habit strength between the stimulus and the response,

D = the drive level of the animal/human,

V = the stimulus intensity,

K = the reward incentive.

All variables had an operational definition and could be expressed in numbers, so that it was possible to *predict* the precise behaviour of an animal in a particular situation.

Independent and dependent variables

The second idea the behaviourists took from the philosophers of science was that a distinction had to be made between independent variables and dependent variables. Independent variables were characteristics of the environment and/or the participant that might have an impact on the behaviour and that could be manipulated by the researcher (e.g. the number of T-junctions in a maze). Dependent variables were behaviour features that could be measured to see whether the independent variable had an effect (e.g. the time the rat needed to find the food in the maze). On the basis of this distinction, psychological research could be defined as the study of the impact of a Stimulus (the independent variable) on the Response (the dependent variable). As a consequence, behaviourism also became known as an S-R-psychology.

The need for verification

verification

principle that up to the 1950s formed the core of the scientific method: a proposition was meaningful (scientific) if its truth could be empirically verified

Finally, a third idea the behaviourists took from the philosophy of science was the necessity of verification in science. Statements were only useful if they could be verified by empirical observation. The requirement of verification ruled out religious statements, such as 'god loves everyone', but according to the behaviourists also ruled out introspective statements such as 'to me this stimulus looks like a combination of . . .'. Verification meant that researchers had to present their evidence in such a way that it could be verified by others (see also Chapter 8).

The incorporation of the above principles considerably increased the objectivity of research in psychology, although the requirement of mathematically expressed laws turned out to be less important than originally thought by the behaviourists (Chapter 10).

Interim summary

- Behaviourism was part of a wider movement within Western society to make science the cornerstone of human progress.

- The philosophers of science tried to define the qualities of a true science. In addition to the ideal of mathematical laws, behaviourists took three ideas from them:
  - Operational definitions are necessary.

Interim summary (continued)

- There is a distinction between independent variables and dependent variables (this got translated into S-R associations).
- Science relies on verification.

What do you think?

If you did a course in research methods, you would immediately see the lasting influence of these insights on the way psychology students are taught to do research. If you have your textbook of research methods with you, look up the different insights and what your present-day book says about them.

Further developments in behaviourism: Skinner versus Tolman

In an ironic twist of fate, Watson's scientific career ended in more or less the same way as it started. Remember that his impact got a major boost when Baldwin was forced to leave Johns Hopkins University. In October 1920, Watson in turn had to leave Johns Hopkins as a result of an extramarital affair with a graduate student (Rosalie Rayner, with whom he had published the famous study of Little Albert). Watson took up a job in advertising where his income apparently was many times higher than what he earned at university.

Skinner and radical behaviourism

Watson's legacy was continued by three heavyweight successors (in addition to hundreds of lesser-known researchers all over the world). The first of them was Clark Hull, whom we described above. The second was Burrhus Frederic Skinner (1904–1990), who is particularly well known for his research on operant conditioning and for his radical behaviourism. Operant conditioning is another name for instrumental conditioning (coined by Skinner) and examines the ways in which behaviour changes as a function of the reinforcement or punishment that follows. **Radical behaviourism** is a strong version of behaviourism, which holds that an organism is nothing but a place where stimuli provoke behaviours on the basis of S-R associations.

Skinner denied the relevance of information processing in the mind. All that happened was the direct activation of responses on the basis of stimulus input. Below you find some quotes from a popular text he wrote on behaviourism, illustrating the point (Skinner 1974; see also Malone and Cruchon 2001):

> The brain is said to use data, make hypotheses, make choices, and so on, as the mind was once said to have done. In a behaviorist account it is the person who does these things [p. 86].

> In all these roles it has been possible to avoid the problems of dualism by substituting 'brain' for 'mind' . . . Both the mind and the brain are not far from the ancient notion of a homunculus—an inner person who behaves in precisely the ways necessary to explain the behavior of the outer person in whom he dwells . . . A much simpler solution is to identify the mind with the person [p. 130].

radical behaviourism

strong version of behaviourism, defended by Skinner, which denies the relevance of information processing in the mind and holds that all human behaviour can be understood on the basis of S-R associations

We do not need to describe contingencies of reinforcement in order to be affected by them . . . Certainly for thousands of years people spoke grammatically without knowing that there were rules of grammar [p. 141].

It is often said that a science of behavior studies the human organism but neglects the person or self. What it neglects is a vestige of animism . . . traces of the doctrine survive when we speak of a *personality*, or an ego . . . of an *I* who says he knows what he is going to do and uses his body to do it . . . [p. 184].

A person is not an originating agent; he is a locus, a point at which many genetic and environmental conditions come together [p. 185].

There are two points noteworthy in Skinner's radical behaviourism. First, in the human brain all that matters is the formation of S-R connections. Second, persons are not responsible for their actions; they simply respond to events in the environment. Nor do they take the initiative. All they do is respond to stimuli from outside. It is fair to say that this strong stance, though it was in line with Watson's views, eventually did behaviourism more harm than good.

Tolman and purposive behaviourism

In introductory books behaviourism is often identified with Skinner's radical behaviourism (and at the same time dismissed). However, as we have indicated a few times already, it is important to dissociate the ideas of an individual from those of the larger movement. Although Skinner was the best known behaviourist, this does not imply that his views were shared by everybody who felt attracted to behaviourism. Hull, for instance, allowed some scope for internal mental processes in the form of internal r-s connections (giving rise to S-r-s-R sequences) and the third main neo-behaviourist, Edward C. Tolman (1886–1959), actually doubted Skinner's interpretation of operant conditioning.

According to Tolman, operant condition could not be understood in simple S-R terms and he devised several experiments to show this. Here we describe only one study, actually carried out by a student of Tolman, Hugh Blodgett, in 1929 (i.e. years before Skinner's radical behaviourism became influential).

In Skinner's view animals acquired behaviours because the association between an environmental cue and a particular behaviour was strengthened by the subsequent reinforcement. So, a rat learned to find its way through a maze because a particular turning at each intersection was followed by food (strengthening the link between the intersection and that turn) whereas others were not. If this reasoning were true, Tolman (1948) argued, then rats that were not reinforced, should not learn. However, this was not what Blodgett observed. He had three conditions: (1) a condition in which hungry rats were placed in a maze that contained food at the end of the maze (figure 4.3), (2) a condition in which hungry rats were placed in the same maze, but the food was only introduced on day 3, and (3) a condition in which food was introduced on day 7.

Blodgett observed that the rats in condition (1) showed a fast learning curve. That is, on successive trials they made fewer errors running towards the food. The rats in condition (2) did not run straight towards the end of the maze on the first two days (when they did not find food there), but showed a very different behaviour on day 4 (after having found food on trial 3): now they ran straight to the food location, making no more errors than the rats that had found food (and hence been reinforced)

Figure 4.3 The maze used by Blodgett in 1929 to show the phenomenon of latent learning.
According to Tolman (1948) rats that were not reinforced by food at the end of the maze, still learned the layout of the maze (i.e. they built a cognitive map of the maze), because as soon as they got food at the end, they ran as fast as a group of rats that had been reinforced on each trial (see figure 4.4).

Source: Tolman (1948). Adapted from Blodgett, H.C. (1929) 'The effect of the introduction of reward upon the maze performance of rats', Univ Calif Publ Psychol., **4**, 8, p. 117.

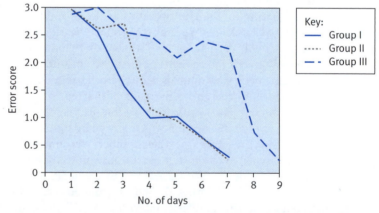

Figure 4.4 The number of errors made by three groups of rats in the study of Blodgett (1929).
The first group always found food at the end of the maze. They showed the usual learning curve. The second group was not fed on the first 2 days and found food on day 3 and each subsequent day. They showed extremely fast learning from day 3 to day 4. The third group was fed from day 7 on. They showed fast learning from day 7 to day 8 and immediately caught up with the performance level of group I. This finding is difficult to explain within Skinner's radical behaviourism.

Source: Tolman (1948). Adapted from Blodgett, H.C. (1929) 'The effect of the introduction of reward upon the maze performance of rats', Univ Calif Publ Psychol., 4, 8, p. 120.

from the first day on. The group that found food on the seventh day showed the same massive and instantaneous learning on day 8. According to Tolman, this showed that the learning of the rats was not due to the fact that the presence of food had reinforced taking the correct turns, but that the rats had learned the layout of the maze and were able to use this knowledge when they had a reason to do so. This is how Tolman described the outcome of the finding:

> It will be observed that the experimental groups as long as they were not finding food did not appear to learn much. (Their error curves did not drop.) But on the days immediately succeeding their first finding of the food their error curves did drop astoundingly. It appeared, in short, that during the non-rewarded trials these animals had been learning much more than they had exhibited. This learning, which did not manifest itself until after the food had been introduced, Blodgett called 'latent learning.' Interpreting these results anthropomorphically, we would say that as long as the animals were not getting any food at the end of the maze they continued to take their time in going through it – they continued to enter many blinds. Once, however, they knew they were to get food, they demonstrated that during these preceding non-rewarded trials they had learned where many of the blinds were. They had been building up a 'map,' and could utilize the latter as soon as they were motivated to do so.
>
> *(Tolman 1948, p. 194–5)*

purposive behaviourism

version of behaviourism, defended by Tolman, which saw behaviour as goal-related (means to an end); agreed with other behaviourists that psychology should be based on observable behaviour

For Tolman, the fact that the animals in Blodgett's study immediately knew where to go to as soon as they had found food once demonstrated that they had learned the layout of the maze during the trials in which no food was given. Together with Blodgett, he called this latent learning, the acquisition of knowledge that is not demonstrated in observable behaviour. More specifically, Tolman argued, the rats acquired a cognitive map of the maze. As soon as they knew where food would be given, they were able to make use of this cognitive map to select the correct alleys.

On the basis of these and other findings Tolman stated that animal and human behaviour was motivated by goals: only when the rats were provided with a goal did they make use of their knowledge. Therefore, Tolman's approach is sometimes called purposive behaviourism. Tolman agreed with Watson and Skinner that psychology should be based on observable behaviour and not seek to understand the animal's 'mind' or 'consciousness', but at the same time he did not see why he should be asked to assume that nothing more than the formation of S-R associations happened in the mind. For him, goals could be studied objectively.

Interim summary

- After Watson's departure from academic life, behaviourism was continued by three heavyweight neo-behaviourists: Hull, Skinner and Tolman.

- Hull: mathematical equations with operationally defined variables that allow detailed predictions of behaviour in specified circumstances.

Interim summary (continued)

- Skinner: radical behaviourism (there is no information processing in the mind; all human actions are the result of S-R connections).

- Tolman: purposive behaviourism (behaviour is motivated by goals; the goal-directedness can be studied in an objective way).

4.2   Adding cognitions to behaviour

Tolman's views turned out to be more fruitful than either Hull's or Skinner's. Although Watson was perfectly right when he asserted that overt behaviours were easier to study than covert cognitions and feelings, the difficulty of investigating what happened in the 'black box' between stimuli and responses did not imply that nothing occurred there at all, as Skinner came to believe.

Shortly after World War II voices against behaviourism grew louder and a new movement became visible, which eventually took the name of cognitive psychology. Probably the best account of the movement's beginning is given by Gardner (1987). This is how the book begins:

> In September of 1948 on the campus of the California Institute of Technology, a group of eminent scientists representing several disciplines met for a conference on 'Cerebral Mechanisms in Behavior' . . . This conference had been designed to facilitate discussions about a classic issue: the way in which the nervous system controls behavior. And yet the discussions ranged far more widely than the official topic had implied. For example, the opening speaker, mathematician John von Neumann, forged a striking comparison between the electronic computer (then a discovery so new that it smacked of science fiction) and the brain (which had been around for a while). The next speaker, mathematician and neurophysiologist Warren McCulloch, used his provocative title ('Why the Mind Is in the Head') to launch a far-ranging discussion on how the brain processes information – like von Neumann, he wanted to exploit certain parallels between the nervous system and 'logical devices' in order to figure out why we perceive the world the way we do.
>
> Less steeped in the latest technological innovations but more versed in the problems of explaining human behavior, the next speaker, psychologist Karl Lashley, gave the most iconoclastic and most memorable address. Speaking on 'The Problem of Serial Order in Behavior,' he challenged the doctrine (or dogma) that had dominated psychological analysis for the past several decades and laid out a whole new agenda for research.
>
> *(Gardner 1987, p. 10–11)*

What was going on and what were the main forces leading to the 1948 meeting described in Gardner's excerpt?

Mathematical and technological advances questioning the behaviourist tenets

As explained in Gardner's text, the most important factors in the developments of the 1940s were technological advances outside the psychological laboratories. Before and during World War II the new spearhead of technology became information handling. There was an increasing need for communication over large distances (e.g. radio and television transmission); the war required the cracking of increasingly sophisticated encryption codes; and engineers became frustrated by the fact that machines, which had given rise to the industrial revolution, could perform only a single operation, and they were looking for ways to make them more flexible by programming them. So, whereas (radical) behaviourism denied information processing inside the human head, the scientific world outside became very much centred on information handling in machines.

Information can be represented as logical operations

By the beginning of the twentieth century it became clear among mathematicians that any mathematical operation, and indeed any type of information, could be expressed by means of logical operations involving the values 0 and 1, known as Boolean operations after their British inventor George Boole (1815–1864). In a matter of years it was realised that electrical circuits could be modelled to enable Boolean operations, so that those circuits effectively were able to *represent* and *compute* all types of information. Furthermore, such an accomplishment was possible for every type of machine that could perform Boolean operations, independently of the way in which the code was put into operation, as was shown by the British mathematician Alan Turing.

Turing proved in 1936 that extremely basic machines working on the basis of Boolean logic would be able to simulate the performance of much more complex and powerful machines working on the same principles, if given enough time. Such a basic machine became known as a **Turing machine** (the machine was not actually built, as the whole argument could be made theoretically).

By the end of World War II, the first practical applications of the new computers became visible. These computers could both *store* information and *transform* it (by means of algorithms). This is what von Neumann referred to in Gardner's text above. He was involved in building one of the first operational computers.

Turing machine

basic (hypothetical) machine operating on the basis of Boolean logic and able to simulate the processing of more complex machines operating according to these principles

? What do you think?

It is sometimes said that computers work on a binary code (bits and bytes). How is this related to Boolean logic?

The brain can do Boolean operations

In 1943 a neurophysiologist, Warren McCulloch, and a logician, Walter Pitts, published an article in which they argued that the human brain could be thought of as a Boolean device as well. They showed that under certain assumptions the operations of a neuron and its connections with other neurons could be modelled in terms of Boolean logic. This meant that in principle the human brain was capable of storing and transforming information in the same way as computers. Both computers and brains could be considered as (complex) Turing machines that performed Boolean operations on stored information. McCulloch was the second speaker at the workshop described by Gardner.

Strings of S-R connections cannot be used to represent human thinking

Once it was realised that a Turing machine on the basis of Boolean logic could simulate all types of information processing, including human thinking and language, researchers started to examine whether the same was true for the S-R models postulated by the behaviourists (in particular Hull). These models accepted only a subset of operations, in particular those in which each element depended on its association with the preceding element (if you want the technical term, these are known as Markov chains).

Karl Lashley (the third speaker at the workshop) was the first researcher to question the viability of the behaviourist S-R models. For instance, he pointed out that in speech the words unfold with such rapidity that it is unlikely that each word can be based upon an S-R association with the previous one. In addition, the speech errors made by individuals often include the anticipation of words that have not yet occurred in the sequence (as in the speech-error in 'you hissed my mistory lecture', where we see an exchange of the m- and the h-sound, although 'history' supposedly is not yet activated at the moment 'missed' is pronounced).

A few years later, it would be shown that human grammar indeed required a Turing machine and could not be captured by a model with S-R connections (or more generally a Markov chain). So, if computers were programmed along the models proposed by the behaviourists, they would never be able to produce the same language as humans did. Only a computer that functioned as a Turing machine could do so.

Interim summary

After World War II experimental psychologists came to include mental processing in their models. This was due to the following developments

- Mathematicians proved that all information could be represented by a Turing machine, working on the basis of binary units and Boolean operations.

- This information is to a large extent independent of the device on which it is implemented (i.e. can easily be transposed on another device).

- Neurophysiologists presented evidence that the brain could be considered as a Turing machine.

- It was shown that the S-R chains proposed by the behaviourists were not powerful enough to be Turing machines and hence to simulate human behaviour.

KEY FIGURES

Key figures in the discovery that information processing can be thought of as device-independent representations consisting of binary units (bits) to which Boolean operations are applied:

- George Boole: British mathematician (1815–1864) who developed Boolean algebra consisting of binary digits and the logical operations AND, OR, NOT and XOR.

- Alfred Whitehead and Bertrand Russell: British-American mathematician (1861–1947) and British philosopher (1872–1970) who in 1910–1913 published a series of books showing that the roots of mathematics lie in logic.

- Alan Turing: British mathematician (1912–1954) who proved that any machine working on the basis of Boolean algebra is able to perform any mathematical and logical operation (Turing machine).

- Claude Shannon (1916–2001): American engineer called 'the father of information theory', who showed that all information can be represented in binary code and that application of Boolean algebra can construct and resolve any relationship.

- Warren McCulloch (1899–1969): American neurophysiologist, famous for his suggestion that the brain can be seen as a Turing machine. Start of neural network research.

The liberating metaphor of the computer

Soon, the 1948 California workshop would be followed by a string of other meetings to discuss the possibilities of the new insights. These grouped mathematicians, engineers, physiologists, psychologists and philosophers, who all took as their point of departure the analogy of human psychological functioning with computer functioning. Leahey (2004, p. 418–21) mentions three further ways in which the availability of computers changed research for psychologists.

A new explanation of the purposiveness of behaviour

homunculus

word (meaning 'little man') used to refer to the difficulty of explaining goal-oriented behaviour without making use of an ultimate intelligent (humanlike) control centre

A problem that had faced psychologists from the start was how to account for the fact that people appear to have clear goals in their life which they deliberately choose and which direct their behaviour. This seemed to require the existence of a **homunculus**, a little man sitting in the brain taking decisions and having a free will to steer behaviour. Even at a lower level, it seemed difficult to avoid the homunculus problem. For instance, when Tolman referred to a cognitive map in rats, he was accused by Skinner of failing to explain who supposedly was reading the map and deciding when to use the knowledge of the map. The homunculus problem was known since the days of Descartes and often referred to as the 'ghost in the machine' (remember that Descartes saw the human body as a machine). For Descartes, and many after him, this was the reason why they made a distinction between the body and the soul (Chapter 2).

Computers, however, showed intelligent functioning that could be described as goal directed. So, why did they not require a homunculus? The answer to this question turned out to be information feedback. When a system is given an end-state, it can reach this state autonomously if it receives feedback about the discrepancy between

information feedback

mechanism in which the current performance level is compared to the desired end-state and the discrepancy is used to bring the performance closer to the end-state aimed for; important for psychology because it explained a great deal of goal-directed behaviour that previously seemed to require a homunculus explanation

the current situation and the end-state. Information feedback was already known long before the computer was invented (it was part of the first steam machines), but its power had never been fully realised until the American mathematician Norbert Wiener during World War II became involved in the attempts to build guided missiles.

The potential of information feedback can easily be illustrated by the role of a thermostat in a heating system: when the temperature is below the indicated level, it sends a signal that switches on the boiler; when the temperature is above the indicated level, it sends a signal to switch off the boiler. From the outside it looks as if the thermostat has a purpose (to keep the temperature in the room at a certain level). However, all that is happening is an automatic information-processing mechanism on the basis of information feedback.

Although informational feedback did not solve the whole homunculus problem (who sets the end-state?), it drastically increased the similarity between man and machine. It allowed psychologists to tackle information-processing issues without being attacked for describing a system that required a homunculus to keep an eye on the goal and to decide which action to take.

Simulation of human thinking

Computers provided psychologists with a second tool: they could start to simulate the hypothesised psychological processes in computer programs, with the ideal being a computer program that would pass the Turing test. This is a test described by Alan Turing and involves a human interacting from a distance with another human and a machine. When the human can no longer decide which of the two partners is the machine, then the machine has passed the Turing test. That is, its performance has reached the human level. (Incidentally, for a machine to pass the test, it would sometimes have to deliberately introduce an error to confuse the interrogator; otherwise, its superior performance – for instance in calculations – would easily betray the machine.) The comparison of human and computer functioning gave rise to a new research field, *Artificial Intelligence*.

Turing test

test described by Alan Turing, which involves a human interacting with a machine and another human without being able to discriminate the machine from the human; machines that pass the Turing test are seen as the goal of artificial intelligence

Psychologists as software engineers

Finally, computers also gave psychological researchers a better idea of their role relative to that of other scientists. They were the programmers working on the software of humans. This could be done to a large extent independently of the electronic circuits in the machine (the anatomy) and knowledge of the way information is coded, stored and retrieved (the physiology). In addition, psychologists could think of information transformation in terms of algorithms that were run on the input. Algorithms are lists of instructions that convert a given input, via a fully defined series of intermediate steps, into the desired output. An example would be an algorithm that turns input speech into a written record of what is said.

algorithm

list of instructions that converts a given input, via a fully defined series of intermediate steps, into the desired output

The role of psychologists as human software engineers can clearly be seen in the following excerpt from the first textbook on cognitive psychology:

> The task of a psychologist trying to understand human cognition is analogous to that of a man trying to discover how a computer has been programmed. In particular, if the program seems to store and reuse information, he would like to know by what 'routines' or 'procedures' this is done.

(Neisser 1967, p. 6)

What do you think?

When you are surfing on the internet, do you ever think of the mechanical operations that present the information on your screen or that execute the operations summoned by your mouse clicks? Do you need to know this when you want to teach someone how to use the internet?

Interim summary

The existence of computers provided psychologists with a new metaphor to understand the mind and the nature of their own research.

- The computer made it easier to understand how an organism can seem to be goal-directed, without there being a homunculus who sets the goals and checks the progress.

- Computers allowed psychologists to simulate human functioning (artificial intelligence).

- Computers needed programmers who dealt with the information processing, independently of the ways in which the processes were realised in the machine.

The emergence of cognitive psychology

Because of the above developments, behaviourism came under increasing pressure. Its framework already felt like an uncomfortable straitjacket to many researchers, and now they were given arguments about why it might be wrong. The year 1956 is seen by most people involved as the turning point. In that year there was another workshop assembling the main proponents of the new movement, and several important books and articles were published (see, e.g., Miller (2003) for a review).

Miller's article on the limits of short-term memory

One of the decisive 1956 publications was George Miller's article on the limits of human short-term memory. Up to the publication of that article, new ideas had largely been 'imposed' on psychology from the outside. The people leading the change were mathematicians, engineers, neuroscientists, a political scientist and a linguist. What psychologists missed were psychological experiments that would convince them of the potential of the new movement. Remember that behaviourists insisted on the importance of verifiable evidence based on experiments with operationally defined variables.

In his publication, Miller reviewed the experimental evidence indicating that humans could report only seven (plus or minus two) unrelated items presented at a rate of about one stimulus per second (precursors of this discovery can already be found in the works of Wundt, James, Ebbinghaus and Binet). This finding was the first empirical evidence that the human mind could be considered as a computer with a limited 'working memory'. Psychologists were particularly sensitive to this argument, because in the 1950s the central processing units of the available computers were very limited, so that only simple operations could be performed. Each time the capacity of the central processing unit was increased, the performance of the computer became much better and more complex operations could be handled. So, the thought of the human brain as a computer with a limited capacity had a strong appeal to psychologists and provided them with new ideas of how to investigate the human mind.

Neisser's (1967) Cognitive Psychology

Another important moment in the new movement was the publication of a book with the title *Cognitive Psychology* by Ulric Neisser in 1967. This book not only summarised the evidence in favour of information processing in the mind, but also helped to establish the name of the new movement. The word cognition itself was defined as follows:

> As used here, the term 'cognition' refers to all the processes by which the sensory input is transformed, reduced, elaborated, stored, recovered, and used. It is concerned with these processes even when they operate in the absence of relevant stimulation, as in images and hallucinations . . . Given such a sweeping definition, it is apparent that cognition is involved in everything a human being might possibly do; that every psychological phenomenon is a cognitive phenomenon.
>
> *(Neisser 1967, p. 4)*

cognitive psychology

movement in psychology arguing that observable behaviours are the result of information processing in the mind; started in the 1950s and currently the dominant form of mainstream psychology

By the mid-1970s academic psychologists identified themselves predominantly with cognitive psychology and not with behaviourism. Although the name **cognitive psychology** originally referred to research on information processing, as described below, it soon became a kind of catch-all term to represent all psychologists who did experimental research and included mental representations in their theorising. Psychologists who were still known as behaviourists mostly did research on learning in animals, where the behaviourist models did a good job of predicting the animal's behaviour under well-controlled circumstances, although in this research area the need for the inclusion of cognitive processes in the models became increasingly felt as well (e.g. Bouton 2007).

Interim summary

Major steps in the emergence of cognitive psychology:

- Miller's 1956 article on the limits of short-term memory, showing that the human brain could be conceptualised as a computer with a limited capacity.

- Neisser's 1967 book *Cognitive Psychology*: Review of the evidence and important for establishing the name.

Figures behind the cognitive revolution:

■ Norbert Wiener: American mathematician (1894–1964) who documented the importance of information feedback in information processing systems.

■ Karl Lashley: American behaviourist (1890–1958), who was one of the first to realise that psychological processes could not be described by a chain of S-R connections. (Also known for his work on brain localisation.)

■ Herbert Simon (1916–2001) and Alan Newell (1927–1992): American political scientist and American computer scientist who pioneered the field of artificial intelligence. They were the first to show that computers could be used for something other than number crunching (e.g. they created a general problem solver program).

■ Noam Chomsky: American linguist (born in 1928) who showed that an S-R chain (Markov chain) is incapable of producing human-like language.

■ George A. Miller: American psychologist (born in 1920) who strongly promoted the cognitive revolution; wrote an influential article on the limitations of short-term memory and was instrumental in translating Chomsky's insights to psychology.

■ Donald Broadbent: British psychologist (1926–1993) working in the British (non-behaviourist) tradition, who was one of the first to use flow diagrams to document the different transformations information had to undergo from input to output. Very influential model of selective attention (filter theory), which stimulated much early research.

■ Ulrich Neisser (born in 1928): wrote the first proper textbook on cognitive psychology.

Specific features of cognitive psychology

The fledgling cognitive psychology differed in two important ways from its predecessors. First, it accepted a separate level of mental representations to which algorithms were applied. Second, it introduced more complex information manipulations than the simple associations that had formed the basis of human knowledge since the days of empiricism and associationism (see Chapter 3). Cognitive psychology also differed from pre-behaviourist psychology (but not from behaviourism) by its insistence on verifiable predictions and experimental tests of the hypothesised mechanisms.

Information processing on the basis of mental representations

Remember that mathematicians had discovered that information could be represented and manipulated by means of logical operations involving binary representations (0s and 1s). That is, information could be thought of as bits (decisions between two equally plausible alternatives), completely divorced from the system on which it was implemented. The sequence 1011001 coded the same piece of information, irrespective of how the 0s and 1s were made real, and could be copied onto every machine

mental representation

information pattern in the mind representing knowledge obtained through observation or the application of an algorithm; forms a realm separate from the brain and could in principle be copied to another brain (or in a more extreme version, to a Turing machine)

information processing

encoding mental representations, transforming them by means of algorithms, and integrating them with existing knowledge; forms the core of cognitive psychology

boxes-and-arrows diagram

flowchart outlining the different information stores (boxes) and information transformations (arrows) involved in the execution of a particular task with observable input and output; used by cognitive psychologists to detail the information processing involved in the task

capable of representing 0s and 1s. This made it possible to think of information as a separate realm, independent of the transmission device and also separate from the outside world. According to Gardner this was the most important advance of cognitive psychology:

> To my mind, the major accomplishment of cognitive science has been the clear demonstration of the validity of positing a level of **mental representation**: a set of constructs that can be invoked for the explanation of cognitive phenomena, ranging from visual perception to story comprehension.
>
> *(Gardner 1987, p. 383)*

Mental representations not only became a layer different from the outside world and the brain; psychologists also started to examine how information could be transformed by means of algorithms. They spoke of information that was encoded, transformed, integrated with previously stored information, and in turn saved. This dynamic aspect of information handling was called **information processing**, and cognitive psychologists started to make models of how this processing could be achieved (i.e. which procedures or routines were involved). Two approaches were taken.

The first approach was to make use of information-processing diagrams, so-called **boxes-and-arrows diagrams**. In these diagrams, the boxes stood for (temporary) stores of information, and the arrows for cognitive processes that transformed the information. As it happened, one of the first influential diagrams did not come from the USA, but from the UK, where the behaviourist tradition had been much weaker (see below). In 1958 the British researcher Donald Broadbent presented a flowchart of how he thought selective attention worked. Selective attention refers to the fact that humans are able to respond to a single stimulus and at the same time ignore distracter stimuli.

Broadbent's model (figure 4.5) included several components. First it assumed that all stimuli were briefly stored in a short-term store. Due to capacity limitations, not all of these stimuli could be further processed; a choice had to be made. This was done by a selective filter. The selected information was further processed on the basis of

Figure 4.5 One of the first boxes-and-arrows diagrams.

Source: Broadbent (1958)

past experiences and, if necessary, the filter was directed to a different sensory channel (e.g. when the information was no longer interesting enough).

The second approach taken by cognitive psychologists was to write a computer program that actually performed the various transformations assumed to occur. In the case of Broadbent's model, for instance, one would try to make a computer program that responded in the same way as humans do to multiple, competing input streams. This approach was much more demanding, but at the same time much more insightful. Boxes-and-arrows models were an interesting starting point but left unspecified much of how the information was stored and transformed. They were similar to an engineer's drawing plans, not to a functioning machine.

By trying to implement the various routines and procedures, psychologists had to be much more specific about the precise mechanisms involved, and that the model guaranteed that the proposed solution worked as predicted (e.g. would Broadbent's boxes-and-arrows model really work if you tried to implement it in a computer, and would it perform the same as humans?). This was the challenge artificial intelligence tried to meet. Another term that is often used for this approach is the building of computational models, computer models that resemble human performance.

computational model

computer program simulating the human information processing assumed to be involved in the execution of a particular task; requires researchers to be much more precise about of what is going on than in a boxes-and-arrows diagram

More complex procedures were needed than foreseen and top-down processes had to be introduced

While trying to make their computer programs work, psychologists were soon confronted by the fact that they had seriously underestimated the complexity of the information processing involved. This became particularly clear in language understanding. For instance, many cognitive psychologists and computer scientists assumed that one of the first straightforward applications of artificial intelligence would be the automatic translation of texts. After all, if you feed a computer with English sentences and a dictionary it must not be too difficult to turn them into correct sentences in whatever other language you choose. However, this turned out not to be the case.

One problem faced by researchers was that the meaning of words often depends on the meaning of the surrounding words (their context). Many words have more than one meaning and use (e.g. bank, coach, swallow) and the meanings of synonyms often differ slightly (e.g. believe, think), so that they are not completely interchangeable. Another problem was that it is often difficult to compute the syntactic structure of sentences and that ambiguities frequently have to be solved on the basis of the plausibility of the different interpretations. To correctly interpret the sentence 'John saw the mountains flying to New York', you must know that John can fly but the mountains cannot.

It soon became clear to everyone involved in machine translation that humans add a lot of background information to the language input they receive, in order to come to the correct interpretation. As long as the computational models were not able to do the same, the quality of the translation remained appalling for all but the simplest sentences. This was a far cry from the conviction in the early days that human knowledge was nothing but associations between elementary sensations (shared by empiricists, structuralists and behaviourists).

One of the new elements the cognitive psychologists had to introduce in their information-processing models was the existence of top-down processes. These refer to the fact that information from higher processing stages is fed back to previous

top-down process

process by which information from a higher processing stage is fed back to previous processing stages and influences the processing at these stages; found to be a helpful (and even essential) element in many computational models processing stages and influences processing at these stages. Information in the human mind does not flow unidirectionally from the input to the output (bottom-up), but requires multiple interactions between the different processing components to solve ambiguities and direct the interpretation in the right direction. Needless to say, the top-down processes were inspired by the information-feedback mechanisms discovered during World War II (see above).

Incidentally, the extent of the challenge faced by cognitive psychologists and computer scientists to build machine translators can be gauged by looking at the quality of current-day software (more than 50 years after the introduction of cognitive psychology and artificial intelligence). What happens if we enter a sentence with a few ambiguities into such a program, translate it in another language and then back to English? Will the program pass the Turing test? Below, you can find out what happened when we asked Google Language Tools to translate an English sentence into a few other languages and then back to English (retrieved on 20 October, 2007, from http://translate.google.com/translate_t):

original sentence: 'I believe the coach on the bank should be moved.'
back translation from Arabic: 'I think that the coach of the World should be moved.'
back translation from German: 'I believe that the coaches on the bench should be postponed.'
back translation from Korean: 'Thinking about the bank's directors must be moved.'
back translation from Spanish: 'I think the coach should go in the bank.'

? What do you think?

Can you see the psychologists' excitement when they discovered all these new tools? At the same time, the computer metaphor pushed aside other research topics such as interest in emotions and motivation. What do you think: can we study the human mind without taking into account motivation and emotion?

Verifiable predictions and experimental tests of the hypothesised processes

To investigate information processing in humans, cognitive psychology gratefully relied on the experimental expertise gathered by the behaviourists. They noticed that other sciences also investigated imperceptible processes and did so by examining the influences of these processes on perceptible phenomena. For instance, astronomers tried to unravel the origin of the universe by looking at the movements of the stellar bodies relative to one another. Similarly, in the biological and physical sciences entities often had to be postulated that could not (yet) be perceived (e.g. the existence of DNA in cells, or the existence of neutrinos in the universe). Usually, when the technology improved sufficiently, these theoretical entities could be laid bare. So, there was nothing wrong with postulating non-observable information algorithms, as long as their impact could be verified in a valid way.

The approach can be illustrated with research motivated by Broadbent's model of selective attention, discussed in figure 4.5. This model predicted the existence of a memory store in which all stimuli are briefly kept, including the ones not attended to by the filter. This assumption seemed to be contradicted by the fact that when people see an array consisting of several elements (e.g. letters) flashed for a short period of time they only manage to see some four elements, a finding already reported by Wilhelm Wundt in 1912.

George Sperling (1960) decided to examine this contradiction. He reasoned that the small number of stimuli reported by the participants might be due to the fact that the traces in the short-term store rapidly fade while the participant is naming the elements, so that only a few can be named before the memory trace is lost. If this is true, Sperling reasoned, then it must be possible to show that people can perceive more stimuli if they are not required to name all of them. To investigate this, Sperling used displays with 12 letters, distributed over three rows, as in the following example:

Q	F	O	I
A	G	N	P
T	L	E	M

Participants did not have to name 'as many letters as they had seen', but they got a tone immediately after the brief stimulus display, telling them which line they had to report. If the tone was high, they had to report the top row; if it was medium they had to report the middle row; and if it was low they had to report the bottom row. With this technique Sperling observed that participants could perfectly report each of the rows requested, as was predicted by Broadbent's model with its full information storage for a brief period of time. To further test the latter part of the model, Sperling introduced a short time delay between the display of the stimulus and the presentation of the tone. As predicted, he noticed that the ability of the participants to report the letters sharply declined as the time between the display and the tone increased. Within a second all memory traces in the visual store were lost.

Sperling's research illustrates how cognitive psychologists combined the various advances made in the first half of the twentieth century to identify and examine cognitive functioning in a much more refined and convincing way. At last, it became possible to look into the functioning of the mind on the basis of the performance of participants under highly controlled circumstances. In the next chapter we will see how this research was supplemented by increasingly sophisticated techniques to directly look at the brain during various tasks.

Interim summary

Specific features of cognitive psychology are:

- The acceptance of a separate level of mental representations, to which transformation algorithms apply.

- Information processing on the mental representations captured by boxes-and-arrows diagrams and computational models.

- Models designed to lead to predictions that can be verified in experiments making use of performance measures.

> ## 4.3   Focus on: Were behaviourism and cognitive psychology revolutionary?

In 1962 (2nd revised edition in 1970) Thomas Kuhn (1922–1996) published a book, *The Structure of Scientific Revolutions*, that would change the notion of scientific progress forever (see also Chapter 8). Kuhn was a physicist who after his PhD turned towards the history and the philosophy of science. He questioned the prevailing view that science is a steady, unidirectional accumulation of knowledge going from ignorance to full understanding. According to Kuhn, a science was characterised by revolutions, sudden theoretical changes that questioned nearly everything believed before.

For Kuhn a science started when the vast majority of researchers agreed on the issues to be addressed and the ways to address them. As long as this was not the case, the research area is better described as a *pre-science* rather than a science. When the researchers reached agreement on the issues and the research methods, they achieved what Kuhn called a *paradigm*, which allowed them to do *normal science*. Normal science consists of solving puzzles set by the paradigm, finding evidence for or against hypotheses that originate from the shared theoretical framework.

Thus far Kuhn's approach still agrees pretty much with the layman's view. However, Kuhn went on to argue that in all sciences the stage of normal science gradually results in a *crisis*, an accumulation of findings that cannot readily be explained by the paradigm and that require an increasing number of unplanned modifications and makeshift extensions of the paradigm. When the crisis reaches its peak, chances are high that a revolution will take place, which calls the whole paradigm into question and replaces it by a new paradigm. This transition is called a *scientific revolution* or a *paradigm shift*. Such a shift is followed by a new stage of normal science resulting in a new crisis and another paradigm shift.

It is not difficult to find examples of revolutionary paradigm shifts in all types of sciences. In astronomy we had the shift from a geocentric universe to a heliocentric universe, effectively called the Copernican *revolution* (Chapter 3). In physics we had the shift from Newton's laws to Einstein's relativity theory and then to quantum physics. In geology we had the acceptance of plate tectonics to explain earthquakes, volcanoes, and the relative position of the continents to one another over time.

Psychologists have been quick to call the rise of behaviourism and cognitive psychology scientific revolutions as well (simply type in 'behavioural revolution' or 'cognitive revolution' in your internet search engine). The story goes more or less as follows. When psychological research started, everyone used introspection to examine consciousness (i.e. this was the shared paradigm). Gradually this research turned into a crisis because knowledge did not advance adequately and the findings required ever more complicated theories to explain them. Then came the behaviourist revolution which slashed the importance of introspection and consciousness and replaced them by experimentation and observable behaviours. After a few decades of normal science, this approach in turn fell into crisis, because its theories grew more complicated without really explaining the essence of human psychological functioning. At that moment, the behaviourist paradigm was replaced by the cognitive paradigm, after which the researchers happily returned to the puzzle solving that is characteristic of periods of normal science. Some authors even have exact dates for the revolutions: 1913 for behaviourism and 1956 for cognitive psychology (see above).

Seeing the introduction of behaviourism and cognitive psychology as scientific revolutions helps us to understand why topics that have been at the forefront of research at one moment, no longer are a few years later and why scientists often do not refer in a positive way to research done in a certain epoch. However, like all approaches, Kuhn's view to some extent distorts reality. It maximises the differences that exist between time periods and minimises the continuity that is present (Leahey 1992). For instance, with respect to the behaviourist revolution, it overlooks the experimental work done since the time of Wundt and the advances in applied psychology (e.g. the development of client-centred therapy and theories of human intelligence), and it ignores the fact that behaviourism has never been an all-dominating paradigm.

In Europe and Canada behaviourism did not have the same impact as in the USA. One of the frontrunners of the 'cognitive revolution', George Miller, recounted a talk he gave at the University of Cambridge in 1963 in which he 'lambasted the hell out of the behaviorists' to a puzzled audience, because, as he was told after the talk, there were only three behaviourists in the UK, none of whom was present (Baars 1986, p. 212). The absence of behaviourist thinking in the UK can easily be supported by the texts published in the heyday of behaviourism. For instance, this is what the director of a major British psychology institute, Kenneth Craik, wrote in 1943 about the function of the mind:

> If the organism carries a small-scale model of external reality and its own possible actions within its head, it is able to try out various alternatives, conclude which is the best of them, react to future situations before they arise, utilize the knowledge of past events in dealing with the present and future, and in every way react to a much fuller, safer and more competent manner to emergencies which face it.
>
> *(Craik (1943) as cited in Mandler (2007) p. 169)*

This clearly is a cognitive text, despite the fact that it was published more than five years before the seminal 1948 workshop described above. Many similar non-behaviourist writings can be found in other parts of Europe and Canada, where the texts of the Gestalt psychologists were read and commented. A case can even be made that the escape of the Gestalt psychologists from Germany to the USA in the wake of World War II was one of the factors contributing to the growth of cognitive psychology in the USA (see Mandler (2007) for a discussion of this possibility). On the other hand, American psychologists were not very impressed by what they saw in Europe, because to them the European work appeared methodologically unsophisticated, not nearly as rigorous as American research (Baars 1986, p. 69).

Even in the USA in the heyday of behaviourism there were many examples of research that did not fit well within the strong behaviourist claims. We already mentioned Tolman, who was very interested in Gestalt psychology and went to study in Germany. Another example was J. Ridley Stroop, who in 1935 published his article on the Stroop effect, which has since become one of the main techniques used in cognitive psychology.

Finally, it must be kept in mind that a number of research traditions started under behaviourism are still very much alive today. Just to name the most glaring examples: research on classical and operant conditioning did not stop with the emergence of cognitive psychology. In addition, there is still a substantial group of researchers who continue the behaviourist tradition and who have their own conferences and journals.

For the above reasons, although the ideas of a behaviourist and cognitive revolution are appealing (and eye-opening), it is good to keep in mind that those terms impoverish the breadth of reality and that there has been more continuity and knowledge accumulation in psychological research than is suggested by the word 'revolution'.

This agrees with what we said at the beginning of this chapter about the 'revolutionary' new psychology in the USA at the end of the nineteenth century, and with the use of the name 'scientific revolution' to indicate the changes of the seventeenth century (Chapter 2).

Interim summary

- Kuhn proposed a theory according to which sciences require the use of a shared paradigm.

- After some time the paradigm ends up in crisis because of anomalous findings. At that moment, there is a paradigm shift or a scientific revolution. Science afterwards continues with the new paradigm until the next crisis.

- The introduction of behaviourism and cognitive psychology can be seen as scientific revolutions within Kuhn's theory.

- At the same time, however, such an approach simplifies the history and overlooks the continuity and accumulation of information that have been present since the onset of psychology.

Recommended literature

We relied heavily on the original resources that are freely available on the internet (in particular on http://psychclassics.yorku.ca and http://books.google.com). Two other very useful sources are: Baars, B.J. (1986) *The cognitive revolution in psychology* (New York: Guilford Press), and Gardner, H. (1987) *The mind's new science: A history of the cognitive revolution* (New York: Basic Books). These books contain a discussion about the rise of behaviourism in addition to its replacement by cognitive psychology.

Further worthwhile reading are the special issues of the *American Psychologist*, published in 1992 (Vol. 47(2) on the occasion of the 100th birthday of the American Psychological Association) and in 2000 (Vol. 55(3) at the start of the new millennium). For the rest, all the history books recommended in Chapter 3 contain chapters on behaviourism and cognitive psychology.

References

Baars, B.J. (1986) *The cognitive revolution in psychology*. New York: Guilford Press.

Benjafield, J.G. (2005) *A history of psychology*. Oxford: Oxford University Press.

Benjamin, L.T., Jr. (2000) 'The psychology laboratory at the turn of the 20th century', *American Psychologist*, 55: 318–21.

Blodgett, H.C. (1929) 'The effect of the introduction of reward upon the maze performance of rats'. Univ Calif Publ Psychol, 4: 113–34.

Bouton, M.E. (2007) *Learning and behavior: A comtemporary synthesis*. Sunderland, MA: Sinauer Associates.

Bridgman, P.W. (1927) *The logic of modern physics*. Chicago: University of Chicago Press.

Broadbent, D.E. (1958) *Perception and communication*. Elmsford, NY: Pergamon Press.

Coon, D.J. (1992) 'Testing the limits of sense and science: American experimental psychologists combat spiritualism 1880–1920', *American Psychologist*, 47: 143–51.

Fuchs, A.H. (2000) 'Teaching the introductory course in Psychology circa 1900', *American Psychologist*, 55: 492–5.

Galef, B.G. (1998) 'Edward Thorndike: Revolutionary psychologist, ambiguous biologist', *American Psychologist*, 53: 1128–34.

Gardner, H. (1987) *The mind's new science: A history of the cognitive revolution*. New York: Basic Books.

Jansz, J. and Van Drunen, P. (eds.) (2004) *A social history of psychology*. Oxford: Blackwell.

Kuhn, T.S. (1962) *The structure of scientific revolutions*. Chicago: University of Chicago Press.

Leahey, T.H. (1992) 'The mythical revolutions of American psychology', *American Psychologist*, 47: 308–18.

Leahey, T.H. (2004) *A history of psychology (6th edn.)*. Upper Saddle River, NJ: Pearson Prentice Hall.

Mackenzie, D.B. (1977) *Behaviorism and the limits of scientific method*. London: Routledge & Kegan Paul.

Malone, J.C. and Cruchon, N.M. (2001) 'Radical behaviorism and the rest of psychology: A review/précis of Skinner's *About Behaviorism*', *Behavior and Philosophy*, 29: 31–57.

Mandler, G. (2007) *A history of modern experimental psychology*. Cambridge, MA: The MIT Press.

McCulloch, W.S. and Pitts, W.H. (1943) 'A logical calculus of the ideas immanent in nervous activity', *Bulletin of Mathematical Biophysics*, 5: 115–33.

Miller, G.A. (1956) 'The magical number seven, plus or minus two', *Psychological Review*, 63: 81–97.

Miller, G.A. (2003) 'The cognitive revolution: A historical perspective', *Trends in Cognitive Sciences*, 7: 141–4.

Neisser, U. (1967) *Cognitive psychology*. New York: Appleton-Century-Crofts.

Richards, G. (1996) *Putting psychology in its place: An introduction from a critical historical perspective*. London: Routledge.

Skinner, B.F. (1974) *About behaviorism*. New York: Knopf.

Sperling, G. (1960) 'The information available in brief visual presentations', *Psychological Monographs*, 74: 1–29.

Stevens, S.S. (1935) 'The operational definition of psychological concepts', *Psychological Review*, 42: 517–27.

Stroop, J.R. (1935) 'Studies of interference in serial verbal reactions', *Journal of Experimental Psychology*, 18: 643–662. (Reprinted 1992 in *Journal of Experimental Psychology: General*, 121: 15–23.)

Thorndike, E.L. (1911) *Animal intelligence*. New York: Macmillan.

Tolman, E.C. (1948) 'Cognitive maps in rats and men', *Psychological Review*, 55: 189–209 (available on http://psychclassics.yorku.ca).

Watson, J.B. (1907) 'Studying the mind of animals', *The World Today*, 12: 421–6 (available on http://psychclassics.yorku.ca).

Watson, J.B. (1913) 'Psychology as the behaviorist views it', *Psychological Review*, 20: 158–77 (available on http://psychclassics.yorku.ca).

Watson, J.B. and Rayner, R. (1920) 'Conditioned emotional reactions', *Journal of Experimental Psychology*, 3: 1–14 (available on http://psychclassics.yorku.ca).

05 The input from brain research

This chapter will cover

Questions to consider

Historical issues addressed in this chapter

- What was assumed in Ancient Egypt about the function of the brain?
- What were the main beliefs about brain functioning in Ancient Greece?
- Why is the nineteenth century a critical century in neuroscience?
- Which developments in neuropsychology and neuroscience took place in the twentieth century?
- Which methods to study the brain were developed in the twentieth century?

Conceptual issues addressed in this chapter

- How could Aristotle be so wrong about the seat of the soul?
- Why were the ventricles thought to be so important for communication between the soul and the body?
- Why were psychologists attracted to the notion of the reflex arc to explain brain functioning?
- Why was it necessary to have good staining techniques before the organisation of brain tissue could be understood?
- Why were the world wars important for the development of brain research?
- What does knowledge about the localisation of brain functions tell us about the nature of the functions?
- What are the commonalities and differences between cognitive neuropsychology, cognitive neuroscience and cognitive neuropsychiatry?

Introduction

A 25-year-old male presented himself to the Psychiatry Outpatients Department with symptoms of restlessness, irritability, and episodic anger outburst, delusions of reference and persecution, auditory and visual hallucinations (hearing divine voices and seeing snakes/fires, etc.) and disturbed sleep for a period of about one year. On exploration, it became clear that he had a history of severe headache off and on, for which he was treated at the local hospital with analgesics . . .

X-rays of the right upper limb showed multiple calcified spots. A CT scan revealed multiple calcified brain lesions with surrounding oedema . . . Histopathological examination confirmed the diagnosis of cysticercosis. Cysticercosis is a condition that has been known about since the Hippocratic era and is the commonest infection of the human central nervous system. It is an infection brought about by the larvea of *T. solium*, the pork tape worm. The tape worms are acquired by ingesting undercooked pork containing cysticerci. . . . The ingested tape worm eggs, activated by gastric and duodenal secretions, develop into invasive larvae in the small intestines. They then migrate across the intestinal wall and are carried by the bloodstream to the sites where they settle and mature into cysticerci. The process can take place anywhere in the body but it is more prevalent in the subcutaneous tissue, muscle and the central nervous system. This process takes approximately two months. Epilepsy is the most common presentation of neurocysticercosis (cysticercosis in the brain); psychosis may be seen in up to 5 per cent of the patients.

(based on Mahajan et al. *2004)*

In Chapters 1–4 we discussed the start of psychology as a scientific discipline. In particular we considered the contributions of philosophy and the general turn of society towards science. At the same time, there was another stream of input, consisting of the growing insights into the workings of the brain and its consequences for mental life. This is the topic of the present chapter (as illustrated by the case study opening this chapter).

The chapter consists of six sections. First, we discuss the views about the seat of the soul and the role of the brain in Ancient Egypt and Greece. Next, we review the few developments that were made before the nineteenth century. In section 5.3 we talk about five discoveries in the nineteenth century that are generally seen as the major breakthroughs towards the current understanding of the brain. Sections 5.4 and 5.5 deal with developments in twentieth century psychology, in particular the appearance of (cognitive) neuropsychology and cognitive neuroscience. As usual, we end with a section *Focus on*, this time about cognitive neuropsychiatry.

? What do you think?

Do you know someone who had a brain examination or took part in a brain study? What was the reason? What was the outcome? What did the study comprise?

5.1   Ideas in Ancient Egypt and Ancient Greece

Beliefs of the Ancient Egyptians

The Edwin Smith papyrus

In 1862 an American collector, Edwin Smith, bought a papyrus scroll in the Egyptian city of Luxor (figure 5.1). Over half a century later, it would be deciphered by the Egyptologist James Breasted (1930). What was recorded on the manuscript perplexed the medical world (Changeux 1997; Gross 1998). In the text, written around 1,700 BCE

Figure 5.1 Cases 47 and 48 in the Edwin Smith Surgical Papyrus.

(Plate XVII and XVIIA from Breasted (1930), Vol. 1). Reproduced with permission.

but probably a copy of an older papyrus from 3,000 BCE, a series of 48 cases were described dealing with the consequences of head and neck injuries. Each case included a title, details of the examination, a diagnosis and an indication of the treatment. The diagnosis consisted of one of three conclusions: 'this is an ailment that I will treat', 'this is an ailment that I will try to treat' or 'this is an ailment that I will not treat'.

The following is what the papyrus said about case 6:

Title: Instructions concerning a gaping wound in his head, penetrating to the bone, smashing his skull, (and) rending open the brain of his skull.

Examination: If thou examinest a man having a gaping wound in his head, penetrating to the bone, smashing his skull, (and) rending open the brain of his skull, thou shouldst palpate his wound. Shouldst thou find that smash which is in his skull [like] those corrugations which form in molten copper, (and) something therein throbbing (and) fluttering under thy fingers, like the weak place of an infant's crown before it becomes whole – when it has happened there is no throbbing (and) fluttering under thy fingers until the brain of his (the patient's) skull is rent open – (and) he discharges blood from both his nostrils, (and) he suffers with stiffness in his neck . . .

Diagnosis: [Thou shouldst say concerning him]: 'An ailment not to be treated.'

Treatment: Thou shouldst anoint that wound with grease. Thou shalt not bind it; thou shalt not apply two strips upon it: until thou knowest that he has reached a decisive point.

(Breasted (1930) retrieved on 23 October, 2007 from http://www.
neurosurgery.org/cybermuseum/pre20th/epapyrus.html*)*

This case includes the first known description of the brain's exterior. In case 8 we read about a smash in the skull, that was accompanied by a deviation of the eyes and the fact that the patient 'shuffled' while walking. The latter bewildered the author, because he repeated four times that this happened, despite the fact that 'the wound was in the skull'. He could not understand why a wound to the head could affect the functioning of the legs.

The Edwin Smith papyrus, as the manuscript became known, illustrates how physicians treating wounded soldiers quite early became convinced of the importance of the head (brain) in controlling behaviour.

Edwin Smith papyrus

papyrus from Ancient Egypt that contains short descriptions of the symptoms and treatment of different forms of brain injury; named after the person who bought the papyrus in Egypt and had it analysed

Beliefs in the wider society

The existence of the Edwin Smith papyrus did not imply that the knowledge contained in it was widespread. As a matter of fact, in Ancient Egypt most scholars were convinced that the heart was the seat of the soul. This can easily be concluded from the finding that many efforts were made to conserve the heart (and other internal organs) at mummification, whereas the brain was picked out through the nostrils by means of hooks. As Gross (1998, p. 7) concluded: 'Dead Pharaohs were prepared for their next life with everything but a brain.'

What do you think?

Is the communication between medical/psychological practitioners and lecturers nowadays better than it was in Ancient Egypt? Or is it still possible that lecturers teach knowledge to students which practitioners know is wrong? How much experience do your lecturers and textbook writers have with real cases?

The roles of the heart and the brain in Ancient Greece

Plato

The discussion over whether the soul was in the heart or in the brain continued in Ancient Greece. Hippocrates placed the soul in the brain, as did Plato, although the latter also saw a function for the heart. According to Plato, the soul was divided into three parts. The highest part, responsible for reasoning, was situated in the brain. It came directly from the soul of the universe, was immortal, separated from the body, and it controlled the body. The second part of the soul dealt with sensation, was mortal and situated in the heart. To avoid it polluting the divine soul a neck separated the two. Finally, the lower part of the soul dealt with appetite and was placed in the liver, far away from the other two.

Aristotle

In contrast, Aristotle was convinced that the heart was the seat of the soul. He gave a series of arguments for this conclusion, summarised in table 5.1. The function of the brain in Aristotle's view was to counterbalance the heat of the heart. The heart and the brain formed a functional unit in which the brain, which was cold, tempered the heat and seething of the heart. The human brain relative to the body was larger than that of other animals because man's heart was hotter and richer and needed a stronger counterbalance for good performance.

Table 5.1 Aristotle's arguments for the heart as the centre of sensation and movement

Heart	Brain
1. Affected by emotion.	1. Not affected.
2. All animals have a heart.	2. Only vertebrates and cephalopods have one, and yet other animals have sensations.
3. Source of blood which is necessary for sensation.	3. Bloodless and therefore without sensation.
4. Warm, characteristic of higher life.	4. Cold.
5. Connected with all the sense organs and muscles, via the blood vessels.	5. Not connected with the sense organs or the connection is irrelevant.
6. Essential for life.	6. Not so.
7. Formed first, and last to stop working	7. Formed second.
8. Sensitive.	8. Insensitive: if the brain of a living animal is laid bare, it may be cut without any signs of pain.
9. In a central location, appropriate for its central role.	9. Not so.

Source: Gross (1998) *Brain, vision, memory: Tales in the history of neuroscience.* Table from p. 21. Copyright © Massachussets Institute of Technology, by permission of the MIT Press.

Galen

According to Gross (1998), Aristotle's views would have been different if he had been interested in medicine and in particular in the study of the effects of brain damage, which is the reason why many physicians did not follow him on this particular topic. A decisive moment in demonstrating the importance of the brain for sensation and movement control came when Galen (*c.* 130–*c.* 200 CE) six centuries after Aristotle started to experiment on animals. In one of his experiments Galen found that a pig stopped squealing, but kept breathing, immediately after he severed nerves in the throat, thus demonstrating that the voice came from the brain and not from the heart. This finding was subsequently repeated in several more experiments of a similar nature. Galen also dissected brains and published drawings of them. For a long time, researchers were puzzled about the poor quality of these drawings, until it was realised that they were based on ox brains, which Galen resized to fit into a human skull.

Another question Galen had to solve was how the brain communicated with the rest of the body. The heart was connected to all parts of the body through the blood in the veins, but how did the brain communicate? It was known that white cables – nerves – connected the brain with the body, but there did not seem to be any liquid flowing through them.

It is important to understand that Galen, in line with thinkers before him, did not think the brain itself was important for reason or emotion but for the soul residing inside the brain. The soul lived in the solid parts and produced and stored **animal spirits**

animal spirits

spirits that were thought by Galen to travel over the nerves between the ventricles in the brain and the body

What do you think?

Why would someone like Galen assume that the brains of humans look the same as those of oxes? Have a look at the pictures: What differences do you see? (Left: human brain; right: brain of an ox.)

Source: (left) Heidi Cartwright/Wellcome Images; (right) Daniel Templeton/Alamy. Reproduced with permission.

ventricles

apertures in the middle of the brain, which for a long time were thought to contain perceptions, memories and thoughts; seat of the animal spirits

in the apertures in the middle of the brain, called the **ventricles**. By means of these spirits the soul communicated with the rest of the body. The spirits travelled between the soul and the organs via the nerves, which were assumed to be hollow tubes. Because of the higher importance attached to the ventricles, they were depicted with much more accuracy and detail in Galen's plates than the brain itself. The convolutions on the surface of the brain were drawn like intestines rather than the way they really looked.

Interim summary

- The Edwin Smith papyrus illustrates that practising physicians rapidly made a link between injuries to the brain and mental and behavioural consequences.

- In the Ancient Egyptian and Greek societies at large, however, the link between the heart and intelligence was stronger (e.g. mummification, Aristotle; but see Hippocrates and Plato).

- Galen's experiments clearly established the primacy of the brain and the nerves, rather than the heart and the veins, for the control of movement (e.g. in the squealing of pigs).

- Galen thought that the soul was located in the solid parts of the brain and commanded animal spirits in the ventricles, which travelled through the nerves to the body parts to be influenced.

KEY FIGURE

Galen

- Greek physician (*c.* 130–*c.* 200 CE) working in Rome after 162 (Latin name: Galenus).

- Previously worked for 3–4 years as a physician in a gladiator school, where he gained much experience with treating injuries, which he called 'windows into the body'.

- Performed operations on humans and animals; also did vivisections on the latter to study the functions of various body parts.

- Established the primacy of the brain for sensation and movement. Located the soul in the solid parts of the brain and animal spirits in the ventricles. The animal spirits travelled to the body via the nerves.

- Wrote extensively, so that he is a link with the medical knowledge of Ancient Greece.

- Works translated in Arabic in the ninth century and in Latin in the sixteenth century (by Vesalius). Legacy continued until the eighteenth–nineteenth centuries.

5.2 Further insights into the anatomy and functioning of the nervous system in the Renaissance and the seventeenth–eighteenth centuries

Research about the brain came to a complete standstill in the Middle Ages and only really took off again in the nineteenth century. Below we discuss the few developments that happened in the era in between.

Developments in the Renaissance

The continuing primacy of the ventricles

Galen's views remained the norm until well into the eighteenth century. When Andreas Vesalius (1514–1564) resumed dissections and extended them to humans, he persisted in Galen's preoccupation with the correct drawing of the ventricles and did not care much about the convolutions of the brain, which he carried on depicting as intestines (the upper part of figure 5.2).

Differentiation between the ventricles

Vesalius further established for certain that there were three ventricles (this was not clear from Galen's writings, probably because there is a difference in this respect

Figure 5.2 Dissections of the brain by Vesalius in 1543.
Notice how the ventricles receive more attention and detail than the brain. In many drawings the convolutions on the outside of the brain were drawn like intestines rather than the way the brain really looks (lower part, also from Vesalius). This bias is in line with the conviction that the ventricles contained the animal spirits.

Source: Vesalius: *De corporis humani fabrica libri septem*. National Library of Medicine.

(a)   (b)

Figure 5.3 The three ventricles of the brain as depicted by (a) Gregor Reisch in 1503 and (b) Leonardo da Vinci around 1490.

Source: (a) Reisch, G. (1503) *Margarita philosopica* reprinted in Gross (1998); (b) Rue de Archives / Mary Evans Picture Library.

between the ox brain and the human brain). Gradually, the function of the three ventricles became differentiated. The front ventricle was assumed to receive information from the senses and, therefore, was called the *common sense*. It also included fantasy and imagination. The second ventricle, in the middle of the head, comprised thought and judgement. Finally the third ventricle, at the back of the head, contained memory. This can clearly be seen in the pictures shown in figure 5.3, respectively from the German prior Gregor Reisch (1467–1525) and the Italian polymath Leonardo da Vinci (1452–1519).

? What do you think?

Do you see the correspondence between the ideas about the roles of the ventricles and the saying 'to have something at the back of the mind'?

Speech problems can be caused by brain injury

With the rediscovery of Galen's texts, researchers also regained interest in the relationship between brain injuries and behaviour. A particularly influential publication was the book *Observationes medicae de capite humano* (Medical Observations on the Human Head), published in 1585 by the German physician Johann Schenk von Grafenberg. In this book von Grafenberg reported clinical observations of brain injuries ranging from the ancient writings to new cases from contemporaries. On the basis of these studies Schenk von Grafenberg concluded, among other things, that after brain damage patients sometimes could no longer speak even though their tongue was not paralysed. Rather, what seemed to happen was that the memory of words had disappeared or at least could no longer be accessed.

Developments in the seventeenth–eighteenth centuries

The brain instead of the ventricles

Gradually the investigators turned their focus to the solid parts of the brain rather than the ventricles. In the seventeenth century they started to pay attention to the difference between the outer layer of the cerebral hemispheres (the parts of the brain with the convolutions), which looked greyish, and the layer underneath, which had a white appearance. The former became known as the rind or the cortex; the latter as the white matter. One of the first researchers to implicate the grey part of the brain in the functions of memory and will was the British anatomist Thomas Willis who published an influential book *Cerebri Anatome* in 1664. At the same time, an increasing number of scholars started to doubt the existence of spirits in the nerves. Instead, they hypothesised that fluids flowed in them.

What do you think?

The influence of the new ideas about the functioning of the brain on the general culture can also be traced in the language. Ever heard of 'the grey cells'?

A problem with the new view, however, was that the brain seemed to be numb. How then could it be involved in sensation and movement? If you exposed the grey matter and touched it, the animal did not seem to be disturbed. However, if you touched the white matter or went into the ventricles, the animal screamed, sometimes showed involuntary movements, and often died. This point against the involvement of the grey matter was strongly made, for instance, by the influential German/Swiss anatomist Albrecht von Haller in a series of book volumes around 1750.

Increased interest in reflexes

A topic that also started to gain momentum in the seventeenth–eighteenth centuries was the insight that some behaviours were elicited automatically, without voluntary intervention. When you step on something sharp, you at once withdraw your foot. Galen had already noticed that sometimes animals performed involuntary acts, which he ascribed to 'sympathy' between the various body parts, so that one could respond sympathetically to another's distress. This view still has an impact on our language, because a part of the autonomic (vegetative) nervous system became known as the *sympathetic nervous system*.

René Descartes was interested in reflexive movements as well, because they fitted within his mechanistic view of the body (Chapter 2). He discussed the idea in 1633 (figure 5.4) and argued that a reflex consisted of a sensory impression which rushed to the brain and subsequently was reflected back (as in a mirror) into a motor command to bring about the required action. The event occurred unconsciously, independently of the will.

Figure 5.4 Drawing from Descartes illustrating the withdrawal reflex when a foot risks being burnt by the fire.
Notice that there is only one nerve tract, carrying the sensory signal to the brain and bringing the motor command back.

Source: The withdrawal arc by Descartes, Stock Montage Inc. Reproduced with permission.

In 1784 the Czech physiologist Jiří Procháska published a book in which he argued that reflexes were not controlled by the brain but involved the spinal cord and the structures just above it. As we will see below, this was the start of one of the great breakthroughs of the nineteenth century.

A proposed treatment for brain injury

It is important to remember that the greater insights into the workings of the nervous system for a long time did not lead to improvements in the treatment of brain injuries, as is exemplified by the following remedy recommended in the seventeenth century to the Archduchess of Austria, who suffered from an apoplexy (stroke):

A most secret and certain remedy against the apoplexy is to take a lion's dung, powdered, two parts, pour spirit of wine till it be covered three fingers breath, let them stand in a vial stopped three days. Strain it and keep it for use. Then take a crow, not quite pinfeathered, and a young turtle, burn them apart in an oven, powder them, pour on the above said spirit of wine, let them stand in infusion for three days. Then take berries of a linden tree, an ounce and a half. Let them be steeped in the aforesaid spirit, then add as much of the best wine and six ounces of sugar candy, boil them in a pot till the sugar be melted. Put it up. Let the patient take a spoonful of it in wine, often in a day, for a whole month. In the paroxysm give a spoonful with Aqua Tiliae, and with the same water, rub the forehead, neck, temples and nostrils.

(Bonnet (1684) as cited in Prins and Bastiaanse (2006) p. 772)

What do you think?

An element often present in folk medicine (i.e. remedies for maladies proposed by people who do not systematically examine the effectiveness of the recommended treatments) is the use of revolting substances, as if the 'evil' should be repelled from the body. Can you see how this applies to the treatment presented here? What other elements do you typically find in folk remedies?

Interim summary

Advances in the understanding of the brain in the Renaissance and the seventeenth–eighteenth centuries

■ In the Renaissance, Vesalius and peers followed Galen's belief that the soul was located in the solid parts of the brain and commanded animal spirits that resided in the ventricles and travelled through the nerves to the other body parts.

■ There was also a renewed interest in the behavioural consequences of brain injury.

■ In the seventeenth–eighteenth centuries there was a gradually increasing focus on the brain itself. A distinction was made between the grey and the white matter in the cerebral hemispheres.

■ There was also growing interest in the reflex, as a type of response that seemed to escape voluntary control.

■ The new insights did not (yet) lead to improved treatment.

5.3   The breakthroughs of the nineteenth century

A series of five breakthroughs in the nineteenth century irrevocably altered the model of brain functioning and made modern neurophysiology possible (Clarke and Jacyna 1987). They were:

1. the discovery of the cerebrospinal axis,

2. the growing impact of the reflex,

3. the localisation of brain functions,

4. the discovery of the nerve cell,

5. the disentangling of the communication between neurons.

Below we discuss the findings one by one. While you read them, keep in mind that their timelines largely overlap and that the discoveries occurred shortly before (and sometimes after) psychology was founded as an independent discipline. Think of the ways in which these developments increased the likelihood of the scientific study of the human mind.

The discovery of the cerebrospinal axis

The body remains functioning when the cerebral hemispheres are disconnected

The first breakthrough in the nineteenth century was the discovery of the role of the cerebrospinal axis in the regulation of physical functions. The received wisdom since Galen was that only the brain was the origin of nerve signals. The spinal cord, in line with the nerves, was seen as a transmission channel of the spirits or – later – the brain fluid. This view started to be questioned when researchers began to realise that a body remained functioning in a vegetative state when the cerebral hemispheres were taken away or disconnected from the structures at the top end of the spinal cord (nowadays called the subcortical structures). So, there were many bodily functions that did not seem to require the cerebral hemispheres. In addition, the work of Procháska (see above) strongly pointed towards the possibility that reflexes were mediated by the spinal cord and not by the cerebral hemispheres.

Clarke and Jacyna (1987, p. 30–1) summarised the outcome of this change of view as follows:

> Ideas of the structure of the cerebrospinal axis underwent a revolution between 1800 and 1840. Quite literally, an inversion of previous modes of conceiving the axis took place: instead of proceeding from above downwards and seeing the spinal cord as a process of the brain, anatomists began to go from below upwards and to describe the brain as the culmination of the spinal cord.

The new view of the precedence of the spinal cord and the subcortical structures in the control of physical functions agreed with the finding that some animal species had a spinal cord but no brain, whereas the reverse was never observed. It looked as if the spinal cord had evolutionary precedence over the brain and that the brain had grown increasingly larger in mammals (with humans as the apex).

What do you think?

Ideas about the evolutionary precedence of the spinal cord over the brain only made sense after the publication of the *Origin of Species*. Can you explain why?

Growing focus on reflexes

The reflex arc

Researchers also started to pay more attention to the nature and function of reflexes in brain functioning. An important figure in this respect was the British physician and

DIAGRAM OF A SIMPLE REFLEX ARC IN A BACKBONELESS ANIMAL LIKE AN EARTHWORM

1. A sensory nerve-cell (S.C.) on the surface receives a stimulus.
2. The stimulus travels along the sensatory nerve-fibre (S.F.)
3. The sensory nerve-fibre branches in the nerve-cord.
4. Its branches come into close contact (SY^1) with those of an associative or communicating nerve-cell (A.C.)
5. Other branches of the associative cell come into close contact (SY^2) with the branches or dendrites of a motor nerve-cell (M.C.).
6. An impulse or command travels along the motor nerve-fibre or axis cylinder of the motor nerve-cell.
7. The motor nerve-fibre ends on a muscle-fibre (M.F.) near the surface. This moves and the reflex action is complete.

Figure 5.5 Diagram of a reflex arc as seen in the early twentieth century.
Signals are picked up by a sensory nerve-cell, travel along a 'sensatory' nerve-fibre to the nerve cord (or spinal cord). There the signal is transmitted to a communicating nerve-cell, from which it activates a motor nerve-cell. Next, it travels over the motor nerve-fibre to the muscle, and finally initiates the reflex reaction. Notice that the distinction between the afferent sensory nerve-fibre and the efferent motor nerve-fibre was not known until the early 1800s. Before, scientists thought there was only one fibre in which the signals travelled back and forth (see figure 5.4).

Source: Thomson (1922)

reflex arc

notion introduced in the nineteenth century to describe the processes underlying a reflex: a signal is picked up by sensory receptors, transmitted to the spinal cord through an afferent nerve, transferred to interneurons, which activate motor neurons that send a motor command over an efferent nerve to initiate the withdrawal movement

physiologist Marshall Hall (1790–1857). He introduced the notion of the **reflex arc** to refer to the mechanisms involved in involuntary movements elicited by sensory stimuli (figure 5.5). Hall profited from the discovery made shortly before that there exist two different types of nerves: one set that carries information from the senses to the spinal cord and the brain (afferent nerves), and another set that carries motor information from the brain and the spinal cord to the muscles (efferent nerves). Previously it had been thought that the nerves worked in both directions (see Descartes' drawing in figure 5.4).

Hall further extended the reflex concept from a simple physiological phenomenon to a biological principle that formed one of the pillars of nervous activity. He insisted that all muscular function other than that owing to volition, respiration, cardiac activity and irritability depended on reflexes controlled by the spinal cord. In the first decades of the twentieth century the British physiologist Charles Scott Sherrington would describe the precise mechanisms of the spinal reflex, for which he was awarded the Nobel Prize for Medicine in 1932.

The reflex arc as the basis of mental functioning

Some time later, researchers extended Hall's reflex arc from the spinal cord to the complete brain. For them, the reflex was no longer one mode of action in the nervous system among others, but the basal unit from which the remaining nervous functions evolved. One of the scholars who took this view was the Russian physiologist Ivan Sechenov. In 1863 he published a theoretical treatise under the title *Reflexes of the Brain*, in which he claimed that all higher functions of the brain were of a reflex nature. Sechenov's treatise was important because it influenced Pavlov, who was a student of his. As we saw in Chapter 4, Pavlov was studying the reflex mechanisms in the digestive system, when he noticed that the dogs started to secrete digestive fluids before food arrived in their mouth. This was the start of the research on classical conditioning, which Pavlov saw as a psychic reflex.

The idea of the reflex arc as the basis of psychological functioning also reached the first psychologists in the United States. For instance, in the *Principles* (1890, Vol. 1, Chapter 3) William James asked the following question:

> The conception of reflex action is surely one of the best conquests of physiological theory; why not be radical with it? Why not say that just as the spinal cord is a machine with few reflexes, so the hemispheres are a machine with many, and that that is all the difference? The principle of continuity would press us to accept this view.
>
> *(James (1890) Vol. 1, p. 129)*

James himself did not go as far as to accept that all thoughts consisted of reflexes, because in his view this would be incompatible with the existence of human consciousness and free will (see Chapter 6), but the excerpt clearly shows that from the very beginning of American psychology the reflex arc was considered as a model of brain functioning.

A similar ambivalence towards the reflex arc can be seen in John Dewey's 1896 article 'The reflex arc concept in psychology' published in the *Psychological Review*. In this article Dewey criticised the reflex concept as too elementaristic and mechanistic, but he proposed a version that remained quite close to the original (in Dewey's version the stimulus and the response mutually influenced each other). As we saw in Chapter 4, none of James's or Dewey's hesitations were shared by Watson when he introduced behaviourism as the science of the S-R reflex arc, or by Skinner in his radical behaviourism.

Localisation of brain functions

The brain equipotentiality theory

Another major discussion taking place in the nineteenth century was whether different psychological functions were localised in different parts of the brain or whether

brain equipotentiality theory

theory saying that all parts of the brain have equal significance and are involved in each task; first thought to apply to the complete brain; since the nineteenth century limited to the cerebral hemispheres

localisation theory

theory saying that brain processes are localised, meaning that only part of the brain underlies a particular mental function

the whole brain was involved in all of them. Before, it had been widely assumed that the brain was a single organ, without further subdivisions (although a few scattered reports can be found of physicians who noticed that certain symptoms were more likely after some brain injuries than other).

The view that the brain functions as a whole with all parts having an equal significance is known as the brain equipotentiality theory. A series of findings in the nineteenth century convinced an increasing number of investigators that this theory was wrong and had to be replaced by the localisation theory, which states that mental functions are localised in specific parts of the brain. In this section we review some of the early evidence; later we will describe more recent evidence on the basis of brain imaging techniques.

Language production is controlled by the front parts of the brain

In 1825 the French professor of clinical medicine, Jean-Baptiste Bouillaud, presented evidence which according to him proved that speech was controlled by the front parts of the brain, the parts of the left and the right brain half touching the forehead (figure 5.6). In a paper read to his colleagues he reviewed the data from 14 autopsies. The eight patients with speech problems all had lesions in the frontal lobes of the brain, whereas these lobes appeared to be intact in the six other patients without speech disorder. In 1848 he presented a large number of new cases to support his theory.

Figure 5.6 The frontal lobes.
This picture shows the frontal lobe of the left brain half. The right hemisphere also has a frontal lobe. In 1825 Bouillaud claimed that speech production was controlled by the two frontal lobes, because patients with speech problems all had an injury here, whereas people without speech problems had injuries in other parts of the brain. In 1861 Broca claimed that only the left frontal lobe controlled language production.

Source: BSIP, JACOPIN / Science Photo Library Ltd.

Bouillaud's message was strongly opposed by his fellow-countryman, Marie Jean Pierre Flourens, who was one of the great brain physiologists of his time. On the basis of ablation and stimulation studies, Flourens agreed that the big structures of the nervous system had divergent functions. For instance, he concluded that the spinal cord was vital for the conduction of brain signals, that the cerebellum was involved in movement, and that a structure above the spinal cord – the medulla – was vital for vegetative functioning (when this structure was severed the animal died at once). Finally, he argued that perception, memory and will were controlled by the cerebral hemispheres. Importantly, however, he strongly defended the equipotentiality of the cerebral hemispheres. These consisted of a single organ. If a small part of them was removed, there was no isolated function lost (as long as the lesion was not too large, so that the remaining tissue could take over).

A similar stance about the equipotentiality of the cerebral hemispheres was taken by the German physiologist, Johannes Peter Müller, who wrote that:

> the mind is a substance independent of the brain and hence . . . a change in the structure of the brain cannot produce a change in the mental principle itself, but can only modify its actions . . . The loss of portions of the cerebral substance . . . cannot deprive the mind of certain masses of ideas, but diminishes the brightness and clearness of conceptions generally.
>
> *(Müller (1838) as cited in Tizard (1959) p. 134)*

Language production is controlled by the left frontal lobe

In April 1861, however, Paul Broca, professor of pathology in Paris, repeated and extended Bouillaud's work and presented evidence to the *Société d'Anthropologie* that speech production was controlled by one frontal lobe only. A patient with a long-standing, severe speech problem had just died. The autopsy showed widespread damage to the left frontal lobe only. In subsequent years, Broca provided more cases showing the importance of a region in the left frontal lobe for language production. This region has since been called Broca's area (figure 5.7).

As an illustration of our observation in Chapter 1 that scientific discoveries are rarely due to the genius of a single person, but are the result of the collective insight of a group of researchers (i.e. the Zeitgeist), Broca shortly after his announcement was accused of having stolen his idea from someone else. Gustav Dax presented evidence that his father, Marc Dax, in 1836 had presented a paper on the left hemisphere dominance for speech control at a medical congress in Montpellier. Furthermore, the same son had submitted a paper of his father's findings to the *Académie de Médecine* in Paris a few months before Broca presented his evidence. The paper had been rejected for publication. It is not known whether Broca saw it. In addition, two weeks before Broca provided his evidence to the *Société d'Anthropologie*, a colleague of his, Ernest Auburtin (who collaborated with Jean-Baptiste Bouillaud), had given a talk to the same *Société*, suggesting the possibility of language localisation at that exact location. Broca repeatedly acknowledged Auburtin's input (Thomas 2007).

Language understanding and the posterior part of the brain

Stimulated by Broca's findings, the German physician Karl Wernicke in 1874 presented evidence that language problems could also occur after damage to the rear part of the

Figure 5.7 Broca's area.
Damage to the coloured part of the brain often leads to speech problems. This part is called Broca's area, after the man who first described it. In most people, it is situated in the left hemisphere. For some people, it is situated in the right hemisphere (in about 5% of right-handers and about 25% of left-handers).

Source: Adapted from Geschwind (1972, p. 78). Courtesy of the Estate of Bunji Tagawa.

Figure 5.8 Wernicke's area.
Damage to the coloured part of the brain leads to problems with speech understanding. This part is called Wernicke's area, after the man who first described it. It mostly is in the left hemisphere, but occasionally can be in the right hemisphere.

Source: Adapted from Geschwind (1972, p. 78). Courtesy of the Estate of Bunji Tagawa.

left hemisphere (figure 5.8). These problems, however, had nothing to do with speaking, but rather with the understanding of language. The patients at first sight gave the impression of fluent speakers, until you tried to make sense of what they were saying; there was no meaning in their language.

The impetus from phrenology

Research on the localisation of brain functions in the nineteenth century was partly motivated by the claims made in the early 1800s by Franz Joseph Gall (1758–1828) and Johann Spurzheim (1776–1832) regarding phrenology. As you may remember

CASE STUDY: Broca's and Wernicke's aphasias

Samples of speech in aphasic patients asked to describe the Cookie Theft Picture

Source: Goodglass and Kaplan (1983). Reproduced with permission.

Patient with Broca's aphasia

Well...see...girl eating no...cookie...no...ah...school no...stool...ah...tip over...and ah... cookie jar...ah...lid...no...see...water all over...spilled over...yuck...Mother...daydreaming.

Patient with Wernicke's aphasia

Well this . . . mother is away here working her work out o'here to get her better, but when she's looking, the two boys looking in the other part. One their small tile into her time here. She's working another time because she is getting, too.

*Source: Goodglass (1983) and Helm-Estabrooks et al.
(1981, p. 425); as cited in Andrewes (2002, p. 310)*

physiognomy

belief that the personality of an individual can be deduced from their appearance, in particular from the shape of the head and the face

from Chapter 4, phrenology is a view that mental functions are localised in the brain and that the capacity of a function depends on the size of the brain part devoted to it. This gave rise to personality assessment on the basis of scalp analysis (by locating the bumps and the troughs on the head). As such, phrenology was part of a much wider and earlier belief that an individual's personality could be deduced from his or her physical appearance, in particular from the head and the face. This belief is known as **physiognomy** and can be traced back to Ancient Greece. At the end of the eighteenth century it was made popular again by the Swiss pastor Johann Kaspar Lavater.

Although phrenology is above all associated with an invalid form of personality assessment, it must not be forgotten that one of its basic messages was the localisation of brain functions. Gall and Spurzheim were convinced that the brain was composed of many organs, each dedicated to a particular skill. Gall initially made a distinction between 27 independent mental faculties, including the instinct of reproduction, love of offspring, self-defence and courage, cleverness, pride and arrogance, caution and forethought, memory of words, sense of language and speech, kindness, morality and compassion, and religion. Later Spurzheim added eight more (figure 5.9).

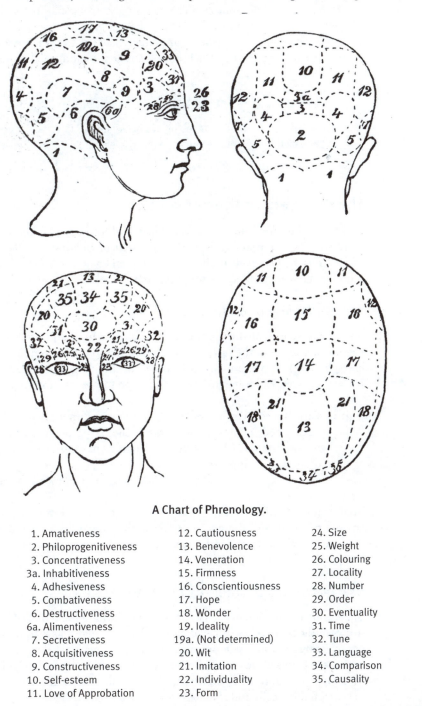

A Chart of Phrenology.

1. Amativeness
2. Philoprogenitiveness
3. Concentrativeness
3a. Inhabitiveness
4. Adhesiveness
5. Combativeness
6. Destructiveness
6a. Alimentiveness
7. Secretiveness
8. Acquisitiveness
9. Constructiveness
10. Self-esteem
11. Love of Approbation

12. Cautiousness
13. Benevolence
14. Veneration
15. Firmness
16. Conscientiousness
17. Hope
18. Wonder
19. Ideality
19a. (Not determined)
20. Wit
21. Imitation
22. Individuality
23. Form

24. Size
25. Weight
26. Colouring
27. Locality
28. Number
29. Order
30. Eventuality
31. Time
32. Tune
33. Language
34. Comparison
35. Causality

Figure 5.9 A drawing of the head with an indication of the various faculties according to Spurzheim (1834).

Because of their teachings, Gall and Spurzheim ran into difficulties with the Roman Catholic Church in Vienna (which opposed the idea that the divine soul could be fractioned into different faculties) and in 1807 moved to Paris (after two years of travelling through Europe). They parted company in 1812, arguably because Gall did not feel at ease about Spurzheim's increasingly strong claims for the diagnostic value of phrenology. Although Gall and Spurzheim's particular scheme rapidly was proven to be wrong, their more general argument that the brain is divided into specialised parts was a strong impetus for brain researchers to address the subject matter.

What do you think?

Are there still people believing in physiognomy? If not, what has undermined the belief? If yes, what evidence is there for its validity/usefulness?

The discovery of the nerve cell

The fourth big breakthrough in the nineteenth century was the finding that the grey matter of the cerebral hemispheres consisted of billions of cells and that the white matter and the nerves were the 'tails' (later called axons) of these cells. Two technical innovations were needed for this development.

The availability of better microscopes

First, microscopes of sufficient quality had to be built and used correctly. These only become available in the nineteenth century. Before, the magnification was not strong enough and there were major distortions in the images obtained, leading the British researcher Everard Home in 1798 to come to the conclusion that:

> It is scarcely necessary to mention, that parts of an animal body are not fitted for being examined by glasses of a great magnifying power; and, wherever they are shown one hundred times larger than their natural size, no dependence can be placed upon their appearance.
>
> *(Home (1798) as cited in Clarke and Jacyna (1987) p. 59)*

Technical innovations in the beginning of the nineteenth century, however, hugely increased the quality of the microscopes, so that researchers (including Home) within a few decades could confidently conclude that the brain, just like all other tissue, was composed of minute 'globules'.

New techniques to stain the brain tissue

The second innovation needed to understand the functional units of the brain was a way to colour the brain cells with all their fine details. There was little to be noticed about the organisation of brain tissue as long as the researchers had to look at the raw material. A major step forward was realised by the Italian physician Camillo Golgi in 1873 when he used silver to colour the brain tissue. This technique made the neurons stand out against the surrounding cells and revealed that they not only consisted of globules (cell bodies) but in addition comprised a highly interconnected network of branches (figure 5.10).

Figure 5.10 Staining techniques used to discover the basic structure of neurons.
After he was able to stain nerve cells, Golgi discovered that the grey matter of the brain consisted of a network of branches and globules. Golgi was convinced that the network formed a single unit; Ramón y Cajal argued that it consisted of separate neurons communicating with each other.

Source: Clarke and Jacyna (1987). Reproduced with permission.

Disentangling communication in the nervous system

Individual neurons instead of a continuous network

The big question among brain physiologists after Golgi's discovery of the network of globules and branches was whether the network was a continuous structure or whether it consisted of individual cells. Golgi strongly argued in favour of the former, and it would take nearly half a century before it became generally accepted that the network was composed of individual cells, called **neurons**, which communicated with each other without being attached to one another (Shepherd 1991). An important name in this development was the Spanish researcher Santiago Ramón y Cajal. Golgi and Ramón y Cajal would share the Nobel Prize for Medicine in 1906.

Once it was accepted that the nervous system consisted of billions of independent neurons, the next challenge was to explain how they stored and exchanged information. Remember that the natural philosophers for centuries had been mystified by how the nerves were able to transmit information from and to the brain (soul). First they thought that animal spirits rushed through hollow tubes, and when this was no longer tenable, they proposed brain fluids. However, the latter explanation had difficulty accounting for the speed of neural transmission (which easily exceeds 100 km per hour). In addition, there was the problem that no-one was able to show the presence of fluid in the nerves.

neuron

brain cell; basic unit of the nervous system; contains a cell body, dendrites and an axon

Electricity within neurons

A new idea emerging at the end of the eighteenth century was that communication in the nervous system might resemble the transmission of electrical signals. Around 1650 the first electricity generator was built, followed in 1745 by the first usable device to store electricity, the so-called *Leyden jar* (invented in the Dutch University of Leyden, hence the name). With the help of a generator and a Leyden jar scientists could study the characteristics of electrical currents. Physiologists were struck by the similarities between electrical signals and what happened in the nerves (a signal was transmitted at a high speed and at the end made something happen). Could it be that brain activity was electrical activity?

The first to find clear empirical evidence for the involvement of electricity in the nervous system was the Italian physician Luigi Galvani. In 1786, while operating on frogs, he noticed that a dissected leg of a frog contracted each time his assistant touched a bare nerve with his scalpel and the electricity generator nearby produced a spark. Galvani decided to test the phenomenon more in detail and in 1791 published a text on his findings. Although in hindsight he misinterpreted quite a lot of findings, it was undeniable that body movement could be generated by an electric current applied to a nerve. This is how a colleague described the reception of Galvani's findings:

> The storm among physicists, physiologists and physicians, which the appearance of the commentary created, can only be compared to the one that appeared on the political horizon of Europe at that time [1791]. It can be said that wherever frogs were to be found, and where two different kinds of metal could be procured, everyone wished to see the mutilated limbs of frogs re-animated in this remarkable manner; the physiologists believed that at last the dream handed down from their ancestors of a vital power was within their grasp; the physicians, whom Galvani somewhat thoughtlessly encouraged to attempt the treatment of all manner of nervous disorders, such as sciatica, tetanus, and epilepsy, began to believe that no cure was impossible, and it was considered certain that in the future no one in a trance could be buried alive, provided only that he were galvanized!
>
> *(du Bois-Reymond (1848) as translated by Clarke and Jacyna (1987) p. 169)*

The next question, of course, was how the brain could generate electricity. In the worst case scenario all Galvani had shown was that a frog's leg contracted if you sent electricity through it. He had not shown that brain signals were electrical signals, a criticism made most poignantly by Galvani's Italian colleague Alessandro Volta (who as part of his endeavour to refute Galvani stumbled across the first battery, a device to produce electricity on the basis of chemical reactions). It would take another 50 years before Emil du Bois-Reymond, a Prussian physicist with Swiss roots, would make enough headway to firmly establish that nerve signals indeed involved electricity. He was able to do so with the use of electric fishes (fishes that are capable of discharging electricity on prey and predators) and much improved techniques to measure small electrical signals.

Another question was whether nerves were like real electrical wires or whether the electrical signal generated was based on chemical processes within the nerve. Were the nerves simple, passive transmitters of electrical signals generated in the brain or did they actively continue a chemical process initiated at the level of the brain (or the spinal cord)? This was the background against which von Helmholtz in 1852 decided to measure the speed of signal transmission in the nerve. If nerves were like electric wires, the

Axon terminals (contain chemicals, which are released when an axon signal arrives; these neurotransmitters cross the small cleft between the axon terminal and the dendrite of the next neuron; in this way a signal is transferred from one cell to the next)

Dendrites (receive information from the axon terminals of other neurons)

Cell body (with nucleus)

Myelin sheath (insulates axon and speeds up information transfer; gives white matter and nerves their colour)

Axon (transmits information of the neuron to other neurons or to organs)

Axon hill (initiation of the electrical signal in the axon)

Figure 5.11 Functioning of neurons.
Neurons receive chemical signals from other cells via their dendrites. These signals are grouped in the axon hill from which an electrical signal starts when a threshold is exceeded. The electrical signal travels through the axon, on the basis of chemical changes in the axon, and causes neurotransmitters to be released in the terminals. These neurotransmitters are the signals for the next cell. Most axons have a myelin sheath which is white; hence the colour of the nerves and the white matter in the brain.

Source: Brysbaert (2006). Reproduced with permission from Academia Press.

signal speed should be astronomically high (close to the speed of light). Alternatively, if the signal was based on chemical processes, as von Helmholtz assumed, it would be much slower. As we saw in Chapter 2, the latter was the case: the speed of the nerves in the leg of a frog was only some 30 metres per second (or 108 km per hour).

In the twentieth century the exact mechanisms of signal transmission in the nerves would be unravelled (figure 5.11), largely on the basis of the neurons of the giant squid, which were so big that they could be seen with the naked eye.

Communication between neurons: the synapse

neurotransmitter

chemical substance used to communicate between neurons; is released from the synapse when a signal arrives through the axon; can be affected by drugs

In the twentieth century the communication *between* neurons also became understood. Although a small part of this communication is electrical, the bulk is achieved chemically, by means of neurotransmitters. Towards their end, the axons branch out in a multitude of terminals, called synapses, which contain chemicals and lie close to the dendrites (and bodies) of other cells. When the electrical signal reaches a synapse, it induces chemicals to be released, which make contact with the next cell. These chemicals are called neurotransmitters and they can be influenced by chemical substances, which opened the door to the creation of medicines that either block or increase the availability of neurotransmitters and that have an impact on brain-related disorders going from epilepsy to depression (see Chapter 11).

Interim summary

Five big breakthroughs in the nineteenth century:

1. Understanding that the spinal cord was an integral part of the central nervous system and was involved in the control of many bodily functions.

2. Discovery that many processes in the central nervous system were reflexes that did not need voluntary initiation; question to what extent higher cognitive functions could be considered as reflexes as well (e.g. Pavlov, behaviourism).

3. Intense discussions between proponents of brain equipotentiality and adherents of brain localisation; initially the former were dominant; increasingly, however, evidence for the latter position was found.

4. Discovery that the brain consisted of a network of individual neurons that communicated with each another; required good microscopes and techniques to stain neurons.

5. Discovery that the neurons store and transfer information by means of electro-chemical signals; electrical information mainly involved in intra-cell communication, chemical information transfer important for communication between neurons.

KEY FIGURES

Understanding the workings of the nervous system

■ Galen (c. 130–c. 200): ventricles and animal spirits; legacy until well into the eighteenth century.

■ Andreas Vesalius (1514–1564): translated Galen's anatomical works in Latin and extended them by new dissections, including on humans.

■ René Descartes (1596–1650): proposed the idea of automatic, reflexive reactions that did not involve the will.

■ Thomas Willis (1621–1675): published an influential atlas of the brain in which he attached more importance to the solid brain parts.

■ Luigi Galvani (1737–1798): discovered that electricity is involved in signal transmission in the nerves.

■ Jiří Procháska (1749–1820): importance of the spinal cord and the subcortical structures for the control of reflexes.

■ Franz Joseph Gall (1758–1828) and Johann Gaspar Spurzheim (1776–1832): proposed idea of localisation of functions in the brain, against the equipotentiality idea. Nowadays mostly associated with phrenology.

- Marshal Hall (1790–1857): stressed the importance of reflexive actions and initiated the term 'reflex arc'.

- Marie Jean Pierre Flourens (1794–1867) and Johannes Peter Müller (1801–1858): strong defenders of the brain equipotentiality theory on the basis of empirical studies.

- Jean-Baptiste Bouillaud (1796–1881): localisation of language in the frontal lobes; first empirical evidence for localisation of function in the brain.

- Paul Broca (1824–1880): localisation of speech in the left frontal lobe.

- Camillo Golgi (1843–1926): staining technique that made neurons visible.

- Carl Wernicke (1848–1905): localisation of language understanding in the rear part of the left hemisphere.

- Santiago Ramón y Cajal (1852–1934): established the neuron doctrine, which says that the brain consists of individual neurons that communicate with each other.

- Charles Scott Sherrington (1857–1952): described the mechanisms of the spinal reflex.

5.4 The emergence of neuropsychology in the twentieth century

Much of the research discussed in section 5.3 was based on animals (remember that the workings of the neuron were largely unravelled by examining the nervous 'system' of the giant squid). This was highly informative because there is a great similarity between the brain functioning in humans and animals. Research on animals continued at an ever faster speed in the twentieth century. However, in the rest of this chapter we will focus on the research into the human brain, in particular on the relationship between brain functioning and mental and behavioural performance.

Localisation studies in the world wars

Localisation studies continued in the twentieth century. In particular the world wars resulted in new insights. The invention of high-velocity bullets had the unforeseen consequence that brain wounds were more focused than before, allowing researchers to get a sharper image of function loss after damage to small parts of the brain.

Vision problems after shot wounds at the back of the head

One of the most famous series of case studies in World War I was published by the British neurologist, Gordon Holmes. He examined the consequences of small-scale wounds at the back of the head. Here is the first case study he reported in his 1918 article:

> CASE 1. – Private R–, 15104, was wounded on September 26, 1916, by a shrapnel ball which penetrated his steel helmet. He was unconscious for an hour or so, and stated that he was completely blind till the next day. He never noticed any subjective visual phenomena. He was admitted to a Base Hospital on the day following the infliction of the wound.
>
> *Wound*. – There was a small penetrating wound from which softened brain extruded, immediately to the right of the middle line of the skull and 1 inch (2-5 cm.) above the inion. A radiograph revealed much depressed bone, but no foreign body. An operation was performed next day, and several fragments of bone as well as clots and pulped brain tissue were removed from the occipital pole. The recovery was rapid and uneventful. His visual fields were taken by a perimeter and a screen scotometer six days after the infliction of the wound, and again a week later. There was then a large left homonymous paracentral scotoma to an object $7mm^2$ which reached the fixation point and extended outwards from it to about 25°. Its mesial border coincided with the vertical above the fixation point, but receded from it below this. Peripheral vision was unaffected, and the colour fields were normal in the right halves, but there was no perception of either red or green to the left of the middle line line [figure 5.12].
>
> *(Holmes 1918, p. 354–5)*

Figure 5.12 The first figure given in Holmes (1918) about the consequences of shot wounds. The soldier got a shrapnel ball at the back of the head (exact position in the lower part of the figure). As a result, he lost vision in the left half of his central visual field (the black areas in the upper figures, representing vision in the left and the right eye).

Source: Holmes (1918) Disturbance of vision by cerebral lesions, *British Journal of Opthalmology,* **2**, p. 355, (retrieved on 24 October 2007 from http://www.pubmedcentral.nih.gov/articlerender.fcgi?artid=513514). Reproduced with permission from the BMJ Publishing Group.

World War II and prosopagnosia

Similar observations were made in World War II. A particularly important paper here was that of the German physician, Joachim Bodamer (1947), describing soldiers who lost their ability to recognise faces as a consequence of brain injury at the rear of the brain. The author called this condition *prosopagnosia*. Subsequent literature searches revealed that similar cases had been described by French, British and German neurologists in the second half of the nineteenth century (Ellis and Florence 1990). The following are excerpts from Bodamer's text:

CASE 1: S (24 Years old)

On 11.9.44 S went into a special hospital for brain injuries . . . After the injury, S was completely blind for several weeks. His sight returned gradually, in defined phases . . . But all impression of colour was missing – he could distinguish only light and dark, black and white. . . .

He said he had had difficulties with objects for a long time after his injury but he had gradually got to know objects again – he made mistakes now only with those objects he had not seen since his injury . . .

Also S had . . . a disorder of the recognition of faces and, in a wider sense, of expressions . . . S recognized a face as such, i.e. as different from other things, but could not assign the face to its owner. He could identify all the features of a face, but all faces appeared equally 'sober' and 'tasteless' to him . . .

25.11.44. S is told to look at own face in the mirror. At first he mistakes it for a picture but corrects himself. He stares for a long time as though a totally strange object is before him, then reports he sees a face and describes its individual features . . .

30.12.44. A picture of a long-haired dog, from the front, sitting [is shown]: S identifies it as human but with 'funny' hair.

(Bodamer (1947) as translated in Ellis and Florence 1990)

neuropsychology

branch of psychological research and practice that looks at the relationship between brain and behaviour; research traditionally focused on understanding the consequences of brain damage and localising the affected tissue; practice aimed at assessing the behavioural and mental consequences of the injury and administering the rehabilitation programme

The start of neuropsychology

The mission of neuropsychology

Increasingly, in the second half of the twentieth century psychologists rather than physicians became involved in studying the behavioural consequences of brain injury. They started to call themselves **neuropsychologists** and established their own journals and societies (e.g. the first issue of the journal *Neuropsychologia* was published in 1963). Initially, their research was a continuation of the existing research and aimed at gaining further insight in the localisation of different functions in the brain. They also wanted to get a more detailed picture of the consequences of brain injury for higher mental functions, such as perception, language and action.

This is how the mission statement of the first issue of *Neuropsychologia* read:

At Mond See in Austria, in 1951, a small group of European neurologists and psychologists met to discuss disorders of higher mental function associated with injury or disease of the brain. The specific themes of the Conference were disorders of spatial perception and psychic symptoms associated with lesions of the third ventricle . . .

The papers given at these conferences have never been published, the aim being above all to stimulate discussion and to provoke the expression of widely different points of view. None the less, in view of the fact that a certain unity of subject matter and approach has emerged which goes beyond the limits of the individual disciplines (neurology, psychology, neurophysiology) involved, the members of the group believe that the time is now ripe for the launching of a new journal, dedicated to the idea of 'neuropsychology' . . .

Under the term 'neuropsychology', we have in mind a particular area of neurology of common interest to neurologists, psychiatrists, psychologists and neurophysiologists. This interest is focused mainly, though not of course exclusively, on the cerebral cortex. Among topics of particular concern to us are disorders of language, perception and action.

(Editorial, Neuropsychologia, *1963, Vol. 1, p. 1)*

Neuropsychology was presented as a new link between psychologists and the medical world (in addition to the links that already existed through clinical psychology and counselling). The assessment and treatment of the effects of brain damage became a joint enterprise of physicians and psychologists.

A change of focus: Cognitive neuropsychology

Dissent among neuropsychologists

In the 1970–1980s, a number of neuropsychologists became dissatisfied with the way in which the subject matter was investigated. They had two grievances. First, the localisation issue turned out to be difficult to address on the basis of human brain injuries. All that could be done was to establish a correlation between symptoms measured while the patient was alive and brain damage observed much later, after the patient had died. Furthermore, the damage caused by brain injuries and strokes most of the time is widespread and not limited to one specific brain structure, making it difficult to decide which part of the damage was at the origin of the symptoms.

What do you think?

Another reason why the traditional neuropsychologists gave up the localisation issue was the development of better techniques to localise brain functions. Can you think of examples?

The second reason why neuropsychologists felt dissatisfaction was that the results of the examinations rarely went beyond a list of symptoms displayed by various patients (case studies). There was little theory behind the enterprise, little effort to link the various findings and draw implications for normal, healthy functioning. What neuropsychology had to do, the dissenters argued, was to use observations from patients with brain damage to test and amend the information-processing models proposed by the cognitive psychologists (Chapter 4). Instead of looking for anatomical localisations, neuropsychologists should investigate the functional implications of injuries: which cognitive processes were affected by the brain damage?

A new name

**cognitive
neuropsychology**

part of neuropsy-
chology aimed at
understanding and
treating the behav-
ioural conse-
quences of brain
damage within the
information pro-
cessing models
proposed by cogni-
tive psychologists

To emphasise the difference between the new type of research and the traditional neuropsychological approach, a new name was coined: cognitive neuropsychology. It referred to research dealing with the consequences of brain injuries for the information-processing models proposed by the cognitive psychologists. This is how one of the textbooks described the need for cognitive neuropsychology:

> For 100 years, it has been well known that the study of the cognitive problems of patients suffering from neurological diseases can produce strikingly counterintuitive observations . . . However, in general, neuropsychology has had little impact on the study of normal function.
>
> With any knowledge of the history of clinical neuropsychology, it is easy to understand why this neglect occurred. The standard of description of the psychological impairments of patients was low, often being little more than the bald statement of the clinical opinion of the investigator. There was frequently a dramatic contrast between the vagueness of the psychological account of the disorder and the precision with which anatomical investigation of the lesion that had given rise to it was carried out post-mortem.
>
> *(Shallice 1988, p. 3)*

By relating the consequences of brain damage to the theories of normal functioning, the cognitive neuropsychologists explicitly aimed to increase the impact of their research within the departments of psychology.

Deep dyslexia

A landmark publication in the history of cognitive neuropsychology was a book on deep dyslexia, edited by Coltheart, Patterson and Marshall (1980). Dyslexia refers to reading problems, which can either be due to developmental factors (making it hard for children to learn to read) or to brain damage (disrupting the performance of previously fluent readers). *Deep dyslexia* is a condition of strongly impaired reading after brain injury with a very particular symptom: sometimes, when the patients try to identify a word, they do not read the word itself but a semantically related word. For instance, when asked to read the word *storm*, they might say *thunder*; or the stimulus word *uncle* might be read as *nephew*. When first discovered, this phenomenon baffled psychologists: how can the meaning of written words become activated when the patient is not capable of recognising the words?

To explain the semantic reading mistake, Morton and Patterson (1980) postulated a distinction between a logogen system and a cognitive system (figure 5.13). The logogen system could be compared to a mental dictionary; it contained all the words known to a patient (later the name *lexicon* was used for this system). The logogen system did not contain information about the meaning of the words; this was stored in a central cognitive system with which the logogen system interacted. Written words were recognised by first activating their entry in the visual logogen system and then by activating the corresponding meaning in the cognitive system.

Morton and Patterson (1980) argued that there were three different logogen systems: a visual logogen system for the recognition of written words, an auditory logogen

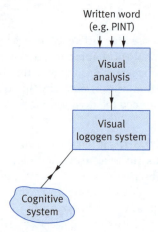

Figure 5.13 Figure illustrating the distinction between the logogen and the cognitive system made by Morton and Patterson (1980).
According to Morton and Patterson, a distinction had to be made between processing the word forms and processing the word meanings. To read the written word PINT, first the sequence of letters must be recognised as a known word form (this happens in the visual logogen system). Only then can the meaning of the word become activated in the cognitive system.

Source: based on Morton and Patterson (1980). Reproduced with permission. (See also figure 5.14)

system for the recognition of spoken words, and an output logogen system for the production of speech (figure 5.14). Within the full model there were three routes for a normal reader to read aloud a written word. The first route directly converted the letters into sounds; this one was called the grapheme phoneme conversion route. It allowed readers to name non-words, such as *dom* and *pham*. The second route consisted of a direct connection between the visual logogen system and the output logogen system. The existence of such a route predicted that there would be patients who were able to name words with irregular pronunciations (e.g. *yacht*, *pint*) without knowing their meaning. Such patients have subsequently been described (see Coltheart 2004). Finally, the third route to name written words was one via the visual logogen system, through the cognitive system, to the logogen output system. In this route the visual logogen activated its meaning and on the basis of this meaning candidate output logogens were activated.

According to Morton and Patterson (1980), the third route was the origin of the semantically related errors observed in deep dyslexia patients. In these patients the grapheme phoneme conversion route and the direct route between the visual logogen system and the output logogen system were severed (figure 5.14). All they had left was the route mediated by the cognitive system. Because this route was not very accurate, a lot of words failed to be read altogether and other words gave rise to semantically related responses. For instance, the input word *storm* activated the meanings associated with storms and tempests, but these meanings were not specific enough to activate the correct output logogen *storm* and instead a related word (*thunder*) got activated.

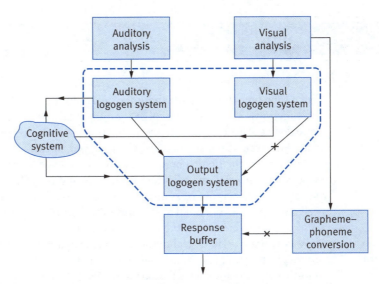

Figure 5.14 Morton and Patterson's (1980) full model and its explanation of deep dyslexia. In this model for the naming of spoken and written words, three different logogens are distinguished, together with a grapheme phoneme conversion system for the naming of unknown words and non-words. For a normal reader, there are three routes to name a written word. For a patient with deep dyslexia, two of these routes are severed and the only remaining route is the one via the cognitive system. This route gives rise to the semantically related errors observed in these patients.

Source: based on Morton and Patterson (1980). Reproduced with permission.

By integrating neuropsychological research in the mainstream of cognitive research, the cognitive neuropsychologists not only advanced the cognitive information processing models, but also ensured that the findings from the clinic became central to psychological thinking and teaching.

Interim summary

Neuropsychology

■ Examination of bullet wounds in the world wars provided physicians with more detailed knowledge about the behavioural consequences of brain injuries. Two famous examples were the partial loss of vision after shot wounds above the neck and the inability to recognise faces (prosopagnosia).

■ Research and treatment of the consequences of brain damage were increasingly taken over by psychologists, who called themselves neuropsychologists.

■ In the 1970–1980s a number of neuropsychologists started to study the implications of brain damage for the information-processing models proposed by cognitive psychologists; this was the start of cognitive neuropsychology.

■ One of the first topics addressed by the new approach was deep dyslexia.

5.5   Brain imaging and the turn to neuroscience

For a long time the evidence about the neurophysiology of the brain and the localisation of functions was based on post-mortem analyses. Needless to say, such analyses revealed very little about the actual functioning of the living brain. In the twentieth century, however, scientists increasingly managed to extract information from a working brain. One of the first techniques used was single-cell recording. In this technique electrodes were planted in individual brain cells and recorded when the cells fired. By presenting different types of stimuli researchers could determine in which processes each cell took part. Unfortunately, because this technique involved brain surgery and the insertion of electrodes in the brain, its use with humans was very limited. Eventually, however, brain imaging techniques became available that did not require the researchers to touch the brain. These are called non-invasive techniques. Below we summarise the most important and give a flavour of some of the results they have provided.

non-invasive techniques

methods in neuroscience that allow the study of the workings of the brain without surgery or the use of irreversible interventions

Measuring electrical signals from groups of cells

EEG-recording

In 1928 the German physician and psychologist Hans Berger published an article that would dramatically change brain research. He reasoned that if brain activity was electrical activity, he might be able to pick up some signals if he put electrodes on the human scalp (there was some evidence that brain activity could be measured on the exposed brain surface of animals). Berger indeed found very weak signals that seemed to oscillate at a frequency of some 10 cycles per second, at least when the person was at rest with their eyes closed. As soon as the person opened their eyes or was touched on the skin, the regular signal disappeared and was replaced by smaller and faster oscillations, which disappeared again when the person closed their eyes and returned to rest (figure 5.15).

Figure 5.15 EEG-recording of Hans Berger.
This shows one of Berger's first recordings. First the participant was awake but resting with the eyes closed. The EEG consists of an alpha wave (a slow, regular wave of 10 cycles per second; the underlined segment represents half a second). At the point indicated by the arrow, the hand of the participant was touched. Immediately the recording becomes irregular, with lower amplitude and a faster rhythm, a pattern Berger called a beta wave. After some time without stimulation the alpha wave returns.

Source: Berger (1969; as cited in Changeux) (1997)

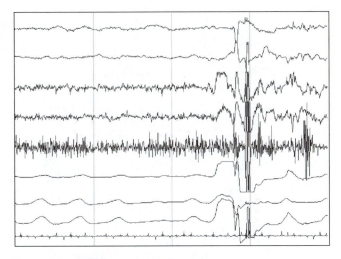

Figure 5.16 EEG-recording during an epileptic seizure.
This recording shows that an epileptic seizure is often accompanied by a strong electrical discharge, making lots of neurons fire in an uncontrolled manner. Each line represents the recording of a different electrode placed at a different location on the head.

EEG

electroencephalo-gram: outcome of measurement of electrical brain activity by means of sensors placed on the scalp; routinely used in hospitals for the detection of epilepsy

Berger called the print-out of the electrical brain activity as a function of time an electroencephalogram, better known under its abbreviation **EEG**. He further called the slow, regular waves at rest *alpha waves*, and the fast, irregular waves under situations of alertness *beta waves*. These waves are the result of the firing of millions of neurons underneath the skull. If the neurons fire at a slow pace in synchrony, the waves are large; if they fire rapidly and independently, the waves become small and fast. The former is the case under rest conditions, the latter under conditions of information processing and alertness.

One of the first applications of the EEG-measurement was the demonstration that epileptic seizures involved uncontrolled electrical discharges (figure 5.16). Another application was the discovery of different sleep stages.

Event Related Potential (ERP)

signal obtained by averaging the EEG-signals to stimuli that are repeated a number of times; allows researchers to look for differences in the signal as a function of characteristics of the stimulus

Event Related Potentials and magnetoencephalography

As the accuracy of the EEG-recordings grew, two further applications became available. The first was the measurement of changes in the electrical signal as a function of specific stimuli. In this type of research, two types of stimuli are presented repeatedly and researchers examine in what respects the brain response to one type of stimulus differs from that to the other. This research is called **Event Related Potential (ERP)** research, because the electrical responses to individual events are registered and compared.

Figure 5.17 illustrates the ERP technique. The left part shows the EEG-recordings on trials when nothing was presented; the right part shows the recordings on trials when an auditory click was presented. When the average is calculated across different trials, a smooth curve is obtained with peaks and troughs. This is the ERP-signal. It

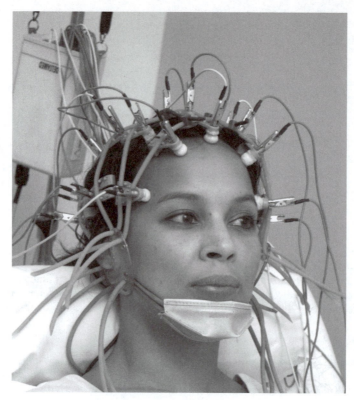

Making an EEG-recording.

Source: AJ Photo / Hop Americain / Science Photo Library Ltd

Mean EEG-signal of the   Mean EEG-signal of the
trials without stimulus   trials with an auditory click

Figure 5.17 Calculating an ERP-signal.
This figure shows the EEG-signal of an electrode on 10 trials without stimulus (left column)
and 10 trials when an auditory click was presented (right column). By taking the mean of
the trials, the random noise in the signal (the jitter) is averaged out and the remaining
smooth curve is the ERP-signal.

Source: Brysbaert (2006). Reproduced with permission from Academia Press.

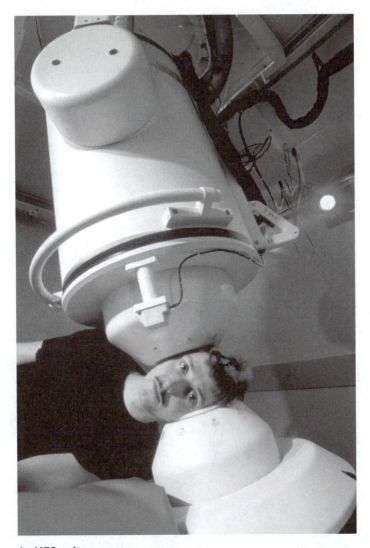

An MEG unit.

Source: Dr Jurgen Scriba / Science Photo Library Ltd

can be used to determine how fast the brain responds to various types of signals and how the response differs as a function of the stimulus.

The second new use of EEG-recordings was the fact that one could try to localise the source of the electrical signal. In a recording different electrodes are placed on the head (up to 128). Not all of these electrodes return an equally strong signal. Depending on the distribution of signals, it is possible to have an estimate of the part of the brain that was at the origin of the signal. Unfortunately, because of the limit to the number of electrodes that can be placed on the head (and because of the small errors involved in the placement itself), localisation on the basis of EEG-recordings is not very accurate.

A much better resolution can be obtained if instead of measuring the electrical activity on the scalp, researchers measure the magnetic field around the head. The electrical signals in the brain produce magnetic fields, which can be picked up by sensitive sensors. This forms the basis of **magnetoencephalography (MEG)**, a technique which is still in its early stages but which is expected to have a very significant impact.

Measuring blood flow in the brain

Brain activity is very energy demanding. It is estimated that the brain requires some 20 per cent of the blood in the body and 25 per cent of the oxygen to function properly. A short interruption in the blood flow to the brain results in massive and irreversible damage. By looking at the blood flow it is thus possible to know which brain regions are particularly active during a task.

PET and fMRI

There are several ways to determine the blood flow, depending on how precise the measurement has to be. One of the first techniques consisted of injecting a radioactive tracer into the blood circulation and detecting the radioactive signal. The more blood a certain region requires, the more tracer goes to that area. This was the basis of **PET** (positron emission tomography), a technique that now is used infrequently because of the need to use radioactive material and because the precision of the measurement is limited.

magnetoencephal-ography (MEG)

measurement of the electrical brain activity by means of measurement of the magnetic field around the head; is one of the most promising brain imaging techniques, because it has the potential of both a high temporal and spatial resolution

positron emission tomography (PET)

brain imaging technique based on measurement of radioactive tracer injected into the bloodstream

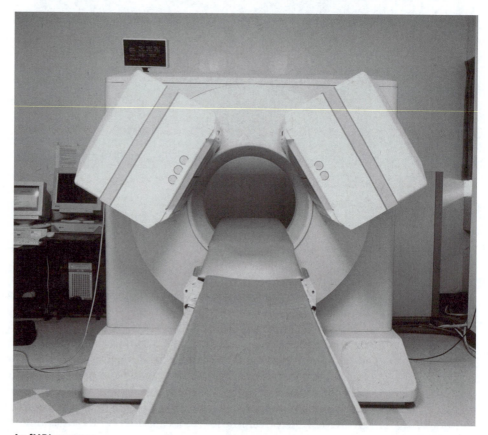

An fMRI-scanner.

Source: Raymond Koch / Photonica / Getty Images

(a)

(b)

Figure 5.18 fMRI signal of people generating words that start with a particular letter.
The upper part shows the brain activity in the majority of people; the lower part shows the activity in people with right brain dominance. The left side in each part gives a view from behind, the right side a view from above.

Source: Hunter *et al.* (2007), © 2007 by the Massachusetts Institute of Technology

fMRI

brain imaging technique based on the measurement of blood with oxygen vs. blood without oxygen; currently the most popular imaging technique because of its high spatial resolution (allows good localisation); has rather low temporal resolution (cannot trace what is happening at a speed of hundreds of registrations per second)

Another technique is to measure the magnetic resonance of the blood. This differs between blood with oxygen and blood without oxygen. Measurement of the magnetic resonance makes it possible to determine which regions of the brain are using a lot of oxygen (and thus are very active). Further advantages of the technique, which is called **fMRI** (functional magnetic resonance imaging), are that more accurate measurements can be made and that the investigation takes place without the need for an injection. A limitation of the technique is that at present the oxygen use can only be registered at a rate of a few times per second, so that researchers cannot measure the detailed processing that is going on (e.g. an ERP-signal is based on 1,000 measurements per second).

An example of an fMRI-study is a study in which people are put in the scanner and asked to generate as many words as possible that start with a particular letter (e.g. S). Given that this task deals with word generation, we can assume that Broca's area will be involved (figure 5.7). In addition, we can assume that for the majority of people the area will be in the left hemisphere. However, for some people it will be in the right hemisphere. The latter is more likely in left-handed people than in right-handed people, as it is known from neuropsychological research that some 25 per cent of left-handers have their speech area in the right hemisphere compared with less than 5 per cent of the right-handers.

The upper part of figure 5.18 displays the fMRI output of four participants who showed the typical pattern of brain activity in the word generation task; they had their language production neatly lateralised to the left hemisphere. The lower part of the figure shows the data of two left-handers, who turned out to rely on their right hemisphere for word generation. So, the localisation of Broca's area can easily be picked up with an fMRI scanner and the word generation task.

Measuring effects of 'virtual lesions'

TMS

Whereas the previous techniques allow researchers to measure how active different brain regions are during the performance of specific tasks, a final technique allows them to interfere temporarily with the activity in a restricted brain area. Because brain activity is electrical activity, it is possible to interfere with it by inducing a weak

TMS is delivered by a coil.
The resulting electric current briefly interferes with the activity of the neurons underneath the coil.

Source: University of Durham/Simon Fraser/Science Photo Library Ltd

transcranial magnetic stimulation (TMS)

stimulation of a brain region by means of a coil placed on the head; allows temporary interference with the processing of a small part of the brain

electric current in the neurons. Interference with the electrical activity of neurons in a restricted brain area is the basic mechanism behind transcranial magnetic stimulation (TMS). A coil is placed on the head of the person and a focused electric current is sent to the grey matter underneath. If the current is sent to the region in the brain that controls arm movements, for instance, the participant will feel an involuntary trembling in the arm on the other side of the body. If the current is sent to the location of the shrapnel wound described in figure 5.12, then the person will experience unstructured light sensations (phosphenes) in the corresponding part of the visual field.

The intensity of the electric current is so low that the interference with the brain activity is too small to elicit involuntary actions, but is strong enough to interfere slightly with the ongoing activity. This can be picked up by looking at the speed with which the activity is performed (e.g. the time needed to respond to a stimulus). With the use of TMS, psychologists can establish which brain areas are needed for the completion of particular cognitive processes, just like cognitive neuropsychologists are able to test cognitive theories on the basis of brain injuries. The advantages of TMS over lesion research are that the effects are transitory and that the interference can be limited to a restricted brain area.

TMS is complementary to fMRI, because fMRI only allows researchers to see a correlation between activity in certain brain regions and performance on a particular task. It does not tell researchers whether the brain activity is necessary for the behaviour. Such a conclusion is only possible with TMS. By interfering with the activity of an area, the researchers can examine whether the region is critical for good task performance. The usual line of investigation in brain imaging studies, therefore, is first to use fMRI to identify a potentially interesting brain area and then to turn to TMS to confirm the critical involvement of the area in performance.

What do you think?

If you were given the opportunity to conduct research with one of the above techniques, which one would you prefer? Why? Do you have reasons for not wanting to do this type of research? Which technique do you object to?

cognitive neuroscience

the scientific study of the biological mechanisms underlying cognition; largely based on brain imaging techniques, TMS and the measurement of electrical activity

The birth of cognitive neuroscience

Cognitive neuroscience: testing the cognitive information-processing models with brain imaging techniques

The availability of techniques to measure human brain activity while participants are performing mental operations opened a completely new field of research for psychologists. Just as neuropsychological information was used to test cognitive models of information processing (see above), so did psychologists increasingly rely on brain imaging data to test their theories. This branch of research became known as cognitive neuroscience, the scientific study of the biological mechanisms underlying cognition.

Is cognitive neuroscience more than high-tech localisation?

Not everyone is convinced, however, that brain imaging and TMS allow the researcher to really test the information-processing models proposed by cognitive psychologists. One major limitation of most techniques, in particular those based on blood flow measurement (such as fMRI), is their low temporal resolution. Activity must be measured over seconds, making it difficult to get insight into the detailed information processing going on and the ways in which this is influenced by minor variations in the stimulus materials. According to some authors (e.g. Coltheart 2006; Uttal 2001), the findings of fMRI are more comparable to the localisation efforts of traditional neuropsychology (sometimes mockingly referred to as 'blob spotting') than to the testing of cognitive models done in cognitive neuropsychology. This criticism has probably been formulated most cogently by Uttal (2001):

> Even if we could associate precisely defined cognitive functions in particular areas of the brain (and this seems highly unlikely), it would tell us very little if anything about how the brain computes, represents, encodes, or instantiates psychological processes.
>
> *(Uttal 2001, p. 217)*

Kihlstrom (2007) went even further and argued that the conclusions based on brain imaging have a strong resemblance to the claims made by the nineteenth-century phrenologists. He took social cognition (i.e. knowledge about oneself and others) as an example. First, he noticed that many of the faculties identified by Spurzheim had to do with social functioning (see the blue parts of figure 5.19). Then he pointed out how similar a modern picture based on brain imaging looks (figure 5.20). Placing the two pictures next to one another, Kihlstrom wondered how much more information the modern brain imaging pictures have provided for the understanding of social cognition than Spurzheim's picture from 1834.

What do you think?

Do we know anything more about how people think when we know which precise brain parts are involved?

In defence of cognitive neuroscience

Despite the doubts about whether brain imaging studies are able to provide anything more than the localisation of brain activity, even the strongest critics cannot deny that cognitive neuroscience deeply influenced psychological thinking and is likely to do so in the future as well. These are some of the arguments.

First, there is a difference between empirically showing the brain regions involved in a particular task and speculating about them. Though the overlap between figures 5.19 and 5.20 may be striking, Spurzheim's broad claims were based on speculation and scattered brain injury findings, whereas figure 5.20 is the result of a detailed analysis of activity in well-controlled tasks. As a result, the amount of reliable information is much higher in figure 5.20 than in figure 5.19.

Figure 5.19 Faculties of social functioning.
According to some authors, localisation based on brain imaging is nothing more than an improved version of phrenology, without real impact on our insight in underlying mechanisms. They claim the information provided by cognitive neuroscience comes closer to that provided by traditional neuropsychology than that provided by cognitive neuropsychology. This figure shows the parts of the brain that were involved in social cognition according to Spurzheim (1834). Compare this with the parts of the brain involved in social cognition according to the latest brain imaging results.

Source: Gross (1998) *Brain, vision, memory: Tales in the history of neuroscience.* Figure from p. 54. Copyright © Massachussets Institute of Technology, by permission of the MIT press.

Second, the low resolution of current methods does indeed constrain the type of questions that can be answered. However, this is a practical limitation, which is likely to improve in the future, rather than a theoretical impediment. In addition, some of the limitations are being circumvented by combining methods. For instance, the low temporal resolution of fMRI can be addressed by adding EEG measurements to the study. The latter allow time measurement with an accuracy of 1 ms (one-thousandth of a second).

Third, localisation of the brain activity while a person is performing a task does provide information about the processes involved. For instance, in Chapter 6 we will see that the brain regions normally involved in moving the feet are activated when participants see a picture of a person kicking something or are asked to read the word 'kick'. This strongly suggests that activation of movement commands is part of the understanding of actions and words referring to actions. This information (and the ensuing changes in theories of how people understand concepts) would not have been there without brain imaging.

Finally, another important understanding that has arisen from brain imaging studies, is the finding that, although the brain is compartmentalised into regions with specialised functions (as defended by the localisers), even performance of the simplest tasks requires the interaction of several areas distributed over distant parts of the brain (see figures 6.3 and 6.5 for examples). This too was not realised before the start of cognitive

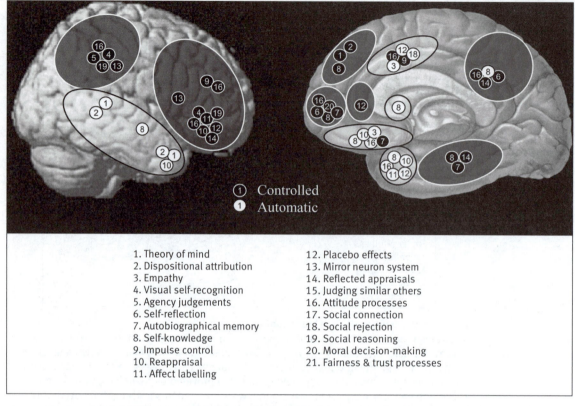

Figure 5.20 Localisation of social cognition functions on the basis of brain imaging studies.
For instance, the regions numbered 6 are the ones that are particularly active when people reflect about themselves. Kihlstrom (2007) wondered how much more informative this picture is than Spurzheim's picture shown in figure 5.19.

Source: Lieberman (2007). Reproduced with permission.

neuroscience. In addition, although brain areas are specialised, they are involved in several tasks with different stimuli. For instance, it has been found that Broca's area is involved not only in speech production but also in language understanding and music perception, possibly because it plays a role in grammar processing.

The overlap of functions in brain areas and the cooperation of different, distant parts of the brain were not recognised in the traditional localisation theories or indeed in the early days of cognitive neuroscience. These are genuine insights resulting from brain imaging studies. It might even be argued that the discussion about equipotentiality vs. localisation has been settled to a large extent by these two findings. Different parts of the brain are indeed specialised in the processing of different types of information, but task performance requires innumerable interactions between various areas all over the cerebral hemispheres. There is also evidence that the extent of a brain region is not fixed but depends on practice. For instance, it has been found that music-related brain areas are substantially more developed in professional musicians than in control people (Peretz and Zatorre 2005).

Interim summary

Advances in studies of the working brain

- Single-cell recording allows researchers to find out to which type of information individual neurons respond; it is an invasive technique, however.

- EEG-recordings allow researchers to pick up the summed electrical activity of groups of cells non-invasively. They allow researchers to detect cases of epilepsy and to discover different stages in sleep.

- ERP-studies are based on EEG-recordings and allow researchers to find out how the brain response changes as a function of different types of stimuli.

- MEG-scanning also measures the electrical activity of groups of neurons and allows researchers to add localisation to the ERP-studies.

- PET-scanning allows researchers to see which brain areas require extra blood during the performance of tasks by tracing a radioactive substance injected into the blood.

- fMRI-scanning also allows researchers to localise brain activity on the basis of oxygen use. Produces more detailed images than PET and does not require an injection of substance into the participants.

- TMS allows researchers to interfere briefly with the activity of a small region of the grey matter and to examine the effects of this interference on the time needed to complete a particular task. Makes it possible to ascertain that the brain region is crucial for performance.

- The above techniques have allowed researchers to measure brain activity while participants are performing mental tasks. This created a new research field, known as cognitive neuroscience.

- Not everyone is convinced that brain imaging techniques allow researchers to examine the detailed cognitive processes involved in correct task performance.

- On the other hand, brain imaging findings have resulted in several innovative insights. For instance, it has become clear that although brain areas are specialised in different functions, correct task performance always requires the collaboration of several areas often over large distances. For that reason, brain areas are usually involved in more than one task (e.g. the brain tissue involved in controlling body movements is also involved in understanding the words referring to those movements).

5.6   Focus on: Can delusions be investigated with the cognitive neuropsychological approach?

Cognitive neuropsychiatry as a new research area

In the previous sections we saw how neuropsychology and neuroscience shifted from the question 'where in the brain do different processes take place' to the question 'how does brain functioning constrain cognitive theories of information processing'.

To stress the change of focus, the new disciplines called themselves *cognitive* neuro-psychology and *cognitive* neuroscience.

At the end of the twentieth century a group of researchers argued that a similar approach could be used in the study of faulty thinking in mental disorders, in particular with respect to delusions. Delusions are strong erroneous beliefs that are not supported by empirical evidence. They are present in approximately 75 per cent of people diagnosed with schizophrenia, but also happen sometimes after brain injury and even seem to be experienced by some 5–10 per cent of the general population at least once in their life. For instance, in a large-scale longitudinal study over two years, Hanssen *et al.* (2005) reported that 2 per cent of their interviewees in the general population experienced one or more delusions.

The most common delusions in acutely hospitalised psychiatric patients are (Appelbaum *et al.* 1999):

- persecutory (e.g. someone is trying to harm me) 51 per cent,
- body/mind control (e.g. my thoughts are controlled by an alien) 27 per cent,
- grandiose (e.g. I have achieved something big but nobody realises it) 23 per cent,
- religious (e.g. I am in direct contact with an important religious figure) 18 per cent.

The new subfield that tries to understand delusions (and other consequences of mental disorders) in terms of breakdowns within the cognitive models of normal psychological functioning is called **cognitive neuropsychiatry**. We illustrate the approach with the Capgras delusion.

cognitive neuropsychiatry

subfield that tries to understand consequences of mental disorders in terms of breakdowns in the cognitive models of normal psychological functioning

The case study of Joseph Capgras

On a summer day in 1918, Mme. M. went to a Parisian police station to alert the authorities that her children had been imprisoned by a gang. She urgently asked the police officers to help her. Upon further questioning she added that in several other places in Paris people had been kidnapped as well and were kept in underground prisons. It soon turned out that Mme. M. had a long history of mental problems. In 1906, after the death of her twins, she had delusions of grandeur, thinking she was the illegitimate daughter of an extremely wealthy man from South America. In 1914, she suddenly stopped recognising her daughter and was convinced that the child had been replaced by a double. She also thought that her husband in reality might be a look-alike.

Instead of being helped to free her children, Mme. M. was brought to a psychiatric emergency clinic and from there to a psychiatric institute. She was taken into care by a psychiatrist, called Joseph Capgras (1873–1950). He was a famous French psychiatrist, specialising in delusions. So, none of the beliefs of grandeur and persecution really surprised him (as indicated above, they are quite common among psychotic patients). However, he was struck by the strength of this woman's conviction that her child and her husband had been replaced by imposters. She still recognised them, but they did not feel 'real' to her. They had lost all their warmth and familiarity, hence her conviction that they were look-alikes and that her real relatives had been kidnapped (and maybe killed). In 1923 Capgras wrote an article on this delusion, together with his collaborator Reboul-Lachaud.

A Freudian interpretation of the delusion

The following year Capgras published two more papers on the case. However, by this time he had retracted his original interpretation that the delusion was the result of a discrepancy between rationally recognising the family member and no longer feeling any sense of familiarity. Instead, he advanced a psychoanalytic explanation in line with the growing dominance of Freudian thinking in (French) psychiatry. Capgras now proposed that the source of the delusion was an incestuous desire for the father. This led to ambivalence in the feelings for other relatives, resulting in a mixture of love and hate. If the conflict escalated too much, it was 'solved' by making a dissociation between the real, beloved person, who was absent, and the look-alike that could be hated.

Arguably, in his revision Capgras was influenced by the similarity of Mme. M. with the Paul Schreber case, which Freud analysed in 1911. Paul Schreber had been a judge in Dresden, who in his autobiography described his descent into paranoia and wrote how he was surrounded by '*flüchtig hingemachte Männer*' (evanescent, makeshift men). On the basis of Schreber's writings, Freud linked the paranoia to anxieties surrounding homosexuality and questions of paternity, caused by a 'father complex'. Capgras may have seen an analogy between the evanescent men in Schreber's world and the imposters of Mme. M., from which he deduced that Mme. M.'s delusion could be attributed to a 'father complex' as well.

It soon turned out that the delusion described by Capgras was not a unique case (although rather rare) and the term *Capgras delusion* became used to refer to the condition, together with Capgras's revised Freudian interpretation. The interpretation seemed to make sense, because patients only complained about family members being replaced by doubles.

The cognitive neuropsychiatry alternative

Cognitive neuropsychiatrists got interested in the Capgras delusion when it became clear that the delusion sometimes started after a brain injury. Ellis and Lewis, for instance, described the following case:

> A recent well-publicized UK court case of Capgras delusion involved a teacher named A.D. who, following a car crash, developed the belief that his wife had died in the incident and that the woman living with him was an impostor, someone with whom he is now uncomfortable. He still insists that his real wife died in the accident and he successfully sued the driver of the other vehicle for the distress caused. In court a consultant psychiatrist explained that Mr D. was suffering from Capgras delusion.
>
> *(Ellis and Lewis 2001, p. 149)*

Apart from the Capgras delusion, the man did not seem to have other symptoms of an underlying Freudian conflict.

The Capgras delusion further attracted interest because cognitive models of face processing had pointed to the conclusion that face recognition involved two different routes. This conclusion was based on neuropsychological research of prosopagnosia (see above). Bauer (1984) showed pictures of famous people and family members to a 39-year-old male college graduate who had been involved in a serious motorcycle accident, leaving him unable to recognise faces, including his own. On each trial of Bauer's experiment, a picture was shown and five names were read to the patient. The patient had to indicate which of the names represented the picture. At the same time, the skin conductance was measured. This is a variable that is influenced by the autonomous (i.e. involuntary) nervous system and that in people without face processing difficulties shows an increased activity when a familiar person is encountered.

As expected, the patient was unable to match the names to the faces. However, on many trials the skin conductance response increased when in the series of names the correct name was mentioned. So, it seemed as if the patient on an unconscious, emotion-related level *did* recognise the face. Bauer's finding was subsequently repeated in several other experiments: individuals with prosopagnosia do not recognise faces consciously, but show an unconscious emotional reaction when they are confronted with a familiar face.

Relating the prosopagnosia findings to the Capgras delusion, Ellis and Young (1990) put forward the hypothesis that what might be happening in the Capgras delusion is that the unconscious, emotion-based, face processing route has been severed. Such a disconnection would result in the patients still recognising the person at a conscious, rational level but failing to experience the emotional response associated with the person (figure 5.21). To test the hypothesis, Ellis *et al.* (1997) measured the skin conductance of five patients with Capgras delusion and five control patients to known and unknown faces. As expected, the control patients showed enhanced skin conductance responses when a known face was presented than when an unknown face was presented, but the Capgras patients did not, giving credence to the hypothesis.

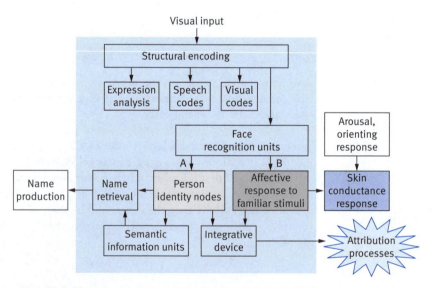

Figure 5.21 A cognitive model to explain face recognition and the occurrence of prosopagnosia and Capgras delusion.
There are two routes in which faces are recognised: one leads to the conscious recognition of the person (via a person identity node) and one leads to an unconscious emotional response (an affective response). A disruption in the first route (A) leads to prosopagnosia; a disruption in the second route (B) leads to a Capgras delusion.

Source: Based on Ellis and Lewis (2001). Reproduced with permission.

What do you think?

Have cognitive psychiatrists been too fast trying to reject the Freudian interpretation of the Capgras delusion? What evidence would you use to support your claim?

The research on the Capgras delusion is an example of the growing interactions between cognitive psychology and psychiatry. Just as in cognitive neuropsychology and cognitive neuroscience, researchers are seeing merit in combining psychological models of information processing with biological processes (for more examples, see Coltheart 2007; Halligan and Marshall 1996). This is a theme to which we will return in Chapter 11.

Interim summary

Cognitive neuropsychiatry

■ Cognitive neuropsychiatry states that symptoms of mental disorders (such as delusions) can be understood as the result of errors in the cognitive information-processing model that accounts for normal psychological functioning.

■ The Capgras delusion refers to a situation in which a person still recognises close relatives, but is convinced that these have been replaced by look-alikes.

■ The Freudian interpretation of the delusion refers to conflicting feelings towards the relatives, which result in a dissociation between the absent loved persons and the present hated look-alikes.

■ Cognitive neuropsychiatry argues that the condition results from blocked information transfer in an unconscious, emotion-related processing route that under normal circumstances elicits an emotional response each time we encounter a familiar person. As a result, the relatives feel strange, even though we recognise them.

Recommended literature

Most handbooks of neuropsychology contain a chapter on the history of the discipline. In addition, an increasing number of the original publications are becoming available on the internet. A further interesting compilation of studies is Code, C., Wallesch, C.W., Joanette, Y. and Lecours, A.R. (eds) (1996) *Classic cases in neuropsychology* (Hove, England: Psychology Press). Two interesting books on the history of neurophysiology are Gross, C.G. (1998) *Brain, vision, memory: Tales in the history of neuroscience* (Cambridge, MA: The MIT Press) and Clarke, E. and Jacyna, L.S. (1987) *Nineteenth-century origins of neuroscientific concepts* (Berkeley: University of California Press). Good books about cognitive neuroscience are Gazzaniga, M.S. (2006) *Cognitive neuroscience: The biology of the mind.* (London: W.W. Norton & Co.) and Ward, J. (2006) *The student's guide to cognitive neuroscience* (Hove, England: Psychology Press).

References

Andrewes, D.G. (2002) *Neuropsychology: From theory to practice*. Hove: Psychology Press.

Appelbaum, P.S., Robbins, P.C. and Roth, L.H. (1999) 'Dimensional approach to delusions: Comparisons across types and diagnoses', *American Journal of Psychiatry*, **156**: 1938–1943.

Bauer, R.M. (1984) 'Autonomic recognition of names and faces in prosopagnosia: A neuropsychological application of the guilty knowledge test', *Neuropsychologia*, **22**: 457–69.

Berger, H. (1969) 'Hans Berger on the electroencephalogram of man: The fourteen original reports on the human electroencephalogram', *EEG & Clinical Neurophysiology*, Supp. 28.

Breasted, J.H. (1930) *The Edwin Smith surgical papyrus*. Chicago: University of Chicago Press (2 vols).

Brysbaert, M. (2006) *Psychologie*, Belgium: Academia Press.

Capgras, J. and Reboul-Lachaux, J. (1923) 'L'Illusion des "sosies" dans un délire systématisé chronique', *Bulletin de la Société de Médecine Mentale*, **11**: 6–16. Translated into English in Ellis, H.D., Whitley, J. and Luauté, J.-P. (1994) 'Delusional misidentification. The three original papers on the Capgras, Frégoli and intermetamorphosis delusions', *History of Psychiatry*, **5**: 117–46. If you read Dutch, also available in Draaisma, D. (2006) *Ontregelde geesten*. Groningen: Historische Uitgeverij.

Changeux, J.P. (1997) *Neuronal man: The biology of mind*, translated by Laurence Garey. Princeton, NJ: Princeton University Press.

Clarke, E. and Jacyna, L.S. (1987) *Nineteenth-century origins of neuroscientific concepts*. Berkeley: University of California Press.

Coltheart, M. (2004) 'Are there lexicons?' *Quarterly Journal of Experimental Psychology*, **57A**: 1153–71.

Coltheart, M. (2006) 'What has functional neuroimaging told us about the mind (so far)?', *Cortex*, **42**: 323–31.

Coltheart, M. (2007) 'The 33rd Sir Frederick Bartlett Lecture: Cognitive neuropsychiatry and delusional belief', *Quarterly Journal of Experimental Psychology*, **60**: 1041–62.

Coltheart, M., Patterson, K. and Marshall, J.C. (eds.) (1980) *Deep dyslexia*. London: Routledge & Kegan Paul.

Dewey, J. (1896) 'The reflex are concept in psychology', *Psychological Review*, **3**: 357–70. Retrieved on 12 November 2007 from http://psychclassics.yorku.ca

Ellis, H.D. and Florence, M. (1990) 'Bodamer's (1947) paper on prosopagnosia', *Cognitive Neuropsychology*, **7**: 81–105.

Ellis, H.D. and Lewis, M.B. (2001) 'Capgras delusion: A window on face recognition', *Trends in Cognitive Sciences*, **5**: 149–56.

Ellis, H.D. and Young, A.W. (1990) 'Accounting for delusional misidentifications', *British Journal of Psychology*, **157**: 239–48.

Ellis, H.D., Young, A.W., Quayle, A.H. and de Pauw, K.W. (1997) 'Reduced autonomic responses to faces in Capgras delusion', *Proceedings of the Royal Society London: Biological Sciences*, **264**: 1085–92.

Geschwind, N. (1972) 'Language and the brain', *Scientific American*, **226**, 4: 76–83.

Goodglass, H. (1983) 'Linguistic aspects of aphasia', *Trends in Neuroscience*, June: 241–3.

Goodglass, H. and Kaplan, E. (1983) *The assessment of aphasia and related disorders*. Philadelphia: Lea & Febiger.

Gross, C.G. (1998) *Brain, Vision, Memory: Tales in the history of neuroscience*. Cambridge, MA: The MIT Press.

Halligan, P.W. and Marshall, J.C. (1996) *Method in madness: Case studies in cognitive neuropsychiatry*. Hove: Psychology Press.

Hanssen, M., Bak, M., Bijl, R., Vollebergh, W. and van Os, J. (2005) 'The incidence and outcome of subclinical psychotic experiences in the general population', *British Journal of Clinical Psychology*, **44**: 181–91.

Helm-Estabrooks, N., Fitzpatrick, P.M. and Barresi, B. (1981) 'Response of an agrammatic patient to a syntax stimulation program for aphasia', *Journal of Hearing and Speech Disorders,* **46:** 422–7.

Holmes, G.M. (1918) 'Disturbance of vision by cerebral lesions', *British Journal of Ophthalmology,* **2:** 353–84.

Hunter, Z.R., Brysbaert, M. and Knecht, S. (2007) 'Foveal word reading requires interhemispheric communication', *Journal of Cognitive Neuroscience,* **19:** 1373–87.

James, W. (1890) *The principles of psychology,* New York: Henry Holt.

Kihlstrom, J.F. (2007) *Social neuroscience: The footprints of Phineas Gage.* Retrieved on 11 November, 2007 from http://socrates.berkeley.edu/~kihlstrm/SocialNeuroscience07.htm.

Lieberman, M.D. (2007) 'Social cognitive neuroscience: A review of the core processes', *Annual Review of Psychology,* **58:** 259–89.

Mahajan, S.K., Machhan, P.C., Sood, B.R., Kuman, S., Sharma, D.D., Mokta, J. and Pal, L.S. (2004) 'Neurocysticercosis presenting with psychosis', *Journal of the Association of Physicians in India,* **52:** 663–66.

Morton, J. and Patterson, K. (1980) 'A new attempt at an interpretation, or, an attempt at a new interpretation.' In M. Coltheart *et al.* (eds.), *Deep dyslexia.* London: Routledge & Kegan Paul.

Müller, J.P. (1838) *Elements of physiology* (Translated by W. Baly). London.

Peretz, I. and Zatorre, R.J. (2005) 'Brain organization for music processing', *Annual Review of Psychology,* **56:** 89–114.

Prins, R. and Bastiaanse, R. (2006) 'The early history of aphasiology: From the Egyptian surgeons (c. 1700 BC) to Broca (1861)', *Aphasiology,* **20:** 762–91.

Shallice, T. (1988) *From neuropsychology to mental structure.* Cambridge: Cambridge University Press.

Shepherd, G.M. (1991) *Foundations of the neuron doctrine.* New York: Oxford University Press.

Spurzheim, J.G. (1834) *Phrenology of the doctrine of the mental phenomenon* (3rd edn). Boston: Marsh, Caper and Lyon.

Thomas, R.K. (2007) 'Recurring errors among recent history of psychology textbooks', *American Journal of Psychology,* **120:** 477–95.

Thomson, J.A. (1922) *The outline of science: A plain story simply told.* New York: G.P. Putnam's Sons.

Tizard, B. (1959) 'Theories of brain localization from Flourens to Lashley', *Medical History,* **3:** 132–45.

Uttal, W.R. (2001) *The new phrenology: The limits of localizing cognitive processes.* Cambridge, MA: MIT Press.

06 The mind–brain problem, consciousness and free will

This chapter will cover

Questions to consider

Historical issues addressed in this chapter

■ When did dualism, materialism and functionalism (in philosophy) start? Which developments were at their origin?
■ When did scholars realise that not all thought processes were conscious?

Conceptual issues addressed in this chapter

■ How does the mind relate to the brain?
■ Why did the psychologists in the first half of the twentieth century struggle with dualism?
■ Do humans have free will?
■ Is it possible that humans exist only to continue the life of their genes?
■ Why was the invention of the computer important for the mind–brain problem?
■ Can you copy the mind of a person? Can you transport it by means of teleportation?
■ In what respects does information processing in the human brain differ from information processing in a computer?
■ What is the function of consciousness? When do we have a conscious experience?
■ When can we rely on our intuitions?

Introduction

The Astonishing Hypothesis is that 'You,' your joys and your sorrows, your memories and your ambitions, your sense of personal identity and free will, are in fact no more than the behavior of a vast assembly of nerve cells and their associated molecules. As Lewis Carroll's Alice might have phrased it: 'You're nothing but a pack of neurons.'

(Crick 1995, p. 3)

The citation that opens the present chapter comes from a book by the British scientist and co-discoverer of the DNA structure, Francis Crick (1916–2004). In that book Crick argued that the spectacular advance of modern science made the concepts of the soul and consciousness redundant. In his view, we should no longer be satisfied with the religious guesses of yesterday, however charming they may be.

The present chapter also deals with the question how we can reconcile the biological workings of the brain with the feeling we all have of being more than a mere pack of nerve cells. Throughout history, humans have been impressed by their ability to reflect about themselves and the world around them. Asked what they consider to be the essence of their life, most people refer to their self, the feeling they have of being an individual with private experiences, feelings and beliefs, who interacts in a coherent and purposeful way with the environment. The existence of such a feeling begs the question where the self comes from. What gives us the power to experience ourselves as consistent entities with goals and values? Even stronger, what gives us the power to think, to have a mind? This is arguably the biggest conceptual issue in psychology. How do the brain and the mind relate to each other? This issue is known as the mind–brain problem.

Three different views of the interaction between mind and brain will be discussed in the sections below. The first is the oldest and intuitively the most appealing. It says that the mind (or the soul) is something independent of the body. This view is called dualism. The second approach states that the mind is nothing but a by-product of the biological processes taking place in a particular brain. This view is called materialism. Finally, the third approach says that the mind is indeed realised in a brain, but that it could be copied to any other brain, just like information on a computer can be copied to other machines. This is the functionalist view.

After the discussion of the three views, we will continue with a review of present-day research about consciousness and end by looking at the evidence suggesting that unconscious processing is the automatic pilot that guides us through life and that may help us to reach better decisions.

As with all the topics in this book, we can only paint the broad brushstrokes of what are much richer themes with heated discussions (albeit more among philosophers of the mind than among psychologists). We have made a selection of the big historical developments and the contemporary ideas that have particular appeal to psychologists, accepting that for many of the players involved our discussion may do injustice to the richness of their proposals.

self

the feeling of being an individual with private experiences, feelings and beliefs, who interacts in a coherent and purposeful way with the environment

mind–brain problem

issue of how the mind is related to the brain; three main views: dualism, materialism and functionalism

Interim summary

- The mind–brain problem refers to the relationship between the mind and brain.

- Three main approaches are discussed in this chapter:
  - dualism: mind and brain are two independent entities,
  - materialism: the mind is a by-product of the biological workings of the brain,
  - functionalism: the mind is realised in the brain, but the information can be copied to another machine with the same structure.

What do you think?

Before you continue reading it may be good to ask yourself what your opinion of the mind–brain problem is. Which approach appeals most to you? Why? Is this the first time you have thought about this question?

6.1   Dualism: The mind is independent of the brain

---

mind

aggregate of faculties humans (and animals) have to perceive, feel, think, remember and want

When scholars refer to the **mind**, they mean the faculties humans (and animals) have to perceive, feel, think, remember and want. The oldest and intuitively most appealing view of the mind is that it is something completely different from the body (in particular the brain). The mind and the body are two different realms. This view is known as **dualism**.

dualism

view about the relationship between the mind and brain that considers them as two different realms; in general the mind is seen as immaterial and in control of human behaviour (free will)

Dualism in religion and traditional philosophy

Religion

Dualism is central to religions. They are grounded in the belief that people possess a divine soul, which was created by God, temporarily lives in the body, and leaves the corpse upon its death. The soul is what gives people their purpose and values in life. It usually aims for the good, but can be tempted and seduced by evil forces. This belief gave rise to the so-called demonologist view of psychopathology, the conviction that mental disorders are due to possession by bad spirits. Indeed for a long time it seemed more acceptable that mental disorders were due to evil ghosts than to physiological malfunctions.

Plato and Descartes

Dualism was also central in the philosophies of Plato and Descartes. Plato (Chapter 1) maintained that the soul existed before, and survived the body. Human souls were made of the leftovers of the soul of the cosmos and travelled between their companion stars and the human bodies they temporarily inhabited. Because human souls were part of the cosmos-soul, they had knowledge of the perfect realm that contained the eternal, ideal forms of which the worldly objects were but imperfect reflections filled with error. By focusing on the innate knowledge of their immortal soul, humans could get access to the true ideas.

A very similar view was defended by Descartes who was strongly influenced by Plato and the teachings of the Roman Catholic Church. According to Descartes, humans were composed of a divine soul in a sophisticated body (sometimes referred to as 'the ghost in the machine'). The soul was immaterial and formed the thinking part of the person. Just like Plato, Descartes believed that the soul brought divine information to humans and, therefore, that people had innate knowledge, which they could recover through deductive reasoning. As we saw in Chapter 2, the conjecture that people have innate skills and abilities is known as nativism.

Because Descartes was the first modern philosopher to address the relationship between the body and the mind and because he strongly defended the dualist view, current-day philosophers use the term Cartesian dualism to refer to theories in which the mind is seen as radically different from the body and as independent of the biological processes in the brain.

What do you think?

Do you think that humans are born with some forms of innate knowledge? And is heavenly or divine information the only possible source of such knowledge?

Dualism in early psychology and lay thinking

Dualism in early psychology

For reasons that will be outlined below, since the second half of the nineteenth century a growing number of scientists started to question the dualistic view. They felt increasingly uncomfortable with the emphasis religions placed on the immortality of the soul, the connection of the soul to a divine entity and its independence of the body. At the same time, they were unwilling to reduce the human mind to nothing but brain tissue, so that in practice most defended some kind of implicit dualistic view. Lyons (2001) gives several examples of such ambivalence among early psychologists, as can be seen in the following citation from a much used textbook, *A Manual of Psychology*, authored by G.F. Stout (1924):

> It thus appears that even if the being which is a mind is also supposed to be a body, yet the mental aspect of its nature is so distinct from its bodily aspect that each requires separate and independent investigation. Knowledge concerning the mind does not of itself include or conduct to knowledge concerning the body as such. Knowledge concerning the body does not of itself involve or conduct to knowledge concerning the mind as such. Hence Physiology and Psychology are radically distinct sciences, each dealing with its own subject matter.
>
> *(Stout (1924) as cited in Lyons (2001) p. 18)*

The distinction between the body and the mind was additionally attractive to early psychologists because it provided them with their own study area that could not be invaded and taken over by brain scientists. It also resulted in the development of research methods that differed from those of the neurophysiologists.

Dualism in spontaneous thinking

The Australian philosopher David Chalmers (1996, p. 125) argues that dualism nowadays still is the fundamental attitude people have about the relationship between the mind and the brain. Very few people spontaneously say that the mind is a biological brain process, even though they readily accept that such processes form the basis of mental operations. They feel more comfortable with statements like: 'The mind arises from the brain', showing that deep down the mind is experienced as something different from the brain. There is a gap between the mind and the body. What could be the origin of this feeling?

What do you think?

Chalmers claims that dualism is the fundamental attitude people have about the relationship between the mind and the brain. Does this agree with your own feelings? Does your intuition tell you that your thinking forms a separate reality from your body?

Dualism puts consciousness at the centre of human functioning and gives humans free will

Dualism has an intuitive appeal because it puts conscious information processing at the centre of our functioning and it gives us the feeling of being in control of our actions.

In dualist models consciousness is the core of human existence

Dualism not only makes a clear distinction between the mind (soul) and the brain, in general it also gives priority to the mind. Our conscious, deliberate thinking is the centre of our existence and controls our actions. Because of this conscious control, we experience ourselves and the world around us as rich and coherent. We see ourselves as individuals with particular appearances and traits, who respond in a reasonably consistent way, are guided by goals and values, and have a strong feeling of continuity. Similarly, our experience of the world around us is rich, meaningful and much more than simply knowing what is there and what it is for. Our private experiences are so rich that we often feel we cannot fully describe them to someone else (see the notion of qualia below).

consciousness

word referring to the private, first-person experiences an individual lives through; contains all the mental states a person is aware of; part of the mind that can be examined with introspection

Our self-perception and the explicit experiences we have of the world around us are part of what is usually referred to as our **consciousness**, a word that has different meanings within different theories but that in general refers to the private, first-person experiences we live through (our 'I'). It contains all the mental states and psychological functions we are aware of, such as thoughts, beliefs, desires, feelings and intentions. It is the part of the mind that psychologists try to examine with introspection (Chapter 3).

Dualism puts consciousness at the centre of the person, because the mind (or the soul) is the acting unit and the mind coincides with consciousness. The actions of an individual are guided by the private, first-person experience of that individual.

Dualism gives humans free will

Because in the dualist view consciousness is the centre of the mind, nothing happens unless it is licensed by the mind. This puts humans in full control over their actions

free will

situation in which individuals can choose their course of action from a number of alternatives; choice is the outcome of a rational deliberation

and decisions. They can choose their course of action from a number of alternatives, a phenomenon that is referred to as free will. Individuals with free will are motivated by intentions they set themselves. They try to achieve goals and they are guided by reason. Having free will also means that the individuals are responsible for their actions: they could have chosen to behave otherwise.

Three conditions must be met before an action can be ascribed to free will (e.g. Walter, 2001):

1. The agent must have been able to do otherwise. Free will only exists when there is a choice.

2. The act must originate in the agent, not in some external force.

3. The act must be the outcome of rational deliberation (acts that are erratic and unpredictable are not seen as free).

What do you think?

Can you think of an instance in which you decided to do something different from everyone else? And can you think of an instance in which you did something without really wanting to do it? How do these relate to your free will?

Problems with dualism

Although dualism strongly agrees with human intuitions (and we mostly rely on it in our everyday social functioning), it has come under severe attack since the second half of the nineteenth century, to such an extent that it is no longer a viable approach within the philosophy of mind. It also has been banned from models of cognitive functioning (although Chalmers (1996) argues that this is usually done by sweeping the mind–brain problem under the rug rather than by explicitly denying dualism). Several factors contributed to the downfall of dualism. We discuss the most important.

The interaction problem

A first problem for dualism was how to explain the mechanisms by which an independent mind (or soul) can influence the body. This 'interaction problem' already arose in Descartes' day, when the 25-year-old Princess Elizabeth of Bohemia sent Descartes the following question: 'How can the soul of man, being only a thinking substance, determine his bodily spirits to perform voluntary actions?' (Lyons 2001, p. 25). Because the soul cannot be perceived, Descartes thought of it as an immaterial substance that did not occupy volume in the material world. The soul had no length, no width, no depth. How, then, could such an immaterial soul steer the human body into action? Similarly, how can a non-physical, spiritual mind control physical brain processes? Descartes and the dualists after him have never found a satisfactory answer to this problem.

The existence of unconscious control processes

A second factor that was difficult to account for in dualism was the finding that many mental functions happened outside consciousness. In Chapter 5, we discussed how neurophysiologists discovered that reflexes and bodily functions were controlled by the spinal cord and the subcortical structures, not by the cerebral hemispheres. A lot seemed to be happening in a person without conscious control. In addition, it was not difficult to find other examples of unconscious functioning. For instance, what happened during sleep, when organisms arguably 'lost' their consciousness? And what happened under hypnosis (a phenomenon popularised in the eighteenth century by the Austrian physician Franz Anton Mesmer)? And what about the memories a person was not thinking of, but that could easily be brought into consciousness?

The understanding that a large part of mental life may be unconscious is usually credited to Sigmund Freud. Freud indeed did much to raise awareness of this type of processing (see Chapter 3). However, already well before Freud, philosophers and scientists were considering the existence of unconscious mental processes. For instance, this is what was written about the Scottish philosopher William Hamilton in 1858:

> Sir William Hamilton . . . thinks that in order to explain certain phenomena of memory, and of association of ideas, it is necessary, as far as we are able, to take account of the unconscious modifications of the mind. It is a curious speculation, and as it is rather novel in our country, though we are assured, familiar to the Germans, we shall take a glance at it.
>   . . . the mind 'contains certain systems of knowledge, or certain habits of action which it is wholly unconscious of possessing in its ordinary state, but which are revealed to consciousness in certain extraordinary exaltations of its powers.' For evidence of this, we are referred to the class of cases . . . where knowledge is revived in fever, delirium or somnambulism, which apparently had become extinct.
> (Blackwood's Edinburgh Magazine, *October 1858, pp. 506–7; retrieved on 3 November 2007, from http://www.google.co.uk/books).*

Needless to say, the more mental processes seemed to escape conscious control, the less central the position of consciousness in human functioning became.

The disappearance of mystery forces in the scientific world

Another reason why dualism lost its appeal was that it needed the existence of an immaterial, mysterious, animistic 'soul'. Scientists had bad experiences with such entities, which to them looked more like relics from the pre-scientific world with its animistic explanations than building blocks of a sound scientific theory. There were two prime examples of such mysterious 'substances' that had been postulated in science before but which in the end turned out to be materialistic phenomena that could be measured and manipulated by the scientists.

The first substance was phlogiston. This had been invoked in the seventeenth century to explain why some materials easily caught fire (wood, certain types of gas), whereas others did not catch fire at all (stone, water). The idea was that flammable materials contained a substance, called phlogiston, which was released during burning.

phlogiston

substance that was believed to make materials flammable before the chemical processes of combustion were understood

Materials without the substance were not combustible. Experimentation, however, called the phlogiston theory into question. For instance, it was found that materials sometimes weighed more after being burned than before. This was difficult to reconcile with the idea that phlogiston provided the fuel for the flames. It was also found that fire depended on the availability of oxygen. These findings gradually brought researchers to the insight that fire and heat were by-products of particular chemical changes involving the elements carbon, oxygen, hydrogen and nitrogen (although a bit of sulphur helps as well). The process needed a certain temperature (flash point) to get going, but afterwards it was self-perpetuating as long as the base elements were present.

Once the combustion processes were known, the phenomenon of fire was understood and could be controlled. It became possible to determine how flammable new chemical compounds would be. It was even possible to develop fire-repellents, materials that were impenetrable to flames (and did not weigh too much). Researchers also started to realise that the processes involved in combustion showed similarities to what happened in respiration. As a result, fire lost its mystery.

vital force

animistic substance thought to be present in living matter before the chemical and biological differences between living and non-living matter were understood

The second mystery substance that in the end turned out not to exist, was the **vital force**. This force had been postulated to explain why some organisms were living and others not. Living matter was supposed to have a 'vital force', which non-living matter lacked. Like many other animistic explanations, the vital force stayed nearly unquestioned until the seventeenth century. A defining moment in its demise was the realisation that it was possible to make living (organic) matter out of non-living (inorganic) components. This finding was reported in 1828 by the German chemist Friedrich Wöhler, who synthesised urea (an organic substance found in urine) from the inorganic compounds potassium cyanate and ammonium sulphate. Suddenly it became clear that the distinction between organic and inorganic matter was not as sharp as had always been assumed. The main difference turned out to be the central role of the chemical element carbon in organic material.

Wöhler's finding was but the first in a long series of discoveries that disentangled the essence of living matter. Another important insight was that all living things were composed of cells that grew out of previous cells. This discovery was made possible by the invention and optimisation of the microscope. Once the cell was isolated as the basic unit, researchers started to unravel the processes taking place in it. Among other things, they discovered that the instructions to build the cell were stored in the DNA of the cell nucleus and that DNA consisted of a sequence of four bases. Currently researchers think they are on the brink of creating a new life form by inserting a newly designed sequence of DNA bases into the nucleus of existing cells. They are adamant that the resulting organism will be a living organism, capable of reproducing itself (see the opening of Chapter 1).

Given that mysteries like phlogiston and the vital force in the end turned out to be chemical and biological processes that could be manipulated, an increasing number of scholars began to claim that something similar would happen to the mind. Once all the brain processes were understood, what humans experienced as their mind would simply turn out to be a by-product of the working brain, just like fire was a by-product of certain chemical reactions and the vital force was a consequence of a particular arrangement of molecules. At some point it would be discovered what biochemical processes were involved in the human mind and the mystery would be solved. This belief gave rise to materialism, which we discuss in the next section.

Interim summary

- The mind refers to a person's faculties to perceive, feel, think, remember and want.

- In religions the mind is often equated with an immaterial, divine soul. This is an example of dualism. A similar view was defended by Descartes and, therefore, in philosophy is often called Cartesian dualism.

- Dualism is an intuitively attractive model of the mind–brain relationship because it gives humans free will (i.e. control over their actions and decisions) and it readily accounts for the existence of consciousness in humans. The latter refers to the rich and coherent, private, first-person experience people have about themselves and the world around them.

- Dualism does have problems explaining how an immaterial mind can influence the body, and how it is possible that so much information processing in humans occurs unconsciously. It also does not agree with a scientific world view, where there is no place for mysterious and animistic substances.

6.2   Materialism: The mind is the brain

The alternative: Materialism

The idea of an independent, incorporeal mind (soul) as the core of a human being already struck British empiricists in the eighteenth and the nineteenth centuries as quite implausible, although they had to be careful not to upset the church too much. After one of them, David Hume (1711–1776), openly declared that he saw no good reason why one should believe in a soul (and in God), he was prevented from getting an academic post in the UK (Jahoda 2007, p. 29) and had to make a living as a tutor and secretary to embassies, despite the fact that his writings were (and still are) among the best of their time.

materialism

view about the relationship between the mind and brain that considers the mind as the brain in operation; predicts that the mind depends on the specific brain in which it is realised; denies the existence of free will

The idea of the mind as nothing other than a brain in operation really took off towards the end of the nineteenth century. This view is usually called materialism, although some prefer the names *physicalism* (to stress that everything is physical), *monism* (to stress the difference with dualism) or *reductionism* (because the mind is reduced to more basic biological processes). As we saw in Chapter 5, the end of the nineteenth century was the time when it was discovered that many brain processes were reflexes. It was also the time when Darwin's evolutionary theory started to have a considerable impact on philosophy and psychology (Chapters 2 and 11).

Within psychology, the rise of materialism was one of the reasons why the behaviorists wanted to get away from the study of 'consciousness' (Chapter 4). Although psychologists were still at a loss to come up with ideas about how human consciousness could be the emanation of biological processes, it was not done to keep defending the idea of a non-materialistic mind. Even Boring, who as a student of Titchener started his career studying the structure of consciousness (Chapter 3), wrote in the 1930s that:

> While there is no possibility of disproving or proving dualism, the exposition of the present book is based on the assumption that it is scientifically more useful to consider that all psychological data are of the same kind and that consciousness is a physiological event.
>
> *(Boring 1933, p. 14)*

The consequences for consciousness and free will

The replacement of dualism by materialism was not without consequences for the ideas of consciousness and free will. Whereas dualism put them at the centre of human functioning, materialism did not require either of them. Below we give examples of the most extreme positions this led to. Crick's book cited at the beginning of this chapter is another example.

Consciousness is folk psychology

folk psychology

collection of beliefs lay people have about psychological functioning; no efforts made to verify them empirically or to check them for their internal coherence

The Canadian philosopher Paul Churchland (1981) argued that consciousness as the centre of the human mind and the controller of human actions was not only an illusion but also a dangerous idea, because it gave individuals a misunderstanding of what makes them tick. For Churchland, consciousness and the associated opinions were examples of folk psychology, unsubstantiated convictions of lay people, similar to 'folk medicine' and 'folk science', which are also incoherent collections of beliefs and superstitions that are void of empirical verification. This is how Churchland introduced his view:

> Eliminative materialism is the thesis that our commonsense conception of psychological phenomena constitutes a radically false theory, a theory so fundamentally defective that both the principles and the ontology of that theory will eventually be displaced, rather than smoothly reduced, by completed neuroscience. Our mutual understanding and even our introspection may then be reconstituted within the conceptual framework of completed neuroscience, a theory we may expect to be more powerful by far than the common-sense psychology it displaces, and more substantially integrated within physical science generally.
>
> *(Churchland 1981, p. 67)*

It is not so difficult to find examples of strongly held opinions in most people's consciousness that turn out to be wrong when they are properly tested. For instance, most people are adamant that they would help other people in need and that they would never deliberately harm someone else. Darley and Latané (1968) examined the first claim and found that people quite often fail to assist others in emergency situations. One of the most counterintuitive findings was that the chances of helping someone decreased in proportion to the number of people who witnessed the situation. Apparently, when there are other people who could intervene, we feel less compelled to do it ourselves, a phenomenon the authors called the *bystander-effect*. Another finding is that people are less likely to help others who differ from them (e.g. in race, clothing, or language), as predicted by the Darwinist account that we are more likely to help someone who shares many genes with us.

Milgram (1963) examined the claim that we would not harm others. He invited ordinary participants to a laboratory where they were introduced to another person (supposedly another participant but actually a confederate of the experimenter). The other person had to learn a particular task and would be punished by electric shocks of increasing intensity each time he made an error. The shock was to be administered by the participant. The confederate (who had gone to another room and interacted with the participant via an intercom) made many mistakes and so the participant was forced to administer ever increasing shock intensities. On the control panel the induced pain and the associated risks were clearly indicated. Beforehand, psychologists and psychiatrists predicted that every participant would stop as soon as the intensity became too high. However, as is now well known, this was not what Milgram observed. Even though the experimenter did not insist too much, all participants gave much higher shock intensities than they had thought themselves capable of and 65 per cent went up to the highest level, which was clearly indicated as lethal.

The above findings agree with Churchland's (and the other materialists') claim that the conscious human mind is not the controller of human behaviour, but a delusion that can have damaging consequences.

Is there still room for free will?

If our conscious mind is not the controller of our actions, does this then also imply that we have no free will, that our actions are basically governed by our biological make-up? A view very close to this has been defended by the British biologist Richard Dawkins (1976/2006). According to Dawkins, the evolutionary theory has been mis-understood in the first century after its introduction by Darwin. Whereas everyone assumed natural selection was about the survival of individuals (in their offspring) and species, the selection actually concerns the survival of DNA-molecules. Dawkins points out that the contribution of individuals to their offspring rapidly dilutes after a few generations, making it impossible that something 'biological' of an individual is preserved. Similarly, he points out that throughout history life forms have come and gone, replaced by others that were better adapted to the (changed) circumstances. So, species do not survive either. The only things that have remained constant throughout are the genes that make up the living organisms. They are the true survivors and they have managed to mobilise a whole range of survival machines that keep them alive and enable them to get multiplied.

The overlap in genetic material among the many species on Earth is indeed remarkable. For instance, the similarity in genetic material between mice and humans is estimated to be around 85 per cent. If anything comes close to eternity, Dawkins argues, it is the genes. The present-day genes are very similar to the genes of a million years ago and in all likelihood will have a high resemblance to the genes found on earth in a million years' time. In Dawkins's view, humans are nothing more than survival machines for the genes they carry around, on equal par with mice, bacteria and plants, which are also survival machines for very similar genes. In his own words:

> We are survival machines, but 'we' does not mean just people. It embraces all animals, plants, bacteria, and viruses. The total number of survival machines on earth is very difficult to count and even the total number of species is unknown. Taking

just insects alone, the number of living species has been estimated at around three million, and the number of individual insects may be a million million million. Different sorts of survival machine appear very varied on the outside and in their internal organs. An octopus is nothing like a mouse, and both are quite different from an oak tree. Yet in their fundamental chemistry they are rather uniform, and, in particular, the replicators that they bear, the genes, are basically the same kind of molecule in all of us – from bacteria to elephants. We are all survival machines for the same kind of replicator – molecules called DNA.

(Dawkins 1976/2006, introduction of Chapter 3)

If one day humans fail, that will be bad for the genes in them, but other carriers with very similar genes will take over and continue the journey of the genes

Needless to say, a vision of humans as mere survival machines for the genes they contain is a far cry from the dualist conjecture of the conscious mind being the control centre of humans and characterised by free will. This shift of emphasis is exemplified in the terminology used to describe humans in a materialistic world. They are variously described as *survival machines*, *slaves*, *robots* or *automata*. On the other hand, close reading of the writings on materialism leaves some scope for freedom. For instance, although Dawkins sees humans as survival machines, nowhere does he state that this means humans (or other animals) have no choice at all. Although their genes make sure that they feel an urge to reproduce and to defend themselves and their next of kin in case of danger (at the expense of others), the genes do not control day-to-day life. Indeed, according to Dawkins the survival machines have been created to relieve the genes from the everyday survival struggle. A similar argument had been made several centuries before by Descartes (see Chapter 2), when he argued that God created the world as a perfect machine, so that he did not have to attend to it any more.

The same idea can also be found in Dennett (2003), who argues that humans need some form of freedom, because they have to avoid harm in their environment. This is only possible if they are able to make 'rational choices' on the basis of previous experiences.

What do you think?

How does it feel to assume that your life is nothing but a means to continue the existence of the genes that made you? How do you reconcile this with the efforts you are currently doing to become a psychologist and the joy you experience learning new things?

Problems with materialism

How can we reconcile what feels like the power and the richness of the human mind with the materialistic view?

A first limitation of materialism is that nobody has a convincing idea of how the human mind can be a by-product of the biological processes in the brain. Proponents of materialism have the firm belief that in the end the human mind will be of the same order as phlogiston and the vital force, but attempts to outline specific mechanisms thus far have been elusive.

How can different experiences be compared?

Another problem is that according to materialism experiences completely depend on the way in which they have been realised in a specific brain at a specific time. If two people experience the same event, but use different physiological changes to encode it, then strictly speaking these encodings are incompatible. The same is true when a person experiences a similar event twice. Given the complexity and the flexibility of the human brain (involving over 100 billion neurons and trillions of connections), it is next to impossible for these experiences to be encoded in exactly the same way. As a result, the encodings will be incompatible and cannot be matched to each other in a materialist model. This problem is known as the **problem of the identity theory**.

problem of the identity theory

difficulty the materialistic theory of the mind–brain relationship has to explain how two events can be experienced as the same despite the fact that their realisation in the brain differs

Materialism had a too simplistic view about information processing

Materialism was particularly strong in the middle of the twentieth century, when behaviourism and logical positivism were in their heydays (Chapters 4 and 8). Not surprisingly, the development of real robots – computers – was a major turning point for the philosophy of science as well. Suddenly, there was the opportunity to compare humans with real information-processing devices. What were the commonalities? And what were the differences? It soon turned out that the robot world was slightly different from that foreseen by the materialists. In particular it turned out that information is not as closely tied to the machine on which it is implemented as assumed by the materialists. Some rethinking was on its way, as we will see in the next section.

Interim summary

- Materialism holds that, just as previous mysterious forces were by-products of chemical and biological processes, so will the mind in the end turn out to be a by-product of the workings of the brain.

- Materialism started with the scientific revolution, but only really took off towards the end of the nineteenth century. It was one of the developments that made behaviourism possible.

- According to the strongest versions of materialism, there is no mind and no consciousness. Consciousness is an illusion, a form of folk psychology.

- Materialism also erodes the free will of humans, who are described as robots or machines.

- Materialism is more a faith than a fact, as nobody knows how the human mind could be a by-product of biological processes; in addition, some of the stronger claims by materialism have been pre-empted by developments in artificial intelligence.

6.3   Cybernetics: The new eye-opener leading to functionalism

cybernetics

the study of communication and control in machines

Because humans in the materialistic approach were increasingly compared with robots, controlled by their biology, it was normal for philosophers of mind to keep a close eye on the developments in artificial intelligence. The study of communication and control in machines is known as cybernetics. One particular finding in this discipline had far-reaching consequences for the understanding of the human mind.

Information transcends its medium

Something few researchers had foreseen at the outset of cybernetics was that the efforts to make machines intelligent would confront them with the discovery that information can be thought of as an abstract representation independent of the medium upon which it is realised. Information that is stored and processed on a computer indeed depends on the functioning of the computer, but can easily be copied to other computers (even computers of a different brand that operate differently). This contradicts the basic tenet of materialism that the information is unique to the machine (brain) upon which it has been realised.

As we saw in Chapter 4, according to cybernetics all intelligence can be represented by binary symbols (zeros and ones) upon which Boolean transformations (algorithms) operate. Every medium that is capable of doing so is a Turing machine and can process the same information. This is how Alan Turing described his insight:

> The idea of a digital computer is an old one. Charles Babbage, Lucasian Professor of Mathematics at Cambridge from 1828 to 1839, planned such a machine, called the Analytical Engine, but it was never completed . . . The fact that Babbage's Analytical Engine was to be entirely mechanical will help us to rid ourselves of a superstition. Importance is often attached to the fact that modern digital computers are electrical, and that the nervous system also is electrical. Since Babbage's machine was not electrical, and since all digital computers are in a sense equivalent, we see that this use of electricity cannot be of theoretical importance.
>
> *(Turing 1950, p. 439)*

The insight that information transcends the medium upon which it is realised was not only a big breakthrough for computer scientists (because it meant that computer programs could be run on many different types of machines without compatibility problems), it also had major implications for the way in which the mind was conceived. In Chapter 4 we saw how it led to the emergence of cognitive psychology. Here we discuss its impact on the philosophy of mind.

A solution to the identity problem

The first outcome of the understanding that information forms a device-independent realm was that it provided an answer to the problem of the identity theory. Because information in cybernetics is independent of the precise ways in which it has been realised (as long as it retains the binary symbols and the Boolean transformations), the physical changes by which computers code zeros and ones and work with them, do not really matter. Similarly, the minute physiological changes that accompany a particular human experience are not important, as long as they preserve the information code. The same information can be realised and communicated in multiple ways.

Functionalism in philosophy

functionalism

in philosophy, view about the relationship between the mind and brain that considers the mind as a separate layer of information implemented on a Turing machine; predicts that the mind can be copied onto another Turing machine

The conclusion that not the exact implementation but the functional organisation determines the nature of the information gave rise to a school in philosophy called functionalism (also sometimes called *machine functionalism*), not to be confused with functionalism in psychology (see Chapter 3). Just as functionalists in psychology around 1900 studied the functions of the mind rather than the nature of the mind, so functionalists in philosophy from the 1970s onwards examined the functions of information, rather than the precise ways in which the information was realised. To understand what hunger is, they argued, it is not necessary to know what neurophysiological mechanisms make the phenomenon possible but what it *does* to the organism.

This is how one of the most famous proponents, the American philosopher Jerry Fodor, summarised the movement:

> In the past 15 years a philosophy of mind called functionalism that is neither dualist nor materialist has emerged from philosophical reflection on developments in artificial intelligence, computational theory, linguistics, cybernetics and psychology. All these fields, which are collectively known as the cognitive sciences, have in common a certain level of abstraction and a concern with systems that process information. Functionalism, which seeks to provide a philosophical account of this level of abstraction, recognizes the possibility that systems as diverse as human beings, calculating machines and disembodied spirits could all have mental states. In the functionalist view the psychology of a system depends not on the stuff it is made of (living cells, metal or spiritual energy) but on how the stuff is put together.
>
> *(Fodor 1981, p. 124)*

Beam me up, Scotty

thought experiment

hypothetical scenario that helps with the understanding of a philosophical argument

The British philosopher Derek Parfit presented an interesting thought experiment that illustrates the difference between functionalism on the one hand and Cartesian dualism and materialism on the other. A thought experiment is a hypothetical scenario that helps us understand things. In Parfit's case, it is even a very easy thought experiment, because most of us have already seen it 'in action' in the science fiction series *Star Trek*. The actors in this series can be transported from their ship, the *Enterprise*, to nearby planets and back by teleportation, operated by the transport chief Montgomery 'Scotty' Scott (hence, the catch-phrase at the beginning of this paragraph). The teleportation works by disassembling the particles of the person's body at the place of departure and reinstating them at the location of destiny.

Now, the interesting question about such teleportation is what it would do to the mind. In Descartes' approach, we would probably have to predict that the mind would not survive such a process. Given that the mind (soul) does not come from biological brain processes and forms an independent, non-material entity, it cannot be teleported with the rest. So, teleportation would result in the reinstatement of the body without the accompanying mind. In contrast, within the functionalist framework, teleportation should work fine (as it did in the series). The mind is nothing but the information stored within the physiological network of the brain and if the latter is restored, the mind should be back as well.

In the materialist view the mind would survive the teleportation without any loss of information only when exactly the same brain is re-instantiated. Because the mind depends on the specific brain operations that give rise to it, only a reinstatement of the original particles in their initial positions would result in a flawless transportation of the mind. In contrast, within the functional view, the mind will be transported as soon as the information code can be implemented on the new brain. Because we have seen teleportation 'work' so often in *Star Trek*, we may have overlooked its implications for the mind–brain problem.

Information as the saviour of free will?

Information allows humans to rebel against the genes

Given that information in the cybernetic world can be considered as independent of the matter on which it is realised, does this mean that information escapes the control of the genes? Is it possible that humans escaped the tyranny of the biological make-up, because they assembled matter-independent information? One of the most outspoken scholars defending this position is the Canadian psychologist Keith Stanovich in his book *The robot's rebellion: Finding meaning in the age of Darwin*. This is how he phrases his view:

> People who do not like the idea of genetic determinism do in fact have an escape route. However, the escape route is not to be found in denying the known facts about the heritability of human behavioral traits, or in denying their evolutionary origins . . .
>
> The first step in conceptualizing the escape route involves focusing on the startling fact . . . that the interests of replicators [genes] and vehicles [survival machines] do not always coincide. When a conflict occurs, short-leashed response systems will prime the response that serves the genes' interests (replication) rather than those of the vehicle. However, as humans, we are concerned with our own personal interests, not those of the subpersonal organic replicators that are our genes. The presence of our analytic processing systems makes it possible to install the mental software . . . that maximizes the fulfillment of our own interests as people. This mindware ensures a mental set to give primacy to the person's fulfillment (to side in favor of the vehicle and against the replicators when their interests do not coincide). That mental set is the proclivity for rational thought.
>
> *(Stanovich 2004, p. 81–2)*

In other words, the fact that humans can encode, store, retrieve and manipulate information enables them to pursue intentions that need not coincide with those of the genes. As Stanovich sees it, the robots have a potential to rebel, if they are willing to use rational thought aimed at their own personal interests.

Memes

Not everybody is convinced, however, that information is liberating humankind. Dawkins (1976) was probably the first to spot that information shows many similarities with DNA molecules. According to him, DNA need not be the only replicator in the universe. There may be others, which also work on the principles of *variation* (the introduction of spontaneous small changes when existing material is copied), *selection* (of the changes that fit well within the environment) and *replication* (of the successful variations).

Dawkins argues that the build-up of information by humans fulfils all the principles of Darwinism. A few variations find a storage facility and a way to get copied. During the copying small changes are introduced. Many of these changes are uninteresting and fail to get reproduced. However, the few ideas that fit well in the environment copy themselves copiously and spread throughout the territory. Dawkins calls the individual ideas that make up information and try to replicate themselves, memes.

meme

information unit proposed by Dawkins that reproduces itself according to the principles of the evolutionary theory (variation, selection and replication)

Although Dawkins did not write this explicitly, the picture of memes he paints is not one of a medium that liberates people, but rather one of a medium that also uses humans as 'survival machines'. So, it might be that humans are not only 'programmed' to spread genes, but also to spread information in the form of memes. The main difference between genes and memes at present is that the former have managed to harness many organisms, so that they can survive the extinction of a species, whereas the latter (still) largely depend on the human race for their growth and distribution. Such a view would predict that memes will push for the development of forms of information multiplication other than humans (e.g. by means of computers, robots and neural networks).

? What do you think?

One prediction of the meme theory is that memes need not be helpful to get copied. Some memes may even be harmful to humankind and still get copied. An example of an unhelpful meme that gets copied endlessly is a chain letter; an example of a harmful meme is the belief that you have to kill individuals who do not share your opinions (memes). Can you think of other examples?

Telecopying

Needless to say, the above ideas find fruitful soil in science fiction (which to some extent can be compared with thought experiments, as we have seen in the example of Parfit). For instance, it is not so difficult to take the teleportation example a few steps further on the basis of what we have seen. Let us suppose teleportation does not require that the very same particles disassembled at the point of departure are reinstated at the destination location but that other particles with similar features would do as well (cybernetics allows that). Then, we would not only be able to teleport a person but also to telecopy them. And if we can do that once, then in principle we can repeat it indefinitely (as long as we have the resources to make the particles). Each copy would have the same information and thus would start off with the same mind.

Furthermore, nothing requires the tissue to be biological tissue. If we manage to assemble a silicone network with the same layout as the human brain, then in principle it should be possible to copy human knowledge onto that network. An interesting question at this point is whether such a network also would inherit the human mind, complete with consciousness and free will.

Interim summary

- Cybernetics has shown that information transcends the medium on which it is realised. It can be copied from one Turing machine to another.

- This insight provides a solution to the identity problem, the fact that it is unlikely that two identical thoughts are realised physiologically in exactly the same way.

- This insight also led to functionalism in the philosophy of mind, the conviction that philosophers of mind had to investigate the functions of information, and not the precise ways in which the information was realised in the brain.

- Functionalism (and materialism) can explain how the mind is not lost in the thought experiment of teleportation, unlike dualism.

- Some authors see the fact that information is a realm separate from the machine upon which it is implemented as a way in which humans can reclaim their free will; others claim it simply implies that humans are not only slaves of their genes but also slaves of the information realm (composed of memes).

6.4   Consciousness again

Has functionalism demystified the human mind, as materialism predicted would happen? Is the mind nothing but a by-product of information stored and manipulated in a Turing machine? For some philosophers, functionalism indeed has crossed the big gap between mind and brain. Others, however, doubt whether the real mystery has been solved now and that only the further tightening of a few loose ends is required. They point to continuing differences between information processing in computers and conscious experiences in humans.

More thought experiments

The Chinese room thought experiment and the Mary thought experiment

A series of thought experiments are classically given as evidence that functionalism may be missing something crucial of the human mind. A first thought experiment was

Chinese room

thought experiment proposed by Searle to illustrate the difference between information processing in humans and information processing in computers

conceived by the American philosopher John Searle (1980) and is called the Chinese room thought experiment. Suppose you don't know any Chinese and you are locked up in a room where you regularly receive a Chinese character through a slot and have to supply another character in return. In order for you to be able to select the right answer, you have a book full of rules that for each character you receive, tells you which character to return. Gradually you become more and more practised in the task, so that you can return the required character rapidly. Also, now and then you get a batch of additional rules, which allow you to process a larger number of symbols. Could we then say that you have come to master Chinese, because you are able always to provide the right answer to each question you get (and hence would be able to fool a Chinese speaker in a Turing test; see Chapter 4)?

Searle used this thought experiment to make clear that the operations of a computer do not by themselves lead to the experience of consciousness as we humans know it. A processing entirely based on the application of rules (algorithms) on shapes (symbols) stays devoid of meaning. This is very unlike human thinking, where the symbols have extensive and rich meanings, grounded in the interactions with the world. When we read about a tree, we have a rich image of what this word stands for, where we can expect to find it, what characteristics it has, what actions it affords, and so on. Philosophers refer to these quality-feelings of conscious thoughts as phenomenal qualities or qualia.

qualia

qualities of conscious thoughts that give the thoughts a rich and vivid meaning, grounded in interactions with the world

> ## ? What do you think?
>
> To illustrate the importance of qualia in consciousness, Nagel (1974) suggested you try to imagine what it is like to be a bat. How does the experience of the environment differ between you and a bat as a consequence of differences in qualia?

Because of the qualia, Searle argued, seeing human consciousness as information processing in a Turing machine overlooks a fundamental property of human thinking and cannot be a full account of the human mind. The same argument can be found in the following famous thought experiment, proposed by the Australian philosopher Frank Jackson:

Mary is a brilliant scientist who is, for whatever reason, forced to investigate the world from a black and white room *via* a black and white television monitor. She specializes in the neurophysiology of vision and acquires, let us suppose, all the physical information there is to obtain about what goes on when we see ripe tomatoes, or the sky, and use terms like 'red', 'blue', and so on. She discovers, for example, just which wavelength combinations from the sky stimulate the retina, and exactly how this produces via the central nervous system the contraction of the vocal chords and expulsion of air from the lungs that results in the uttering of the sentence 'The sky is blue' . . .

What will happen when Mary is released from her black and white room or is given a color television monitor? Will she *learn* anything or not? It seems just obvious that she will learn something about the world and our visual experience of it. But then it is inescapable that her previous knowledge was incomplete. But she had *all* the physical information. *Ergo* there is more to have than that, and Physicalism is false.

(Jackson 1982, p. 130)

The zombie thought experiment

Another thought experiment suggesting that functionalism may not (yet) have solved the complete mystery of the human mind, was presented by the Australian philosopher, David Chalmers (1996), and is known as the zombie thought experiment. Chalmers argued that we can perfectly imagine a twin of ourselves, who is molecule for molecule identical to us, but who lacks conscious experience. Chalmers called this twin a zombie. Usually zombies refer to reanimated corpses (or corpses made undead), but in Chalmers's view the only difference between the zombie and us is that it does not have the consciousness we have. All the rest, including the appearance and the behaviours, is identical to what we are and do. Our zombie would respond in exactly the same way as we do, but it would lack the qualia that make up our phenomenal world. When it is stabbed, it would show the same overt reactions as we do (groan, grimace, try to defend itself), but it would feel no pain. We could even imagine a zombie world, a world physically identical to ours, but in which there are no phenomenal experiences.

The fact that we can imagine a word that is physically and functionally identical to ours, but lacks consciousness, Chalmers argues, means that we cannot reduce consciousness to materialism and functionalism. Consciousness is something more, and trying to grasp this something is what Chalmers calls the hard problem. According to Chalmers, trying to explain why we have phenomenal experiences with qualia is the problem cognitive psychologists skirt when they draw their flow diagrams or write their computational models. They limit their efforts to the so-called easy problems of detailing the processes and functions of cognitive functioning, without worrying about what makes our minds different from those of zombies.

zombie thought experiment

thought experiment proposed by Chalmers to illustrate that consciousness is more than the working of the brain or the implementation of information on a Turing machine because it involves a subjective component with qualia

hard problem

name given by Chalmers to refer to the difficulty of explaining in what respects consciousness is more than accounted for on the basis of materialism and functionalism

Psychological research on the nature of consciousness

As it happened, by the time Chalmers published his book with the zombie thought experiment (1996), consciousness was a very active topic of research in psychology again. As a result of the methodological advances since the beginning of the twentieth century, the scientific study of consciousness was no longer a utopia.

Evidence for unconscious information processing

Experimental research on consciousness started when researchers discovered hard evidence for the existence of unconscious processing. One of the first experiments proving that humans can be influenced by stimuli they do not perceive consciously was published by Kunst-Wilson and Zajonc (1980). The experiment consisted of two phases. In the first phase, participants were asked to watch a screen and try to discern what was presented. Ten irregular polygons were presented five times for 1 millisecond, too short to be seen by the participants (all they saw were light flashes). In the second phase, participants were shown two polygons and had to decide which one

Figure 6.1 The effect of stimuli that cannot be perceived consciously.
When participants in a first phase are exposed to stimuli they cannot perceive consciously, they are unable in the next phase to indicate which stimulus of a pair was presented in the first phase and which one is new, but they show a reliable preference for the stimuli they were exposed to in the first phase. This was the first evidence for unconscious stimulus processing.

Source: Kunst-Wilson and Zajonc (1980). Reproduced with permission.

they thought they had seen in phase 1 and which one they liked most. One of the polygon pairs had been presented in the first phase, the other was new. Figure 6.1 shows the findings. As expected, the participants could not indicate which polygon had been presented in the first phase (because they were not aware of having seen them). However, the participants more often than predicted by chance preferred the polygon shown in the first phase. This was the first strong evidence that emotional responses could be based on unconscious information processing.

Shortly after the study of Kunst-Wilson and Zajonc (1980), Marcel (1983) presented evidence that cognitive processing could be unconscious as well. He made use of a technique known as *semantic priming*. In this technique two stimuli are presented immediately after one another: the prime and the target. The usual finding is that the target is recognised faster when it succeeds a semantically related prime than when it succeeds an unrelated, neutral prime. So, the target word *boy* is recognised faster after the prime word *girl* than after the prime word *goal*. In Marcel's experiments, target word recognition time was measured by means of a lexical decision task. In this task participants have to decide on each trial whether a presented string of letters is a word (e.g. *boy*) or not (e.g. *doy*). The target stimuli (both words and non-words) were preceded by primes to which the participants did not have to respond. In a first condition, Marcel presented the primes long enough for them to be clearly visible. In this condition, as expected he found a nice semantic priming effect (left part of figure 6.2). That is, participants indicated faster that *boy* was an existing English word if it had been preceded by the prime *girl* than if it had been preceded by the prime *goal*. In a second condition, Marcel limited the presentation time of the primes to a few milliseconds, so that participants could no longer see them consciously. Still

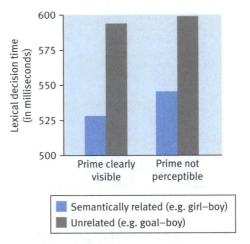

Figure 6.2 Evidence for unconscious cognitive processing.
Target words are recognised faster when they are preceded by a semantically related prime than when they are preceded by an unrelated prime. This is so both when the primes are clearly visible and when they are presented too briefly to be seen consciously.

Source: Marcel (1983). Reproduced with permission.

he found a priming effect that was nearly as strong as the effect with the clearly visible primes (right part of figure 6.2). This indicated that the prime word did not have to be perceived consciously in order to be processed and to influence the subsequent recognition of the target word.

Free will and the initiation of movement

In 1985, Libet argued that not only perception to a large extent escapes conscious control, but that the same is true for action control. To perform an action, a lot of processing is needed that we are unaware of. As a matter of fact, Libet argued, even the initiation of a deliberate action happens outside consciousness.

Libet based his claim on a fairly simple but straightforward experiment (as has been the case for many classic findings in scientific research). He asked participants to deliberately make a finger movement from time to time. Participants saw an analogue clock face in front of them with a light going round the face every 2.56 seconds. Participants were asked to indicate after each trial when they had decided to initiate the movement by telling the experimenter at what position the light had been at the moment they made their decision. Libet measured two extra things: (1) the time at which the movement was initiated, and (2) the electrical brain activity of the participants. The latter was registered because it had been shown in the 1960s that voluntary movements are preceded by a readiness-potential in the brain, a change in the EEG-signal very similar to the Event Related Potentials discussed in Chapter 5 (figure 5.17).

What everyone expected would happen was that the participants would first decide to make a movement, then after some delay would show a readiness-potential in their EEG, and after some more delay would initiate the movement. However, this

Figure 6.3 The findings of Libet (1985).
Libet showed that when participants deliberately make a movement, brain responses needed for the movement are initiated well before the participant has the conscious impression of being about to initiate the movement. This strongly suggests that consciousness is informed of the upcoming movement rather than consciousness being the initiator of the movement.

Source: Libet (1985). Reproduced with permission.

was not what Libet observed. His data clearly showed that the brain signalled its readiness for the response (as seen by the onset of the readiness-potential) well before the participant had the conscious impression of starting the movement! Rather than consciousness deciding it would make a movement, it looked as if consciousness was informed by the brain that a movement was about to be initiated. Figure 6.3 shows the timeline of the events.

What Libet's (1985) experiment showed was that under the conditions tested consciousness did not control the initiation of the movement, as the participants thought, but that it was notified by the unconscious part of the brain when everything was ready for a movement. In other words, there was no free will involved in the initiation of the movement. In a later publication Libet (1999) conceded that free will might still play a role, because it could stop a programmed movement once it was ready to be launched.

The global workspace model

Since the seminal studies of Kunst-Wilson and Zajonc (1980), Marcel (1983) and Libet (1985), many more instances of unconscious processing have been documented, to such an extent that unconscious information processing nowadays is generally accepted in cognitive psychology. As a matter of fact, this should not surprise us. Unconscious information processing is a mystery within a dualist vision, where the conscious human mind controls everything, but is perfectly acceptable within a materialistic or functionalistic view. There is nothing untoward in sense receptors that fire automatically when they are activated by an appropriate stimulus, or in motor neurons that are mobilised for an upcoming movement. There is also nothing strange in signals being passed through the various nerves and brain centres and activating representations that are related to the original stimulus. What is difficult to explain within materialism and functionalism is why this processing from a certain point on gives rise to a *conscious* experience of the event, including qualia. So, with respect to Marcel's experiment there is no problem explaining how briefly presented primes are processed by the brain. What is more difficult to grasp, however, is why from a certain presentation time on the participant has a clear, conscious, vivid image of the word that is presented. Remember, this is what Chalmers called the hard problem.

A metaphor that is increasingly used within cognitive psychology to understand the role of consciousness is that of a theatre (e.g. Baars 1997). According to this metaphor, the brain can be compared to a big theatre where many processes are needed in the background for the play to take place (preparation of the decors, costumes, new players ready to come on stage, etc.). These processes work to a large extent independently but they need to be informed about what is going on in the play, in order to synchronise their activities with those of the central event. This is the role of consciousness: making information available to the global workspace, so that the activities of the automatic processes can be tuned to each other.

global workspace model

model that explains the role of consciousness by analogy to a theatre: consciousness is meant to make some information available to the whole brain (i.e. the play), so that the various background processes can align their functioning to what is going on centrally

The French neuroscientist Dehaene and his colleagues (2001) presented brain imaging evidence for the global workspace model. They measured brain activity to visual stimuli that were presented either too briefly to be consciously perceptible or long enough to be clearly visible. When the stimuli were presented below the consciousness threshold, some activity was noticed in areas at the back of the brain that are normally associated with object and word recognition (figure 6.4a). However, as soon as the participants started to see the words consciously, a large network distributed all over the brain became active (figure 6.4b), making the stimulus available everywhere in the cerebral hemispheres.

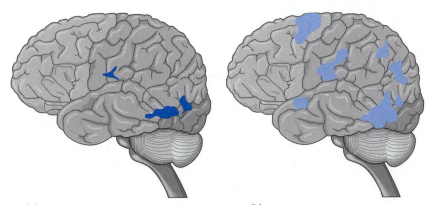

(a) Briefly presented visual stimul   (b) Consciously visible stimul

Figure 6.4 Brain activity for unconscious and conscious visible stimuli.
(a) Brain activity (measured with fMRI) when stimuli are presented too briefly to be consciously perceptible; the activity is largely limited to those brain areas that are responsible for visual object identification.
(b) Brain activity when the stimuli are clearly visible; now the object recognition areas are supplemented by activity in a large network that is distributed all over the cerebral hemispheres.

Source: Based on Dehaene *et al.* (2001)

KEY FIGURES

Philosophy of science

- Descartes: Cartesian dualism (mind is immaterial and independent of the body, a 'ghost in a machine').

- Paul and Patricia Churchland: staunch defenders of materialism.

- Richard Dawkins: humans are survival machines for genes and memes.

- Alan Turing: information forms an independent realm that can be copied from one Turing machine to another.

- Jerry Fodor: strong supporter of functionalism in the philosophy of science.

- Derek Parfit: the Star Trek thought experiment.

- Keith Stanovich: matter-independent information provides humans with a chance to rebel against their genes.

- John Searle: Chinese room thought experiment (importance of qualia).

- Frank Jackson: Mary thought experiment (importance of qualia).

- David Chalmers: zombie thought experiment and formulation of the 'hard problem' in the explanation of consciousness (importance of qualia).

- Benjamin Libet: impression of free will in the initiation of action is an illusion.

- Bernard Baars: global workspace model.

Dehaene *et al.* (2003) argued that the global workspace model is based on three assumptions:

1. Most information processing takes place automatically without consciousness.

2. Attention processes enhance and integrate part of the ongoing information processing, and bring it into consciousness.

3. Conscious awareness is required for operations involved in controlled processing, based on planning and evaluation.

Lamme (2006) argued that information is brought into consciousness by means of a continuous exchange of information between different brain areas. Incoming information not only activates bottom-up processes from the perceptual input regions to the higher cortical regions but also top-down processes back from the higher cortical areas to the perceptual input areas. This sustained information exchange between brain areas allows the organism to become aware of the stimulus. The bottom-up processes only allow the organism to respond automatically to a stimulus, without being conscious of the stimulus.

This is how Lamme described the process related to the perception of visual stimuli:

> When a new image hits the retina, it is processed through successive levels of visual cortex, by means of feedforward connections, working at an astonishing speed . . . Thus, the *feedforward sweep* enables a rapid extraction of complex and meaningful features from the visual scene, and lays down potential motor responses to act on the incoming information.
>
> Are we conscious of the features extracted by the feedforward sweep? Do we *see* a face when a face-selective neuron becomes active? It seems not. Many studies, in both humans and monkeys, indicate that no matter what area of the brain is reached by the feedforward sweep, this in itself is not producing (reportable) conscious experience. What seems necessary for conscious experience is that neurons in visual areas engage in so-called recurrent (or re-entrant or resonant) processing, where high- and low-level areas interact. This would enable the widespread exchange of information between areas processing different attributes of the visual scene, and thus support perceptual grouping.
>
> *(Lamme 2006, p. 495–7)*

Unconscious processing is not special

When the first experimental evidence for unconscious information processing was published, it received quite a lot of attention in the media, because many people tended to be wary of information processing beyond their conscious control. This was partly due to Freud's claims that the unconscious is a dark force, aiming at instant gratification of its sexual and aggressive desires without regard for social or ethical considerations, which constantly tries to control humans and has to be restrained by the ego. Another reason why people did not like the idea of unconscious processing was that several urban legends about the powers of unconscious information processing were around. One of these legends was that it is possible to manipulate people's actions through subliminal advertising. Another was that unconscious messages, intermixed in music or sea sounds, can be used to heal. Still another was that hidden backward messages in songs can take control of the listeners and, for instance, incite them to commit murder or suicide.

What do you think?

Have you ever heard of a story about unconscious influences? Which one? What evidence was given in favour of it? Was this enough? What type of evidence would you need to really be sure about the truth of the story?

Psychologists have been unable to find empirical support for any of the above strong claims (see Greenwald 1992; Kreiner *et al.* 2003; Loftus and Klinger 1992; Mayer and Merckelbach 1999). For instance, Greenwald *et al.* (1991) examined the effects of 'subliminal messages' (i.e. messages below the consciousness threshold) in records that otherwise sounded like normal soothing sounds. According to the makers, some records were good for improving memory; others were good for improving self-esteem. Greenwald *et al.* gave half of their participants a record to improve their memory and half a record to increase their self-esteem (this was clearly indicated on the record). Participants listened for a month at least once a day to the records. At the end of the study, they completed questionnaires about their memory performance and their self-esteem (they had done the same at the beginning of the study).

As predicted by the makers of the tapes, the participants who had listened to the self-esteem enhancing records reported higher self-esteem, and the participants who had listened to the memory enhancing records reported better memory skills. However, unknown to the participants, Greenwald *et al.* had changed the labels of half of the records, so that half of the participants who thought they were listening to self-esteem enhancing messages, actually heard memory enhancing messages. Similarly, half of the participants who thought they were listening to memory enhancing messages, in reality were exposed to self-esteem enhancing messages. Greenwald *et al.* found no difference whatsoever between the types of the *actual* records used; they only obtained an effect of the type of message the participants *thought* they had been listening to. On the basis of these findings, Greenwald *et al.* concluded that the positive effects participants reported were due to a placebo effect (participants expected to do better after the treatment), and not to the actual 'messages' they had been hearing. This finding agrees with the limited results of therapies based on subliminal messages.

What is possible, however, is to subtly increase the activation of certain goals and feelings with subliminal primes (e.g. Dijksterhuis *et al.* 2005). Just as non-visible prime words can activate target words, so it is possible to use non-conspicuous cues in the environment to make participants more likely to perform certain actions. For instance, Johnston (2002) showed that participants took more ice in a consumer test, when the person before them (a confederate of the experimenter) had taken a large sample than if the person had taken a small sample. None of the participants was aware of this influence. Similarly, Lowery *et al.* (2007) showed that they could increase the academic performance of students by increasing their self-confidence and motivation to perform well. The authors had half of their participants look at subliminally presented words that either primed for intelligence (intelligent, smart, brilliant, bright) or that were neutral (smock, birch, bring, tale). Subsequently the participants took part in a practice exam. Those who had seen the intelligence-related words performed better on the exam than those who had been exposed to the neutral words. Interestingly, the effect persisted on a true midterm exam a few days later, possibly as a result of the better results on the practice exam.

With respect to the above findings, it is important that they are not peculiar to unconscious processing. Exactly the same priming effects are found when participants perceive the information consciously, for instance as part of a word searching task with the words hidden in a letter matrix (e.g. Bargh *et al.* 2001). The similarity between conscious and unconscious priming is in line with the conjecture of the global workspace model that unconscious processing is the same type of information processing as conscious processing. It is processing that happens in the background, assists adequate performance, enters consciousness when important enough, and occasionally influences the line of thought or action. It does not have mythical powers, though.

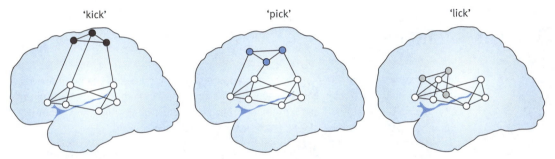

Figure 6.5 Brain regions active when participants read the word 'kick', 'pick' and 'lick'.
These regions not only involve Broca's area (figure 5.7) and Wernicke's area (figure 5.8), but also brain regions that are active when respectively a leg movement is made ('kick'), a hand movement is made ('pick'), or a tongue movement is made ('lick'). This suggests that the motor information related to the actions becomes co-activated as part of the meaning of the word. This may provide an explanation of why conscious experiences are characterised by qualia.

Source: Based on Pulvermüller (2005)

Embodied cognition and qualia

Another question experimental psychology has started to address is why conscious processing is phenomenally so rich, meaningful and full of qualia. A possibly ground-breaking finding here came from brain imaging and has to do with the discovery that in every task vast, interconnected networks in the brain become active. In particular, it has been found that the brain areas normally activated when people perceive visual stimuli or perform motor actions, also become active when people think about these stimuli or actions, or read words related to them.

Figure 6.5 shows the brain areas that were active when participants read the words 'kick', 'pick' and 'lick'. As expected, these areas included Broca's area (figure 5.7) and Wernicke's area (figure 5.8). However, in addition, the word 'kick' activated the brain region that is normally active when the participants move their legs. Similarly, the word 'pick' activated the brain region related to the control of hand movements, and the word 'lick' activated the brain region related to the control of tongue movements.

The fact that perceptual and motor areas become co-activated when we say or hear perceptually or motor-related words may be the reason why conscious experiences are so rich. The word 'tree' has a phenomenally vivid meaning, because it activates memories of actual experiences with trees (both visual and motoric) when it is read. The fact that consciousness is able to bind information from different parts of the brain makes it possible to interconnect everything. With reference to Searle's thought experiment, we may conclude that such co-activation allows the brain to exceed the poorness of the information processing in the Chinese room. The brain does not normally manipulate meaningless symbols; upon encountering a familiar symbol it co-activates a big chunk of our previous experiences with that particular stimulus. This certainly is a line of research to keep an eye on in the coming years. The fact that the meanings of words include actually experienced, body-related information is called embodied cognition (see also Chapter 11).

embodied cognition

view about the meaning of events and words that stresses their dependence on body-related perceptual and motoric experi-ences; information is not abstract, independent of the personal experiences of the information carrier

Interim summary

- Information as currently implemented in computers does not possess the phenomenal richness (qualia) of human consciousness and also does not seem to result in coherent information processing based on meaning. This can be concluded from three famous thought experiments: the Chinese room, Mary and the zombie world.

- Because of the remaining differences between human consciousness and information processing in computers, Chalmers claims that the hard problem of consciousness has not yet been solved.

- Recent advances in scientific psychology have shown that:
  - Unconscious processing occurs in the brain and largely resembles conscious processing; it mainly is less rich and integrated than conscious processing.
  - When a stimulus becomes conscious, many additional areas in the brain become active; this is in line with the global workspace model, which says that conscious information is available for all the automatic, unconscious processes that are going on in the background, so that they can tune their activities to the central processing.
  - None of the sensational myths of unconscious processing has been corroborated by experimental evidence.
  - When conscious thoughts involve perceptions or motor actions, the parts of the brain that normally subserve these functions become active. This could be the reason why consciousness is so vivid and feels so lively.

6.5   Focus on: Can automatic processing help us to make better decisions?

In the previous section we saw that automatic, unconscious processing is not the dangerous entity Freud imagined. As a matter of fact, researchers are starting to consider it more and more as a kind of 'automatic pilot' that keeps us alive (as far as the vegetative functions such as breathing and heart beating are concerned, even in a very literal sense!) and in good shape. It is the type of background processing that is required for us to function properly.

Type 1 thinking

The automatic system involves all types of information processing that do not require focused attention and that produce an output without any apparent effort or awareness. It is based on innate knowledge that has been inherited from previous generations as a result of natural selection (e.g. caution for snakes, automatic attention capture by angry voices or approaching noises) and on knowledge that has been

associative learning

learning of simple associations (corre- lations) between all types of events; thought to be the basis of automatic, type 1 thinking

acquired on the basis of **associative learning**. The latter refers to the learning of simple associations (correlations) between events. It not only includes associations between elements that we have deliberately memorised, but also associations between stimuli co-occurring in the environment (which we have picked up through classical condi- tioning; e.g. certain smells and the availability of food), and associations between stimuli and actions (learned on the basis of operant conditioning; e.g. being given a present and saying 'thank you'). The automatic processing system forms the basis of our motor skills, but also of our practical, everyday functioning and the knowledge we typically call intuition or gut feeling (Lieberman 2000).

Type 2 thinking

In humans, the automatic type 1 thinking is supplemented with a second form of rea- soning that is controlled, serial and conscious. This type of thinking allows us to go beyond what is physically present in the environment. We can think of people and events that are absent, and we can try out hypothetical, counterintuitive solutions and evaluate what outcomes they would produce. As such it is the core of scientific thinking (see Chapter 8). It is also related to the intelligence of people as measured by IQ-tests or school results.

Table 6.1 provides an overview of the main differences that have been postulated between type 1 and type 2 thinking.

A focus on type 2 thinking

In the first decades of cognitive psychology most research was geared towards type 2 thinking. For instance, a lot of effort went into the questions regarding how good people are at reasoning and problem solving. Do people follow the rules of logic when they reason? Are they thinking like intuitive scientists? Do they take all evidence into consideration when making a decision? Are their evaluations and explanations of events error-free and unbiased?

Table 6.1 Characteristics associated with automatic (type 1) and controlled (type 2) thinking

System 1	System 2
Unconscious/implicit	Conscious/explicit
Automatic	Controllable
Evolved early	Evolved late
Shared with other animals	Uniquely human
Independent of language	Related to language
Pragmatic/contextualised	Logical/abstract
High processing capacity, parallel	Constrained by working memory, sequential
Driven by learning and innate modules	Permits hypothetical thinking
Independent of general intelligence	Correlated with general intelligence

Source: Based on Evans (2002)

What do you think?

How good are people at reasoning? Do you approach a problem like an intuitive scientist? If yes, what exactly does your approach involve and why is this scientific? If no, in what ways does your approach differ from the scientific method as discussed in Chapter 2?

Out of this research came the conclusion that without formal training people do not reason like intuitive scientists. They do not strictly follow the strategies that in science have proven to lead to the most reliable knowledge (Chapters 3, 4 and 8). Instead, they spontaneously make use of heuristics, rules of thumb that do not require as much effort as a full-blown scientific evaluation and that most of the time result in good decisions, but that occasionally go wrong.

A typical example of this type of research makes use of the following problem (from Swinkels 2003):

Dr. Swinkels's cousin, Rudy, is a bit on the peculiar side. He has unusual tastes in movies and art, he is married to a performer, and he has tattoos on various parts of his body. In his spare time Rudy takes yoga classes and likes to collect 78 rpm records. An outgoing and rather boisterous person, he has been known to act on a dare on more than one occasion. What do you think Rudy's occupation most likely is?

A) Farmer   B) Trapeze Artist

What do you think?

Which occupation is most likely in the example of Swinkels? Why?

A scientific approach to the problem of Swinkels would require knowledge of (1) the probability of each of the occupations and (2) the predictive value of the different traits for each of the occupations. So, if farmers makeup 5 per cent of the population and if the features described in the story are present in 10 per cent of the farmers, one can conclude that 0.5 per cent of the population (i.e. one person in every 200) will be a farmer and show the characteristics described in the example. Similarly, if 0.0001 per cent of the population is a trapeze artist (these people tend to be rather rare) and 60 per cent of the trapeze artists show the characteristics described, one can conclude that 0.00006 per cent of the population (i.e. roughly one person in every 17,000) will be a trapeze artist and show the described characteristics. In other words, chances are much higher that Dr. Swinkels's cousin is a farmer than that he is a trapeze artist.

As you may have experienced, the above type of reasoning is not what the participants in Swinkels's (2003) study did. They simply reasoned that more elements of the story agreed with the stereotypical image of a trapeze artist than with the stereotypical image of a farmer, and they predominantly – but wrongly – opted for the trapeze alternative as the most probable one.

On the basis of studies like the one just described, cognitive psychologists came to see humans as suboptimal, heuristic-based thinkers cursed with a list of biases towards reasoning errors (e.g. Kahneman and Tversky 1974, 1979; Nisbett and Wilson 1977; Nisbett and Ross 1980). Good psychology students were taught about these pitfalls and warned to avoid them. Within this research, type 1 thinking did not figure predominantly, and was seen as the main origin of the reasoning biases. For instance, the reasoning error in the Swinkels example could be attributed to an unwarranted reliance on associative learning between personality characteristics and occupations (giving too much weight to the correspondence of the features described and the prototypical image of a trapeze artist).

heuristic-based thinkers

those who think based on heuristics, rules of thumb that do not require as much effort as the scientific method and that most of the time result in good decisions, but that are subject to a number of biases

The revival of system 1 thinking

In the last decade, however, researchers have started to re-appreciate system 1 thinking. Automatic thinking is not always inferior to controlled thinking and may even turn out to be superior. To understand when this could be so, it is important to keep in mind that type 1 thinking consists of the automatic detection of correlations between the events in everyday life (including books, films, stories told, etc.). As a result, some stimuli become associated with an automatic approach response and others with an automatic avoidance response. These automatic evaluations can activate the wrong answer in 'artificial' situations, such as the Swinkels example, but they should be reliable in often-experienced, everyday situations.

An example of a theory that defends the superiority of type 1 thinking in certain everyday situations is the so-called *theory of unconscious thought* proposed by Dijksterhuis and colleagues (e.g. Dijksterhuis and Nordgren 2006). In this theory, three main differences are postulated between conscious and unconscious thought:

1. Unconscious thinking, unlike conscious thinking, is completely determined by the stimuli. They automatically activate stored associations, without the interference of hypothetical thinking. On the negative side, this means that important considerations may be overlooked in unconscious thinking (such as the probability of the different occupations in Swinkels's experiment). On the positive side, it means that the response will be in line with what has worked in the past.

2. Conscious thinking is able to follow strict rules, whereas unconscious thought only results in a gist or a hunch. To know the answer to the problem 13×14 you need conscious thought. However, on the basis of unconscious thinking you can rapidly decide that it will not be equal to 4,000,000 without having to do the detailed calculations.

3. The main limit of conscious thought is that it has a low capacity. Without making use of systematic data analysis and written notes, conscious processing can only take into account the contribution of some four, rather easy-to-understand variables. As soon as a problem becomes more complex, the processing effort increases so rapidly that it exceeds the capacities of most individuals. In contrast, unconscious thinking can take into account the simultaneous contribution of a large number of influences. The outcome will still be a hunch, but not less accurate than for a simple problem.

Figure 6.6 Conscious deliberation in decision making is not always the best strategy. This figure shows the percentage of participants who chose the most desirable car as a function of the complexity of the decision and the mode of thought. When the choice was relatively easy, a careful comparison of the two alternatives produced the best results. In contrast, when the complexity of the choice exceeded the limited capacity of conscious processing, it was better for some time not to think about the problem and to trust the hunch of unconscious thought.

Source: Dijksterhuis *et al.* (2006). Reproduced with permission.

To test the theory of unconscious thought, Dijksterhuis and colleagues (2006) presented their participants with vignettes of real life choices. For instance, the participants had to decide which car or apartment to buy. One of the alternatives was significantly worse than the other, though not on all attributes. There were two different conditions: information was given about 4 attributes (easy condition) or about 12 attributes (difficult condition). Participants either had to make an immediate decision based on conscious thinking, or they first had to complete a distracter task that prevented them from further thought about the choice. If the theory of unconscious thought was correct, Dijksterhuis and collaborators predicted an interaction between the mode of thinking and the difficulty of the problem, as they indeed observed (figure 6.6). Participants made better decisions if they were allowed to think consciously about the easy alternatives, whereas they performed better if the complex alternatives could be put aside for some time and mulled over by the unconscious brain. On the basis of their findings, Dijksterhuis *et al.* advised 'sleeping on' complex problems, so that unconscious thought can evaluate the alternatives and contribute to the final decision.

Interim summary

- There is increasing evidence for two thinking systems: one that is automatic and based on associative learning (type 1), and one that is controlled, explicit and based on hypothetical thinking (type 2).

- For a long time, cognitive psychology was only interested in type 2 thinking, which was seen as heuristic-based and prone to reasoning errors; type 1 thinking was largely overlooked and considered as the origin of some of the reasoning errors.

Interim summary *(continued)*

- Currently there is a redressing of the balance, because it is realised that system 1 thinking forms the basis of much of everyday interaction and intuitive thinking.

- According to the theory of unconscious thought, it is possible to evaluate information without consciousness. Such evaluation is less susceptible to the capacity limitations of conscious thought. It does not lead to precise conclusions, but to rough estimates of the desirability of the alternatives and can be used when complex decisions must be made.

Recommended literature

The argument in the first three sections of this chapter has been inspired by the line of thought developed in Lyons, W. (2001) *Matters of the mind* (New York: Routledge). Another interesting book on consciousness is Dietrich, A. (2007) *Introduction to consciousness* (Basingstoke: Palgrave Macmillan). If you are interested in the more detailed discussions within the philosophy of mind, good introductions are Heil, J. (1998) *Philosophy of mind: A contemporary introduction* (London: Routledge) and (at a more advanced level) Stich, S.P. and Warfield, T.A. (eds.) (2003) *The Blackwell guide to philosophy of mind* (Oxford: Blackwell Publishing).

References

Baars, B.J. (1997) *In the theater of consciousness: The workspace of the mind.* New York: Oxford University Press.

Bargh, J.A., Gollwitzer, P.M., Lee-Chai, A., Barndollar, K. and Trötschel, R. (2001) 'The automated will: Nonconscious activation and pursuit of behavioral goals', *Journal of Personality and Social Psychology*, **81**: 1014–27.

Boring, E.G. (1933) *The physical dimensions of consciousness.* New York: Appleton-Century.

Chalmers, D.J. (1966) *The conscious mind: In search of a fundamental theory.* New York: Oxford University Press.

Churchland, P. (1981) 'Eliminative materialism and the propositional attitudes', *The Journal of Philosophy*, **78**: 67–90.

Crick, F. (1995) *The astonishing hypothesis: The scientific search for the soul.* London: Touchstone Books.

Darley, J.M. and Latané, B. (1968) 'Bystander intervention in emergencies: Diffusion of responsibility', *Journal of Personality and Social Psychology*, **8**: 377–83.

Dawkins, R. (1976 / 2006) *The selfish gene: 30th anniversary edition – with a new Introduction by the Author.* Oxford: Oxford University Press.

Dehaene, S., Naccache, L., Cohen, L., Le Bihan, D., Mangin, J.F., Poline, J.B. and Riviere, D. (2001) 'Cerebral mechanisms of word masking and unconscious repetition priming', *Nature Neuroscience*, **4**: 752–58.

Dehaene, S., Sergent, C. and Changeux, J.P. (2003) 'A neuronal network model linking subjective reports and objective physiological data during conscious perception', *Proceedings of the National Academy of Sciences of the United States of America*, **100**: 8520–5.

Dennett, D.C. (2003) *Freedom evolves*. New York: Penguin.

Dijksterhuis, A., Bos, M.W., Nordgren, L.F. and van Baaren, R.B. (2006) 'On making the right choice: The deliberation-without-attention effect', *Science*, **311**: 1005–7.

Dijksterhuis, A. and Nordgren, L.F. (2006) 'A theory of unconscious thought', *Perspectives on Psychological Science*, **1**: 95–109.

Dijksterhuis, A., Smith, P.K., van Baaren, R.B. and Wigboldus, D.H.J. (2005) 'The unconscious consumer: Effects of environment on consumer behavior', *Journal of Consumer Psychology*, **15**: 193–202.

Evans, J.S.B.T. (2002) 'Logic and human reasoning: An assessment of the deduction paradigm', *Psychological Bulletin*, **128**: 978–96.

Fodor, J.A. (1981) 'The mind–body problem', *Scientific American*, **244**(1): 124–32.

Greenwald, A.G. (1992) 'New look 3: Unconscious cognition reclaimed', *American Psychologist*, **47**: 766–79.

Greenwald, A.G., Spangenberg, E.R., Pratkanis, A.R. and Eskenazi, J. (1991) 'Double-blind tests of subliminal self-help audiotapes', *Psychological Science*, **2**: 119–22.

Jackson, F. (1982) 'Epiphenomenal qualia', *Philosophical Quarterly*, **32**: 127–36.

Jahoda, G. (2007) *A history of social psychology*. Cambridge: Cambridge University Press.

Johnston, L. (2002) 'Behavioral mimicry and stigmatization', *Social Cognition*, **20**: 18–35.

Kahneman, D. and Tversky, A. (1974) 'Judgment under uncertainty: Heuristics and biases', *Science*, **185**: 1124–31.

Kahneman, D. and Tversky, A. (1979) 'Prospect theory: Analysis of decision under risk', *Econometrica*, **47**: 263–91.

Kreiner, D.S., Altis, N.A. and Voss, C.W. (2003) 'A test of the effect of reverse speech on priming', *Journal of Psychology*, **137**: 224–32.

Kunst-Wilson, W.R. and Zajonc, R.B. (1980) 'Affective discrimination of stimuli that cannot be recognized', *Science*, **207**: 557–8.

Lamme, V.A.F. (2006) 'Towards a true neural stance on consciousness', *Trends in Cognitive Sciences*, **10**: 494–501.

Libet, B. (1985) 'Unconscious cerebral initiative and the role of conscious will in voluntary action', *Behavioral and Brain Sciences*, **8**: 529–39.

Libet, B. (1999) 'Do we have free will?' *Journal of Consciousness Studies*, **6**: 47–55.

Lieberman, M.D. (2000) 'Intuition: A social cognitive neuroscience approach', *Psychological Bulletin*, **126**: 109–37.

Loftus, E.F. and Klinger, M.R. (1992) 'Is the unconscious smart or dumb?' *American Psychologist*, **47**: 761–5.

Lowery, B.S., Eisenberger, N.I., Hardin, C.D. and Sinclair, S. (2007) 'Long-term effects of subliminal priming on academic performance', *Basic and Applied Social Psychology*, **29**: 151–7.

Lyons, W. (2001) *Matters of the mind*. New York: Routledge.

Marcel, A.J. (1983) 'Conscious and unconscious perception: Experiments on visual masking and word recognition', *Cognitive Psychology*, **15**: 197–237.

Mayer, B. and Merckelbach, H. (1999) 'Unconscious processes, subliminal stimulation, and anxiety', *Clinical Psychology Review*, **19**: 571–90.

Milgram, S. (1963) 'Behavioral study of obedience', *Journal of Abnormal and Social Psychology*, **67**: 371–8.

Milgram, S. (1974) *Obedience to authority: An experimental view*. New York: Harper & Row.

Nagel, T. (1974) 'What is it like to be a bat?' *Philosophical Review*, **4**: 435–50.

Nisbett, R. and Ross, L. (1980) *Human inference: Strategies and shortcomings of social judgment*. Englewood Cliffs, NJ: Prentice-Hall.

Nisbett, R. and Wilson, T. (1977) 'Telling more than we can know: Verbal reports on mental processes', *Psychological Review*, **84**: 231–59.

Pulvermüller, F. (2005) 'Brain mechanisms linking language and action', *Nature Reviews Neuroscience*, **6**: 576–82.

Searle, J. (1980) 'Minds, brains, and programs', *Behavioral and Brain Sciences,* **3:** 417–57.

Stanovich, K.E. (2004) *The robot's rebellion: Finding meaning in the age of Darwin.* Chicago: The University of Chicago Press.

Swinkels, A. (2003) 'An effective exercise for teaching cognitive heuristics', *Teaching of Psychology,* **30:** 120–22.

Turing, A. (1950) 'Computing machinery and intelligence', *Mind,* **59:** 434–60.

Walter, H. (2001) *Neurophilosophy of free will.* Cambridge, MA: MIT Press.

Wilson, T.D. and Dunn, E.W. (2004) 'Self-knowledge: Its limits, value, and potential for improvement', *Annual Review of Psychology,* **55:** 17.1–17.26.

07 How did psychology affect everyday life?
The history of applied psychology

This chapter will cover

Questions to consider

Historical issues addressed in this chapter

■ When were the first psychological clinics established? What opposition existed?
■ Why was research about shellshock so important in the early years of applied psychology?
■ When did client-centred therapy start? In what respect was the time ripe for such a development?
■ Which events increased the status of clinical psychology during and after World War II?
■ When did psychoactive drugs become available? What impact did they have?
■ When were the first achievement tests used?
■ What triggered the start of the research on work and organisation at the beginning of the twentieth century?
■ How have the views on work motivation changed over the twentieth century?

Conceptual issues addressed in this chapter

■ To what extent has psychological research changed the way people see each other?
■ Is it possible to do research about the efficacy of psychotherapy?
■ What has the welfare state to do with the development of clinical psychology?
■ What are tests used for?
■ Why should a test be reliable and valid?
■ Why do psychologists need tests?
■ What needs to be done to have a useful test?
■ Why is Western society becoming increasingly individualised?
■ Why have text writers a tendency to idealise classic experiments? What is the outcome of this practice?

Introduction

What every educator, every jail-warden, every doctor, every clergyman, every asylum-superintendent, asks of psychology is practical rules. Such men care little or nothing about the ultimate philosophical grounds of mental phenomena, but they do care immensely about improving the ideas, dispositions, and conduct of the particular individuals in their charge.

(James 1892, p. 148)

Another way of looking at the history of psychology is to see what impact it has had on society. In his book *Modernizing the Mind: Psychological Knowledge and the Remaking of Society*, the American sociologist Steven C. Ward (2002) argues that the discipline of psychology, over the course of the twentieth century, grew from a marginal academic field to a discipline that has done more than any other to transform the routines and experiences of everyday life. In his own words:

> Today, psychological knowledge is present in such diverse places as the discourse of TV talk shows, the organization and production in factories and the self-esteem workshops in public schools. Its practitioners and representatives are found not only at traditional centers of knowledge production, such as universities and research laboratories, but also in courtrooms, at disaster scenes, in advertising agencies, in sports training camps and corporate education centers. In fact, it can be argued that psychological knowledge is so pervasive that to think and feel in the early twenty-first century inevitably means utilizing and activating its terminology, classifications and modes of understanding.
>
> *(Ward 2002, p. 1)*

A similar conclusion was reached by the Dutch authors Jansz and Van Drunen (2004). Both they and Ward talked about the *psychologisation* of society to refer to the growing impact of psychological theories and findings on everyday life in our society. We will discuss the socio-political issues of this psychologisation in Chapter 12. Here we deal with the knowledge itself. What did psychology have to offer?

A noteworthy observation is that most of psychology's influences on society have to do with applied aspects of psychological knowledge, the application of psychological knowledge and research methods to solve problems in other areas. This is interesting because for a long time applied psychology hardly figured in the history books of psychology, as if it were a branch of secondary importance (see our discussion of Boring in Chapter 3). Applied psychology is rapidly expanding nowadays (e.g. in the areas of health, sport, law, business management and product design). However, as in the other chapters we must limit our coverage. Only three areas with histories going back to the late nineteenth century will be discussed. First, we review the developments in clinical psychology. Next, we discuss why psychological testing took such a high flight, and we end by tracing the history of the psychology of work and organisation.

applied psychology

the application of psychological knowledge and research methods to solve practical problems

7.1   Changes in the treatment of mental health problems

In Chapter 3 we saw the history of mental health care up to the twentieth century. We ended with the appearance of neurologists at the end of the nineteenth century signalling the beginning of a new era in the treatment of psychopathology. Neurologists were physicians who treated milder forms of mental disorders in private settings using methods such as communication, hypnosis and suggestion. They were the initiators of psychotherapy and had a strong influence on their medical colleagues in the asylums, the psychiatrists, who took over their ideas. The best-known neurologist was Freud, partly inspired by developments in France (e.g. Charcot).

Evolutions before World War II

Mental health problems must be treated by practitioners with a medical degree

Although psychologists are keen to present Freud as the person who introduced the psychological treatment of mental health problems, they usually fail to mention that Freud saw himself in the first place as a medical doctor and psychoanalysis as a medical treatment. Likewise, psychiatrists in various countries lobbied to have psycho-analysis acknowledged as a medical treatment and, therefore, confined to practitioners with a medical degree (e.g. Ward 2002, p. 48–51). Psychologists were not allowed to provide unsupervised therapies in official settings and their private practices were not covered by health insurance. As a result, psychologists involved in mental health care had a subordinate function (reporting to the psychiatrist) and were mainly hired to administer psychological tests (see below).

The first clinical psychology centres

Treatment centres run by psychologists started in the USA and were university-related. The facility that is considered to be the first psychology health centre was opened by Lightner Witmer in 1896 at the University of Pennsylvania. Tellingly, it was aimed at helping behavioural and learning problems in school children, building upon the growing impact of educational psychology (Chapter 12) and keeping away from what happened in psychiatric clinics.

In subsequent years the growth of psychology clinics was slow (in 1914 there were only 19 of them in the USA) and up to World War II limited to problems in school children (McReynolds 1987). The founding of clinical psychology centres was further impeded by the lack of support from the academic psychologists. This was partly because the psychology departments at the universities were dominated by experimental psychologists, who wanted to promote psychology as a science (Chapters 4 and 9), and partly because the academics did not want to upset their medical colleagues, whose help they needed for the expansion of their departments (Chapter 12). Even in 1921, the American Psychological Association (APA) made it publicly known that its objective was the advancement of psychology as a science, not as a profession (Abma 2004, p. 108). Although Witmer was a founding member of the APA, he withdrew from it bitterly in the early 1900s (McReynolds 1987).

In the meantime mental health problems and psychoanalysis became popular courses in psychology. In 1907, Witmer used the term clinical psychology to refer to the branch of psychology applying psychological knowledge to the assessment and treatment of mental disorders. These were his words:

clinical psychology

branch of psycho-logy applying psychological knowledge to the assessment and treatment of mental disorders

> Although clinical psychology is clearly related to medicine, it is quite as closely related to sociology and to pedagogy . . . An abundance of material for scientific study fails to be utilized, because the interest of psychologists is elsewhere engaged, and those in constant touch with the actual phenomena do not possess the training necessary to make the experience and observation of scientific value . . . While the field of clinical psychology is to some extent occupied by the physician, especially by the psychiatrist, and while I expect to rely in a great measure upon the educator and social worker for the more important contributions to this branch of psychology, it

is nevertheless true that none of these has quite the training necessary for this kind of work. For that matter, neither has the psychologist, unless he has acquired this training from sources other than the usual course of instruction in psychology . . . The phraseology of 'clinical psychology' and 'psychological clinic' will doubtless strike many as an odd juxtaposition of terms relating to quite disparate subjects . . . I have borrowed the word 'clinical' from medicine, because it is the best term I can find to indicate the character of the method which I deem necessary for this work.

(Witmer (1907) as cited in McReynolds (1987) p. 852)

The first clinical psychology centre in the UK was set up in 1920 in a private house in Tavistock Square, London. It was named the Institute for Medical Psychology (later renamed the Tavistock Clinic). This is how Wooldridge (1994) described it:

The clinic, the first of its kind in the country, aimed at treating patients who suffered from hysteria, abnormal fears and obsession, neurasthenia, and behaviour disorders. Its general approach was eclectic, embracing all the known methods of psychotherapy, such as various forms of suggestion, re-education and mental analysis, but it laid particular emphasis on Freudian psychoanalysis.

(Wooldridge 1994, p. 140)

As was the case for Witmer's centre, the Tavistock Clinic had a particular interest in child psychology. The first patient was a child.

The impact of World War II

An urgent need for psychological advice and treatment

World War I had taught the military that the new fighting techniques (with more devastating weapons and less physical contact) put heavy mental strain on the soldiers. A phenomenon that became documented was shellshock, an anxiety response that prevented soldiers and officers from functioning properly despite the usual disciplinary actions. This finding gave rise to two developments. First, there was a need for increased psychological testing to predict who would be prone to shellshock and hence should not be employed by the paid armed forces. Second, there was increased pressure to treat personnel who suffered from shellshock. As a result, when the USA decided to join World War II, they also decided to properly staff the military psychiatric service. Because the demand vastly outstripped the number of available psychiatrists, a crash course in the treatment of mental disorders was offered to all medical officers, and clinical psychologists were taken on board, both for testing and treatment. Given that the USA after World War II became involved in other wars (e.g. Korea 1950–1953, Vietnam 1965–1975), the service remained.

shellshock

anxiety response on battlefield that prevents soldiers from functioning properly; was one of the first topics addressed by applied psychology

The beginning of client-centred therapy

The rising demand for psychological help also formed fertile soil for new developments in therapy. Psychoanalysis required a long series of treatment sessions and was not experienced by all therapists as effective. In 1942, Carl Rogers published *Counseling and Psychotherapy*, in which he proposed client-centred therapy as an alternative. In this therapy, the clients searched for solutions to their current problems by talking them through with a listening, understanding and supporting therapist. This is how Rogers (1942) introduced it:

> There are a great many professional individuals who spend a large portion of their time in interviewing, bringing about a constructive change of attitude on the part of their clients through individual and face-to-face contacts. Whether such an individual calls himself a psychologist, a college counselor, a marital advisor, a psychiatrist, a social worker, a high-school guidance counselor, an industrial personnel worker, or by some other name, his approach to the attitudes of his client is of concern to us in this book . . .
>
> There are various names which may be attached to such interviewing processes. They may be termed treatment interviews, which is a simple and descriptive term. Most frequently they are termed counseling, a word in increasingly common use, particularly in educational circles. Or such contacts, with their curative and remedial aim, may be classed as psychotherapy, the term most frequency used by social workers, psychologists, and psychiatrists in clinics. These terms will be used more or less interchangeably in these chapters, and will be so used because they all seem to refer to the same basic method – a series of direct contacts with the individual which aims to offer him assistance in changing his attitudes and behavior.
>
> *(Rogers 1942, p. 3)*

In the light of the power struggle between psychiatrists and psychologists about the right to give psychotherapy it is interesting to see how cleverly Rogers downplayed the requirement of a medical degree for his 'treatment interviews'. What characterised a

KEY FIGURE

Carl Rogers

Source: Roger Ressmeyer/CORBIS

- American psychologist (1902–1987).

- Best known for his client-centred therapy in which people search for solutions to their current problems by talking them through with a listening, understanding and supporting therapist or counsellor.

- Rogers's therapeutic approach was based on a personality theory, which stressed that humans are driven by a positive force to move forward and to realise themselves, a force Rogers called self-actualisation. This was a reaction against Freud's negative view of humans (who saw individuals as being in a never-ending struggle between unconscious factions).

- Rogers was also one of the founders of humanistic psychology in the 1950s, a movement that emphasised the fact that humans are individuals, unique beings who should be recognised and treated as such by mental health practitioners. The humanistic approach was presented as the third way, a counterweight against psychoanalysis (which reduced humans to unconscious drives and wishes), and behaviourism (which reduced persons to behaviours controlled by environmental contingencies).

good counsellor in Rogers's eyes was not knowledge of physical diseases and their cures, but:

- unconditional positive regard: the counsellor supports the client unconditionally and non-judgementally,

- empathic understanding: the counsellor ensures that he/she understands the client's thoughts, feelings and meaning from the client's point of view,

- congruence: the counsellor is genuine in their support and understanding, it is not a mere implementation of a therapeutic technique.

After World War II: antipsychiatry, scientific input and psychoactive drugs

Three major developments after World War II further strengthened the status of clinical psychologists. The first was unease with the way in which patients were treated by psychiatrists in asylums. The second was the input from scientific research into psychotherapy. The third was the fact that psychiatrists increasingly turned to medicines for the treatment of mental disorders.

Antipsychiatry

As part of a wider cultural movement against the establishment in the 1960–1970s, the treatment of patients in mental hospitals began to be questioned. It was seen not only as ineffective, but also as dangerous and demeaning for the patients. In the previous decades, psychiatry had experimented with a number of controversial and invasive biological treatments, such as lobotomy and electroshocks, which had adverse consequences.

Lobotomy consisted of cutting the nerve tracts between the frontal lobes and the thalamus. It had been proposed by the Portuguese neurologist Egas Monitz as an efficient treatment of violent behaviour and it was applied on a massive scale in the USA (Monitz in 1949 received the Nobel Prize for the procedure). However, gradually it became clear that the procedure resulted in massive side effects, as described by Hoffman (1949):

> These patients are not only no longer distressed by their mental conflicts but also seem to have little capacity for any emotional experiences – pleasurable or otherwise. They are described by the nurses and the doctors, over and over, as dull, apathetic, listless, without drive or initiative, flat, lethargic, placid and unconcerned, childlike, docile, needing pushing, passive, lacking in spontaneity, without aim or purpose, preoccupied and dependent.

Electroshocks consisted of applying electrical shocks to the brain, resulting in a massive discharge of neurons. Although this procedure has been shown to be effective for the treatment of otherwise incurable depression (UK ECT Review Group 2003), its use in mental hospitals for a long time was much wider and without empirical support.

The use of electroshocks and lobotomy to subdue unruly psychiatric patients became known to the public after the publication of the cult novel *One Flew Over the Cuckoo's Nest* by Ken Kesey in 1962 (based on his experiences as an orderly at a mental-health institute). The novel was subsequently turned into an equally successful play and film.

antipsychiatry movement

a pressure group
starting in the
1960s that called
the usefulness of
the prevailing psy-
chiatric treatments
into question

Lobotomy, electroshocks and other demeaning treatments (such as the use of straitjackets and isolation cells to discipline patients) exposed psychiatry to anti-establishment protests in the 1960s–1970s. This resulted in the antipsychiatry movement, a pressure group that called the usefulness of psychiatry into question. Psychiatry was not seen as a profession helping patients with mental health problems, but as a way of controlling the patients and expelling them from society (see the discussion of Foucault in Chapter 12). This criticism did not only come from outside. Within universities it was driven by the publications of a number of psychiatrists who felt unhappy with the prevailing treatments (Rissmiller and Rissmiller 2006). For example, in 1960 the American psychiatrist Thomas Szasz published *The Myth of Mental Illness*, in which he argued that most psychiatric disorders were not incurable mental diseases, but transient problems with life and difficulties fitting in with society. He argued that this should be reflected in the treatment. A similar case was made by the Scottish psychiatrist Ronald Laing (e.g. Laing 1960).

Another milestone in the realisation that the existing psychiatric institutions did not help patients with mental problems, came with the publication of the article *On being sane in insane places* in 1973 by the psychologist David Rosenhan. In this study, eight healthy volunteers (including Rosenhan and a few other psychologists) went to mental hospitals complaining that they heard voices saying 'empty, hollow, and thud'. All 'patients' were admitted and essentially left to their own devices. Even though the complaint about the voices was the only symptom ever mentioned and the pseudopatients immediately ceased simulating any more symptoms of abnormality once they were admitted, they were institutionalised for between 7 and 52 days and eventually discharged with the diagnosis 'schizophrenia in remission' (meaning that they were thought to be schizophrenic, but at that moment did not display symptoms). None of the staff noticed that the patients behaved 'normally', although the nurses did mention in their reports that the patients' behaviour was exemplary (i.e. not disruptive).

On the basis of incidents like the ones just described, the antipsychiatry movement contended that the treatment of mental disorders had to change. For a start, there had to be much more respect for the rights and the dignity of the patients. Second, hospitalisation had to be as short as possible and geared towards reintegration in society. And, finally, many more initiatives had to be taken to prevent hospitalisation and to treat people with mental problems outside clinics. All of these recommendations went in the direction of the positions defended by clinical psychologists (e.g. Rogers's client-centred approach) and, as a result, improved the standing of clinical psychologists within mental health organisations.

? What do you think?

The idea put forward by the antipsychiatry movement (treating people with mental problems in the society, outside clinics) very much resembles the informal care that existed before the state started to intervene with its asylums (Chapter 3). In what respects does the new care differ from the old, informal care? Does it make any difference to you whether you can work as a psychologist in a mental health centre or whether you take care of a relative with a mental health problem? Why?

Input from science

Another evolution after World War II that improved the standing of clinical psychologists was the fact that researchers started to evaluate the efficacy of therapies. It was no longer enough to believe the founders' claims about the usefulness of their therapies; value had to be shown empirically. In this respect, one of the first studies turned out to be a severe wake-up call. Hans Eysenck (1952/1992) reviewed the available evidence about the effectiveness of talking cures for non-psychotic patients (i.e. patients without hallucinations and delusions). He compared the improvement of persons who were given psychotherapy, with the improvement of persons who did not see a therapist but were put on a waiting list (and remained in contact with their general practitioner). Eysenck observed that in *both* groups about two-thirds of the patients were significantly better two years later. The therapy group did not outperform the control group, indicating that the effect due to the therapy had been minimal or even absent. All progress could be explained by a general improvement in the condition of the patients since the moment they sought therapeutic help. On the basis of this finding Eysenck concluded that:

> ...certain conclusions are possible from these data. They fail to prove that psychotherapy, Freudian or otherwise, facilitates the recovery of neurotic patients. They show that roughly two-thirds of a group of neurotic patients will recover or improve to a marked extent within about two years of the onset of their illness, whether they are treated by means of psychotherapy or not. This figure appears to be remarkably stable from one investigation to another, regardless of type of patient treated, standard of recovery employed, or method of therapy used. From the point of view of the neurotic, these figures are encouraging; from the point of view of the psychotherapist, they can hardly be called very favorable to his claims.
>
> (Eysenck 1952/1992, p. 661–2)

Although Eysenck (1952/1992) could have concluded from his findings that all forms of psychotherapy were worthless, his message was subtler. He argued that the therapies in the 1950 were ineffective, because they were not based on scientific research. If therapists wanted their therapies to be helpful, they had to systematically examine which techniques worked and which did not, and adapt their approach as a function of the feedback. Indeed, Eysenck would later become a strong supporter of therapies grounded in psychological research, such as behaviour therapy (based on the principles of operant and classical conditioning; see Eysenck 1976) and cognitive therapy (based on research in cognitive psychology about debilitating thoughts and convictions).

Eysenck's (1952/1992) study also gave rise to much more research on the effectiveness of therapies, both existing ones and new ones that were introduced. Thankfully for the mental health sector, these new results were considerably more reassuring: more clients who were given psychotherapy recovered than clients who were denied psychotherapy; they also improved more rapidly (see e.g. Wampold *et al.* 1997). As all this research was done by psychologists, it once again increased the status of clinical psychologists in the mental health services.

The availability of medicines for mental disorders

Another reason why clinical psychologists became more involved in psychotherapies was that the psychiatrists lowered their resistance against treatment by non-medical

psychoactive drugs

medicines prescribed for mental disorders

practitioners. This was partly because of the influence of psychology pressure groups, but also because of the fact that psychiatrists increasingly turned towards medicines as the preferred treatment for mental health problems. Given that only medical practitioners were allowed to prescribe medicines, this gave psychiatrists a new edge over psychologists.

The first psychoactive drugs, medicines that relieve the symptoms of mental disorders, were discovered by chance, as side-effects of existing medicines. The emergence of these drugs can be traced back to antihistamines synthesised in the 1940s (i.e. medicines against allergic reactions). From these, in 1950 chlorpromazine was developed, which turned out to be a sedative (i.e. it made animals and people calm). It was tested in a French hospital on patients with debilitating psychotic episodes and turned out to be unexpectedly effective for most of them, significantly diminishing their delusions and hallucinations. In a few years, chlorpromazine swept across the mental hospitals, and pharmaceutical companies tried to improve on it, which among other things, gave rise to new applications. One of the derivatives of chlorpromazine, for instance, turned out to be an antidepressant.

Together with the altered views of society, the psychoactive drugs radically changed the treatment of mental disorders. First, they contributed to non-residential therapies, greatly reducing the number of patients who had to be hospitalised for long periods. Second, they lowered the threshold for treatment of mental health problems. In most developed countries psychoactive drugs nowadays account for 15 per cent of all medicines taken (a number that is still rising), with antidepressants and anti-anxiety medicines figuring among the top-10 of the medications taken.

social management

management and control of deviant individuals and individuals in need by official social services

welfare state

socio-political system in which individuals insure themselves against setbacks via taxes, which are used by the state to provide welfare services

individualisation

trend in a society towards looser social relations and a greater focus by individuals on themselves than on the groups they belong to

Social management and individualisation

The growing impact of clinical psychology over the twentieth century was also linked to the enhanced role of social management in society. As we saw in Chapter 3, from the sixteenth century onwards authorities increasingly replaced the family and relatives for the control of individuals who did not adhere to the existing norms and for the care of those who could not maintain themselves. This process continued in the twentieth century, giving rise to the so-called welfare state, a situation in which individuals insured themselves against setbacks via taxes with the state providing welfare services.

The reliance on public services, including mental health organisations, grew not only because people wanted to have professional help, but also because social structures became looser. Due to increased social mobility, social relationships were more and more limited to work contacts and people often found themselves in situations in which they did not trust their acquaintances enough to confide in them. At the same time, people developed a growing awareness of their individuality and defined themselves increasingly in terms of their own qualities, achievements and emotions rather than on the basis of the groups they belonged to. The greater focus on the self further increased the likelihood that people would want to talk to a professional counsellor about their functioning. Both evolutions (looser social relations and a greater focus on the self) are summarised in the sociological literature under the name individualisation.

CASE STUDY

Working in the Healthcare Unit of a prison

When I finished my BSc Psychology, I applied for a position of Prison Officer working on a healthcare unit that caters for women with varying mental health needs. I always had a passion for forensic psychology and in my final year of university elected to study various units pertaining to this subject. Post graduation I wanted to gain practical experience working with mentally disordered offenders and saw the Prison Service as a perfect opportunity to achieve this. To my delight, I got recruited. This was two years ago.

Now I work as part of a multidisciplinary team caring for women with all manner of mental health needs in the prison environment. We aim to help these women reintegrate themselves into the generic prison population or where necessary arrange for their transfer to medium or high security psychiatric hospitals.

All things tend to be very different in practice than they are in theory. This was exactly what I found when I was first exposed to individuals who were diagnosed with the mental illnesses I had read so much about. At times this proved to be incredibly stressful and upsetting. Dealing with repeated acts of serious self-harm, restraining violent patients or even just listening to women recount tales of an abusive past or talk about their crimes can be mentally and physically draining.

However, the experiences have been invaluable and far surpass any negative aspects. In prison many of these women were provided with the treatment and care that had not been afforded to them in the community. It may be a cliché but by working in this type of environment you really do feel like you are making a positive difference to the lives of many.

In the meantime I have also started a Masters in Forensic Mental Health with the intention of exploring the subject further at a doctoral level.

(C.J., personal communication, 24 April 2008)

Increased knowledge about psychology in the population

A final reason why clinical psychology became increasingly pervasive in society towards the beginning of the twenty-first century was that this type of knowledge got integrated into mainstream education and became part of everyday interactions. As for the former, an increasing number of degree programmes involving communication with clients started to pay attention to psychological ideas and findings. The majority of teachers, nurses, social workers, clergy and secretaries nowadays take at least one introductory psychology course as part of their education. As Jansz put it:

> ...as important was the gradual adoption of psychological methods and more generally, a psychologized perspective, by other professionals. Almost without exception, psychology was introduced as part of the training in the 'helping' professions. In particular, the basic technique of 'counseling', developed . . . by the psychologist Carl Rogers, became a widely used tool among professionals of various disciplines. Focusing on the articulation of clients' needs and encouraging a supportive and advisory, rather than directing, role of professionals, it fitted perfectly with the change from an authoritarian, disciplinary style of intervention to more subtle ways of influencing behavior.

(Jansz 2004, p. 39)

At the same time, psychological research findings have become part of general knowledge. People who today read newspapers and magazines have a weekly supply of the newest psychological findings; psychology and psychological problems are discussed in television talk shows; and psychology has become by far the most popular topic of self-study. Even everyday conversations are full of words borrowed from psychology: people are said to be nervous, unconscious, extrovert, intelligent, depressed, self-conscious, neurotic, emotionally stable, dependent, etc. This does not mean that all the information is correct and that everyone has a coherent picture of what is known in psychology. It does mean, however, that knowledge of basic psychological findings and psychological vocabulary slowly but surely has become public property, as indicated by Ward (2002) at the beginning of this chapter.

Interim summary

Twentieth-century changes in the treatment of mental health problems:

■ Before World War I psychologists were largely excluded from treatment; their main task was administering psychological tests; there were a few university-related centres.

■ Because of the increased need for advice and treatment during World War II, psychologists became involved in treatment.

■ After World War II, the position of psychologists in the treatment of mental disorders was further strengthened by
  ■ the antipsychiatry movement,
  ■ scientific research on the efficacy of psychotherapies,
  ■ the fact that psychiatrists became more involved with the prescription of psychoactive drugs,
  ■ the increase of social management and individualisation in society.

■ Knowledge of psychology also became of public interest.

7.2   Psychological testing

The need for tests in society

Throughout recorded history, people have used tests in three types of situations: to establish a person's honesty, to select the best person and to diagnose illness.

Authenticity tests to expose dishonesty

Humans can deceive. They can present themselves differently from whom and what they are. To counteract this tendency, social groups have devised a long tradition of techniques to see through lies and to reveal the underlying truth. These techniques

authenticity test

test to determine whether a person is who he/she pretends to be and to ascertain guilt or innocence

were called authenticity tests, tests to establish whether individuals were who they claimed to be. An early example of such a test can be found in Homer's epic poem, *The Odyssey* (written around 700 BCE). In this poem the queen Penelope set two authenticity tests to find out whether the person who turned up after 20 years' absence was indeed her husband Odysseus. One of the tests was to string a particular bow and shoot an arrow through 12 axe-handles, a feat only Odysseus could accomplish.

Authenticity tests were also used to ascertain guilt and innocence. One such test was trial by ordeal. For instance, in Europe between 500 and 1200 CE the innocence of people was sometimes determined by throwing them into a river with hands and feet bound. The assumption was that God would reveal his judgement by letting the innocent drown and making the guilty float (the latter was believed to be particularly true for witches).

Qualifying tests to measure aptitude and competence

qualifying test

test to find the best person for a task

Authenticity tests were only useful when someone was suspected of wrongdoing. Another situation asking for tests occurred when the best person for a task had to be designated. Then, a so-called qualifying test was required. This happened, for instance, in the legendary, medieval world of King Arthur. Only the person who was able to draw the magic sword Excalibur from the rock would be the rightful king.

Tests to diagnose disease

diagnostic tests

tests to determine which condition a person has

A final use of tests was to determine which adverse condition people had. These are the so-called diagnostic tests. For instance, papyri from Ancient Egypt minutely described the symptoms that pointed to various diseases. Similarly, Byzantine doctors (*c.* 300 – *c.* 1450 CE) had an extensive system to assess illnesses on the basis of a visual analysis of the patient's urine (a technique known as uroscopy, not to be confused with the current-day chemical analysis of urine, known as urinalysis). This technique was passed on to the Arabs and medieval Western Europe.

What is a test?

Although most people have an implicit understanding of what a test is, the American sociologist Alan Hanson claims that few are aware of the fact that tests actually involve three basic conditions (Hanson 1993):

1. A test contains the condition of intent: tests are planned, arranged and given by someone with a purpose in mind; they are never random events.

2. A test is not administered to collect information about performance on the test itself, but as an indication of some other condition: for instance, uroscopy was not meant to collect information about the urine, but to make statements about possible illnesses in the person.

3. A test involves a difference in status between the test giver and the test taker: the test giver draws conclusions on the basis of the test which the test taker has to undergo. Usually test givers represent organisations, whereas the test takers are individuals. (The importance of this aspect will become clearer in Chapter 12.)

Psychologists and tests

From the outset psychologists were adamant that they could provide society with good tests about mental functioning. They could make authenticity tests (e.g. for lie detection), qualifying tests (e.g. for personnel selection) and diagnostic tests (e.g. for the assessment of learning difficulties) that went far beyond what was available. These tests would be based on scientific research, inspired by the belief that human nature depended on invariable laws, which science could discover and bring into use. (You may have noticed that none of the pre-scientific, historical examples given above has stood the test of time.) Psychology would do for mental functioning what medical science was doing for physical functioning: provide practitioners with scientifically validated tests they could rely on.

The need for reliable and valid assessment

A first major achievement of psychologists was that they were able to define what good tests were and how this could be assessed in an objective way. Two issues were of importance: reliability and validity.

Reliability

reliability

in test research the degree to which the outcome of a test is the same if the test is repeated under unchanged circumstances or if an equivalent test is used

By reliability, psychologists mean that the assessment will be the same if it is repeated under unchanged circumstances. For instance, reliable scales imply that you get the same weight if you step on them twice with a few seconds in between or if you weigh yourself on two different scales. Similarly, a reliable psychological assessment means that you will get the same outcome if the assessment is repeated without any intervention or if the assessment is repeated by another professional.

The reliability of a test can be measured by calculating the correlation between two different measurements. For instance, a group of people is given a test twice with a few weeks in between. Then, a mathematical formula is used to express the relationship between the measures. This results in a *correlation coefficient*, which can in theory vary from -1.00 (when the measurements are each other's opposite), over 0.00 (when the two measurements are not related to each other), to $+1.00$ (when the measurements indicate the same ordering of participants). In practice, the correlation coefficient in reliability research will be between 0.00 (a useless test) and $+1.00$ (a perfect test). This is illustrated in figure 7.1. Over the years, test construction has become so professionalised that only test–retest correlation coefficients higher than $+.80$ are still acceptable.

The concept of test reliability was introduced in 1904 by the British psychologist Charles Spearman, shortly after his colleague Karl Pearson developed the first useful technique to calculate correlations. Spearman's work was picked up by the American psychologist Edward L. Thorndike, who at that time was writing his highly influential book *An Introduction to the Theory of Mental and Social Measurements*. From there it spread rapidly throughout the group of psychologists interested in test construction.

Validity

validity

in test research the degree to which a test measures what it claims to measure; determined by correlating the test results with an external criterion

A valid assessment means that the assessment measures what it claims to measure. Validity implies reliability but goes beyond that. For instance, you can imagine that Byzantine physicians were quite reliable in establishing the colour of urine, but that very often there was no correlation between the colour of the urine and the disease

(a) Scenario 1: A perfect test

	Score 1	Score 2
person 1	15	15
person 2	20	20
person 3	18	18
person 4	10	10
person 5	16	16

correlation coefficient =   1.00

(b) Scenario 2: A good test

	Score 1	Score 2
person 1	15	13
person 2	20	22
person 3	18	14
person 4	10	11
person 5	16	16

correlation coefficient =   0.82

(c) Scenario 3: A bad test

	Score 1	Score 2
person 1	15	14
person 2	20	11
person 3	18	20
person 4	10	14
person 5	16	22

correlation coefficient =   0.03

(d) Scenario 4: A weird test

	Score 1	Score 2
person 1	15	15
person 2	20	10
person 3	18	16
person 4	10	20
person 5	16	18

correlation coefficient =   −0.83

Figure 7.1 The reliabilities of tests expressed as correlation coefficients.
Five people take the same test twice in 3 weeks. The first scenario depicts the ideal situation. Each person gets exactly the same score on the second test taking as on the first test taking. This is expressed by the correlation coefficient of +1.00. Scenario 2 depicts a more realistic situation: there are some small differences in the scores, but participants who scored high the first time also score high the second time, and people who scored low the first time score low the second time. This is expressed in the correlation coefficient of +0.82. Scenario 3 points to a very bad test: there is no relationship whatsoever between the scores obtained on the first test taking and the scores obtained on the second test taking. This is captured by the correlation coefficient of +0.03. Finally, scenario 4 illustrates a situation that would be very alarming: the participants who performed worst on the first test taking, score best on the second test taking and vice versa. This is represented by the correlation coefficient of −0.83. Such a situation never occurs in reliability research, because it would imply that the first test taking had a profound impact on those who took it.

they diagnosed. A similar situation would be present if you tried to predict people's intelligence by measuring the strength of their hand grip. Although you can get reliable measurements of grip strength (which remain stable on repeated tests), knowing this value for a particular person would tell you nothing about that person's intelligence. People with a strong hand grip can be low, medium or high in intelligence. Similarly, people with a weak grip can have all possible levels of intelligence. So, knowledge about the grip strength of a person gives you no information about the person's intelligence. It is not a valid measure of intelligence. Indeed, as we saw in Chapter 3, many of the first attempts to measure intelligence turned out to be invalid (see the efforts of Galton and Van Biervliet, and the first attempts of Binet).

Validity concerns were present from the very beginning of test construction. For instance, Binet and Simon (Chapter 3) made sure that the items of their intelligence test could be answered by all children up to a certain age (and not, for example, by 5-year-olds but no longer by 11-year-olds). This age-differentiation criterion was based on the assumption that intelligence increases with age through childhood and that this should be reflected in the performance on the items. In addition, the scores on the intelligence tests were compared with the judgements of teachers (or the school results) to see whether they showed the expected relationship with school performance.

Most of the early validation attempts were done in an unorganised way, however, with every test constructor using their own home-made method. This changed when the American Psychological Association at the end of the 1940s supported a task force to streamline the various attempts and to write a proper manual on how to establish the validity of psychological tests (which was published in 1954).

Clinical impressions and unstructured interviews do not score high on reliability and validity

A second important finding by psychologists was that the intuitively most appealing way to obtain information about other people, a face-to-face interview, did not score high on reliability and validity. We start with one of the first studies on this topic and then continue with some more recent theorising.

Differences between raters

Hollingworth (1922) ran a study in which 12 experienced sales managers interviewed 57 applicants for 'positions involving personal salesmanship of a well-known service'. The managers were free to discuss anything they pleased with the applicants during the interviews. After the interviews, the sales managers were asked to rank the candidates as a function of their suitability for the job (1 = best candidate, 57 = worst candidate). Table 7.1 shows the results Hollingworth obtained for the first 10 candidates. In this figure you can clearly see the disagreement between the different managers with respect to the suitability of the various candidates. (If you are interested, the correlations between the various managers varied from +0.62 between managers 3 and 11 to −0.48 between managers 7 and 9! The mean correlation coefficient over all managers was a meagre +0.15.)

This is what Hollingworth concluded on the basis of his findings:

The facts shown by the table are instructive enough. Almost any given applicant is likely to receive ratings placing him at any point in the scale, from first position to last. Applicant C, for example, is given position 1 by one judge, 57 by another, 2 by a third, and 53 by a fourth judge; in general he occupies positions all along the scale of 'suitability.' Much the same result is to be observed with all of the applicants. Occasionally an applicant is found whom all the judges tend to judge more or less favorably. Thus applicant I may be said to be favorably rated, on the whole, although even here the positions assigned him range all the way from 2 to 36. . . .

When it is borne in mind that these judges were not casual people who were enlisted in the investigation, but expert sales managers, experienced interviewers and directors of personnel, and that the position (salesmanship) for which they were

Table 7.1 Ranks assigned to applicants by interviewers

Lack of agreement of sales managers concerning the suitability of candidates for a sales position. Managers were asked to rank the candidates on the basis of an unstructured interview with them (1 = best candidate; 57 = worst candidate).

Applicant	Sales managers											
	1	2	3	4	5	6	7	8	9	10	11	12
A	33	46	6	56	26	32	12	38	23	22	22	9
B	36	50	43	17	51	47	38	20	38	55	39	9
C	53	10	6	21	16	9	20	2	57	28	1	26
D	44	25	13	48	7	8	43	11	17	12	20	9
E	54	41	33	19	28	48	8	10	56	8	19	26
F	18	13	13	8	11	15	15	31	32	18	25	9
G	33	2	13	16	28	46	19	32	55	4	16	9
H	13	40	6	24	51	49	10	52	54	29	21	53
I	2	36	6	23	11	7	23	17	6	5	6	9
J	43	11	13	11	37	40	36	46	25	15	29	1

Source: Hollingworth (1922, p. 65)

rating the applicants was precisely in the line of work in which they had developed expertness and acquired positions of responsibility, the inference is clear. However much the interview may be improved by better methods of inquiry and report, in its traditional form it is highly unreliable. No better evidence is required than the spectacle of two different expert interviewers, one rejecting an applicant as the most unsuitable of the group of fifty-seven, another selecting him as the choice specimen of the lot.

(Hollingworth 1922, p. 64–6)

Subsequent research confirmed Hollingworth's finding about the low reliability of unstructured interviews and extended it to validity issues. It has been shown over and over again that on the basis of unstructured interviews there is little correlation between scores given by personnel managers at job interviews and subsequent performance levels (McDaniel *et al.* 1994); there is little correlation between how positively students are evaluated on university intake interviews and their subsequent exam results (Hell *et al.* 2007); and there is little correlation between the impression inmates make on probation panels and their subsequent risk of reoffending (Monahan 1981). Binet around 1900 already reported that teachers were not able to assess a pupil's intelligence on the basis of an interview (as mentioned in Hollingworth 1922).

First impression and the implicit personality theory

It took psychologists quite some time to find out why decisions on the basis of interviews turned out to be so unreliable and invalid. A major breakthrough came

**implicit
personality
theory**

mixture of stereo-
types and individu-
ating information
about the associa-
tions of person
characteristics that
people use to make
predictions about
how others will
behave in social
relations

when it was shown that the decisions on the basis of interviews largely depended on the first impression candidates make. This impression is based on the so-called **implicit personality theory** of the assessors, a mixture of stereotypes and individuation information every person has and uses to make predictions about how others will behave (Kunda and Thagard 1996; Schneider 1973). Stereotypes are simplistic views about groups of people based on categories such as gender, race, age, place of birth, profession and appearance. For instance, when you hear that your new room-mate will be a Spanish exchange student called Manolo, this activates a number of expectations about what type of person he will be and how he will act. Stereotypes are mostly acquired through observational learning, on the basis of how various groups are treated and how they are represented on television and in the other media. For instance, it has been shown over and over again that physically attractive people are considered to be more interesting and competent than less attractive people (e.g. Eagly *et al.* 1991; Hosoda *et al.* 2003). Along the same lines, it has been observed that overweight people make a less positive first impression, which they must overcome in subsequent contacts (Puhl and Brownell 2001).

Individuation information refers to everything known about a person as an individual. The more contact one has with a particular person, the more the individuating information replaces the stereotypical views, which are particularly strong on first encounters.

Dougherty *et al.* (1994) showed that if recruiters are not careful, job interviews are to a large extent coloured by first impressions. Candidates who make a positive first impression on the interviewer receive easier questions on which they have more chances of making a good impression than candidates who make a less favourable first impression. Other research has shown that candidates can improve the first impression they make by paying attention to their appearance and their behaviour (as shown in figure 7.2). This phenomenon is known as *impression management* (Leary and Kowalski 1990). Such impression management again reduces the validity of an unstructured interview, because fundamentally nothing has changed; the candidate has just learned to make a better first impression on the interviewer.

? What do you think?

Sometimes people find it hard to believe that their first impression has such a strong influence on their expectations and judgements of others. One situation you may be familiar with, however, is when you first see a person for some time and then hear them talk. Have you ever experienced surprise because the voice was so different from what you expected? The reverse is also true. Often people are astonished when they see a photograph of a radio presenter they know well. They had imagined them completely differently. Can you find other examples of how you automatically seem to activate expectations of people on the basis of small bits of information? For instance, with whom would you prefer to collaborate: Michael or Hubert? And why?

Figure 7.2 Which doctor would you prefer to look after you?
Patients in an Accident and Emergency Unit were shown a card with pictures of different physicians and asked who they wanted to look after them. Eighty per cent of the patients preferred to be treated by a doctor in a white coat. This was particularly true when the pictures were of female physicians. This figure shows four pictures of the same person that were used on the different cards.

Source: Rehman *et al.* (2005). Reproduced with permission.

Psychological tests as the alternative

Having found ways to measure the quality of a test and having found that face-to-face interactions with unknown people did not score well, psychologists set out to develop and scrutinise better alternatives.

Structured vs. unstructured interviews

On the basis of their initial experiences, psychologists realised that they had to take away the variability due to assessors and contexts if they wanted to improve the reliability of their assessments. Reliability was adversely affected by factors that varied randomly from observation to observation. For instance, given that the type of questions asked in job interviews depended on the first impression the candidate made, one way to increase the reliability of the procedure was to have a standard set of questions asked of each candidate, so that all applicants could be judged on the same core of information. Such a procedure became known as a **structured interview**, as opposed to an unstructured interview, in which the questions depended on the answers the applicants gave. Research later indeed confirmed that structured interviews were a more reliable and valid way of assessing job applicants than unstructured interviews (McDaniel *et al.* 1994; Schmidt and Hunter 1998).

structured interview

interview in which all interviewees receive the same set of questions

Standardised tests

standardised psychological test

test that psychologists have examined for reliability and validity, for which they have information about the expected perform- ance, and which is administered in a uniform way

A still better way to limit the influence of biasing factors was to develop and use standardised psychological tests. These were tests that psychologists had examined for reliability and validity, for which they had information about the expected perform- ance, and which were administered in a uniform way (so that the performance was not affected by the test giver). Many of these insights were in a rudimentary form present when psychologists started to develop their first tests at the beginning of the twentieth century, but required decades of test development and test research before they were fully understood and implemented. As a consequence, the quality of the tests improved throughout the twentieth century and in all likelihood will continue to do so for some time to come (as psychologists are still working on further improvements of many tests currently used). Below, we discuss the main developments in three of the most frequently used standardised tests: intelligence tests, achievement tests and personality tests.

Intelligence and achievement tests

IQ-tests

IQ-test

test which is sup- posed to measure the intelligence of a person; focuses on learning potential; results correlate with school performance and suitability for intellectually demanding occupations

In Chapter 3 we saw how Binet and Simon designed the first valid intelligence test. It was no coincidence that the test was proposed around the time when primary school education became compulsory. Suddenly schools were confronted by the fact that not all children were doing well, even though many of them did not show obvious signs of mental limitations. It was not clear whether these children performed badly because they were 'feeble-minded' or because they did not get enough support at home, hence the need for an intelligence test and its enormous popularity once it became available.

Although the IQ-test was primarily meant for schools, its aim was not to duplicate school exams. It was not intended as an evaluation of what *had been learned*, but as an indication of the *potential to learn*, independent of the circumstances in which the test taker had grown up. Although the latter seems quite obvious to us now, it took psychologists many years to realise that information-related questions very often showed cultural biases, which advantaged some groups of participants over others. These biases became painfully visible when IQ-tests were administered on a very large scale to army recruits in World War I (in which the USA entered in 1917) and to immigrants. There was a massive difference in test scores between white people with an English-speaking background and those with another background. Although at first this was used as an argument to limit the immigration of people with a non-English background, it gradually became clear that part of the difference was due to the questions used. For instance, in one test participants were given a picture of a ten-nis court without a net and asked what was missing. Needless to say, those who had never heard of tennis (and there were many of them at the beginning of the twentieth century) failed on this particular item. Awareness of cultural biases resulted in in-creased efforts to make the IQ-tests culture-neutral.

Another development in the construction of IQ-tests was the finding that intelli-gence did not consist of a single ability, but of a group of abilities (see any textbook on intelligence for this). This led to a greater diversity of tasks in the IQ-tests (most of Binet's tasks had to do with verbal material). The researcher who arguably was the most instrumental in this change was the American psychologist David Wechsler, who developed the *Wechsler Adult Intelligence Scale* in 1939. In this test he measured at the same time the so-called verbal intelligence and performance intelligence, the latter being measured with tasks such as picture completion, block design and matrix reasoning. By comparing the verbal IQ with the performance IQ, psychologists could see whether the test taker had a particular weakness in language functions or in performance functions. The distinction between verbal and performance intelligence was retained in the later tests Wechsler developed for children and preschool children, and encouraged the use of a larger diversity of tasks in other intelligence tests as well.

Achievement tests

achievement test

standardised test which measures the knowledge of a particular topic or set of topics

Quite soon (American) test developers saw that the approach of IQ-tests could be combined with that of traditional exams to make so-called standardised **achievement tests**. Seven years after Lewis Terman finished the *Stanford–Binet Intelligence Test* (the first truly standardised intelligence test in the USA, published in 1916), he was co-author of the *Stanford Achievement Test*. Achievement tests probed the participants' knowledge of a preset series of topics, to measure the intellectual progress of the participants and their suitability for intellectually demanding positions. To increase their reliability, the tests mostly made use of multiple-choice questions (i.e. for each question a limited number of possible answers is given and the candidate has to indicate which one is correct).

Achievement tests rapidly conquered the educational system. They became the instrument of choice to compare the performance of pupils. In many countries they also started to play a role in the entrance to universities and government positions. For instance, in the USA the *Scholastic Aptitude Test* was introduced in 1926 and is still administered (under a different name) to almost 2 million students every year. These students see their university options affected by the results they obtain. Similarly, future employees of the European Union have to pass an entry exam that largely consists of an achievement test.

Achievement tests also became part of the quality control set up by political administrations. For instance, in 1989 the British government not only introduced minimum standards of what had to be taught in primary and secondary schools in England and Wales, it also introduced a system of nationwide achievement tests to assess the pupils' performance regularly in the different schools (the so-called *Standard Attainment Tests* or SATs, taken by pupils at the age of 7, 11 and 14 years. However, from 2009, the tests for 14-year-olds will be abolished and students will be assessed by their teachers instead.).

? What do you think?

Discuss the importance of reliability and validity for achievement tests. Can you see why parents in England and Wales would be upset if it turned out that the SATs were unreliable or invalid?

Achievement tests were also used to compare whole nations. Table 7.2 shows the results of one such evaluation, looking at science education in different countries. All participants sat the same science achievement test and on the basis of their results,

Table 7.2 Standardised achievement tests

Standardised achievement tests are used to compare the performance of schools across countries. In this table you find the results of 15-year-olds on a science test administered in different countries, ranked from highest to lowest.

Country	Mean score	Country	Mean score
Finland	563	Slovak Republic	488
Hong Kong – China	542	Spain	488
Canada	534	Lithuania	488
Chinese Taipei	532	Norway	487
Estonia	531	Luxembourg	486
Japan	531	Russian Federation	479
New Zealand	530	Italy	475
Australia	527	Portugal	474
Netherlands	525	Greece	473
Liechtenstein	522	Israel	454
Korea	522	Chile	438
Slovenia	519	Serbia	436
Germany	516	Bulgaria	434
United Kingdom	515	Uruguay	428
Czech Republic	513	Turkey	424
Switzerland	512	Jordan	422
Macao – China	511	Thailand	421
Austria	511	Romania	418
Belgium	510	Montenegro	412
Ireland	508	Mexico	410
Hungary	504	Indonesia	393
Sweden	503	Argentina	391
Poland	498	Brazil	390
Denmark	496	Colombia	388
France	495	Tunisia	386
Croatia	493	Azerbaijan	382
Iceland	491	Qatar	349
Latvia	490	Kyrgyzstan	322
United States	489		

Source: Based on figure 2.11b 'Multiple comparisons of mean performance on the science scale', p. 56, *PISA 2006 Science competencies for tomorrow's world*, **1**. OECD 2007. Reproduced with permission.

average scores per country were calculated. Each time the results of such a comparison are published, they are followed by lengthy discussions in government and in the media about the relative position of their own country and what can be done to improve it (or retain it).

Achievement tests in China

It may be good to know that the Western society is not the only society that uses achievement tests for entry to highly esteemed positions. Nor for that matter was it the first. Some 2000 years ago the Chinese Han Dynasty (206 BCE–220 CE) used a standardised test battery to select and promote civil servants in an objective way. The administration of these tests became better and better organised (involving a hierarchy of local, regional and national testing centres) to reach the maximum number of candidates. Only those who passed the final (national) set of tests were eligible for office.

There is good evidence that the Western world learned about achievement tests through the Chinese (Kaplan and Saccuzzo 2005, p. 12). Reports by British missionaries and diplomats in the nineteenth century encouraged the English East India Company to use the Chinese system for the selection of their personnel. From there the practice spread to the British government, the governments of mainland Europe and the USA. Standardised achievement tests still are a central element in Chinese education and the civil service.

Personality tests

personality test

test to measure relatively stable and distinctive patterns of behaviour that characterise individuals and their reactions to the environment

Personality tests are another widely used type of test. They are meant to probe relatively stable and distinctive patterns of behaviour that characterise individuals and their reactions to the environment.

The Woodworth Personal Data Sheet

One of the first personality tests was the *Woodworth Personal Data Sheet*, published by Robert S. Woodworth in 1920 to identify soldiers who would be susceptible to shellshock (remember that this became a problem in World War I). The test consisted of 116 questions, such as:

- Does the sight of blood make you sick or dizzy?
- Are you happy most of the time?
- Do you sometimes wish you had never been born?
- Do you drink whisky every day?
- Do you wet the bed at night?

There were two features of Woodworth's questionnaire that soon turned out to need improvement. First, the questions were mainly based on Woodworth's clinical judgement without properly testing whether they did indeed make a distinction between soldiers who would develop shellshock and those who would not (although Woodworth did reject questions that in a pretest had been endorsed by 25 per cent or more of a normal sample in the scored direction). The second feature was that the test started from the assumption that participants would answer all questions faithfully, even though the available response alternatives often differed in social desirability.

Going beyond face validity

Woodworth's approach of using his own judgement to decide which questions were informative rapidly turned out to be insufficient. A study by Langner (1962) illustrates this point. Langner also wanted to develop a test that would indicate who was likely to develop psychiatric impairment. He started from a total of 120 questions that looked interesting to him. However, unlike Woodworth, he tested the usefulness of the questions by administering them to a group of 72 participants without psychiatric symptoms and a group of 139 hospitalised psychiatric patients and outpatients. Only 21 questions made a clear difference between the two groups and were retained in the test. Subsequently, these questions were administered to a community sample of 1,660 adult residents to determine from which score on there was an increased risk of psychiatric problems. So, rather than deciding which questions looked all right, Langner gathered empirical evidence about the usefulness of his questions. He not only took into account the face validity of the test (whether the questions looked valid to him and his colleagues), but also empirically tested this validity. Such evidence-based validation rapidly became the norm for psychology tests.

face validity

estimating the validity of a test by estimating to what extent the items of the test agree with one's own beliefs; is not evidence-based

The problem of social desirability

Another problem that became clear with the publication of Woodworth's *Personal Data Sheet* was that often the aim of the questions was clear and that participants could adapt their answers as a function of what they thought was socially desirable. One big difference between IQ-tests and personality tests is that in the former case the results depend on the test taker's abilities, whereas in the latter case candidates can choose whatever alternative they prefer, even when it does not (really) apply to them. Social desirability refers to the bias people have to present themselves in a manner they think will be viewed favourably by others (in particular the psychologist who gives the test). This is especially the case in high-stakes situations, where the outcome of the test has implications for the candidate's future (as in job applications; see Ones *et al.* (1996) and Morgeson *et al.* (2007) for the issue of social desirability in this situation).

social desirability

bias people have to present themselves in a manner they think will be viewed favourably by others

Psychologists have explored various ways to circumvent the problem of social desirability. These include making the questions subtler, including a scale to measure the bias in the test taker, and using formats other than self-report questionnaires. The first two measures were included in the *Minnesota Multiphasic Personality Inventory (MMPI)*, published in 1943 and arguably the first high-profile personality questionnaire used in clinical settings. This test consisted of 566 items selected from an original pool of 1,000. They had to be marked 'true' or 'false' by the test-taker. In the validation process, the test was administered to eight different groups of 50 psychiatric patients each (including 'hypochondriacs', 'depressives' and 'schizophrenics') and a group of 700 control participants. On the basis of the answers of the various groups, items were selected that made a distinction between them and were included in a scale for the different clinical profiles (e.g. hypochondria, depression, schizophrenia). In addition, three so-called validity scales were compiled. Two of these validity scales addressed whether the participants were presenting themselves too favourably, for instance by not wanting to acknowledge minor flaws that are present in virtually everybody (e.g. 'I sometimes lose control of myself'). The third validity scale included items that were virtually never endorsed (e.g. 'I am aware of a special presence that others cannot perceive') and, therefore, could indicate whether someone wanted to make a particularly negative impression.

The validation efforts and the measures to come to grips with the social desirability problem illustrate why psychological tests are more than simply 'collecting a few questions' and why they are capable of returning more information than can be obtained on the basis of a simple interview.

Measuring personality differences in the non-pathological range

Personality tests were not only used to distinguish between the normal and the pathological range. They also became used to distinguish between people in the normal range. Particularly influential in this respect was the trait theory of personality. According to this theory, people differ from one another on the basis of a limited number of personality traits, or relatively enduring ways in which they interact with their environment.

personality trait

basic dimension used to describe differences in personality between people; is often bipolar with opposites at the extremes (e.g. introvert vs. extrovert)

The search for personality traits started when the American psychologist Gordon Allport in the 1930s tried to discover the structure that underlies the adjectives people use to describe each other (e.g. 'my left-hand neighbour is polite, helpful and modest, whereas my right-hand neighbour is rude, obstructive and boastful of his wealth'). Allport started from a total of 4,504 adjectives in the English language and set out to see how this number could be reduced. Some adjectives were close synonyms or had largely overlapping meanings (e.g. friendly, cordial, welcoming, amiable, warm). These could be grouped. Other adjectives were opposites (e.g. friendly vs. unfriendly, warm vs. cold). These could be placed at opposite ends of bipolar traits. Allport's main problem, however, was how to do this grouping in an objective way, so that it went beyond his own personal judgement.

Although Allport made some headway (Allport and Odbert 1936), the real breakthrough came when the British psychologist Raymond Cattell joined him for some time at Harvard University. Cattell was a specialist in a new statistical technique to find relationships between stimuli, called factor analysis (see Chapter 10), and he managed to achieve what had eluded Allport. Using a series of studies, he claimed that each person could be described adequately on the basis of 16 bipolar traits, such as reserved–warm, serious–lively, expedient–conscientious, shy–bold and trusting–vigilant. Cattell developed a questionnaire to measure these traits, called the *Sixteen Personality Factors Questionnaire* (Cattell 1956, see figure 7.3).

Cattell's conclusions were opposed by Hans J. Eysenck, who argued that Cattell's 16 traits were not independent dimensions and that people only differed on three traits: introversion–extroversion, neuroticism–emotional stability and psychoticism (without antipole). These were measured with the *Eysenck Personality Questionnaire* (Eysenck and Eysenck 1975; Eysenck *et al.* 1985). Further analyses of the data obtained with the different personality questionnaires suggested that Cattell indeed had overestimated the number of personality traits needed to accurately describe people, but that Eysenck had underestimated them. In the early 1980s researchers more or

A simplified version of the Sixteen Personality Factors Questionnaire

Indicate your position on each scale by placing a mark on each line indicating your position between the extremes.

Reserved	Warm
Reasoning: Concrete	Abstract
Emotionally reactive	Emotionally stable
Deferential	Dominant
Serious	Lively
Expedient	Rule-conscious
Shy	Socially bold
Utilitarian	Sensitive
Trusting	Vigilant
Grounded	Abstracted
Forthright	Private
Self-assured	Apprehensive
Traditional	Open to change
Group-oriented	Self-reliant
Tolerate disorder	Perfectionistic
Relaxed	Tense

Figure 7.3 An example of a personality test.
Score yourself and a friend by placing marks on each line to indicate your positions on each bipolar trait (e.g. where do you see yourself and your friend on the continuum going from reserved to warm?). Ask your friend to do the same and compare your answers.

Source: Simplified version of Cattell's Sixteen Personality Factors Questionnaire based on the bipolar traits identified by Cattell (the personality test itself is protected by copyright)

less settled on a total of five fundamental traits, called the Big Five (e.g. Goldberg 1990). They are:

- Openness to experience
- Conscientiousness
- Extroversion
- Agreeableness
- Neuroticism

Since 1980, a large number of personality questionnaires have been developed based on this categorisation (which can easily be remembered by using the acronym OCEAN). For instance, in personnel selection it has repeatedly been found that employees who score low on conscientiousness ('I rarely plan my work', 'I tend not to be very organised', 'I rarely check the quality of my work') do not get the best appraisals from their supervisors.

What do you think?

Make a list of the occasions on which you were given psychological tests (IQ, achievement, personality, other). Did you perceive these tests as informative? How would you as a psychologist make use of tests?

Development of personality tests

- Robert S. Woodworth (1869–1962)
  - American psychologist and author of very influential textbooks of psychology in the first half of the twentieth century.
  - Author of one of the first personality tests, the Woodworth Personal Data Sheet (measured vulnerability to shellshock).

- Gordon W. Allport (1897–1967)
  - American psychologist who initiated the trait approach in personality research.
  - Sought to find the minimum number of dimensions (traits) needed to describe the personalities of people by analysing the relevant adjectives in the English language.

- Raymond B. Cattell (1905–1998)
  - British born psychologist working in the USA.
  - Used factor analysis to find the minimum number of dimensions needed to describe the personality of people on the basis of adjectives.
  - Settled on 16 dimensions that were measured with the 16 Personality Factors Questionnaire.
  - Also used factor analysis to look at the structure of intelligence as measured with IQ-tests (leading to a distinction between fluid intelligence and crystallised intelligence).

- Hans J. Eysenck (1916–1997)
  - German-born psychologist working in the UK.
  - Argued that personalities were adequately described on the basis of three dimensions: introversion–extroversion, neuroticism–emotional stability and psychoticism.
  - Also known for his strong support of behaviour therapy after having shown that the psychotherapies of the 1950s were ineffective.

Hans J. Eysenck
Source: Popperfoto/
Getty Images

- Various test researchers at the beginning of the 1980s
  - Came to the conclusion that five dimensions are needed to describe personality: openness, conscientiousness, extroversion, agreeableness and neuroticism.

Tests have become increasingly popular due to the individualisation of society

Since their inception the number of psychological tests administered has steadily increased (Hanson 1993). There are several reasons for this. One is that psychological tests are the best we have to make assessments and predictions about human functioning, even if they are not infallible. Another is that society increasingly turned to science-based evidence to make decisions (Chapters 8 and 12), if only so as not to be found legally liable in case the decision was called into question. Finally, the growing individualisation of society also enhanced the need for information about individuals.

Growing individualisation

As we saw above, individualisation involves looser social relations and a greater focus on the self. This process started several centuries ago (arguably when more and more people left their villages and moved to the emerging cities), but further intensified in the twentieth century. At the beginning of that century, more people agreed with statements like 'Children must stay with their parents until they are married' and 'I respect the decisions taken by my family' than at the end of the century. Conversely, more people at the end of the twentieth century agreed with statements like 'If a social group hinders my development, it is better to leave the group' and 'I want to be judged on the basis of my own achievements.'

Within an individualised society, members are more interested in what distinguishes them from others than in what they have in common. Applied to achievement and personality, they are more interested in what is unique to them than in what they share with others. Personality research has followed this shift. Whereas at the beginning of the twentieth century personality theories were about what defined humans in general (e.g. Freud's and Rogers' theories), towards the end of the century research became dominated by individual differences, as measured by ability and personality tests.

Why is society becoming increasingly individualised?

An intriguing question is why Western society has become increasingly individualised and whether such a shift will be true for other cultures as well. One idea was mentioned in Kagitcibasi (2002). According to her, researchers in the 1970s thought collectivism depended on the fear parents had that their children would not take care of them in their old age. As a result, children were not encouraged to show initiative and independence. They were expected to obey their parents and stay in close contact with them. However, after the welfare state became established, the elderly were able to rely less on their children, for example because they received a retirement pension. Consequently, the younger generation was given more freedom and was able to become more autonomous and to optimise their individual potential. This tendency may have been reinforced by the dominance of the countries where the individualisation happened first (UK, USA).

Another idea about growing individualisation was proposed by Foucault (1976). According to him, individualisation was a consequence of the fact that society gathered and stored more and more information about individuals, which in addition was reported back to the citizens. This gave everybody the feeling of standing out of the crowd.

Finally, Richards (2002: 150) conjectured that individualisation was a consequence of the increasing diversity in occupations and complexity of social relations. As long as people stayed in the region and class they were born in, they were content to describe themselves in terms of age, gender, appearance and occupation. At most Hippocrates' four temperaments (phlegmatic, choleric, melancholic and sanguine) were needed for some further refinement of character. However, industrialisation and the increased urbanisation put people in a more complex and competitive social network in which everyone struggled to maintain a sense of dignity and meaning. This intensified the need for instruments to position oneself relative to others, a need that was filled by the ability and personality tests presented by psychologists.

What do you think?

Which explanation of the growing individualisation seems more plausible to you? Could they all apply? Can you think of other explanations?

Interim summary

Psychological testing

- Psychologists needed reliable and valid assessments. These were not provided by unstructured interviews, due to problems with first impressions and the implicit personality theories people have.

- Standardised tests were proposed as an alternative. These tests were administered to a test group in a uniform way, so that the users knew how new test takers scored relative to the test group. In addition, the reliability and validity became empirically verified.

- IQ-tests allowed psychologists to assess an individual's intellectual potential. Achievement tests allowed them to test the acquired knowledge about a particular topic in a reliable and valid way.

- Good personality tests required empirical validation (i.e. they had to go beyond face validity) and measures to tackle the problem of social desirability.

- In the non-pathological range, most personality tests are self-report questionnaires that measure traits. At the moment most researchers believe that the personality can be described accurately on the basis of five traits (Big Five). Previously, Cattell defended a minimum number of 16 and Eysenck a number of 3.

- Tests have become popular partly because of the increased individualisation of society.

7.3   The psychology of work and organisation

An aspect of life that changed beyond recognition in the twentieth century was the type of work people did and the ways in which they interacted at work. Again psychology had a strong involvement in this evolution, not only because an increasing number of psychologists were part of it (e.g. as human resource managers), but also because the different players, from the lowest to the highest level, were inspired by psychological findings. In the previous section we talked about the increased use of standardised tests in personnel selection. In this section we will see how ideas of work motivation changed and what the contribution of psychology was.

Industrial psychology at the beginning of the twentieth century

The industrial revolution in the eighteenth and nineteenth centuries (see Chapter 2) introduced a separation between work and family. Whereas before, family life and work responsibilities had been closely intertwined on the small farms and in the housebound craftsmen's businesses, the new factories broke up that bond. In addition, the growing size and complexity of the companies meant that many workers no longer turned out finished products, but were a link in a much longer production chain.

For most of the nineteenth century and the first half of the twentieth century, employees were considered as 'the hands of the factory'. They were thought to be motivated by physiological needs (to eat, drink, have shelter) and money was seen as the only incentive. Industrial psychology, as it became known at the beginning of the twentieth century, was geared towards improving the efficiency of the work processes and selecting the best applicant for the job. Typical research topics were the minimum number of breaks needed by workers, the most efficient lighting level, or the best organisation of the workplace. In this endeavour, industrial psychology was inspired by the American engineer and inventor Frederick W. Taylor (1856–1915), who improved the productivity of companies by dividing production into a sequence of stages and searching for ways to speed up the stages (this was done, among other things, by measuring the time needed to finish various operations). Taylor (1911) called this approach scientific management. Complex tasks (such as building a machine) were split into a sequence of simple actions that could be performed rapidly and easily. This led to the well-known assembly line.

In Taylor's view, there was a distinction between thought and action: the management thought and the employee carried out the orders. The management's aim was to simplify the various actions, so that there was no problem finding suitable candidates for the jobs. Wages were set in such a way that the individual worker was motivated to work as hard as possible (e.g. by using a bonus system). One of Taylor's convictions was that a lack of individual monitoring and rewarding encouraged the forming of 'gangs', which tended to oppose productivity, because they feared higher productivity would lead to higher performance standards and eventually loss of jobs. Taylor's basic philosophy was that employees would have no problems performing simple, routine jobs in isolation, if they were paid enough. This formed the foundation for the first view about work and organisation, usually indicated with the name industrial psychology.

industrial psychology

first theory about how work should be organised; strongly influenced by Taylor's scientific management: employees were the hands of the company that would accept any work if remunerated enough; tasks had to be made simple so that everyone could do them without much practice

The Hawthorne studies and the human relations movement

Between 1924 and 1932 a number of studies were run at the Hawthorne plant of the Western Electric Company near Chicago, which would have a profound influence on the psychology of work and organisation. They started off as technical optimisation studies, fully in line with the prevailing scientific management approach. One of the factors the researchers examined was the lighting level for the assemblage of telephone relays. Another study looked at the effect of changes in the work hours.

Although the studies were not particularly well designed or well performed (Adair 1984; Kompier 2006; also see below), they led one of the researchers, Elton Mayo, to draw a very far-reaching conclusion. On the basis of the studies, Mayo (1945) decided that it was not so much the physical circumstances or the pay that determined productivity, but the extent to which the workers found themselves valued and esteemed. The various changes the authors introduced had a limited impact, while at the same time the employees involved in the studies outperformed their colleagues. On the basis of these findings, Mayo concluded that the performance was higher because the participants knew they were part of a study and because they had a say in the course of the study.

Mayo used the findings in the Hawthorne plant to argue that industrial psychology was wrong in its emphasis on the physical environment and the pay. What counted in the workplace were the social relations the employees had and the fact they belonged to a group. Informal groups in a company had a strong influence on the workers' well-being and productivity, and good companies looked after these groups. This was the start of the human relations movement. Companies were encouraged to acknowledge the humanity of their employees (rather than seeing them as disposable equipment) and make them feel part of a social organisation (e.g. by supporting informal group activities).

human relations movement

second main theory of how work should be organised; stressed the humanity of the employees and the importance of social relations

The human relations movement also pointed to the importance of the ways in which supervisors interacted with their subordinates. They took inspiration from Kurt Lewin's research on attitude changes in youth groups (e.g. Lewin *et al.* 1939). In particular, Lewin had looked at the consequences of three types of leadership: autocratic (imposing commands), democratic (leading through negotiations) and laissez-faire (giving no leadership). Lewin and his colleagues concluded that there was more originality, group-mindedness and friendliness in the democratic groups, whereas there was more aggression, hostility, scapegoating and discontent in the laissez-faire and autocratic groups. This message agreed well within the wider change that was taking place in Western culture from a 'command society' to a 'negotiating society' (Van Drunen *et al.* 2004: 157).

? What do you think?

The citation below suggests that virtual informal groups are becoming increasingly important in companies. Do you agree? How do they complement face-to-face gatherings? What are their advantages? And can something that is written and visible to everyone be informal?

This year London became the biggest city on Facebook, and more than 1.8 million people now identify it as their primary geographic network – about a quarter of London's official real world population.

Businesses, too, are increasingly finding that their workers are gathering in ad hoc groups on the site.

'It's a bit like an electronic smoking room, but one that's spread across the whole company,' says Giles Deards, a spokesman for BT, where about 8,000 workers are registered on the company's Facebook network. The group was set up by employees rather than corporate bosses, but workers are not blocked from logging on to social networking sites while in the office.

'It's not an official network; it was set up by staff to discuss issues. We've had some surprisingly liberal conversations on there, but that's because people have taken an adult and responsible approach to it.'

(B. Johnson, The Guardian, *15 December 2007. Copyright Guardian News & Media Ltd 2007*)

Human resource management

human resource movement

third main theory of how work should be organised; stressed the desire for self-actualisation in employees; employees will perform best if given autonomy and authority

In the 1980s a new approach replaced the human relations movement: **human resource management**. It stressed more than before that a company's main assets were its employees, who had to be retained and nurtured. The emergence of the human resource management approach was embedded within other major societal changes, such as a change in the type of work that had to be done, and an overall increase of the level of affluence among employees. Most of the monotonous jobs that made up the bulk of factory work at the beginning of the twentieth century were taken over by robots and computers and were replaced by more intellectually demanding jobs in the service sector. In addition, for many of the new jobs, the relationship between productivity and salary became less straightforward than it had been for manufacturing goods.

Table 7.3 Evolution of the psychology of work and organisation

A comparison of industrial psychology and human resource management shows how much ideas about the relations between organisations and their employees changed in the twentieth century.

Industrial psychology	Human resource management
Technology comes first.	Social and technical systems are optimised together.
People are extensions of machines.	People complement machines.
People are expendable spare parts.	People are resources to be developed.
Tasks are narrow and individual: skills are simple.	Related tasks make an optimum grouping; skills are multiple and broad.
Controls are external – for example by supervisors, staff, procedures, books	Individuals are self-controlled; work groups and departments are self-regulating.
Organisation chart has many levels; management style is autocratic.	Organisation chart is flat; management is participative.
Atmosphere is competitive and characterised by gamesmanship.	Atmosphere is collaborative and cooperative.
Only the organisation's purposes are considered.	Individual and social purposes, as well as the organisation's, are considered.
Employees are alienated: 'It's only a job.'	Employees are committed: 'It's my job!'
Organisation is characterised by low risk taking.	Organisation is innovative: New ideas are encouraged.

Source: Weisbord (1985) reproduced by permission from Elsevier. Adapted and reproduced with permission from Trist (1981). Copyright © Queen's Printer for Ontario, 1981.

Influenced by Rogers and humanistic psychology, psychologists started to consider employees as individuals who sought self-actualisation in their work. It became acceptable to give autonomy and authority to the workers and to trust them in terms of discipline. Employees became seen as people who would respond positively to challenges if these contributed to their needs for self-actualisation and autonomy. Management did not have to impose control but give the employees enough trust and responsibility so that they controlled themselves.

Weisbord (1985) published a table that nicely summarizes the changes between industrial psychology and human resource management (table 7.3). With some exaggeration, this table can be considered as the legacy of what the psychology of work and organisation achieved in the twentieth century.

Interim summary

The psychology of work and organisation

- At the beginning of the twentieth century, industrial psychology was under the influence of scientific management which considered workers as dispensable 'hands of the factory', motivated solely by money to address physiological needs.

- Based on the Hawthorne studies, Mayo pointed to the importance of social and psychological factors for the well-being and motivation of employees. This was the start of the human relations movement (e.g. importance of democratic leadership).

- In the 1980s, human resource management stressed that the employees were the central asset of a company. Workers should not be controlled but given autonomy and responsibility so that they come to self-discipline. Work is no longer a chore, but an opportunity that can help self-actualisation.

7.4   Focus on: The lure of idealising classic studies

Without doubt, the Hawthorne studies have played a major role in the history of the psychology of work and organisation. As such, this study is part of all introductory books to this area of research. It even figures in many general introductions to psychology and educational science, because it shows how knowledge of taking part in a study can have a profound effect on the participants' behaviour (this is known as the 'Hawthorne effect'). However, it is becoming increasingly clear that the Hawthorne studies were of a much lower quality than most people are aware of. There are even questions as to whether anything was found in the Hawthorne studies at all!

What actually happened at the Hawthorne plant

The discussion below is based on Kompier (2006). A very similar message can be found in Adair (1984) and other critical reviews. Kompier first described what actually happened in the Hawthorne research (references are omitted):

> The Western Electric Factory was the supplier of telephone equipment to the last American Bell System. The Hawthorne plant was its main factory. At the start of the studies, it offered employment to some 29 000 men and women, many of them immigrants. The Hawthorne research consisted of the following six, partly overlapping, studies: (i) three illumination experiments (November 1924–April 1927), (ii) the first relay assembly test room (April 1927–February 1933), (iii) the second relay assembly group (August 1928–March 1929), (iv) the mica splitting test room (October 1928–September 1930), (v) the interview program (September 1928–early 1931), and (vi) the bank wiring observation room study (November 1931-May 1932).
>
> *(Kompier 2006, p. 403)*

Next Kompier described how the Harvard business professor, Elton Mayo, became known as the main interpreter of the Hawthorne studies (in many later accounts referred to as 'the director of the studies'), even though for the first years he was not involved at all (his first visit to the factory was in 1928) and the bulk of his publications were based on five reports by the real researchers. By the time he published his book *The Social Problems of an Industrial Civilization* (1933), the study was not only suspended because of the economic recession but most of the participants involved in the study had been laid off as well.

More importantly, Mayo gave a much embellished version of what actually happened. Kompier (2006, p. 403–4) listed the following flaws in the first relay assembly study from 1927 till 1933:

- The group consisted of five young women operators and a sixth lay-out operator who distributed the materials among the operators; her income was dependent on the output of the five operators.

- Two operators had initially been selected because they were 'thoroughly experienced' and 'willing and cooperative' and not soon to be married; next these two operators invited the three other operators.

- The two independent variables (rest pauses and duration of work) were manipulated in a very complicated order, depending on unmotivated decisions by the experimenters and influenced by economic circumstances (e.g. breaks were introduced in period 4, removed in period 12, and then re-installed); in addition, at a certain point in time an additional variable was introduced, consisting of a piecework system based on the average output of the experimental group and not, as before, on the output of the entire department.

- No control group was established.

- At the beginning of period 8 (January 1928) operators 1a and 2a were removed from the experimental group because they were too busy 'talking and fooling'.

In particular the last event illustrates how differently the study was reported by Mayo than it was perceived by those participating in it. Whereas the researcher involved wrote that an obstructive minority had been rejected, Mayo noted that operators 1a and 2a 'dropped out' and were 'permitted to withdraw'. There is good evidence that the former was the correct interpretation, because Mayo himself had previously written of operator 2a in a letter: 'One girl, formerly in the test group, was reported to have "gone Bolshevik" and had been dropped.' Although the two girls had been warned repeatedly and threatened with disciplinary action, they 'did not display that wholehearted cooperation desired by the investigators' (as cited in Kompier 2006, p. 404).

The above problems are only part of those identified by Kompier. His list made up several pages, making him conclude that the scientific worth of the studies was next to nil and that their impact was solely due to the myth Mayo managed to spread. If the studies were submitted to a journal nowadays, they would be rejected outright because of the many methodological flaws.

Why did the low quality of the Hawthorne studies not prevent them from being taught to students?

Another issue Kompier pondered is why these studies keep being cited and praised in introductory books, despite the fact that the devastating methodological problems have been described many times before. He suggested five reasons:

1. *The story is too good not to be true:* The story that employees worked harder because they received human attention is too seductive not to include in an introductory psychology book. In this respect, the Hawthorne effect resembles an urban legend. Once you have heard the story, you never forget it.

2. *The original researchers published biased and selective reports; later generations simply referred to them without checking the evidence:* A lot of scientific writing is based on secondary sources. Once a 'good story' gets into the literature, it is likely to be quoted without consultation of the original sources (which sometimes are difficult to get hold of, certainly if they are old studies).

3. *The underlying message is correct:* The Hawthorne studies also keep being cited because the basic message of the human relations movement – that social and psychological factors are important in the workspace – was correct. The Hawthorne studies should not have been used to promote the human relations movement (and certainly no longer can be, now that we know what really happened!), but this does not detract from the message of the human relations movement that scientific management was flawed in its conceptions of workers' motivation. As such the Hawthorne message seems to have been 'confirmed' by the subsequent findings and developments.

4. *The story is good for psychologists:* The Hawthorne message (attention and social influences are important on the work floor; supervisors should learn social skills) suits the psychologists' interests. Therefore, they love to teach the story to students.

5. *The story is good for management:* Finally, Mayo's message that social factors prevail over the physical environment was also good news for the management level. The roles of management are to ensure worker productivity and to control the social process in the factory, and Mayo reassured the managers that these are indeed important responsibilities. As a result, the Hawthorne studies became included in management books as well.

Because of the above features, a second take-home message of the Hawthorne studies is that you must remain sceptical when you read a glowing text about a 'classic' study that without a shred of doubt seemed to prove a particular point or theory. Writers of scientific textbooks have a tendency to idealise 'old' studies that became turning points in history. They want to present a straightforward and convincing story and as a result lower their guard when it comes to describing the classics.

Other examples of idealised reporting of 'classic' studies

We wish we could tell you that the Hawthorne studies are a one-off as far as idealised reporting is concerned, but it is becoming clear that such reporting is widespread. Further examples in psychology are the ways in which introductory books write about Rayner and Watson's classic study on the conditioning of fear in Little Albert (Albert was not so easy to condition and was also less afraid of other furry things than often reported; Harris 1979), the case study of the murder of Kitty Genovese (there were not 38 witnesses who saw the murder happen and who could have intervened; Manning *et al.* 2007), the first study 'showing' a positive effect of psychotherapy on the survival rates of cancer patients (the effect could not be replicated; Coyne and Palmer 2007), the impact of snow words on the perception of white in Eskimos (no such study took place; Martin 1986), the apparatus used by Pavlov in his salivation experiments with dogs (Pavlov rarely used a bell [it scared the dogs] and the picture usually given to illustrate Pavlov's dog shows the apparatus of someone else; Goodwin 1991), and the remarkable case study of what happened to Phineas Gage after his frontal lobes were pierced by a rod (there is actually very little known of what happened to him; Kotowicz 2007). Allchin (2003) reported similar biases in the reporting of studies in biology and medicine.

**pseudohistory
of science**

text that looks like a history of science, but that contains systematic errors because of a desire to present the research as more impressive and important than it was and to depict the scientist as a genius who has to battle against the lack of understanding and appreciation by the peers

Given the above examples, it is important to keep in mind that scientific issues have rarely been settled by a single study and that the so-called 'classics' often are idealised crystallisations and hindsight reinterpretations on the basis of much additional research (see also our discussion of Mendel's findings in Chapter 1). Sometimes it is better not to see textbook descriptions of classic studies as reports of what actually happened but as portrayals of 'what ought to have happened' given what we know (believe) now.

The danger of establishing a pseudohistory of science

Allchin (2004) is less lenient in his appraisal of idealised classic studies in introductory books. He calls them examples of a **pseudohistory of science**. Although the heroic stories of the discoveries are meant to convey enthusiasm for science and are based on historical events, they are flawed and promote false ideas about how science works (such as: science is faultless, science is entirely fact-driven, discoveries come out of the blue and are met with disbelief, big discoveries are simple findings).

? What do you think?

Have you ever read a historical text about a scientific subject? Was this one that presented the materials matter-of-factly, or one that tried to engage you by making the findings more surprising, sensational, important and unbelievable than they probably were? What is better: that people read a popularised history, even though it includes elements of pseudoscience, or that they read no history at all?

Figure 7.4 summarises the features Allchin discerns in the pseudohistory of science. They may help you to spot them in the literature. In the next chapter we will have more to say about how science works and what status it has.

Warning Signs of Pseudohistory

romanticism
flawless personalities
monumental, single-handed discoveries
'Eureka'-type insight
'crucial' experiments only
sense of the inevitable (plot trajectory)
rhetoric of truth-versus-ignorance
absence of any error
unproblematic interpretation of evidence
general oversimplification or idealization
ideology-laden conclusions
author with a narrow agenda

Context is missing:
- no cultural or social setting
- no human contingency
- no antecedent ideas
- no alternative ideas
- uncritical acceptance of new concept

Figure 7.4 **Warning signs identified by Allchin (2004) that may help you to identify and avoid pseudohistory.**

Source: Allchin (2004). Reproduced with permission.

Interim summary

The weak methodology of the Hawthorne studies

- The Hawthorne studies were not well done, because many aspects were changed simultaneously, so that the authors could not conclude for sure which factor was the origin of the effects they observed.

- Still, strong conclusions were drawn on the basis of the findings.

- These conclusions have been perpetuated in textbooks, because:
  - writers do not read the original sources (certainly if these are difficult to obtain),
  - the story is too good not to be true,
  - the basic message of the human relations movement was correct,
  - the story strengthened the positions of psychologists and managers

- The idealised depiction of the Hawthorne studies is an example of the pseudohistory of science, an attempt to excite enthusiasm for science by narrating simplified and heroic stories that promote false ideas of how science works.

Recommended literature

The present chapter was inspired by three books: Jansz, J. and Van Drunen, P. (eds.) (2004) *A social history of psychology* (Oxford: Blackwell Publishing); Ward, S.C. (2002) *Modernizing the mind: Psychological knowledge and the remaking of society* (Westport, CT: Praeger Publishers); and Hanson, F.A. (1993) *Testing testing: Social consequences of the examined life* (Berkeley: University of California Press). If you are interested in the history of clinical psychology, a good book is Reisman, J.M. (1991) *A history of clinical psychology* (2nd edn) (Taylor & Francis). Also try to find a text on the history of the mental health services in your country. For the UK this can be Rogers, A. and Pilgrim, D. (2001) *Mental health policy in Britain* (2nd edn) (Basingstoke: Palgrave Macmillan). If you are interested in test research, two good books are Gregory, R.J. (2007) *Psychological testing: History, principles, and applications* (5th edn) (Boston: Pearson Education); and Kaplan, R.M. and Saccuzzo, D.P. (2005) *Psychological testing: Principles, applications, and issues* (6th edn) (Thomson Wadsworth). A good book on the psychology of work and organisation is Arnold, J. *et al.* (2005) *Work psychology: Understanding human behaviour in the workplace* (4th edn) (Harlow: Pearson Education).

References

Abma, R. (2004) 'Madness and mental health.' In J. Jansz and P. van Drunen (eds.), *A social history of psychology.* Oxford: Blackwell, pp. 93–128.

Adair, J.G. (1984) 'The Hawthorne effect: A reconsideration of the methodological artifact', *Journal of Applied Psychology,* 69: 334–45.

Allchin, D. (2003) 'Scientific myth-conceptions', *Science Education,* 87: 329–51.

Allchin, D. (2004) 'Pseudohistory and pseudoscience', *Science & Education,* 13: 179–95.

Allport, G.W. and Odbert, H.S. (1936) 'Trait-names, a psycho-lexical study', *Psychological Monographs,* 47(1).

Cattell, R.B. (1956) 'Validation and intensification of the Sixteen Personality Factor Questionnaire', *Journal of Clinical Psychology,* 12: 205–14.

Coyne, J.C. and Palmer, S.C. (2007) 'Does anyone read the classic studies they cite? Reflections on claims that psychotherapy promotes the survival of cancer patients', *The European Health Psychology,* 9: 46–9.

Dougherty, T.W., Turban, D.B. and Callender, J.C. (1994) 'Confirming first impression in the employment interview: A field-study of interviewer behavior', *Journal of Applied Psychology,* 79: 659–65.

Eagly, A.H., Ashmore, R.D., Makhijani, M.G. and Longo, L.C. (1991) 'What is beautiful is good, but . . .: A meta-analytic review of research on the physical attractiveness stereotype', *Psychological Bulletin,* 110: 109–28.

Eysenck, H.J. (1952/1992) 'The effects of psychotherapy: An evaluation', *Journal of Consulting Psychology,* 16: 319–24. Reprinted in *Journal of Consulting and Clinical Psychology,* 60: 659–63.

Eysenck, H.J. (1976) 'Learning theory model of neurosis: New approach', *Behaviour Research and Therapy,* 14: 251–67.

Eysenck, H.J. and Eysenck, M.W. (1975) *Manual of the Eysenck Personality Questionnaire.* San Diego: Educational and Industrial Testing Service.

Eysenck, H.J., Eysenck, S.B.G. and Barrett, P. (1985) 'A revised version of the psychoticism scale', *Personality and Individual Differences,* 6: 21–29.

Foucault, M. (1976) *Surveiller et punir: Naissance de la prison.* Paris: Gallimard. [English translation: Foucault, M. (1979) *Discipline and punish: The birth of the prison.* New York: Vintage.]

Goldberg, L.R. (1990) 'An alternative "description of personality": The big-five factor structure', *Journal of Personality and Social Psychology,* **59**: 1216–29.

Goodwin, C.J. (1991) 'Misportraying Pavlov's apparatus', *The American Journal of Psychology,* **104**: 135–41.

Harris, B. (1979) 'Whatever happened to Little Albert?', *American Psychologist,* **34**: 151–60.

Hell, B., Trapmann, S., Weigand, S. and Schuler, H. (2007) 'The validity of admission interviews – a meta-analysis', *Psychologische Rundschau,* **58**: 93–102.

Hoffman, J.L. (1949) 'Clinical observations concerning schizophrenic patients treated by prefrontal leukotomy', *New England Journal of Medicine,* **241**: 233–6.

Hollingworth, H.L. (1922) *Judging human character.* New York: Appleton & Company.

Hosoda, M., Stone-Romero, E.F. and Coats, G. (2003) 'The effects of physical attractiveness on job-related outcomes: A meta-analysis of experimental studies', *Personnel Psychology,* **56**: 431–62.

James, W. (1892) 'A plea for psychology as a "natural science"', *The Philosophical Review,* **1**: 146–53.

Kagitcibasi, C. (2002) 'A model of family change in cultural context'. In *Online Readings in Psychology and Culture.* Retrieved on December 10, 2007 from http://www.ac.wwu.edu/~culture/contents_complete.htm.

Kaplan, R.M. and Saccuzzo, D.P. (2005) *Psychological testing: Principles, applications, and issues* (6th edn). Belmont, CA: Thomson Wadsworth.

Kompier, M.A.J. (2006) 'The "Hawthorne effect" is a myth, but what keeps the story going?', *Scandinavian Journal of Word Environment & Health,* **32**: 402–12.

Kotowicz, Z. (2007) 'The strange case of Phineas Gage', *History of the Human Sciences,* **20**: 115–31.

Kunda, Z. and Thagard, P. (1996) 'Forming impressions from stereotypes, traits, and behaviors: A parallel-constraint-satisfaction theory', *Psychological Review,* **103**: 284–308.

Laing, R.D. (1960) *The divided self: An existential study in sanity and madness.* Harmondsworth: Penguin.

Langner, T.S. (1962) 'A twenty-two item screening score of psychiatric symptoms indicating impairment', *Journal of Health and Human Behavior,* **3**: 269–76.

Leary, M.R. and Kowalski, R.M. (1990) 'Impression management: A literature review and two-component model', *Psychological Bulletin,* **107**: 34–47.

Lewin, K., Lippitt, R. and White, R. (1939) 'Patterns of aggressive behaviour in experimentally created "social climates"', *Journal of Social Psychology,* **10**: 271–99.

Manning, R., Levine, M. and Collins, A. (2007) 'The Kitty Genovese Murder and the social psychology of helping: The parable of the 38 witnesses', *American Psychologist,* **62**: 555–62.

Martin, L. (1986). '"Eskimo words for snow": A case study in the genesis and decay of an anthropological example', *American Anthropologist,* **88**: 418–23.

Mayo, E. (1945) *The social problems of an industrial civilization.* Cambridge, MA: Harvard University Press.

McDaniel, M.A., Whetzel, D.L., Schmidt, F.L. and Maurer, S.D. (1994) 'The validity of employment interviews: A comprehensive review and meta-analysis', *Journal of Applied Psychology,* **79**: 599–616.

McReynolds, P. (1987) 'Lightner Witmer: Little-known founder of clinical psychology', *American Psychologist,* **42**: 849–58.

Monahan, J. (1981) *The clinical prediction of violent behavior.* Washington, DC: Government Printing Office.

Morgeson, F.P., Campion, M.A., Dipboye, R.L., Hollenbeck, J.R., Murphy, K. and Schmitt, N. (2007) 'Reconsidering the use of personality tests in personnel selection contexts', *Personnel Psychology,* **60**: 683–729.

OECD (2007) 'Multiple comparisons of mean performance on the science scale', *PISA 2006: Science competencies for tomorrow's world,* **1**.

Ones, D.S., Viswesvaran, C. and Reiss, A.D. (1996) 'Role of social desirability in personality testing for personnel selection: The red herring', *Journal of Applied Psychology,* **81**: 660–79.

Puhl, R. and Brownell, K.D. (2001) 'Bias, discrimination, and obesity', *Obesity Research,* **9**: 788–805.

Rehman, S.U., Nietert, P.J., Cope, D.W. and Kilpatrick, A.O. (2005) 'What to wear today? Effects of doctor's attire on the trust and confidence of patients', *The American Journal of Medicine*, **118**: 1279–86.

Richards, G. (2002) *Putting psychology in its place: A critical historical overview* (2nd edn). London: Routledge.

Rissmiller, D.J. and Rissmiller, J.H. (2006) 'Evolution of the antipsychiatry movement into mental health consumerism', *Psychiatric Services*, **57**: 863–6.

Rogers, C.R. (1942) *Counseling and psychotherapy*. Boston, MA: Houghton Mifflin.

Rosenhan, D.L. (1973) 'On being sane in insane places', *Science*, **179**: 250–8.

Schmidt, F.L. and Hunter, J.E. (1998) 'The validity and utility of selection methods in personnel psychology: Practical and theoretical implications of 85 years of research findings', *Psychological Bulletin*, **124**: 262–74.

Schneider, D.J. (1973) 'Implicit personality theory: Review', *Psychological Bulletin*, **79**: 294–309.

Szasz, T.S. (1960) 'The myth of mental illness', *American Psychologist*, **15**: 113–18.

Taylor, F.W. (1911) *Scientific management*. New York: Harper & Brothers.

UK ECT Review Group (2003) 'Efficacy and safety of electroconvulsive therapy in depressive disorders: A systematic review and meta-analysis', *The Lancet*, **361**: 799–808.

Van Drunen, P., Van Strien, P.J. and Haas, E. (2004) 'Work and organization.' In J. Jansz and P. Van Drunen (eds.) (2004) *A social history of psychology*. Oxford: Blackwell Publishing.

Wampold, B.E. *et al.* (1997) 'A meta-analysis of outcome studies comparing bona fide psychotherapies: Empirically, "all must have prizes"', *Psychological Bulletin*, **122**: 203–15.

Weisbord, M.R. (1985) 'Participative work design: A personal odyssey', *Organizational Dynamics*, **13**: 4–20. (Table adapted from Trist, E. (1981) *The evolution of socio-technical systems – A conceptual framework and an action research program*. Toronto: Ontario Ministry of Labour.)

Wooldridge, A. (1994) *Measuring the mind: Education and psychology in England, c. 1860–c. 1990*. Cambridge: Cambridge University Press.

08 What is science?
Twentieth-century insights

This chapter will cover

Questions to consider

Historical issues addressed in this chapter

■ When did the shift from an emphasis on deductive reasoning to an emphasis on inductive reasoning take place? Who were the big names in this transition?

■ What impact did World War II have on the philosophy of science?

Conceptual issues addressed in this chapter

■ How certain is scientific information?

■ Is science a cumulative process, in which knowledge constantly increases?

■ Why did the philosophy of science only really start 300 years after the beginning of the scientific revolution?

■ Is passive observation the only way of gaining knowledge according to the empiricists?

■ What did the logical positivists claim was the essence of science?

■ Is it possible to define a set of criteria that demarcate science (i.e. set scientific knowledge apart from other types of knowledge)?

■ What are the shortcomings of the verification principle?

■ What was the new insight of Popper about the nature of science?

■ What does this mean for the status of scientific theories?

■ Why did Popper at a certain moment talk about sophisticated falsificationism?

■ What new insight did Kuhn propose? What did his theory look like?

■ Why did Lakatos make a distinction between a degenerative research programme and a progressive research programme?

■ How did Kuhn's theory inspire the postmodernists?

■ In what ways does pragmatism offer an interesting new approach? Why has it been ignored most of the time by the philosophers of science?

Introduction

Are we living in a sci-fi novel where scientists have taken over the world, and democracy is replaced by a tyranny of men and women in white coats?

It seems that every policy and initiative, from climate change to child obesity, now has to be based on what 'the science tells us'. So the new Intergovernment Panel on Climate Change report is hailed as 'a pocket guide for policy-makers' that will tell governments what harsh measures they must impose to cut our carbon emissions, whether voters like it or not.

Discussions no longer start with a political leader telling us 'This is what I believe in.' Instead a little news report will inform us how 'research shows . . .' that some problem or other is getting worse. And where such supposedly scientific research leads, politicians follow.

Scientists have not really staged a coup. Instead, political leaders lacking ideas or authority of their own are hiding behind scientists, trying to use the status of science to give them something to stand on, rather as tobacco companies once used doctors to advertise cigarettes. And once 'The Science' has spoken on, say, climate change, we are told there is no room for further debate.

(The Times, *20 November 2007)*

In the previous chapters we described the growth of the scientific approach. The time has come to analyse what science stands for. Is it true that 'once "The Science" has spoken, there is no room for further debate', as the author of the cited newspaper article disparagingly writes? Do we have to slavishly follow the white coats? Our exploration has been inspired by Alan F. Chalmers' (1999) book *What is This Thing Called Science?* – a book well worth being read in its entirety.

We start our discussion with the standard view of science as a continuous accumulation of facts based on objective and value-free observation and experimentation. Then, we describe how this view became criticised in the middle of the twentieth century and how it was shown that scientific research proceeds more by venturing possibly wrong ideas that are subsequently tested. Next, we review the evidence that research is influenced by the social norms of the research community and how these norms can change. We end by mentioning the pragmatic proposal that there may be no way of judging the scientific quality of a finding other than by looking in hindsight at whether the finding has been of practical use or not.

You will notice that in this chapter we include no psychology examples. This is deliberate because we want to discuss the ideas about the so-called hard sciences (e.g. physics and medicine) before we apply them to psychology (Chapter 9). Furthermore, you will see that many of the examples we give are 'old' examples, dealing with findings and theories from before 1900. This is deliberate too, because you need distance before you can discern the big evolutions underlying the history of a phenomenon. We do not (yet) know the many conceptual issues underlying current-day research.

Finally, you may wonder why we did not start the book with the present chapter. After all, in the previous chapters we described the growth of the scientific approach.

Did we then not have to start the book with an explanation of what science is and how it works? There is a good reason for postponing the discussion until now. Up to the second half of the twentieth century scientists had little more knowledge about the exact workings of science than the method of the natural philosopher described in Chapter 2 (see section 2.4).

Even in 1969 the Nobel laureate and biologist Peter Medawar described how many successful scientists tend to show an expression of both solemnity and shifty-eyedness when asked to describe what their scientific method is: solemn, because they feel they ought to give a weighty answer, shifty-eyed because they have no clue about what to say. According to Medawar this may be because working scientists are too preoccupied with doing research to have time to contemplate how they do it. Apprentices simply take over the methods of their masters without giving them much thought. Rosenthal and Rosnow (2008) even suggest that too much concern about the scientific method may interfere with the process itself, just like a centipede could become unable to walk if it were able to think about how such a feat can be achieved with 100 legs.

So, maybe it is no wonder that most thinking about the precise ways in which scientific progress is achieved has been done by philosophers rather than by active scientists. In addition, much of the thinking is from well into the twentieth century. That is, it was not known to the historical figures described in the previous chapters. So, starting the historical part of this book with a discussion of what is currently thought about science would have biased our interpretation. The practice of depicting and interpreting events of the past in the light of present-day ideas and knowledge is known as **presentism** in history writings and is to be avoided.

Of course, nothing prevents you from going back to the previous chapters at the end of the present one and rereading them in the light of the new information you will have learned. Also, remember that in Chapter 2 we asked you to write down your ideas about science and the scientific method. This is the right time to dig up that sheet of paper and see how far your intuitions got you in the philosophy of science!

presentism

practice of depicting and interpreting events of the past in the light of present-day ideas and knowledge

8.1   Science is based on observable facts

To set the picture, we start by recapitulating the developments up to the twentieth century, described in the previous chapters.

From deductive reasoning to observation and experimentation

Plato: reasoning on the basis of innate ideas

Plato was among the first to have an explicit opinion of how knowledge is acquired. As we saw in Chapters 2 and 6, in his view learned thinking consisted of reasoning about the way the things were, starting from the innate knowledge the soul had brought with it when it entered the body. Careful observation was not needed. The important branches of knowledge were arithmetic, geometry and astronomy (largely based on the former two). The excerpt below summarises Plato's view:

> The starry heaven which we behold is the finest and most perfect of visible things, but it must necessarily be deemed to be greatly inferior, just because they are visible, to the true motions of absolute swiftness and absolute slowness, which are relative to each other. The true realities of velocities are found in pure number and in every perfect figure. Now, these are to be apprehended by reason and intelligence, but not by sight.
>
> *(Plato,* The Republic*)*

Aristotle and the distinction between deductive and inductive reasoning

deductive reasoning

form of reasoning in which one starts from a number of indisputable premises (known statements), from which new, true conclusions can be drawn if the rules of logic are followed

A (slightly) different view was held by Aristotle. He made a distinction between deductive reasoning and inductive reasoning. **Deductive reasoning**, as we saw in Chapter 2, is a form of reasoning in which one starts from known statements and deduces new conclusions. It is the form of reasoning Plato defended and a form we also often use in our daily interactions. If we know that children younger than 6 months do not yet talk and if we know that the child in front of us, say Harriet, is younger than 6 months, then we know that Harriet will not be able to talk to us (or if you prefer a more formal rendition in the form of a syllogism: 'No children younger than 6 months talk, Harriet is a child younger than 6 months, therefore Harriet does not talk').

inductive reasoning

form of reasoning in which one starts from observations and tries to reach general conclusions; is needed in science to come from observed phenomena to scientific laws; no guarantee that the conclusions are true

Inductive reasoning, on the other hand, is a form of reasoning in which likely conclusions are drawn on the basis of a series of converging observations. If year upon year we observe that the Sun rises higher in the summer than in the winter, then we can postulate a general conclusion (sometimes called a 'law') that the Sun rises higher in summer than in winter. If our observations are done carefully and if they converge over many repetitions, then we can be pretty confident (although not 100 per cent sure) about the legitimacy of the conclusion. Inductive reasoning is a form of reasoning we often use in daily life as well. If a colleague is consistently bad-tempered on Monday morning, then we build up the expectation that this again will be the case on the next Monday and we will, for instance, adapt our behaviour (e.g. by not scheduling an important meeting then).

As indicated in Chapter 2, although Aristotle pointed to the importance of inductive reasoning, there was little doubt in his writings about the primacy of deductive reasoning: if the facts did not comply with the intuitive understanding, then in all likelihood the facts were wrong.

Interim summary

Deductive vs. inductive reasoning

- Deductive reasoning
  - Is a form of reasoning in which one starts from known statements and deduces new conclusions.
  - The conclusions are guaranteed to be true if the known statements are true and if the correct logical rules are followed.

Interim summary continued

- Usually presented in the form of a syllogism, a logical argument consisting of two premises and a conclusion. For instance,

  > If it rains, the street is wet.
  > It rains.
  > Therefore the street is wet.

- This is the type of reasoning stressed in rationalism, according to which reality can be known by reasoning from innate knowledge (e.g. Plato and Descartes).
- Is used in science to formulate hypotheses on the basis of existing theories, so that the theories can be tested.
- Is the type of reasoning used in daily life to make predictions about specific instances on the basis of general information:

  > If I want to get full marks for coursework essays, I have to submit them before the deadline.
  > I want to get full marks for my next essay.
  > Therefore, I have to submit my next essay before the deadline.

- Inductive reasoning

  - Is a form of reasoning in which likely conclusions are drawn on the basis of a series of convergent observations.
  - The conclusion is not necessarily true. As a matter of fact, certainly in the beginning conclusions are often guesses that turn out to be wrong and have to be replaced.
  - Is mostly used to generalise from a limited number of observations to a general conclusion (e.g. concluding that sparrows are brown on the basis of the sparrows we have seen thus far), to detect correlations between events (e.g. noticing that there are more sparrows in the garden after we put food in the feeder), and to make causal inferences (e.g. concluding that there are more sparrows in the garden after we put food in the feeder, *because* the sparrows are hungry and want to get some of the food).
  - Is used in daily life to bring order to our many experiences by noticing the similarities between events, so that general principles can be formulated and mechanisms hypothesised about how these principles operate (see the examples of the sparrows above).
  - Is the type of reasoning stressed in empiricism, according to which knowledge is achieved on the basis of experiences and observations.
  - Is used in science to work out explanations for observed phenomena.

Empiricism and the primacy of observation

The primacy of observation over conviction started to really take off in the seventeenth century with the empiricist movement in Britain (Chapter 2), although as usual there were several forerunners. The British scholar Francis Bacon (1561–1626) is usually credited as being the first important defender of the inductive method. In his view, knowledge should be based on observation and not on obedience to (religious) authorities, as is clearly illustrated in the following excerpt:

In the year of our Lord 1432, there arose a grievous quarrel among the brethren over the number of teeth in the mouth of a horse. For 13 days the disputation raged without ceasing. All the ancient books and chronicles were fetched out, and wonderful and ponderous erudition, such as was never before heard of in this region, was made manifest. At the beginning of the fourteenth day, a youthful friar of goodly bearing asked his learned superiors for permission to add a word, and straightway, to the wonderment of the disputants, whose wisdom he sore vexed, he beseeched them to unbend in a manner coarse and unheard-of, and to look in the open mouth of a horse and find answer to their questionings. At this, their dignity being grievously hurt, they waxed exceedingly wroth; and, joining in a mighty uproar, they flew upon him and smote him hip and thigh, and cast him out forthwith. For, said they, surely Satan hath tempted this bold neophyte to declare unholy and unheard-of ways of finding the truth contrary to all the teachings of the fathers. After many days more of grievous strife the dove of peace sat on the assembly, and they as one man, declaring the problem to be an everlasting mystery because of a grievous dearth of historical and theological evidence thereof, so ordered the same writ down.

(Bacon as cited in Baars (1986) p. 19)

A strong feature of the inductive method is that its starting point (observations rather than personal opinions) can be controlled and replicated by others. According to Chalmers (1999), the idea that science is based on facts is still the main criterion people use to decide whether a statement is scientific or not.

Empiricism and the start of experimentation

Francis Bacon not only stressed the importance of observation and inductive reasoning in knowledge acquisition. He further urged natural philosophers to take an active role and to use experimental histories to find the most likely interpretation of a phenomenon. In these experimental histories the situation was not passively observed, but elements of it were actively manipulated to see which effects this had on the phenomenon.

experimental history

expression introduced by Francis Bacon to indicate that empiricists should not base their knowledge entirely on passive observation, but had to actively manipulate elements of the situation to see what effects this has

A nice illustration of what Bacon meant by experimental histories was published shortly after Bacon's death in 1638 by Galilei in his final book (published in the Netherlands because Galilei had been put under house arrest by the Roman Catholic Church; see Chapter 2). In this book Galilei described how he set out to test whether the velocity of a rolling ball was constant, as claimed by Aristotle, or accelerating, as Galilei thought. He took a board 12 cubits long and half a cubit wide (about 5.5 m by 23 cm) and cut a groove, as straight and smooth as possible, down the centre. He inclined the plane and rolled brass balls down it, timing their descent with a water clock – a large vessel that emptied through a thin tube into a glass. After each run he weighed the water that had run out – his measurement of elapsed time – and compared it with the distance the ball had travelled. On some trials the ball would roll for 3 cubits, on others it would roll for the full length of 12 cubits. Galilei observed that the time required for 12 cubits was not four times longer than the time required for 3 cubits, as predicted by Aristotle, but only about twice as long, in line with his own predictions. On the basis of many measurements with the board, Galilei formulated the law of falling bodies, which stated that the distance travelled was proportional to the square of the time travelled ($d \sim t^2$).

Experimentum crucis

Another early example of the application of the empirical approach can be found in the book *Micrographia*, published in 1665 by the British scholar Robert Hooke about his observations with the microscope. In this book Hooke defended the primacy of observation as follows:

> The Science of Nature has been already too long made only a work of the Brain and the Fancy. It is now high time it should return to the plainness and soundness of Observations on material and obvious things.
>
> *(Hooke (1665) as cited in Gleick (2003) p. 63)*

In his book Hooke further introduced the notion of an *experimentum crucis*, an experimental history that allowed researchers to verify the correctness of their explanation.

Logical positivism and the first attempt to define what exactly constitutes the scientific method

Logical positivism

philosophy of science

branch of philosophy that studies the foundations of scientific research, to better understand the position of scientific research relative to other forms of information acquisition and generation

The seventeenth-century empiricist ideas were extended and refined in the next centuries by subsequent empiricists. In addition, the scientific method was promoted by the positivists as the best form of knowledge acquisition, superseding earlier religious and philosophical explanations (see Chapter 2). However, in terms of ideas about the scientific method nothing fundamental changed until the twentieth century.

In the early twentieth century a group of philosophers began to take the positivist's claim of the superiority of scientific knowledge seriously and argued that philosophy should abandon its metaphysical questions (i.e. questions about the ultimate nature of the universe and human beings) and turn its attention to the question of why the scientific approach had been so successful. By doing so, philosophy could integrate the scientific method in its own endeavour and advise other disciplines that were striving for a scientific approach. This branch of philosophy became known as the philosophy of science.

The new movement was initially associated with a circle of scholars in Vienna around the physicist Moritz Schlick (1882–1936). They were called the *Wiener Kreis* (Vienna Circle) and started to meet in 1922. Well-known attendants were Otto Neurath, Rudolf Carnap and Ludwig Wittgenstein (who was not officially a member but had meetings with the others; in addition many of the early meetings of the Circle were devoted to his book *Tractatus Logico-Philosophicus* published in 1922). In the years leading up to World War II the group became dispersed and many members moved to the USA and the UK, where they continued and extended their work. In addition, there were already close contacts with like-minded philosophers in these countries (e.g. Alfred Ayer and Bertrand Russell in the UK).

logical positivism

philosophical movement in the first half of the twentieth century, claiming that philosophy should stop thinking about metaphysics, and instead try to understand the essence of the scientific approach; central tenet was the verification principle

The movement became known under the name logical positivism (although the British philosophers and Schlick preferred the name 'logical empiricism'). The 'positivism' part referred to the high esteem of the scientific approach shared with Comte's nineteenth-century movement, in particular the idea that scientific knowledge always was true knowledge. 'Logical' referred to the preoccupation with language and meaning (i.e. trying to answer the question 'which statements are meaningful?').

Demarcation of science

The primary question addressed by the logical positivists was what set science apart from other ways of knowledge acquisition and generation. This is known as the search for demarcation criteria, a set of criteria that would distinguish science from non-science (such as religion, voodoo, astrology), so that the scientific standing of new disciplines could be appraised and advice given to those disciplines about how to become more 'scientific'. The logical positivists wanted their definition to be universal (i.e. hold for all sciences) and ahistorical (i.e. applicable to all times).

As an aside, the demarcation ambition clearly shows that at that time it was not yet realised that most of the time it is impossible to find a set of criteria that fully define naturally occurring concepts (e.g. which set of rules includes all possible games and does not include instances from other concepts such as sports and work?). Indeed, the impossibility of finding such a set of criteria for the demarcation of science was the reason why Wittgenstein later in life would claim that many philosophical problems cannot be solved due to the limits of the human language.

Observation, induction and verification

According to the logical positivists science proceeded by means of a cycle consisting of observation, induction and verification. The first step was careful observation of what happened. The logical positivists assumed that there was a direct correspondence between the outside reality and human perception, so that the world could be known by observing it. The assumption of a direct relationship between reality and perception is known as the 'correspondence theory of truth'. As we will see below, this assumption became questioned in the second half of the twentieth century.

The next step in the scientific cycle according to the logical positivists was the translation of individual observations into general conclusions on the basis of inductive reasoning. The ideal here consisted of the mathematical laws of physics generated by Newton. These laws made it possible to have a detailed understanding of all types of movement in the universe.

Finally, the general conclusions (or scientific laws) based on observation and induction had to be verified. Here we see the influence of Bacon's experimental histories and Hooke's *experimentum crucis*. The logical positivists went one step further, however, and claimed that empirical verification could be seen as the demarcation criterion of science: a statement was scientific if and only if it could be verified as true or false through objective, value-free observation. Sometimes the argument was made even more general and implied that knowledge was *meaningful* if and only if it could be verified (if there was no way of verifying a proposition, then it was meaningless). This criterion became known as the verification principle and its requirement for valid knowledge as verificationism.

Next to induction, the logical positivists of course also accepted deductive reasoning on the basis of the principles of logic as a way of making meaningful statements. However, this type of reasoning could only be used to deduce conclusions from what was already known; it did not yield new knowledge. If the reasoning resulted in new knowledge, the ensuing statement had to be verified anew (also see the hypothetico-deductive method below).

In summary, for the logical positivists science consisted of the ever increasing accumulation of knowledge through observation, induction and verification. They

---

demarcation criteria

set of criteria that fully defines a concept (i.e. includes all instances belonging to the concept and excludes all instances not belonging to the concept)

verificationism

adherence to the principle that a proposition is meaningful only if it can be verified as true or false; with respect to science states that a proposition is scientific only if it can be verified through objective, value-free observation assumed an outside reality which could be known by means of objective, value-free observation. Knowledge acquisition went from unbiased observation to understanding. It was enough to carefully observe, in order to know what was going on. Scientifically acquired knowledge could be trusted as a true depiction of reality.

Interim summary

- Originally, knowledge acquisition was associated with deductive reasoning (Plato).

- Aristotle made a distinction between deductive and inductive reasoning, but still gave primacy to deductive reasoning.

- Inductive reasoning based on observation and experimentation became the core of scientific thinking for the empiricists.

- Logical positivism identified verification as the core principle of the scientific method: a statement is scientific only if it can be verified as true or false through value-free observation.

8.2 Problems with the view that scientific knowledge can be produced from facts alone

In this section we will see how the views of the logical positivists became questioned. First we explore how knowledge acquisition does not proceed unidirectionally from perception to understanding. Then we discuss how the observation of verifiable facts nevertheless can lead to erroneous conclusions. Next we consider the finding that the existing scientific theories often include non-observables, and we end by noting that verification is logically impossible.

Perception requires interpretation

Perception is more than sensing stimuli

When the logical positivists claimed that science was special because it was based on facts, then they assumed that facts could be perceived prior to and independently of any theoretical framework and that the perception of facts was the same for all careful observers. Unfortunately, there is quite some evidence that this is not the case. As every introductory psychology textbook will tell you, perception involves the *interpretation* of sensations. To illustrate this, have a look at figure 8.1.

Figure 8.1 very much resembles the fragmented reality researchers are confronted with when they try to understand a phenomenon on the basis of the facts they observe. Each black blob represents an isolated observation. Different groups of researchers try to understand the different blobs. For instance, a group of a few hundred (thousand?) scientists is working on the second blob of the first line in figure 8.1, trying to understand its functioning by carefully observing what happens and using experimental histories to

Figure 8.1 An illustration of the fragmented reality researchers are confronted with when they observe facts.

Source: Edith Brysbaert.

verify whether their understanding is correct. Another group of scientists is trying to understand the blob below. Both groups may inform each other of their findings, although there is no real need to do so, as both phenomena are thought to be independent.

Now suppose someone comes along with a theory of what the overall framework might be, how the different components fit within a larger organisation, as shown in figure 8.2 (overleaf). At that moment, the situation alters dramatically for the scientists. Although the facts are still the same, they suddenly get a completely different meaning, because they are part of a much wider organisation.

A theory changes the perception of the facts

What figure 8.2 illustrates is that the understanding of a scientific phenomenon involves more than simply sensing the isolated facts. It involves an element of interpretation to understand what the different facts mean and how they relate to each other. Once such an interpretation has been found, the meaning of the originally observed facts changes spectacularly. Look back at figure 8.1: Is it possible for you now not to see the girl any more, and to see the figure as you saw it at first?

If you think the situation depicted in the figures 8.1 and 8.2 is exaggerated, just think of the efforts astronomers had to make in order to come up with a model of the universe that would explain the observable movements of the Sun, the Moon, the planets and the stars! Also think of how the perception of the world changed, once it was realised that the Earth was not flat but round. Or how the field of chemistry changed, once the periodic table was discovered.

A theory enables scientists to focus on the important facts

A theory not only changes the perception of the facts, it also allows scientists to search in a more directed way. It helps them to sort out the avalanche of facts and to decide which facts are important and which are not. Figure 8.2, for instance, shows that not all blobs are equally important for the overall interpretation and, therefore, that a better understanding of some blobs is more crucial than the understanding of others.

Without a theory, scientists do not know which observations are important and which are not. For instance, in the nineteenth century much energy was invested in determining the exact weights of the chemical elements. This was done because researchers believed that the relative weights of the elements would provide them with

Figure 8.2 An illustration of how a general theory of a phenomenon may alter the way in which scientists are able to examine the 'facts' (blobs).

Source: Edith Brysbaert.

information about the structure of the elements. In particular, it had been observed that the weights of the chemical elements tended to be multiples of the weight of hydrogen, the lightest element. Therefore, it was hypothesised that all matter consisted of combinations of hydrogen atoms (for example, oxygen was about eight times heavier than hydrogen, suggesting that oxygen consisted of eight hydrogen atoms). Once it was realised that the different chemical elements have their own composition, it became clear that their relative weights were not at all important and that researchers could drop this particular line of investigation.

In conclusion, it is hard to maintain that facts are perceived prior to and independently of background knowledge (theory). In general, the more an observer knows about a particular phenomenon, the richer his or her perception becomes. Botanists see more in meadows and marshlands than people without knowledge of plants; radiologists see more in X-rays than people without such training. So, what we perceive depends on what we know (or think we know, as we will see further on).

Verifiable perceptions are no guarantee for a correct understanding

The fact that scientific understanding involves more than perception and verification can also be illustrated with erroneous scientific conclusions that have been drawn in the past on the basis of verifiable 'facts'. Below we give two examples. You will notice that one of them again involves Galilei. The reason why Galilei figures so prominently in writings about the philosophy of science is that the Copernican revolution has been widely studied by philosophers of science, so that an awful lot is known about the detailed reasoning of that time. In addition, knowing that not everything Galilei wrote turned out to be true is a good antidote against the tendency to see scientists as infallible heroes fighting against the ignorance of the world (see the section on the pseudo-history of science in Chapter 7). Error-stories are part of each scientific discipline and warn us that not all scientific statements have stood the test of time.

Galilei measures the diameters of stars

In one of his writings, Galilei proposed a method to determine the magnitude of the stars (as cited in Chalmers 1999, p. 25). His method was simple and straightforward.

He positioned himself relative to a cord so that the cord just blocked a particular star out of sight. On the basis of the thickness of the cord and the distance of the eye from the cord, Galilei could calculate the visual angle subtended by the cord and therefore, so he thought, the visual angle of the star. What Galilei did not realise, however, was that the apparent size of a star in the sky is largely due to atmospheric scatter (so that stars seem much bigger than they actually are) and that the distances from the stars to the Earth vary widely. As a result, Galilei's estimates of the diameters of the stars turned out to be worthless once they were compared to the measurements corrected for these errors. Still they were based on observable facts that could easily be verified by others.

The discovery of phosphohistidine

In 1963, the highly-respected American biochemist Paul Boyer published an article in the top journal *Science*, in which he claimed that at last he had found the missing substance required according to the prevailing theory for the final stage of the chemical reactions that provide cells with energy (see Allchin 2002 for more details). Chemists had been searching for this substance for more than a decade. Boyer called the substance *phosphohistidine* and described not only how he had observed it using the latest techniques, but also how he had made sure that it indeed fulfilled some of the roles that were ascribed by the theory to the substance.

Phosphohistidine had a huge influence on chemistry for the next 20 years, but in the end turned out to have a different function from what everyone imagined. In 1981, Paul Boyer admitted he had been wrong. By that time he had already started to work on a new theory of energy provision in cells that no longer required the intractable intermediate (for this work, he was awarded the Nobel Prize for Chemistry in 1997).

The two examples above illustrate that verifiable perceptions even by the best scientists are not a fail-safe guarantee that the conclusions based on them will be correct. Scientific understanding is more than a careful observation of facts.

Scientific theories are full of non-observable variables

A further argument against the idea that science proceeds completely from observation to understanding can be found in the fact that many scientific theories include non-observable variables. This can easily be illustrated with one of the laws of physics derived by Newton in his *Principia Mathematica* (1687; Chapter 2). For instance, his second law of motion reads $F = ma$ (force equals mass times acceleration). None of these variables is observable in the sense that they can be directly perceived by the senses.

Trying to define non-observable scientific variables

The logical positivists were soon confronted with the problem of non-observable scientific variables. They circumvented this problem by pointing out that although Newton's variables could not be perceived directly, they still involved magnitudes that could be measured in relatively simple ways: mass could be measured as weight (measured in grams), acceleration as the rate of change of velocity over time (which ultimately boiled down to measuring distances and times).

The logical positivists maintained that as long as it was possible to calculate the values of non-observable variables, it was acceptable to include them in scientific theories. You may remember from Chapter 4 that this refers to the requirement of having *operational definitions* for the variables included in a scientific law. If you could not change the variables into numbers by referring to the way in which you measured them, the resulting law was unverifiable and, hence, meaningless (remember Hutchinson's 'law' of moral importance, stating that moral importance equalled benevolence times abilities: $M = B \times A$).

Although the criterion that non-observable variables should have an operational definition solved some of the problems, it was not watertight. Some variables require complex, indirect methods to be revealed. Does this still count as an operational definition? And if it does, from what point on does a non-observable become non-scientific? Any dividing line between scientific and unscientific non-observables ultimately turns out to be an arbitrary distinction, as was eventually also recognised by Rudolf Carnap, one of the proponents of logical positivism:

> There is no question here of who is using the term 'observable' in a right or proper way. There is a continuum which starts with direct sensory observations and proceeds to enormously complex, indirect methods of observation. Obviously no sharp line can be drawn across this continuum; it is a matter of degree. A philosopher is sure that the sound of his wife's voice, coming from across the room, is an observable. But suppose he listens to her on the telephone. Is her voice an observable or isn't it? A physicist would certainly say that when he looks at something through an ordinary microscope, he is observing it directly. Is this also the case when he looks into an electron microscope? Does he observe the path of a particle when he sees the track it makes in a bubble chamber? In general, the physicist speaks of observables in a very wide sense compared with the narrow sense of the philosopher, but, in both cases, the line separating observable from nonobservable is highly arbitrary.
>
> *(Carnap 1966, Chapter 23)*

Non-observables may become observable

The fuzzy border between observables and non-observables is further evidenced by the fact that over time many initially hypothesised, non-observable phenomena have become observable, because of technical improvements and because the theory allowed the scientists to know what they were looking for (so that they could focus their efforts much more). Probably the best example in this respect is that of an atom. Towards the end of the nineteenth century, leading scientists such as Ernst Mach and Wilhelm Ostwald refused to see the atomic theory as a true description of reality, because atoms were unobservable. Therefore, they claimed, atoms had no place in science and should at best be treated as fictions that were helpful to generate new ideas. Although atoms still are invisible in a literal sense (they are too small to be seen with visible light), in the twentieth century it became possible to observe them indirectly with an electron microscope by scanning atoms with a laser of electrons.

The example of the atoms illustrates that what is unobservable at one point in time can become observable at another point. At the same time, the experiences of Paul Boyer warn us that a hypothesised, non-observable phenomenon may be unobservable because it does not exist. How then to make a distinction between 'true' and 'false' non-observables?

Verification is logically impossible

A final problem with the approach advocated by the logical positivists is that it is logically impossible to prove the truth of a conclusion reached through observation. In order to come from observation to a general conclusion, you need inductive reasoning (see above) and inductive reasoning does not lead to conclusions that are guaranteed to be true according to the rules of logic.

The prime example here is how to prove the truth of the saying 'all swans are white'. For centuries Europeans were 100 per cent sure of the validity of this saying, because all the swans they encountered were white. As a result, many languages had the expression 'black swan' to refer to something impossible. Imagine then the surprise when the Dutch explorer, Willem de Vlamingh, in 1697 came across black swans on his discovery voyage to Australia!

So, even though you have collected hundreds of verifications of a particular inductive statement, it is still possible that the next observation disproves it. As a result, verification cannot be used as the basis of science. In contrast, it is logically possible to falsify a statement based on inductive reasoning. All you have to do is to find one counterexample. As soon as Willem de Vlamingh discovered the existence of a black swan, the saying 'all swans are white' became false. We will return to this asymmetry between verification and falsification in the next section.

Interim summary

Problems with the logical-positivist view that scientific knowledge can be produced from facts alone

■ Facts can only be known through perception, and perception involves an element of interpretation. This means that the facts we observe are influenced by our background knowledge (theory), as can be seen in the historical examples of fallible 'facts'.

■ Also the search for new facts is guided by the existing knowledge.

■ It is impossible to draw a sharp divide between observable and non-observable variables.

■ Many scientific theories make use of non-observables.

■ It is logically impossible to prove that a conclusion based on induction is true.

8.3   Science is theory driven

The more the logical positivists tried to defend observation, induction and verification as the basis of scientific knowledge, the more it became clear that these criteria did not capture the essence of scientific progress, as outlined in the previous section. An alternative view was in the making. This came from Karl Popper (1902–1994), an Austrian-born scholar who had his education in the heyday of the Wiener Kreis (and attended several of the meetings as a student). Popper published his first important work *Logik der Forschung* (The Logic of Scientific Discovery) in 1934. Because of the political situation, he moved to New Zealand in 1937 and to the UK in 1946, where he remained.

Popper: falsification instead of verification

Science constantly questions its explanations

Popper started by accepting the importance of theories in scientific thinking. What distinguishes science from non-science, he argued, is not that the former is based on observable and verifiable facts and the latter not, but that science constantly questions its explanations, whereas non-scientific movements have no such inclination.

Popper was particularly intrigued by the difference between physics and Freudian psychoanalysis. Both claimed to be a science. However, studies in physics were primarily aimed at suspected weaknesses of the theories (remember that physics at the turn of the twentieth century went from Newton's physics to Einstein's relativity and subsequently to quantum physics). In contrast, studies in psychoanalysis mainly consisted of trying to find corroborating evidence for the theory.

Although physics arguably had a sounder basis (given that Newton's ideas had been successful for over 200 years, whereas Freud's were still very much in the making), its researchers predominantly tried to achieve progress by making sure that no error had been overlooked. Psychoanalysts, on the other hand, tried to make progress by gathering observations in favour of their view. Popper noticed a similarity between this approach and the approach advocated by religions and sects. As Chalmers wrote:

> Popper himself tells the story of how he became disenchanted with the idea that science is special because it can be derived from the facts, the more facts the better. He became suspicious of the way in which he saw Freudians and Marxists supporting their theories by interpreting a wide range of instances . . . in terms of their theory and claiming them to be supported on this account. It seemed to Popper that these theories could never go wrong because they were sufficiently flexible to accommodate any instances of human behaviour or historical change as compatible with their theory. Consequently, although giving the appearance of being powerful theories confirmed by a wide range of facts, they could in fact explain nothing because they could rule out nothing.
>
> *(Chalmers 1999, p. 59)*

Falsification instead of verification

Because of the problems related to verification, Popper argued that what distinguishes scientific from non-scientific theories is that the scientific theories are falsifiable. According to falsificationism, statements that cannot be falsified because they make no clear predictions, are not scientific. This is, for example, the case for statements like: 'You may feel better tomorrow' and 'God shows his love in multiple ways'. These are not falsifiable, because all possible outcomes are in line with them.

A theory is falsifiable if it rules out a range of outcomes, if there is agreement about observations that would be inconsistent with the theory and, therefore, refute the theory. A statement like *'It rains more on Wednesdays than on Thursdays'* is falsifiable, because failing to observe a difference in rainfall between Wednesdays and Thursdays would invalidate the statement.

falsificationism

view within the philosophy of science that statements are scientific only if they can be falsified empirically

In later writings Popper pointed to the need not only for falsifiability, but also for a commitment by the proponents to put their ideas to the test effectively. Many statements in psychoanalysis and astrology could in principle be put to the falsification test but, as said above, Popper saw little enthusiasm in their advocates to do so. All they tried to do was to find evidence *in favour of* their statements.

> **?**
>
> ## What do you think?
>
> Is the horoscope below falsifiable? And is it likely ever to be falsified?
> 'You will be feeling more like your old self today, as the influence of the earth element increases, making things a lot more settled.'

The hypothetico-deductive method

hypothetico-deductive method

model introduced by Popper to understand the scientific method; on the basis of observation, induction and educated guess-work, a theory of a phenomenon is formulated; the correctness of the theory is evaluated by the formulation of a testable prediction (hypothesis) on the basis of deductive reasoning; the prediction is subsequently put to a falsification test, which provides new observational data for further theorising

To further illuminate the role of falsificationism in scientific reasoning, Popper introduced the **hypothetico-deductive method** (which he claimed went back to the British scientist William Whewell in the first half of the nineteenth century). According to this method, scientific progress involves a combination of inductive and deductive reasoning (figure 8.3). On the basis of observation, induction and educated guesswork, an interpretation (theory) of a phenomenon is formulated. To check the correctness of the interpretation, the researcher uses deductive reasoning to generate a testable prediction. This prediction (hypothesis) is next put to the test by means of an experiment. The result of such a test provides new observational data for further theorising and new predictions, and so on.

An example of the use of the hypothetico-deductive method is the way in which the French chemist Louis Pasteur (1822–1895) in the nineteenth century discovered why wine, beer and milk turn sour. Through inductive reasoning he came to the tentative conclusion that this might be due to organisms introduced in the liquids from the environment, contrary to the prevailing explanation that the souring was a result of spontaneous generation of changes in the liquid. Pasteur hypothesised that if his interpretation was correct he should be able to prevent the souring by putting a filter between the liquid and the air, which blocked the organisms from entering the liquid. Finding such a filter would falsify the spontaneous generation account and would add evidence to Pasteur's alternative interpretation. Pasteur was able to show that an air filter indeed prevented the souring of wine and beer, but not (quite) of milk (which in addition needed to be boiled to kill the germs already present in it).

In line with the superiority of falsification over verification, Popper stressed that hypothesis testing should not be directed at trying to confirm a theory, but at seeing whether

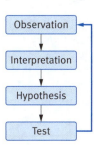

Figure 8.3 The different steps of the hypothetico-deductive method. The step from observation to interpretation is based on inductive reasoning, the step from interpretation to hypothesis on deductive reasoning. The observation and test stages make sure that the scientific explanations are empirically grounded. According to Popper, the hypothesis must be directed at a possible falsification of the interpretation/theory.

the theory could be falsified. If researchers repeatedly tried to reject a theory and failed to do so, they had strong evidence about the correctness of the theory. On the other hand, as soon as a test falsified the theory, they knew the interpretation was a false trail.

What do you think?

If you've taken a course of statistics, you know that a statistical test consists of trying to reject the null-hypothesis. Can you see how this fits in with falsificationism?

Falsification goes against the human intuition: the confirmation bias

The power of falsification relative to verification is further illustrated by an experiment that was published in 1960 by the British psychologist Peter Wason. He presented participants with cards on which a series of three numbers was printed, for instance '2, 4, 6'. Wason told the participants that they could ask as many questions as they thought necessary to find out the rule according to which the numbers had been generated. The rule Wason had in mind was 'each number is larger than the previous one'. This rule could easily be found by generating theories and trying to falsify them. For instance, a participant's initial theory could be that the experimenter added 2 to each number. This theory could be falsified by asking the experimenter whether the sequence '1, 2, 3' was a valid sequence. If this sequence was valid, then the participant knew for sure that his or her initial theory was false and had to be replaced by another theory. On the other hand, if the sequence '1, 2, 3' turned out not to be valid, then the participant had further evidence for the initial theory and could try out another falsification (e.g. by asking 'is 6, 4, 2 a valid sequence?'; see below).

Illustration of how falsification can be used to find out which rule generated the sequence 2, 4, 6

Trying to find the rule that generated the sequence 2, 4, 6

Initial theory: 'each number is generated by adding 2 to the previous number'

Try to falsify the theory. One way of reasoning could be: 'If the theory is correct, then the sequence 1, 2, 3 should be invalid (as each number is generated by adding 1 to the previous number)'. Test this.

Two possible outcomes:
- 1, 2, 3 turns out to be valid: Then the initial theory is wrong and a new theory must be generated (e.g. that each number is generated by adding the same amount to the previous number; this new theory can be falsified by asking whether 1, 2, 5 is a valid sequence)
- 1, 2, 3 turns out to be invalid: This is in line with the initial theory that 2 has to be added to each number and a new attempt to falsify the theory must be made (e.g. by asking whether 6, 4, 2 is valid; this allows the participant to test whether subtracting 2 from the previous number is permitted)

As you can imagine, Wason did not observe many participants using falsification (only 21 per cent found the correct rule). The majority of participants started from the theory 'add 2 to each number' and asked questions to verify this theory, such as 'is 1, 3, 5 a valid sequence' and 'is 14, 16, 18 a valid sequence'. In other words, the participants asked questions on which they expected a yes-answer. They did not ask questions that would have required the experimenter to say no. The tendency people have to search for evidence that confirms their opinions is known in psychology as the confirmation bias. Notice how this bias prevented the participants from finding the correct rule. After a few trials they said they knew the answer and that it was 'add 2 to the previous number' (because all the evidence they had gathered was in line with this rule).

confirmation bias

tendency people have to search for evidence that confirms their opinion; goes against falsificationism

What do you think?

Try to find evidence in favour of the opinion 'smoking is good for your health'. Can you see how such selective evidence gathering may strengthen health-hazardous opinions in people who use the confirmation bias? How could you use falsification to test the correctness of this opinion?

Science proceeds by trial and error

Notice how Wason's experiment not only illustrates the weakness of verification (as shown by the confirmation bias). It also shows how strong the falsification test is to unearth the truth. If participants thoroughly try to falsify each rule they come up with and if at some point they generate the correct rule, they are bound to find the solution Wason had in mind at the outset of the experiment. This is in line with Popper's recommendation of how scientists should work: they should generate bold theories as speculative and tentative conjectures, and then ruthlessly put them to the test on the basis of experiment and observation.

Because theories are generated without guarantee of correctness, it is entirely possible for them to be wrong, even when they initially seem to be in line with the collected evidence (i.e. have passed the first few falsification tests). As a matter of fact, it can be argued that scientists are never fully sure of the correctness of their scientific explanations. All they can say is that a particular theory thus far has stood the falsification tests and, therefore, is likely to be correct. They also have a lot of information about explanations that were wrong, because they did not pass the falsification test. Theories can be proven false, but cannot be proven true; they are just the best available, the ones that (thus far) have passed the tests.

Because there is no guarantee that scientific explanations are correct, progress in science is best seen as a trial and error process, in which many possible explanations are ventured and only the fittest survive. On the positive side, the ruthless falsification ensures that scientists are less likely to stick to wrong opinions than people who do not critically evaluate their opinions. At some point in time, a wrong scientific theory will hit on a falsification test it cannot pass and will have to be replaced by a (hopefully) better theory. In this respect, science learns from its mistakes. On the negative side, however, falsificationism implies that scientists can give wrong advice if they base their advice on wrong theories that have not yet been falsified.

> ## What do you think?
>
> Popper's view of science as a trial and error enterprise puts scientific advice in another light. Apply this to the scientific advice below, given by the behaviourist John Watson about how to educate children. He gave this advice in the full conviction that it was right, because it was in line with the latest findings of behaviourism. Try to evaluate the advice within a Popperian framework and within the framework of the logical positivists. In what respects will your evaluations differ?
>
> > Never hug and kiss [children], never let them sit in your lap. If you must, kiss them once on the forehead when they say goodnight. Shake hands with them in the morning.
>
> *(Watson (1928) as cited in Birnbaum (1955))*

Degrees of falsifiability

According to Popper, a statement is scientific if it has been put to the falsification test. However, this is not the only criterion scientists can use to measure the scientific status of a statement. The degree to which a statement or theory exposes itself to falsifiability is also informative. The more falsifiable a theory is, the higher its scientific status. Consider the following two statements:

1. Wine sours because of organisms.
2. Wine sours because of bacteria coming from the air.

Because of its higher specificity, the second statement is more prone to falsification than the first and, therefore, has a higher scientific standing. The clearer and the more precise a theory is, the higher its status if it stands repeated falsification tests. Another important variable is the scope of a theory: the more facts a theory explains, the better it is.

Popper was particularly impressed with Eddington's test of Einstein's theory of general relativity. Einstein had predicted that rays of light would bend as they passed close to a massive object. Eddington decided to make use of a solar eclipse in 1919 to test this prediction (see figures 8.4 (a) and (b)). Expeditions were sent to two different places where the observation conditions were best. One was led by Eddington himself to the island of Principe off the West African coast, and one was to northern Brazil. Each expedition was to take pictures of the sky during the eclipse and also on a night when the stars were at exactly the same position relative to the Earth without the interfering presence of the Sun (Eddington had to wait for several months before these conditions were met at his site). Although the results were less clear-cut than Eddington had hoped for (Coles 2001), they still convinced nearly all researchers involved that the data were in agreement with Einstein's predictions and significantly different from what was predicted by Newtonian physics. There was a significant difference between the perceived location of the stars during the eclipse and the perceived location without the interfering sun. In addition, the magnitude of the deviation was within measurement error of the deviation predicted by Einstein.

This, Popper argued, was science at its best: an extremely falsifiable theory was put to the test. There were hundreds of reasons to expect no difference in the perceived location of the stars at the time of the eclipse and at the time of the reference measurement; there was only one reason to expect the predicted difference, namely that Einstein's theory and his calculations were right. Without Einstein's theory the odds of finding the expected deviation were next to nil.

Figure 8.4a How a solar eclipse looks.
The white part around the occluded sun is called the corona.

Source: © UC Regents/Lick Observatory. Reproduced with permission.

Figure 8.4b Changes in star positions during the eclipse in 1922 in Australia.
How the position of the stars, as viewed from Earth, differs on the day of a solar eclipse and on a comparison night. The eclipsed Sun is represented by the circle in the middle of the diagram. Stars too close to the Sun cannot be seen because of the corona. The recorded displacements of the other stars are represented by lines. The differences observed were only predicted by Einstein's relativity theory. Therefore it was a strong test of the theory, as the chances of the theory being falsified were much higher than its chances of being confirmed.

Interim summary

Popper's alternative to logical positivism

- Science is better considered as the formulation of theories (on the basis of inductive reasoning and educated guessing) that scientists subsequently try to falsify by deriving hypotheses which are put to the falsification test; this is the hypothetico-deductive method.

- There is no guarantee that an initially proposed theory is correct; therefore, science proceeds by trial and error.

Interim summary (continued)

- Science differs from non-science because (1) the theories can be falsified and (2) there is a willingness to do so.

- Falsification is a better criterion than verification, because it is logically possible to falsify a statement based on inductive reasoning.

- The more falsifiable a theory is (depending on its level of detail and scope), the better the theory is.

- Falsification is counterintuitive because people have a bias towards trying to confirm their opinions rather than trying to reject them.

Sophisticated falsificationism

Do not give in too easily

Popper's approach was soon perceived by the philosophers of science as more fruitful to the understanding of scientific progress than logical positivism. However, it had its problems too. In particular the idea that theories should be rejected as soon as they were falsified did not seem to be in line with the way in which scientists worked. Scientists did not throw away a theory as soon as some data contradicted it. First, they investigated whether the data were sound, so that they did not reject a theory on flawed grounds. Second, if they were convinced of the soundness of the evidence, they examined whether the theory could be amended so that it incorporated the new finding. Most of the time theories contain several variables that can be adapted to accommodate a deviating finding.

A particularly compelling example of how a deviating observation may lead to a modification of the existing theory concerns the problems the motion of Uranus caused for Newton's laws of physics. In the nineteenth century it became undeniable that Uranus's path deviated too much from Newton's laws to be acceptable. According to falsificationism, this should have been the signal to give up the theory and look for something new. An alternative, however, was proposed by Leverrier in France and Adams in the UK. They put forward the suggestion that Newton's laws could be saved if there was another planet in the neighbourhood of Uranus that influenced its orbit. The astronomers started to calculate where the new planet should be and what size it should have. On the basis of these calculations it was possible to inspect the designated part of the sky more thoroughly. This eventually led to the discovery of Neptune.

Episodes like the one above illustrate that science is more than simply rejecting falsified bold conjectures and replacing them with equally bold alternative conjectures. Often it is better to change an existing, good theory so that it is no longer contradicted by the available empirical evidence. If scientists had always given up their theories as soon as they were confronted with some negative evidence, they arguably wouldn't have had any left any more! Even Popper eventually agreed that scientists should not give up their theories too easily:

> I have always stressed the need for some dogmatism: the dogmatic scientist has an important role to play. If we give into criticism too easily, we shall never find out where the real power of our theories lies.
>
> *(Popper 1970, p. 55)*

Modifications of theories in the light of counterevidence

If modifications of existing theories are allowed, the next question, of course, is which modifications are acceptable and which are not. Popper himself pointed out that a modification must under no condition make the theory less falsifiable. As a matter of fact, the theory should become more falsifiable as a result of the modification. The postulation of a new planet to save Newtonian physics in the light of the disturbing evidence from Uranus's motion was an acceptable modification, because it led to a new falsifiable prediction, namely that a certain planet should be observed in a certain region of the universe. In contrast, modifications that were not testable or that made a theory less falsifiable, were unacceptable in Popper's eyes. He called them **ad hoc modifications**.

ad hoc modifications

modifications to a theory that according to Popper make the theory less falsifiable; decrease the scientific value of the theory

A clear example of an ad hoc modification was the response of the adherents of the phlogiston theory when it was discovered that some materials weighed more after being burnt than before. Remember from Chapter 6 that the phlogiston theory for some time 'explained' why certain materials were highly flammable and others not. The idea was that highly flammable materials contained a lot of an invisible substance, phlogiston, which was released during the fire. This theory predicted that materials should weigh less after being burnt than before, which was contradicted for some materials by a series of careful observations. In order to save the phlogiston theory, some adherents ventured the possibility that phlogiston could have a negative weight, so that materials could become heavier when the phlogiston was released. According to this view, phlogiston was not only invisible but also had a negative weight! This increased lack of falsifiability is a tell-tale sign of unscientific thinking.

Unfortunately, the situation about allowable and unallowable modifications is not as simple as suggested by Popper. Researchers can go a long way modifying their theories with falsifiable amendments without making any scientific progress. This is illustrated by the following hypothetical scenario from Lakatos, obviously inspired by the events surrounding the discovery of Neptune:

> The story is about an imaginary case of planetary misbehaviour. A physicist of the pre-Einsteinian era takes Newton's mechanics and his law of gravitation (N), the accepted initial conditions, I, and calculates, with their help, the path of a newly discovered small planet, p. But the planet deviates from the calculated path. Does our Newtonian physicist consider that the deviation was forbidden by Newton's theory and therefore that, once established, it refutes the theory N? No. He suggests that there must be a hitherto unknown planet p' which perturbs the path of p. He calculates the mass, orbit, etc., of this hypothetical planet and then asks an experimental astronomer to test his hypothesis. The planet p' is so small that even the biggest available telescopes cannot possibly observe it: the experimental astronomer applies for a research grant to build yet a bigger one. In three years' time the new telescope is ready. Were the unknown planet p'; to be discovered, it would be hailed as a new victory of Newtonian science. But it is not. Does our scientist abandon Newton's theory and his idea of the perturbing planet? No. He suggests that a cloud of cosmic dust hides the planet from us. He calculates the location and properties of this cloud and asks for a research grant . . .

(Lakatos 1970, p. 100–1)

Measuring skulls

If the above hypothetical example looks a bit farfetched to you, see what happened when the great nineteenth-century French scholar Paul Broca (see Chapter 5) encountered data that did not agree with his ideas. Broca was heavily involved in attempts to investigate whether the big differences observed in the brains of people were associated with individual differences in functioning. (The brains of individuals differ as much in their appearance as, for instance, faces. Brain imagers who work with a limited number of patients, know after some time who a particular brain image is from by simply looking at it, just like we can identify people on the basis of their faces.)

One rather straightforward and generally accepted hypothesis was that there would be a positive correlation between the size of a brain and the intelligence of the person: the larger the brain the more intelligent the person. And indeed the pattern of carefully measured specimens initially seemed to bear out the prediction. For instance, an analysis of brains of high performing individuals showed that famous people like Cromwell, Byron and Cuvier had brains of more than 1,800 g, well above the male average. Other measurements showed that males had larger brains than females, that adult people had larger brains than elderly, and that Europeans had larger brains than natives from Africa and America (you can find a review of these findings in the first volume of the *Journal de Médecine Mentale* (1861), in an article entitled *Du volume et de la forme du cerveau*).

However, in 1862 Broca was given a collection of 60 skulls excavated from a cemetery in a poor Basque village in Spain. As can be seen in figure 8.5, the highly unexpected finding was that these people had consistently larger brains than the Parisians! Here is how Broca responded to this finding (translated from Broca (1863) p. 11–13):

> The average skull capacity of the Basque people is … larger than that of the total group of the Parisians. Only inferior to the skulls from the Morgue, it surpasses . . . the capacity of the skulls of the aristocrats from the Middle Ages . . . and even that of the skulls of the bourgeoisie from the nineteenth century.

	NOMBRE de crânes.	CAPACITÉ moyenne.
Crânes de la Cité................	116	1,427.57
Crânes des Innocents............	117	1,409.23
Crânes du { Sépult⁰ˢ. partic⁰ˢ.....	90	1,484.23
xix⁰ siècle { Fosse commune......	35	1,403.14
Les deux séries précédentes.......	125	1,461.53
Crânes de la Morgue............	17	1,517.29
Tous les crânes parisiens réunis...	384	1,437.24
Crânes des Basques.............	60	1,486.88

Figure 8.5 Original table from Broca (1863).
This shows the larger brain capacities in 60 Basque skulls than in 384 Parisian skulls (there were five different sources for the latter). The mean size of the Basque people was 1,487 cm^3; that of the Parisians 1,437 cm^3. Only one small Parisian sample (coming from the Morgue) outperformed the Basques.

What could be the reasons for this unexpected result? The skulls in all samples have been collected without selection, so that the relative proportion of skulls of the two sexes should be more or less the same in all samples. A comparison of the Parisian samples has shown the influence of the social class on the volume of the head. The skull of a modern bourgeois is more voluminous than that of a proletarian; it is also more voluminous than that of an aristocrat from the Middle Ages; this would establish that in the same race, the progress in civilization, comfort and education coincides with a growth of the brain. But this evidently cannot be the reason of the great capacity of the skulls in the Basque people. Those skulls come from a poor village cemetery, from a backward and ignorant populace that vegetated in the darkness . . .

The substantial capacity of the skulls is, therefore, a natural characteristic of this race. However, M. Broca is far from concluding on the basis of this that the Basque people would be more intelligent than the people from Paris. As a matter of fact, the intelligence does not depend solely on the volume of the encephalon; it also depends on the relative development of the different regions of the brain. The brains of the Basque people are, on average, larger than ours; but this would only be an indication of superiority if they had the same shape, if, for instance, the frontal region were in absolute or in relative terms as developed as ours. So, M. Broca has measured separately the main parts of the head, and he has discovered that *the anterior skull is, in absolute terms, smaller in Basque people than in Parisian people*. It is the considerable development of the occipital region that gives the Basque skulls their big capacity. (italics from the original)

So, rather than giving up his theory in the face of falsifying evidence, Broca introduced a modification to salvage the theory: the Basque people had larger skulls, not because they were more intelligent (or because intelligence was not correlated with brain size), but because the brain parts unrelated to intelligence were larger. Notice that this modification would have been acceptable for Popper as it was based on empirical evidence and increased the falsifiability of the theory. All that was needed was to set up a study to test the new claim (which, as far as we know, has never happened).

It is important to realise that Broca is by no means an exception. Everyone reading primary scientific literature (i.e. original research reports) will be familiar with this type of wriggling by authors who are confronted with evidence that does not fit their theory, and who propose all types of modifications without (yet) testing them.

Why researchers do not like to give up theories

The reason why scientists in general do not like to give up their theories is not so much that they have to admit they were wrong (although this sometimes is a problem for the researcher who initially proposed the theory), but that rejecting a theory means the scientists have to start all over again. They have to search for a new, plausible theory that explains everything the previous theory explained plus the novel, contradictory finding. This arguably is one of the hardest challenges in science.

Remember the Wason task we discussed above. There we said that: 'If participants thoroughly try to falsify each rule they come up with and *if at some point they generate the correct rule*, they are bound to find the solution Wason had in mind.' The condition in italics is the bottleneck: someone has to come up with the correct idea, before falsificationism leads to progress. Falsificationism by itself does not lead to the correct explanation; it only eliminates wrong ideas. As long as no-one ventures the right interpretation, falsificationism is a dead-end. This is what Albert Einstein (1879–1955) meant when he wrote: 'A theory can be proved by an experiment; but no path leads from experiment to the birth of a theory' (as cited in Andrews (1987) p. 264). For that reason scientists need convincing evidence before they are willing to give up their favourite theories.

Although Popper's insights of falsificationism and the unacceptability of ad hoc modifications were important steps forward, they did not explain why most of the time researchers tend to cling on to their theories in the light of counterevidence and why at other times they are willing to give up a theory in search for a new conjecture. A model that does a better job in this respect was proposed in the 1960s by Thomas Kuhn.

Interim summary

Sophisticated falsificationism

■ Popper's insistence on replacing falsified theories by bold alternatives as soon as they were contradicted by empirical observations does not agree with scientific practice and would also seem to be too radical.

■ When researchers are confronted with conflicting evidence, they first try to modify the existing theory so that it can account for the contradictory finding.

■ According to Popper, modifications are acceptable as long as they do not make the theory less falsifiable; otherwise, they are unacceptable ad hoc modifications.

■ Problem: Researchers regularly propose modifications they do not test and that are not taken up by other researchers. Is this still science?

8.4   Science is a succession of paradigms

Thomas Kuhn (1922–1996) was an American physicist who after his PhD first turned to the history of science and then to the philosophy of science. His best-known publication is *The Structure of Scientific Revolutions* (first published in 1962; second, revised edition in 1970). Kuhn agreed with Popper about the priority of theory over observation. In his view too, science did not in the first place proceed from fact to theory, but on the basis of conjectures that were mercilessly tested. Even more than Popper, he stressed that all observations and theoretical concepts were dependent on the language of the adopted theory/conjecture. He also emphasised the pressures that are present in the science community to keep individual scientists within the confines of the prevailing research tradition. Only certain research questions are considered to be of interest by the majority of researchers; in addition these questions must be examined in well-specified ways. Researchers that do not adhere to these conventions are seen as mavericks and are ostracised, as we will see below.

The general layout of Kuhn's theory

Pre-science

Figure 8.6 shows the general lay-out of Kuhn's theory. In his view, each research discipline starts with an unorganised amalgam of facts, observations and models to explain small-scale phenomena (i.e. the situation illustrated in figure 8.1). Figure 8.7 shows another example of this situation. Researchers try to understand isolated facts (the black lines) without having an idea of the wider framework. As a consequence, their explanations often contradict each other (e.g. the explanation of one fact is incompatible with that of another fact). They also do not agree about the methods to use.

paradigm

notion introduced by Kuhn to refer to the fact that scientists share a set of common views of what the discipline is about and how problems must be investigated

The creation of a paradigm

At some point in time, a general framework (theory) is proposed (figure 8.8). This not only informs the researchers about the interrelations of the various blobs, they also have an idea of the methods that must be used to properly investigate the different facts. In Kuhn's terms, at that moment the researchers share a paradigm, a set of common views

---

Kuhn's theory of scientific progress

pre-science → normal science → crisis → revolution → new normal science
→ new crisis → . . .

Figure 8.6 Different stages in Kuhn's theory of scientific progress.

Figure 8.7 Pre-science stage of Kuhn's theory.
Researchers have a collection of facts, observations and models to explain these facts. There is not yet a general theory that integrates the different findings within an overall framework. There is also no agreement yet about the precise research methods to be used.

Source: Adapted from Fischer (1968). Reproduced with permission.

Figure 8.8 Normal science stages of Kuhn's theory.
When researchers start to use a common theoretical framework to investigate the different facts (i.e., that the lines represent a swan), according to Kuhn they have a paradigm. This paradigm determines which facts should be examined, how this should be done, and what types of explanations are allowed.

Source: From Isa Brysbaert, based on Fischer (1968).

of what the discipline is about and how the problems must be approached. This is the start of science. The paradigm will determine:

1.   what is to be observed and scrutinised,
2.   which questions should be asked,
3.   how the questions are to be structured,
4.   how the results of scientific investigations should be interpreted.

Normal science

Once the researchers share a paradigm, the discipline finds itself doing *normal science*. This involves attempts to falsify the theory, to see how strong the theory is. If there is a consistent deviation between the theory and a line of findings, a modification or extension is introduced to capture the intractable fact without changing the core of the paradigm (as indicated above). Although there is no explicit ban, researchers are not expected by their colleagues to question the paradigm and to come up with incommensurable, bold conjectures. If they nevertheless do so, they will find themselves ostracised, which will result in difficulties obtaining money for their research and getting their papers published.

Kuhn also called the stage of normal science *puzzle-solving*, because researchers work on familiar topics using well-known techniques and practices. They have confidence that they will be able to solve the puzzle using the available tools. They are guided (governed) by the rules of the paradigm.

Crisis and revolution

Inevitably the phase of normal science will yield results that cannot be accounted for by the paradigm. At first, these findings are seen as *anomalies*, unexplained observations, rather than falsifications, and researchers will question the quality of the

degenerative research programme

notion introduced by Lakatos to indicate a paradigm that does not allow researchers to make new predictions and that requires an increasing number of ad hoc modifications to account for the empirical findings

progressive research programme

notion introduced by Lakatos to indicate a paradigm that allows researchers to make new, hitherto unexpected predictions that can be tested empirically

findings or look for ways in which they can be explained with the use of modifications to the existing theory. Again, inevitably (in Kuhn's view) the anomalies will multiply and become more severe. They will require an increased use of ad hoc modifications and changes to the theory that other researchers do not find interesting enough to test (like Broca's proposal about the magnitude of the different brain regions). Because of the proliferation of ill-substantiated modifications, the original framework will become increasingly incoherent and cluttered, resulting in a state of affairs very similar to the pre-science situation. Scientific progress stalls and confidence in the paradigm is undermined. In Kuhn's term, the discipline finds itself in a state of *crisis*.

At the time of a crisis, a scientific discipline is more open to bold, alternative conjectures that question the core of the paradigm. These alternatives must provide the same level of detail and falsifiability as the existing paradigm and, in addition, provide a better interpretation for the deviating findings. In particular, scientists are looking for a conjecture that allows the discipline to make progress again, to yield new predictions that can be falsified and stand the test.

A particularly interesting distinction in this respect was introduced by the Hungarian born mathematician, Imre Lakatos (1970). He called a paradigm that does not allow its adherents to make new predictions and that requires a growing number of post hoc modifications to explain conflicting findings, a degenerative research programme. In contrast, a paradigm that allows the formulation of novel, hitherto unexpected facts he labelled a progressive research programme. Dienes (2008, p. 48) used the following colourful description to illustrate the difference between the two types of programmes: 'In a progressive programme, theory keeps ahead of the data; in a degenerating programme, theory lags behind the data, desperately trying to adjust itself to keep up.'

Kuhn called the replacement of a paradigm in crisis by an incompatible, new paradigm that makes new predictions and that repeatedly stands the falsification test, a scientific revolution. During a scientific revolution, a *paradigm shift* takes place, in which the old paradigm (the degenerative research programme) is replaced by a new paradigm (the progressive research programme). This is a time of intense scientific progress. Suddenly, a lot of facts which previously were not understood start to make sense and new grounds are captured. It is a time of enormous scientific excitement (because of the major breakthroughs that are made in rapid succession), unlike the everyday ebb and flow that characterise normal science.

To give you an idea of what happens during a scientific revolution, have a look at figure 8.9. It contains the same facts as figures 8.7 and 8.8. However, because of the shift in paradigm, the meaning of the facts has changed emphatically. What researchers previously believed to be a head (metaphorically speaking) suddenly turns out to be a tail! No wonder the scientists did not understand the facts within the previous paradigm and had to revert to increasingly degenerative modifications of their theory.

Examples of scientific revolutions

Astronomy provides several nice examples of degenerative theories that were replaced by incompatible new ones. The most famous, of course, is that of the Copernican revolution, when geocentrism was replaced by heliocentrism (Chapter 2). Another example around the same time was the replacement of circular orbits by ellipsoid orbits. Copernicus had started his model of the universe by assuming that all movements of the celestial bodies

Figure 8.9 Crisis stage in Kuhn's theory.
During the crisis phase in Kuhn's theory, a paradigm in crisis is replaced by an incompatible, new paradigm that enables the prediction of new, hitherto unexpected facts, which subsequently stand the falsification test (i.e., the lines do not come from a swan but a squirrel). Kuhn called this a paradigm shift.

Source: From Isa Brysbaert, based on Fischer (1968).

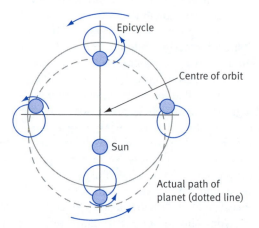

Figure 8.10 The use of epicycles to explain the movement of a planet around the Sun in Copernicus's model of the universe.
To approach the observed path of the planet, Copernicus had to assume (1) that the Sun was not at the centre of the orbit of the planet, and (2) that the planet not only moved in a circle around the Sun, but in addition in a circle around the first circle, a so-called epicycle. Because in some cases the predictions still did not match the observations fully, a further epicycle on the first epicycle was required.

were circular. This required him to work with epicycles, to explain the observed movements of the sun and the known planets (the 'wandering stars'; figure 8.10). Each time a significant deviation was noticed between the predicted movements and the observed movements, a new epicycle had to be added post hoc (i.e. after the deviation had been observed). In the end, Copernicus needed more than 30 of them (which he claimed was still less than the geocentric model of Ptolemy and Aristotle).

At the beginning of the seventeenth century the German astronomer Johannes Kepler proposed a theory according to which the orbit of a planet around the Sun was

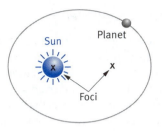

Figure 8.11 Kepler's alternative model.
Based on the idea that the orbit around the Sun is an ellipse with the sun in one of the foci. This model not only was much simpler, it also gave a better account of the speed of the planet.

ellipsoid rather than circular, with the sun in one of the foci of the ellipse (figure 8.11). This model was not only simpler; it also allowed for new predictions about the speed of the planets. Incidentally, both examples (Copernicus and Kepler) also illustrate that scientific revolutions do not always happen overnight, as the name may suggest. As we saw in Chapter 2, Copernicus first wrote about his model in 1514, more than a century before Galilei started to defend it! Similarly, Kepler published his ideas about the orbits of the planets in 1619, but they were largely ignored for the first 50 years (among others, by Galilei and Descartes). To some extent this is understandable. Only when the discipline is in crisis do scientists start to look for alternative explanations. Either these have to be newly found as a result of the crisis, or they are based on a search through the archives for ideas that for a long time were overlooked (because they were not in line with the then prevailing paradigm).

Still related to scientific revolutions, it is important to keep in mind that they consist of a paradigm shift, a shift of the theoretical backbone of a discipline. A scientific revolution means that many existing research topics lose their appeal (either because their mystery has been solved or because it becomes clear that the research on them was misguided). They are replaced by new topics that follow from the novel paradigm and that often require different research methods. When only a minor part of the paradigm needs to be replaced by an alternative explanation, Kuhn did not consider this to be a revolution. Others, however, have been less restrictive in their use of the word paradigm (see, for instance, Chapter 10, where the opening quote talks of a 'paradigm war' in psychology). In particular psychology seems to have been quite generous with the term, using it for nearly every major change in theory and approach, making the anthropologist Geertz (2000) jest that in psychology paradigm shifts come along not by the century but by the decade or even by the month (Driver-Linn 2003).

? What do you think?

In Chapter 4 we saw that the cognitive psychologists in the 1970s thought they were witnessing a paradigm shift from behaviourism to cognitive psychology. Can you think of arguments in favour of this belief? And what are the counter-arguments? (Remember that you always must try to falsify statements, rather than give in to the confirmation bias.)

Return to normal science

Once the paradigm shift has taken place, the new paradigm takes over and forms the new background against which research occurs. After the rapid changes and excitement of the revolution, the situation returns to normal and the scientists go back to their usual activity of puzzle-solving. They will defend the new paradigm and the associated research methods with the same vigour as they defended the previous paradigm.

The pressure a research community in a period of normal science exerts on its members to stay within the limits of the shared paradigm can be illustrated by the ways in which novices (students) are introduced into the field. They are taught a set of 'objective' and 'generally accepted' (i.e. unquestionable) research techniques, and they have to study from textbooks that hide the paradigm shifts of the pasts. The latter is achieved either by reinterpreting the past so that it fits within the current paradigm or by placing the start of the discipline at the moment of the most recent revolution. Everything that happened before is then conveniently summarised as well-meant but ultimately naïve precursors of the current, 'real' science. In this way, the illusion of science as a cumulative enterprise of ever increasing knowledge is maintained. As Gould (1996, p. 25) rightly noted, 'Most scientists don't care a fig about history; . . . they do regard the past as a mere repository of error – at best a source of moral instruction in pitfalls along paths to progress.' Normal science continues until the anomalies once more become too numerous and too severe to remain acceptable, propelling the discipline into its next crisis . . .

What do you think?

Go back to the preface where we defined conceptual issues. Can you see now how the conceptual issues are closely intertwined with the paradigm in a research discipline (the implicit set of rules about what is worthwhile to investigate and how this has to be done)?

Interim summary

Kuhn's theory

- A discipline needs a general theory to become scientific (otherwise it is a pre-science). This theory forms a paradigm against which observations are made, questions posed and answers interpreted.

- During periods of normal science, scientists solve puzzles within the existing paradigm. They defend the paradigm and ostracise colleagues who question it. Modifications of the theory in the light of contradictory findings must stay within the paradigm. Otherwise the finding is an unexplained anomaly.

- During a period of normal science, anomalies accumulate and modifications become increasingly ad hoc. This triggers a crisis.

On the relativity of paradigms and science

Paradigms are ever changing

A disturbing aspect of Kuhn's theory is that each paradigm is considered to be a temporary set of ideas, bound to turn into a crisis and to be replaced by an alternative paradigm. This means that current scientific knowledge cannot be considered as an absolute truth but must be seen as a transition phase from the previous paradigm to the next. The squirrel in figure 8.9 is not the final interpretation. At some point in the future it will be replaced by yet another organisation, which itself will only last for some time, etcetera.

The unbearable lightness of science

A second disturbing factor about Kuhn's theory is that Kuhn has been rather unclear about whether a revolution meant progress or simply a change of paradigm. Whereas scientists feel affinity with the former view (bad theories are replaced by better ones), philosophers of science have been more intrigued by the second possibility. What if science was nothing but an endless parade of paradigms, each throwing a different, limited light on what is essentially a multifaceted reality? This would completely rob science of its aura of objectivity and dethrone it from its supposed superiority over other forms of knowledge! Or as the Austrian philosopher Feyerabend (1975) put it in his anarchistic theory of knowledge, scientific claims would be no different from other kinds of opinions, such as those provided by ancient myths or religions. Science would have no inherent authority and the respect for science in current Western society would be nothing more than the reverence people in the Middle Ages felt for the Catholic Church.

science wars

notion used by the postmodernists to refer to their attacks against the special status of science and their unmasking of scientific knowledge as a social construction

The science wars

Needless to say, the above line of reasoning is strong ammunition for people who question the usefulness and the meaningfulness of science. On the basis of Kuhn's analysis they started to defend the position that current-day science is nothing but a set of stories, shrouded in a secretive language and adorned with an unjustified air of objectivity, which in a hundred years' time is likely to be looked upon as an outmoded paradigm based on wrong assumptions. After all, there are plenty of examples of superseded scientific 'facts' that in the past were defended with the same zeal as scientists nowadays push forward their latest 'data'. Nothing guarantees that the present paradigms in the different sciences are the right ones. Kuhn's theory predicts they are not (and never will be).

postmodernist

in the philosophy of science someone who questions the special status of science and sees scientific explanations as stories told by a particular group of scientists

social construction

notion used by postmodernists to indicate that scientific knowledge is not objective knowledge discovering the workings of an external reality, but a story told by a particular scientific community on the basis of their language and culture

Towards the end of the twentieth century the above conclusion led to a frontal attack against science by a number of philosophers and sociologists, who are often referred to as the postmodernists (although in the literature there are many more names referring to the different positions taken). Important names are the French philosophers Michel Foucault, Jean-François Lyotard and Bruno Latour. In particular, they questioned the claim for realism on which science is based. Realism refers to the assumption that scientific knowledge (and human knowledge in general) aims to discover things in the world, that the concepts used in scientific theories refer to real things. Within a realistic view true statements refer to statements that correspond with the world.

According to the postmodernists, the analyses of Popper and in particular Kuhn show that scientific knowledge has less to do with realism than with the opinions shared by the group of scientists. So-called scientific knowledge is a social construction by the scientific community and is affected by their language and culture. The truth of scientific statements does not depend on how well the statements represent reality, but on how coherent they are with the rest of the paradigm shared by the group. Scientific knowledge is in no way superior to other types of knowledge; scientists have simply managed to acquire a lot of power in Western society by forming alliances with other strong groups (see also Chapter 12).

The discussion between scientists and postmodernists is sometimes referred to in the philosophy of science as the science wars (which is a good term to search for further information on the internet), although very few scientists seem to be aware of these wars (in line with their general indifference towards the efforts to define the essence of the scientific method, as we saw at the beginning of this chapter). For them, the scientific achievements of the past 400 years are so overwhelming that it is inconceivable that anyone would doubt them. As Sokal (1996) wrote, paraphrasing the eighteenth-century philosopher David Hume: 'anyone who believes the laws of physics are mere social conventions is invited to try transgressing those conventions from the windows of my apartment. (I live on the twenty-first floor.)'

KEY FIGURES IN THE PHILOSOPHY OF SCIENCE

- Francis Bacon (1561–1626)
  - British scholar and politician.
  - Among the first to promote the use of observation and experimental histories as the basis of knowledge acquisition, rather than reliance on tradition and authority.

- Charles Peirce (1839–1914)
  - American philosopher.
  - Founder of pragmatism (together with James and Dewey).
  - Maintained that only knowledge of practical value to cope with the world was true.
  - Neglected for most of the twentieth century because pragmatism did not make a distinction between scientific and non-scientific knowledge; currently increasing interest in his views.

- Wiener Kreis (Vienna Circle; 1924–1936)
  - Group of philosophers and scientists in Vienna (Austria) who tried to define the essence of the scientific method.

■ Known as the proponents of 'logical positivism', which saw the scientific method as based on verification through observation (verificationism); also requirement of operational definition of variables.

■ Karl Popper (1902–1994)

Karl Popper
Photo by Keystone/
Getty Images

■ Born in Vienna; attended meetings of the Wiener Kreis.

■ Left Austria because of the growth of Nazism, first to New Zealand, and then to England, where he became professor at the University of London.

■ Argued that science is theory driven: scientists conjecture explanations which they subsequently try to falsify. This is the so-called hypothetico-deductive method. As a result, science proceeds by trial and error.

■ Stressed the importance of falsification over verification.

■ Modifications to theories are only allowed if they make the theory more falsifiable.

■ Thomas Kuhn (1922–1986)

Thomas Kuhn
Photo by Bill
Pierce/Time Life
Pictures/Getty Images

■ American physicist who first became interested in the history of science and then in the philosophy of science.

■ Stressed that science is a social activity, because researchers in a scientific discipline share a paradigm they impose on newcomers.

■ An established science continuously goes through a cycle of normal science → crisis → revolution → normal science . . .

■ During a revolution, a paradigm shift takes place.

■ Because scientific research depends on a paradigm that will change in the future, scientific findings are relative.

■ Postmodernists (end of the twentieth century)

■ Group of philosophers (first in Austria and France, then also in other countries) who on the basis of Kuhn argued that scientific theories were social constructions, no different from other types of knowledge.

Interim summary

■ Paradigm shifts in Kuhn's theory do not imply that the old paradigm is replaced by a better one; it is just replaced by another one.

■ This means that all scientific knowledge is relative and time-dependent, because it is based on a paradigm that is bound to be replaced in the future.

■ The awareness that scientific knowledge is relative has elicited strong criticism from the postmodernists. In their view science is in no way superior to other types of knowledge, because it consists of social constructions made up by the scientists. Scientists have more power because they have formed strong alliances with other powerful groups.

In search of middle ground

In the previous sections we have seen two extreme views of the status of science. On the one hand, there is the claim by many researchers that science is objective, because it is based on observable facts and on theories that have been verified. On the other hand, there are the critics who argue that science is time-dependent because the perception of facts is biased by the scientist's theoretical background (paradigm) that will change in the future. How can these two views be reconciled?

Facts have an objective basis even if there is a subjective component in their perception

A first step towards middle ground is the acceptance that the perception of facts has both an objective and a subjective component. Just as it cannot be denied that the perception of facts is coloured by the theoretical framework within which they are studied, it seems better to accept that observations correspond to 'something' in the world. It is not true that scientists have consistently found what they expected to find. Throughout history, empirical observations have imposed themselves on scientists and forced them to revise their ideas. More than once, their perceptions have baffled scientists because they were so much at odds with the existing expectations.

When Galilei first observed moons around Jupiter with his telescope (Chapter 2), this was not because he expected them there. Neither did his critics when they were invited to have a look through the telescope. Similarly, the Danish scholar Ørsted had no biasing prejudices when in 1820 he suddenly observed that the needle of his compass deflected each time he switched on an electric battery (this was the origin of the research showing a close relationship between electricity and magnetism). Researchers have a name for this type of accidental discovery while they are looking for something entirely different; they call it *serendipity*.

Accidental discoveries illustrate that perceptions have an origin outside the perceiver and at times can enforce themselves. They are more than theory-laden projections by the scientists. Observations may be misinterpreted, but they will never be completely at odds with the events that are at their origin. As such, the constant coupling of scientific statements to observations is an assurance that the statements will not be completely unsubstantiated (as may be the case with unchecked, principle-driven claims), even if there is no guarantee for their full correctness.

Scientific claims must be treated with caution, certainly when they are new

A second step towards middle ground is the acceptance that scientific claims do not have an unquestionable status. We have seen a multitude of reasons why a particular claim may be wrong, why scientific progress should be considered as a process of trial and error rather than a steady accumulation of unquestionable facts. Therefore, it is pivotal to remain critical about the claims made by scientists. It is not true that there is no more room for debate once science has spoken (as suggested in the excerpt that opened this chapter).

The advice for critical thinking is reasonably well known to people who take a scientific course. After all, they are urged to look for possible falsifications. However, in general this advice is limited to questioning the validity of the empirical findings within the existing paradigm (how sound are the data and how justified is the scientist to draw his or her conclusions on the basis of the data that were obtained?). What the present analysis adds is that we should always keep in mind that the starting conjecture may be wrong, either because the researcher had the wrong convictions or because the existing paradigm misconceives the wider context of the issue.

There is no fail-safe advice to be given about how to avoid misleading scientific claims. One helpful rule of thumb, however, is to look at the time period since the claim has been introduced and the amount of research that has gone into it thus far. Most people are particularly impressed by the latest research, but in general this is the most risky part of science. The more falsification tests a statement has passed, the surer we can be of its validity (always keeping in mind that it is impossible to achieve 100 per cent certainty). In this respect, researchers talk about the importance of *converging evidence*, evidence from a long series of different falsification attempts, each aimed at a potential weakness of the statement.

Of all the research that is done and the theoretical modifications that are introduced, only a small fraction survives the first 10 years. Although some of the forgotten ideas may later turn out to be missed critical insights (like Kepler's), the vast majority of them are overlooked because they were false starts or simply not important enough. The short life span of many newly proposed scientific ideas is also the reason why scientific textbooks and lectures should not be limited to the research of the last few years (Sternberg 1999). They should first of all pay attention to the well-established, 'classic' findings and interpretations.

Interim summary

- The strong relative view of scientific knowledge is based on the assumption that the perception of facts is fully dependent on the perceiver's background knowledge.

- If one accepts that the perception of facts has an objective component, grounded in reality, then the constant coupling of ideas to observations by means of verification and falsification is a guarantee that the ideas will not be completely in contradiction with the reality as it can be observed.

- The observation that science proceeds by trial and error and happens within a paradigm that may turn out to be wrong, should warn people always to remain critical about the scientific claims that are made. A helpful rule of thumb in this respect is to always look at how many falsification tests the claim has stood.

8.5   Focus on: Is there room for pragmatism?

Realism vs. idealism

If you know something about philosophy, you may have noticed that the discussion about the status of science touches one of the fundamental questions in philosophy: What are the sources, nature and limits of knowledge? Two opposing views exist: realism and idealism.

realism

view within philosophy that human knowledge tries to reveal real things in the world; the truth of knowledge is determined by the correspondence of the knowledge with the real world

idealism

view within philosophy that human knowledge is a construction of the mind and does not necessarily correspond to an outside world; the truth of knowledge depends on the coherence with rest of the knowledge in the social group

Realism says that:

- human knowledge corresponds to the reality,
- concepts used in human knowledge refer to real things in the world,
- knowledge is discovered rather than created,
- truth is determined by the correspondence between knowledge and the world.

In contrast, idealism holds that:

- the world as we know it is a construction of the mind,
- our knowledge is a subjective or social construction that does not necessarily correspond to an outside world,
- all knowledge is affected by language and culture,
- the truth of statements depends on their coherence with the rest of our knowledge.

The discussion of idealism vs. realism was first raised explicitly by the Irish philosopher George Berkeley (1685–1753). He reasoned that if one assumes that all knowledge is based on perception (as the empiricists did; see Chapter 2), then one has to conclude that there is no real, knowable object behind the perception. The only thing that is real for people is the perception itself.

What do you think?

Look at the different views of scientific knowledge we have discussed. Where do they lie on a continuum going from realism to idealism?

The pragmatic alternative

Both realism and idealism have arguments for and against, making it impossible to convince the die-hard proponents of either view that they may be wrong. Ironically, this may be because the question addressed is less relevant than would seem at first sight. If you asked scientists which scientific insights are worthwhile and likely to be carried on, they might not even refer to the ones that are 'true' (whatever 'true' may mean). They may be more likely to point to the ones that made a difference and that allowed them to put new ideas into practice. Similarly, in Chapter 7 we saw that the largest impact of psychology on society in the twentieth century may not have been based on its 'true' insights, but on the insights that were perceived as useful by the social groups.

pragmatism

view within philosophy that human knowledge is information about how to cope with the world; the truth of knowledge depends on the success one has in engaging with the world, on what works

This alternative view in philosophy is known as pragmatism. Its basic tenet is that knowledge arises from the interactions of the individual with the world. Knowledge is not a passive mirror of reality (as defended by realism), nor a subjective construction (as claimed by idealism). It is information about how to cope with the world. Truth within this view depends on the success one has in engaging with the world, on what works. The truth of a theory (as opposed to its rival) is only of interest if it makes a practical difference. Because the world constantly changes, the truth is not fixed either.

The founder of pragmatism was the American philosopher Charles Peirce (1839–1914). For most of his life Peirce was not connected to a university (he actually had a rather tragic life, which can easily be found on the internet) and his influence was mainly due to a friend of his, William James (yes, him!), and a PhD student he had during a short stint at Johns Hopkins University: John Dewey. Both men were extremely effective in the launch of functionalist psychology in the USA but identified themselves primarily as philosophers trying to advance the cause of the pragmatic movement.

Why pragmatism was overlooked for a long time in the philosophy of science

Despite the fact that the pragmatic approach was formulated well before the advent of logical positivism, it did not have much impact on the latter or on subsequent developments within the philosophy of science. For instance, Chalmers (1999) does not mention it. The reason why the positivists were not impressed by the pragmatic move probably was that it did not draw a clear distinction between scientific knowledge and non-scientific knowledge (remember the demarcation criteria). Peirce made a distinction between four ways of gathering knowledge, of which the scientific method was only one. The other three were:

1. *The method of tenacity*: People hold assumptions and beliefs because they have been around for a long time. Peirce (1877) considered this to be the most primitive form of knowledge. It is the origin of culture-specific customs passed on from generation to generation through observational learning.

2. *The method of authority*: People form opinions by consulting 'experts'. This is usually associated with the influence of various religions on human thinking (cf. Chapters 1 and 2). However, it also applies to the automatic adoption of scientific advice, or to the situation in which scientists rely on the conclusions of other scientists without checking them.

3. *The a priori method*: People use their own reason and logic to reach conclusions. This includes deductive reasoning, but also the type of knowledge that is important in disciplines such as art history, literary criticism, philosophy and theology, where people express opinions and theories without feeling a need to verify them empirically. Arguably this type of knowledge also includes intuitive knowledge, defined as hunches people have about what may work in a particular situation without knowing the reasoning that resulted in the hunch.

According to the pragmatic approach, all knowledge that helps to cope with the world is useful, whether it comes from the scientific method or any of the other three methods (e.g. tradition, religion or philosophy). William James, for instance, was not only a founding member of the American Psychological Association (promoting scientific psychological research), but also a founding member of the American Society for Psychical Research (promoting research into spiritualism; see Chapter 4) and investigator of mind-cure therapies, which were popular in the USA around the turn of the twentieth century.

Only in the last decades of the twentieth century has interest in the pragmatic alternative gained momentum within the philosophy of science, because it may provide answers to questions that are left open by the other approaches, as we will see in the next chapters (see also Bem and Looren de Jong 2006; Rochberg-Halton 1987).

Interim summary

■ A strong component of the discussion within the philosophy of science is the extent to which human perception and understanding correspond to reality. This is known as the realism vs. idealism debate.

■ A third view is that knowledge of reality is derived from successfully coping with the world. Ideas that work are retained; ideas that do not make a practical difference get lost. This is the pragmatic view.

■ The pragmatic view for a long time has been ignored, because it does not give a special status to scientific knowledge, but currently seems to be gaining momentum.

Recommended literature

The introductory book on the philosophy of science we recommend is Chalmers, A.F. (1999) *What is this thing called science?* (Maidenhead, UK: Open University Press). Another interesting book specifi-cally dealing with psychology is Dienes, Z. (2008) *Understanding psychology as a science: An introduction to scientific and statistical inference* (Basingstoke: Palgrave Macmillan).

References

Allchin, D. (2002) 'To err and win a Nobel Prize: Paul Boyer, ATP synthase and the emergence of bioenergetics', *Journal of the History of Biology,* 35: 149–72.

Andrews, R. (1987) *The Routledge dictionary of quotations*. London: Routledge.

Baars, B.J. (1986) *The cognitive revolution in psychology*. New York: Guildford Press.

Bem, S. and Looren de Jong, H. (2006) *Theoretical issues in psychology: An introduction*. London: Sage Publications.

Birnbaum, L.C. (1955) 'Behaviorism in the 1920's', *American Quarterly,* 7: 15–30.

Broca, P. (1863) 'Sur les caractères des cranes basques', *Extrait des Bulletins de la Société d'anthropologie de Paris*. Retrieved on 10 January 2008, from books.google.com.

Carnap, R. (1966) *Philosophical foundations of physics: An introduction to the philosophy of science*. New York: Basic Books.

Chalmers, A.F. (1999) *What is this thing called science?* Maidenhead, UK: Open University Press.

Coles, P. (2001) 'Einstein, Eddington and the 1919 eclipse', *Historical Development of Modern Cosmology, ASP Conference Series, 252*. Retrieved on 11 January 2008 from www. articles.adsabs.harvard.edu.

Dienes, Z. (2008) *Understanding psychology as a science: An introduction to scientific and statistical inference*. Basingstoke: Palgrave Macmillan.

Driver-Linn, E. (2003) 'Where is psychology going? Structural fault lines revealed by psychologists' use of Kuhn', *American Psychologist,* **58:** 269–78.

Feyerabend, P.K. (1975) *Against method: Outline of an anarchistic theory of knowledge.* London: New Left Books.

Geertz, C. (2000) *Available light: Anthropological reflections on philosophical topics.* Princeton, NJ: Princeton University Press.

Gleick, J. (2003) *Isaac Newton.* New York: Pantheon Books.

Gould, S.J. (1996) *The mismeasure of man* (2nd edn). New York: Norton & Company.

Hanson, F.A. (1993) *Testing testing: Social consequences of examined life.* Berkeley: University of California Press.

Lakatos, I. (1970) 'Falsification and the methodology of scientific research programs.' In I. Lakatos and A. Musgrave (eds.), *Criticism and the growth of knowledge.* New York: Cambridge University Press.

Medawar, P.B. (1969) *Induction and intuition in scientific thought.* London: Methuen. As cited in R. Rosenthal and R.L. Rosnow (2008) *Essentials of behavioral research: Methods and data analysis* (3rd edn). Boston: McGraw Hill.

Peirce, C.S. (1877) 'The fixation of belief', *Popular Science monthly,* **12:** (November), 1–15.

Popper, K.R. (1970) 'Normal science and its dangers.' In I. Lakatos and A. Musgrave (eds.), *Criticism and growth of knowledge.* New York: Cambridge University Press.

Rochberg-Halton, E. (1987) 'Why pragmatism now?' *Sociological Theory,* **5:** 194–200.

Rosenthal, R. and Rosnow, R.L. (2008) *Essentials of behavioral research: Methods and data analysis* (3rd edn). Boston: McGraw Hill.

Sokal, A.D. (1996) 'A physicist experiments with cultural studies', *Lingua Franca,* May/June, 62–64. (Also available on http://www.physics. nyu.edu/sokal.)

Sternberg, R.J. (1999) 'Twenty tips for teaching introductory psychology.' In B. Perlman, L.I. McCann and S.H. McFadden (eds.), *Lessons learned: Practical advice for the teaching of psychology* (Vol. 1). Washington, D.C.: American Psychological Society, pp. 99–104.

Thorndike, E.L. (1922) *An introduction to the theory of mental and social measurements.* New York: Teachers College.

Wason, P.C. (1960) 'On the failure to eliminate hypotheses in a conceptual task', *Quarterly Journal of Experimental Psychology,* **12:** 129–40.

09 Is psychology a science?

This chapter will cover

Questions to consider

Historical issues addressed in this chapter

- When did the hermeneutic approach in psychology start?
- Who were the main contributors to this approach?

Conceptual issues addressed in this chapter

- Why did psychologists not break with the past but see their endeavour as a continuation of previous philosophical efforts to understand human functioning?
- Why did psychologists stress the use of the scientific method? What consequences did this have for their education programmes?
- Why do people have difficulty in seeing psychology as a science?
- What is the difference between scientific psychology and hermeneutic psychology?
- Does psychology have an unbiased image of men and women?
- What makes a good history of psychology?

Introduction

On various internet sites you can find the story 'How to identify professors'. Below we give an abbreviated version.

Chemistry Professor: Wears a white lab coat. This may actually be clean but does not have to be. Physical chemistry professors have a brand new coat that has never been in the lab; polymer chemists have strange glop on their coat, and freshman chemistry professors have acid holes.

Physics Professor: Wears blue jeans and a flannel shirt. May sometimes forget to wear shirt altogether. If a professor is wearing blue jeans and suspenders, ten to one he is a physicist. Physics profs often have German accents, but this is not a distinguishing characteristic.

Biology Professor: Sometimes wears a lab coat, though usually this is the sign of a biochemist. Marine biologists walk around in hip boots for no explainable reason, even in the middle of winter. They are apt to wear grey slacks and smell like fish, as opposed to most biologists, who smell strongly of formalin. Microbiology instructors go around in spotless white coats, refuse to drink beer on tap, and wipe all their silverware before using it.

Psychology Professor: Psychologists are not real scientists, and can be easily identified by their screams of protest whenever anyone questions whether psychology is a science. Psychologists have beady little eyes and don't laugh at jokes about psychology. If you are not sure whether a person is a scientist or a comparative religion instructor, he is probably a psychologist.

Funny stories like the one above reflect (and reinforce) stereotypes but often include a true core. In Chapter 4 we saw how behaviourists and cognitive psychologists struggled to get their investigations acknowledged as scientific research. And presently many introductory classes to psychology still start by stressing that psychology is a true science as well (as if otherwise students might finish their course without properly realising this). So, why do academic psychologists feel a need to emphasise that psychology is a science and why does the public at large keep having problems believing this? In what respects does psychology resemble and differ from physics, chemistry and biology?

Now that we have seen what science is (Chapter 8), we can address the question to what extent psychology is a science. We start by reviewing the reasons why psychology is claimed to be science. Then, we discuss the reasons why people do not perceive it as such. We end with a discussion of the movements in psychology that have criticised the exclusive reliance on scientific research methods, and ask whether this implies that the history of psychology ought to be given by neutral historians.

9.1   Reasons why psychology is claimed to be a science

The foundation of psychology as an academic discipline was legitimised on two pillars

Psychology has a long, respectful past and uses the scientific method

In his book *Modernizing the mind*, the American sociologist Steven Ward (2002; see also Chapters 7 and 12) made the case that a new branch of knowledge can establish itself and survive only if it succeeds in convincing the ruling powers of the need for such knowledge as well as reassuring them that it is no threat to their prosperity. This requires rhetoric and alliance formation with powerful groups, as much as (and in

Ward's view even more than) intellectual substance. The founders of psychology promoted it as a new academic discipline by stressing two messages:

1. Psychology was the continuation of the old and respectful tradition of mental and moral philosophy, going back at least to Aristotle.

2. The new element was that the scientific method, so successful in other disciplines, would be applied to the study of the human mind. Because of the use of this method, psychology made a bridge to the natural sciences and derived status from them.

There are many examples of the rhetoric with respect to the first claim. For instance, the German psychologist Hermann Ebbinghaus wrote in 1908 that 'Psychology has a long past but only a short history'. Similarly, James McKeen Cattell asserted in his 1895 presidential address to the American Psychological Association that (cited in Ward (2002) p. 36):

> While the recent progress of our science has been great, we do not admit that psychology is a new science . . . If science is to date from the year of 'the master of those who know', then we may take pride in the beginnings of psychology whose foundations were more securely laid by Aristotle than those of any other science.

A nice example of how the new, scientific method was promoted can be found in the book *Psychology*, published by John Dewey in 1887. In this book Dewey stated that psychological investigation had languished for too long under the metaphysical philosophy associated with the American mental philosophers and that it was time psychology had a treatment of its own. In his own words:

> how shall we make our psychology scientific and up to the times, free from metaphysics – which, however good in its place, is out of place in a psychology . . . ?
>
> *(Dewey 1887, p. iv)*

The adherence to the scientific method was further communicated by putting the start of the discipline at 1879, the year when the first *scientific laboratory* of psychology had been established by Wundt in Leipzig. As we saw in Chapter 3, the teaching of psychology was considerably older.

Consequences for the psychology curriculum

Because psychology was promoted on the basis of its long past and its sound method, both 'history of psychology' and 'research methods' were major components of the curriculum. Students were taught how to run proper studies in the laboratories and had to buy syllabuses or books on research methods. Similarly, students had to study the history of psychology. Shortly after 1910, the first textbooks on the history of psychology appeared, the best known of which probably is that of Baldwin, published in 1913 (which you can find on the internet). Remember this was only some 20 years after the foundation of the very first laboratory of psychology in the USA! Little surprise then that these history books hardly dealt with the new discipline. They were reviews of person-related ideas and insights from philosophy and religion, which were rephrased as precursors of psychological thought. These books were self-legitimisation as much as essential stepping stones for a good psychology education.

What do you think?

An intriguing observation is that the importance of history courses in psychology seems to be questioned more now than a century ago. Could this be because psychology as an independent branch of learning has become more self-confident? Or is it because nowadays much more is known about psychology than 100 years ago, so that more topics are competing for a limited number of time slots? What's your view about the role of history courses in a psychology education: essential or self-glorification?

Science is defined by its method rather than by its subject matter

Every topic studied with the scientific method is a science

To be accepted as a science, psychologists – together with sociologists – had to make the case that what differentiated sciences from non-sciences was the way in which problems were investigated, and not the type of problems addressed. Chemistry at the end of the nineteenth century was a highly successful science not because of its topics, but because it had embraced the scientific method. Indeed, before it did so, it was an obscure and secretive subject matter practised by a group of alchemists who failed to make any noticeable progress. Only when people like Robert Boyle in the seventeenth century began to experiment and publish their findings, did chemistry start to flourish.

The founders of psychology claimed that a similar feat would be achieved by psychologists if they were given the means to start the scientific study of the human mind (Chapters 3 and 4). Although few people spontaneously associated the study of mental life with scientific research (certainly not in the nineteenth century!), the first academic psychologists maintained that there was nothing inherent in the subject matter that prevented it from being studied with the scientific method.

Methodolatry

Because of its emphasis on method in the definition of science, academic psychology invested heavily in developing appropriate research designs and analysis techniques. It is not a coincidence that psychologists since the beginning of the twentieth century have been at the forefront of investigations into increasingly powerful research designs and statistical analyses of complicated datasets. Psychologists had to be the top of the class as far as research methods and statistics were concerned! Even recently this became apparent when psychological researchers in the 1990s started to collaborate with their medical colleagues in cognitive neuroscience. A recurrent complaint among the psychologists (although rarely recorded on paper) was the low level of methodological sophistication in their medical collaborators, making the findings vulnerable to a long line of validity threats.

It has been argued by several authors that psychology throughout its existence has overplayed the role of research methods at the expense of theory building (see Chapter 8 for the importance of theories in science). This, for instance, was the conclusion the eminent American psychologist Sigmund Koch (who would later become president of the APA) drew after he was asked by the American Psychological Association to analyse the status of psychology at the mid twentieth century:

> Ever since its stipulation into existence as an independent science, psychology has been far more concerned with being a science than with courageous and self-determining confrontation with its historically constituted subject matter. Its history has been largely a matter of emulating the methods, forms, symbols of the established sciences, especially physics.
>
> *(Koch 1961, p. 629–30)*

A similar criticism can be heard from Noam Chomsky, the linguist who in the 1960s formulated a theory of language processing that would form the inspiration for thousands of scientific studies in cognitive psychology (Chapter 4):

> Take the phrase 'behavioral sciences.' It's a very curious phrase. I mean it's a bit like calling the natural sciences 'meter-reading sciences.' In fact a physicist's data often consists of things like meter readings, but nobody calls physics 'meter-reading science.' Similarly, the data of a psychologist is behavior in a broad sense. But to call a field 'behavioral science' is to say it's a science of behavior in the sense in which physics is a science of meter reading.
>
> *(Chomsky in Baars (1986) p. 346–7)*

It was also the conclusion Baars (1986) reached in his book about the cognitive revolution:

> Almost every mature science shows a tension between experimentalists and theoreticians. Experimental scientists often complain that the theoreticians ignore inconvenient evidence, whereas theoreticians tend to believe that experimentalists cannot see the larger picture. This tension can be healthy and creative, providing that there is also good communication . . .
>
> But in psychology, only one-half of this dialectic existed. There simply was no credible theory. In the absence of accepted theory, it was never clear which experiments had important implications.
>
> *(Baars 1986, p. 161–2)*

? What do you think?

The last sentence of the excerpt from Baars may be quite detrimental for psychology, because 'in the absence of accepted theory' may be interpreted as meaning that psychology still is in the pre-science phase of Kuhn's framework. Remember from Chapter 8 that this is the stage in which isolated phenomena are investigated without being integrated within a coherent, larger framework (a paradigm). It is the phase in which a discipline is not yet a science according to Kuhn. What do you think? Does psychology have a paradigm? Or is it still a loose amalgam of isolated observations?

Would your answer be any different if you knew that Kuhn (1970) in his book on paradigms mentioned psychology as an example of a discipline in pre-science phase?

The bias towards methodological rigour rather than theory formation has been called
methodolatry or **methodologism** (e.g. Teo 2005). Instead of searching for a theoretical framework that united them, the founders of psychology assumed that as long as they followed the rules of scientific methodology they would contribute to progress in the discipline.

**methodolatry or
methodologism**

tendency to see
methodological
rigour as the only
requirement for
scientific research
at the expense of
theory formation

The shadow of logical positivism

One reason why psychologists tended to stress valid testing rather than theory formation arguably was that they tried too hard to be good scientists. Remember that the first decades of the psychology history were the heyday of positivism and logical positivism. There probably were no keener and more obedient students of these movements than the experimental psychologists (in particular the behaviourists). Just have a look at how well they followed the core advice on how to do proper science:

1. science proceeds from facts to knowledge on the basis of observation, inductive reasoning and verification,

2. non-observables must be excluded, unless they have an operational definition,

3. theories are limited to descriptions of the observed facts, preferentially in the form of a mathematical law; by no means must they include speculation.

What do you think?

Do you agree with the criticism that a psychology degree is more about learning the right research methods rather than useful theories? Or has the situation changed in the last 30–50 years?

The scientific method has not let psychologists down

In the preceding chapters and sections we saw how psychology started as the outcome of the growing impact of scientific thinking in Western society. In the nineteenth century this led to an increasing number of scholars becoming convinced that there was a future in the application of the scientific method to the human mind. At that time, this was a matter of faith, rather than a guaranteed success. The fact that after nearly a century and a half, the majority of academic psychologists still subscribe to this choice is a sign that they have not regretted it. Looking through a variety of sources suggests that the factors below are the main reasons why psychologists keep on using the scientific method.

Systematicity and cumulativeness of knowledge

Science, more than any other method of knowledge acquisition, stresses the requirement that knowledge builds on existing knowledge. New findings and explanations must be coherent with existing information. Therefore, previous knowledge should be available and new knowledge must be made public. Remember from Chapter 1 how in preliterate society knowledge was local and diffuse, so that contradictions were abundant and went unnoticed. In contrast, science is meant to be cumulative: researchers consult what has been found before with respect to a particular topic, so that they can build on it and avoid previous pitfalls. An analogy sometimes used in this respect (among others, by Newton) is that of a scientist 'standing as a dwarf on the shoulders of giants'.

As we saw in Chapter 8, there are limits to the cumulative nature of science, because the accumulation of knowledge depends on the prevailing paradigm, which may change. However, the records of previous attempts should remain available and a proper literature search is seen as the prerequisite of good science. In particular, the historians of a discipline should be able to go beyond the current paradigm and see the continuities and discontinuities in thinking.

The use of well-defined methods

Information must be gathered in line with agreed methods that are clearly outlined. There is systematicity in the collection of observations. The methods used must be accepted by the existing research community and be described in such detail that the observation can be replicated by others. As we have seen in Chapter 8, this does not preclude that research methods comprise an element of relativity (due to the paradigm on which they are based), but they can be repeated by others if they follow the instructions.

Clarity

The findings are stated in such a way that they are interpreted in the same way by different readers. As you may have noticed from some of the quotations in the present book, this requirement was not always met in the philosophical writings (cf. the interpretation problems related to Plato, Aristotle and even Wundt).

Prediction

Science, again much more than any other method of information generation, stresses the importance of prediction. It is not enough to explain phenomena post hoc, after they have happened; a scientist must be able to predict what will happen in the future (under well-controlled circumstances). Such prediction enables control of the event.

Knowledge is revisable

Scientific knowledge is open, can be revised at all times. As we saw in Chapter 8, trying to falsify existing convictions is central to science, to make sure that no wrong beliefs are perpetuated. Knowledge is not person-bound. Opinions are not held on to because of the person who formulated them. They are adhered to because they are not contradicted by the available evidence. This does not mean that all revisions happen instantaneously (remember the fate of anomalies in periods of normal science; Chapter 8), but knowledge that consistently fails to pass the falsification test will eventually lead to a revision of the theory, even if that includes a paradigm shift.

Comparison with pseudoscience

Another way to illustrate the importance of the scientific method for psychology researchers is to compare it with the methods prevalent in pseudoscience, a branch of knowledge that pretends to be scientific but violates the scientific method on essential aspects, such as:

pseudoscience

branch of knowledge that pretends to be scientific but that violates the scientific method on essential aspects, such as lack of openness to testing by others and reliance on confirmation rather than falsification

1. lack of openness to testing by other experts,

2. the use of vague, exaggerated or untestable claims,

3. over-reliance on confirmation rather than falsification,

4. personalisation of issues (intuitions rather than data),

5. use of misleading language (e.g. maintaining ideas that are known to be false).

What do you think?

Can you think of examples of pseudoscience?

Acceptable progress thus far

Another reason why psychological research remains largely scientific is that psychologists themselves are not unhappy with the progress they have made in the past 150 years. They have evidence that standardised tests are better predictors of future performance than unstructured interviews (Chapter 7); they know that people in many situations do not behave in the way that they think they do (Chapters 6 and 10); and experimental research allows psychologists to investigate phenomena that otherwise would be inaccessible. As we have seen in Chapter 6, many phenomena occur outside a person's conscious awareness (for instance, the processes involved in text reading). These cannot be examined by introspection but require careful performance monitoring in controlled situations (e.g. by measuring the speed of word recognition). The 'experimental histories', as Francis Bacon called them (Chapter 8), have enabled psychologists to get a much better understanding of how people achieve good performance in a wide variety of tasks and why performance sometimes goes awry (see the section on cognitive neuropsychology in Chapter 5).

What do you think?

A straightforward objection against the last criterion (acceptable progress) is that psychologists may very well be biased in their perception of the progress they have made (e.g. on the basis of the confirmation bias; Chapter 8). How does this agree with your impression? On the basis of what you have learned thus far, do you think psychology has made genuine progress in understanding the human mind in the past century? Or do you agree with the philosopher Wittgenstein who said more than 50 years ago that in psychology there are experimental methods and conceptual confusion?

The relation to other sciences

By looking at cross-references it is possible to position psychological research relative to the other research disciplines. Is psychology an isolated discipline that does not feed insights into other disciplines and that does not take into account information from other sciences either? How often do researchers from other disciplines refer to findings in psychology and how often do psychologists refer to findings from other disciplines?

Boyack *et al.* (2005) analysed citation data from more than one million journal articles appearing in over 7,000 scientific journals in the year 2000, to see how often researchers in the different disciplines mention each other's findings. Their results are summarised in figure 9.1. In this figure, journals that often make

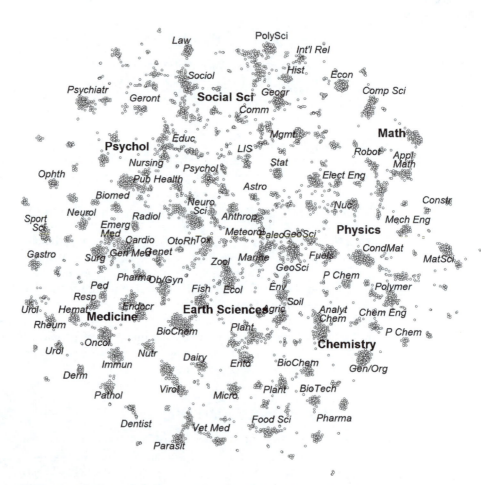

Figure 9.1 Map of science generated on the basis of the number of citations between the different scientific disciplines.
Each dot represents one scientific journal. Large font size labels identify major areas of science. Small labels denote the disciplinary topics of clusters of journals.

Source: Boyack *et al.* (2005). Reproduced with permission.

cross-references are close together. Journals that rarely refer to one another are further apart. Disciplines near the perimeter are more isolated than those near the centre.

The findings of Boyack *et al.* (2005) can best be summarised by quoting their conclusion (p. 366):

> The order of major fields in Figure [9.1] follows an intuitive pattern as one moves clockwise around the map: Mathematics, Physics, Chemistry, Earth Sciences (including Biological, Plant, and Animal Sciences), Medicine, Psychology, and Social Sciences . . . The fine structure of the map is also revealing. Engineering disciplines are near Physics and Chemistry. Interfacial disciplines appear to be reasonably placed. For example, Public Health lies between Medicine and Psychology . . .
>
> In general, the more insular fields lie toward the outside of the map, and those with more interdisciplinary linkages are toward the center . . . Social Sciences are tied to Psychology through various specialties in Psychology; Medicine is tied to Psychology directly and through Neurology; Biochemistry links directly to Medicine and Chemistry; . . .

A particularly interesting feature that comes out of Boyack *et al.*'s (2005) analysis is that psychology does not form an isolated island only referring to itself. As a matter of fact it is one of the seven major areas of research (next to Math, Physics, Chemistry, Earth Sciences, Medicine and Social Sciences), forming a hub for a series of other disciplines related to human functioning, with strong links to two other major areas (Medicine and Social Sciences). This agrees with the claim that psychological research is well embedded within the sciences.

Interim summary

Reasons why psychology is claimed to be a science:

- The founders have defined psychology as the study of the human mind with the scientific method.

- They further argued that whether or not a discipline is a science depends on the research methods used and not on the topic investigated: psychology used the scientific method and, therefore, was a science.

- The scientific method has proven to be a fruitful approach and is fully integrated within mainstream psychological research.

- Psychological research is fully integrated within other scientific research. It is one of the seven major areas with strong links to two other major areas. It forms a hub for a series of less central sciences related to human functioning.

9.2   Reasons why psychology is not seen as a science

In the previous section we have explored the arguments behind the scientific status of psychology. We now address the arguments questioning this status.

There is little overlap between the stereotypical view of a scientist and the stereotypical view of a psychologist

It has been shown repeatedly in social psychology that the perception of unfamiliar groups is largely driven by social stereotypes. These are automatically activated, unsophisticated opinions of other groups (Bargh and Chartrand 1999) that strongly affect the first impression people have when they encounter members of these groups (Chapter 7). Social stereotypes can be overruled by controlled thinking (Chapter 6) or when one has enough individuation information about a group or an individual due to regular contact, but for most people they will be the basis upon which their judgements are made. So, a first aspect to look at is how much overlap there is between the stereotypical views of a psychologist and a scientist. If the overlap is small, then the first impression about a psychologist will not be that of a scientist, no matter how often psychologists repeat their message that psychology is a science.

Stereotypes about science and scientists

So, what are the stereotypical views about science? A look at the literature (e.g. Kessels *et al.* 2006; Sandoval 2005; Vilchez-Gonzalez and Parales Palacios 2006) suggests the following:

1. science is for males,
2. science is difficult,
3. science affords fewer opportunities to be creative than arts and languages, because only one answer is correct; this answer is found by collecting facts,
4. scientific discoveries are made by chance,
5. knowledge accumulation in science is linear (i.e. there no crises, deadlocks, and paradigm shifts in science),
6. science does not offer much variation in work; the only research methods are observation and experimentation.

In addition, there are stereotypes related to scientists (e.g. McDuffie 2001; Yasar *et al.* 2006). These are:

1. scientists are middle aged,
2. male (often with glasses and unconventional hair styles),
3. serious or crazed,
4. work alone,
5. obsessed with their work,
6. do not have good writing, verbal or people skills.

Figure 9.2 Examples of teachers' sketches of scientists, revealing the stereotypical views people have about these individuals.

Source: McDuffie (2001)

When people hear or read about a scientist, the attributes just listed are the ones most likely to be activated. A test sometimes used to study the stereotypical views about scientists is to ask people to draw 'a scientist'. Figure 9.2 shows some of the drawings McDuffie (2001) obtained from teachers (including science teachers!).

Depictions of scientists in books and films

The stereotypical views listed above are the outcome of how scientists are depicted in the wider culture (i.e. the associations that are there to be picked up by the individuals). After a review of the Western literature, Haynes (2003) distilled seven archetypes of scientists that are used as convenient shorthand to include such characters in books (and films):

1. the scientist as an evil and dangerous man (this is by far the most frequent picture),

2. the noble scientist as hero or saviour of society,

3. the foolish scientist (absentminded and nutty),

4. the inhuman researcher,

5. the scientist as adventurer who travels in space and time,

6. the mad, bad, dangerous scientist,

7. the helpless scientist, unable to control the outcome of his work.

What do you think?

Stereotypes figure prominently in cartoons (which in turn are important perpetrators of stereotypes). Go to images.google.com and type in *cartoon scientist*. Analyse the first 100 images you get. How well do they agree with the stereotypical views outlined above?

Stereotypes about psychology and psychologists

In the same way, we can look at the stereotypical views that the words psychology and psychologist evoke. These are the opinions automatically associated with psychology:

1. psychology involves an interaction between a therapist and a client (notice the confounding with psychiatry),

2. psychology is interested in abnormal behaviour,

3. psychology aims at helping others,

4. also sometimes reference to the other applications of psychology, in particular school psychology and work psychology,

5. psychology is easier than the natural sciences.

   When asked about psychologists, the following features are most likely to be activated (Barrow 2000; Hartwig 2002; von Sydow 2007):

1. the image of a psychologist is largely dominated by the 'shrink'-stereotype (male, psychoanalytically oriented, looking like Freud, with a client – often female – on the couch)

2. ambivalence between idealisation (warm, intelligent, understanding, almost mystical powers) and very negative images (neurotic, dangerous, manipulative, lack of common sense)

3. balding, wearing a suit, glasses, sitting with the legs crossed, middle-aged and older.

Figure 9.3 shows some examples of drawings people make of 'typical' psychologists.

What do you think?

Again go to images.google.com and type in *cartoon psychologist*. Analyse the first 100 images you get. How well do they agree with the stereotypical views outlined above?

Depiction of psychologists in books and films

Again the stereotypes people have of psychologists are strongly influenced by the roles psychologists are given in the media. If we zoom in on the image of psychotherapists

Figure 9.3 Drawings of 'typical psychologists'.

Source: Hartwig (2002)

(the image most frequently associated with psychologists), the following four types seem to be used, with the negative depictions outnumbering the positive ones (Gabbard and Gabbard 1999; Orchowski *et al.* 2006):

1.   The oracle: when portrayed positively, the psychologist has brilliant insight into the psyche (e.g. to solve crimes); when portrayed negatively, the psychologist is a pretentious know-it-all who provides misinformation.

2.   The social agent: when portrayed positively, helps patients with social problems; when portrayed negatively, coerces patients into unwanted action (e.g. adherence to dull society norms for creative, nonconforming individuals).

3.   The eccentric and the romantic therapist: when depicted positively, seen as a sign of humanity; when depicted negatively, the result is a dishevelled, clownish and unorganised professional who conducts largely ineffective psychotherapy.

4.   The wounded healer: when depicted positively, again sign of humanity; when depicted negatively, indication of someone who is unfit for the job.

Lack of overlap between the stereotypical image of a scientist and a psychologist

The fact that a psychologist is spontaneously associated with the image of a practising clinical psychologist means that there is virtually no overlap in the stereotypical images of scientists and psychologists. Whereas the former are essentially depicted as loners obsessed with their investigations, the latter are nearly always seen in interaction with other people. There is some overlap in the negative traits (mad, dangerous, lack of social skills and common sense), but these are more part of the effort to keep the image of one's own group high by attributing negative features to other groups rather than essential characteristics of scientists and psychologists. Finally, there is the – ironic – overlap in the fact that both groups are spontaneously associated with older men (whereas the majority of psychologists are women).

Given the small overlap in the stereotypical views of scientists and psychologists, it should come as no surprise that the general public does not spontaneously associate psychologists with scientists. People find it hard to think of psychologists as loners obsessed with their subject matter studied in an uncreative, instrument-reading way.

Psychology researchers vs. psychology practitioners

Professional psychologists largely outnumber psychology researchers

In the previous section we saw that the general population spontaneously associates psychologists with psychology practitioners, in particular clinical psychologists. The fact that the practitioners strongly outnumber the researchers is another feature that distinguishes psychology from sciences such as physics, chemistry and biology. The only real comparison here is that of medical practitioners.

Practitioners, both psychological and medical, rarely see themselves as (stereotypical) scientists. They are users of scientific information, but do not consider it as part of their job to generate new knowledge on the basis of the scientific method. Their scientific training helps them to look critically at the evidence presented in favour of an intervention, and to appreciate whether the claims made have sufficient empirical support or are unsubstantiated conjectures. However, practitioners typically have no ambition to get involved in scientific research themselves. Returning to the types of knowledge acquisition differentiated in Chapter 8, they make much more use of the method of tenacity (this intervention has always been used for this type of problem) the method of authority (this intervention is advised by experts) and the a priori method (this looks like a good intervention to me), than the scientific method (this intervention works because I have tested it empirically and shown its effectiveness with a falsification test).

The fact that psychological (and medical) practitioners are users of science rather than scientists means that there is quite some variety in the scientific standards to which they adhere, as has been observed by the sociologist Ward (2002, p. 223):

Although groups such as the APA and most experimentalists sought to control strictly the type of people who could be called 'psychologists' and the type of knowledge the discipline was to produce, they were never able to establish a monopoly on what would count as legitimate psychological knowledge. As a result, practitioners peddled all types of intellectual wares under the label of 'psychology' throughout most of the twentieth century.

Interestingly enough, Ward (2002) argues that the differentiation between researchers and practitioners has been a strength of psychology rather than a weakness, because each approach meets different needs in the population, an idea we will return to in Chapter 12.

Ways in which psychology researchers have tried to distinguish themselves

Because psychology researchers saw the natural-scientific status of psychological research constantly being misunderstood, they repeatedly tried to distinguish their own work from the mainstream image of psychology. One way of doing this was to adopt a different name. Three names have been used: 'the new psychology' (which was apt up to the middle of the twentieth century but now has become obsolete), 'experimental psychology' (to stress the use of experiments as the basis of information acquisition) and 'scientific psychology' (to stress the more general scientific method).

Another way in which researchers distanced themselves from professionals was by the creation of their own societies. Indeed, in many countries you find psychology societies that are predominantly meant for (university) researchers and societies that are predominantly meant for professionals. These are not always in unison, although they have the shared goal of promoting psychologists' standing in the wider society.

In the USA, for instance, the APA (American Psychological Association) started largely as a gathering of psychology researchers and had little interest in the practitioners' needs (see Witmer's experiences in Chapter 7). The disenchantment of the practitioners (in particular the clinical psychologists) with the way in which they were treated reached its height in 1937, when a number of them walked out and founded the Association for Applied Psychology. Only after the APA promised to do more for the professionals were they willing to become part of the APA again (this happened in 1945). One of the initiatives set up the APA to make amends was a task force on how to establish the reliability and validity of psychological tests (see Chapter 7). The APA was keen to demonstrate that it had something to offer to the professionals.

The efforts of the APA to serve the practitioners were not appreciated by all researchers, who questioned the usefulness of such a society for them. As a result, there twice was a revolt of researchers, leading to the foundation of the Psychonomic Society in 1959 and the American Psychological Society (now called the Association for Psychological Science) in 1988.

A similar tension between professionals and researchers can be seen in the UK, where there is a distinction between the British Psychological Society (established in 1901 mainly by researchers, but increasingly taking on the interests of professional psychologists) and the Experimental Psychology Society (founded in 1946 to better meet the researchers' needs). At the European level there are also societies primarily aimed at practitioners (e.g. the EFPA [European Federation of Psychologists' Associations]) and societies primarily meant for researchers (e.g. the ESCoP [European Society for Cognitive Psychology]).

Unlike scientific results, psychological findings are easy to understand

Everybody understands worthwhile psychological findings

As we have seen above, science is perceived as difficult, a challenge many people try to avoid. In contrast, psychology is seen as accessible. The reason for this is more or less as follows: because we are all humans interacting with others, we all have experience with what works and what does not work in our daily life. Psychological research can give us new insights (ideas of which we had not thought before), but if these insights are worthwhile we will have no difficulty relating to them. There will be a resonance between our own intuition and the new knowledge. This line of thinking has both positive and negative consequences.

A positive consequence is that most people are much more interested in psychological findings than in findings from other sciences. They are not put off by the perceived difficulty. As a result, psychological thinking has had a larger impact on the society than many other sciences (see the psychologisation of the society in Chapters 7 and 12). People are convinced that every sane and sufficiently intelligent person can understand the really important psychological findings.

A negative consequence is that the public in general does not believe psychologists have much specialised knowledge. Psychological findings that are too difficult to understand are not 'real' psychology, and findings that do not agree with the general opinion are likely to be wrong. For instance, Janda *et al.* (1998) asked a representative sample of 100 residents of Virginia (USA) how large the difference was between what an expert (i.e. a college professor or a licensed professional) knows about his or her field and how much an average person knows about the field. Seven disciplines were examined: biology, chemistry, economics, medicine, psychology, physics and sociology. Figure 9.4 shows the findings. From these, it is clear that the natural sciences (chemistry, medicine, physics, biology) are perceived as having much more expert knowledge than the social sciences (psychology, sociology, economics).

 What do you think?

Philosophers of science from time to time claim that psychology is overly complicated, because it lacks a paradigm (see the citations of Kuhn and Wittgenstein in this chapter). Could this be because they spontaneously assume psychology ought to be simple? Is the knowledge in psychology really more complex, specialised and contradictory than the knowledge in, say, physics, medicine, or computer sciences?

Not all psychologists are convinced of the added value of the scientific method

A final reason why psychology has difficulties being seen as a science is that not all psychologists, academics included, are convinced that the turn towards the scientific

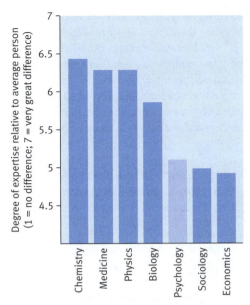

Figure 9.4 Difference in expertise between expert and average person.
When people are asked how much more expertise a college professor or licensed professional
has relative to an average person, they make a distinction between the so-called 'hard
sciences' (chemistry, medicine, physics, biology) and the 'soft' social sciences (psychology,
sociology, economics).

Source: Janda *et al.* (1998)

approach has been the right choice to study the human mind. Remember from
Chapters 2 and 3 that before Wundt started his psychology laboratory, there already
was a flourishing literature on the human mind. This literature grew out of three
sources:

1. an increased philosophical interest in the human mind,

2. interest from teacher education programmes,

3. interest from religious studies.

hermeneutics

approach in psy-
chology according
to which the task of
the psychologist is
to interpret and
understand persons
on the basis of their
personal and socio-
cultural history
(understanding
rather than
controlling)

The hermeneutic alternative

Not everyone agreed with the positivists that psychology ought to jump on the band-
wagon of the natural sciences. Another approach that has been proposed can be described as the hermeneutic approach (although various names have been used
throughout the history). Hermeneutics is a word coming from Ancient Greek referring to the interpretation and translation of messages sent by the gods (these messages
were usually conveyed by the god Hermes, hence the word). In psychology,
hermeneutics refers to the interpretation and understanding of individuals on the
basis of their personal and socio-cultural histories. Hermeneutics will, for instance,
pay close attention to the motives people give for their actions and the purposes they
want to achieve in life.

Throughout the history of psychology, the hermeneutic approach has coexisted with the mainstream natural-scientific approach, often on not very friendly terms (e.g. Park and Auchincloss 2006). The experimental psychologists objected to the fact that the hermeneutic approach kept on questioning the status of psychology as a natural science and, thereby, hindered the attempts to have psychology departments accepted as scientific departments at the universities. The hermeneutically oriented academics in turn maintained that the experimental approach overlooked essential skills practitioners needed for their profession.

Unravelling how the human mind functions versus understanding what the human mind comprises

The main criticism of the proponents of hermeneutics against the experimental study of the human mind has been that it is too much geared towards unravelling the processes of the mind (answering the question 'how does it work?'), in the same way as natural scientists try to understand the workings of the heart, the behaviour of electrons in an atom, or the operation of a computer. What the experimental psychologists overlooked, according to the hermeneutists, was that understanding a person involves not so much knowing *how* the person functions, but *what* the person thinks, believes, feels, wants.

Because the tension between the experimental and the hermeneutic approach has been a central issue throughout the history of psychology, we will devote the rest of this chapter and the next chapter to it. First, we give a short review of the hermeneutic approach (this chapter). Then, we have a look at the methods proposed by both traditions (next chapter).

Interim summary

Reasons why psychology is not seen as a science:

- The stereotypical view people have of a psychologist is that of a clinical psychologist treating patients. This view does not overlap with the stereotypical view people have of a scientist as a loner who is obsessed with his work and which he studies in an uncreative way making use of instruments.

- Professional psychologists largely outnumber psychology researchers, and they are users of scientific knowledge rather than creators of such knowledge.

- People are convinced that they have as much knowledge about psychological issues as psychologists, or at least that they can keep up with psychologists as long as they pay attention to the psychological research that is described in the media.

- Next to the mainstream scientific tradition in academic psychology, there is a hermeneutic approach that is more in agreement with the public's view of psychology as non-scientific.

9.3   The critique of scientific psychology

In the previous section we saw how throughout the history of psychology scientifically oriented psychologists have coexisted with psychologists who questioned the usefulness of the scientific method for the study of mental life. In this section, we explore the evolutions within the hermeneutic movement.

Dilthey: *Naturwissenschaften* vs. *Geisteswissenschaften*

One of the first authors to openly criticise psychology's turn to the natural sciences was the German historian and philosopher Wilhelm Dilthey (1833–1911). In a series of publications in the 1880s and 1890s, he drew a distinction between what he called the *Naturwissenschaften* (natural sciences) and the *Geisteswissenschaften* (the mental sciences or the human sciences). He noted that the natural sciences sought to distil universal laws from a limited set of observations; their main method was the experiment. In contrast, the mental sciences aimed at understanding and interpreting the individual person by an analysis of his or her personal and socio-cultural history. The main research method here was understanding, in the same way as a historian tries to understand what happened in the past.

The four elements of Dilthey's approach

There were four main elements in Dilthey's approach. Firstly, psychology should be *content based*. It should not focus on how the brain functions (the form), but on what the mind comprises (the meaning structure of the person). Because psychology was based on understanding the content of the mind, Dilthey argued, it belonged to the *Geisteswissenschaften*, together with history, political science, law, theory, literature and art.

Secondly, Dilthey argued that the subject matter of psychology was the *human experience in its totality*, including cognition (thoughts), emotion and volition (motivation to act). Psychology should not aim at dissecting the human mind but at describing the complete mind with its constant interplay of cognition, emotion and volition.

The third element was that a person's life was embedded in a *context*. A person could not be studied in isolation, but had to be seen in his/her socio-cultural and historical context. A similar remark was made by Karl Marx (1818–1883), who urged philosophers and psychologists to study the mind of the individual as part of a society, instead of focusing on abstract individuals beyond history and society.

Finally, the natural-scientific research method with its experimentation and bias towards measurement could never grasp the totality of the mental life within its context. Therefore, the appropriate method for psychology was *understanding*. Dilthey distinguished three different levels of understanding:

1. elementary forms of understanding used to solve the simple problems of life,

2. empathy through which an observer can re-experience someone's experiences,

3. the hermeneutic level of understanding, by which an observed person can be better understood than the person understands him/herself.

Psychoanalysis and related schools

Freud

Another major source of inspiration for the hermeneutic approach came from Freud's psychoanalysis and the subsequent evolutions. Although Freud saw his efforts as part of the natural-scientific tradition, the approach he recommended was much closer to that of Dilthey than to that of Wundt and his American students (although Stanley Hall, the founder of the first psychological laboratory in the USA, would invite Freud to the USA in 1909 and award him an honorary degree from Clark University). Freud's method was in line with the hermeneutic approach because it aimed at understanding the contents of a person's mind and was based on the interpretation of visible human products (dreams, memories, slips of the tongue, symptoms, art) with the use of the psychoanalytic theory.

What do you think?

How does Freud's theory relate to the four elements of Dilthey's approach? Which level of understanding is the most important for Freud?

Related schools

In the twentieth century, Freud's ideas inspired a series of other theorists to come up with alternative theories of what constitutes the core of the human mind and how it develops over time. The best known are:

■ Carl Jung (1875–1961)

He made a distinction between the personal unconscious (forgotten and repressed contents of the individual's mental life) and the collective unconscious (acts and images shared by all human beings or by a particular culture; manifest themselves in archetypes – e.g. the archetype of an old, wise man with a white beard). Jung also distinguished several personality types and introduced the characteristic of extroversion versus introversion.

■ Alfred Adler (1870–1937)

He argued that the most important motive for a human being was a feeling of inferiority, originating from the sense of dependence and helplessness felt by infants. The feeling of inferiority resulted in a striving for superiority and perfection.

■ Erik Erikson (1902–1994)

Erikson is best known for his theory of developmental stages. According to this theory the human life comprised eight stages (infant, toddler, preschooler, school-age child, adolescent, young adult, middle adult, old adult) in each of which a new psychosocial crisis had to be solved (e.g. gaining trust in infancy). If the crisis was solved well, it resulted in a psychosocial virtue (e.g. hope and faith in infancy). If the crisis was not solved well, it resulted in maladaptation and malignancy (e.g. withdrawal of the infant).

- John Bowlby (1907–1990)

He is known for his attachment theory, which states that infants seek proximity to a limited number of familiar people (in particular the mother) and use these people for comfort in stressful times and as a secure basis for exploration of the environment. Secure attachment is only possible if the adults are sensitive and responsive to the child's communications; it is also adversely affected by an abrupt and long lasting separation. The quality of the emotional attachment formed in infancy has a lasting influence on the person's later emotional and social development. Bowlby supported falsification tests of his theory, in particular via a long-term collaboration with Mary Ainsworth, who devised 'the strange situation' test (in which the caregiver temporarily had to leave the child in an unfamiliar environment) to measure the attachment style of the child.

Rogers and humanistic psychology

Rogers

The psychoanalysts were not the only ones who on the basis of their treatments formulated theories of human functioning that deviated from the natural-scientific tenets defended by the experimental psychologists. Shortly before World War II, Carl Rogers (see Chapter 7) started to question the tenets of the Freudian therapy and promoted an alternative form of therapy. In his client-centred approach, a therapist still tried to understand the client, but this was done without interpretation on the basis of psychoanalytic theory. Viewed within Dilthey's scheme of understanding, Rogers emphasised the empathic form of understanding, whereas Freud chose the hermeneutic level. The therapist in Rogers's view had to share the client's experiences but not interpret them; his/her role was supportive rather than enlightening.

Interestingly, just like Bowlby, Rogers combined the hermeneutic approach with the natural-science approach when he insisted that the efficacy of his therapy be tested (see also Eysenck's research in Chapter 7). In 1954, he co-edited a book (Rogers and Dymond 1954) in which the results of a four-year programme on the efficacy of the client-centred therapy were examined. In the words of a reviewer:

> Changes in the clients during therapy were measured not against some abstractly defined global criterion or index of success of failure; instead, objective measures were used that would detect changes in certain specific personality variables that could be predicted from the theories of Rogers and operationally defined. These were: changes in self-perception, changes in the total personality make-up as determined by the TAT test, changes in the client's attitude toward others, and changes in scores on an emotional maturity scale.
>
> *(Hulett 1955, p. 369)*

The APA thanked Rogers for this initiative by bestowing on him one of its first Distinguished Scientific Contribution Awards in 1956.

What do you think?

In what respects does Rogers's research qualify as science according to the (logical) positivists? And in what respects does it qualify according to Popper?

Maslow

Rogers was, together with Abraham Maslow (1908–1970), one of the founders of **humanistic psychology** in the 1950s. This movement was promoted as the 'third force', because it offered an alternative to psychoanalysis and behaviourism. In 1966 Maslow published a book, *Psychology of Science*, in which he detailed what he thought was wrong with a psychology exclusively built on the 'classic' scientific method. In his words:

> In my own history this clash in scientific world view first took the form of living simultaneously with two psychologies that had little to do with each other. In my career as an experimentalist in the laboratory, I felt quite comfortable and capable with my heritage of scientific orthodoxy . . . Indeed it was John B. Watson's optimistic credo (in *Psychologies* of 1925) that had brought me and many others into the field of psychology. His programmatic writings promised a clear road ahead. I felt – with great exhilaration – that it guaranteed progress . . .
>
>   But insofar as I was a psychotherapist, an analysand, a father, a teacher, and a student of personality – that is, insofar as I dealt with whole persons – 'scientific psychology' gradually proved itself to be of little use . . .
>
>   It was as if psychologists then lived by two mutually exclusive sets of rules, or as if they spoke two different languages for different purposes. If they were interested in working with animals, or with part-processes in human beings, they could be 'experimental and scientific psychologists.' But if they were interested in whole persons, these laws and methods were not of much help.
>
> *(Maslow 1966, Chapter 2)*

Importantly, Maslow did not conclude from this that science was worthless for the study of the whole person. Rather he stressed the need for a new type of science, which was not exclusively based on Descartes' mechanistic world view (in which everything is interpreted as a machine). This can be seen in the following quote (Maslow 1966, Preface):

> I have been disturbed not only by the more 'anal' scientists and the dangers of their denial of human values in science, along with the consequent amoral technologizing of all science. Just as dangerous are some of the critics of orthodox science who find it too skeptical, too cool and nonhuman, and then reject it altogether as a danger to human values. They become 'antiscientific' and even anti-intellectual. This is a real danger among some psychotherapists and clinical psychologists, among artists, among some seriously religious people, among some of the people who are interested in Zen, in Taoism, in existentialism, 'experientialism,' and the like. Their alternative to science is often sheer freakishness and cultishness, uncritical and selfish exaltation of mere personal experiencing, over-reliance on impulsivity (which

humanistic psychology

psychological movement promoted by Rogers and Maslow as a reaction against psychoanalysis and behaviourism; stressed that people are human, inherently positive, endowed with free will and living within a sociocultural context

they confuse with spontaneity), arbitrary whimsicality and emotionality, unskepti-
cal enthusiasm, and finally navel-watching and solipsism. This is a real danger . . .
I certainly wish to be understood as trying to *enlarge* science, not to destroy it.

So, Maslow's approach must not be confounded with an anti-intellectual stance in
which all systematicity is dropped. In the next chapter we will see how qualitative
research methods tried to address Maslow's view of systematicity without reduction
to a mechanistic world view.

Neglect of individual differences

Another criticism raised against experimental psychology was that it ignored individual
differences and tried to understand the functioning of the 'average' person. All participants of an experimental condition were considered to be equal. The American psychologist Gordon Allport (1947) argued that this was a direct consequence of psychology's
infatuation with physics and technology: humans were made to fit in a machine model.
    As it happened, Allport's criticism struck a chord with the natural-scientific
approach as well as with the hermeneutics approach, partly because around that time
statistical techniques became available that allowed researchers to measure individual
differences. Shortly after Allport's seminal work, quantitative research on individual
personality differences was booming, even to such a degree that it nearly oppressed
the existing research into what people had in common. In line with the tenets of the
natural-scientific approach, however, this research did not treat the participants as
individuals with their own thoughts, emotions and motivations. They were considered as types that differed on a limited number of features (traits), and tests were
devised to measure these differences (see Chapter 7).

Research methods govern research questions

A further criticism of natural-scientific psychology was that the method determined
the research questions to be addressed. Research questions that did not fall within the
realm of the natural-scientific approach were not examined and, by consequence,
were not thought to be of interest. According to Giorgi (1970), this included all
knowledge that could not be characterised as empirical, positivistic, reductionistic,
quantitative, deterministic or predictive. The requirement of operationally defined
variables meant that a large number of phenomena could not be investigated and,
therefore, were excluded from psychology's discourse. As Maslow (1966) observed in
the excerpts above, the topics of experimental psychology worked well as long you
did not have to respond in a role as psychotherapist, father or teacher.
    Books on research methods often make a distinction between facts and values (e.g.
Stangor 2006, p. 8–9). Facts are defined as 'objective statements determined to be accurate through empirical study' (e.g. smoking increases the incidence of cancer and heart
disease). In contrast, values are defined as 'personal statements that cannot be considered to be true or false' (e.g. it is important for me to quit smoking; or, I'd better not start
drinking alcohol). Values cannot be proved or disproved by science; all science can do is
provide facts that help people select their values. Within this perspective it could be argued that the direct impact of experimental psychology on everyday life is limited
because many human choices and interactions are centred on values rather than facts.

Psychology has been confined too long to white Western males

Scientific psychology has also been criticised for being interested only in topics and research approaches that were of concern to Western males. The history of psychology indeed for a large part reads as a history of middle-class males in Western Europe and Northern America. This is the result not only of the group's dominance in academic life over the past centuries, but also the fact that the white men have largely ignored the contributions of other groups and sometimes even actively suppressed them. For instance, Titchener excluded women from the 'experimental club' he founded to discuss psychological research. This impeded the careers of women researchers such as Mary Whiton Calkins, Margaret Floy Washburn and Christine Ladd-Franklin. The bias against female and non-Western values has respectively been studied in feminist psychology and postcolonial psychology.

feminist psychology

movement in psychology aimed at understanding women; is particularly concerned with the way in which women are treated in mainstream psychology

postcolonial psychology

movement in psychology addressing the issues of racism and the ways in which dominant groups treat other groups

We will say more about racism in psychology in Chapter 12. The objections feminist psychology raised against traditional scientific psychology can be summarised as follows (Gross 2003):

- Men are taken as the standard/norm from which women deviate.
- Men decide what is worth investigating and how it should be investigated.
- There is a bias to publish the results of studies that show a difference between the genders.
- Results regarding gender differences are regularly interpreted in line with stereotyped expectations.
- Results regarding gender differences are interpreted as due to the individual and not to the social context.

Although not all feminist critiques question the value of the natural-scientific method, they do take issue with the fact that it is seen as the only acceptable research method, and they point out that such an approach is a typical Western white male approach. According to feminist psychologists, the way in which gender differences have been examined and interpreted clearly shows that science is not an objective and value-free enterprise, as claimed by the positivists, but a value-laden approach related to the socio-cultural context in which it occurs. Psychological researchers would do better acknowledging these influences, so that they do not continue the ongoing prejudice and discrimination against women under the guise of impartial scientific inquiry. A summary of this critique can be found in the following excerpt:

> feminist researchers have joined with other voices within philosophy and science . . . to challenge some of the traditional tenets of 'objectivity' in science. There appear to be two major thrusts to the feminist challenge. The first is the recognition that values are an integral part of science, that they influence all phases of the process, and that they should be acknowledged and made explicit in the same way that we recognize that scientific truths are not independent of time and place . . . The second challenge to traditional scientific thinking goes further and argues more explicitly that the language, objectives, and methods of individual disciplines, and of science itself, particularly as defined by the experimental method, have been shaped by 'masculine' concerns, interests, and personality.

(Lott 1985, p. 158–9)

What do you think?

Currently there are many more female psychology students than male psychology students. Is this translated into the teaching you get and the type of research you are allowed to do, or are the criticisms raised by feminist psychology still valid today?

The scientific claims of objectivity and universal validity are exaggerated

A final criticism against the natural-scientific approach in psychology has been that it promises more than it can deliver. One promise, for instance, is that evidence-based opinions are guaranteed to be objective and true. In Chapter 8 we saw that this is not so. All scientific research is embedded within a paradigm, which determines the questions asked and the type of answers that are allowed. In addition, the postmodernists have pointed out that scientists are influenced by the society in which they work.

Ward (2002, p. 87–92) gives some eye-opening examples of the relativity of scientific opinions (see also Chapter 12). These examples are related to the late-nineteenth-century teenage-sex panic that took over the USA after it became an issue that teenagers engage quite regularly in masturbation. Psychologists were more than willing to offer scientific advice to the worrying parents and educators. G. Stanley Hall – student of Wundt, founder of the first psychological laboratory in the USA, first president of the APA, and leading child psychologist of the day – wrote in his influential 1904 book series *Adolescence* that:

> Sex asserts its mastery in field after field, and works its havoc in the form of secret vice, debauch, disease, and enfeebled heredity . . . dangerous malady . . . most liable to occur in individuals who lack stamina . . . the very saddest of all the aspects of human weakness . . . bought at the cost of the higher life.
>
> *(as cited in Ward 2002, p. 88)*

Hall was by no means the only psychologist giving scientific advice. Another well-known PhD in psychology, trained with Wundt in Germany, was Elwood Worcestor. He was involved in a Boston-based religious and psychotherapy group known as the Emmanuel Movement. His appreciation in 1908 was:

> no one can deny that serious moral and nervous affections follow the habitual practice of masturbation, and these are more serious in early life, and when, as is often the case, the victim is temporarily nervous and delicate. The physical symptoms are weakness, pallor, and backache and general debility. The effects on the brain and nervous system are more serious.
>
> *(as cited in Ward 2002, p. 89–90)*

Although it is tempting to ascribe these unsubstantiated pieces of advice as the outcome of a lack of empirical data at the beginning of the twentieth century, the postmodernists warn us that they are much more a testimony of the fact that opinions ventured by scientists are influenced by the socio-historical context in which they live. Psychologists who nowadays are asked to give advice about masturbation, are as much influenced by the prevailing morals about sexuality as their colleagues were in the early 1900s. According to the postmodernists the same is true for advice on autism, ADHD, OCD, global warming, the smacking of children, testing children from an early age, and so on.

Critical psychology

The latest development within the hermeneutic approach has been the emergence of a number of positions that became known as critical psychology (or rather critical psychologies, as the different positions do not see themselves as fully compatible; Teo, 2005). Critical psychology is based on the following three tenets.

Idealism instead of realism

As we saw in Chapter 8, there are two opposing views in philosophy about the nature of human knowledge. On the one hand, there is *realism*, saying that knowledge corresponds to reality, which must be discovered; its truth depends on the correspondence with the real world. On the other hand, there is *idealism*, saying that knowledge is a social construction, which does not necessarily correspond to an outside world; the truth of statements depends on their coherence with the rest of knowledge. Critical psychologists argue that scientific psychology (which they usually call 'mainstream psychology') wrongly believes in realism. According to them, human language does not represent things in the world but is meant to facilitate social interaction. For the same reason, mainstream psychology is wrong in the emphasis it puts on the individual in isolation; what matters is the person as a social being.

Science is a social construction

The idealistic world view of critical psychologists also has implications for their perception of science. They agree with the postmodernists (Chapter 8) that science is not a progressive uncovering of reality, but a social construction in which scientific statements are primarily determined by the language and the culture of the scientists. As a result, scientific statements are not fixed 'truths', but ever changing stories that reflect the socio-political and cultural world of the scientists. Scientific writings must be read like history texts: as one of the possible accounts of what is/was going on. Indeed, one of the first writings in critical psychology was entitled 'Social psychology as history' (Gergen 1973). This implies that to understand psychology, it is important not to see it in isolation but to examine the context in which it takes part as an academic discipline.

Psychologists have a moral responsibility

Because the (social) reality is constantly changing as a function of what happens, psychologists must be aware of the fact that their research affects reality. Psychological theories change the perception of people and, as a result, the world in which they live. For instance, psychology research can condone a social injustice and promote its continuation by giving it a 'scientific' justification. Because of concerns about the implications of research, there is usually a larger degree of social and political engagement among critical psychologists than among mainstream psychologists. This, for instance, can be seen in the close ties that exist between the critical psychology movement, feminist psychology and postcolonial psychology. According to critical psychology, psychologists cannot pretend they are studying their subject matter in a detached way from the outside; they are part of the subject matter and have to act accordingly, as shown in the citation below:

> One bottom-line lesson which I feel to be important is really a moral one: the psychologist is not outside the things that he or she studies, not an external 'objective' observer of the human psyche, but an active participant in the collective psychological life of their community, culture and, ultimately, species. This means that what psychologists say and do, the theories, images and models of the psychological that they devise and promote, have real consequences for everybody else. They are in an even weaker position than the physical scientists to disclaim responsibility for what society does with what they produce, for even in producing it they are participating in this collective social psychological process.
>
> *(Richards 2002, p. 5)*

We will return to the ways in which psychological research changes society in Chapter 12.

What do you think?

Above we saw that according to feminist psychology the ways in which psychology researches gender differences colour the perceptions people have of such differences. Can you find a specific example? And can you think of other examples in which psychological research has had an impact on the way in which people perceive a particular phenomenon?

Conclusion

Ever since psychology carved itself a niche in academia as a science, there has been the feeling that the scientific method does not provide all the information psychologists need. This has been felt in applied contexts, but also in academic psychology. Remember from Chapter 3 that Wundt already made a distinction between three research methods: experimental methods, introspection and the historical method. Only the first one qualified as scientific according to the behaviourists.

A similar ambiguity towards experimental psychology can be found in James and his successor at Harvard University, Hugo Münsterberg, who published a textbook in 1915 under the title *Psychology: General and applied*. In this book Münsterberg drew a distinction between causal psychology (the natural-scientific approach) and purposive psychology (the hermeneutic approach), which he saw as complementary:

> [In the causal psychology] we shall resolve the personality into the elementary bits of psychical atoms and shall bring every will act into a closed system of causes and

effects. But in the purposive part we shall show with the same consistency the true inner unity of the self and the ultimate freedom of the responsible personality. Those two accounts do not exclude each other; they supplement each other, they support each other, they demand each other.

(p. 17; as cited in Cahan and White, 1992)

Also nowadays introductory textbooks of psychology include a discussion of ideas from the hermeneutic tradition, even if in the introduction they define psychology as a *scientific study*.

Although it is fair to say that the natural-scientific and the hermeneutic approaches in general have not been comfortable with each other, there have been many attempts to find common ground and to see how each could strengthen the other. Unfortunately, those attempts have not been very fruitful, possibly because the two traditions represent diametrically opposing world views: positivism vs. romanticism (see Chapter 2). For the positivist psychologist, the fact that not everything can be addressed with the scientific method is an indication that the available scientific tools are not yet powerful enough or that it is not yet known how to measure certain phenomena properly. For the romantically inclined psychologist, the fact that not everything can be addressed with the scientific method is a sign that the scientific rationalisation of life and the depiction of the world as a soulless machine miss the most fundamental aspect of (human) life.

On the other hand, there is evidence that the two approaches inspire each other indirectly, through their respective influences on society and because psychologists study both traditions in their education. The psychoanalyst Bornstein (2005) calls this type of implicit influence **unconscious plagiarism**. Table 9.1 lists some of the terms used in cognitive psychology that according to Bornstein have such an overlap with Freudian ideas that they have to be inspired by them. An influence the other way round is the growing discussion within psychoanalysis about the desirability of empirical research on the psychoanalytic tenets (e.g. Luyten *et al.* 2006).

unconscious plagiarism

term used by Bornstein to indicate how the scientific and the hermeneutic approach in psychology have influenced each other without the proponents being aware of it

Table 9.1 Revisions and reinventions of psychoanalytic concepts
Cognitive terms that have a large resemblance to ideas put forward by Freud more than half a century earlier.

Psychoanalytic concept	Revision or reinvention
Unconscious memory	Implicit memory
Primary process thought	Spreading activation
Object representation	Person schema
Repression	Cognitive avoidance
Preconscious processing	Preattentive processing
Parapraxis	Retrieval error
Abreaction	Redintegration
Repetition compulsion	Nuclear script
Ego	Central executive
Ego defence	Defensive attribution

Source: Bornstein (2005)

Interim summary

The critique of experimental psychology:

- Dilthey: psychology belongs to the *Geisteswissenschaften* (mental sciences) because:
  - it deals with the *content* of the human mind,
  - it describes the *human experience in its totality* (including cognition, emotion and volition),
  - it sees a person's life within its *context*,
  - only the method of *understanding* can study the full human experience (different levels of understanding).
- Psychoanalysis used the hermeneutic approach because it tried to understand the contents of the human mind through interpretation on the basis of the psychoanalytic theories.
- The client-centred approach also stressed the importance of understanding the other in psychotherapeutic relations; in this tradition, however, understanding was defined as empathy and not as an interpretation within a theoretical framework.
- Allport criticised experimental psychology because it ignored individual differences.
- In the natural-scientific approach the interesting research questions are too much defined as a function of what can be examined with the scientific method.
- Experimental psychology is partly the result of the dominance of white Western males in psychological research. Gave rise to feminist and postcolonial psychology.
- The natural-scientific approach ignores the fact that all knowledge is relative, depending on the prevailing research paradigm and influences from society.
- The strongest criticism against experimental psychology currently comes from critical psychology. This movement points to the facts that (1) knowledge is not a mirror of reality, (2) science is a social construction and (3) psychologists have a moral responsibility because their research changes the social reality.
- Criticism of experimental psychology has had an influence on research, but mostly indirectly (through unconscious plagiarism).

9.4 Focus on: Can the history of psychology be taught by psychologists?

Traditional vs. new history of psychology

In this chapter we saw how history became part of the curriculum of psychologists, not only because it was essential for their education but also because it legitimised psychology as a young science. This history had a number of characteristics:

- It stemmed from psychologists themselves, who did it 'on the side'.
- It was undertaken out of curiosity, for celebratory reasons, or for didactic purposes.

- It took the contemporary state of psychology as the starting point and saw history as the anticipation of that state (often with hindsight bias of what had been important in the history and what had been false starts).

- Saw psychology as a progressive, cumulative process that over time came closer to the truth.

- Was basically a review of the achievements of the 'great men' of psychology.

In 1989, the American historian Laurel Furumoto called for a different (new) approach to the history of psychology. According to her, the new history:

- investigates the assumptions that gave rise to contemporary psychology,

- tries to understand the historical events within the knowledge that existed at the time of the event,

- has an eye for the influences of the wider society and the relativity of knowledge,

- is done by independent and specialised historians,

- takes a detached and often critical stance towards psychology.

Vested interests

The advantage of independent history teachers is that they are not associated with one particular approach. A danger associated with psychology teachers is that they may be biased (implicitly or explicitly) towards their own stance. For instance, the fact that this book has been written by two cognitive psychologists could make you expect that:

- mainstream psychology will be described in a positive way,

- the scientific approach will be presented positively,

- psychological knowledge will be seen as cumulative (we know more now than we ever did before),

- there will be more detailed information about the natural-scientific approach than about the other approaches,

- there will be a bias towards academic research at the expense of applied psychology.

What do you think?

How is the book doing with respect to the criticisms above? How would the book differ if it was written by authors from the hermeneutic approach?

Because of the vested interests of psychologists, some psychology departments have decided to outsource the teaching of the history of psychology to the history departments. Unfortunately, this raises other issues. Just to cite a few:

- The attitude towards psychology is influenced by the attitude a lecturer has towards science in general, and this is true for historians as much as for psychologists.

■ Although the wider social influences are important, there remains a sequence of events that have shaped psychology and that must be included in any course. So, historians teaching the history of psychology need to have a good grasp of what happened in the field if they want to teach a relevant course.

■ There is no 'true' history of psychology. Many different histories can be written (and have been written). The history of psychology consists of everything that has ever been recorded in relationship to psychology (or the study of the human mind in general), including a myriad of ambiguities, inconsistencies and contradictions between different actors and, quite often, within the same actors on different occasions. Every history is a simplified summary of the raw material on the basis of the materials that are easily available and the opinions held within the social groups to which the authors belong. The only distinction one can make is between blatantly biased histories and histories that are perceived by the different actors at a particular time as 'reasonably (un)biased'. Whether or not the narrator is a psychologist is of secondary importance.

? What do you think?

How would you tell the story of your life? And how would someone else tell it? Someone you get on with and someone you do not get on with? Your parents? What would be the true story of your life? And how long should it be before it is 'complete'? And would that then still be interesting to anyone?

Other possible points of view

To illustrate the relativity of each approach, we list a number of ideas about history books we have encountered in our research for this book but that in the end did not (quite) make it. Maybe one of you wants to pursue a few of them?

■ Psychology has generated no useful knowledge thus far, but has managed to impose itself on society by making clever alliances and by creating problems for which it subsequently pretended to offer solutions. (This is an approach often found in postmodernistically inspired sociological writings; e.g. Achterhuis 1979; Ward 2002.)

■ Psychology has had no ideas by itself, but has always borrowed ideas from other disciplines and from developments within society.

■ History is a constant recycling of ideas that thrive for some time, get forgotten and are then returned to.

■ A history of psychology should focus on the scientists that made the discipline.

■ A history should be organised in terms of the main problems and ideas that have been addressed.

■ A history should divide the past into periods.

■ A history must give due attention to the biographies of the main actors; how their ideas were shaped by their life experiences.

- A history should focus on the distribution of powers in the society and show how dominating groups oppressed the ideas of others.

- A history of psychology should not be limited to the history of Western psychology.

- The history of psychology cannot be understood without a detailed analysis of the changing attitudes toward religion in Western society.

Interim summary

- Each history is relative and conveys only part of the rich raw material that is available.

- In the history of psychology a distinction is often made between the traditional approach (largely seen as a legitimisation of the current state of affairs) and the new approach (more critical, has an eye for the relativity of knowledge, tries to expose the assumptions that gave rise to current opinions).

- An extra problem is that book authors and lecturers may have vested interests, which bias the coverage of the history.

- The history described in the present book is not THE history of psychology. It is only one of the possible stories, which we hope will not be perceived as being too biased.

Recommended literature

The scientific tradition in psychology is well described in the first chapters of most research books in psychology. We in particular used Christensen, L.B. (2004) *Experimental methodology* (9th edn) (Boston: Pearson Education) and Rosenthal, R. and Rosnow, R.L. (2008), *Essentials of behavioral research: Methods and data analysis* (3rd edn) (Boston: McGraw-Hill).

For the critical part we found much information and many ideas in Teo, T. (2005) *The critique of psychology: From Kant to postcolonial theory* (New York: Springer Science+Business Media, Inc.); and in Gross, R. (2003) *Themes, issues and debates in psychology* (2nd edn) (Abingdon: Hodder Arnold).

References

Achterhuis, H. (1979) *De markt van welzijn en geluk [The market of well-being and happiness]*. The Netherlands: Uitgeverij Ambo.

Allport, G.W. (1947) 'Scientific models and human morals', *Psychological Review*, 54: 182–92.

Baars, B.J. (1986) *The cognitive revolution in psychology*. New York: Guilford Press.

Bargh, J.A. and Chartrand, T. (1999) 'The unbearable automaticity of being', *American Psychologist*, 54: 462–79.

Barrow, R. (2000) 'Determining stereotypical images of psychologists: the Draw A Psychologist Checklist', *College Student Journal,* **34**: 123–33.

Bornstein, R.F. (2005) 'Reconnecting psychoanalysis to mainstream psychology: Challenges and opportunities', *Psychoanalytic Psychology,* **22**: 323–40.

Boyack, K.W., Klavans, R. and Börner, K. (2005) 'Mapping the backbone of science', *Scientometrics,* **64**: 351–74.

Cahan, E.D. and White, S.H. (1992) 'Proposals for a second psychology', *American Psychologist,* **47**: 224–35.

Dewey, J. (1887) *Psychology.* New York: Harper & Brothers.

Ebbinghaus, H. (1908/1973) *Psychology: An elementary textbook.* New York: Arno Press.

Furumoto, L. (1989) 'The new history of psychology.' In I. Cohen (ed.), *The G. Stanley Hall Lecture Series* (Vol. 9). Washington, DC: APA.

Gabbard, G.O. and Gabbard, K. (1999) *Psychiatry and the cinema* (2nd edn). Washington, DC: American Psychiatric Press.

Gergen, K.J. (1973) 'Social psychology as history', *Journal of Personality and Social Psychology,* **26**: 309–20.

Giorgi, A. (1970) *Psychology as a human science.* New York: Harper & Row.

Gross, R. (2003) *Themes, issues and debates in psychology* (2nd edn). Abingdon: Hodder Arnold.

Hartwig, S.G. (2002) 'Surveying psychologists' public image with drawings of a "typical" psychologist', *South Pacific Journal of Psychology,* **14**: 69–75.

Haynes, R. (2003) 'From alchemy to artificial intelligence: Stereotypes of the scientist in Western literature', *Public Understanding of Science,* **12**: 243–53.

Hulett, J.E. (1955) 'Book review of *Psychotherapy and personality change: Coordinated research studies in the client-centered approach,* by Carl R. Rogers and Rosalind F. Dymond', *American Sociological Review,* **20**: 369–70.

Janda, L.H., England, K., Lovejoy, D. and Drury, K. (1998) 'Attitudes toward psychology relative to other disciplines', *Professional Psychology: Research and Practice,* **29**: 140–3.

Kessels, U., Rau, M. and Hannover, B. (2006) 'What goes well with physics? Measuring and altering the image of science', *British Journal of Educational Psychology,* **76**: 761–80.

Koch, S. (1961) 'Psychological science versus the science-humanism antinomy: Intimations of a significant science of man', *American Psychologist,* **16**: 629–39.

Kuhn, T.S. (1962) *The structure of scientific revolutions.* Chicago: Chicago University Press.

Lott, B. (1985) 'The potential enrichment of social personality psychology through feminist research and vice versa', *American Psychologist,* **40**: 155–64.

Luyten, P., Blatt, S.J. and Corveleyn, J. (2006) 'Minding the gap between positivism and hermeneutics in psychoanalytic research', *Journal of the American Psychoanalytic Association,* **54**: 571–610.

Maslow, A.H. (1966) *Psychology of science.* New York: Harper and Row.

McDuffie, T.E. (2001) 'Scientists – geeks & nerds? Dispelling teachers' stereotypes of scientists', *Science and Children,* **38**: 16–19.

Münsterberg, H. (1915) *Psychology: General and applied.* New York: D. Appleton & Co.

Orchowski, L.M., Spickard, B.A. and McNamara, J.R. (2006) 'Cinema and the valuing of psychotherapy: Implications for clinical practice', *Professional Psychology: Research and Practice,* **37**: 506–14.

Park, S.W. and Auchincloss, E.L. (2006) 'Psychoanalysis in textbooks of introductory psychology: A review', *Journal of the American Psychoanalytic Association,* **54**: 1361–80.

Richards, G. (2002) *Putting psychology in its place: A critical historical overview.* London: Routledge.

Rogers, C.R. and Dymond, R.F. (eds.) (1954). *Psychotherapy and personality change: Coordinated research studies in the client-centered approach.* Chicago: The University of Chicago Press.

Sandoval, W.A. (2005) 'Understanding students' practical epistemologies and their influence on learning through inquiry', *Science Education,* **89**: 634–56.

Stangor, C. (2006) *Research methods for the behavioral sciences.* Boston, MA: Houghton Mifflin.

Vilchez-Gonzalez, J.M. and Parales Palacios, F.J. (2006) 'Image of science in cartoons and its relationship with the image in comics', *Physics Education,* **41**: 240–9.

Von Sydow, K. (2007) 'The public image of psychologists, psychotherapists, and psychiatrists', *Psychotherapeut,* **52**: 322–33.

Ward, S.C. (2002) *Modernizing the mind: Psychological knowledge and the remaking of society.* Westport, CT: Praeger.

Yasar, S., Baker, D., Robinson-Kurpius, S., Krause, S. and Roberts, C. (2006) 'Development of a survey to assess K-12 teachers' perceptions of engineers and familiarity with teaching design, engineering, and technology', *Journal of Education,* **95**: 205–16.

10 The contribution of quantitative and qualitative research methods

Questions to consider

? Conceptual issues addressed in this chapter

- What are the assumptions upon which quantitative research methods in psychology are based?
- Why do quantitative researchers see a hierarchy of evidence going from descriptive research, over relational research, to experimental research?
- What are the assumptions upon which qualitative research methods in psychology are based?
- Why is discourse analysis more in line with social constructionism than grounded theory?
- What are the arguments psychologists use to defend the idea that qualitative and quantitative research methods cannot coexist?
- What are the arguments psychologists use to defend the idea that qualitative and quantitative research methods complement each other and that progress in psychology is best guaranteed by a combination of both types of methods?
- What implications does the coexistence of quantitative and qualitative methods in psychology have for philosophy of science?

Introduction

Collecting and editing the manuscripts have reminded me of the rapidity of change in our world and our scholarly work. Ten years ago, after I completed one of the first qualitative dissertations done in my college, I was a participant in the great paradigm war between positivists and constructivists – the Quantoids and the Smooshes . . . There were few qualitative sessions at the American Education Research Association (AERA) meetings, and the Educational Researcher was full of salvos fired across the paradigm lines.

It feels to some of us like we won the war. Has qualitative research taken over the high ground and become what Kuhn (1970, p. 10) called "normal science"?

(Hatch 1995, p. xvi)

In Chapter 9 we saw that psychology can be divided into two research lines. On the one hand, there is the traditional, natural-science oriented approach, on which psychology as an academic discipline was founded. On the other hand, there is the hermeneutic approach, which argues that the traditional scientific method is unsuitable to study mental life, because the method of the natural sciences makes it impossible to access to the richness of the human experience. As the quote above shows, this discussion is not limited to psychology, but can be found in all human and social sciences (e.g. education, social work, management, sport, health, . . .).

In recent years, the discussion has crystallised into the question to what extent the traditional quantitative methods should be supplemented (or replaced) by qualitative research methods. In the quote at the opening of this chapter this is referred to as the 'paradigm war'. Below we will have a look at the various positions and see whether the situation is indeed as grave as suggested in the citation. First we discuss the essence of the quantitative and the qualitative methods.

10.1   The essence of quantitative research

quantitative research methods

research methods based on quantifiable data; are associated with the natural-science approach based on the hypothetico-deductive model

Quantitative research methods are research methods based on quantifiable data, findings which can be represented as numbers either because their magnitude can be measured or because their frequency of occurrence can be counted. They usually involve statistical analysis and are the methods preferred by the traditional, natural-science oriented psychology researchers. Their application depends on a number of assumptions, which we first outline.

Assumptions underlying quantitative research methods

There is an outside reality that can be discovered

Quantitative psychologists start from the assumption that phenomena in the world have an existence outside people's minds. That is, they believe in realism (Chapter 8). In addition, they defend the idea that humans can discover reality by using the scientific method. This does not mean they subscribe to the positivist view that reality can be known simply by means of observation, induction and verification, and that scientific knowledge is always true. They are well aware of the fact that science is not a linear accumulation of facts but proceeds through trial and error (with theories and paradigms that do not stand the falsification test and that after some time have to be abandoned). However, they are convinced that in the long term the scientific method based on the hypothetico-deductive model (Chapter 8) leads to an understanding of reality; scientific knowledge is cumulative.

The main aim of scientific research is to find universal causal relationships

Researchers who subscribe to quantitative research methods are primarily interested in discovering relationships between causes and effects. They want to know *how* humans function: how various variables interact and how particular functions are accomplished. In addition, they want to know how general the principles are. Ideally they hope the mechanisms they discover will apply to all humans. If this turns out not to be the case, they search for the causes underlying individual differences and try to integrate them into a wider pattern that covers the entire spectrum.

Trying to avoid confounds and sources of noise

Users of quantitative research methods are extremely vigilant about the possible intrusion of undesired factors into their designs. Because they are looking for 'true' cause–effect relations, they try to avoid the presence of so-called *confounding variables*, variables that were overlooked but that could be the true causes of the effects observed (see below for an example). As a result, quantitative researchers try to maximally control the circumstances under which they run their studies, even if this leads to artificial situations (i.e. so-called laboratory situation).

Quantitative researchers also try to eliminate the impact of random variables. These are elements that vary randomly from one study to the next and that may lead to findings which are not replicable (because the effect was due to a random variable that only in one particular study had the value causing the effect). These random variables are called *noise*.

Suspicion about the researcher's input

A source of confounding and noise that is of particular interest to quantitative psychology researchers is the researcher him- or herself. Humans are known to have fallible perceptions and opinions, meaning that they can be a source of bias (confound) or randomness (noise). A biased researcher is a researcher who consistently obtains 'evidence' other people cannot find. This usually consists of evidence in line with the researcher's convictions (see Chapter 8 for the ways in which opinions shape the perception of facts). A random researcher is a researcher who in a study obtains evidence no-one else (including the researcher him/herself) can replicate, because it was a fluke.

To protect themselves against biases and noise, quantitative researchers make use of standardised measurements and instruments. For instance, they will make use of generally accepted questionnaires to measure aspects of people and they will analyse the data with generally accepted statistical tests. In this way, they have more certainty that the findings they obtain can be replicated by others using the same methods.

Progress through falsification

One final feature of the quantitative research approach is that researchers continuously evaluate the truth of their conclusions, theories, hypotheses and instruments. This is part of the falsification element in scientific research. Researchers constantly try to prove each other wrong, which often bewilders non-scientific spectators who cannot understand why scientists rarely seem to agree with one another. As a rule of thumb, an effect will only be accepted as 'probably true' when there is a great deal of converging evidence for it, coming from different measurements and falsification attempts.

Now that we have seen the assumptions underlying quantitative research methods, we can have a closer look at the various techniques that are available. These are usually divided into three broad orientations (e.g. Rosenthal and Rosnow 2008): descriptive research, relational research and experimental research.

Descriptive research

Observation of numerical data

In descriptive research, the focus is on observation, a careful charting of the situation. As we have seen several times in this book, detailed observation is the start of scientific research. Certainly with respect to psychology, this is not a platitude. Just think of how long philosophers thought they could study human functioning without looking at what people were actually doing. The same is true for many everyday conversations, in which people vent opinions based on their hunches. How often do you hear someone say they cannot discuss a particular psychological topic (e.g. the influence of divorce on the well-being of children) because they would first need to have a look at the empirical evidence?

What do you think?

Why do you think many people have little problem discussing psychological topics without first seeing empirical evidence?

Would there be a difference between different types of topics?

Can you answer the above two questions without having data on how many people are willing to discuss various topics without empirical evidence?

Typical for quantitative research is that the data are gathered in a numerical form, either by collecting measurements or by counting frequencies of occurrence. Quantitative researchers will not observe 'violence', but will measure aspects of violence (e.g. the number of incidents reported to the police, the number of incidents reported in diaries or interviews, the amount of violence as rated by participants on a Likert scale, etc.). In Chapter 4 we called this the requirement of *operational definitions*. In addition, before the researchers collect data, they have a good idea of how they will analyse it: what types of measurements they will obtain and what types of statistics they can apply to summarise and evaluate the data.

Large samples and a few data points per participant

Although this is not an absolute rule, the vast majority of descriptive quantitative studies involve the collection of a limited amount of data from a reasonably large group of participants. There are two main reasons why researchers want to include large groups in their studies. The first is that the larger the sample examined, the more representative it becomes for the population (i.e. the more it resembles the population). As indicated above, quantitative researchers usually want to generalise their findings from the sample studied to the complete group of people involved in the study, so that universal conclusions can be reached. Although quantity is only one aspect of representativeness, it is an important one and one that is taught to all psychology students.

The second reason why descriptive quantitative studies usually involve many participants is that large numbers of observations yield more precise statistics. In all likelihood, the mean of a sample is closer to the population mean when it is based on a large sample than when it is based on a small sample. When social services want to know how many teenagers are unhappy, they will feel more confident about an estimate if it is based on a sample of 1,000 respondents than if it is based on a sample of 20 respondents, even when every precaution has been taken to make both samples equally representative. The reason why the mean of 1,000 observations is more reliable than the mean of 20 observations is that the mean of 1,000 observations is likely to be very much the same if the study were repeated with another sample of the same size, whereas there can be a serious difference in estimates based on two different samples of 20 participants only.

Descriptive research usually is but the first step of a quantitative research programme, because the researchers want to know what caused the data they observe. How did the figures come about? To discover cause–effect relations, a first move is to find out which events (variables) are related. If a survey indicates that 15 per cent of the teenagers call themselves unhappy, the logical next question is which variables are related to being (un)happy. Is it the case that teenagers who call themselves unhappy have less money to spend than teenagers who call themselves happy? Are they less supported by their parents? Do they have fewer peers who like them? This is addressed in relational research.

Relational research

Correlations

The way to find out whether two variables are related according to quantitative psychologists is to collect measures of both variables and to correlate them. There are various statistical techniques to calculate a coefficient that indicates how closely two variables co-vary. These techniques not only provide information about whether or not two variables are correlated, but also how strong the correlation is (see Chapter 7).

Quantitative researchers point to the importance of calculating and using statistical correlation coefficients to decide which variables are correlated and which are not, because people do not seem to be good at detecting them (at least not at a conscious level; see Chapter 6). For instance, since the seminal publication of Paul Meehl (1954) there has been a continuous stream of studies showing that decisions based on standardised interviews/questionnaires and statistical correlations outperform clinical judgements by psychologists. This is true, for example, for the prediction of academic performance, psychotherapy outcome, success in military training, probation success, business failure and detection of malingering (for a review, see Grove *et al.* 2000).

There are two problems involved in the intuitive detection of correlations by humans. The first is the failure to detect genuine correlations. In particular negative correlations (where the variables vary in opposite directions) seem to be difficult to perceive. The most notorious example in this respect is the time it took before people realised that there was a negative correlation between smoking and longevity (the more you smoke, the younger on average you will die; figure 10.1).

illusory correlation

perception of a correlation between events for which no independent evidence can be found

The second problem with the detection of correlations by humans is that in some cases people tend to perceive correlations that do not exist. These are called **illusory correlations**. For instance, in Chapter 9 we mentioned that for many people there is a positive correlation between being a scientist and being a middle-aged man with untidy hair. Similarly, King and Koehler (2000) showed that graphologists tend to conclude that people who write fast have an impulsive personality, whereas people who write slowly are supposed to have a cautious personality. There are no such correlations to be detected in quantitative data, but people are prone to believing in them because the meanings of the variables are associated: slowness seems to go along with caution and speed with impulsivity. In general, people are prone to illusory correlations when two variables overlap in meaning (e.g. red hair and hot temper) or when the correlation is good for the self-esteem (e.g. members of one's own group are perceived as more interesting than members of other groups).

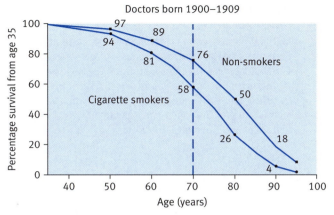

Figure 10.1 The negative correlation between smoking and age at death.
In this study, a cohort of male British medical doctors was followed from the age of
35 years on. The graph shows the survival rate for smokers and non-smokers. Of the
smokers, 58% were still alive at the age of 70, against 76% of the non-smokers.

Source: Doll *et al.* (2004) 'Mortality in relation to smoking: 50 years observations on male British doctors', *British Medical Journal*, **328**, p. 1519–28. Reproduced by permission of the BMJ Publishing Group.

Factor analysis

Statistical correlations are interesting not only because they allow researchers to
assess the relationship between two variables, but also because they make it possible
to investigate the pattern of correlations between any number of variables. A statistical
technique often used in this respect is factor analysis. We will illustrate the technique
with a small example. Suppose you want to know what the correlations are between
the marks psychology students obtain on their exams in statistics, research methods,
social psychology, and historical and conceptual issues. Are students who are good at
stats also good at the three other courses? Or is it the case that someone who gets a
high mark on stats obtains a relatively low mark on historical and conceptual issues?
Or could it be that the courses are not related to each other and that knowing the
stats score of a student does not help you to make a better prediction about their
score on historical and conceptual issues?

To find out, you collect the exam marks of all students at a particular university
and you calculate the correlations between the various scores. Suppose Table 10.1
summarises your findings.

In this figure you see an interesting pattern of findings. There is a high positive
correlation (.80) between the exam marks of Statistics and Research Methods, and
between Social Psychology and Historical and Conceptual Issues. In contrast, there are
no correlations between Statistics and Research Methods on the one hand and Social
Psychology and Historical and Conceptual Issues on the other hand. This means, for
instance, that a student who scores high on the Stats exam in all likelihood will also have
a high mark on the Research Methods exam, and can have a high, medium or low score
on Social Psychology and Historical and Conceptual Issues. Such a pattern suggests that
the exam scores are determined by two independent factors: one for Statistics and
Research Methods and one for Social Psychology and Historical and Conceptual Issues.

Table 10.1 Fictitious example of correlations between exam marks of four courses in a psychology degree

In this table you see that there is a high correlation (.80) between the exam marks of Statistics and Research Methods, and between Social Psychology and Historical and Conceptual Issues. In contrast, there are no correlations between Statistics and Research Methods on the one hand and Social Psychology and Historical and Conceptual Issues on the other hand. This suggests that the exam scores are determined by two independent factors: one for Statistics and Research Methods and one for Social Psychology and Historical and Conceptual Issues.

	Stats	**ResMeth**	**SocPsy**	**HisConcep**
Stats	1.00	.80	.00	.00
ResMeth	.80	1.00	.00	.00
SocPsy	.00	.00	1.00	.80
HisConcep	.00	.00	.80	1.00

Now suppose that your correlations looked as shown in table 10.2. Here you see that there are high positive correlations between all courses. A student who scores high on the Statistics exam also on average scores high on the three other exams, and a student who scores low on one exam scores low on the other exams as well. This is not in line with the idea that there would be two factors underlying the scores. Rather, all scores seem to be due to a single factor, which we could call an intelligence/motivation factor: students who score high on this factor get good marks on all exams, students who score low on this factor score low on all exams.

Factor analysis is a statistical technique calculating how many factors are needed to account for the correlations between the variables measured and how these variables relate to the factors. For instance, for the data of Table 10.1 it would extract two factors, one with Statistics and Research Methods loading on it, and one with Social Psychology and Historical and Conceptual Issues loading it. For Table 10.2 it would return one factor on which all courses load.

Table 10.2 Another fictitious example of correlations between the exam marks of four courses in a psychology degree

In this table you see that there are high correlations (.80) between all four exams. This suggests that the exam scores are determined by a single factor.

	Stats	**ResMeth**	**SocPsy**	**HisConcep**
Stats	1.00	.80	.80	.80
ResMeth	.80	1.00	.80	.80
SocPsy	.80	.80	1.00	.80
HisConcep	.80	.80	.80	1.00

Experimental research

Correlations do not allow researchers to be sure about causes

Relational research makes it possible for quantitative researchers to assess which variables are related and which are not, but does not allow them to be certain about the origin of the correlation (i.e. the underlying cause–effect relation). For instance, several studies have shown that there is a negative correlation between the presence of children and marital satisfaction: couples with children show less marital satisfaction than couples without children (Twenge *et al.* 2003). Although it is tempting to conclude from this correlation that the presence of children does decrease the degree of marital satisfaction experienced by parents (i.e. the children are the cause of the decrease in satisfaction), there is nothing in the correlation itself that allows the researchers to draw this conclusion. There could be tens of other reasons why couples with children rate their marital satisfaction lower than couples without children. Maybe couples without children split up sooner, so that the remaining ones score high on satisfaction? Or it might be that couples who score high on satisfaction do not feel a need for children? Or that people who enjoy their job score high on marital satisfaction and do not feel a need for children?

?

What do you think?

To help you appreciate that correlations often have a more complicated explanation than simply one variable being the cause of the other, try to explain the following correlations.

1. There is a positive correlation between the number of ice creams sold at the seaside and the number of people that need to be saved from drowning: the more ice-creams sold, the more people need to be saved.

2. There is a positive correlation between the number of churches in a town and the number of murders in that town: the more churches, the more murders.

3. There is a positive correlation between the weight of a person and their net income: the more a person weights the higher their income.

Variables responsible for the correlation: (1) temperature, (2) size of the town, (3) age

---

Experiments to determine cause–effect relations

To be able to draw firm conclusions about cause and effect, quantitative psychologists will set up an experiment in which they manipulate the suspected cause and see whether this has an effect on the phenomenon they are examining. For instance, if psychologists suspect that tea helps students to remember texts, they will design an experiment in which half of the participants get a cup of tea and the other half get nothing or something else (e.g. a glass of water) while they are studying. If the experiment is run properly and if the predicted difference between both conditions is observed, the psychologist can be pretty sure that the tea indeed caused the difference in performance.

Controlling for confounding variables

An important aspect of experiments is that only the suspected causes are manipulated and the resulting changes in the phenomenon registered. Everything else must be held constant. The latter stipulation is critical. If researchers want to be sure that the manipulated variable really is the cause of the effect, then they must make sure that no other variables can be the origin of the change detected. As indicated above, this requirement is known as the problem of the confounding variable.

confounding variable

variable that was not taken into account in the study and that may be the origin of the effect observed

To illustrate the problem of confounding variables we again take the example of a psychologist wanting to know whether a cup of tea helps students memorising a text. Suppose two groups of participants took part in the experiment. One group (in the morning) studied a text with a cup of tea and after an hour took part in a multiple choice quiz. The second group (in the afternoon) studied the same text and completed the same quiz, but was not given tea. Suppose the group with tea answered 20 per cent more questions correctly than the group without tea. Can the psychologist then conclude that tea is helpful for studying?

As you may have noticed, the problem with the study, as it has been described, is that one group was seen in the morning and the other in the afternoon. Maybe people study better in the morning than in the afternoon: could that be the reason for the difference in performance? The time of test is a confounding variable of the availability of tea and prevents the psychologist from being able to conclude for certain that tea is good for studying. In addition, when you come to think of it, there are other possible confounding variables in the design. Maybe the first group consisted of more motivated participants than the second. Could there be a difference between people who take part in a morning experiment and people who take part in an afternoon experiment?

To address the criticism of possible confounds, experimental psychologists introduce an increasing number of controls (e.g. by testing both groups at the same time, by testing four groups on two different days with the availability of tea counterbalanced over the days, and by randomly allocating the participants over conditions). Unfortunately, each control adds an extra constraint to the situation and puts the testing into an increasingly artificial setting. To counter this problem, quantitative researchers usually run several experiments on the same topic (involving different manipulations, measurements and controls) and look for *converging evidence* across studies.

Experiments are not always possible

Needless to say, not all issues in psychology can be addressed experimentally. For instance, although it easy to think of a hypothetical experiment addressing the question of whether the presence of children is the cause of the drop in marital satisfaction, such an experiment could never be run in practice. It would involve the selection of two matched samples of couples, one of which would be forced to have children and the other prevented from having children. Both groups of couples would then be followed for several years to see how their marital satisfaction evolves. If the presence of children indeed is the cause of the drop in marital satisfaction, such a drop should be observed in the sample with children only.

The fact that many psychological experiments are impossible may be one of the reasons why progress in psychology is harder to achieve than in sciences such as physics, chemistry or botany, where researchers are less often confronted with practical and ethical limits.

Analogy with the hierarchy of evidence in medical science

The status of the different approaches in quantitative research can be illustrated by relating them to the so-called *hierarchy of evidence* in medical science (cf. Greenhalgh 1997). This hierarchy indicates how strong the evidence is for a particular therapy or pathogen (figure 10.2).

At the low end of the hierarchy we find case reports, consisting of anecdotal evidence related to individual patients. They have the same status as descriptive research: they may point to interesting phenomena but do not provide much information about the underlying causes.

At the second level we find cross-sectional surveys. They form the first step of relational research. A group of participants is asked to complete a questionnaire about health-related topics. Afterwards the researchers look for correlations between the answers to the various questions (e.g. is the consumption of a certain food related to a higher/lower risk of cancer?). This type of research enables epidemiologists to find potential relationships. However, there is little control of confounding variables (e.g. the relationship between the food and cancer could be due to other lifestyle differences between the people eating the food and those who do not).

In case-control studies (level 3) patients with a particular disease are matched on a series of possible confounding variables (age, gender, socio-economic status . . .) with participants who do not have the disease. The medical histories of both groups are compared in search for differences that can be the origin of the ailment observed.

In follow-up studies (level 4) two matched groups, one with the disease/treatment and one without, are followed for a certain period of time, to see how they evolve.

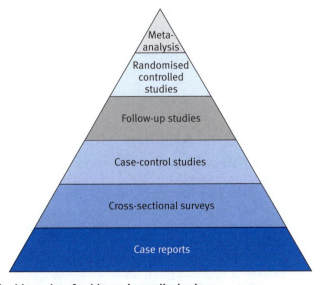

Figure 10.2 The hierarchy of evidence in medical science.

Any difference between the groups is likely to be due to the disease/treatment, as the groups were originally matched on possible confounding variables.

At level 5 we find the randomised controlled trials. These are the equivalent of experimental studies and are often used to assess the efficacy of therapies. Patients are randomly distributed over two conditions, so that both conditions are equivalent in terms of possible confounding variables. Then, one group (determined at random) receives the experimental treatment, whereas the other group receives a placebo treatment that looks exactly like the experimental treatment but without the critical agent (e.g. a pill of the same size and colour as the experimental pill but only consisting of the binding and colouring agents used for the experimental pill). Further controls are introduced to make sure that any effect observed cannot be due to other variables. For instance, the patients and the practitioners do not know which type of pill has been administered, so that the results are not biased by the expectations people have when they know they only received a placebo pill rather than the 'real' pill (such studies are called *double blind studies*, because neither the patients nor the treating practitioners know which condition the patient is in).

Finally, at the top of the hierarchy we find the meta-analysis. This is a review of all the available evidence concerning a particular treatment or pathogen coming from many different sources. For each study the relevant features and the accompanying effects are collected. On the basis of these figures, an overall estimate of the effect size is calculated. Because the analysis is based on many different studies, coming from different labs and using different procedures, this type of evidence exceeds the limitations of each individual study. In addition, because it is based on a large sample of participants, the conclusions are stable.

What do you think?

Suppose you want to answer the question 'does watching violence on TV increase the aggression of the viewers?' Which studies could you run at each level of the hierarchy? Can you see how the evidence becomes stronger as you get higher in the hierarchy?

Strengths of quantitative research methods

Because quantitative research makes use of the scientific method applied to psychological topics, it inherits all the strengths of the method we have discussed in the preceding chapters. The application of powerful statistical analyses enables researchers to detect nearly every pattern of association in large datasets, and the merciless application of the falsification test prevents wrong ideas and weak theories from thriving for too long.

Because the strengths of quantitative research have been extensively discussed before, we will not dwell on them any longer. Instead, we will have a look at the weaknesses of the approach.

Limits of quantitative methods

No interest in the person behind the participant

With some exaggeration, participants in quantitative research can be described as number providers. The research is designed in such a way that each participant returns one or a few numbers, which can be used in statistical analyses. As a consequence, quantitative studies are usually brief. In addition, participants are confronted with researchers who shun close interactions during the data gathering because they fear such interactions might invalidate the study (e.g. by betraying the research question or by biasing the participants in their responses). To make sure that no situation factors could turn into confounding variables, good researchers are taught to act as uninvolved, dispassionate observers.

This is how one critic summarised the way in which participants are treated in quantitative research:

> In the first half of the twentieth century the investigative practice of American psychology came to rely increasingly on the construction of 'collective subjects' for the generation of its knowledge products . . . Three types of these artificial collectivities were distinguished: those that were the result of averaging the performance of individuals subjected to similar experimental conditions, those that were constituted from scores obtained by means of some psychometric testing instrument, and those that were produced by subjecting groups of individuals to different treatment conditions.
>
> *(Danziger 1990, p. 113)*

The lack of interest in the person behind the participant is of particular concern when the research concerns real life situations (e.g. the psychology of health), because in these situations psychologists can learn a lot by listening to the experiences and opinions of the people involved (practitioners, patients, support staff, relatives).

Research is too much driven by what can be measured numerically and tested experimentally

quantitative imperative

a bias only to find measurable topics interesting because quantitative research methods require numerical data

Because quantitative analyses require the data to be represented as numbers, quantitative psychologists have a bias to limit their research to topics that can easily be measured. According to the hermeneutic critique, this has resulted in the quantitative imperative, the conviction that you cannot know what you cannot measure.

Furthermore, because experiments provide the strongest information within the quantitative paradigm, much research has been geared towards questions that can be addressed experimentally. The aspects of mental life that cannot be captured by numbers and that cannot be manipulated in an experiment have been considered of secondary importance.

The falsification test lends itself better to destroying ideas than to finding practical solutions for specific problems

Another limitation of quantitative research is that the falsification test, on which the method rests, is primarily geared towards erasing wrong theories rather than generating new ones. It is much easier to set up an experiment showing that someone is

Table 10.3 Differences between the quantitative and the pragmatic approaches
Some differences between the quantitative psychological approach and the pragmatic engineering approach.

Artificial intelligence/psychology	Engineering
Motivated by long-term goal (exhaustive understanding)	Motivated by short-term goals (so that progress can be measured)
Seeks breakthroughs and radically new perspectives	Tends to proceed by improving existing systems
Tries to solve problems in their most general form (general-purpose system)	Looks for solutions for specific problems
Makes recourse to introspection about human capabilities and about what seems intuitively likely	Designs and tunes systems to work on average; focuses on the desired input–output behaviour and designs algorithms to achieve this

Source: Ward (1998)

wrong than to come up with a new theory that is worthwhile. As a result, it is not unusual to see theories that have been discredited for some time still being 'rejected' on a regular basis in scientific journals, just because it is so easy to set up an experiment to disprove them.

The negative tone underlying falsification tests can easily be illustrated by comparing the ways in which automatic speech recognition (speech recognition by computers) has been approached by quantitative psychologists and engineers. Table 10.3 summarises the differences as perceived by one of the players (Ward 1998). While the psychologists tried to solve the problem by generating and testing general theories of how humans (and by extension machines) function and spent a lot of time showing each other that their respective theories and ideas were wrong (as indicated by falsification tests), the engineers concentrated on the problem at hand and searched for concrete steps that would bring the solution closer. The psychologists were looking for the truth, the engineers searched for algorithms that would improve the performance of the machine. Ward noticed that the latter, pragmatic approach over a period of 40 years resulted in significantly more progress.

The above example is not meant to question the value of the falsification test for scientific progress (Chapter 8). However, it does remind us that falsification only leads to progress when there are worthwhile proposals to be tested. An exclusive reliance on the falsification test involves the danger that more knowledge is gathered about what is not 'true' than about what works. Falsification tests without equally strong efforts to try to understand what is going on, risk ending up in a situation where rival views are more interested in showing each other they are wrong, than in contemplating whether the resulting discussion brings the solution any closer. An informative book in this respect is Eysenck and Keane (2005), because for each topic it nicely summarises the different points of view and the evidence *against* them.

Interim summary

The essence of quantitative research

- Quantitative research methods refer to research methods based on quantifiable data and the following assumptions:
    - There is an objective reality to be discovered.
    - The main aim of scientific research is to find universal cause–effect relations.
    - To do this one has to rely on the hypothetico-deductive method and to avoid confounds and sources of noise.

- A distinction can be made between descriptive, relational and experimental research.
    - Descriptive research: trying to express variables in numbers, usually involves a few measures from a large group of participants.
    - Relational research: searching for statistical correlations in order to understand relationships between variables; use of factor analysis to find the structure in datasets with many variables.
    - Experimental research: searching for cause–effect relationships by excluding confounding variables; experiments often not possible.
    - Status of the different types of research can be understood by analogy with the hierarchy of evidence in medical science.

- Strengths:
    - Inherits the strengths of the natural sciences (in particular of the falsification criterion).
    - Application of powerful statistical techniques enables researchers to detect every pattern of association in large datasets.

- Weaknesses:
    - No interest in the person behind the participant.
    - Research too much driven by what can be measured numerically and tested experimentally.
    - The falsification test is not primarily geared towards the generation of new ideas and finding practical solutions to specific problems.

10.2   The essence of qualitative research

Qualitative research methods are directed at understanding phenomena (including people) in their historical and socio-cultural context. They are favoured by the hermeneutic approach in psychology, because they allow researchers to understand the complete situation they find themselves in. In line with our discussion of quantitative research methods, we start with the general assumptions underlying this type of research, before we describe specific techniques and their strengths and weaknesses.

Assumptions underlying qualitative research methods

In psychology there is little or no evidence for a reality outside people's minds

Unlike quantitative psychologists, most qualitative psychologists are not convinced that in psychology there is an objective reality, which can be discovered with the scientific approach. For them the only reality that matters is the reality as perceived and constructed by people. There are differences in the degree to which the various methods question the existence/importance of an objective reality, as we will see below, but they all agree that it is more important to understand people's views rather than their responses to aspects of the environment.

Attempts to control the situation make the setting artificial and impoverished

According to qualitative psychologists, quantitative researchers are misguided in their attempts to try to measure 'reality' in unbiased ways. The attempts to control for confounding variables and noise do not help to make the 'real world' visible, but turn the environment into an artificial setting that robs the participants of their usual ways of interacting and coping in meaningful situations. For instance, when Milgram (1963; Chapter 6) saw participants punish other humans with increasingly harmful electrical shocks in his experiments, he did not observe 'true' obedience, but participants pressing buttons in one particular social environment that was perceived and interpreted by the participants in ways unknown to Milgram.

Similarly, the attempts to restrict and streamline the interactions between the researcher and the participants do not in the first place increase the chances of making the 'true' world visible, but seriously limit the information the researcher can get from the study. Rather than being an uninvolved, distant observer, the investigator should become an active participant and listen to what the participant has to say. He or she should not be guided by fear of drawing wrong conclusions but by a constructive desire to understand the meaning of what is going on.

Qualitative researchers acknowledge that the approach they promote entails the danger of the conclusions being influenced by the researcher, but argue that:

1. This danger is offset by the expected gains due to an understanding of the situation.

2. All conclusions, even those reached on the basis of quantitative research and falsification tests, are relative (because they depend on the prevailing paradigm).

3. The most obvious biases can be avoided by being aware of them and by doing the analysis in such a way that it can be repeated and checked by others.

Immersion and understanding

The point of departure of qualitative psychology is the immersion of the researcher in the situation that is being studied, so that the *meaning* of the situation can be understood. The researcher will not approach the situation with a preconceived list of variables that need to be scored and that constrain the outcome of the study. Instead, the researcher approaches the situation open-mindedly and sees what comes out. This is how Willig described the essence of the qualitative methodology:

> Qualitative researchers tend to be concerned with meaning. That is, they are interested in how people make sense of the world and how they experience events. They aim to understand 'what it is like' to experience particular conditions (e.g. what it means and how it feels to live with chronic illness or to be unemployed) and how people manage certain situations (e.g. how people negotiate family life or relations with work colleagues). Qualitative researchers tend, therefore, to be concerned with the quality and texture of experience, rather than with the identification of cause–effect relationships. They do not tend to work with 'variables' that are defined by the researcher before the research process begins. This is because qualitative researchers tend to be interested in the meanings attributed to events by the research participants themselves. Using preconceived 'variables' would lead to the imposition of the researcher's meanings and it would preclude the identification of respondents' own ways of making sense of the phenomenon under investigation.
>
> (Willig 2008, p. 8–9)

Ideographic vs. nomothetic

ideographic approach

the conclusions of a study stay limited to the phenomenon under study

The emphasis on immersion in and understanding of a particular situation implies that qualitative research methods are not in the first place interested in generalisable knowledge. In principle their analysis is limited to the situation and the participant(s) at hand. This is called an ideographic approach, a study of what is relevant to the subject under study, as opposed to a nomothetic approach, a search for universal principles that exceed the confines of the study (i.e. the approach that is prominent in quantitative research).

Induction rather than deduction

nomothetic approach

a study is run in search for universal principles that exceed the confines of the study

Quantitative researchers often make use of predetermined variables because they have specific hypotheses to test as part of the hypothetico-deductive model they follow. In their research, theories are tested over and over again by deriving hypotheses from them and putting them to a falsification test. Each hypothesis deals with a particular detail of the theory. As a result, most research within the quantitative approach consists of testing details that have been produced on the basis of *deductive reasoning* (i.e. reasoning from theory to fact, in which one starts from known – or at least assumed – statements and deduces new conclusions).

bracketing

requirement in qualitative research to look at a phenomenon with an open mind and to free oneself from preconceptions

Qualitative researchers object to this approach because it entails a serious risk of the scientist missing the essentials of the situation. By constantly focusing on details, researchers easily lose sight of the wider picture. According to the qualitative psychologists, it is much more important to look with an open mind at the complete situation, rather than always homing in on a single detail. Instead of constantly using deductive reasoning, psychologists should pay more attention to *inductive reasoning* (i.e. reasoning from fact to theory, in which one tries to draw adequate conclusions on the basis of a series of convergent observations). The advice of qualitative psychologists to start an investigation by looking at the complete situation with an open mind and freeing themselves from their preconceptions is called bracketing (cf. Lemon and Taylor 1997).

Qualitative research is evidence-based

The above characteristics do not mean that data are less important for qualitative than for quantitative researchers. In qualitative research too a study depends on collecting and analysing empirical findings. In addition, these data must be gathered and made available in such a way that the conclusions can be verified by others. It is not the case that qualitative research is based on the researcher's intuitions and opinions. The main difference in data with quantitative research is that the findings typically are not coded in a numerical format. They comprise an organised set of verbal statements that in the researcher's eyes summarises the examined situation. Below we will see three examples of such analysis.

Data collection

Qualitative researchers stress the importance of 'rich information'. By this they mean information that in the participants' eyes adequately describes the situation. Rather than the researcher defining beforehand what aspects are of importance, the participants determine what will be found.

semi-structured interview

interview in which each interviewee gets a small set of core questions, but for the rest is encouraged to speak freely; achieved by making use of open-ended, non-directive questions

The most frequently used technique of data collection is the semi-structured interview. In such an interview, the interviewer uses a limited set of core questions, so that the answers of the participants can be compared, but for the rest encourages participants to speak freely. This is done by using open-ended and non-directive questions. Open-ended questions are questions that invite the interviewees to give their meaning rather than their agreement with the question (e.g. one would ask 'What do you think of qualitative research methods' rather than 'Do you think qualitative research methods are good?'). Non-directive questions are questions that do not give the participant an indication of the desired answer (e.g. a qualitative researcher would never ask 'Do you agree that qualitative research methods are useful?').

focus group

technique in which a group of participants freely discuss a limited set of questions

Another technique increasingly used in qualitative research is that of focus groups. In this technique the questions of the semi-structured interview are given as the basis of a discussion by a group of participants rather than by individual participants. This creates a different dynamic to face-to-face interviews and is more likely, for instance, to bring out differences in point of view between the participants.

Transcription and analysis of the data

Transcription

The raw materials of semi-structured interviews usually consist of auditory or visual recordings. These have to be transcribed in written form, so that they can easily be referred to. By making use of standardised codes, the transcription not only contains what was said, but also the non-verbal signals, such as hesitations, gestures and intonations. This part of the research is usually very time-intensive, but ensures the easy availability of the raw materials.

After the transcription, the written records are numbered. The text is torn apart into its constituent parts, which are numbered. Usually, the numbering is very detailed, going down to the level of individual sentences and even single phrases. Before researchers start doing this, it is recommended they go through the texts/interviews a few times, so that they have a good feel of the topics that are covered.

Data analysis

In a qualitative analysis the investigator rewrites the raw materials as a flow chart of core ideas, based on multiple close readings and guided by the questions emphasised by the different approaches (see below). The analysis requires an adequate classification of the various statements into a number of (recurring) themes and clear ideas of how the components are interconnected. The researcher tries to encompass the data as comprehensively and systematically as possible. The analysis keeps cycling through the materials, until saturation is reached. All the time the researcher remains vigilant not to overlook elements or to bias the interpretation towards a preconceived theory. Software programs are available to number and rephrase the various statements and integrate them within the coding scheme.

In the remainder of this section, we discuss three main approaches used in qualitative research (see Willig (2008) and Smith (2008) for further details and more techniques). They are: grounded theory, interpretative phenomenological analysis (IPA) and discourse analysis.

Grounded theory

grounded theory

qualitative research method that tries to understand what is going on in a particular situation and that on the basis of a qualitative analysis and induction tries to come to a theoretical insight grounded in the data

Grounded theory is the oldest of the techniques described here. It is based on the book *Discovery of Grounded Theory* (1967) by the Chicago sociologists Glaser and Strauss. Its name derives from the explicit goal of coming to theoretical insights that are grounded in the data. Glaser and Strauss wrote their book as a reaction against the then dominant sociological approach of formulating large, abstract theories without much empirical input.

In a grounded theory analysis, the investigator rewrites the raw materials on the basis of questions such as 'What is going on here?', 'What are the main problems of the participants?', 'How do they try to solve them?' On the basis of these questions, the participants' answers are recoded into a sequence of themes, which are then grouped into higher-order categories. According to Glaser and Strauss (1967) this makes it possible for a theory to emerge from the data through inductive reasoning.

The best way to have a feeling for what is going on in a grounded theory analysis is to look at a case study. The example we describe uses a grounded theory analysis to find out why students procrastinate.

CASE STUDY

An example of grounded theory: Why do students procrastinate?

Schraw *et al.* (2007) examined academic procrastination with the grounded theory. Their goal was to get a complete picture of the phenomenon, starting from the conflicting observations that many people view it as a negative personality trait but at the same time that the majority of students seem to do it. The available quantitative data were largely in line with the negative view, as questionnaire data pointed to negative correlations with health, long-term learning and self-esteem, and positive correlations with anxiety and fear of failure. As a consequence, most researchers conceptualised procrastination as a combination of three components: fear of failure, task aversiveness and laziness.

▶

CASE STUDY *(continued)*

Schraw *et al.* described the reasons for starting their study as follows (pp. 12–13):

The purpose of the present research was to construct a grounded theory of procrastination on the basis of college students' reports about their own procrastination. We did so for several reasons. One is that there is relatively little research on procrastination, even though it is a commonly occurring phenomenon among college students. Second, most of the existing research has reported correlations between self-reported procrastinatory behavior and academic outcomes, such as grades and study time. We hoped to expand on this research by providing a more in-depth descriptive account of academic procrastination. Third, and most important to us, there is no existing theory or process model of procrastination. We conducted the present research to examine the process by which procrastination occurs and to propose a preliminary paradigm model . . . that can be tested in future research.

The study involved 67 students over a total of four phases (table 10.4). In the first phase a combination of focus groups and semi-structured interviews was used to identify the themes students found important with respect to procrastination. The general instructions were (p. 15):

I'm going to ask you about academic procrastination. I'm interested in how you define it, factors that affect whether you procrastinate, and whether there are positive or negative consequences. I have a structured interview with some follow-up probes after each question. Please take your time when responding and focus on your own procrastination behavior rather than other students. If you would like to return to a point that you discussed earlier, feel free to do so.

Table 10.4 Phases involved in the Schraw *et al.* (2007) study

Phase	Coding	Semester	Purpose	Participants (*n*)
1	Open	1	Identify codes within categories for further analysis.	26 (20 in focus groups; 6 individual interviews)
2	Axial	2–6	Explore codes in detail; relate codes to one another to construct themes.	18 individual interviews
3	Selective	6 and 7	Construct paradigm model and discuss themes in relation to model; establish story line that integrates paradigm model.	12 individual interviews
4	Selective	8	Test, validate and explicate paradigm model until saturated; identify emergent principles consistent with paradigm model; conduct member checks.	11 individual interviws

CASE STUDY *(continued)*

Answers were sought for the following open-ended questions:

1. How would you describe academic procrastination?
2. What do you do when you procrastinate?
3. Are there situations where you are most likely to procrastinate?
4. How do you cope when you do procrastinate?
5. What are some of the positive and negative consequences of procrastination?

   Table 10.5 lists the 33 codes that were extracted from phase 1, together with the five categories in which they were classified. In phase 2 structured in-depth interviews were held with students to get a better

Table 10.5 Codes extracted from phase 1 in the Schraw *et al.* (2007) study

Category	Code
Antecedents of procrastination	1. Lack of personal interest
	2. Lack of task-relevant knowledge
	3. Aversive task
	4. Better use of resources to delay work
	5. Competing interests
	6. Lack of focus
	7. Laziness
	8. Low motivation
	9. Poor instruction
Definitions of procrastination	10. Putting things off that need to be done
	11. Deferring necessary work
	12. Postponing important tasks
Contexts and conditions that affect procrastination	13. Busy with other activities
	14. Grades
	15. Belief that effort doesn't help
	16. Help from others
	17. Low study self-efficacy
	18. Poor study strategies
	19. Teacher doesn't hold students accountable
	20. Poor teaching
	21. Stress
Coping strategies	22. Make a schedule
	23. Manage time
	24. Plan and prioritise
	25. Work with other students
	26. Monitor negative self-talk
	27. Use a variety of study strategies
Consequences	28. Guilt
	29. Less effort put into schoolwork
	30. Greater productivity
	31. Increased stress
	32. Procrastination does not affect quality of work
	33. Increased confidence

▶

CASE STUDY *(continued)*

understanding of each of the five categories. On the basis of these interviews, the structure was refined by inserting macrothemes between the categories and the initial codes (now reduced to 29 themes). Phase 3 was used to further check and polish the structure distilled from phase 2 by means of a new set of structured interviews. Table 10.6 shows the structure resulting from phases 2 and 3.

Table 10.6 Refined structure resulting from the interviews of phases 2 and 3 in the Schraw *et al.* (2007) study

Category	Macrotheme	Theme
Antecedents of procrastination	1. Task	1. Low background knowledge
		2. Task difficulty
	2. Self	3. Interest
		4. Organisational skills
	3. Teacher	5. Clear expectations for course
		6. Well-organised course materials
		7. Tests and graded assignments
Definitions of procrastination phenomenon	4. Adaptive aspects of procrastination	8. Cognitive efficiency
		9. Peak work experience
	5. Maladaptive aspects of procrastination	10. Laziness
		11. Fear of failure
		12. Postponement of work
Contexts and conditions that affect procrastination	6. Unclear directions	13. Ill-defined course content
		14. Unclear criteria for grading
	7. Deadlines	15. Lack of due dates for assignments
	8. Lack of incentives	16. Low intrinsic motivation: high self-efficacy
		17. Low impact of procrastination on grades
Coping strategies	9. Cognitive	18. Identifying clear learning goals
		19. Planning and organising future work
		20. Budgeting resources (time and effort)
	10. Affective	21. Reframing
		22. Protective self-talk
		23. Stress reduction (physical and psychological)
Consequences of procrastination	11. Quality of life	24. Cognitive efficiency
		25. Improved quality of work
		26. Peak work experience
	12. Quality of work	27. Increased efficiency
		28. Cognitive incubation
		29. Less revision of work

CASE STUDY *(continued)*

In phase 4, 11 new students were interviewed individually and asked to respond to the model as displayed in table 10.6. This step helped to ensure, according to the authors, that the final model was fully saturated, dependable and credible.

On the basis of the model in table 10.6, Schraw *et al.* (2007) distilled six emergent principles that affected students' procrastination:

1. *Minimum time:* Students have busy lives with the following sequence of priorities: personal relationships, work and study. The amount of study time is minimised to maximise the time available for friends and work. Procrastination enables students to delay as much study as possible until the last weeks of the semester. This is done more to safeguard personal time than to avoid failure or indulge laziness.

2. *Optimum efficiency:* A concentrated effort late in the semester increases productivity, creativity and quality of work, and reduces wasted time due to boredom and false starts.

3. *Peak affective experience:* Working hard towards a deadline creates a state of 'flow' by increasing motivation and eliminating distractions.

4. *Early assessment of work requirements:* Procrastination often is the result of planning. Students at the beginning of term gauge the efforts that will be needed for a particular course and adapt to them. As a result, procrastination tends to increase as students become senior, because they can better assess the demands of the courses.

5. *Open escape routes:* Students protect themselves against the negative psychological consequences of procrastination by engaging in three self-handicapping thoughts: (1) it is a necessary evil, (2) I am satisfied with a B rather than an A, and (3) I learn the big ideas and forget the rest.

6. *Rewards:* There are rewards associated with procrastination, such as more rapid feedback, and the sudden and intense release of stress once the deadline is met.

Schraw *et al.* (2007) stressed that their conclusions, which deviated substantially from the available conclusions on the basis of quantitative, correlational research, were interpretative in nature and required further investigation.

Phenomenological analysis

Unease with grounded theory

Although grounded theory was warmly received by the hermeneutically oriented psychologists, it soon turned out to have limitations. The first was that grounded theory largely assumed the existence of an objective reality that was there to be discovered. In this respect, grounded theory stayed close to mainstream psychology based on quantitative research. The findings that emerged from a grounded theory analysis were meant to describe 'reality'.

A second problem was that grounded theory stressed the importance of inductive reasoning (from data to theory) and verification (up to the saturation point). As you may remember from Chapter 8, these were exactly the criteria identified by the logical positivists for good scientific research. Scientists had to begin with careful observations, from which theories would emerge, and the truth of theories could be established by means of empirical verification. Given that these tenets of logical positivism were completely overthrown by twentieth-century philosophy of science, they are shaky foundations for good research. Even Glaser and Strauss in later writings disagreed as to what extent a grounded theory analysis could be completely theory-neutral, with Strauss being less convinced that data could be gathered and analysed adequately without making use of some pre-existing theoretical framework. One way in which grounded theory has responded to this criticism was by accepting that the outcome of an analysis is not a description of reality, but a social construction by the researcher (see Willig 2008). Other researchers, however, sought a more radical alternative.

A final problem with grounded theory for psychological research was that it did not take into account the fact that the data provided by the participants actually comprised their perceptions and interpretations of what was happening. In this respect, it became clear that grounded theory had found its origin in sociology where the research topics may be less dependent on the participants' views than in psychology.

Inspiration from Husserl

To address the problems with grounded theory, hermeneutically inspired psychologists stressed that the primary aim of qualitative research was to examine what reality looked like for the participants, leaving open the question whether in psychology there is something of an objective, person-independent reality.

A main source of inspiration came from the phenomenology of the Austrian-German philosopher Edmund Husserl (1859–1938). Husserl's phenomenology stressed that psychology should be a reflective study of consciousness as experienced from the first-person point of view. With respect to mainstream psychological research, Husserl warned that it had turned away from the concrete human experience too rapidly. Psychology had been too eager to study the 'objective reality', rather than the world as perceived by people. By developing abstract and unexamined concepts to describe this 'reality', psychological research risked to address spurious issues because the concepts they used were not properly grounded in experience. In Husserl's eyes it was much better for psychology to return to the experience itself. The human experience was not in the first place a matter of lawful responses to events in the environment, but a system of interrelated meanings, which Husserl called a Gestalt or *Lebenswelt* ('lifeworld'; see also Ashworth 2003).

Husserl's views gave rise to the so-called *phenomenological analysis* in qualitative research. A widely used variant of such analysis in psychology is the interpretative phenomenological analysis (IPA; Smith, 1996, 2008), which we will use in the rest of our discussion.

interpretative phenomeno- logical analysis

qualitative research method in psychology that tries to understand how a phenomenon is experienced by the people involved

How does IPA work?

IPA resembles very much the analysis in grounded theory (cf. Willig 2008, p. 72–3). Both proceed by systematically going through the transcriptions identifying themes that can be clustered into higher-order categories, which capture the essence of the phenomenon under investigation. They are both based on a limited number of single-case studies which are combined to get a more complete picture.

The main difference between IPA and grounded theory is that IPA is centred on how participants make sense of their personal and social world. It attempts to explore the personal experience and is concerned with the participant's personal account, not with an understanding of the phenomenon itself. Therefore, guiding questions are

'How is this perceived by the participant?', 'What meaning does the participant attach to this event?' and 'How does the participant make sense of this situation?'

In addition, IPA acknowledges the input from the researcher, who tries to make sense of the participants trying to make sense of their world. Possible guiding questions in this respect are 'What is the person trying to achieve here?' and 'Is something leaking out here that was not intended?' The researcher's involvement does not mean that the researcher is allowed to introduce obvious biases. As a matter of fact, as in all other qualitative methods, investigators are advised to bracket as much as possible and to approach the new situation open-mindedly. However, because this is not totally possible IPA accepts that some form of meta-interpretation from the part of the researcher is inevitable.

Reid *et al.* (2005, p. 20) identified the following key elements of IPA:

- It is an inductive approach going from data to understanding (i.e. it is 'bottom-up' rather than 'top-down'). It does not test hypotheses, and prior assumptions are avoided.

- IPA aims to capture and explore the meanings that participants assign to their experiences. Participants are experts on their own experiences and can offer researchers an understanding of their thoughts and feelings.

- Researchers reduce the complexity of the raw data through rigorous and systematic analysis.

- The analysis is primarily focused on what is specific for the phenomenon studied (cf. the ideographic approach), although it usually also attempts to take into account what is shared by the various participants in the study (i.e. it includes an element of the nomothetic approach).

- The resulting analysis is interpretative (i.e. it does not have the status of fact).

- A successful analysis is transparent (grounded in the data of the study) and plausible (to the participants, co-analysts and readers).

- Researchers should reflect upon their role in the process.

To give you a clearer picture of what an IPA involves, we again include a case study, this time on how the chronic fatigue syndrome is experienced by patients.

CASE STUDY

An example of IPA: How is the chronic fatigue syndrome experienced?

Dickson, Knussen and Flowers (2008) examined the experiences of people living with the chronic fatigue syndrome (CFS). They had semi-structured, in-depth interviews with 14 patients. Each participant was interviewed individually. The researchers had prepared a number of non-directive, open-ended questions which were used in a flexible way. Typical questions included 'Tell me about your experience with CFS', 'What aspects of your life has CFS impacted on most?', 'In what ways?' and 'How have other people reacted to your condition?'

▶

CASE STUDY *(continued)*

Transcripts were analysed manually for recurrent themes using IPA. When the same themes appeared in at least half of the transcripts, they were categorised as being recurrent (i.e. offered some scope for nomothetic conclusions). Analysis was centred on capturing the meaning of the phenomenon to the participant, taking into account the inevitability of the researchers' interpretative engagement with the transcripts.

Three recurrent, inter-related themes were identified:

1. *Identity crisis, agency and embodiment:* This theme comprised a feeling of personal loss characterised by profound diminishing personal control and agency, as exemplified by the following statement: 'CFS is a dictator. It dictates my everyday life. It determines what I can and cannot do. It controls my body and my mind and every part of my being.'

2. *Scepticism and the self:* This theme referred to difficulties in social interactions because of scepticism about the wider society. It is exemplified in the following excerpt: 'Well, people thought you were a malingerer . . . That you were "at it" and there was this idea that you were just lazy'. This led to a sense of crisis of the self: 'I started to think to myself "Am I just making this up? Is it all in my head?".'

3. *Acceptance, adjustment and coping:* This theme referred to the attempts made by the patients towards acceptance, adjustment and coping with their situation, as shown in the following statement: 'It's all about accepting the illness and learning to deal with it. Accepting it stops you from feeling down in the dumps and it helps you just to take each day as it comes. That helps a lot. You know that you're going to have good days and bad days and that people don't understand what you have, you've just got to get through it.'

Discourse analysis

The linguistic turn in the philosophy of science and in critical psychology

discourse analysis

qualitative research method that aims to discover how social relations between people are determined by the language they use

The final qualitative analysis we discuss is discourse analysis. This analysis investigates the ways in which language constructs social reality. It is a direct consequence of the linguistic turn in the philosophy of science and in critical psychology, which claims that reality is nothing but a social construction based on language and culture (Chapters 8 and 9). On this view, language is the only topic worth investigating because it makes the world in which humans live.

According to Alvesson (2000) the linguistic turn in postmodernist writings influenced the development of qualitative research in three ways:

1. Researchers turned their attention from reality to language and examined the possibilities and impossibilities language brought with it.

2. Researchers became particularly interested in language use in real-world or naturally occurring settings (as opposed to artificial, research-related settings).

3. Finally, there was an enhanced reflexivity on the part of the researchers regarding their own language use. Research reports were no longer seen as dispassionate, transparent accounts of social reality, but as stylised, rhetorical and constructed accounts intended to have an impact.

How are relations between people determined by the language they use and how do people try to achieve goals by means of their language?

As was the case for grounded analysis and phenomenological analysis, there are several variants of discourse analysis (see, e.g. Willig 2008). They all have in common that they try to determine how participants use discursive resources and what effects this has. How do participants use language to manage social interactions? How do they use language to achieve objectives? In which roles are participants pushed by the language they use and how does this relate to the power balance between them? What can be said by whom, where and when?

A comparison of discourse analysis with grounded theory and phenomenological analysis

To illustrate the specific character of discourse analysis, we make use of a study by Starks and Trinidad (2007), who not only applied discourse analysis but also grounded theory and phenomenological analysis to the same set of raw materials. The materials consisted of interviews with 25 general practitioners (GPs) about prostate cancer screening. In this situation a difficult choice exists between on the one hand recommending a screening (which involves a rather distressing examination in addition to the likelihood of a false alarm and even the unnecessary treatment of a benign ailment) and on the other hand not recommending such a screening (involving the risk of the patient developing a lethal cancer).

The GPs were asked a number of open-ended, non-directive questions meant to elicit rich discussions of the problems involved in raising the issue of prostate cancer screening (PCS) with patients. Starks and Trinidad analysed the transcripts of the interviews along the dimensions advocated by grounded theory, phenomenological analysis and discourse analysis.

Grounded theory was used to build a theory of what was going in discussions between GPs and patients on the desirability of a PCS-test and how these visits could be improved. It concerned an analysis of the circumstances leading to such a discussion and how GPs and patients engaged in the discussion. Starks and Trinidad used the 'six Cs' of social processes as guiding principles in the analysis of the transcripts (what are the causes, contexts, contingencies, consequences, covariances and conditions of a discussion about a PCS-test?). As part of this analysis, they discovered that an important factor deciding whether a discussion would take place consisted of the limitations imposed by the appointment schedule on the GP (mostly 10 to 15 minutes per patient). Another important variable was the patients' expectations about such screening. GPs were most likely to give full information when patients had not yet made up their mind and showed an interest in the pros and cons of the alternatives. On the basis of the grounded theory analysis, Starks and Trinidad were able to formulate a theory about the logistical, professional and personal constraints that limited the GP's likelihood of giving enough information so that patients could make an informed decision about which action to take in their particular case.

The purpose of *phenomenological analysis* was to understand how GPs experienced an uncertain clinical decision-making process within the larger context of the doctor–patient relationship. For instance, many interviewees expressed their discomfort with the fact that they could not meet their patients' expectations because there are no clear recommendations for prostate cancer screening. A typical comment was: 'It's hard [to have these discussions with patients] because the data stinks, and there's so much misinformation and so much promotion of prostate cancer screening that it puts the primary care physician who wants to be evidence-based in a very difficult position . . . And so, you leave the patient with, this "Well, I have no clue what to do," kind of a handout' (Starks and Trinidad 2007, p. 1378).

Finally, the *discourse analysis* was concerned with the question how the discourse in medicine and public health constructed the roles, identities and interactions between patients and GPs in PCS discussions. For instance, the discourse of medicine strongly pushes GPs into the roles of expert diagnostician, scientist practising evidence-based medicine, and advisor to the patients. This gives GPs a high status and helps them, for instance, when they want to have a PCS-test done on a particular patient. However, it also puts them in a difficult position when they want to explain to patients that prostate cancer screening is not always indicated, certainly if at the same time they want to convey the message that regular cancer screenings in general are a good idea. Under these circumstances the GPs often found themselves confronted with the fact that their knowledge was more limited than expected from their role, as can be seen in the following comment: 'What I would really like to have – and I know these exist, so I guess it's mainly my own fault that I don't have it, honestly – is the accepted age-based normal range for PSA [prostate specific antigen testing], and secondly, the likelihood of prostate cancer based on PSA reading and age' (Starks and Trinidad 2007, p. 1378). [Notice how the GP in this statement tried to affirm his/her role as expert diagnostician, evidence-based scientist and advisor, even in the light of faltering knowledge.]

By analysing the communication between doctors and patients, the discourse analysis aimed to discover what these individuals did while they were communicating, how they created a common reality by means of language, and how their communication coordinated their activities. According to Starks and Trinidad such an analysis can be used to shed light on why GPs fail to give enough information for patients to make an informed decision.

Table 10.7 summarises the specificities of the three different approaches for the study of Starks and Trinidad.

Table 10.7 Informed Decision Making (IDM) as seen through the different approaches

A comparison of three qualitative research approaches to the question of how general practitioners (GPs) discuss prostate cancer screening with their average-risk patients.

	Grounded theory	**Phenomenology**	**Discourse analysis**
Research question	How does IDM about prostate cancer screening happen between GPs and their average-risk patients?	What is the lived experience of GPs as they discuss prostate cancer screening with their patients?	What discourses are used in IDM, and how do they shape GP and patient roles and identities in the doctor–patient relationship?
Purpose	To develop effective training and education for GPs about how to approach prostate cancer screening discussions	To understand GPs' experience of decision making with patients under conditions of clinical uncertainty	To shed light on the reasons for the limited or incomplete adoption of IDM by GPs

Source: adapted from Starks and Trinidad (2007)

What do you think?

If you had to choose one qualitative approach for a study, which one would you take? Why?

Strengths of qualitative research

Directly focused on understanding situations and solving problems

Qualitative research is directly aimed at understanding a problem and working towards a solution. This is different from the detour quantitative research makes by trying to reach the truth via rejecting false explanations. In this respect, it is no coincidence that the major drive behind qualitative research has come from applied psychology, where psychologists are confronted with specific cases that need to be solved (see the engineers' approach in table 10.3). In such situations, the search for generalisable, universal principles is often secondary to a focused intervention. A client interacting with a counsellor is not interested in the counsellor compulsively trying to falsify wrong accounts, but is helped by a counsellor who tries to understand what is going on and helps find ways to cope with the situation. Similarly, a company consulting a psychologist about a publicity campaign is more interested in what would work than in hearing what would be ineffective.

Stratton (1997) described how his group became involved in research, paid for by British Airways, into the needs of long-haul air passengers. The research was one of the studies the company repeatedly ran to discover what its customers wanted, so that they not only could improve their service, but also knew how best to advertise and whether there was scope for 'new product development', finding a market for something that did not yet exist. Stratton argued that in particular the last two goals could not easily be studied with quantitative research and profited from an in-depth qualitative approach.

Generation of new ideas and elaboration of theories

Because qualitative studies involve intensive investigations, they are particularly well suited for finding new ideas. Quantitative studies, in which a specific hypothesis is tested, constrain the situation to such an extent that only a yes/no-answer is expected. This type of study is perfect for the deductive part of the hypothetico-deductive method, but does not provide much inspiration for the theory-building part. A qualitative study like Schraw *et al.*'s (2007) on procrastination in students can result in a series of new ideas to be tested. In the same vein, a qualitative study can lead to an extensive elaboration of a theory if it shows that the existing quantitative research has measured only a small part of a much wider phenomenon.

An interesting analogy in this respect was reported by Vandenbroucke (2008). He noticed that the hierarchy of evidence in medical science (figure 10.2) was a hierarchy to decide whether a treatment or pathogen had the expected effect (i.e. to evaluate a hypothesis). When it came to discovery of new facts or explanations, the hierarchy actually had to be inversed. A new discovery was least likely on the basis of a meta-analysis and most probable as part of a case report.

More perceptive to the needs of the participants

Because qualitative researchers want to understand events as they are perceived by the participants, they will have a much better feeling for the participants' needs. This decreases the risk of advice that is perceived as unhelpful by the participants. Given that science proceeds by trial and error (see Chapter 8), a potentially erroneous intervention is extra painful if it has not been experienced as helpful by the persons involved.

Limits of qualitative research

Limits of inductive reasoning and verification

Qualitative research stresses the importance of inductive reasoning (from data to theory) and verification (up to the saturation point). As we saw above, these problems were raised in particular with respect to grounded theory. However, they apply to all the methods we discussed. Although qualitative researchers took their inspiration from postmodernist critiques of the scientific method, it cannot be denied that they in fact returned to the very first scientific method recommended by philosophers of science and since successfully criticised by Popper and Kuhn.

Less well suited to decide between theories

Because qualitative methods stress the inductive part of research, they are extremely well suited for charting new grounds and infusing new ideas in a discipline (i.e. theory generation and elaboration). However, they fare less well when it comes to deciding between ideas and theories. Suppose that other researchers find the topic of experiences in the chronic fatigue syndrome interesting and decide to repeat Dickson *et al.* (2008). Should they then start from the findings of Dickson *et al.* or should they bracket themselves and start anew from scratch? Furthermore, if they find deviating results, what conclusions are they to draw? That their study differed from the original one and that both conclusions have equal value given that they were never meant to be nomothetic? Suppose 50 groups of researchers ran a study equal to Dickson *et al.*'s. Who would be able to make sense of the various differences reported by the different groups? Or would that be a pointless question, given that each study was ideographic and not meant to be compared with the others?

Qualitative methods are based on introspection

The reason why qualitative methods create difficulties in deciding between competing conclusions is that in the end they go back to introspective opinions, formulated by participants (in face-to-face interviews or in focus groups) and interpreted by researchers. In the absence of an external criterion, it is impossible to decide between conflicting opinions of people.

When evaluating the conclusions of introspective research (both qualitative and quantitative), it may be good to keep in mind that introspection still has the same precarious status it had in the early days of psychology (Chapters 3 and 4). People have no knowledge of many things they do and factors that influence them (Chapter 6). In addition, a century of psychological research has shown that even if people have strong opinions, they do not always agree with their actions. This is not the place to go into this literature, but the quotes below may be a good reminder of what is at issue (they also contain pointers for those who want to explore this literature in more depth).

Recent developments in the behavioral-, cognitive- and neurosciences indicate that, more often than not, we act in an automatic and unaware fashion, making up reasons only as we go along . . . We are not directly aware of what drives our actions but infer reasons on the basis of a priori causal theories, confabulating them if we cannot find reasonable explanations . . . So many causal factors escape consciousness that confabulation seems to be the rule rather than the exception . . . Even our moral judgments seem to be based on intuitions that are not, or are only partially, accessible to introspection. The reasons we come up with to justify these judgments are post hoc rationalizations that had no role in their generation . . .

(Sie and Wouters 2008, p. 3)

. . . the vast adaptive unconscious is dissociated from conscious awareness and can never be directly viewed via introspection. Introspection reveals the contents of consciousness, such as at least some of people's current thoughts and feelings. It cannot, however, no matter how deeply people dig, gain direct access to nonconscious mental processes. Instead, people must attempt to infer the nature of these processes, by taking what they know (e.g. their conscious states) and filling in the gaps of what they do not know (their nonconscious states) by constructing a coherent narrative about themselves.

(Wilson and Dunn 2004, p. 505)

The researcher's involvement may be a disadvantage in high-stakes situations

Finally, qualitative researchers acknowledge that the outcome of a study to some extent depends on the person who does the study. The researcher has an impact on the interview and colours the analysis. Although such a state of affairs may be acceptable in fundamental research and in some areas of applied psychology (e.g. when the intervention can be tailor-made to the individual client), there are other situations in which psychologists may find themselves vulnerable to criticism. In general, society is not too happy when high-stakes decisions like personnel selection, university admissions or probation judgements differ too much from one psychologist to another. In those situations psychologists have to show that they adhere to standardised instruments that have a high inter-rater reliability and that have proven their validity (Chapters 7 and 12).

Interim summary

The essence of qualitative research

- Qualitative research methods are directed at understanding phenomena in their historical and socio-cultural context. They are based on the following assumptions:
  - In psychology there is little or no evidence for a reality outside people's perception and experience.
  - Attempts to control the situation make the setting artificial and no longer meaningful.

Interim summary (continued)

- Researchers must immerse themselves in the situation so that they can understand the meaning of the situation.
- Qualitative research is in the first place meant to understand specific situations (ideographic), not to come to general rules (nomothetic).
- Induction is more important than deduction; the researcher must approach the situation open-mindedly and accept the input from the participants.
- Qualitative research must remain evidence-based, starting from a careful and verifiable collection of data.

- Data collection usually occurs by means of semi-structured interviews with a limited number of participants; increasingly also use of focus groups.

- The data need to be transcribed and analysed up to saturation along the lines proposed by the qualitative method that is used.

- Three methods were described:
  - Grounded theory: introduced by sociologists, tries to understand the phenomenon.
  - Interpretative phenomenological analysis (IPA): inspired by phenomenology (Husserl), tries to understand the ways in which the phenomenon is perceived and experienced by the participants.
  - Discourse analysis: inspired by postmodernism, tries to understand how language constructs human interactions.

- Strengths:
  - Directly focused on understanding situations and solving problems.
  - Generation of new ideas and elaboration of theories.
  - More attention to the participants' needs.

- Weaknesses:
  - Based on induction and verification.
  - No external criterion to decide between theories.
  - Based on introspection (with the risk of participants confabulating).
  - Input from the researcher may be a problem in high-stake situations.

10.3 How do quantitative and qualitative research methods relate to each other?

Now that we have discussed the two types of research methods, we can ask ourselves how they relate to each other. As you can imagine, the existence of two types of methods related to two different views about the nature of psychology (natural-science oriented vs. hermeneutics oriented) has given rise to a great deal of controversy. The various positions can be divided into two groups. On the one hand, there are psychologists who strongly feel that the two types of research cannot coexist and, therefore, that psychology must make a choice. On the other hand, there are psychologists who see both types of methods as complementary, each with their own weaknesses and strengths, and that psychology gains by combining them. Below we discuss the two stances.

What do you think?

Before you start reading about the different sides of the controversy it may be interesting for you to establish for yourself where you stand at this moment. After having read the essentials of the quantitative and the qualitative research methods, to what extent do you see them as incompatible or complementary?

The two types of research are incompatible

Incompatibility of the underlying paradigms

Psychologists who stress the incompatibility of quantitative and qualitative research methods emphasise the different world views underlying them: objective reality vs. social construction, natural sciences vs. humanities, hypothetico-deductive research vs. hermeneutics, mainstream psychology vs. critical psychology, and above all positivism vs. postmodernism. According to these authors, the approaches are so contradictory that trying to integrate them results either in an oxymoron or a stealthy attempt to win back lost ground. This is the 'paradigm war' referred to in the opening of this chapter. Below we discuss some examples.

Quantitative psychology's arguments against the need for qualitative psychology

A first argument fervent quantitative psychologists use against qualitative methods is that the hermeneutic and postmodernist movements throw away all the progress that has been made in the past 150 years and catapult psychology back to the early 1800s, before psychology became seen as the scientific study of mental life (Chapter 3).

> Psychology would become, as it is in some parts of Europe, an arts-based discipline; its funding would decline; and scientific psychologists would leave to take up appointments in departments of cognitive science or neuroscience . . .
>
> There are some issues which can be solved by finding a middle way, and others where one has to make a choice. My opinion is that we have to reject postmodernism from scientific psychology, if only to have a coherent teaching programme. We cannot have one set of lecturers explaining to students how to study psychology scientifically, and another set of lecturers telling the same students that when studying people, the methods of science are no use. It won't work, and psychology departments won't work.
>
> *(Morgan 1998, p. 481–2)*

Another argument against qualitative research methods is that they reject the existence of an objective reality, which is the *raison d'être* of science.

> I began this debate by suggesting that qualitative psychologists pose a threat to traditional notions of psychology as a science. The problem is not that they use single case studies; it is not that they may find no use for statistics; it is not even that they reject the goal of quantitative laws. The real problem is that they reject the notion of something 'out there' which can be studied objectively.
>
> *(Morgan 1998, p. 488)*

A final criticism heard from proponents of the quantitative research methods is that qualitative research methods do not provide researchers with new information and devalue psychological research to pop-psychology. Again, Morgan (1998) phrased this most cogently:

> [They seem] to be making the claim that the aim of psychology should be to understand people, and that one can only understand people by forming social relationships with them, to which scientific objectivity is a barrier. To this one could reply that we have been forming social relationships with one another for some half a million years, and have indeed got to understand one another quite well at a certain level as a result.
>
> But it is unlikely that qualitative psychology will improve this intuitive understanding unless it brings some new technique to the job, and I have yet to be convinced that the techniques go beyond those of good investigative journalism. 'Forming relationships' with people is the job of everyone; I see no reason to pay researchers to do it. Something a bit different is expected from scientists.
>
> *(Morgan 1998, p. 482)*

Qualitative psychology's arguments against the need for quantitative psychology

For each of the arguments put forward by quantitative researchers, a similar argument can be found among ardent qualitative supporters. They too see quantitative and qualitative research as incompatible, but argue that quantitative psychology should be dropped. They question the superiority of scientific knowledge and hold that mainstream psychologists clutch at the scientific method not because it has brought understanding of human functioning, but because it has brought status and money to psychology departments. This has been formulated most eloquently by Stevenson and Cooper (1997) in an otherwise more moderate paper.

> The adoption of a positivist position allows psychology to maintain 'scientific' respectability. Psychology as a discipline and profession therefore has a vested interest in maintaining the dominance of objectivity in relation to the production of psychological knowledge.
>
> The emergence of constructivist approaches creates a particular form of knowledge that appears to challenge the nature of psychology itself by suggesting that knowledge (and therefore psychology) is socially constructed, and that knowledge

is associated with power. Perhaps because of the potentially far-reaching conse-quences for the discipline of adopting a qualitative inquiry position, the legitimacy of qualitative research is frequently questioned.

(Stevenson and Cooper 1997, p. 159)

Qualitative psychologists further argue that quantitative research is misguided in its search for the 'objective reality': If something like an objective reality existed in psy-chology, one would have expected quantitative psychology to be more successful after 150 years.

What about the claimed solidity of traditional psychological knowledge? It has become characteristic of our discipline that different theories, each equally empiri-cally confirmed according to prevailing standards, exist side by side. We are point-ing here to more than a mere multiplicity of theories. Rather, they make universal claims about identical objects on the basis of incompatible (or at least mutually problematic) concepts, and we are in no position to be able to decide which of the theories is tenable and which ought to be rejected. (A comparable situation would exist in physics if there were half a dozen permanently competing theories about the free fall of objects.)

(Maiers 1991, p. 33)

Finally, the hardcore qualitative psychologists argue that if there is no objective reality, quantitative research methods have nothing to tell us about human func-tioning. All they can do is give us replicable, useless information.

I am far less sanguine about the predictions of artificial and culturally isolated behaviors often used in testing abstract hypotheses about mental function. The question is not whether such hypotheses are true or false in any ultimate sense but whether the particular predictions have any utility outside the local game of truth. As I see it, a postmodern empiricism would replace the 'truth game' with a search for culturally useful theories and findings with significant cultural meaning.

(Gergen 2001, p. 808)

Attempts to reconcile quantitative and qualitative research methods are stabs to regain lost ground

Psychologists who consider qualitative and quantitative research as incompatible often mistrust efforts to unite them, because they see these efforts as disguised attempts to regain lost ground. The quantitative researchers consider those efforts as the latest attempt of hermeneutics to grab a slice of the cake after the status of psy-choanalysis declined in the second half of the twentieth century. The qualitative researchers fear that the integration attempts by quantitative psychology are meant to seize the qualitative research methods under the umbrella of positivist psychology, oppressing everything that is typical for the qualitative methods, such as the convictions that participants should be studied in rich contexts of history, society and culture, that people should be studied in meaningful situations which form part of their life worlds, and that mental life consists of social constructions on the basis of language and culture.

Marecek (2003) described four myths about qualitative methods that are prevalent among quantitative researchers who treat qualitative research methods as just another type of research:

1. Qualitative and quantitative psychology are complementary methods and lead to the same type of understanding.

2. Qualitative research is an adjunct to quantitative research; its findings are an interesting first step but they require further quantitative exploration.

3. Qualitative research only consists of inductive reasoning.

4. Qualitative research is nothing but psychology without numbers.

According to Marecek, if one opts for qualitative research, one should also opt for the values that underlie this approach.

The two types of research complement each other

The other view, which is rapidly gaining popularity (e.g. Todd *et al.* 2004), is that qualitative and quantitative research methods can be used in tandem depending on the question one wants to answer. Such a view is found, for instance, in Lee *et al.* (1999, p. 164), who wrote about the use of qualitative research in organisational and vocational psychology that:

> Summarizing across these major characteristics and themes, [we conclude] that qualitative research is *well* suited for the purposes of description, interpretation, and explanation. In particular, it can effectively address questions such as 'What is occurring?' and 'How is it occurring?' In contrast, qualitative research is *not well* suited for issues of prevalence, generalizability, and calibration. For example, it cannot effectively answer a question such as 'How much—of whatever it is—is occurring?' Thus, the kinds of questions that are answered by qualitative and quantitative research methods differ. Perhaps needless to say, organizational and vocational psychologists should apply the method that best fits their theoretical question and analytical situation. In our judgment, qualitative methods simply offer additional and more specialized tools that seem likely to be useful for *some* of our research.

Similar statements can be found in many other recent texts, making it likely that in the future quantitative and qualitative research methods will be used in combination. Psychologists who defend this position are less concerned with the contradictions in the underlying philosophies but focus on what the methods themselves deliver in terms of information. They point out that those who argue for incompatibility exaggerate the differences between the approaches at the expense of the commonalities, and that each method to some extent compensates for weaknesses in the other.

Quantitative research is more than a positivist search for physical laws

Quantitative psychologists are depicted by hardcore qualitative psychologists as positivists in search of scientific laws of behaviour. This description contains three strong statements: (1) quantitative psychology defends a positivist view of the world,

(2) quantitative psychology is looking for laws similar to Newton's laws of physics, and (3) quantitative psychology is only interested in behaviour.

The first claim suggests that quantitative psychologists subscribe to positivism. Certainly in the last decades such a claim has a negative connotation, because positivism is taken to mean that only scientific knowledge is worthwhile and that scientific knowledge is never wrong (because it is a constant accumulation of knowledge). As explained in Chapter 8, this view has been rejected in the second half of the twentieth century, and claiming that quantitative psychologists still subscribe to it assumes they are unaware of these developments. A more realistic view of the attitude of quantitative psychology towards the merits of the natural science approach is given by Smith (1994):

> What I see as most unfortunate, however, is the tendency, abetted by Gergen, to give up the conception of science—natural or human, historical or ahistorical—as an evidential, public, self-critical social enterprise, an enterprise that has successfully sought progressively more adequate and comprehensive understanding of the phenomena in its domain—an enterprise committed to an ideal of truth, the approach to which can be evaluated pragmatically. I find little justification in the postmodernist literature for the claim that scientific constructions, fallible as they are and always subject to disconfirmation and revision, are simply optional myths on all fours with religious or political dogmas and ideologies.
>
> *(Smith 1994, p. 408)*

The second claim, that quantitative psychology is only interested in laws similar to those of physics, is outdated as well. It is true that scientific psychology in its early days was infatuated with physics, like all other sciences at that time. However, this is no longer the case. Scientists nowadays make a distinction between deterministic and stochastic processes. A *deterministic process* is a process in which the variability is so small that you can predict with high accuracy what the outcome will be when you know the precursors. In contrast, a *stochastic process* is a process where the variability in the possible determinants and the contribution of the random noise is so big that it becomes impossible to exactly predict the next outcome. All you can do is to estimate the probability with which various outcomes may occur and search for variables that (slightly) change this probability. A typical example is trying to predict which clubs of a sports league will win the next round of matches. Although some clubs may be better than others, and therefore more likely to win their match, there never is certainty, only differences in probability. Psychology deals with stochastic processes, as opposed to Newtonian physics.

The changed nature of quantitative psychological research has been documented nicely by Teigen (2002). He made an analysis of the use of the notion 'law' in the psychological literature of the twentieth century and observed a steady decline. The term was used almost exclusively to refer to ideas of the nineteenth and the early twentieth centuries (such as Weber's law, the law of effect or the Gestalt laws). In the course of the twentieth century psychologists increasingly described regularities as principles, effects, trends or functions. In particular the word 'model' came into vogue.

> More complex regularities in the second half of the century are often called models, a term practically unknown in psychology until the publication of Rosenblueth and Wiener's (1945) seminal article. Subsequently, the popularity of this term has increased sharply from decade to decade; today it can be found in about 10% of all

PsycLit journal abstracts . . . The term has the advantage of flexibility, it does not claim universality or definitiveness, and can be embraced by scientists regardless of their position on the realism vs. relativism issue.

(Teigen 2002, p. 113)

Finally, the claim that quantitative psychology is only interested in behaviour is overstated as well. Some qualitative psychologists have the tendency to equate quantitative research with the collection of numbers in artificial, impoverished and restrained situations that no longer have a meaning for the participants. Usually this is connected to problems with *external validity* (the degree to which the findings of a study can be generalised to other participants, measurements and contexts) and *ecological validity* (the degree to which findings in laboratory studies can be generalised to the real world). Most of the time, however, this criticism is not substantiated. It is presented as a truism, something that can be taken for granted. However, a search through the literature does not reveal a string of publications showing that quantitative psychology findings deviate consistently from the way people live in real life. As a matter of fact, there is a rather substantial literature indicating that quantitative data based on standardised tests for some topics predict performance better than clinical judgement based on interviews (Meehl 1954; Grove *et al.* 2000; Chapter 7).

A particularly instructive case in this respect was published by Van Strien and Dane (2001). They described a personnel recruitment and selection agency in the mid-twentieth century that operated on the basis of the then dominant phenomenological psychology in the Netherlands. This phenomenological psychology was promoted by the physiologist and psychologist Frederik Buytendijk and maintained that humans could not be understood by means of standardised tests and techniques. Such understanding required a 'meeting of minds', a personal relationship between a 'you' and 'me'. Observations could only result in information after they had been contemplated and understood by the interviewer. Consequently, the bureau recruited personnel on the basis of a day's meeting of minds including the contemplation and understanding of in-depth interviews and observed behaviours on home-made tasks. The agency was one of the leading consultants in the Netherlands, until a collaborator started to analyse the recommendations and correlated them with outcome measures obtained from the companies that had taken on the personnel. The result was a disappointing correlation of +.15 (Modderaar 1966), hardly better than if the agency had tossed a coin to decide which candidates could be employed (in which case one would expect a correlation of .00).

This example illustrates that having the intention to talk about meaningful situations by itself is no guarantee that the outcome will be more useful than numbers obtained under more constrained circumstances (Schmidt and Hunter (1998) report correlations up to +.58 between test results and performance measures in personnel selection). An interesting development in this respect will be to see whether findings based on current-day qualitative methods (such as grounded theory, IPA, or discourse analysis) do better than the hermeneutic attempts of the past.

Qualitative research is more than a chat with participants

Qualitative research is often misrepresented in texts that question its usefulness. Probably the most common misunderstanding is that qualitative methods involve nothing but a few interviews with people, after which the interviewer writes down his or her impressions. As we have indicated above, data collection in qualitative research methods is as rigorous as in quantitative research. The transcripts must be made available to everyone who wants to verify the outcome of the analysis. In addition, researchers are taught to be careful not to let their views bias the interview or the interpretation, and to incorporate controls to increase the validity of the findings. These include the following checks (cf. Silverman 2005):

1. **Representativeness.** Researchers must provide the criteria they used for their data analysis, so that the representativeness of the reported instances can be gauged.

2. **Confirmability.** Would someone else come to the same conclusions on the basis an equivalent data analysis?

3. **Credibility.** Do the conclusions sound credible to the participants involved in the study?

4. **Comparison of situations that differ on one critical aspect.** Another way to check the validity of conclusions is to compare the data with those of similar cases that deviate in a critical aspect. Silverman (2005, p. 212–14), for instance, described a qualitative study that investigated what happened to Down's syndrome children in a heart hospital. In order to make sure that the study really addressed the concerns of those children, a comparison was made with consultations at the same clinic involving children without the syndrome.

5. **Alternative explanations.** Could the data be explained differently?

6. **Refutability.** Is there evidence that refutes the conclusions? This principle very much resembles the falsification test in quantitative psychology.

Personally, when preparing this chapter we were struck by the many similarities between what qualitative researchers do and what quantitative researchers do in a literature review. In both cases researchers:

1. Try to leave their preconceptions behind and look with an open mind at the documents available.

2. Start by reading through the various documents to get a feeling for the main themes and their connections.

3. On the basis of several close re-readings, build up and refine a coding scheme that adequately summarises the various statements, always making reference to the original materials so that colleagues can check the conclusions.

4. Look up extra sources in case of doubt, ambiguity or possible new leads.

5. Make sure that no issues have been overlooked.

6. Try to reach conclusions that go beyond the obvious but increase the understanding of the phenomenon and/or provide ideas for further exploration.

7. Have the credibility of the synopsis checked by getting reviews from experienced people.

8. Accept that the end product is to some extent influenced by the creator and limited in the degree to which the conclusions can be generalised.

The only difference is that in a literature review the raw materials are journal articles and book chapters, whereas in qualitative research one is dealing with transcripts of human interactions. So, if quantitative researchers question the value of qualitative methods, they also question the value of their own literature reviews that try to bring order to the many scattered findings and conjectures about a particular topic.

Weaknesses in quantitative research that can be addressed by the qualitative approach

If one accepts that there is no inherent incompatibility between quantitative and qualitative research (remember that not everybody does so!), it becomes worthwhile to search for ways in which one method can compensate for weaknesses in the other. As we have seen above, three weaknesses of quantitative psychology are (1) not enough interest in the participants, (2) research is too much driven by what can be measured and tested experimentally, and (3) too much focus on falsification at the expense of a pragmatic solution to the problem at hand. It is not so difficult to see how a qualitative approach can be fruitful here: (1) participants are the centre of focus in qualitative research, (2) qualitative research deals primarily with variables that are hard to quantify and that cannot be manipulated, and (3) given the correspondence between a qualitative analysis and the traditional literature review, one can see how the former can be used successfully for theory building and the solution of practical problems.

Weaknesses in qualitative research that can be addressed by the quantitative approach

Again the three weaknesses we discussed with respect to qualitative research coincide with strengths of the quantitative approach. The quantitative approach is focused on falsification, which may form a welcome addition to the induction and verification of qualitative research, at least if the conclusion can be tested. Similarly, the quantitative approach is well suited to decide between theories (if they can be tested), and the quantitative approach has a wide arsenal of techniques to test whether the introspections of participants agree with their actions in relevant situations. Finally, statistical methods are much more powerful than the human mind to detect differences and correlations in large-scale datasets. This is interesting for qualitative researchers because quite often the data from a qualitative analysis exceed the human reasoning capacity. For instance, Lee *et al.* (1999) argued that qualitative research can be compared to an informal exploratory factor analysis. In their own words:

> Through a variety of qualitative techniques, for example, large amounts of qualitative data are subjectively evaluated (cf. intuitively correlated), simplified (cf. judgmentally combined into factors), and reconstituted (cf. subjectively rotated). If this is successful, the net result is greater understanding of the empirical evidence (cf. latent and causal traits are identified and defined).
>
> *(Lee* et al. *1999, p. 164)*

If this is true (and we see little reason to doubt their assessment), then whenever the data can be analysed statistically, there is overwhelming evidence that such an analysis will produce a more stable and detailed picture than human assessment. This is also the case when the data come from a qualitative study.

For the above reasons, an increasing number of psychologists have become convinced that progress in psychological research is better served by combining quantitative and qualitative methods rather than by trying to force research in one or the other direction. An interesting development in this respect will be what consequences this has for the underlying philosophies (the 'paradigms' of the opening citation).

? What do you think?

Did the review of the different positions about the relationship of qualitative and quantitative research methods make you change your mind? In what ways? Or why not? What is your position now?

Interim summary

How do quantitative and qualitative research methods relate to each other?

- Some psychologists (both quantitative and qualitative) see them as incompatible and argue that psychology must make a choice:
  - The underlying philosophies (positivism vs. postmodernism) are mutually exclusive.
  - Attempts to combine both approaches are disguised attempts to improve the standing of the natural-science oriented research line or the hermeneutics oriented research line at the expense of the other.

- Other psychologists see both types of research methods as complementary; they focus more on the type of information provided by each method rather than on the philosophies that underlie them:
  - Fervent supporters of each approach tend to depict an exaggerated view of the other approach.
  - The weaknesses of one approach are the strengths of the other.

10.4   Focus on: Is too much respect for the philosophy of science bad for morale?

Psychology's rough treatment by philosophy of science

In Chapter 9 we saw how psychologists in the first half of the twentieth century turned to philosophers of science for inspiration on how to increase the scientific standing of their research. More than any other research discipline they slavishly implemented the recommendations of the then prevailing positivists and logical positivists, only to find themselves criticised 50 years later for a lack of theory.

Repentantly, they listened to Popper and started to build cognitive theories that would enable them to test hypotheses, again to find themselves criticised 50 years later for not having an open mind. By the same time they also started to receive the 'gleeful' message that science after all was nothing special and that psychology had deluded itself thinking that adherence to the scientific method made any difference. This reignited the discussion between the natural-sciences oriented and the hermeneutics oriented movements. One would forgive those psychologists who start doubting whether philosophy of science has done any good for them!

Can we predict what governs scientific progress?

One of the reasons why it may be difficult to set up guidelines about how to achieve scientific progress is that doing good research is not a deterministic process that can be summarised in a few rules. As we saw above, a deterministic process is a process where the variability is so small that you can predict with high accuracy what the outcome will be when you know the precursors. Its alternative is a stochastic process, a process where the variability in the possible determinants and the contribution of random noise is so big that it becomes impossible to exactly predict the next outcome. All you can do is estimate the probability with which various outcomes may occur.

Scientific creativity can hardly be considered a deterministic process, meaning that it is impossible to isolate a few factors that govern it. All you can do is point to a series of factors that (slightly) increase or decrease the probability of a new worthwhile finding. In addition, many of these factors are simply correlations, not causal influences. For instance, most scientists are hardworking people. However, this by itself does not mean that forcing people to work long hours will result in extra scientific progress. Only if the number of working hours is a causal factor of scientific progress, will such a policy make a difference.

The evolutionary model of scientific progress

Interestingly, there is an account of scientific progress that fits within the view that there are very few ways in which progress can be stimulated. According to the evolutionary account, scientific progress follows Darwin's evolutionary principles of random variation followed by natural selection (e.g. Campbell 1960; Simonton 1999). In this view, scientific discoveries are nothing but blind (i.e. random) variations, similar to gene mutations. The subsequent selection determines whether a discovery will have an increasing number of descendants or whether it will be one of the many mutations that rapidly die out without leaving offspring.

According to the evolutionary account, the most important factor in scientific progress is the extent to which the environment favours reproduction. In an environment that stimulates reproduction, a lot of new variants will appear and start their struggle for life; an environment that stifles reproduction will only see a few variants come out with low chances of success. A secondary variable that affects scientific progress is the fit between the offspring and the environment. A mutant that fits well in the environment will have more chances of reproduction than a mutant that does not fit in the environment. Within this view, the only contribution philosophy of science can make is to help create an environment that favours the reproduction of ideas.

Worthwhile ideas in a pragmatic world

An attempt to explain the recent rise of qualitative research within the evolutionary account of scientific progress would refer to an accidental confluence of events that gave rise to these ideas and to an environment that was fruitful to them, so that they could multiply fast. Although it is tempting to see a decisive role for philosophy of science here (in particular the introduction of the postmodernist idea of science as a social construction), in the long run the viability of the approach depends on its reception by the culture at large. Because research requires sponsorship from outside, only ideas that are seen as interesting by sufficiently large groups will keep being supported and will survive.

Indeed, in both the quantitative and qualitative literature we see increasing reference being made to the practical impact of a finding as an index of its quality rather than a strict adherence to methodology. So, in the editorial of a mainstream, quantitative journal we read that:

> A former editor of the journal, Endel Tulving, recently recounted a rule he set for reviewing: Ask yourself, 'What did I learn from reading this paper? Was it worth learning?' If you get a positive response, accept; if not, reject. Tulving thought his admonition had little impact. I'm happy to contradict him. Most reviewers, most of the time, take the message to heart.
>
> *(Bock 2008, p. 2)*

Similarly, in a text describing the worth of qualitative research we read that:

> The decisive criterion by which any piece of research must be judged is, arguably, its impact and utility. It is not sufficient to develop a sensitive, thorough and plausible analysis, if the ideas propounded by the researcher have no influence on the beliefs or actions of anyone else.
>
> *(Yardley 2000, p. 223)*

According to these citations, the impact of a study depends not in the first place on whether the study followed each and every methodological prescription but on whether the insights are judged interesting by others. This also seems to agree with a review of the most eminent psychologists of the twentieth century (Haggbloom *et al.* 2002). The six psychologists with the most impact were respectively: Skinner, Piaget, Freud, Bandura, Festinger and Rogers. Of these, at least three (Piaget, Freud and Rogers) would be classified as qualitative researchers in present-day terms. They did not come to their theories on the basis of rigid adherence to the hypothetico-deductive method, but on the basis of trying to understand their own functioning and that of a few others. Their ideas survived not because they were 'scientifically sound' or 'obviously true', but because a lot of people found them interesting and inspiring.

So, the ultimate criterion of scientific development might be whether or not a finding has relevance for the research community and society at large (i.e. fits within the prevailing environment). Needless to say, such a conclusion is nauseatingly ironic for psychologists, because it undeniably points to the pragmatic criterion put forward by William James and John Dewey in the nineteenth century, when they founded American functionalism! The criterion has been ignored by the philosophers of science for most of the twentieth century, because it did not allow them to demarcate science from other ways of knowledge acquisition (Chapter 8), but it may come to the foreground now.

Interim summary

Is philosophy of science useful for psychology?

- Psychology has tried to follow the directives from philosophers of science on how to do 'proper' science, but has been confronted with changing and at times conflicting advice.

- The problem may be that philosophy of science in vain tries to distil a limited set of rules that would govern a process which is not deterministic.

- An alternative view that may be more in line with the stochastic nature of scientific discovery is the evolutionary account. According to this model, the rise and fall of scientific ideas follow Darwinian principles of random variation and natural selection.

- Because natural selection depends on the fit of an idea in the environment and because science depends on the wider culture to be financed, the ultimate criterion determining whether an idea will survive, may be whether society at large finds the idea interesting and useful.

- This entails a return to the pragmatic criterion put forward by James and Dewey at the beginning of psychology.

Recommended literature

Information about both quantitative and qualitative research methods can be found in Howitt, D. and Cramer, D. (2008) *Introduction to Research Methods in Psychology* (2nd edn) (Harlow: Prentice Hall).

Further information about qualitative research methods can be found in Willig, C. (2008) *Introducing qualitative research in psychology* (2nd edn) (Maidenhead: McGraw Hill Open University Press), or in Smith, J.A. (ed.) (2008) *Qualitative psychology: A practical guide to research methods* (2nd edn) (London: Sage Publications).

References

Alvesson, M. (2000) 'Taking the linguistic turn in organizational research', *Journal of Applied Behavioral Science,* **36**: 136–58.

Ashworth, P. (2003) 'The origins of qualitative psychology.' In J.A. Smith (ed.), *Qualitative psychology: A practical guide to research methods.* London: Sage, pp. 4–24.

Bock, K. (2008) Editorial. *Journal of Memory and Language,* **58**: 1–2.

Campbell, D.T. (1960) 'Blind variation and selective retention in creative thought as in other knowledge processes', *Psychological Review,* **67**: 380–400.

Danziger, K. (1990) *Constructing the subject: Historical origins of psychological research.* Cambridge: Cambridge University Press.

Dickson, A., Knussen, C. and Flowers, P. (2008) '"That was my old life; it's almost like a past-life now": Identity crisis, loss and adjustment amongst people living with Chronic Fatigue Syndrome', *Psychology & Health,* **23**: 459–76.

Doll, R., Peto, R., Boreham, J. and Sutherland, I. (2004) 'Mortality in relation to smoking: 50 years' observations on male British doctors', *British Medical Journal,* **328**: 1519–28.

Eysenck, M.W. and Keane, M.T. (2005) *Cognitive psychology: A student's handbook* (5th edn). Hove: Psychology Press.

Gergen, K.J. (2001) 'Psychological science in a postmodern context', *American Psychologist,* **56**: 803–13.

Glaser, B.G. and Strauss, A.L. (1967) *Discovery of grounded theory: Strategies for qualitative research.* New York: Aldine de Gruyter.

Greenhalgh, T. (1997) 'How to read a paper: Getting your bearings (deciding what the paper is about)', *British Medical Journal,* **315**: 243–46.

Grove, W.M., Zald, D.H., Lebow, B.S., Snitz, E. and Nelson, C. (2000) 'Clinical versus mechanical prediction: A meta-analysis', *Psychological Assessment,* **12**: 19–30.

Haggbloom, S.J. *et al.* (2002) 'The 100 most eminent psychologists of the 20th century', *Review of General Psychology,* **6**: 139–52.

Hatch, J.A. (ed.) (1995) *Qualitative research in early childhood settings.* Westport, CT: Greenwood Publishing Group.

King, R.N. and Koehler, D.J. (2000) 'Illusory correlations in graphological inference', *Journal of Experimental Psychology: Applied,* **6**: 336–48.

Lee, T.W., Mitchell, T.R. and Sablynski, C.J. (1999) 'Qualitative research in organizational and vocational psychology 1979–1999', *Journal of Vocational Behavior,* **55**: 161–87.

Lemon, N. and Taylor, H. (1997) 'Caring in casualty: The phenomenology of nursing care.' In N. Hayes (ed.), *Doing qualitative analysis in psychology.* Hove: Psychology Press, pp. 227–43.

Maiers, W. (1991) 'Critical psychology: Historical background and task.' In C.W. Tolman and W. Maiers (eds.), *Critical psychology: Contributions to an historical science of the subject.* Cambridge: Cambridge University Press.

Marecek, J. (2003) 'Dancing through minefields: Toward a qualitative stance in psychology.' In P.M. Camic, J.E. Rhodes and L. Yardley (eds.), *Qualitative research in psychology: Expanding perspectives in methodology and design.* Washington DC: American Psychological Association, pp. 49–69.

Meehl, P.E. (1954) *Clinical vs. statistical prediction: A theoretical analysis and a review of the evidence.* Minneapolis: University of Minnesota Press.

Milgram, S. (1963) 'Behavioral study of obedience', *Journal of Abnormal and Social Psychology* **67**: 371–8.

Modderaar, J. (1966) 'Over de validiteit van de selectie voor bedrijven [On the validity of selection for companies]', *Nederlands Tijdschrift voor de Psychologie,* **21**: 573–89.

Morgan, M. (1998) 'Qualitative research: Science or pseudo-science?' *The Psychologist,* **11**: 481–3 (and Postscript on p. 485).

Reid, K., Flowers, P. and Larkin, M. (2005) 'Exploring lived experience', *The Psychologist,* **18**: 20–23.

Rosenthal, R. and Rosnow, R.L. (2008) *Essentials of behavioral research: Methods and data analysis* (3rd edn). Boston: McGraw-Hill.

Rosenblueth, A. and Wiener, N. (1945) 'The role of models in science', *Philosophy of Science,* **12**: 316–21.

Schmidt, F.L. and Hunter, J.E. (1998) 'The validity and utility of selection methods in personnel psychology: Practical and theoretical implications of 85 years of research findings', *Psychological Bulletin,* **124**: 262–74.

Schraw, G., Wadkins, T. and Olafson, L. (2007) 'Doing the things we do: A grounded theory of academic procrastination', *Journal of Educational Psychology,* **99**: 12–25.

Sie, M. and Wouters, A. (2008) 'The real challenge to free will and responsibility', *Trends in Cognitive Sciences,* **12**: 3–4.

Silverman, D. (2005) *Doing qualitative research: A practical handbook* (2nd edn). London: Sage Publications.

Simonton, D.K. (1999) 'Creativity as blind variation and selective retention: Is the creative process Darwinian?' *Psychological Inquiry*, **10**: 309–28.

Smith, J.A. (1996) 'Beyond the divide between cognition and discourse: Using interpretative phenomenological analysis in health psychology', *Psychology and Health*, **11**: 261–71.

Smith, J.A. (ed.) (2008) '*Qualitative psychology: A practical guide to research methods* (2nd edn). London: Sage Publications.

Smith, M.B. (1994) 'Selfhood at risk: Postmodern perils and the perils of postmodernism', *American Psychologist*, **49**: 405–11.

Starks, H. and Trinidad, S.B. (2007) 'Choose your method: A comparison of phenomenology, discourse analysis, and grounded theory', *Qualitative Health Research*, **17**: 1372–80.

Stevenson, C. and Cooper, N. (1997) 'Qualitative and quantitative research', *The Psychologist*, **4**: 159–60.

Stratton, P. (1997) 'Attributional coding of interview data: Meeting the needs of long-haul passengers.' In N. Hayes (ed.), *Doing qualitative analysis in psychology*. Hove: Psychology Press, pp. 115–42.

Teigen, K.H. (2002) 'One hundred years of laws in psychology', *The American Journal of Psychology*, **115**: 103–18.

Todd, Z., Nerlich, B., McKeown, S. and Clarke, D.D. (2004) *Mixing methods in psychology: The integration of qualitative and quantitative*
methods in theory and practice. Hove: Psychology Press.

Twenge, J.M., Campbell, W.K. and Foster, C.A. (2003) 'Parenthood and marital satisfaction: A meta-analytic review', *Journal of Marriage and the Family*, **65**: 574–83.

Vandenbroucke, J.P. (2008) 'Observational research, randomised trials, and two views of medical science', *PLoS Medicine, 5, e67,* doi:10.1371/journal.pmed.0050067.

Van Strien, P.J. and Dane, J. (2001) *Driekwart eeuw psychotechniek in Nederland: De magie van het testen* [Three-quarter century of psychotechnics in the Netherlands: The magic of testing]. Assen: Koninklijke Van Gorcum.

Ward, N. (1998) 'Artificial intelligence and other approaches to speech understanding: Reflections on methodology', *Journal of Experimental and Theoretical Artificial Intelligence*, **10**: 487–93.

Willig, C. (2008) *Introducing qualitative research in psychology*. Maidenhead: McGraw-Hill/Open University Press.

Wilson, T.D. and Dunn, E.W. (2004) 'Self-knowledge: Its limits, value, and potential for improvement', *Annual Review of Psychology*, **55**: 493–518.

Yardley, L. (2000) 'Dilemmas in qualitative health research', *Psychology and Health*, **15**: 215–28.

11 The precarious balance between biological, psychological and social influences

This chapter will cover

Questions to consider

Historical issues addressed in this chapter

- When did researchers start to include the impact of social relations in their theories?

Conceptual issues addressed in this chapter

- What does the biopsychosocial model of medicine imply? Does this have a psychological counterpart?
- Can human behaviour be explained on the basis of instincts?
- What evidence supports the view that mental life depends on biological factors?
- What has contributed to the current popularity of evolutionary psychology?
- What evidence supports the view that mental life depends on psychological factors?
- What evidence supports the view that mental life depends on socio-cultural factors?
- In what way does the diathesis–stress model relate to the biopsychosocial model?
- In what ways do people of various cultures differ?
- What causes aggression?

Introduction

For far too long, behavioral genetics and socialization theory have been viewed as necessarily in opposition to one another. Researchers in both 'camps' have very rarely referred to studies from the other 'camp', other than to attack their concepts and findings. The result has been much fruitless dispute and serious misunderstandings of what each body of research has to contribute.

(Rutter 2006, p. vi)

In many introductory psychology books it is stressed that human functioning is affected by biological, psychological and socio-cultural factors. A person's actions, thoughts and feelings are influenced by his or her biological constitution, the way he or she perceives, interprets and remembers events, and the interactions the person has with other people. In this discussion, often reference is made to Engel's (1977) **biopsychosocial model** of medicine. According to this model, medicine must take into account the psychological and social contributions to disease, as well as the biological involvement, if it wants to treat an illness properly. Similarly, according to the biopsychosocial model in psychology, mental functioning cannot be understood without taking into account the three types of influences (e.g. Peterson 1997).

However, a look at the literature beyond introductory books shows that although authors theoretically subscribe to the three sources of input, in practice they assign widely divergent weights to them. Most authors seem to pick out one influence (or at most two, as in the extract that opened this chapter), which they claim has not been given the full weight it deserves. So, throughout the history of psychology there have been psychologists stressing that the biological component of mental functioning is underestimated. Similarly, there have been psychologists emphasising that cognitive processes are the main forces behind human behaviour, both normal and abnormal, and that these processes overrule the biological and social constraints. Finally, there have been psychologists arguing that the social situation is a much stronger determinant of human behaviour than the opinions an individual has or the traits the individual inherited.

Because of the enduring quarrel between the three groups of researchers, the balance between biological, psychological and social forces is continuously shifting (hence the title of the chapter: 'the precarious balance'). At different times and within different branches of psychology, each group of variables has been given primacy. Sometimes the biological variables are on the winning hand; then the psychological factors are in the spotlight; and finally there are epochs in which the social influences are centre stage. Some of the shifts follow cyclic movements with one group of variables getting most attention at one time, followed by a countermovement pointing to one of the other groups, again followed by a countermovement returning to the initial bias, and so on.

In this chapter we will review the arguments of the three groups, so that you have more background when you read books or articles of individual authors. In line with the historical slant of the book, we start with a historical example, before we have a look at the current situation. In that way we hope to make clear that the discussion is not new, but has existed from the beginning of psychology.

biopsychosocial model

model according to which the understanding of medical and psychological phenomena requires attention to biological, psychological as well as socio-cultural factors

? What do you think?

On the basis of what we have already covered in this book (and other lectures you attended), you can probably indicate some of the biases that are present. Which line of approach has dominated, for instance, in functionalism, behaviourism, neuropsychology, feminist psychology, cognitive psychology, critical psychology?

Interim summary

■ According to the biopsychosocial model, psychology has to take into account biological, psychological, and socio-cultural factors if it wants to understand a topic fully.

11.1   What drives people? McDougall and his critics

McDougall's instincts and sentiments

You may remember William McDougall from Chapter 4. He was the British psychologist who was not allowed to start a laboratory in Oxford and eventually moved to the USA. One of his main contributions was that he brought research on motivation and emotion to the foreground. Before him, experimental psychologists examined intellectual processes such as sensation, perception, learning, memory and thinking, but eschewed issues like motivation and emotion, which according to McDougall were essential aspects of mental life. Why did people do the things they did? Why did they live in groups? Why did they follow leaders? The answers to such questions were left to anthropologists, sociologists, economists and historians.

McDougall is best known for his book *An introduction to social psychology*, first published in 1908. Despite its title, the main message was that humans were motivated by a limited set of innate motives from which all the other motives were derived as a result of an individual's experience. (Like nearly all English psychologists of his time, McDougall was deeply influenced by Darwin's writings.) At first, McDougall called the primary motives instincts. He later regretted this, because most students interpreted them as automatic reflexes, whereas McDougall saw them as strivings to achieve particular goals. Therefore, he later called them *propensities*. In 1908, he listed 12 primary instincts (which in the subsequent revisions of the book he extended to 17). They were the instincts:

instinct

innate and fixed response that is automatically elicited by an appropriate stimulus; used around the turn of the twentieth century to explain motivation

1. to desire food periodically (hunger)

2. to reject certain substances (disgust)

3. to explore new places and things (curiosity)

4. to escape from danger (fear)

5. to fight when frustrated (anger)

6. to have sex (mating propensity)

7. to care for the young (mothering propensity)

8. to seek company (gregarious propensity)

9. to seek dominance (self-assertive propensity)

10. to accept inferiority (submissive propensity)

11. to make things (constructive propensity)

12. to collect things (acquisitive tendency)

McDougall further theorised that as a result of experience the primary instincts became modified. They could become activated upon thinking of a relevant object rather than seeing it, and they could be co-activated with other instincts as part of a blend, which McDougall called a *sentiment*. For instance, a husband's love for his wife was a sentiment including the mating propensity, the mothering propensity, and possibly others as well. Similarly, McDougall saw patriotism as a sentiment in which a man's native land had become the object of several instincts. McDougall argued that adult behaviours were primarily motivated by sentiments, rather than by instincts. Nevertheless, because the sentiments were derived from the instincts, they still possessed the emotional striving of the instincts. Social behaviour, for instance, was based on loyalties and interests resulting from the instincts combined into sentiments.

McDougall was not the first to use instincts – James had done so extensively in his *Principles* – but his system was the first in which instincts were seen as the basis of a coherent and structured set of motives that drove human actions. As McDougall himself wrote:

> Take away these instinctive dispositions with their powerful impulses, and the organism would become incapable of activity of any kind; it would lie inert and motionless like a wonderful clockwork whose mainspring had been removed.
>
> *(McDougall (1948) as cited in Jahoda (2007) p. 159)*

The reactions to McDougall

Woodworth (1948) describes the responses to McDougall's book. At first, they were largely positive. The book was a source of inspiration for the creation of social psychology as a separate branch of psychological research, rather than as part of sociology. Also the social sciences took inspiration from the book, trying to show how a society emerged as a means to meet the instinctive demands of the individuals, and how the instinctive cravings of the individuals could be adapted to fit into an industrialised society.

Soon, however, McDougall's doctrine of instincts ran into what Woodworth called the 'professional bias of sociologists'. This is how he described the evolution:

> With their eyes fixed on the social group as the important object of study, [the sociologists] were less impressed with the natural demands of the individual than with another line of facts suggesting that the individual was molded by society. The individual derives his language, his manners and customs, and to a large extent his beliefs from the social environment . . . While to the psychologist it may be self-evident that society is composed of individuals and must meet their demands, to the sociologist the main fact is that society is there before any given individual and imposes on him its demands and standards. We behave alike and 'behave like human beings,' not in the main because of our instincts, but because of the culture we all receive.
>
> *(Woodworth 1948, p. 223)*

The sociological critique to McDougall reached its height in 1924 when Luther L. Bernard published a book entitled *Instinct, a study of social psychology*, in which he rejected instincts as the basis of human behaviour. He pointed out that no two psychologists agreed on the list of instincts and that instincts referred to complex activities that differed from culture to culture. Bernard argued, for instance, that a mother's care of her baby was not instinctive mothering behaviour but a complex activity taught by people in the environment. In his view, the highly artificial environment humankind had developed in the twentieth century was not primarily motivated by a desire to meet an individual's biological needs. Rather the opposite was true: society expected individuals to adapt themselves to the existing customs and institutions.

Not only sociologists took issue with McDougall's doctrine. Behaviourists attacked the theory, because they saw the instincts as too broad, unlikely to be a driving force throughout a person's life, and improbable as an explanation of the complex behaviour patterns shown by humans. How could complex behaviours be the result of inheritance? This, for instance, is what John Watson had to say about instincts:

> The behaviorist has found by his study that most of the things we see the adult doing are really learned. We used to think that a lot of them were instinctive, that is 'unlearned.' But we are now almost at the point of throwing away the word 'instinct.' Still there are a lot of things we do that we do not have to learn – to perspire, to breathe, to have our heart beat, to have digestion take place, to have our eyes turn toward a source of light, to have our pupils contract, to show a fear response when a loud sound is given. Let us keep as our second classification then 'learned responses,' and make it include all of the our complicated habits and all of our conditioned responses; and 'unlearned' responses, and mean by that all of the things that we do in earliest infancy before the processes of conditioning and habit formation get the upper hand.
>
> *(Watson 1925, p. 15)*

In Watson's eyes instincts were limited to the biological functions that were present at birth; all other behaviour was acquired through conditioning and habit formation.

The significance of the example: What are the weights of biological, psychological and social factors?

We discussed McDougall's views at some length, not because they are unavoidable in the history of psychology, but because they nicely illustrate the shifting balance of biological, psychological and socio-cultural contributions. McDougall started out with a predominantly biological view: motivations were based on innate instincts. This was questioned by the behaviourists, who emphasised that psychological processes (learning) should carry more weight. They also included socio-cultural influences (e.g. other people as the source of reinforcement and punishment), but these influences did not figure strongly in their thinking (as most of their theories were about the performance of individuals). Finally, the sociologists pointed to the importance of socio-cultural norms and expectations in human behaviour, at the expense of biological and psychological factors. As we will see in the following sections, the discussion about the relative weights of the different types of influence is still very much alive today.

Interim summary

- McDougall argued at the beginning of the twentieth century that humans are motivated by innate drives (instincts or propensities), which become modified and grouped into sentiments as a result of experience.

- At first, the reactions to McDougall's book were positive, but soon sociologists criticised it because it overlooked the social factors in human behaviour. At the same time, behaviourists criticised it because in their view behaviour was learned, not innate.

- McDougall's book and the reactions it provoked are typical of the constant discussion in psychology about the relative importance of biological, psychological and socio-cultural influences on human behaviour.

What do you think?

Now that you have read the McDougall case, how do you feel about the relative importance of biological, psychological and social factors? Are they equally important, or do you see a ranking of them? Discuss this with others. Do you all agree?

11.2   The biological perspective

According to the biological perspective, mental life is primarily determined by the biological processes in the brain. This perspective goes back at least as far as Hippocrates in Ancient Greece (Chapter 5). However, for most of recorded history its role was very limited, under the influence of the dualistic view defended by Plato and the Catholic Church. As you may remember from Chapter 6, dualism draws a sharp divide between the mind and the body. As a result, biological influences on mental functioning were seen as very minor. There was some surge in their perceived contribution in the nineteenth century and at the beginning of the twentieth century, when the relationship between aphasia and brain lesions was discovered (Chapter 5) and when Darwin's evolutionary theory started to have an impact (Chapter 3; see also McDougall above). However, within psychology the ascent of the biological perspective was blocked by the advent of behaviourism, which stressed the importance of learning.

Currently the biological perspective is gaining rapidly in power. Arguably its impact has never been as strong as now. Four main developments have led to this state of affairs: the discovery of psychoactive medication, the finding of a hereditary component in many psychological functions, the observation that certain types of human behaviour can be understood from an evolutionary point of view, and recent advances in neuroscience. Given that the last development has been dealt with extensively in Chapter 5, we discuss only the first three here.

The impact of psychoactive medication

Antipsychotics

An important argument for the influence of biological factors on mental life is the finding that chemical substances can affect psychological functions. Such influence was already known for many centuries in a negative way, particularly with respect to alcohol. However, in the middle of the twentieth century, as a result of the advances in medical science, medication became available that actively alleviated mental problems. One of the first drugs available was chlorpromazine for the treatment of hallucinations and delusions in schizophrenia (Chapter 7). Currently the contribution of antipsychotics in the treatment of schizophrenia is no longer questioned, despite their risk of side-effects such as drowsiness, involuntary movements and weight gain (e.g. Lehman and Steinwachs 1998).

Epilepsy

The biological approach had even more success in the treatment of some other mental disorders. A typical example is epilepsy. Epilepsy is a group of syndromes that have in common that part of the brain becomes active in an uncontrolled way. It affects up to 2 per cent of the population at some point in their life (e.g. sometimes in old age). Symptoms during a seizure differ depending on the location of the source and the extent of the discharge. In the worst case patients faint and have convulsions (uncontrolled limb movements because of discharges in the motor cortex).

Because of the sudden onset of seizures, epilepsy for a long time was associated with demonic possession. As a result, the disorder carried a strong stigma (i.e. was socially discrediting for the patient). With the emergence of neurology in the nineteenth century, epilepsy increasingly became seen as a brain disorder and bromide was introduced in 1857 as the first effective anti-epileptic drug. Research received a further impetus when scientists were able to measure the brain's electric activity with the use of EEG recordings (Chapter 5). This confirmed the presence of electrical discharges during a seizure and allowed researchers to better localise the site of the discharges. Bromide as the main drug for treatment was replaced by phenobarbitone (first used in 1912) and phenytoin (first used in 1938).

The increased understanding of the workings of the brain accelerated the development of still better drugs, which currently control seizures effectively in 70–80 per cent of newly diagnosed patients. The remaining cases increasingly profit from high-precision surgery, helped by brain imaging, to remove or control the affected part of the brain. As a result of these evolutions, the treatment of epilepsy nowadays fully falls under the realm of biological treatments.

Ulcers

Another condition that for a long time was thought to have a strong psychological component but over time shifted to a biological treatment is that of stomach and intestinal ulcers. For a long time it was thought that lifestyle factors, in particular psychological stress, caused ulcers. As part of his research on the biological reactions to stress, the endocrinologist Hans Selye (1907–1982) noticed that rats he put under duress developed ulcers. For him, this seemed to agree with the correlation physicians observed between stress and stomach ulcers in humans. Consequently the proposed treatment of ulcers primarily included attempts to diminish the patients' stress.

In 1982, however, two Australian scientists, Robin Warren and Barry Marshall, discovered the presence of a new type of bacterium, *Helicobacter pylori,* as the cause of stomach and intestinal ulcers in the majority of patients. Warren and Marshall subsequently demonstrated that ulcers could be induced by injection of the bacteria into the stomach and could be cured with a treatment of antibiotics. In 2005 they were awarded the Nobel Prize for Medicine for their discoveries.

The importance of heredity in psychology

Heredity

Another finding that points to the impact of biological processes on mental functioning is the demonstration that differences between people are inherited to a large extent. There are two main ways to estimate the impact of heredity. The first is to compare identical twins with fraternal twins. Identical twins share the same genes, whereas fraternal twins do not share more genes with each other than brothers and sisters. So, if a trait is inherited, identical twins ought to resemble each other more than fraternal twins. The second method is to look at adopted children. If a trait is inherited, an adopted child should be more similar to the biological parents than to the adoptive parents. As you may remember from Chapters 7 and 10, similarity is expressed as a correlation coefficient. By comparing the correlations in different groups of individuals (e.g. identical twins vs. fraternal twins), it is possible to estimate how much of the variance is due to heredity and how much to the environment.

Needless to say, researchers have to make sure that there are no confounding variables biasing their figures. This has given rise to quite some discussion in the literature about how best to do this, although one cannot escape the impression that the controls nowadays tend to be much less strict than they were in the 1980–1990s, in line with the increased status of the biological perspective. Researchers seem to have accepted a strong genetic component in psychological variables and are no longer questioning to what extent, for instance, the environment of identical twins can be compared to that of fraternal twins (e.g. it is likely that the environment is more similar for identical twins than for fraternal twins, given their similarity in appearance; in a good study, this should be controlled for).

Table 11.1 lists some of the heredity estimates that have been reported. In this figure, 0 per cent variance explained means that all differences between individuals are due to differences in their environments (including biological factors such as the hormones to which the foetuses are exposed in the womb); 100 per cent variance explained means that all individual differences are due to genetic variation.

Although there are interesting differences in estimated heritability between the characteristics (with a stronger genetic component in disorders such as ADHD and schizophrenia than in disorders such as alcohol dependence and major depression), the most conspicuous finding is that for all characteristics there is a clear impact of genetic factors. There are even data on a strong genetic component in feeling lonely and being satisfied with one's life! Such findings are in line with the predictions of the biological perspective.

Table 11.1 Heredity estimates reported (percentage of variance explained by the genetic constitution)

Although there are some differences between the characteristics (ADHD (Attention Deficit Hyperactivity Disorder) and schizophrenia have a stronger genetic component than alcohol dependence and life satisfaction), there is a clear contribution of heredity for all characteristics. This is in line with the biological perspective.

Characteristic	Percentage of variance	Source
ADHD	60–91%	Thapar *et al.* (2007)
Aggression	40–53%	Miles and Carey (1997)
Alcohol dependence	25–49%	Liu *et al.* (2004)
Depression (major)	31–42%	Sullivan *et al.* (2000)
Dyslexia	47–60%	Raskind (2001)
Feeling of loneliness	44–53%	Boomsma *et al.* (2005)
Intelligence	30–70%	Mackintosh (1998)
Life satisfaction	20–44%	Stubbe *et al.* (2005)
Obesity	64–84%	O'Rahilly and Farooqi (2006)
Personality disorders	50–60%	Torgersen *et al.* (2000)
Personality traits	41–51%	Bouchard (1994)
Schizophrenia	73–90%	Sullivan *et al.* (2003)
Sexual orientation	28–65%	Kendler *et al.* (2000)

The importance of variation and selection: evolutionary psychology

Not only are the differences between individuals influenced by their biological make-up; human behaviours in general also seem to have a genetic component. There is a growing body of evidence indicating that many human behaviours are in line with what would be predicted on the basis of natural selection: behaviours that increase the chances of survival have a higher chance of being passed on to the next generation than behaviours that are less helpful. This message was first conveyed by the Harvard biologist Edward O. Wilson (1975) in a book called *Sociobiology: The new synthesis*. In this book, Wilson claimed that most social behaviours would eventually be understood on the basis of the reproductive advantage they give.

The message was picked up by a group of psychologists and translated into a new research area, **evolutionary psychology**, which attempts to explain mental and psychological traits as a result of the 'struggle for life'. This was not a new perspective (see the functionalists in Chapter 3 and McDougall above), but the advances in evolutionary theory and the degree of knowledge available at the end of the twentieth century allowed the supporters to go well beyond what was achieved before. We summarise some of the most important claims and findings.

evolutionary psychology

approach in psychology that aims to understand human behaviour on the basis of natural selection and the evolutionary theory

Long-term partner selection

In order to pass on one's genes, it is important to choose a mate who not only produces viable offspring but is also willing to invest in the offspring until they can reproduce themselves. Humans in the past who were discerning in this respect have multiplied their genes, the others not. Buss (2004, p. 109) mentions the following features that help to increase the chances of viable offspring:

■ choose a mate who is able to invest,

■ choose a mate who is willing to invest,

■ choose a mate who is able to protect the children,

■ choose a mate who will help raise the children,

■ select a mate who is compatible with yourself,

■ select a mate who is healthy.

Because humans for the most part of their history were hunter-gatherers with a clear division of labour between the sexes (men = hunting and achieving wealth and power in the group, women = bearing and raising children, gathering fruit and vegetables), the selection criterion for successful reproduction differed for men and women. For men the most important selection criteria were:

■ identify a woman with high fertility and reproductive value (young, healthy, attractive),

■ identify a woman who will stay loyal to you, so that you are not raising another man's children.

For women the following have been the most important criteria:

■ make sure the man has the resources to raise the children or is likely to acquire them,

■ make sure the man will commit himself to you and your children,

■ make sure the man can protect you and your children (i.e. is healthy and has sufficient status in the group).

Buss (1989) noticed that these indeed were the main criteria men and women used to find a long-term partner in all 37 cultures he investigated. Men were particularly looking for youth, attractiveness (as an indicator of health) and signs of loyalty. Women were more interested in wealth, status, power and commitment. Buss further noted that the uncertainty a man has about the paternity of the children he is raising, will lead to sexual jealousy in men, because husbands who in the past guarded their wives had more chances of passing on their genes than husbands who did not care. Other authors, however, have found less convincing evidence for these claims (Buller 2005; Richardson 2007).

parental investment theory

hypothesis in evolutionary psychology holding that the gender investing the most in the upbringing of offspring is more discriminating about mating

In 1972, after comparing mate selection in different species, Robert Trivers noticed another regularity. He observed that in general the gender investing more in the upbringing of children is more discriminating about mating than the gender investing less. He called this the **parental investment theory**. For instance, among the Mormon crickets, where the males produce large, nutritious spermatophores at a considerable cost, the females compete with each other for access to the males who then select which females they want.

In most other species, where the females bear the larger brunt of gestation and feeding, the roles are reversed: females are more selective and prudent with whom they will mate than males. According to Trivers, the parental investment theory also applies to humans. He further noticed that species in which the offspring requires a lot of care are likely to be monogamous (with the male and the female staying together), whereas species in which the offspring requires little effort are usually characterised by polygyny (in which a relatively small number of males impregnate the females). Polygyny is present among nearly all mammal species. Monogamy is widespread among birds and humans.

Short-term partner selection

DNA-research in bird colonies has shown that monogamy should be understood as 'male and female raise the offspring together', rather than as 'males and females are sexually loyal to each other'. In particular, partners of males with a low status tend to have intercourse with higher ranked males, presumably because this improves the quality (and hence the reproduction chances) of their offspring. Geary *et al.* (2004) suggested a similar pattern in humans. They pointed to studies showing 1 per cent extramarital children in a rich quarter of a Swiss city against 30 per cent in a disadvantaged British estate. Apparently, women who have ended up with a partner who does not rank high in the hierarchy are more likely to have an extramarital child than women with a highly desirable man. Along the same lines, McNulty *et al.* (2008) noticed that couples in which the husbands are rated as more attractive than the wives tend to be less stable.

What do you think?

For some years paternity tests have allowed fathers to be sure about their relationship to the children they are raising. Do you think this makes any difference to short-term partner strategies? Is having better offspring the only reason for short-term partnerships?

Inclusive fitness

inclusive fitness

hypothesis in evolutionary psychology that behaviour is motivated not only by the organism's own survival but also by the survival of organisms that are genetically related; the motivation depends on the degree of relatedness

William D. Hamilton (1964) launched a second idea that would be of importance to evolutionary psychology. He argued that individuals are not only motivated to promote their own genes, but also to help individuals with shared genes. The higher the genetic overlap, the more likely the support. Trivers called this **inclusive fitness**. It refers to the likelihood of passing on genes not only by direct reproduction but also by helping relatives to produce offspring. So, it is the sum of an individual's own reproductive success (the classical fitness in Darwin's theory) plus the effects of the individual's actions on the reproductive success of his or her next of kin (Buss 2004). Inclusive fitness enables evolutionary psychologists to understand altruistic behaviour. A parent who dies to save his/her child increases his/her inclusive fitness, especially if the parent is unlikely to have more children.

Inclusive fitness makes a number of interesting predictions, which have been borne out by the data (Buss 2004; but also see Buller 2005). One of them is that the probability of a human helping someone else depends on their genetic similarity. Another is that step-parents will be more likely to abuse and kill children than biological parents. The reason for this is the conflict that exists between the child, who is motivated to profit as much as possible from the parent, and the parent who is motivated to reproduce their own genes. In the case of biological children, inclusive fitness forms a counterweight which is absent in step-parents. Similarly, inclusive fitness predicts that parents will be more likely to kill their children when they themselves still have good chances of reproduction than when such chances are absent.

Inclusive fitness also explains why individuals will protect their next of kin (their own group) in case of danger. This is true in war and conflict. However, Van Vugt *et al.* (2007) showed that it is also true in a virtual world. Male students were more likely to cooperate with their own group in an internet game, when there was a perceived competition from a rival group at another university than when there was no such competition.

Cooperative alliances

Another question evolutionists have considered is what implications the struggle for life has for alliances between individuals who do not share many genes. At first sight, one would expect the struggle to result in selfishness. After all, individuals who constantly help others at the expense of their own reproduction fail to pass on their genes. In contrast, those who make sure they always get as much as possible out of the others are able to have many offspring and to multiply their genes. However, such a view overlooks the fact that most of the time individuals obtain more when they cooperate. Trivers (1971) called this *reciprocal altruism*, cooperation between two or more individuals for mutual benefit. As long as the individuals cooperate, the gains accrue. When one of them cheats and takes advantage of the others' cooperation, the gains for that person increase rapidly at the expense of the others. How to make sure then that the cheaters do not get the upper hand in a group?

With the use of computer simulations Axelrod and Hamilton (1981) showed that a simple but very efficient strategy is the so-called tit-for-tat strategy. It consists of two simple rules:

tit-for-tat strategy

strategy proposed in evolutionary psychology to explain how evolutionarily motivated individuals cooperate in situations of mutual dependency and benefit

1. start by cooperating,

2. thereafter, do the same as the other does (i.e. if they cooperate, continue cooperating; if they refuse cooperation, refuse as well).

The strategy basically means that individuals will tend to cooperate when they encounter someone else for the first time, but will refuse cooperation as soon as the other does not reciprocate. This refusal will continue until the other breaks the spell and offers collaboration. As long as individuals act according to the tit-for-tat strategy, they maximise their long-term profit (although there always will be the temptation of big short-term gains, offset by the prospect of possible ostracism). According to evolutionary psychologists, individuals who followed the tit-for-tat strategy had a higher overall reproduction rate and, therefore, became more and more frequent in subsequent generations. Hence, many social interactions in current society can be understood on the basis of this strategy.

KEY FIGURES IN TWENTIETH-CENTURY EVOLUTIONARY THEORY

David Buss
© David M. Buss,
all rights reserved.

Edward O. Wilson
- American biologist who started sociobiology with the publication of his book *Sociobiology: The new synthesis* (1975), in which he claimed that many social behaviours can be understood on the basis of the reproduction advantage they have had for humans.

David Buss
- American psychologist who applied the evolutionary theory to mating strategies and was one of the founders of evolutionary psychology.

Robert Trivers
- American biologist who introduced the theories of parental investment and reciprocal altruism (which forms the basis of cooperative alliances).

William D. Hamilton
- British biologist who proposed the importance of inclusive fitness to understand altruism in the evolution theory. He also proposed the tit-for-tat strategy in collaboration with Robert Axelrod.

Innate knowledge

Evolutionary theory also provides an answer to a question that has vexed philosophy since the invention of empiricism, namely how the mind can absorb and structure empirical facts when it starts off as a blank slate. To translate this into a contemporary problem: why do human babies after a few years fluently understand human speech, whereas thus far it has proven impossible to implement such a feat on a computer? The computational power of computers easily outperforms that of the human brain. Still this does not suffice to turn the blank slate of the computer into a talking machine. The cause probably is that the human brain processes speech information in a way we have not worked out yet. As a result, we don't know yet how to program a computer so that it learns like a human. However, this begs the question: how is the brain capable of doing so?

The German philosopher Immanuel Kant (1724–1804; see also Chapter 2) was the first to realise this. He argued that the only way in which the soul could absorb and structure empirical information was not by being a blank slate but by being an entity that from the onset on imposed some organisation on the incoming information. Kant postulated 'innate categories' (e.g. of time, space and causality) as the foundation of such organisation. In his view, humans were able to perceive cause–effect relations because they had an innate category for them.

A frustrating aspect of Kant's theory was that he referred to divine or metaphysical input to explain the origin of the innate information. Evolutionary theory provides a scientifically more appealing answer. Just as the eye evolved to respond to certain electromagnetic rays emitted by the environment, so did the brain evolve to respond to certain stimuli emanating from the surroundings. Genes that caused a defence reaction upon seeing a snake or upon hearing a looming noise, increased the chances of survival and hence of reproduction. So, after they emerged they were likely to stay and to pervade the species. Similarly, genes that increased the amount of information the brain could pick up from the environment, resulted in a survival advantage and were likely to be passed on, once they had appeared on the basis of random variation. Eventually, this process of random variation and natural selection led to the brains we currently have, made in such a way that they are able to rapidly tune to important signals in the surroundings and to learn from them. The learning component will be discussed in the next section.

Interim summary

The biological perspective

- According to the biological perspective, mental life is primarily determined by the biological processes in the brain.

- Four developments have increased the impact of the biological perspective in recent years:

  - the discovery of psychoactive medication,
  - the finding of a hereditary component in many psychological functions,
  - the observation that certain types of human behaviours can be understood from an evolutionary point of view (partner selection, inclusive fitness, cooperation, innate knowledge),
  - advances in neuroscience.

11.3   The psychological perspective

Adherents of the psychological perspective agree with the proponents of the biological perspective that some innate knowledge and behaviours may be the starting point of mental life. However they disagree about the possibility of understanding human behaviour primarily on the basis of biological factors. In their view, to appreciate an individual's current functioning, it is much more important to know his or her ways of thinking. After all, a fundamental characteristic of people is that they gather knowledge all their life, which they use to carry on and improve their fate. Very few behaviours are purely instinctive, in the sense that they are elicited reflexively by the presence of a stimulus and need no learning. Organisms capable of learning have an enormous survival advantage, because they can take profit from their past experiences. They can avoid stimuli that previously caused negative sensations and approach stimuli that in the past led to positive experiences.

In addition, supporters of the psychological perspective point to the many aspects of human life that cannot be understood without assuming sophisticated psychological processes. This is true for the information processing emphasised by cognitive psychologists (Chapter 4), for emotions beyond reflexive fear and happiness (e.g. regret, shame, disappointment), and for the understanding of meaningful situations as stressed in the hermeneutic approach.

Although we could have opted for examples in which psychological processing is pivotal, in the sections below we focus on functions close to biological and social functioning. In this way, we stay closer to the true message of the biopsychosocial model that biological, psychological and socio-cultural variables are involved in *each and every* aspect of human functioning.

Olfaction

Innate odours and survival

It is not difficult to find evidence for biological influences on olfaction. In line with evolutionary theory, researchers have found that some responses to odours are innate (e.g. Kobayakawa *et al.* 2007). From their first contact rodents are repulsed by the odours of spoiled food and by odorants associated with predators (e.g. the scent secreted from the anal gland of a fox). In contrast, they show instinctive attraction towards food smells and odours associated with their own species (e.g. urine of females). Similarly, people show stable individual differences in their preferences for body odours, which have been linked to the immune system (Jacob *et al.* 2002).

At the same time, research on olfaction has provided some of the strongest evidence concerning the influences of learning and cognition on human behaviour. People respond differently to odours as a consequence of their learning histories and as a function of what they think the origin of the smell is.

Odours and associative learning

Odours that have been associated with negative events become conditioned stimuli that evoke an avoidance response; odours associated with positive events elicit an approach response. This is nicely illustrated by a study of Li *et al.* (2008). Participants smelled sets of three bottles (two containing the same odorant, one containing a barely distinguishable different odorant). At first, participants could not discriminate between the odours. However, after one of the odorants had repeatedly been paired with electrical shocks, participants' ability to discriminate the smells improved dramatically. Also their neural processing of the smells, as assessed with fMRI, changed.

Associations between odours and feelings or cognitions are capitalised upon by the fragrance industry, which aims to influence people's moods and buying behaviour with odours (cf. Chebat and Michon 2003). For instance, Spangenberg *et al.* (2006) observed that customers had a more favourable impression of a shop and bought more when the scent in the shop was congruent with the clothing sold (Vanilla for women and Rose Maroc for men) than when it was not.

Odours and labelling

Interestingly, people's responses to odours do not require a lengthy learning process. Simply labelling an odour already has a strong impact. Djordevic *et al.* (2008) asked participants to rate the pleasantness of an odour. Participants were presented with a total of 15 odours under three conditions: same odours were presented at different times with a positive, negative or neutral name. For example, in the positive name condition, participants were told for one of the odours that it came from Parmesan cheese, in the negative name condition they were told that the same odour came from

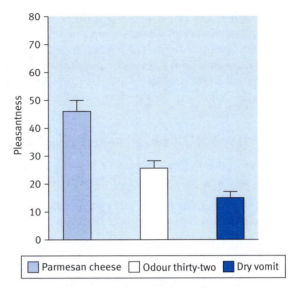

Figure 11.1 The influence of cognition on odour perception.
When participants are given an odour and asked to rate its pleasantness (0 = extremely unpleasant, 100 = extremely pleasant), they give much higher ratings when they are told the odour comes from Parmesan cheese than when they are told it comes from odour thirty-two. Similarly, they give much lower ratings when they are told it comes from dry vomit. So, simply labelling the odours induces huge changes in perception.

Source: Adapted from Djordevic *et al.* (2008), with permission.

dry vomit, and in the neutral name position that it came from odour thirty two. Figure 11.1 shows the dramatic differences in experience these labels induced. In another study, De Araujo *et al.* (2005) reported that a label (Cheddar cheese vs. body odour) not only had an impact on the subjective ratings of the participants but also on their brain responses as measured with fMRI.

The fact that simple sensory responses to odours so strongly depend on the way in which they are interpreted shows the impact of psychological factors on human functioning. In addition, responses to odours are not the only emotional responses subject to cognitive control. There is a considerable literature on how emotional responses to a wide variety of stimuli are influenced by cognitive processes (e.g. Ochsner and Gross 2005).

Cognitive modulation of pain

The gate control theory of pain

Another biological response that is modulated to a considerable extent by cognition is pain perception. Quite rapidly researchers noticed that there was very little correlation between the amount of tissue damage and the degree of pain experienced. Some people complain of unbearable, chronic pain with non-noticeable damage, whereas others continue to function at a high level despite obvious pain-inducing wounds. To account for these findings, Melzack and Wall (1965) proposed the **gate control theory of pain**. According to this theory, the nerve signals carrying the pain message have to pass

gate control theory of pain

theory of pain perception which assumes that the nerve signals carrying the pain message have to pass through a gate before they reach the brain; at this gate the signals can be made stronger or weaker through a gate before they reach the brain. At this gate they can be modulated. One source of inhibition consists of the endorphins released in the brain in emergency situations to help with the fight or flight response. The other attenuation occurs through cognitive modulation, in particular the attention paid to the pain signal and the interpretation of the pain signal. Sportspeople, for instance, endure a considerable amount of pain to improve their performance level.

Psychological factors in pain modulation

Three psychological factors have been reported to increase the level of physical disability and psychological distress provoked by pain (Keefe *et al.* 2004):

1. pain catastrophising, defined as the tendency to focus on pain and negatively evaluate one's ability to deal with pain,

2. pain related anxiety and fear of pain, resulting in a high degree of fear avoidance behaviour, which further weakens the person,

3. helplessness, defined as the tendency to view all attempts to try to manage pain as ineffective.

In contrast, four psychological factors have been described that decrease the impact of pain on a person's functioning:

1. self-efficacy, defined as the person's confidence in their ability to find a way to deal with the pain,

2. pain coping strategies, defined as the variety of strategies used to deal with the pain,

3. readiness to change, defined as the willingness to take an active role in learning to manage the pain,

4. acceptance, defined as an active willingness to engage in meaningful activities in life regardless of the experience of pain; this is particularly needed in situations of persistent pain that cannot be controlled.

As a result of these findings, it is becoming clear that the treatment of chronic pain requires as much psychological help as biological interventions to decrease the impact of the pain signal. This is another argument in favour of the importance of psychological factors in human functioning. Even a biological process such as pain perception is more than a mere physiological registration of a biological change.

Cognitive processes in depression

Thoughts are an important factor in the origin and maintenance of mental health problems as well.

Irrational thoughts and maladaptive schemas

In particular with respect to depression there is good evidence for pathogenic thoughts as the core of the problem. Two independently working American cognitive therapists were central in this realization: Albert Ellis (1913–2007) and Aaron Beck (born in 1921). Ellis stressed that many patients with depression and generalised anxiety have irrational thoughts, such as 'everyone should love me and approve of me' and 'I should always be able, successful, and on top of things'. Beck pointed to the existence of maladaptive schemas in patients dealing with themselves, their future and the world. In Beck's view, the schemas (mostly the result of experiences in childhood and adolescence) become activated under the influence of situational stress and interfere with the person's coping strategies. Both Ellis and Beck showed that cognitive psychotherapies directed at correcting the irrational and maladaptive thoughts were highly effective in the treatment of the disorder.

Rumination

Another researcher stressing the importance of cognitive processes in depression is the American psychologist Susan Nolen-Hoeksema (2000). Her research focused on the relationship between mood regulation strategies and vulnerability to depression and other mental health problems. In particular she examined the effects of rumination, the tendency to respond to distress by focusing on the causes and consequences of the problems, without trying to actively solve the problems. Rumination exacerbates negative thinking and interferes with good problem-solving.

Treatment of depression

The relative contribution of biological and psychological factors in depression can be gauged by looking at the outcome of the therapies proposed by the two approaches. The biological perspective holds that depression is due to a biological imbalance in the brain and should be treated with medication. The psychological perspective maintains that medication is only indicated in the most severe cases (when the patients are too depressed to work on their problems) and that nothing much will change as long as patients do not alter their irrational and maladaptive thoughts. The latter is the explicit goal of the cognitive therapies of Ellis and Beck, but is also implicitly present in all other forms of psychotherapy.

An interesting study comparing the biological and the psychological approach was run at the outpatient psychiatric clinics of the University of Pennsylvania and Vanderbilt University (DeRubeis *et al.* 2005; Hollon *et al.* 2005). Patients were divided into three matched groups: the first group received medication; the second, cognitive psychotherapy. The third group was a placebo group that was treated in exactly the same way as the medication group, except for the fact that there was no active substance in the pills. For all patients, the severity of the depression was assessed biweekly by independent assessors (who were blind to the treatment condition). Figure 11.2a shows the improvement of the three groups over the first 8 weeks. As in the other studies published on this topic, the improvement was three-quarters due to a placebo effect and one-quarter due to the treatment used (see also Kirsch *et al.* 2008; Wampold *et al.* 2005). As for the treatment, no difference was observed between psychotherapy and medication.

The patients of the medication group and the psychotherapy group received treatment for 16 weeks and were subsequently followed for a year to see what happened to them. The patients in the medication condition were divided into two groups: one half

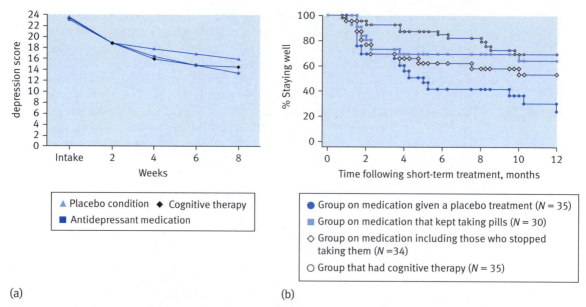

(a) (b)

Figure 11.2 (a): Decrease of depression scores as a function of time in therapy and treatment group.
All three conditions show an improvement, including the placebo condition. After 2–4 weeks, the improvement in the conditions with antidepressant medication (ADM) (N = 120) and cognitive therapy (CT) (N = 60) starts to become bigger than in the placebo condition (N = 60).
(b): Percentages of patients who stay well in the year after the treatment.
Patients in the medication condition put on a placebo pill relapsed in 76% of the cases (i.e. only 24% stayed well). Of the patients in the cognitive therapy condition 76% stayed well; of the patients who continued to receive medication 53% stayed well. Part of this figure was due to participants who stopped taking their medication (see the difference between the curve with the filled squares – patients who continued to take their pills – and the curve with the open diamonds – patients who did not adhere to the medication).

Source: (a) DeRubeis *et al.* (2005); (b) Hollon *et al.* (2005). Both copyright © 2005 American Medical Association. All rights reserved. For full credit see p. xvi.

was gradually placed on a placebo treatment, and the other half continued with the active substance. The patients in the cognitive therapy condition stopped their therapy and were allowed a maximum of three booster sessions when they felt a need for them. Each patient was seen once a month by an independent assessor who decided whether the treatment still worked or whether the patient had relapsed and needed more intensive therapy. Figure 11.2b shows the percentage of patients who stayed healthy in the different conditions. Of the group that received medication followed by a placebo, 76 per cent relapsed, against 24 per cent of the patients who had been given psychotherapy. The group of patients who continued their medication fell between both groups, partly because a number of patients stopped taking their pills.

The above study is representative of the other studies on the treatment of depression: More than half of the improvement is due to a placebo effect and when patients on pills stop taking their medication, there is high percentage of relapse. Both findings point to the importance of the psychological perspective in explaining and treating depression. The placebo effect is understandable in terms of cognitions (patients have renewed hope and force to tackle their problems) and the risk of relapse upon termination of medication is in line with the claim that persons remain vulnerable as long as they do not improve their irrational and maladaptive thoughts.

What do you think?

What is your way of coping when you feel down? Do you look for pills (biological perspective), do you try to change your thoughts (psychological perspective) or do you seek support from friends and family (socio-cultural perspective)? Why?

Social cognition

The importance of the implicit personality theory

The power of psychological processes is also exemplified by the way in which our perceptions of others influence our interactions with them. We have seen how the implicit personality theory governs our first impressions (Chapter 7). The implicit personality theory refers to the network of associations each person has about the correlations between various personal characteristics. They include characteristics related to the appearance of people (e.g. the presence of glasses, the clothes worn), information related to them (e.g. their name), the way they talk and behave, and the groups they belong to. All these factors determine the impression people will make on us and the way we will interact with them.

For instance, we are more likely to initiate contact with people who resemble us than with people who are different from us, a phenomenon called the *similarity-attraction hypothesis*. Nass and colleagues (1995) showed that this bias even works in interactions with computers. On the basis of a questionnaire they distinguished between a group of dominant college students and a group of submissive students. The students had to interact with a computer to solve problems. Half the students worked with a 'dominant' computer, called Max, who used strong language consisting of assertions and commands (e.g. 'You should definitely rate the flashlight higher. It is your only reliable night signalling device.'). The other half interacted with a 'submissive' computer, Linus, who used weaker language consisting of questions and suggestions (e.g. 'Perhaps the flashlight should be rated higher? It may be your only reliable night signalling device.'). After the task the participants were asked to indicate how much they appreciated the help from the computer. The computer received higher ratings when its personality matched that of the participant; it was also judged more competent.

Interim summary

The psychological perspective

- According to the psychological perspective, mental life (both normal and abnormal) is primarily determined by psychological processes. We have seen three examples of this:

  - the importance of learning and cognition in perception (olfaction),
  - the importance of cognitive modulation in pain perception,
  - the role of irrational and maladaptive thoughts in depression.

- Psychological processes are also important in social interactions (social cognition).

11.4   The socio-cultural perspective

In the previous sections we saw evidence that human experiences and behaviour are influenced by biological factors and the way in which individuals perceive and process information. In addition to these two influences, people are also affected by the groups to which they belong and in which they move. Just think of it: how much of your time do you interact with others? And how much of the time you spend alone is actually devoted to thoughts of others, or to trying to meet their expectations (e.g. with respect to your academic performance)? Social factors were first emphasised within sociology, but in the course of the twentieth century became important in psychology as well (see the part on McDougall above). Below we discuss a few examples of social influences.

The first studies of social influences

The birth of sociology

Given that humans so often interact with others, it is surprising to see how long it took philosophers and scientists to pay attention to the influences people have on each other. Although there were a few isolated forerunners, the incorporation of social factors in thinking had to wait until the beginning of the nineteenth century when French scholars tried to understand what had happened during the French revolution. The best known among them was Auguste Comte (1798–1857; see Chapter 2), who coined the name 'sociology'. According to Comte, sociologists had to study the existing (Western) society by means of the scientific method and try to steer it towards improvement. (Just as in psychology, Comte's scientific, positivist dogma would later be questioned by a hermeneutic line of thought.) The early French sociologists were joined by similarly minded scholars in Germany, Italy, Great Britain and – towards the end of the nineteenth century – the USA.

Although sociologists were interested in social structures, for most of them the people inhabiting society were of secondary importance. Society was their primary unit of analysis. It produced the individual through the process of socialisation and it provided individuals with roles, positions, relationships and structures within which they had to function.

social Darwinism

belief in Victorian England and the USA that progress in a society could be made by allowing the strong members to flourish and the weak members to die

Impact of the evolutionary theory on sociological thinking

At the turn of the twentieth century sociological thinking found itself confronted with Darwin's evolutionary theory. On the one hand, the theory offered interesting points of view for the organisation of society (cf. McDougall's ideas discussed above). On the other hand, some conclusions went so diametrically against the sociological tenets that they were bound to elicit a negative response. Two lines of reasoning in particular provoked criticism.

The first development was social Darwinism, first propagated by Darwin's contemporary, Herbert Spencer (1820–1903). (For the sake of historical accuracy, it must be noted that the name 'social Darwinism' was rarely used in Spencer's day; it is a name that was given later to refer to this line of thought.) Spencer defended the idea that a society evolved in the same way as living creatures did, on the basis of natural selection. However, in his view natural selection improved the rough material with which it set out (you may remember from Chapter 2 that the idea of cumulative progress is a common misunderstanding of the evolution theory). So, according to Spencer, societies were constantly improving under the influence of natural selection. They should not be tampered with. In particular, Spencer claimed that a society should not help individuals who were struggling, because these were the ones on the verge of being eliminated by the 'survival of the fittest' (a phrase coined by him). In the same vein, individuals who were doing well should not be hindered because they were the ones scoring high on the fitness scale. Although Spencer later softened some of his writings, the following quote illustrates what social Darwinism in its raw form implied:

> Fostering the good-for-nothing at the expense of the good, is an extreme cruelty. It is a deliberate stirring-up of miseries for future generations. There is no greater curse to posterity than that of bequeathing to them an increasing population of imbeciles and idlers and criminals . . . The whole effort of nature is to get rid of such, to clear the world of them, and make room for better.
>
> *(Spencer, cited in Ritzer and Goodman (2004) p. 43)*

eugenics

social philosophy claiming that the fate of a nation can be improved by selective breeding of the inhabitants

Social Darwinism was swiftly joined by an even stronger version of how evolutionary theory could (or should) be applied to social issues: eugenics. According to this view, society should not be left free to do the natural selection, but it should be actively helped to produce more desirable individuals and get rid of the unwelcome elements. Originating in Britain with Francis Galton, eugenics would quickly capture the USA (Chapter 4) and be put into practice. It is estimated that several tens of thousands of people in the USA and Germany were sterilised against their will in the 1930s on the basis of the eugenic principle (Rutter 2006, p. 8).

Appalled by these excesses and influenced by the behaviourist manifesto that all behaviour is learned behaviour, psychologists would start to examine how human functioning was influenced by the presence of others. They became known as social psychologists. Below we list some of their main findings and tenets.

Social learning of cultural differences

Observational learning

observational learning

learning as a result of observing others performing actions and being rewarded or punished

A first important finding to help understand the influences people have on each other is the observation that automatic learning is not limited to classical conditioning and operant conditioning (see Chapter 4). For humans and animals it often is enough to observe others in order to learn. This form of learning is called observational learning or *social learning* and was introduced by the Canadian-American psychologist, Albert Bandura (born in 1925).

Observational learning means that individuals in a society learn the society's customs not by being rewarded for good behaviour and punished for bad behaviour, or by associating some activities with positive feelings and others with negative feelings, but simply by watching what others do and what consequences their behaviour has. As you may remember from Chapter 2, on the basis of his experiments Thorndike thought observational learning was impossible in cats. Since Thorndike's writings it has become clear, however, that this type of learning is quite prevalent and happens in all types of species.

A typical example of contemporary research on observational learning is Saggerson *et al.* (2005). In this study, naïve pigeons observed other pigeons that had been trained to peck or step on a panel to obtain food. Two lights indicated when food would be delivered. If the red light went up, the 'expert' pigeon stepped on the panel to obtain food; if the green light went on, the 'expert' pigeon pecked on the panel to get food. The observers were in an adjacent cage and could see the demonstrator through walls of transparent plastic. They did not have a response panel in their cage (and they were hungry). The observers received repeated cycles of observational training and testing. For the latter, they were placed in the chamber of the 'expert' pigeon in the absence of the demonstrator and received presentations of the two lights. Saggerson *et al.* reasoned that if the naïve pigeons had learned by observing the demonstrators, they should show the appropriate behaviour. This was indeed what happened.

Cultural differences

Observational learning explains many social phenomena, such as why people in different cultures prefer different types of food and why they eat more in some cultures than in others (Geier *et al.* 2006). It is also an important factor in perpetuating gender differences in accepted behaviour. Davis (2003), for instance, showed that the traditional division of roles between men and women is strongly promoted in television commercials targeted at children.

At a more general level, one of the most widely used schemes to understand cultural differences was proposed by the Dutch organisational psychologist Geert Hofstede (e.g. 2001). He distinguished four main dimensions along which cultures differ. They are:

1. *Power distance:* the extent to which the less powerful members (also in the family) accept and expect that power is distributed unequally; how much they are willing to honour the more powerful and show respect to them.

2. *Individualism vs. collectivism:* the degree to which individuals are integrated in groups. On the individualist side we have societies in which individuals primarily look after their own development. On the collectivist side, we have societies in which individuals primarily look at the interests of the group(s) to which they belong.

3. *Masculinity vs. femininity:* whether the values of the culture (in particular those for men) are biased towards assertive and competitive or towards modest and caring. On the masculine side of the dimension, there usually is a large gap between men's and women's values.

4. *Uncertainty avoidance:* the degree to which the society tolerates uncertainty. It indicates the extent to which individuals feel comfortable in unstructured, novel situations. Uncertainty avoiding cultures highly value traditions with strict laws and rules; they also prefer superiors from within their own cultures. Uncertainty accepting cultures are more tolerant of opinions different from those they are used to; they have fewer rules and more easily accept superiors from abroad.

Table 11.2 Degrees to which different countries accept differences in power, stress individualism, stress masculinity and try to avoid uncertainty

Country	Power	Individualism	Masculinity	Uncertainty avoidance
Arab world	80	38	52	68
Australia	36	90	61	51
Brazil	69	38	49	76
Canada	39	80	52	48
China	80	20	66	30
France	68	71	43	86
Germany	35	67	66	65
India	77	48	56	40
Japan	54	46	95	92
Mexico	81	30	69	82
Netherlands	38	80	14	53
Poland	68	60	64	93
Russia	93	39	36	95
Sweden	31	71	5	29
United Kingdom	35	89	66	35
United States	40	91	62	46

Source: Adapted from Hofstede, G. (2005) *Cultures and Organizations: Software of the Mind,* 2nd Edition, McGraw Hill Professional. With permission.

Table 11.2 lists the values of the four dimensions for some countries. Go to the website http://www.geert-hofstede.com to find them for other countries. According to the social perspective these values will have strong effects on how the individuals in different societies function.

Nature vs. nurture

nature–nurture debate

discussion about the respective contributions of genes and environment in the development of (human) qualities

The social perspective is adamant that many individual differences are not due to inherited, genetic traits, but to the social experiences people have had. The resulting discussion between the social and the biological perspective is known as the nature–nurture debate. At a general level (see below for provisos), the variance not accounted for by heredity in table 11.1 can be ascribed to differences in the environment. In addition, proponents of the social perspective will question to what extent the heredity figures have been overestimated because of environmental confounds (e.g. because the environments of identical twins are more similar than those of fraternal twins).

Adoption and intelligence

One way to gauge the importance of the environment is to look at the consequences of adoption into a different environment. A particularly informative study in this respect was published by Capron and Duyme (1989). They looked at the intelligence of 14-year-old French children who had been adopted before the age of 6 months. On the basis of archives the authors were able to locate four groups of individuals. The

Table 11.3 The combined effects of nature and nurture on the IQ-scores of adopted children

This table shows that both heredity and environment have a substantial effect on the IQ-scores of children who had been adopted before the age of 6 months.

	Adoption family	
Biological parents	**Low intelligence**	**High intelligence**
Low intelligence	92	104
High intelligence	108	120

Source: Capron and Duyme (1989). Reprinted by permission from Macmillan Publishers Ltd: Assessment of effects of socioeconomic status on IQ in full cross-fostering design. *Nature*, **340**, p. 552–3 (Capron, C. and Duyme, M. (1989) copyright © 1989.

first group had biological parents with low intelligence and went to adoption families with low intelligence. The second group of children had biological parents with low intelligence and were adopted by families with high intelligence. The third group of children had intelligent biological parents, and were adopted by less intelligent families. Finally, the fourth group had intelligent biological parents and were adopted by intelligent families. Table 11.3 shows the IQ-scores of the four groups.

Table 11.3 clearly illustrates that both nature and nurture have a considerable impact on the intelligence of adoptive children. The children of biological parents with low intelligence scored on average 16 IQ-points lower than the children of biological parents with high intelligence. At the same time, children who came into an adoptive family with high intelligence scored 12 IQ-points higher than children who were adopted by a family with a low intelligence.

A paradox in the nature–nurture debate

Within the nature–nurture debate, it is important to know that the relative importance of heredity and environment, as shown in table 11.1, is not fixed, but depends on the way in which the society is organised. This can easily be illustrated with intelligence. Imagine a society where 10 per cent of the population is extremely rich and can afford the best education for their children; the other 90 per cent is extremely poor, is not nourished properly, and cannot afford schooling for their children. In such a society, the environment (i.e. the socio-economic status of the parents) will have much more impact than the genes of the parents. That is, there will be a high correlation between the intelligence of the children and the socio-economic status of their parents, and a low correlation between the intelligence of the children and environment-free intelligence measures of the parents. Now imagine a society in which each child has access to exactly the same type of good education, where each child is supported to attain his or her full potential. In such a society, the intelligence differences between the children will have a low correlation with the socio-economic status of their parents (the environment) but will have a high correlation with the genetic intelligence of the parents.

The above situation leads to a counterintuitive paradox in the nature–nurture debate. It is the following: *The more a society tries to give each child proper education, the higher the variance explained by heredity will be and the more it will look as if the environment has little impact on intelligence.* It may be good to keep this paradox in mind if in the future you read articles about the relative impact of genes and environment. A low correlation with the socio-economic status of the parents does not necessarily mean that the environment has no influence on the intelligence of children; it may also mean that society has managed to wipe out the impact of the parents' socio-economic status by providing first class education to all the children. A similar paradox applies to all topics that form the subject of a nature–nurture debate.

Interactions in the nature–nurture debate

Although the contributions of nature and nurture are often presented in a simplified, either–or way, recent insights have depicted a much richer picture, full of interactions between genes and environment (Rutter 2006). For a start, very few genes have a deterministic outcome (i.e. invariably lead to a certain characteristic when they are present in one form, and to another characteristic when they are present in another form). Instead, most of the time genetic influences operate probabilistically. That is, they slightly increase or decrease the chances of having a certain condition or they slightly increase or decrease the severity of the condition (see the difference between stochastic and deterministic processes in Chapter 10 for an analogy).

Second, the influences of the environment are also probabilistic. They too slightly increase or decrease the likelihood and/or severity of a certain characteristic. Third, the influences of nature and nurture do not simply add on, but can reinforce each other. For instance, in each cell only a small percentage of the genes are active. The genes involved in forming a nose, for example, are only active in one part of the body. Otherwise the whole body would consist of nose-like structures. So, every cell not only contains the DNA needed for the formation of all the different body parts, but also a complicated system of keys that determine which genes in a cell will become active and which not. In recent years, it is becoming clear that the activation of genes in cells may also depend on the environment in which a person grows up. Some gene-related personality features only become active in certain environments. In this way, genes and environment interact. Finally, a person's genes to some extent determine the environment in which the person will dwell. People shape and select their environment partially as a function of their genetic constitution (e.g. people with high energy levels are more likely to find themselves in risky and demanding environments).

Notice that the interactions currently being investigated between nature and nurture are unlikely to be the only ones. If psychological processes are equally important for human functioning, as proposed by the biopsychosocial model, then we can expect interactions between all three types of influences.

strong social situation

a situation in which nearly all individuals act virtually the same, despite differences in biological make-up and differences in learning history

Strong social situations

Another argument in favour of the social perspective is that in some social situations nearly all individuals act very much the same, despite differences in biological make-up and differences in learning history. Such situations are sometimes called strong social situations, because the situation overwhelms the differences in personal traits that people assume to be the controller of social behaviour. In Chapter 6 we saw an example of such a situation when we described Milgram's obedience research (1974).

Another classic study is the Stanford Prison Experiment (Haney *et al.* 1973). In this study, students who had volunteered to take part in a psychological experiment, were 'arrested' without warning and 'jailed' in a basement of Stanford University, which looked like a real prison. They were guarded by peer students, who also had been selected randomly and been imparted this responsibility. The study was an attempt to examine what conformity pressures would do to groups of people functioning within the institutional setting of a prison, what the power of institutional environments was to influence those who passed through them.

This is how Haney and Zimbardo (1998) summarised the findings 25 years later:

Twenty-five years ago, a group of psychologically healthy, normal college students (and several presumably mentally sound experimenters) were temporarily but dramatically transformed in the course of six days spent in a prison-like environment, in research that came to be known as the Stanford Prison Experiment . . . The outcome of our study was shocking and unexpected to us, our professional colleagues, and the general public. Otherwise emotionally strong college students who were randomly assigned to be mock-prisoners suffered acute psychological trauma and breakdowns. Some of the students begged to be released from the intense pains of less than a week of merely simulated imprisonment, whereas others adapted by becoming blindly obedient to the unjust authority of the guards. The guards, too— who also had been carefully chosen on the basis of their normal–average scores on a variety of personality measures—quickly internalized their randomly assigned role. Many of these seemingly gentle and caring young men, some of whom had described themselves as pacifists or Vietnam War 'doves,' soon began mistreating their peers and were indifferent to the obvious suffering that their actions produced. Several of them devised sadistically inventive ways to harass and degrade the prisoners, and none of the less actively cruel mock-guards ever intervened or complained about the abuses they witnessed. Most of the worst prisoner treatment came on the night shifts and other occasions when the guards thought they could avoid the surveillance and interference of the research team. Our planned two-week experiment had to be aborted after only six days because the experience dramatically and painfully transformed most of the participants in ways we did not anticipate, prepare for, or predict.

(Haney and Zimbardo 1998, p. 709)

Haney and Zimbardo (1998) still subscribed to the conclusion they had drawn from the study 25 years earlier:

The negative, anti-social reactions observed were not the product of an environment created by combining a collection of deviant personalities, but rather the result of an intrinsically pathological situation which could distort and rechannel the behaviour of essentially normal individuals. The abnormality here resided in the psychological nature of the situation and not in those who passed through it.

(Haney and Zimbardo 1998, p. 710)

Indeed, Zimbardo (2004) referred to the same findings when he explained five years later why American soldiers had tortured Iraqi prisoners of war:

> The horrifying photos of young Iraqis abused by American soldiers have shocked the world with their depictions of human degradation, forcing us to acknowledge that some of our beloved soldiers have committed barbarous acts of cruelty and sadism. Now there is a rush to analyze human behavior, blaming flawed or pathological individuals for evil and ignoring other important factors. Unless we learn the dynamics of 'why,' we will never be able to counteract the powerful forces that can transform ordinary people into evil perpetrators.

Psychological research as a social enterprise?

Psychological research depends on the social context in which psychologists work

Social factors are particularly emphasised in critical psychology (Chapter 9), not only with respect to the participants in the studies but also with respect to the researchers themselves. Remember that according to postmodernists scientific knowledge is a social construction. Scientists do not study reality but construct reality (see also Chapter 12). This is how the American scholar Stephen Jay Gould formulated it:

> . . . science must be understood as a social phenomenon, a gutsy, human enterprise, not the work of robots programmed to collect pure information . . . Science, since people must do it, is a socially embedded activity.
>
> *(Gould 1996, p. 53)*

According to Gould, social embeddedness is particularly true for a discipline like psychology, because:

> . . . some topics are invested with enormous social importance but blessed with very little reliable information. When the ratio of data to social impact is so low, a history of scientific attitudes may be little more than an oblique record of social change.
>
> *(Gould 1996, p. 54)*

An argument in favour of this view is that psychological research knows a good deal of faddism: research issues come, are popular for some time, and go without leaving a trace. As noticed by Hunt (2005):

> mainstream experimental research in psychology can appear curiously faddish. Research central to one decade is all but gone from leading journals in the next, replaced by topics often entirely independent and noncumulative . . . Further, and in marked contrast to the usual energization of research in the physical sciences resulting from consensual resolution of major debates, in psychology research topics often seem to disappear precisely after research consensus has been reached.
>
> *(Hunt 2005, p. 360)*

According to critical psychologists, social factors will (co-)determine which view psychologists promote. There is some evidence for this. For instance, Gould (1996) noticed that biological factors in intelligence research tend to come to the fore each time there is a political turn to the right with promises of fewer taxes and fewer social services. Such a political shift is usually justified by a rhetoric stressing that people are born into their social classes because of their genetic endowment. Consequently, there is little point in helping those of the low classes. In contrast, social factors in psychological theories are dominant when there is a massive economic expansion and upward social mobility (as in the USA at the beginning of the twentieth century, and Europe and the USA after World War II).

A critique of evolutionary psychology

According to critical psychologists, social factors are involved in the current popularity of evolutionary psychology as well. The argument is that evolutionary psychology has many followers, not because the evidence for it is stronger or scientifically more convincing, but because social factors make psychologists more inclined to adopt this view. The following social reasons have been mentioned (Buller 2005; Fausto-Sterling *et al.* 1997; Jackson and Rees 2007):

- evolutionary psychology is popular because it focuses on the origin and history of humankind, which easily catches people's interest (e.g. it is the theme of most popular science books),
- the focus on sex and reproduction also has a strong appeal, certainly when the individual organism is seen as unconsciously engaged in strategies to maximise its opportunity to mate and to ensure survival of its offspring,
- the main principles of evolutionary psychology are simple just-so stories that can be understood without much effort,
- evolutionary psychology has benefited from attracting a highly talented group of popular-science writers (e.g. Robert Wright and Steven Pinker),
- evolutionary psychology affirms existing gender inequalities and stereotypes (females are more sexually reserved than males, women are only interested in sex until they have children, women have less of men's innate ambition and willingness to take the risks needed for professional success),
- evolutionary psychology suggests an 'explanation' for why many people are unhappy (their body and mind are not adapted to modern society).

In Chapter 12 we will see more examples of how society and research interact.

What do you think?

How do you now feel about the relative importance of biological, psychological and socio-cultural factors? Has our discussion made you change your mind? In what way? Or why not?

Interim summary

The socio-cultural perspective

- First accentuated by sociologists (nineteenth century, Comte).

- Ambivalent relationship with evolutionary theory:
  - On the one hand, evolutionary theory provides interesting ideas.
  - On the other hand, evolutionary theory gives rise to claims sociologists do not believe in (social Darwinism, eugenics).

- The influence of socio-cultural factors is due to the learning of cultural differences:
  - Observational learning (form of associative learning).
  - According to Hofstede, cultures differ on four dimensions:
    - power distance,
    - individualism vs. collectivism,
    - masculinity vs. femininity,
    - uncertainty avoidance.

- Nature–nurture debate: to what extent are individual differences in processing due to genes and to environment?
  - Intelligence: adoption study showing impact of both.
  - Genes and environment are not each other's opposite; both influences are probabilistic (i.e. increase or decrease likelihoods) and interact with each other.

- The importance of social factors also clear in strong social situations, where the situation overwhelms the differences in biological constitution and learning history.
  - Examples are Milgram's obedience studies and the Stanford Prison Experiment.

- Socio-cultural factors are emphasised in critical psychology, in particular with respect to the ways in which socio-cultural factors influence the hypotheses psychologists (and other scientists) are interested in.

11.5   Focus on: Why are people aggressive?

In the sections above we reviewed the arguments psychologists have used to argue that mental life is the result of biological, psychological and social forces, and, therefore, requires a biopsychosocial model of explanation. We also mentioned that the balance between the three types of variables is a precarious one, constantly shifting as a function of the latest findings. For instance, in the past 10 years the biological perspective has gained considerably in strength, under the influence of brain imaging techniques, evolutionary psychology, and the biological treatment of mental disorders. A look at the past suggests that this surge in biological interest is likely to be followed by a rebound of the psychological and/or the social perspective at some point in the future.

So far we have illustrated the three perspectives with different topics. However, it is also possible (and instructive) to illustrate them with respect to the same topic. For instance, why are people aggressive? Why do they enforce harm on others who try to escape this? (For reviews, see Anderson and Bushman 2002; Geen 2001).

Biological factors

The death drive in Freud's theory

One of the first explicit theories about aggression was presented by Freud. In some of his later writings he saw humans as driven by two innate drives: eros and a death drive (*Todestrieb*; later called *thanatos*). Eros was geared towards pleasure and the preservation of life; the death drive was directed towards destruction. The latter resulted in aggression and the refusal of pleasure. Both drives accumulated over time and needed to be discharged periodically, giving rise to a catharsis. As a result, both pleasure seeking and aggression were inherent features of humans.

Lorenz's evolutionary theory

The idea of aggression as an innate feature, a drive, was also put forward by the Austrian animal researcher, Konrad Lorenz (1903–1989), and integrated within an evolutionary perspective. According to him, aggression was essential for the survival of the fittest because fighting for mates ensured that the offspring came from the strongest exemplars. Another advantage was that chased-off animals increased the dispersion of the species. Aggression built up over time and fired off whenever an appropriate stimulus was encountered. The resulting violence freed the energy, which was followed by a new accumulation.

Evidence for a biological component

Evidence for a biological contribution can be found in the fact that humans show individual differences in their degree of aggressiveness and that these differences are to a considerable extent inherited. As shown in table 11.1, heredity is estimated to account for 40–53 per cent of the variance in aggression encountered in humans. Other evidence for a biological contribution comes from the critical role of the limbic system in the regulation of aggression. This is an evolutionarily old part of the brain that is also involved in the regulation of emotions. An imbalance in the chemical substances that regulate the communication in this part of the brain results in an increased degree of aggression. A final biological factor is the availability of the male hormone testosterone. When female-to-male transsexuals were injected with testosterone as part of their gender changing treatment, they reported a surge of aggressive feelings. The opposite happened when male-to-female transsexuals received testosterone-lowering medication (Van Goozen *et al.* 1995).

Implications for treatment

Knowing about biological risk factors increases the possibility of medical treatment. At the same time, an exclusive reliance on the biological component drastically reduces the range of treatments, because the biological perspective does not offer much more than medicines to influence the communication in the limbic system and to lower the availability of testosterone in individuals with a high genetic risk. It also supplies tests to assess who has an enhanced risk, so that they can be watched (and maybe incarcerated preventively). For the others, Freud and Lorenz recommended hard work and competitive sports to channel the aggressive energy towards more acceptable outlets.

Psychological factors

Learning aggressive behaviour

The psychological perspective stresses the importance of learning, perception and interpretation in aggression. Individuals who are reinforced for aggressive behaviour, will increase it; individuals who are not reinforced (or punished), will decrease it. Patterson (1982), for instance, described circumstances in which children learn to behave aggressively, either because this leads to positive results or because it stops negative situations (which may happen, for instance, when a child notices that it is no longer bullied when it responds aggressively). According to the psychological perspective, much aggression (theft, fraud, extortion) is not elicited by aggression-provoking stimuli, as Freud and Lorenz claimed, but is due to the profit the perpetrator expects to extract from it.

Aggression is learned not only on the basis of one's own experiences, but also on the basis of what is observed in others. These can be real life models, but also characters from movies and videogames. There is a long tradition of research showing observational learning of aggression by watching violent films or taking part in brutal videogames (Anderson *et al.* 2003). Observational learning is one of the main reasons why individuals who as children suffered from domestic violence are more likely to continue this behaviour in their new families (continuing a familial cycle of violence).

The importance of a person's perceptions

There is also good evidence that aggressive people have different perceptions from less aggressive individuals. They perceive more events as threatening, insulting or provocative. Dodge and Coie (1987) gave a review of the attributions that are likely to provoke aggression. An aggressive response is more likely,

- when a social situation is perceived as intentional rather than accidental,
- when a social situation is perceived as foreseeable rather than unforeseeable,
- when a social situation is perceived as freely chosen by the other rather than constrained.

A person who is biased to perceiving actions of others as intentional, foreseeable and of their own choice is more likely to respond aggressively than a person who is inclined to see actions as accidental, unforeseeable and due to circumstances.

The role of social skills

Finally, there is evidence that people with a high degree of aggression have more limited social skills. They have learned to solve their problems by resorting to violent behaviour and do not seem to have the normal range of responses. Nangle *et al.* (2002) reported that aggression is less likely in persons with skills:

- to negotiate conflict and influence peers,
- to participate and cooperate,
- to communicate (e.g. knowing that a listener ought to remain silent as long as a speaker is making a statement),
- to generate alternative solutions,
- to think of the consequences of actions,
- to pair solutions and consequences (both short term and long term),
- to appreciate that others have thoughts, feelings and motives in problem situations (i.e. perspective taking),
- to contain their anger and make use of self-instruction, relaxation and self-regulation.

Implications for treatment

The more individuals learn about possible causes of aggression and how to deal with them in a non-violent way, the more likely they are to resort to ways of settling their disagreements other than violence. Most children learn this from their natural environment (family, peers, school), but psychologists maintain that those skills can be learned throughout life and, therefore, should be part of rehabilitation programmes. Violent individuals often come from families where the parents were bad examples.

Social factors

Evidence for a social contribution

Because of the learning mentioned above, children who grow up in a social group with a high level of violence will be exposed to more aggression-related learning than children who grow up in more serene circumstances. An interesting study in this respect was published by Bohman (1996), who examined adopted children in Sweden. For each child, Bohman had information about the antisocial behaviour in the biological and the adoptive parents, and records about whether or not the children as adults came into trouble with the police. Table 11.4 lists the results.

When both the genes and the environment were aggression-free, only 3 per cent of the adopted children ran into trouble with the police by the time they were adults. Violence in the biological parents increased the percentage to 12 per cent; violence in the adoption family to 7 per cent. However, the strongest effect was seen when both the biological and the adoption parents were prone to antisocial behaviour. Then, 40 per cent of the children were known to the police for troublesome behaviour

Table 11.4 Aggression in adopted children as a function of antisocial behaviour in the biological and adoptive parents

These data show the combined effects of nature and nurture on aggression. When both influences were peaceful, only 3% of the children got in trouble with the police. The percentage rose both when either nature or nurture was a risk factor, and spiralled to 40% when both were negative.

Antisocial behaviour in adoptive parents	Antisocial behaviour in biological parents	
	Yes	No
Yes	40%	7%
No	12%	3%

Source: Bohman (1996)

(which incidentally is an example of the interactions between genes and environment discussed above; they can reinforce each other).

The diathesis–stress model

A model that has been proposed to explain the interaction between biological and social factors, as found by Bohman, is the **diathesis–stress model** (Zubin and Spring 1977). According to this model, the likelihood of a person having a disorder depends on the vulnerability of that person (the diathesis) and the amount of stress in the environment. The vulnerability is the outcome of genetic risk-factors and previous experiences (e.g. child abuse). A highly vulnerable person will show the disorder even under low levels of stress. An individual with low vulnerability may still succumb to the disorder when the life circumstances are excessively stressful.

Other environmental factors that increase the probability of violence

Apart from the social environment, there are other factors that can increase the occurrence of violence. They are: frustration (being hindered in the achievement of a goal), provocation, threat, heat, noise, pain, the availability of weapons, alcohol and drugs. Social groups that are more exposed to these factors have a higher chance of acting violently. Finally, aggressive individuals will shape their environment so that it better fits their behaviour. A common phenomenon is that aggressive adolescents become isolated within their normal social groups (family, school, usual nightlife) and seek the company of gangs that highly value aggressive behaviour. Within these groups, the use of violence is further reinforced by the increase in status and power it brings.

Implications for treatment

Knowledge about the importance of social factors helps to organise communities in order to prevent violence, and is extremely useful in rehabilitation programmes to avoid relapse.

In summary, uncovering the various factors that contribute to aggression helps communities to deal with this problem. As the above review shows, progress is most likely not by focusing on a single perspective at the exclusion of the others, but by taking into account all three types of factors: the biological, the psychological and the social.

Interim summary

Why are people aggressive?

■ Biological contributions:

  ■ evolutionary advantage of aggressiveness,
  ■ individual differences that to a large extent are inherited,
  ■ chemical imbalances in the limbic system,
  ■ impact of testosterone,
  ■ points to a medical treatment (also preventive).

■ Psychological contributions:

  ■ learning aggressive behaviour on the basis of observational learning and operant conditioning (positive results or the termination of a negative situation),
  ■ biases in the perception, so that more social situations are seen as provocative,
  ■ limited social skills, so that there is no other response than a violent one,
  ■ points to the importance of teaching new perceptions and responses in the treatment of aggression.

■ Social contributions:

  ■ degree to which the environment exposes children to aggression-related learning,
  ■ interacts with the person's vulnerability (diathesis–stress model),
  ■ series of other violence-provoking features in the environment,
  ■ aggressive individuals seek the company of gang members that reinforce their behaviour,
  ■ points to the need to change social influences in the treatment of aggression.

? What do you think?

Given the many sources of evidence for the biopsychosocial model, it is surprising how little impact this model has in practice (both in research and in the treatment of diseases and disorders). Can you think of reasons? Why do more people seem to focus on the impact of a single factor than on the combined impacts of the different factors?

Recommended literature

A good book about evolutionary psychology is Buss, D.M. (2004) *Evolutionary psychology: The new science of the mind* (2nd edn) (Boston: Pearson Education).

At the same time it may be interesting to read a more critical evaluation, such as Buller, D.J. (2005) *Adapting minds: Evolutionary psychology and the persistent quest for human nature* (Cambridge, MA: MIT Press).

A good book about learning and conditioning is Bouton, M.E. (2007) *Learning and behavior: A contemporary synthesis* (Sunderland, MA: Sinauer Associates Inc.).

An interesting book about the social and cultural influences on human behaviour is Matsumoto, D. and Juang, L. (2004). *Culture and psychology* (3rd edn) (London: Thomson Wadworth).

References

Anderson, C.A. and Bushman, B.J. (2002) 'Human aggression', *Annual Review of Psychology*, 53: 27–51.

Anderson, C.A. *et al.* (2003) 'The influence of media violence on youth', *Psychological Science in the Public Interest*, 4: 81–110.

Axelrod, R. and Hamilton, W.D. (1981) 'The evolution of cooperation', *Science*, 211: 1390–6.

Bernard, L.L. (1924) *Instinct: A study of social psychology*. New York: Henry Holt & Co.

Bohman, M. (1996) 'Predisposition to criminality: Swedish adoption studies in retrospect.' In G.R. Bock and J.A. Goode (eds.), *Genetics of criminal and antisocial behaviour*. Chichester: Wiley, pp. 99–114.

Boomsma, D.I., Willemsen, G., Dolan, C.V., Hawkley, L.C. and Cacioppo, J.T. (2005) 'Genetic and environmental contributions to loneliness in adults: The Netherlands Twin Register study', *Behavior Genetics*, 35: 745–52.

Bouchard, T.J. (1994) 'Genes, environment, and personality', *Science*, 264: 1700–1.

Buller, D.J. (2005) *Adapting minds: Evolutionary psychology and the persistent quest for human nature*. Cambridge, MA: MIT Press.

Buss, D.M. (1989) 'Sex differences in human mate preference: Evolutionary hypotheses testing in 37 cultures', *Behavioral and Brain Sciences*, 12: 1–49.

Buss, D.M. (2004) *Evolutionary psychology: The new science of the mind* (2nd edn). Boston, MA: Pearson Education.

Capron, C. and Duyme, M. (1989) 'Assessment of effects of socioeconomic status on IQ in a full cross-fostering design', *Nature*, 340: 552–3.

Chebat, J.C. and Michon, R. (2003) 'Impact of ambient odors on mall shoppers' emotions, cognition, and spending: A test of competitive causal theories', *Journal of Business Research*, 56: 529–39.

Davis, S.N. (2003) 'Sex stereotypes in commercials targeted toward children: A content analysis', *Sociological Spectrum*, 23: 407–24.

De Araujo, I.E. Rolls, E.T., Velazco, M.I., Margot, C. and Cayeux, I. (2005) 'Cognitive modulation of olfactory processing', *Neuron*, 46: 671–9.

DeRubeis, R.J. *et al.* (2005) 'Cognitive therapy vs. medications in the treatment of moderate to severe depression', *Archives of General Psychiatry*, 62: 409–16.

Djordevic, J. *et al.* (2008) 'A rose by any other name: Would it smell as sweet?' *Journal of Neurophysiology*, 99: 386–93.

Dodge, K.A. and Coie, J.D. (1987) 'Social-information-processing factors in reactive and proactive aggression in children's peer groups', *Journal of Personality and Social Psychology,* **53**: 1146–58.

Engel, G.L. (1977) 'The need for a new medical model: A challenge for biomedicine', *Science,* **196**: 129–36.

Fausto-Sterling, A., Gowaty, P.A. and Zuk, M. (1997) 'Evolutionary psychology and Darwinian feminism', *Feminist Studies* **23**: 403–18.

Geary, D.C., Vigil, J. and Byrd-Craven, J. (2004) 'Evolution of human mate choice', *The Journal of Sex Research,* **41**: 27–42.

Geen, R.G. (2001) *Human aggression* (2nd edn). Buckingham, UK: Open University Press.

Geier, A.B., Rozin, P. and Doros, G. (2006) 'Unit bias: A new heuristic that helps explain the effect of portion size on food intake', *Psychological Science,* **17**: 521–5.

Gould, S.J. (1996) *The mismeasure of man* (2nd edn). New York: W.W. Norton & Co.

Hamilton, W.D. (1964) 'The genetical evolution of social behavior I and II', *Journal of Theoretical Biology,* **7**: 1–52.

Haney, C. and Zimbardo, P. (1998) 'The past and future of US prison policy: Twenty-five years after the Stanford Prison Experiment', *American Psychologist,* **53**: 709–27.

Haney, C., Banks, W. and Zimbardo, P. (1973) 'Interpersonal dynamics in a simulated prison', *International Journal of Criminology and Penology,* **1**: 69–97.

Hofstede, G. (2001) *Culture's consequences: Comparing values, behaviors, institutions, and organizations across nations.* Thousand Oaks, CA: Sage Publications.

Hofstede, G. (2005) *Cultures and organizations: Software of the mind* (2nd edn). London: McGraw-Hill Professional.

Hollon, S.D. *et al.* (2005) 'Prevention of relapse following cognitive therapy vs medications in moderate to severe depression', *Archives of General Psychiatry,* **62**: 417–22.

Hunt, H.T. (2005) 'Why psychology is/is not traditional science: The self-referential bases of psychological research and theory', *Review of General Psychology,* **9**: 358–74.

Jackson, S. and Rees, A. (2007) 'The appalling appeal of nature: The popular influence of evolutionary psychology as a problem for sociology', *Sociology,* **41**: 917–30.

Jacob, S. *et al.* (2002) 'Paternally inherited HLA alleles are associated with women's choice of male odor', *Nature Genetics,* **30**: 175–9.

Jahoda, G. (2007) *A history of social psychology.* Cambridge: Cambridge University Press.

Keefe, F.J., Rumble, M.E., Scipio, C.D., Giordano, L.A. and Perri, L.M. (2004) 'Psychological aspects of persistent pain: Current state of the science', *The Journal of Pain,* **5**: 195–211.

Kendler, K.S., Thornton, L.M., Gilman, S.E. and Kessler, R.C. (2000) 'Sexual orientation in a U.S. national sample of twin and nontwin sibling pairs', *American Journal of Psychiatry,* **157**: 1843–6.

Kirsch, I., Deacon, B.J., Huedo-Medina, T.B., Scoboria, A., Moore, T.J. and Johnson, B.T. (2008) 'Initial severity and antidepressant benefits: A metaanalysis of data submitted to the Food and Drug Administration', *PLoS Med 5(2): e45.* doi:10.1371/journal.pmed.0050045 Received 23 January 2007.

Kobayakawa, K. *et al.* (2007) 'Innate versus learned odour processing in the mouse olfactory bulb', *Nature,* **450**: 503–8.

Lehman, A.F. and Steinwachs, D.M. (1998) 'At issue: Translating research into practice: The Schizophrenia Patient Outcomes Research Team (PORT) treatment recommendations', *Schizophrenia Bulletin,* **24**: 1–10.

Li, W., Howard, J.D., Parrish, T.B. and Gottfried, J.A. (2008) 'Aversive learning enhances perceptual and cortical discrimination of indiscriminable odor cues', *Science,* **319**: 1842–5.

Liu, I., Blacker, D.L., Xu, R., Fitzmaurice, G., Lyons, M.J. and Tsuang, M.T. (2004) 'Genetic and environmental contributions to the development of alcohol dependence in male twins', *Archives of General Psychiatry,* **61**: 897–903.

Mackintosh, N.J. (1998) *IQ and human intelligence.* Oxford: Oxford University Press.

McNulty, J.K., Neff, L.A. and Karney, B.R. (2008) 'Beyond initial attraction: Physical attractiveness in newlywed marriage', *Journal of Family Psychology*, 22: 135–43.

Melzack, R. and Wall, P.D. (1965) 'Pain mechanisms: A new theory', *Science*, 150: 971–9.

Miles, D.R. and Carey, G. (1997) 'Genetic and environmental architecture of human aggression', *Journal of Personality and Social Psychology*, 72: 207–17.

Milgram, S. (1974) *Obedience to authority: An experimental view.* New York: Harper & Row.

Nangle, D.W., Erdley, C.A., Carpenter, E.M. and Newman, J.E. (2002) 'Social skills training as a treatment for aggressive children and adolescents: A developmental-clinical integration', *Aggression and Violent Behavior*, 7: 169–99.

Nass, C., Moon, Y., Fogg, B.J., Reeves, B. and Dryer, D.C. (1995) 'Can computer personalities be human personalities?' *International Journal of Human–Computer Studies*, 43: 223–39.

Nolen-Hoeksema, S. (2000) 'The role of rumination in depressive disorders and mixed anxiety/depressive symptoms', *Journal of Abnormal Psychology*, 109: 504–11.

Ochsner, K.R. and Gross, J.J. (2005) 'The cognitive control of emotion', *Trends in Cognitive Sciences*, 9: 242–9.

O'Rahilly, S. and Farooqi, I.S. (2006) 'Genetics of obesity', *Philosophical Transaction of the Royal Society B – Biological Sciences*, 361: 1095–105.

Patterson, G.R. (1982) *Coercive family process.* Eugene, OR: Castalia.

Peterson, C. (1997) *Psychology: A biopsychosocial approach.* (2nd edn). New York: Addison Wesley Longman.

Raskind, W.H. (2001) 'Current understanding of the genetic basis of reading and spelling disability', *Learning Disability Quarterly*, 24: 141–57.

Richardson, R.C. (2007) *Evolutionary psychology as maladapted psychology.* Cambridge, MA: MIT Press.

Ritzer, G. and Goodman, D.J. (2004) *Modern sociological theory* (6th edn). Boston: McGraw Hill.

Rutter, M. (2006) *Genes and behavior: Nature–nurture interplay explained.* Oxford: Blackwell Publishing.

Saggerson, A.L., George, D.N. and Honey, R.C. (2005) 'Imitative learning of stimulus–response and response–outcome associations in pigeons', *Journal of Experimental Psychology: Animal Behavior Processes*, 31: 289–300.

Spangenberg, E.R., Sprott, D.E., Grohmann, B. and Tracy, D.L. (2006) 'Gender-congruent ambient scent influences on approach and avoidance behaviors in a retail store', *Journal of Business Research*, 59: 1281–7.

Stubbe, J.H., Posthuma, D., Boomsma, D.I. and De Geus, E.J.C. (2005) 'Heritability of life satisfaction in adults: A twin-family study', *Psychological Medicine*, 35: 1581–88.

Sullivan, P.F., Neale, M.C. and Kendler, K.S. (2000) 'Genetic epidemiology and major depression: Review and meta-analysis', *American Journal of Psychiatry*, 157: 1552–62.

Sullivan, P.F., Kendler, K.S. and Neale, M.C. (2003) 'Schizophrenia as a complex trait: Evidence from a meta-analyis of twin studies', *Archives of General Psychiatry*, 60: 1187–92.

Thapar, A., Langley, K., Owen, M.J. and O'Donavan, M.C. (2007) 'Advances in genetic findings on attention deficit hyperactivity disorder', *Psychological Medicine*, 37: 1681–92.

Torgersen, S. *et al.* (2000) 'A twin study of personality disorders', *Comprehensive Psychiatry*, 41: 416–25.

Trivers, R.L. (1971) 'The evolution of reciprocal altruism,' *Quarterly Review of Biology*, 46: 35–57.

Trivers, R.L. (1972) 'Parental investment and sexual selection.' In B. Campbell (ed.), *Sexual selection and the descent of man: 1871–1971.* Chicago: Aldine, pp. 136–79.

Van Goozen, S.H.M., Cohen-Kettenis, P.T., Gooren, L.J.G., Frijda, N.H. and Van de Poll, N.E. (1995) 'Gender differences in behaviour: Activating effects of cross-sex hormones', *Psychoneuroendocrinology*, 20: 343–63.

Van Vugt, M., De Cremer, D. and Janssen, D.P. (2007) 'Gender differences in cooperation and competition: The male-warrior hypothesis', *Psychological Science*, 18: 19–23.

Wampold, B.E., Minami, T., Tierney, S.C., Baskin, T.W. and Bhati, K.S. (2005) 'The placebo is powerful: Estimating placebo effects in medicine and psychotherapy for randomized clinical trials', *Journal of Clinical Psychology*, **61**: 835–54.

Watson, J.B. (1925) *Behaviorism*. New York: People's Institute Publishing Company. (Reprinted in 1997 by Transaction Publishers.)

Wilson, E.O. (1975) *Sociobiology: The new synthesis*. Cambridge, MA: Harvard University Press.

Woodworth, R.S. (1948) *Contemporary schools of psychology* (Revised edn). New York: The Ronald Press.

Zimbardo, P.G. (2004) 'Power turns good soldiers into "bad apples".' Editorial in *The Boston Globe*, May 9.

Zubin, J. and Spring, B. (1977) 'Vulnerability: A new view of schizophrenia', *Journal of Abnormal Psychology*, **86**: 103–26.

12 Psychology and society
The socio-political side

This chapter will cover

Questions to consider

Historical issues addressed in this chapter

- Is the rise of psychology related to changes in religious convictions?
- Why does psychology today attach more interest to ethics in research and practice than in the first half of the twentieth century?

Conceptual issues addressed in this chapter

- Why are metaphors important in psychological research? Where do they come from?
- How has research on intelligence testing been influenced by social values in society?
- Are psychologists involved in power struggles between socio-political groups?
- In what way may postmodernism have contributed to the rise of pseudo-science?
- In what ways can psychological knowledge be misused?
- Does psychological research have an influence on the way in which people view themselves and interact with others?
- Could it be that psychologists create needs rather than solve problems?
- Are psychologists politically neutral?
- Why does mental illness carry a stigma?

Introduction

Many of the fundamental categories of twentieth-century psychology are, to all intents and purposes, twentieth-century inventions. Such concepts as 'intelligence', 'behaviour' and 'learning' were given such radically changed meanings by modern psychology that there simply are no earlier equivalents.

(Danziger 1997, p. 36)

In the previous chapters we saw how psychology has developed and how it has been affected by a number of basic questions (conceptual issues). In this final chapter we look at the ways in which psychology and society influenced each other. Psychology would not be around if the society had not felt a need for this type of knowledge, and the Western world would look different without psychology. In the first part of the chapter we review a number of ways in which psychology has been influenced by socio-political tendencies in society. In the second part we see how psychology has changed society and has influenced the ways in which people perceive each other and interact with one another.

12.1 Ways in which society has influenced psychology

Science overtakes religion in Western society

Initial strong links between psychological thinking and religion

As sketched in the first chapters, psychology as a separate branch of knowledge grew out of the rising role of scientific thinking in Western society. Without the scientific revolution and the increasing status of the natural sciences in the eighteenth and nine-teenth centuries, there would never have been sufficient critical mass to start the scientific study of mental life. In all likelihood, psychology would have remained a religious or philosophical subdiscipline, clearly secondary in status. Education for a long time was controlled by the churches, which did not look favourably upon those who tried to examine the soul. This was the case in Europe, but also in the USA. As Fuchs (2000, p. 6) wrote:

> Seminaries provided the only graduate education available in the pre-Civil War period. Those who attended seminaries were prepared and chosen not only for the ministry but also for college professorships.

Unsurprisingly, many early psychologists had strong connections with religion. Carl Jung and Edward Thorndike, for instance, were sons of ministers. G. Stanley Hall and Carl Rogers came from very religious families and initially studied for the ministry. In 1904 Hall created the *Journal of Religious Psychology*. Another early psychologist who stayed close to religion was William James, who in 1902 wrote the bestseller *The Varieties of Religious Experience*.

Alliance formation with the expanding sciences

Rapidly, however, the experimental psychologists distanced themselves from religion, because it jeopardised their scientific credentials. They sought to align themselves with the rapidly growing natural sciences, by denouncing weaker fields that might contam-inate them, such as religion, philosophy and sociology (Ward 2002, p. 53). The main exception was William James, who his whole life felt as much attraction to mysticism as to scientific research, and in the end was felt by many of his colleagues to be an embarrassment rather than an asset to psychology (Hood 2000). Within this perspective, psychology would never have sought to affiliate itself with the natural sciences if they had been perceived as weak by society (which they very much were until the seventeenth century; see Chapters 1 and 2).

Psychologists replace pastors

Another reason why the decline in religion contributed to the emergence of psychology is that fewer people felt comfortable discussing their mental health problems with religious authorities. Whereas the churches for a long time were the first port of call (and for many people still are), the growing secularisation increased the need for non-religious counselling. At the same time, a growing number of clergy started to study psychology to improve the help they were able to provide.

Society as a metaphor provider

metaphor

in science stands for an analogy from another area that helps to map a new, complex problem by making reference to a better understood phenomenon

Another way in which the wider world has influenced psychology is by the provision of metaphors. Metaphors in science are analogies from other areas that help to map a new, complex problem by making reference to a better understood phenomenon. A typical example of a metaphor in science is that of electricity as a fluid streaming through the cables and appliances and exerting a power against elements that resist the flow.

Examples of metaphors in psychology

Metaphors have had an influential role in psychological thinking as well. For instance, they have strongly shaped the ideas scholars had about memory (Draaisma 2000). Plato had already used the metaphor of a wax tablet to understand memory (a good memory consisted of a clear impression in the tablet and memories faded just like impressions on a tablet). From the Middle Ages on, memory was often seen as a library, full of books. In the nineteenth century and the first half of the twentieth century, this metaphor became supplemented with those of new inventions that were made, such as the switchboard (from telephone exchanges), the mechanical piano (that 'remembered' a song and played it automatically), the phonograph and the photograph. In the mid-twentieth century, a completely new and exciting metaphor was found in the computer, giving rise, for example, to research about the difference between a short-term memory (a central processor) and a long-term memory (a hard disk on which information was stored and from which it was retrieved).

Metaphors have played a role in other areas of psychology as well (Leary 1995). For instance, when psychodynamic therapists attempt to relieve the pressure built up in a patient, they are following Freud's metaphor of the mind as a hydraulic device.

More generally, Gentner and Grudin (1985) argued that psychologists have used four types of metaphors:

1. the mind as an animal (e.g. ideas struggle or compete with each other),

2. the mind as a neural system (e.g. ideas are inhibited; disturbance of thought arises because of over-excitation in the brain),

3. the mind as a spatial container (e.g. memories that are in the background, fear that inundates the sympathetic nervous system),

4. the mind as a mechanical or computational system (e.g. serial, iterative operations going on in the brain).

What do you think?

Socrates compared memories with birds that you try to catch in a cage. To what extent does this metaphor differ from the library metaphor? And in what way does it differ from the computer metaphor?

The power of metaphors

It is important to realise that metaphors in science are not just comparisons. They allow researchers to formulate and test hypotheses on the basis of the analogy, which otherwise would have remained elusive. For instance, the library metaphor of memory made researchers alert to the way in which books are located in such a system. Each book has a particular location, which can be found by means of an index system (e.g. the author's name or a few keywords). Could it be that something similar was operating in the brain and that people needed memory cues in order to 'find' the memory traces? This type of question gave rise to a completely new area of memory research in the 1970s (e.g. Tulving and Thomson 1971).

Without doubt, the most influential metaphor in the history of psychology has been the computer. As we saw in Chapters 4 and 6, this metaphor was the catalyst both in the replacement of behaviourism by cognitive psychology, and in the ways psychologists and philosophers looked at the relationship between the mind and the brain.

Metaphors work because they transfer a complex knowledge system from a known theme to an unknown topic. At the same time, they include a danger, because often the phenomenon to be understood does not completely fit into the metaphor. The metaphor does not replace the reality; it only allows the researchers to get a grasp of some aspects of the phenomenon. The danger of overinterpreting metaphors can be illustrated with the library metaphor. In a library, as soon as the location of a book is known, all the information contained in the book becomes available. This is not the case in memory. Most of the time, only partial information can be retrieved from an address, and memory must continue its search. In addition, quite often it has to fill in missing gaps. The latter can be compared to the work of an archaeologist who tries to reconstruct a complete animal on the basis of a few recovered bones, another metaphor that has been used to grasp the workings of memory (Larsen 1987).

Throughout the history of psychology, scientific innovations have been a source of metaphors to understand the mechanisms of the mind. By applying them, psychologists got a better grip on the phenomena they tried to understand. At the same time, metaphors restrict understanding, because the phenomenon to be explained is rarely exactly the same as the analogy used.

Socio-political biases in psychological theories

In Chapters 9 and 11 we saw how scientific research does not happen in a void but is influenced by the culture in which the researchers live. In Chapter 9 we mentioned the type of advice psychologists gave on masturbation at the beginning of the twentieth century. In Chapter 11 we saw how the current popularity of evolutionary psychology might have other origins than the mere scientific supremacy of the theory.

The American scientist Stephen Jay Gould (1996) provided a series of other eye-opening examples related to the history of intelligence testing. He showed how socio-political biases twisted the conclusions that were drawn. Below we present a summary of his findings.

Intelligence testing in the French welfare state

As you may remember from Chapters 3 and 7, the first useful intelligence test was developed in France. This was no coincidence. On the one hand, there was the tradition of brain research initiated by scholars like Paul Broca (see Chapters 5 and 8). On the other hand, there was the political organisation of the French state, which not only aimed for a strong central authority but also felt responsible for the well-being of its citizens. The French state, together with other countries in Western Europe, was a strong proponent of the welfare system, in which inhabitants paid relatively high taxes as an insurance against adversity. Within this context, the Paris psychologists Alfred Binet and Théodore Simon were asked to design a test that would help to diagnose children who needed extra help in teaching.

In line with their assignment and the socio-political system in which they lived, Binet and Simon saw their intelligence as based on three principles:

1. The scores of the test were a practical device, showing how well a child grasped the skills needed within the education system. The scores did not define what intelligence was, because the tasks had simply been chosen because they worked better than anything else that was available.

2. The measure was meant as a rough guide for identifying mildly retarded and learning-disabled children who needed special help. It was not meant to rank children within the normal range.

3. The purpose of the scale was to provide extra help for the children at risk. Mild retardation was not seen as a sign that the children were incapable of studying.

Translation to the American context

Binet and Simon's intelligence test was brought to the USA, when Henry H. Goddard, the director of a School for Feeble-Minded Girls and Boys in New Jersey, heard about the test on a study visit to Belgium. He decided to translate and use the test, at first in his school, but soon in other contexts (e.g. with pupils of regular schools and with immigrants). His popularisation efforts eventually led to the Stanford–Binet test, published by Lewis Terman in 1916, and to the Army Tests (Alpha and Beta), started under the direction of Robert M. Yerkes in 1917 (with the help of Goddard and Terman) and published in 1921.

The philosophy of the American tests, however, was not to identify children at risk so that they could receive extra help. The aim was to optimise the organisation of society by testing which children were intelligent enough for various types of schooling, and which adults were intelligent enough for various types of employment. For instance, in 1923, Terman (together with Yerkes and Thorndike) advertised a group of national intelligence tests on the basis of the Stanford–Binet and the Army Tests, to be used in schools for Grades 3–8. This is what the advert said:

> The direct result of the application of the army testing methods to school needs . . . The tests have been selected from a large group of tests after a try-out and a careful analysis by a statistical staff. The two scales prepared consist of five tests each (with practical exercises) and either may be administered in thirty minutes. They are simple in application, reliable, and immediately useful in classifying children in Grades 3 to 8 with respect to intellectual ability. Scoring is unusually simple.
>
> *(Terman, as cited in Gould (1996) p. 208–9)*

As for the use with employees, Terman wrote in 1916:

> Industrial concerns doubtless suffer enormous losses from the employment of persons whose mental ability is not equal to the tasks they are expected to perform . . . Any business employing as many as 500 or 1000 workers, as, for example, a large department store, could save in this way several times the salary of a well-trained psychologist.
>
> *(Terman as cited in Gould (1996) p. 211)*

More generally, within the American socio-political context, Binet and Simon's principles became translated into the following tenets:

1. The various tasks identified by Binet and Simon and further extended by other researchers, all measure one single capacity, called 'general intelligence'.

2. The amount of intelligence in a person can be expressed by a single number (called IQ).

3. Individuals can be ranked linearly according to their IQ. This is true over the whole range of intelligences, not just in the subnormal range.

4. The IQ refers to an inborn quality, inherited from the previous generations.

5. A person's IQ is stable and permanent; that is, it will not change noticeably by a programme of social and educational intervention.

6. The IQ of a person correlates not only with the type of tasks the person can do, but also with his or her moral reasoning.

As for the latter claim, Goddard wrote in 1919:

> The intelligence controls the emotions and the emotions are controlled in proportion to the degree of intelligence . . . It follows that if there is little intelligence the emotions will be uncontrollable and whether they be strong or weak will result in actions that are unregulated, uncontrolled and, as experience proves, usually undesirable.
>
> *(Goddard as cited in Gould (1996) p. 190–1)*

Given that black Americans on average scored substantially below white Americans, the IQ findings also had sweeping racial implications, as can be seen in the following excerpt from Terman (1916). It is part of a chapter in which Terman discussed the findings about people with IQ scores between 70 and 80 (i.e. the feeble-minded):

> Among laboring men and servant girls there are thousands like them . . . The tests have told the truth. These boys are ineducable beyond the merest rudiments of training. No amount of school instruction will ever make them intelligent voters or capable citizens . . . They represent the level of intelligence which is very, very common among Spanish-Indian and Mexican families of the Southwest and also among negroes. Their dullness seems to be racial, or at least inherent in the family stocks from which they came. The fact that one meets this type with such extraordinary frequency among Indians, Mexicans, and negroes suggests quite forcibly that the whole question of racial differences in mental traits will have to be taken up anew and by experimental methods . . . Children of this group should be segregated in special classes and be given instruction which is concrete and practical. They cannot master abstractions, but they can often be made efficient workers, able to look out for themselves. There is no possibility at present of convincing society that they should not be allowed to reproduce, although from a eugenic point of view they constitute a grave problem because of their unusually prolific breeding.
>
> *(Terman as cited in Gould (1996) p. 220–1)*

When reading the above excerpts, it is important to keep in mind that the change in tone from the French to the American approach was not due to an increase in scientific knowledge in the first decades of the twentieth century. It was virtually all to do with the difference in socio-political context between France and the USA. Many Americans were convinced that the white race was far superior to Native Americans and black people. They also had a much more competitive and individualistic approach to the organisation of the state.

What do you think?

Gould (1996) noted that the tenets of Goddard and Terman regain in popularity each time the politics make a turn toward the right and the social services are slimmed down in order to reduce taxes. Can you find examples of this? Can you think of counterexamples?

Even measurements and data are not safe in the light of strong socio-political opinions

One objection scientists usually make against the criticism that their statements may be socio-politically biased, is that the conclusions are based on sound empirical evidence (Chapters 8 and 9). Gould (1996) devoted a large part of his book to showing how easily the 'objective' findings get distorted by the researchers' expectations. Of the many examples he gave, we only mention the case of Samuel George Morton (1799–1851). Morton was an American physician and natural scientist, who was famous for his skull collection. In 1839, he published a volume on the brain sizes of Americans from different descent. As can be seen in table 12.1, Morton's table clearly 'proved' that the mean skull size of white people (of Caucasian origin) was larger than that of Native Americans and black people.

Table 12.1 Morton's summary table of cranial capacity by race

This table clearly 'shows' that the brain size of American from Caucasian descent was larger than that of the other races.

Race	N	Internal capacity (in³)		
		Mean	**Largest**	**Smallest**
Caucasian	52	87	109	75
Mongolian	10	83	93	69
Malay	18	81	89	64
American	144	82	100	60
Ethiopian	29	78	94	65

Source: Morton (1839) as cited in Gould (1996, p. 86)

From the lower cranial capacity of Native Americans (and the other races), Morton drew sweeping conclusions, such as: 'the benevolent mind may regret the inaptitude of the Indian for civilization' and '[Indians, i.e. Native Americans] are not only averse to the restraints of education, but for the most part are incapable of a continued process of reasoning on abstract subjects' (as cited in Gould (1996) pp. 88–9). Throughout the nineteenth century and the first part of the twentieth century Morton's data were used as the decisive argument for race differences in intelligence.

Interestingly, Morton not only provided a summary table, but full information on each and every skull in his collection. Gould set out to reanalyse the data. These were his findings:

1. The 144 skulls of the Native Americans belonged to many different groups, which differed in cranial capacity. Morton's sample was strongly biased towards the Inca Peruvians, who had smaller brains than the others but also smaller statures (just like with the other body parts, the size of the brain depends on the overall stature of a person). There were three skulls of Iroquois, who had brain sizes very close to those of the Caucasians.

2. Morton excluded the skulls of the Hindus from his Caucasian sample, because they were 'too small to be acceptable'.

3. Morton measured the cranial capacity by pouring mustard seed in the skulls and measuring the amount that was required. This worked reasonably well, except for two problems. The first was that the seed was a bit sticky and sometimes did not fill cavities completely. The second was that mustard seed can be compressed. Because of these drawbacks, Morton later decided to redo his analyses with lead shot. However, he never published a clear summary table of these data. When Gould did so more than a century later, he found that the Caucasian cranial capacity stayed at 87 in³, but that of the Native Americans increased to 86 in³ and that of Africans to 83 in³. That is, Morton had more rigorously shaken and pressed the mustard seeds for his Caucasian skulls than for the other skulls.

When Gould corrected for the various biases, his estimates almost wiped out the racial differences in skull sizes as reported by Morton (the same was true for the other data reported by Morton in later publications on a total of 623 skulls). Gould thought it unlikely that manifest fraud was involved. Otherwise, Morton would never have published a full account of his raw materials. What probably happened was that Morton happily accepted the data that were in line with his expectations, whereas he double-checked and 'corrected' the data he did not understand. The end result was a set of 'scientific' measures that seemed to 'prove beyond doubt' the existence of racial differences in skull sizes (and, hence, intelligence).

Money and Ehrhardt (1972): The trainability of gender identity

Socio-political biases in scientific conclusions are not limited to the biological per-spective. The 1960s and 1970s were a time during which the social perspective dom-inated. The economy expanded rapidly, technological advances were breathtaking, and there was general optimism in the American society. Suddenly it did not seem im-probable that further gains could be made by improving the education system and providing better services to those in need. Maybe there was more merit in the social powers than initially acknowledged by Goddard and Terman in the heydays of eugenics? (Gould (1996) describes how these geneticists recanted some of their views towards the end of their careers.)

Within this period it was not surprising to see a book appear in which it was claimed that a person's gender identity was strongly influenced by education (Money and Ehrhardt 1972). A baby boy turned into a man, not only because of his Y-chromosome but also because of the way in which he was reared. The same was true for a baby girl. Again the conclusion was backed with 'sound' empirical evidence. A particularly revealing case in this respect was that of identical male twins of whom one had his penis severed at 8 months during a medical operation. The penis eventually was removed and replaced by a vulva, and the parents were advised to further raise the boy as a girl. Money and Ehrhardt concluded that after these simple changes the boy happily grew up as a girl, proving that gender identity was not primarily due to the genes, but to the ways in which education depended on the anatomical differences with which boys and girls were born.

Money and Ehrhardt's finding was seized upon by textbook authors who present-ed it as the decisive evidence for the power of social factors in mental and social life. However, with the growth of the biological perspective towards the end of the twentieth century, the case was revisited and found to have been misrepresented (Diamond and Sigmundson 1997). 'Brenda' (previously 'Bruce') Reimer did not remember her childhood as a happy one. From the beginning she had difficulties with the fact that her parents treated her as a girl. She walked like a boy, fought with other boys, and had to change schools a few times because of bullying and behaviour problems. The crisis reached its peak when at puberty she had to take hormones and needed a new operation to continue her female development. In the end, at the age of 14 she was told the truth about what had happened, and she experienced this as a huge relief. Later she had a sex change operation and became 'David', a name chosen for its analogy with the fight between David and Goliath. He married a single mother with three children and was happy with his renewed role. In the end, however, the story took a tragic turn. David's twin brother (who had mental health problems) committed suicide in 2002. Shortly afterwards David lost his job and savings, and was told by his wife that she wanted to separate. In 2004, he committed suicide as well.

By that time David's case had become famous again, because it had been seized upon by a journalist first to write a story in *Rolling Stone* magazine (in 1997), later to publish a book on it (in 2000), which was followed by an acclaimed BBC Horizon documentary (also in 2000). In line with the changed social climate, the case was now presented as evidence against the social perspective and in favour of a strict biological interpretation of the development of gender identity.

> ## ? What do you think?
>
> There is a lot of information available on Money and Ehrhardt's case study on the internet, under the titles 'David Reimer' and 'The boy who was turned into a girl'. Go and search for it, and see how it fits in with a changing socio-political context. Also notice the impact of the socio-political context on the media.

An example of current social influences: hidden racism

Socio-political influences are conspicuous for examples from the past, because the change in context makes the extent of the impact clearer. One cannot help but cringe and feel vicarious shame when reading some of Goddard's and Terman's texts. Surely such practices no longer exist in current-day psychological writings? Or do they, and are we simply not noticing them?

Teo (2005) acknowledges that blatant scientific racism, as found in the texts of Goddard and Terman, is no longer present in the current literature. However, in his view this does not preclude psychologists from still being influenced by the *in-group bias*, the belief that one's own group is superior in knowledge and skills to other groups. This bias shows itself in the fact that other groups are no longer explicitly denigrated, but they are ignored. Scientists from non-dominant groups find it harder to get their manuscripts accepted for publication and, if they do manage this, very few colleagues from the dominant group take notice of their articles. Teo calls this 'hidden colonial thinking' or hidden racism. As he writes:

hidden racism

advancing one's own race by non-conspicuous biases against other groups (usually by ignoring their contribution)

> I suggest that most contemporary psychologists view scientific racism and blatant racial prejudices and actions as aberrations of the discipline's past. However, from a post-colonial perspective the major problem nowadays is not scientific racism . . . but hidden colonial thinking. Hidden colonial thinking in psychology, as hidden culture-centrism in general, expresses itself in terms of exclusion or disregard of non-Western psychologies.
>
> *(Teo 2005, p. 166)*

As a result, psychological research in all countries is dominated by what is thought to be interesting in the Anglo-Saxon world, as was observed by Gulerce (2006, p. 76) for Turkish psychology:

> The interpellation and normalization of American psychology is so strong in Turkish society . . . that Turkish psychologists do not get to study systematically and think

about the long historical period prior to the common celebratory historical marker of the establishment of a Western chair of experimental psychology at a Turkish university. Furthermore, Turkish psychology is even more ahistorical, acultural, and asocial than American psychology, so that even the very idea of critical and cultural history of psychology in Turkey seems oxymoronic, as a good example of overidentification.

A similar criticism was raised by Rogers and Pilgrim (2005) about the treatment of mental health problems. They argue that currently a universal treatment based on Western research and values is being promoted throughout the world, irrespective of the cultural, social or economic context of the people involved.

Socio-political influences on psychological practice

The socio-political context not only influences the theories psychologists build, it also affects the conditions under which they work. Below we list two examples.

An increased interest in ethical issues

One of the developments of the last decades is an increased concern for ethical issues. Two big social changes lie at the basis of this shift. First, there was the acknowledgement that some experiments in the past (in particular medical experiments) were run despite knowledge that they would harm the participants. An important catalyst in this respect was the large-scale medical research done in World War II, which came to light during the Nuremberg Medical Trial (1946–1947; Weindling 2004). The ethical issues raised at this trial (e.g. to what extent the forced sterilisations and experiments on inmates in Germany differed from those in the USA) resulted in the Nuremberg Code on the conduct of experiments with humans. A central principle in this code was **informed consent**. This principle stipulates that participants can only take part in an experiment after they have been informed about what will be involved (including the risks) and after they have explicitly and voluntarily given their consent to participate. Because of the vulnerable position in which individuals may find themselves when asked to give consent, it later became pivotal that an experiment not only involved informed consent from the participants, but also was approved by an independent body, an ethics committee.

The second social trend that made ethical issues central in research was the increased probability of legal action in case of a participant making a complaint. As a result, all official institutions introduced measures to ensure that no research could be done under their responsibility without proper ethical controls. **Ethical codes of conduct** were established and individual applications were checked to make sure they adhered to the code.

A typical example is the code of conduct established by The British Psychological Society, which can be downloaded from their website www.bps.org.uk. It contains the following general principles for research with human participants (as recorded in The British Psychological Society, 2004, and valid in 2008):

1. *Ethical approval for all research.* All research requires ethical approval by an independent body. This body makes sure that the research proposal adheres to the code.

informed consent

central principle in ethics, saying that people can only take part in a study after they have been informed of what will be involved and after they have explicitly and voluntarily agreed to participate

ethical code of conduct

protocol that includes all the ethics-related conditions to which a study must adhere

2. *Protection of participants.* This not only involves protection from possible harm, but also preservation of the dignity and rights of the participants, and safeguards to ensure anonymity and confidentiality. Protection also requires competent supervision.

3. *Informed consent.* No research on a person may be carried out without the informed, free, express, specific and documented consent of the person. If the research cannot be done without concealing its true purpose, the ethics committee will make sure that the deception involved does not prevent the participants from giving informed consent.

4. *No coercion.* No participant should feel coerced to take part in a particular study.

5. *The right to withdraw.* Participants have the right to withdraw from any given research if they no longer feel comfortable. They can do so at any time without penalty and without providing reason. Participants can also require that their data be withdrawn from the study.

6. *Anonymity and confidentiality.* Participants must be assured that all information they give will be treated with the utmost confidentiality and that their anonymity will be respected at all times unless otherwise determined by the law. Procedures for data storage must conform to the Data Protection Act.

7. *Appropriate exclusion criteria.* Researchers must make clear which participants cannot take part in the study (e.g. on the grounds of a pre-existing condition).

8. *Monitoring.* Researchers are obliged to monitor ongoing research for adverse effects on participants and to stop the research if there is cause for concern.

9. *Duty of care.* There is a duty of care on researchers to ameliorate any adverse effects of their study. This involves the need for a debriefing at the end of the experiment. The debriefing consists of the explanation of the goals and the procedures of the study to the participants; it must also correct any form of deception that may have been included in the study.

10. *Additional safeguards for research with vulnerable populations.* Vulnerable populations include schoolchildren under the age of 18, people with learning or communication difficulties, patients, people in custody and probation, and people engaged in illegal activities. No research on these populations can be done without the additional written consent of the people responsible for them.

11. *Appropriate supervision.* Student investigators must be under the supervision of a member of Academic Staff and must be made aware of the relevant guidelines and of the need to observe them.

Codes of conduct are not only for those doing research. Similar codes have been established by professional societies to regulate the interactions between psychologists and clients. For instance, The British Psychological Society has a *Code of Ethics and Conduct* based on the following four domains of responsibility: respect, competence, responsibility and integrity. Each domain involves a number of values and is further defined by a set of standards (for further information, see The British Psychological Society, 2006).

Litigation and the importance of documented evidence

One of the conclusions you may have drawn from the book thus far is that scientific knowledge is not to be trusted, because it is too tainted by the prevailing paradigm and the socio-political pressures that impinge on scientists. Such a conclusion can be defended and would put you in line with Feyerabend (who saw science as just another religion) and the postmodernists (who claimed that scientific knowledge is nothing but a social construction by the scientific community; see Chapter 8).

On the other hand, it is important to keep in mind that the very same biases apply to all kinds of knowledge and that the non-scientific approaches arguably have even fewer defences against them. Although scientists do make errors and from time to time draw wrong conclusions on the basis of their findings, there are a number of mechanisms that allow others to evaluate the claims and to present counterevidence. These are (see also Chapter 9):

- the requirement that the knowledge is coherent and cumulative,
- the requirement that the knowledge is made available, so that it can be checked,
- the requirement to use well-defined and widely accepted methods of information gathering,
- the requirement of clarity of exposition (i.e. ambiguous statements are not accepted),
- the requirement that the knowledge is primarily based on prediction and falsification attempts,
- the requirement that the knowledge is not set in stone, but will be revised in the light of contradictory evidence.

Because of the above requirements, scientific knowledge is among the most trustworthy we have (though not fail-safe, as we have seen). Therefore, it is increasingly relied upon in Western society to make important decisions and to settle disagreements (e.g. in courtrooms). This brings us to a rather paradoxical situation: even though we are becoming increasingly aware of the relativity of scientific knowledge, we nevertheless rely more and more on it to make decisions, simply because the alternatives are more questionable. Although intelligence tests and achievement tests have their disadvantages, it is more acceptable to be excluded from a university on the basis of an achievement test taken by everyone, than on the basis of the whim of a single person deciding about the entry. Students who have reason to believe the test was biased against them can search in the scientific literature for evidence to back their suspicion and can use this in their dispute. Similarly, groups that have good reason to question the usefulness of a test can campaign for another admission procedure (e.g. no longer involving the initial selection of students) or for the use of another, better test.

On balance, the rising reliance on scientifically gathered evidence has been beneficiary for psychologists, as their expertise has increasingly been called upon in situations that could give rise to appeals (Chapter 7). This had led, for instance, to an explosion of the use of tests and psychological assessments in the judiciary system. An increasing number of verdicts are based on documented evidence by independent assessors rather than on subjective judgement alone.

Psychologists as pawns in power games

A main theme in sociology is the struggle for power between the various groups in society. Each group tries to increase its share of resources and its control over the others. Sometimes this results in an open conflict, but most of the time the tensions are sorted out by means of alliance formation. Psychologists as a group are entangled in this process. They try to improve their standing by manipulating others (see below), but at the same time they are constantly being used by others as part of their power struggle. An interesting thinker about the use of power in societies was the French social historian and philosopher Michel Foucault (1926–1984).

Foucault and the power of discipline

In 1976 Foucault published a book, *Surveiller et punir [Discipline and Punish]*, in which he discussed how rulers discipline their inferiors. Until the eighteenth century, power was applied by brute force: by torturing, executing and burning those who defied the king's authority. This was often done in public to set an example. However, despite the use of brutality, the strategy was rather inefficient, because power was applied only sporadically, when the situation got out of hand.

A much better system was a constant surveillance system, in which minor deviances were immediately detected and corrected. An additional advantage of such a system was that it disciplined the subjects to such an extent that they automatically and unthinkingly followed the rules imposed upon them. Such an organisation became more and more dominant from the eighteenth century on, because in the industrial and the postindustrial world production started to depend on smooth interactions between large numbers of people who all performed specialised tasks.

One of the first examples of a surveillance system was the *Panopticon* proposed in 1785 by the British philosopher Jeremy Bentham. It consisted of a building with individual cells that could permanently be observed from a central tower. Bentham saw this as the ideal organisation for prisons, penitentiary houses, houses of industry, workhouses, poor-houses, factories, mad-houses, hospitals and schools. For efficiency purposes, he further proposed that the inmates must not be able to see into the observation tower, so that it was not necessary to permanently man the tower.

Another form of surveillance is to regularly check the workers. Medical (and later psychological) practitioners were brought in as part of this surveillance. The American sociologist F. Allan Hanson (1993) discussed two techniques that have been used in this respect. The first consisted of regular screenings with a lie detector. From time to time employees were required to take part in an interview about their functioning, while they were connected to a lie detector. Such a machine registers the physiological responses that accompany anxiety about lying (such as differences in blood pressure, sweating and changes in the voice). It was made clear to the employees that there was no point in trying to lie, because the machine would expose them. Lie detection tests became part of the working conditions in the USA in the 1980s. Hanson reported estimates of up to two million tests per year, until they were banned in 1988 for most purposes in the private sector (but not in the public sector), because they were experienced as too demeaning.

The second surveillance technique mentioned by Hanson (1993), and still in use, consisted of random drug tests, whereby the urine of employees is tested at random time intervals for the presence of illegal substances. Because of the unpredictable timing and the fact that they were able to trace drugs taken a few days before, these tests are extremely efficient within a surveillance system.

Within Foucault's world view it is a small step to see the primary role of psychologists as being responsible for the surveillance of mental health patients, students, employees and everyone else they are asked to assess and advise. The main task of psychologists is not to help clients, but to keep them in line with the prevailing social organisation. This also explains (part of) the popularity of their tests. As Hanson wrote:

> What is unique about [medical and psychological] testing is that it has brought knowledge, control, and the social definition of the person to a new level of perfection and totality. Never before has any society deployed such a rich and ingenious panoply of dedicated techniques to scan, weigh, peruse, probe, and record the minutiae of its members' personal traits and life experiences. Never before has science, with all the power and prestige that have come to be associated with it, been brought so fully to bear on the problem of generating, storing, and retrieving precise knowledge about so many facets of the human individual. As a result of so much testing, it is certainly fair to say that more knowledge has been accumulated about individuals in contemporary society than at any previous time in history. This knowledge is used to control the behavior of individuals and also to characterize them in terms of their achievements and talents, their physical and mental characteristics, their normalities and abnormalities as measured along innumerable dimensions, many of which were not even recognized a century ago.
>
> *(Hanson 1993, p. 5)*

Foucault's views on madness

Foucault's views about the treatment of mental disorders were even clearer in a previous book: *Folie et déraison [Madness and civilization]*, published in 1961. In this book Foucault described how societies need outcasts, because their exclusion makes everyone else feel better. At first, the outcasts in the Western world were the people with contagious diseases, in particular leprosy. When they disappeared, society searched for a new group to exclude, which turned out to be the insane. Before, these people had been left alone, as they did not cause major problems. Under the new regime, however, they were locked up together with common criminals (Chapter 3).

With the rise of scientism and the fall of religion, mad people were no longer considered as criminals, possessed by devils. However, this did not make them free again. Instead, the notion of mental *illness* was invented. The insane became subjects for diagnosis, discussion and regulation. They were locked up in asylums and put in the hands of hospital directors and psychiatrists. As happened in the society at large, the way in which they were disciplined changed as well. They began to be managed through fear rather than through physical constraint. The wardens became the new social authority, both as judge and as representative of sanity. The insane were made aware of their madness by repeatedly being told of the irrationality of their fellow inmates. Again, in Foucault's world view, psychologists entered this system, not to change it but to continue it, to keep the insane obedient and tranquil at the outskirts of society.

? What do you think?

Foucault's strength was the introduction of new points of view, not the balance of his literature reviews or the internal consistency of his writings. What do you think of his treatment of psychologists?

KEY FIGURE

Michel Foucault

Source: SIPA Press / Rex Features

- French philosopher and historian (1926–1984).

- Best known for his critical studies of social institutions, which he defined in terms of power seeking (e.g. the prison system, psychiatry and medicine).

- *Folie et déraison* [*Madness and Civilization*]: Book published in 1961, in which Foucault claimed that people suffering from mental disorders became treated as outcasts in the fifteenth–seventeenth centuries, because society needed such a stigmatised group after the gradual disappearance of the contagious illness leprosy.

- *Surveiller et punir* [*Discipline and Punish*]: Book published in 1976, in which Foucault argued that in current society power is no longer exerted by brute force but by constant surveillance and correction. Claimed that psychologists were part of the surveillance and correction machine.

- Also one of the first postmodernists who questioned the special status of science and argued that scientific statements were social constructions, part of the constant power game in society.

The misuse of psychological knowledge by pseudoscientists

Another way in which psychologists have been used by society is that their knowledge has been hijacked by groups who did not subscribe to the scientific approach. Arguably the most visible form of such misuse is the exploitation of psychological findings and tests by various types of alternative 'healers' and 'advisors' to strengthen their own claims, to give them credibility and to help them make money. Just as in many other sciences, psychological knowledge has been recycled by individuals who were not primarily interested in the truth of the findings (or at least in the fact that they were evidence-based), but in the extent to which they advanced their own case. In particular with respect to psychological tests, this has required psychologists to organise themselves and, for instance, make sure that the tests can only be administered by properly trained psychologists.

The knowledge spread by people who do not subscribe to the scientific ethos has variously been described as pop-psychology, pseudopsychology and – more generally pseudoscience, counterknowledge (Thompson 2008), mumbo-jumbo (Wheen 2004) or bullshit (Frankfurt 2005). The essential element of this type of knowledge is that evidence-based statements are freely combined with made-up statements, statements from dubious sources, and statements that are known to be wrong. As Frankfurt (2005) argued, such knowledge is worse than lying, because the user does not know what the truth is and does not care (unlike a liar). All that matters is whether a statement advances the case the person wants to make.

What do you think?

Thompson (2008) holds that the internet has made the spreading of pseudoscience easier. As a result, he claims, this type of knowledge can rapidly gain power nowadays and turn into a 'counterknowledge industry', in which (big) money is made out of bogus science. Do you agree with this? Or do you think the internet helps people to become more critical, because they can more easily check the status of claims?

A claim made as part of the 'science wars' (Chapter 8) is that a turn to pseudoscience is exactly what happened to the postmodernists in their criticism of scientific knowledge. Because they saw scientific knowledge as a social construction, they no longer made a distinction between evidence-based statements and made-up statements. The criticism was formulated most strongly by the American physicist Alan Sokal in 1996 when he submitted a manuscript for a special issue of the postmodernist journal *Social Text* devoted to the science wars. The manuscript, entitled 'Transgressing the boundaries: Toward a transformative hermeneutics of quantum gravity', defended an extreme form of cognitive relativism. It claimed that there was no external world, whose properties were 'independent of any individual human being and indeed of humanity as a whole'. As a result, it arrived at the conclusion that mathematical and physical notions such as Euclid's π (used for calculating the area and the circumference of a circle), formerly thought to be constant and universal, should be seen in their 'ineluctable historicity'.

The manuscript was accepted for publication without the need for any major revision and published (Sokal 1996a). Sokal immediately wrote an accompanying article, in which he revealed the parody and showed how unfounded and nonsensical his claims were (Sokal 1996b). The original manuscript had been written with such leaps of logic 'that any competent physicist or mathematician (or undergraduate physics or math major) would realize that it is a spoof' (Sokal 1996b, p. 62).

Sokal's evaluation of the postmodernist response to his manuscript contained many of the accusations that are usually geared towards pseudoscience (or any of the other words mentioned above), as can be seen from the following excerpts:

> to test the prevailing intellectual standards, I decided to try a modest (though admittedly uncontrolled) experiment: Would a leading North American journal of cultural studies . . . publish an article liberally salted with nonsense if (a) it sounded good and (b) it flattered the editors' ideological preconceptions?
>
> The results of my little experiment demonstrate, at the very least, that some fashionable sectors of the American academic Left have been getting intellectually lazy. The editors of *Social Text* liked my article because they liked its *conclusion*: that 'the content and methodology of postmodern science provide powerful intellectual support for the progressive political project.' They apparently felt no need to

analyse the quality of the evidence, the cogency of the arguments, or even the relevance of the arguments to the purported conclusion.

(Sokal 1996b, p. 62)

In a later publication with the Belgian physicist, Jean Bricmont, Sokal stepped up his criticism. In particular Sokal and Bricmont (1997) accused the postmodernists of abusing concepts and terminology coming from mathematics and physics by:

■ referring to scientific theories about which they have, at best, an exceedingly hazy understanding; scientific terminology is used without bothering what the words actually mean,

■ importing concepts from the natural sciences without the slightest conceptual or empirical justification,

■ displaying a superficial erudition by shamelessly throwing around technical terms in a context where they are completely irrelevant, with the sole goal to impress and intimidate the non-scientist reader.

A similar objection can be made against postmodernist revisions of psychology. 'Freeing psychology from its shackles of methods and theories' may be appealing (e.g. to students in exam times), but is unlikely to improve the quality of the services psychologists provide (APA Presidential Task Force on Evidence-based Practice, 2006). There is no evidence that untrained managers are able to select personnel as well as qualified psychologists (quite on the contrary, as we have seen in Chapters 7 and 10) and the thought of having untutored people give therapy simply on the basis of their own intuitions and whims is not particularly reassuring either. There is a good deal of evidence that bona fide treatments (i.e. treatments based on therapies that have been validated and accepted in mainstream psychology) are better than non bona fide treatments (Wampold *et al.* 2002; see also Messer 2004). In addition, many countries have had to pass legislation precisely to protect clients from bogus therapists.

The misuse of psychological knowledge in times of war

An even more worrying risk is that psychological knowledge may become misused against people. An alleged example of such exploitation is the use of interrogation techniques based on *learned helplessness* in war prisoners (for a review, see Mayer 2008). Research in the 1960s showed that subjecting dogs to a series of electric shocks from which they could not escape destroyed them emotionally, so that they no longer tried to escape when later there was a possibility to do so. This research on learned helplessness was extremely important for the understanding of feelings of depression in individuals who no longer had control of their situation. Gradually it also became incorporated in the training of soldiers, to warn them in case they were captured.

At some point, however, according to Mayer the knowledge was reverse-engineered (by CIA psychologists) and used against so-called 'enemy combatants' in the American War on Terror. Needless to say, this charge immediately provoked a sturdy response from the American Psychological Association, which issued a resolution reaffirming its position against torture or other cruel, inhuman or degrading treatment of enemy combatants (Resolution Adopted by APA on 19 August 2007). However, the incident is a wake-up call that psychology is not immune to abuse of its knowledge and that psychologists may be actively involved in such mistreatment.

What do you think?

Can you think of other examples in which psychologists may get involved in power struggles between social groups? Is there anything that can be done against this?

Interim summary

The ways in which society has influenced psychology

- A first factor in the growth of psychology was the decline of the impact of religion and the increase of scientific thinking in Western society.

- Society also provided metaphors to the psychological researchers, analogies that helped them to better understand the phenomena they were investigating (e.g. the mind as a computer).

- Because science is a social enterprise, socio-political values have influenced the ideas psychologists put forward and the theories they examined. We illustrated this with the different views on intelligence testing and the changing roles of social and biological factors in gender identity.

- Society also influences the daily practice of psychologists. For instance, it has led to more interest in ethical issues and to an increased used of psychological tests in courtrooms.

- According to sociologists, psychologists have been used in the power games that are going on in the society. According to Foucault, psychologists were used for the surveillance of various groups. Psychology's findings have also been used by pseudo-scientists, who freely combined evidence-based statements with made-up claims. Finally, there is the concern that psychological knowledge can be misused against people (e.g. prisoners).

12.2   Ways in which psychology has influenced society

The psychologisation of society

Psychologists often do not realise it, but the impact psychology has had on the way in which people interact is enormous. This is not only due to the number of students who each year finish their studies (at most universities psychology degrees are among the most popular), but also to the number of students who have psychology courses as part of their degrees, the number of articles devoted to psychology in newspapers and magazines, the number of radio and television programs dedicated to psychological topics, and the number of times people talk to each other about psychological issues (see Chapter 7).

De Graaf and Kalmijn (2006) interviewed a large cohort of Dutch men and women who had been divorced, about their reasons for divorce. They found that the most frequently given reasons were psychology-related, such as 'we grew apart' (78 per cent of the respondents), 'we didn't pay enough attention to each other' (74 per cent) and 'we were not able to talk' (73 per cent). These reasons were given much more frequently than sexual problems (42 per cent), physical violence (16 per cent), alcohol or drugs problems (22 per cent), infidelity of the spouse (37 per cent) and division of household chores (22 per cent). In addition, the impact of the psychology-related reasons showed a steady increase over the second half of the twentieth century: more people who had divorced toward the end of the century mentioned them than people who had divorced in the middle of the century.

The authors related these findings to what they called the psychologisation of society, the fact that economic ties in primary relationships have become less important over time, whereas emotional ties have grown in importance. The sociologist Steven Ward (2002), who critically reviewed the development of psychology, used the word in a slightly different way. In his view, psychologisation refers to the growing impact of psychology on society. This is how he started his final chapter, entitled 'The psychologization of the United States':

psychologisation

word used with two different meanings referring to: (1) the fact that emotional ties and personal well-being become important in primary social relations, or (2) the growing impact of psychology on the way people see themselves and interact with others

> Throughout this book I have tried to illustrate how over the course of the last century psychological categories and practices became 'naturalized.' As this happened, psychology, like other naturalized ideas and categories, 'disappeared into infrastructure, into habit, into the taken for granted' . . .
>
> Psychology's presence in schools, workplaces and homes is now an ordinary and seemingly indispensable feature of the cultural landscape. As a result of its presence we are now aware that there are children with varying IQ levels, that motivation can be enhanced through certain psychological techniques, that healthy marriages necessitate open communication, that people have certain psychological needs that require fulfillment, that aptitude can be gauged through psychological measurements and that self-esteem determines how we interact with others . . . As a result of this naturalization process, psychology is now 'part of the order of the universe'
>
> *(Ward 2002, p. 217)*

A similar definition was used by Gulerce (2006; see above), who argued that psychologisation is not limited to the Western world, but is becoming a global phenomenon. It is also the definition we will use in this chapter. In the sections below we review some more examples of the ways in which psychology has influenced society.

Psychology has changed how people perceive each other

Labels introduced by psychology become real

One of the big social changes in the past centuries has been the growing individualisation (Chapter 7), the fact that people organise their lives more in terms of their own characteristics and ambitions rather than the groups they belong to. Psychology has been an important element in this transition, because many of the concepts along which people differentiate themselves come from psychological writings. For example, before Jung made a distinction between introverts and extroverts, nobody perceived people in these terms. Similarly, only after the concepts were introduced could people be seen as 'neurotic', 'depressed', 'intelligent', 'resilient' and so on.

Many psychological concepts became part of everyday life, once they were coined. After psychiatrists and psychologists defined the concept 'depression' (actually major depression), people started to interpret their feelings with respect to this entity. The question no longer was whether people were sad or down, but whether they 'were depressed'. This was done first by psychiatrists and psychologists, later by popular psychology magazines, and in the end by everyone.

Another example is the concept of 'intelligence'. It can be argued that the present-day meaning of this word in terms of mental capacity did not exist before Galton and Binet started their research (Chapter 3). Indeed, in societies not yet influenced by Western thought there is no word for 'intelligent' with this particular meaning, in contrast to words referring to wise, handy and socially skilful. In Western society, however, the word has come to refer to what arguably one of the most important features of an individual.

Labels introduced by psychology change the subject of psychology

The fact that new concepts introduced by psychologists change the social reality has an extra twist for psychology, because it not only changes the reality for other people but also for (future) psychologists (Jones and Elcock 2001; Richards 2002). Just like everyone else, new psychology students wrongly believe that the concepts currently used in psychology and the wider culture refer to 'natural personal qualities', which have always been there (because they are part of the person observed) and not to qualities that – to some extent – are the result of prior developments in psychological research.

In other words, as a result of previous research the subject matter observed by psychologists today is different from the subject matter observed in the past. Richards (2002) called this psychology's *reflexive relationship* with its subject matter (in sociology, reflexivity refers to a situation in which the act of examining changes the event that is examined). An example of this reflexive relationship can be seen in the research on performance differences between races. Before the concept 'racism' became used in the 1930s, researchers could comfortably examine such differences and interpret them as the outcome of innate differences (which some happily did, as we saw above). However, as soon as the concept of 'racism' became used as a person trait to explain the atrocities committed in the name of racial superiority, race-related research became charged and shifted from studying performance differences to studying prejudice (Teo 2008).

What do you think?

One of the purposes of this book is to show you the historical and socio-cultural relativity of (psychological) knowledge. Of the examples given, which one struck you as the most revealing? Can you think of others?

Psychological labels are to some extent arbitrary

The sociologist Hanson (1993) pointed out that new psychological concepts not only make new realities, but also define them in arbitrary ways, because the concepts have been introduced without a good understanding of what was involved. He argued that when Binet and Simon selected a few tasks to measure intelligence, they could not suspect that these tasks would become part of the definition of intelligence for the coming century. As Boring (1923) famously declared: 'intelligence is what an intelligence test measures'.

Hanson illustrated the arbitrariness of psychological concepts by giving the example of an alternative way in which intelligence could have been tested (Hanson 1993: 279–80). He called this test the *New Intelligence Test* (NIT). Instead of Binet and Simon's tasks (Chapter 3), the NIT contained the following scales:

1. *A name recall scale*: ability to remember the names of persons to whom one has just been introduced.

2. *A mathematics scale*: measures the subject's ability to do problems of arithmetic and algebra.

3. *The first impression scale*: measures the first impression the subject makes by having a panel of ordinary people evaluate him/her.

4. *An exposition of ideas scale*: the subject is given 5 minutes to read a page of text and 30 minutes to present a clear and accurate written account of it, including original examples and applications. A possible example of such a text is a page from the French philosopher Rousseau describing his distinction between self-love (*amour de soi*) and selfishness (*amour propre*).

5. *A small-talk scale*: evaluates the subject's ability to carry on an interesting conversation with someone he/she has never met.

6. *A bullshitting scale*: evaluates the subject's skill at participating in a discussion with two other people on a topic about which he/she knows nothing.

7. *A follow-the-directions scale*: the subjects is told once, at the speed of ordinary conversation, to do a task that consists of six distinct steps and is evaluated on how well the task is accomplished.

8. *The adult sports scale*: measures the subject's ability to play golf or tennis.

9. *The SES scale*: is a rating of the subject according to the parental socio-economic status.

Hanson argued that if this scale (which he purposely called the NITWIT-scale) had attained the same status as Binet and Simon's, then this is how intelligence would have been defined by society. The resulting NITWIT-score would have indicated whether a student was given entry to various schools and universities, whether s/he would be given access to particular jobs, and how much on average s/he would earn. As a result, people would see the NITWIT-score as an indication of a unitary trait, representing the worth of a person. A further exciting development would be a distinction between culture-free NITWIT-tests (measuring a person's potential and making it possible for psychologists to measure the heredity of the trait) and NITWIT achievement tests (making it possible to assess how well students master NITWIT).

Society adapts to the label

Hanson further argued that once a psychological label has become reality, society starts to adapt itself to the new measure, thereby further increasing the reality of the concept. With respect to the *New Intelligence Test*, Hanson mused how parents would agonise whether their children are nitwitty enough, how they could be helped to attain their maximum NITWIT potential, and how to make sure that children do not underestimate the importance of doing well on NITWIT-tests. As Hanson wrote:

> They would review arithmetic and algebra, they would master techniques for re-membering the names of strangers, they would practice bullshitting, they would take golf and tennis lessons, they would groom themselves to appear more likable on first sight. High school and college curricula would shift in the direction of more training in the areas covered by the NIT (if they did not, irate parents would demand to know why their children were not being taught something useful).
>
> *(Hanson 1993, p. 280)*

A complete industry of NITWIT study guides and training courses would come off the ground, supervised by NITWIT specialists and also seized upon by pseudo-psychologists, who would simply try to make a good living out of it (possibly helped by their high scores on the scales of first impression, small-talk and bullshitting).

This, Hanson argued, is what has happened to the IQ-test and the derived achieve-ment tests. They have become all-invasive in the Western society without anybody knowing what they were measuring and whether they really mattered for the worth of a person. However, as a result of society's eagerness to adapt, year after year the test becomes more inescapable, because it measures one of the most important aspects of the Western society.

? What do you think?

Sociologists have their own view of society. In sociological writings groups try to achieve power, *despite the fact that they have nothing to offer*. So, with respect to psychology, sociologists claim that society has been psychologised, not because this was good for society (or because society chose it), but because psychologists were instrumental in keeping the masses well behaved and within their social classes, because psychologists were good at befriending those in power, or be-cause they were good at convincing people of the need for psychological advice. What answer would you give to the sociologists' assumption that psychology has nothing to offer? Is it true, for example, that IQ-tests are completely arbitrary and in no way helpful to the individuals who take them?

Psychologists make friends

To make your way in society, according to sociologists it is imperative to have influ-ential friends who can assist you. This is important not only for individuals and groups (e.g. the inhabitants of a village), but also for new branches of learning. As illustrated several times in this book, psychologists have vigorously tried to associate themselves with the natural sciences, despite the fact that most individuals did not perceive them that way (see Chapter 9). In turn, the natural sciences saw enough advantage in these advances to tolerate them (e.g. because a coalition with psychology increased the weight of the sciences in the culture, or because psychology brought many students to the science faculty, given that it was a popular study option). However, the position of psychology relative to the natural sciences was rarely one of equals. Therefore, according to Ward (2002), it was desirable for psychology to find other allies, preferably ones over which it had some say, ones who would agree that psychology had something they wanted and needed.

Educational psychology

The first group that welcomed input from psychology consisted of the educationalists. In the late nineteenth century, the educational sector had a low status. The schooling of teachers was rudimentary and they were virtually not represented at university level. At the same time, the number of pupils was rising exponentially as a consequence of the compulsory education introduced in one country after the other. As Ward noted:

> With such a rapid expansion, educators yearned to obtain professional status, public respect and a means for managing the onslaught of new students. Psychologists were in the unique position of being able to offer assistance in all three of these objectives.
>
> *(Ward 2002, p. 60)*

Psychologists, eager to prove their usefulness, swiftly became involved in educational matters. Already in 1892, William James had given a series of public lectures to teachers. He was soon followed by Stanley Hall and, above all, by Edward Thorndike, who in 1906 published *The principles of teaching based on psychology* and in 1910 founded the *Journal of Educational Psychology*. Rapidly, psychologists and teachers agreed that psychology was a core component of a teacher's qualification. In addition, psychology started to introduce its intelligence tests in schools and began to lobby for school counsellors. As Ward (2002) noted, schools were the first arena in which society was psychologised.

Advising parents

From the stronghold in schools, it was a small step to also raid the fledgling literature of parenting. Psychologists became involved in manuals about how to raise children. The pioneer here was Stanley Hall, who widely published about adolescents (Chapter 9). Another well-known psychologist venturing in the domain was the behaviourist John Watson, who urged parents to raise children according to behaviourist principles (Chapter 8). The end result was that new mothers felt less and less secure in relying on the advice of their own mothers, but took for granted that they needed real 'expert' advice for a proper education of their children.

Psychologists create needs

Institutions strive for monopolies by creating needs

A considerable part of the socio-political literature is devoted to the ways in which groups of people and institutions try to gain power. They do so by exaggerating the problems for which they claim to have a solution and by sending out alarming messages.

When a government establishes a new institute to tackle a problem, one of the first things the institute will do is look for ways to increase the chances of its survival and prosperity (some sociologists would argue that most of the time this even comes before the real brief of solving the problem). So, the institute will initiate a number of actions stressing the gravity of the situation and the urgent need for action. It will organise workshops, publish flyers and reports, and lobby for extra funds. In a nutshell, it will do its best to convince others of the need for widespread action upon the problems it comes to identify and for which it is providing solutions. (The same is true for charities and initiatives in the private sector.)

An interesting writer in this literature is the Austrian born scholar Ivan Illich (1926–2002), who most of the time travelled between America (including Mexico and Latin America) and Europe. In a series of books, Illich (1971, 1973, 1976) argued that the greed for power is not limited to small-scale, starting initiatives, but is true for all sections of the society. Once they are established, they try to increase their slice of the economy by creating new needs. They are not in the first place concerned with helping people, but with trying to make individuals dependent on their services. The following quote is typical of Illich's approach:

> Intensive education turns autodidacts into unemployables, intensive agriculture destroys the subsistence farmer, and the deployment of police undermines the community's self-control. The malignant spread of medicine has comparable results: it turns mutual care and self-medication into misdemeanors or felonies.
>
> *(Illich 1976, p. 42)*

Illich's account of medicine

Most interesting for us here is the 1976 book *Limits to Medicine – Medical Nemesis: The Expropriation of Health*. In this book Illich argues that the medical world enormously overstates its significance for the health of people. It is true that life expectancy has increased substantially in the twentieth century, parallel to the development of medicine. However, the most important factors for this evolution, according to Illich, were the reduction of famine, the availability of clean water and fresh air, and improved sanitation (e.g. by the installation of sewers and by pointing doctors to the importance of washing their hands before attending to patients). Figure 12.1 shows one of the arguments Illich used for his claim. Though medicine is thought to have had a very substantial impact on the incidence of tuberculosis, the mortality due to tuberculosis decreased long before the origin and the cure for the disease were found. Neither of these events had a major influence on the drop rate.

On the basis of findings like these, Illich claimed that the best treatment of diseases would consist of (a) creating the conditions that prevent diseases (i.e. good hygiene, food and – as we now know – enough exercise), and (b) having a slimmed-down health service for emergencies in which it is known that short-term interventions can alleviate a lot of suffering. Illich reckons that a few dozens of medicines would suffice for this.

However, this is not how the medical world has developed. Instead of a modest profession, it has grown into a Moloch that makes doctors and pharmaceutical companies rich and that takes away nearly one-fifth of the resources of a country.

Figure 12.1 The drop in mortality from tuberculosis.
Notice how the decline started before the origin of the disease was discovered and before different types of treatment became available. According to Illich, this shows that the decline had little to do with the medical treatment of the disease, but rather with better hygiene and improved nutrition.

Source: McKeown (1979). Reproduced with permission.

This was achieved in large part by doing needless tests and by inventing ever new illnesses for which cures were sold. Although Illich does not deny that medicine has known some successes, he claims that these are offset entirely by the following hidden costs:

1. medicine causes a lot of suffering in terminal patients,

2. medical gains are largely offset by doctor-inflicted injuries (e.g. side-effects of drugs, infections and accidents in hospitals, growth of new, more resistant organisms as a result of treatments),

3. medical practice promotes sickness by reinforcing a morbid society, which encourages people to become consumers of curative and preventive medicine,

4. health professionals have a health-denying effect insofar as they destroy the potential of people to deal with their human weakness, vulnerability and uniqueness in a personal and autonomous way.

Or as Illich summarised it:

After a century of pursuit of medical utopia, and contrary to current conventional wisdom, medical services have not been important in producing the changes in life expectancy that have occurred. A vast amount of contemporary clinical care is incidental to the curing of disease, but the damage done by medicine to the health of individuals and populations is very significant. These facts are obvious, well documented, and well repressed.

(Illich 1976, p. 14–15)

The extension to psychology

The extension to psychology is obvious: psychologists are not in the first place interested in helping people, but in creating needs so that they can expand their industry. This thinking can be found in several places, for instance in the following quote:

> In recent times, we have witnessed a marked rise in the discovery of numerous psychopathologies and syndromes. A wide variety of psychological difficulties and problems are now recognized as constituting identifiable symptoms or characteristics of syndromes previously unheard of. Premenstrual syndrome (PMS), battered woman syndrome, and attention-deficit disorder are just some of the disorders lately 'discovered' and offered up for public attention. Alongside this increase in the discovery and categorization of these types of problems is a parallel rise in the provision of counselling and therapy. Of course, if these syndromes are indeed unmitigated discoveries, the rise in therapy provision is an unambiguous blessing. However, it can be argued that the therapy industry, like any other, creates as well as serves a need.
>
> *(Burr and Butt 2000, cited in Dwight p. 186)*

What do you think?

Again, the critique depends on the extent to which medicine and psychology have nothing to offer to other groups. Can you think of examples where medicine and psychology have made a genuine difference? Or do you think Illich has a point when he says that a lot of needless costs are made by the health sector, simply to grab a bigger slice of the wealth?

Psychologists promote values

Psychologists are not politically neutral

The American lawyer and psychologist Richard Redding (2001) observed that although psychologists celebrate diversity, recognise the value and legitimacy of diverse beliefs and by their own admission strive to be inclusive, conservatives are a vastly underrepresented and marginalised minority in psychology (see table 12.2 for ways in which conservative and liberal views differ). In an analysis of two social journals, Redding found that only 1 in 30 articles reflected conservative values; the others all advanced liberal themes and policies. Similarly, he noticed that in America psychology departments rank fifth in the percentage of staff who call themselves politically liberal.

Ways in which liberal values are promoted

Redding (2001) argued that as a consequence of their bias, psychology departments are a force in the promotion of left and liberal values in the society. He listed several ways in which this happens, the most important of which are:

- *Research biases in policy research.* Given that the way in which one defines a problem has an influence on the type of response one finds, Redding argues that if one asks liberal questions, one is likely to get liberal answers.

Table 12.2 Some differences between conservative (right-wing) and liberal (left-wing) worldviews

	Conservative	Liberal
Individual differences	Mainly innate	Mainly the result of education
Remedies for social problems	Responsibility of the individual and his/her family	Responsibility of society
Responsibility for life circumstances	Individual	Society
Source of moral authority	Extrinsic (e.g. reliance on natural law or God)	Intrinsic (own morals)
Interpersonal relations	Ideal of tough-mindedness	Ideal of tender-mindedness
Ideal family model	Authoritarian – paternalistic	Egalitarian – nurturing

Source: based on Redding (2001)

- *Discrimination against students and scholars who do not share the liberal attitudes and values.* Redding lists examples of biases against students who mentioned their conservative convictions in the application forms to universities, and against researchers who apply for grants or submit manuscripts that are in line with conservative positions.

- *Biases in the educational contents.* Students are not equally exposed to the different political perspectives on social issues and find it hard to defend conservative points of view in classroom debates. Given the strong influence lecturers have on students, this directs initially neutral students to the left.

- *Biases in values promoted by psychotherapists.* Partly because of their left-biased education, psychologists will promote liberal views in their own work. According to Redding (2001, p. 208): 'because a shifting process often occurs in therapy whereby the client's values gravitate toward those of the therapist . . . , there is the ethical concern that therapists may impose their liberal values on conservative clients.'

Consequences for psychology

Redding (2001) further argued that the liberal bias of psychologists has consequences for psychology's standing in the society. In particular, he argued:

- Psychologists have less influence on socio-political issues under conservative rule.

- Psychologists have less to offer to individuals with conservative socio-political values. For instance, given that the success of psychotherapy depends on the match between the client and the therapist, psychotherapists will be less good when it comes to treating conservative clients.

- Researchers are not critical enough when it comes to evaluating liberal policies. In contrast, they are hypercritical about the worth of rightward proposals.

Which socio-political values are promoted by psychologists?

By analysing why most psychologists feel little affinity with conservative policies, we can gain insight into the type of values psychologists implicitly promote. Which features are typical for people who feel comfortable with political conservatism and against which psychologists react? Jost *et al.* (2003) provide an overview. By taking their opposites, we get a picture of what psychologists stand for. These then would be the socio-political tenets of psychologists:

1. You must not be afraid of death.

2. You must accept that the society is constantly changing, that the social system is unstable.

3. You must always look for new experiences.

4. You must not let others tell you what to do (danger of dogmatism).

5. You must tolerate uncertainty and ambiguity.

6. You must accept complexity and not be tempted to search for easy order, structures and closure.

? What do you think?

Do you agree with Redding that psychologists have a bias against right-wing ideas and opinions? Or is his view too strong? Why would such a bias exist? Try to think of a conservative proposal that might throw a different light on an issue discussed in one of your psychology courses and that could be an interesting starting point for thought or for an empirical study.

Interim summary

The ways in which psychology has influenced society

■ Psychology has contributed to the psychologisation of society. This word refers to two phenomena: first, to the fact that individuals have become seen as persons with their own thoughts and emotions, second, to growing impact of psychology on the way people interact.

■ Labels introduced by psychology have become social realities, because they influenced the way people saw themselves and others, and because society adapted itself to the new labels, despite the fact that they were to some extent arbitrary.

■ Psychologists have tried to increase their power by making alliances with established groups, such as the natural sciences, and by extending their reach to new, upcoming groups (e.g. educationists).

Interim summary (continued)

■ Psychologists also tried to increase their power by creating new needs for which they claimed to have solutions (Illich).

■ Psychologists are not politically neutral, but promote liberal values. This decreases the help they can give to people with conservative values.

12.3 Focus on: Trying to make the public views of mental disorders more realistic

Psychologisation is not steered by psychologists

When sociologists write about the psychologisation of society, this to some extent evokes a wrong image, because it suggests that the process is steered by psychologists. This is not quite right. The psychologisation is due as much to what the public thinks psychology is, as it is to what actually happens in psychological research. As we saw in Chapter 9, the public does not even have a correct image of who psychologists are. Similarly, the opinions people have about the roles of psychologists in society are a ragbag of information from the media, stereotypes promoted in the culture and social biases. The difference between popular psychology and evidence-based psychology becomes distressingly clear when we look at the ideas the public has about mental disorders.

The stigma of mental disorders

One way to investigate the perception of a particular social group is to work with vignettes. A vignette is a short story describing a particular person, such as:

> Becky is a 2nd year psychology student. She comes from Hampshire and her parents are both teachers. Most of the time she enjoys her studies, but some weeks are really hard due to the many deadlines that must be met. She has a part-time job in the College Shop, to pay for her day-to-day expenses. Last year she broke with her boyfriend, who had been her childhood sweetheart.

After reading the vignette, participants get a number of questions and have to indicate on a Likert scale (e.g. 1 = very much, 4 = not at all) how interested they would be in interacting with this person. Typical questions could be:

■ How willing would you be to move next door to Becky?

■ How willing would you be to spend an evening socialising with Becky?

■ How willing would you be to make friends with Becky?

■ How willing would you be to work closely with Becky?

■ How willing would you be to see Becky marry into the family?

Link and colleagues (1999) asked these questions to a large representative sample as part of a general social survey. However, they did not depict well-adjusted psychology students with middle-class backgrounds, but different types of mental disorders. This was their vignette for schizophrenia:

Mary is white woman with a college education. Up until a year ago, life was okay for Mary. But then, things started to change. She thought that people around her were making disapproving comments and talking behind her back. Mary was convinced that people were spying on her and that they could hear what she was thinking. Mary lost her drive to participate in her usual work and family activities and retreated to her home, eventually spending most of her day in her room. Mary was hearing voices even though no one else was around. These voices told her what to do and what to think. She has been living this way for six months.

When Link *et al.* (1999) asked the questions about the willingness to interact with Mary, the answers they got shifted toward the alternative 'rather not' (mean score of 2.75), indicating that the participants preferred to keep distance from Mary. Similar data were found for alcohol dependence (2.85), major depressive disorder (2.54) and cocaine dependence (3.20). On the basis of their findings, the authors concluded that the situation at the end of the twentieth century was still very much as Star had described it nearly half a century before:

Mental illness is a very threatening, fearful thing and not an idea to be entertained lightly about anyone. Emotionally, it represents to people a loss of what they consider to be the distinctively human qualities of rationality and free will, and there is kind of a horror in dehumanization. As both our data and other studies make clear, mental illness is something that people want to keep as far from themselves as possible.

(Star (1950) as cited in Link et al. *(1999) p. 1331)*

stigma

attribute that is deeply discrediting and that reduces the bearer to a tainted and discounted person

Many studies have since confirmed that ill mental health carries a **stigma**, defined by Goffman (1963) as an attribute that is deeply discrediting and that reduces the bearer from a whole and usual person to a tainted, discounted one (see also Link *et al.* 2004). To some extent this is surprising given that the lifetime prevalence of mental disorders in the Western world is estimated at more than 40 per cent (Kessler *et al.* 2005), meaning that nearly half the population at some point in their life may be diagnosed with a mental disorder, for which they are likely to seek help. The most prevalent disorders are major depressive disorder (17 per cent), alcohol abuse (13 per cent), specific phobia (12 per cent) and social phobia (12 per cent). It also shows that, whatever influence psychology has on society, at present it is not enough to counterbalance the deep, negative attitude the public has toward individuals with mental problems.

Mechanisms behind the negative image

If psychologists want to address the stigma associated with ill mental health, they need to know what mechanisms underlie it. For instance, they could follow Foucault's argument that mad people have been singled out by society as outcasts, to make everyone else feel better and as a surveillance threat ('if you don't behave well, you will end up in the group of the mad'). In that case, the conclusion would have to be that no matter how much effort psychologists pour into the case, it will be wasted energy. The group of the mad is needed for the other groups to feel better, and if the madness stigma were to disappear, a replacement group would have to be found.

A more positive view is that the stigma of mental illness is a social stereotype and can be tackled like all other stereotypes. For a start, it would imply that, despite all the talk, the public has little veridical information about mental illnesses. There is quite some evidence for this. For instance, the public makes few distinctions between the different types of disorders and their impact on a person's life. When Angermeyer and Matschinger (2005) phoned a representative sample of 1,000 Germans with the question what a bipolar disorder was and gave four response alternatives, only 5 per cent of the group knew the disorder referred to a mental health problem. The majority of the interviewees (61 per cent) thought it had to do with global warming and the melting of the North and the South Pole.

A second finding is that few people indicate that they have direct experience with mental health patients (which incidentally suggests how much mental health problems are hidden). Most information seems to come from the media, in particular television and newspapers. They seem to be the major sources of the negative image, because they portray people with mental health problems as devoid of interesting attributes, severely affected and above all as dangerous (Nairn 2007). It starts as early as children's cartoons (Wilson *et al.* 2000), where characters with mental illnesses serve comic roles or act as evil villains, and where commonly occurring terms such as 'crazy', 'mad' and 'losing your mind' consistently denote loss of control.

Also in prime television series and films, people with mental health problems are predominantly portrayed as dangerous individuals. Of the 20 characters Wilson *et al.* (1999) randomly selected, 15 were portrayed as violent, unpredictable, unproductive, asocial, incompetent and unreliable. Corrigan *et al.* (2005) analysed American newspapers. Of the articles referring to mental health problems, 39 per cent contained an association with violence. These usually figured on the front pages of tabloids (e.g. when a murder had been committed by someone who had been treated by the mental health services). The ones that gave a more representative picture usually were in the scientific sections of the more serious newspapers.

Nairn and Coverdale (2005) further observed that most articles related to mental health problems were stories *about* people and not stories *of* people: There were few first-person stories based on the experiences and the perspectives of persons with mental health problems themselves. In a survey of more than 5,000 respondents, Angermeyer *et al.* (2005) observed that the stigma of mental illness was particularly strong among those who watched a lot of television and read tabloid newspapers.

This is how the mother of a son with schizophrenia experienced it:

Just look how often and in what sort of magazines you can read something about Cholesterol, for instance. Even in the tabloid press, and so often that you're getting sick and tired of it! And when you want to know something about a mental disorder, you only hear about it when a patient has committed a crime, and that's all. And this is a really big mistake!

(Schulze and Angermeyer 2003, p. 306)

The association in the media between mental health problems and danger is by far the strongest reason why the public wants to keep its distance from individuals with a mental illness (Link *et al.* 1999). This is the more unfortunate because there is little empirical evidence for such a link (which also provides scope for change). It is true that some mental disorders are associated with a higher probability of aggression and violence, but these are mostly limited to the antisocial personality disorder and dependence on various substances (in particular related to the need for money to buy the substance). Most other disorders (e.g. mood disorders, anxiety disorders) do not lead to a higher risk (e.g. Arboleda-Florez 1998), sometimes even the reverse (e.g. Bonta *et al.* 1998). Schizophrenia is associated with some increase in risk of violence, but this is largely confined to a subgroup with co-morbid substance misuse, medication noncompliance, active psychotic symptoms and a history of violence (e.g. Walsh *et al.* 2004). Walsh and Fahy (2002) reported that 2 per cent of the arrests in the USA involved schizophrenic patients (they make up about 1 per cent of the population and are overrepresented in lower socio-economic groups). This can be compared with the fact that 16 per cent of the men aged 18–24 years and from low economic classes in the USA are reported as involved in violence.

The fact that mental illnesses are so often associated with violence in the media means that new patients themselves are scared of others on their first admissions. This is what a psychiatrist reported in her daily practice:

Or what you see in crime series on tv. It seems there is a particular trend at the moment. Nearly every week, one of the perpetrators portrayed in these films ends up in a psychiatric hospital, because he's committed a horrific crime. And this shapes the public image, also among the patients. They're afraid they might find themselves attacking someone one day, and they'd rather not stay at the hospital because they're scared of the other patients.

(Schulze and Angermeyer 2003, p. 305)

Finally, there are suggestions that part of the reason why people with poor mental health are doing less well is precisely the way in which the other people treat them. This is how the American anthropologist Tanya Luhrmann (2007) described it:

The primary conclusion of the ethnographic research on subjects with schizophrenia is that the daily experience of survival with serious psychotic illness is one of repeated social failure . . .

You would expect individuals to experience social defeat when they have an encounter with another person who demeans them, humiliates them, subordinates them . . . Social defeat is not so much an idea that someone holds but a human encounter—an important distinction, because to alter individuals' ideas you can use psychotherapy, but to alter their encounters, you must change their social world.

(Luhrmann 2007, p. 149, 151–2)

Luhrmann (2007) described how a considerable percentage of patients diagnosed with schizophrenia end up being homeless and dependent on charity and shelter care houses. In her view, the reaction ex-patients receive from others is one of the reasons why the prospects of recovery are lower in Western countries than in Africa and India, where the extended family remains more involved in the treatment, where individuals do not have to be primary breadwinners or caretakers to be useful members of a household, and where fewer jobs are in fast-paced, high people-contact settings.

What do you think?

To what extent have your psychology studies formed a counterweight against the stigma of mental illness? Or do you see very much the same stereotypes among psychology students as in the general public?

Quo vadis, *psychology?*

The analysis of people's reactions to mental health problems arguably confronts us with the biggest conceptual issue underlying the present book: *Does psychology matter?* This issue can be translated into various sub-questions, such as: Is the knowledge that psychology generates helpful? Does psychology make a difference for those who appeal to it (clients, relatives, schools, hospitals, companies, politicians)? Does it provide students with useful information and skills? Does it require a dedicated degree? And maybe above all: Can we imagine a twenty-first-century society without psychologists? Could the explosion of scientific knowledge in the past 300–400 years have taken place without the emergence of psychology as an independent discipline? And if so, how would our culture differ from the one we know now? These are the questions we happily leave you with at the end of this book.

Interim summary

The stigma of ill mental health

- The public's view of psychology and mental disorders differs from the reality of these disorders.

- The public has a negative image of mental disorders and tries to keep a distance from people with such disorders (i.e. ill mental health carries a stigma).

- The mechanisms underlying this perception are probably:
  - limited knowledge of the different types of disorders with their different degrees of severity,
  - most people have little direct experience with mental health patients,
  - constant negative portrayal in the media and association with danger,
  - reactions patients get from others, leading to repeated social defeat, making it difficult for these patients to have good social relations.

- These reactions confront us with the biggest conceptual issue underlying this book: Does psychology matter? Does it make a difference to those who make an appeal against it?

Recommended literature

The influence of the socio-political context on psychology (in particular intelligence testing) is well described in Gould, S.J. (1996). *The mismeasure of man* (New York: W.W. Norton & Co.).

Good examples of the influences of psychology on society are Ward, S.C. (2002) *Modernizing the mind: Psychological knowledge and the remaking of society* (Westport, CT: Praeger) and Hanson, F.A. (1993) *Testing testing: Social consequences of the examined life* (Berkeley: University of California Press).

For the ways in which social groups try to increase their power, see in particular Illich, I. (1976) *Limits to medicine – Medical nemesis: The expropriation of health* (London: Marion Boyars Publishers).

Finally, for those who wonder whether at the end of the day psychology still has something to offer, an interesting article may be Zimbardo, P.G. (2004) 'Does psychology make a significant difference in our lives?' (*American Psychologist, 59*: 339–51).

References

Angermeyer, M.C. and Matschinger, H. (2005) 'What is a bipolar disorder? Results of a representative survey of the German population', *Psychiatrische Praxis, 32*: 289–91.

Angermeyer, M.C., Dietrich, S., Potl, D. and Matschinger, H. (2005) 'Media consumption and desire for social distance towards people with schizophrenia', *European Psychiatry, 20*: 246–50.

APA Presidential Task Force on Evidence-based Practice (2006) 'Evidence-based practice in psychology', *American Psychologist, 61*: 271–85.

Arboleda-Florez, J. (1998) 'Mental illness and violence: An epidemiological appraisal of the evidence', *Canadian Journal of Psychiatry – Revue Canadienne de Psychiatrie, 43*: 989–96.

Bonta, J., Law, M. and Hanson, K. (1998) 'The prediction of criminal and violent recidivism among mentally disordered offenders: A meta-analysis', *Psychological Bulletin, 123*: 123–42.

Boring, E.G. (1923) 'Intelligence as the tests test it', *New Republic*, 6 June 1923, 35–7.

Burr, V. and Butt, T. (2000) 'Psychological distress and postmodern thought.' In F. Dwight (ed.), *Pathology and the postmodern*. London: Sage Publications, pp. 186–206.

Corrigan, P.W. *et al.* (2005) 'Newspaper stories as measures of structural stigma', *Psychiatric Services, 56*: 551–6.

Danziger, K. (1997) *Naming the mind: How psychology found its language*. London: Sage.

De Graaf, P.M. and Kalmijn, M. (2006) 'Divorce motives in a period of rising divorce: Evidence from a Dutch life-history survey', *Journal of Family Issues, 27*: 183–205.

Diamond, M. and Sigmundson, H.K. (1997) 'Sex reassignment at birth: Long-term review and clinical implications', *Archives of Pediatrics and Adolescent Medicine, 151*: 298–304.

Draaisma, D. (2000) *Metaphors of memory. A history of ideas about the mind*. Cambridge: Cambridge University Press.

Foucault, M. (1961) *Folie et déraison. Histoire de la folie à l'âge classique*. Paris: Librairie Plon. [English translation in 1965: *Madness and civilization: A history of insanity in the Age of Reason*; new translation in 2006: *History of madness*, Routledge.]

Foucault, M. (1976) *Surveiller et punir: Naissance de la prison*. Paris: Editions Gallimard. [English translation: Foucault, M. (1979). *Discipline and punish: The birth of the prison*. New York: Vintage.]

Frankfurt, H.G. (2005) *On bullshit*. Princeton, NJ: Princeton University Press.

Fuchs, A.H. (2000) 'Contributions of American mental philosophers to psychology in the United States', *History of Psychology, 3*: 3–19.

Gentner, D. and Grudin, J. (1985) 'The evolution of mental metaphors in psychology: A 90-year retrospective', *American Psychologist*, **40**: 181–92.

Goffman, E. (1963) *Stigma: Notes on the management of spoiled identity*. Englewood Cliffs, NJ: Prentice Hall.

Gould, S.J. (1996) *The mismeasure of man* (2nd edn). London: W.W. Norton & Co.

Gulerce, A. (2006) 'History of psychology in Turkey as a sign of diverse modernization and global psychologization.' In A.C. Brock (ed.), *Internationalizing the history of psychology*. New York: New York University Press, pp. 75–93.

Hanson, F.A. (1993) *Testing testing: Social consequences of the examined life*. Berkeley and Los Angeles: University of California Press.

Hood, R.W. (2000) 'American psychology of religion and the "Journal for the Scientific Study of Religion"', *Journal for the Scientific Study of Religion*, 39: 531–43.

Illich, I. (1971) *Deschooling society*. London: Penguin Education (also available on http://reactor-core.org/deschooling.html).

Illich, I. (1973) *Tools for conviviality*. New York: Harper & Row (also available on http://clevercycles.com/tools_for_conviviality).

Illich, I. (1976) *Limits to medicine – Medical nemesis: The expropriation of health*. London: Marion Boyars (also available on www.soilandhealth.org).

Jones, D. and Elcock, J. (2001) *History and theories of psychology: A critical perspective*. London: Arnold.

Jost, J.T., Glaser, J., Kruglanski, A.W. and Sulloway, F.J. (2003) 'Political conservatism as motivated social cognition', *Psychological Bulletin*, **129**: 339–75.

Kessler, R.C., Berglund, P., Demler, O., Jin, R. and Walters, E.E. (2005) 'Lifetime prevalence and age-of-onset distributions of DSM-IV disorders in the national comorbidity survey replication', *Archives of General Psychiatry*, **62**: 593–602.

Larsen, S.F. (1987) 'Remembering and the archaeology metaphor', *Metaphor and Symbol*, **2**: 187–99.

Leary, D.E. (ed.) (1995) *Metaphors in the history of psychology*. Cambridge: Cambridge University Press.

Link, B.G., Phelan, J.C., Besnahan, M., Stueve, A. and Pescosolido, B.A. (1999) 'Public conceptions of mental illness: Labels, causes, dangerousness, and social distance', *American Journal of Public Health*, **89**: 1328–33.

Link, B.G., Yang, L.H., Phelan, J.C. and Collins, P.Y. (2004) 'Measuring mental illness stigma', *Schizophrenia Bulletin*, **30**: 511–41.

Luhrmann, T.M. (2007) 'Social defeat and the culture of chronicity: Or, why schizophrenia does so well over there and so badly here', *Culture, Medicine and Psychiatry*, **31**: 135–72.

Mayer, J. (2008) *The dark side: The inside story of how the war on terror turned into a war on American ideals*. Garden City, NY: Doubleday.

McKeown, T. (1979) *The role of medicine: Dream, mirage or nemesis?* (2nd edn). Oxford: Basil Blackwell.

Messer, S.B. (2004) 'Evidence-based practice: Beyond empirically supported treatments', *Professional Psychology: Research and Practice*, **35**: 580–8.

Money, T. and Ehrhardt, A. (1972) *Man and woman, boy and girl, the differentiation and dimorphism of gender identity from conception to maturity*. Baltimore, MD: Johns Hopkins University Press.

Nairn, R.G. (2007) 'Media portrayals of mental illness, or is it madness? A review', *Australian Psychologist*, **42**: 138–46.

Nairn, R.G. and Coverdale, J.H. (2005) 'People never see us living well: An appraisal of the personal stories about mental illness in a prospective print media sample', *Australian and New Zealand Journal of Psychiatry*, **39**: 281–7.

Redding, R.E. (2001) 'Sociopolitical diversity in psychology: The case for pluralism', *American Psychologist*, **56**: 205–15.

Richards, G. (2002) *Putting psychology in its place: A critical historical overview* (2nd edn). London: Routledge.

Rogers, A. and Pilgrim, D. (2005) *A sociology of mental health and illness* (3rd edn). Maidenhead, UK: Open University Press.

Schulze, B. and Angermeyer, M.C. (2003) 'Subjective experiences of stigma. A focus group study of schizophrenic patients, their relatives and mental health professionals', *Social Science & Medicine,* **56**: 299–312.

Sokal, A.D. (1996a) 'Transgressing the boundaries: Toward a transformative hermeneutics of quantum gravity', *Social Text,* **46/47** (spring/summer): 217–52 (also available on http://www.physics.nyu.edu/sokal/).

Sokal, A.D. (1996b) 'A physicist experiments with cultural studies', *Lingua Franca,* May/June, **62–64** (also available on http://www.physics.nyu.edu/sokal/).

Sokal, A. and Bricmont, J. (1997) *Impostures intellectuelles*. Paris: Editions Odile Jacob. Translated into English (1998, 2003) as *Intellectual impostures*. London: Profile Books Ltd.

Teo, T. (2005) *The critique of psychology: From Kant to postcolonial theory*. New York: Springer Science+Business Media, Inc.

Teo, T. (2008) 'Race and psychology.' In W.A. Darity (ed.), *International encyclopedia of the social sciences* (2nd edn). Detroit, MI: Macmillan, Vol. 7, pp. 21–4.

Thompson, D. (2008) *Counterknowledge: How we surrendered to conspiracy theories, quack medicine, bogus science and fake history*. London: Atlantic Books.

The British Psychological Society (2004) *Guideline for minimum standards of ethical approval in psychological research*. Leicester, UK: The British Psychological Society. (Retrieved in March 2008 from www.bps.org.uk.)

The British Psychological Society (2006) *Code of ethics and conduct*. Leicester, UK: The British Psychological Society. (Retrieved in March 2008 from www.bps.org.uk.)

Tulving, E. and Thomson, D.M. (1971) 'Retrieval processes in recognition memory – Effects of associative context', *Journal of Experimental Psychology,* **87**: 116–24.

Walsh, E. and Fahy, T. (2002) 'Violence in society: Contribution of mental illness is low', *British Medical Journal,* **325**: 507–8.

Walsh, E. *et al.* (2004) 'Predicting violence in schizophrenia: A prospective study', *Schizophrenia Research,* **67**: 247–52.

Wampold, B.E., Minami, T., Basking, T.W. and Tierney, S.C. (2002) 'A meta-(re)analysis of the effects of cognitive therapy versus "other therapies" for depression', *Journal of Affective Disorders,* **68**: 159–65.

Weindling, P.J. (2004) *Nazi medicine and the Nuremberg Trials: From medical war crimes to informed consent*. Basingstoke: Palgrave-Macmillan.

Wheen, F. (2004) *How mumbo-jumbo conquered the world: A short history of modern delusions*. London: Harper Perennial.

Wilson, C., Nairn, R., Coverdale, J. and Panapa, A. (1999) 'Mental illness depictions in prime-time drama: Identifying the discursive resources', *Australian and New Zealand Journal of Psychiatry,* **33**: 232–9.

Wilson, C., Nairn, R., Coverdale, J. and Panapa, A. (2000) 'How mental illness is portrayed in children's television: A prospective study', *British Journal of Psychiatry,* **176**: 440–3.

Epilogue

We have come to the end of our journey through the historical and conceptual issues in psychology. We hope you enjoyed it and found it intellectually stimulating. We have tried to strike a fair balance between two types of approaches that prevail in the literature. On the one hand, there are the celebratory reviews of psychology's achievements exalting the many precious gifts psychology has bestowed on society; on the other hand, there are the hypercritical reviews calling into question everything psychologists feel proud of and leaving students bewildered and depressed at the end of the reading.

For the record, we authors are both happy with our careers in psychology and never regretted our choice. However, this does not take away from the fact that from time to time it is good to stand back and take a critical look at what we are doing.

We are very well aware that similar reviews could be written in all the other academic disciplines. The fact that they do not seem to feel the same urge to put themselves into perspective may be seen as an illustration of a masochistic tendency in psychologists, although we ourselves tend to perceive it as an indication that psychologists are interested in all types of human functioning, including their own. We hope you will find the outcome of our enterprise helpful and inspiring for the continuation of your career!

Glossary

achievement test: standardized test which measures the knowledge of a particular topic or set of topics.

ad hoc modifications: modifications to a theory that according to Popper make the theory less falsifiable; decrease the scientific value of the theory.

Age of Enlightenment: name given to the Western philosophy and cultural life of the eighteenth century, in which autonomous thinking and observation became advocated as the primary sources of knowledge, rather than reliance on authority.

algorithm: list of instructions that converts a given input, via a fully defined series of intermediate steps, into the desired output.

animal spirits: spirits that were thought by Galen to travel over the nerves between the ventricles in the brain and the body.

animism: explanation of the workings of the world and the universe by means of spirits with humanlike characteristics.

anthropomorphic interpretation: interpreting behaviour of non-human living creatures by attributing human motives and human-like intelligence to them.

antipsychiatry movement: a pressure group starting in the 1960s that called the usefulness of the prevailing psychiatric treatments into question.

applied psychology: the application of psychological knowledge and research methods to solve practical problems.

associationism: speculation that the mind learns by associating the elements obtained through perception; two main principles of association are similarity (similar elements get associated) and contiguity in time and space (elements that co-occur get associated).

associative learning: learning of simple associations (correlations) between all types of events; thought to be the basis of automatic, type 1 thinking.

asylum: name given to the institutions for the insane established from the eighteenth century on; first modelled after prisons, later after hospitals for chronic patients.

authenticity test: test to determine whether a person is who he/she pretends to be and to ascertain guilt or innocence.

behaviourism: movement in psychology arguing that observable behaviours are the most important aspect of human functioning to be understood; denies to various extents the relevance of information processing going on in the mind; particularly strong in the USA in the first half of the twentieth century.

biopsychosocial model: model according to which the understanding of medical and psychological phenomena requires attention to biological, psychological as well as socio-cultural factors.

boxes-and-arrows diagram: flowchart outlining the different information stores (boxes) and information transformations (arrows) involved in the execution of a particular task with observable input and output; used by cognitive psychologists to detail the information processing involved in the task.

bracketing: requirement in qualitative research to look at a phenomenon with an open mind and to free oneself from preconceptions.

brain equipotentiality theory: theory saying that all parts of the brain have equal significance and are involved in each task; first thought to apply to the complete brain; since the nineteenth century limited to the cerebral hemispheres.

Cambrian explosion: sudden presence of fossils in geological records starting some 542 million years ago; often presented as the beginning of 'real' life.

case study: within medicine and clinical psychology, the intensive study of an individual patient within the context of his/her own world and relations, to understand and help the individual patient.

Chinese room: thought experiment proposed by Searle to illustrate the difference between information processing in humans and information processing in computers.

classical conditioning: form of learning discovered by Pavlov in which an association is made between two events in the environment; usually studied with a stimulus that elicits a reflex-like response (e.g. food in mouth → salivation) to which a second, initially neutral stimulus is coupled.

clinical psychology: branch of psychology applying psychological knowledge to the assessment and treatment of mental disorders.

cognitive neuropsychiatry: subfield that tries to understand consequences of mental disorders in terms of breakdowns in the cognitive models of normal psychological functioning.

cognitive neuropsychology: part of neuropsychology aimed at understanding and treating the behavioural consequences of brain damage within the information processing models proposed by cognitive psychologists.

cognitive neuroscience: the scientific study of the biological mechanisms underlying cognition; largely based on brain imaging techniques, TMS and the measurement of electrical activity.

cognitive psychology: movement in psychology arguing that observable behaviours are the result of information processing in the mind; started in the 1950s and currently the dominant form of mainstream psychology.

comparative psychology: study of behaviour of animals, usually with the intention to shed light on human functioning within the framework of the evolutionary theory.

computational model: computer program simulating the human information processing assumed to be involved in the execution of a particular task; requires researchers to be much more precise about of what is going on than in a boxes-and-arrows model.

confirmation bias: tendency people have to search for evidence that confirms their opinion; goes against falsificationism.

confounding variable: variable that was not taken into account in the study and that may be the origin of the effect observed.

consciousness: word referring to the private, first-person experiences an individual lives through; contains all the mental states a person is aware of; part of the mind that can be examined with introspection.

critical psychology: movement in psychology that criticises mainstream psychology for failing to understand that knowledge does not refer to an outside reality (idealism), that scientific knowledge is not cumulative but consists of social constructions, and that psychological theories and claims have an impact on the world in which people live.

cybernetics: the study of communication and control in machines.

Dark Ages: name given in the Renaissance to the Middle Ages, to refer to the lack of independent and scientific thinking in that age.

deduction: form of reasoning in which one starts from a number of indisputable premises, from which new, true conclusions can be drawn if the rules of logic are followed.

deductive reasoning: form of reasoning in which one starts from a number of indisputable premises (known statements), from which new, true conclusions can be drawn if the rules of logic are followed.

degenerative research programme: notion introduced by Lakatos to indicate a paradigm that does not allow researchers to make new predictions and that requires an increasing number of ad hoc modifications to account for the empirical findings.

demarcation criteria: set of criteria that fully defines a concept (i.e. includes all instances belonging to the concept and excludes all instances not belonging to the concept).

diagnostic tests: tests to determine which condition a person has.

discourse analysis: qualitative research method that aims to discover how social relations between people are determined by the language they use.

dualism: view of the mind–body relation according to which the mind is immaterial and completely independent of the body; central within religions and also in Descartes' philosophy.

dualism: view about the relationship between the mind and brain that considers them as two different realms; in general the mind is seen as immaterial and in control of human behaviour (free will).

Edwin Smith papyrus: papyrus from Ancient Egypt that contains short descriptions of the symptoms and treatment of different forms of brain injury; named after the person who bought the papyrus in Egypt and had it analysed.

EEG: electroencephalogram: outcome of measurement of electrical brain activity by means of sensors placed on the scalp; routinely used in hospitals for the detection of epilepsy.

efficacy of therapies: measure to indicate how much improvement a therapy brings to patients.

embodied cognition: view about the meaning of events and words that stresses their dependence on body-related perceptual and motoric experiences; information is not abstract, independent of the personal experiences of the information carrier.

empiricism: view according to which knowledge is obtained by means of perceptual experiences; usually involves idea of associations between ideas to combine the individual perceptions; also emphasis on inductive reasoning.

ethical code of conduct: protocol that includes all the ethics-related conditions to which a study must adhere.

eugenics: social philosophy claiming that the fate of a nation can be improved by selective breeding of the inhabitants.

Event Related Potential (ERP): signal obtained by averaging the EEG-signals to stimuli that are repeated a number of times; allows researchers to look for differences in the signal as a function of characteristics of the stimulus.

evolutionary psychology: approach in psychology that aims to understand human behaviour on the basis of natural selection and the evolutionary theory.

experimental history: expression introduced by Francis Bacon to indicate that empiricists should not base their knowledge entirely on passive observation, but had to actively manipulate elements of the situation to see what effects this has.

experimentation: method of investigating a phenomenon by means of experiments; in these experiments aspects of the phenomenon are systematically manipulated to observe their consequences; usually done to test predictions that have been derived from the existing understanding by means of deductive reasoning.

face validity: estimating the validity of a test by estimating to what extent the items of the test agree with one's own beliefs; is not evidence-based.

falsificationism: view within the philosophy of science that statements are scientific only if they can be falsified empirically.

feminist psychology: movement in psychology aimed at understanding women; is particularly concerned with the way in which women are treated in mainstream psychology

Fertile Crescent: region in the Middle East with a high level of civilisation around 3,000 BCE; included the Ancient Mesopotamian and the Ancient Egyptian civilizations.

fMRI: brain imaging technique based on the measurement of blood with oxygen vs. blood without oxygen; currently the most popular imaging technique because of its high spatial resolution (allows good localisation); has rather low temporal resolution (cannot trace what is happening at a speed of hundreds of registrations per second)

focus group: technique in which a group of participants freely discuss a limited set of questions.

folk psychology: collection of beliefs lay people have about psychological functioning; no efforts made to verify them empirically or to check them for their internal coherence.

folk science: intuitive theories people have about the workings of the world, based on a combination of scientifically gathered and non-scientifically gathered information.

free will: situation in which individuals can choose their course of action from a number of alternatives; choice is the outcome of a rational deliberation.

functionalism: name given to an approach in early American psychology research, that examined the practical functions of the human mind inspired by the evolutionary theory.

functionalism: in philosophy, view about the relationship between the mind and brain that considers the mind as a separate layer of information implemented on a Turing machine; predicts that the mind can be copied onto another Turing machine.

gate control theory of pain: theory of pain perception which assumes that the nerve signals carrying the pain message have to pass through a gate before they reach the brain; at this gate the signals can be made stronger or weaker.

geocentric model: model of the universe in which the Earth is at the centre; was dominant until the seventeenth century.

Gestalt psychology: group of psychologists who argued that the human mind could not be understood by breaking down the experiences into their constituting elements; perception is more than the sensation of stimuli, it involves organisation.

global workspace model: model that explains the role of consciousness by analogy to a theatre: consciousness is meant to make some information available to the whole brain (i.e. the play), so that the various background processes can align their functioning to what is going on centrally.

grounded theory: qualitative research method that tries to understand what is going on in a particular situation and that on the basis of a qualitative analysis and induction tries to come to a theoretical insight grounded in the data.

hard problem: name given by Chalmers to refer to the difficulty of explaining in what respects consciousness is more than accounted for on the basis of materialism and functionalism.

heliocentric model: model of the universe in which the Sun is at the centre; started to dominate after Galilei's seventeenth-century book.

hermeneutics: approach in psychology according to which the task of the psychologist is to interpret and understand persons on the basis of their personal and socio-cultural history (understanding rather than controlling)

heuristic-based thinkers: those who think based on heuristics, rules of thumb that do not require as much effort as the scientific method and that most of the time result in good decisions, but that are subject to a number of biases.

hidden racism: advancing one's own race by non-conspicuous biases against other groups (usually by ignoring their contribution).

historical method: one of the three research methods introduced by Wundt; consists of studying the human mind by investigating the products of human cultures; according to Wundt particularly well suited to investigate the 'higher' functions of the mind.

Homo sapiens: species to which present humans belong; started in Africa some 200K years ago; nearly decimated some 100–50K years ago.

homunculus: word (meaning 'little man') used to refer to the difficulty of explaining goal-oriented behaviour without making use of an ultimate intelligent (human-like) control centre.

humanistic psychology: psychological movement promoted by Rogers and Maslow as a reaction against psychoanalysis and behaviourism; stressed that people are human, inherently positive, endowed with free will and living within a socio-cultural context

human relations movement: second main theory of how work should be organised; stressed the humanity of the employees and the importance of social relations.

human resource movement: third main theory of how work should be organized; stressed the desire for self-actualization in employees; employees will perform best if given autonomy and authority.

hypothetico-deductive method: model introduced by Popper to understand the scientific method; on the basis of observation, induction and educated guess-work, a theory of a phenomenon is formulated; the correctness of the theory is evaluated by the formulation of a testable prediction (hypothesis) on the basis of deductive reasoning; the prediction is subsequently put to a falsification test, which provides new observational data for further theorising.

idealism: view within philosophy that human knowledge is a construction of the mind and does not necessarily correspond to an outside world; the truth of knowledge depends on the coherence with rest of the knowledge in the social group.

ideographic approach: the conclusions of a study stay limited to the phenomenon under study.

illusory correlation: perception of a correlation between events for which no independent evidence can be found.

implicit personality theory: mixture of stereotypes and individuating information about the associations of person characteristics that people use to make predictions about how others will behave in social relations.

inclusive fitness: hypothesis in evolutionary psychology that behaviour is motivated not only by the orgnism's own survival but also by the survival of organisms that are genetically related; the motivation depends on the degree of relatedness.

individualisation: trend in a society towards looser social relations and a greater focus by individuals on themselves than on the groups they belong to.

induction: form of reasoning in which one starts from observations and tries to reach general conclusions; is needed in science to come from observed phenomena to scientific laws.

inductive reasoning: form of reasoning in which one starts from observations and tries to reach general conclusions; is needed in science to turn observed phenomena into scientific laws; no guarantee that the conclusions are true.

industrial psychology: first theory about how work should be organised; strongly influenced by Taylor's scientific management: employees were the hands of the company that would accept any work if remunerated enough; tasks had to be made simple so that everyone could do them without much practice.

industrial revolution: name to refer to the socio-economic and cultural changes in the nineteenth century caused by the invention of machines; involved, among other things the replacement of the labour of peasants and craftsmen by mass production in factories and the resulting massive relocation from the countryside to the town.

information feedback: mechanism in which the current performance level is compared to the desired end-state and the discrepancy is used to bring the performance closer to the end-state aimed for; important for psychology because it explained a great deal of goal-directed behaviour that previously seemed to require a homunculus explanation.

information processing: encoding mental representations, transforming them by means of algorithms, and integrating them with existing knowledge; forms the core of cognitive psychology.

informed consent: central principle in ethics, saying that people can only take part in a study after they have been informed of what will be involved and after they have explicitly and voluntarily agreed to participate.

instinct: innate and fixed response that is automatically elicited by an appropriate stimulus; used around the turn of the twentieth century to explain motivation.

instrumental conditioning: name introduced by Thorndike to refer to learning on the basis of the law of effect; called operant conditioning by Skinner.

interpretative phenomenological analysis: qualitative research method in psychology that tries to understand how a phenomenon is experienced by the people involved.

introspection: one of the three research methods introduced by Wundt; consists of a person looking inside and reporting what he/she senses, thinks or feels.

IQ-test: test developed by psychologists to measure the intelligence of a person; first useful test published by Binet and Simon in 1907.

IQ-test: test which is supposed to measure the intelligence of a person; focuses on learning potential; results correlate with school performance and suitability for intellectually demanding occupations.

law of effect: behavioural law introduced by Thorndike to refer to the fact that behaviours followed by positive consequences are strengthened and more likely to be repeated.

localisation theory: theory saying that brain processes are localised, meaning that only part of the brain underlies a particular mental function.

logical positivism: philosophical movement in the first half of the twentieth century, claiming that philosophy should stop thinking about metaphysics, but should try to understand the essence of the scientific approach; central tenet was the verification principle.

magnetoencephalography (MEG): measurement of the electrical brain activity by means of measurement of the magnetic field around the head; is one of the most promising brain imaging techniques, because it has the potential of both a high temporal and spatial resolution.

materialism: view about the relationship between the mind and brain that considers the mind as the brain in operation; predicts that the mind depends on the specific brain in which it is realised; denies the existence of free will.

Matthew effect: the tendency to give more credit to well-known scientists than they deserve; increases the perceived impact of these scientists.

mechanistic view: world view according to which everything in the material universe can be understood as a complicated machine; discards the notion that things have goals and intentions as assumed by the animistic view; started with Descartes.

meme: information unit proposed by Dawkins that reproduces itself according to the principles of the evolutionary theory (variation, selection and replication).

mental chronometry: using reaction times to measure the time needed for various mental tasks; on the basis of a comparison of different tasks, models of the mental processes involved in the tasks are postulated.

mental representation: information pattern in the mind representing knowledge obtained through observation or the application of an algorithm; forms a realm separate from the brain and could in principle be copied to another brain (or in a more extreme version, to a Turing machine).

metaphor: in science stands for an analogy from another area that helps to map a new, complex problem by making reference to a better understood phenomenon.

methodolatry or methodologism: tendency to see methodological rigour as the only requirement for scientific research at the expense of theory formation.

mind: aggregate of faculties humans (and animals) have to perceive, feel, think, remember and want.

mind–brain problem: issue of how the mind is related to the brain; three main views: dualism, materialism and functionalism.

natural selection: process in Darwin's evolutionary theory by which the environment results in the continuation and multiplication of organisms with certain genetic features and hinders the reproduction of organisms with other genetic features; the first type of features are called favourable (within the prevailing environment), the second type unfavourable.

nature–nurture debate: discussion about the respective contributions of genes and environment in the development of (human) qualities.

neolithic revolution: the transition from a nomadic hunter-gatherer society to farming and settlement around 10,000 BCE.

neurologist: name used at the end of the nineteenth century by physicians who were interested in the treatment of milder forms of mental problems outside the asylum; the term was later used to refer to specialists of the nervous system, when the original neurologists merged with the psychiatrists and took up the latter's name.

neuron: brain cell; basic unit of the nervous system; contains a cell body, dendrites and an axon.

neuropsychology: branch of psychological research and practice that looks at the relationship between brain and behaviour; research traditionally focused on understanding the consequences of brain damage and localising the affected tissue; practice aimed at assessing the behavioural and mental consequences of the injury and administering the rehabilitation programme.

neurotransmitter: chemical substance used to communicate between neurons; is released from the synapse when a signal arrives through the axon; can be affected by drugs.

nomothetic approach: a study is run in search for universal principles that exceed the confines of the study.

non-invasive techniques: methods in neuroscience that allow the study of the workings of the brain without surgery or the use of irreversible interventions.

observational learning: learning as a result of observing others performing actions and being rewarded or punished.

operational definition: definition of a variable in terms of how the variable has been measured; allows description of the variable in quantitative form.

paradigm: notion introduced by Kuhn to refer to the fact that scientists share a set of common views of what the discipline is about and how problems must be investigated.

parental investment theory: hypothesis in evolutionary psychology holding that the gender investing the most in the upbringing of offspring is more discriminating about mating.

personality test: test to measure relatively stable and distinctive patterns of behaviour that characterise individuals and their reactions to the environment.

personality trait: basic dimension used to describe differences in personality between people; is often bipolar with opposites at the extremes (e.g. introvert vs. extrovert).

philosophy: critical reflection on the universe and human functioning; started in Ancient Greece.

philosophy of science: branch of philosophy that studies the foundations of scientific research, to better understand the position of scientific research relative to other forms of information acquisition and generation.

phlogiston: substance that was believed to make materials flammable before the chemical processes of combustion were understood.

phonogram: a sign that represents a sound or a syllable of spoken language; forms the basis of writing systems.

phrenology: view that mental functions are localised in the brain and that the capacity of a function corresponds to the size of the brain part devoted to it; gave rise to personality assessment by means of analysing bumps on the skull; initiated by Gall and Spurzheim at the beginning of the nineteenth century.

physiognomy: belief that the personality of an individual can be deduced from their appearance, in particular from the shape of the head and the face.

pictogram: an information-conveying sign that consists of a picture resembling the person, animal or object it represents.

place coding system: system in which the meaning of a sign not only depends on its form but also on its position in a string; is used for instance in Arabic numerals.

positivism: view that authentic knowledge can only be obtained by means of the scientific method; saw religion and philosophy as inferior forms of explanation.

positivism: philosophy stating that only empirically obtained and verifiable information is authentic information; started by Comte in the eighteenth century; also often used to refer to an opinion according to which science and scientifically obtained information are the motors of progress.

positron emission tomography (PET): brain imaging technique based on measurement of radioactive tracer injected into the bloodstream.

postcolonial psychology: movement in psychology addressing the issues of racism and the ways in which dominant groups treat other groups.

postmodernist: in the philosophy of science someone who questions the special status of science and sees scientific explanations as stories told by a particular group of scientists.

pragmatism: view within philosophy that human knowledge is information about how to cope with the world; the truth of knowledge depends on the success one has in engaging with the world, on what works.

preliterate civilisation: civilisation before writing was invented.

presentism: practice of depicting and interpreting events of the past in the light of present-day ideas and knowledge.

Principia Mathematica: book in which Newton presented his laws of physics (1687); considered to be the primary reason of the increased status of science.

problem of the identity theory: difficulty the materialistic theory of the mind–brain relationship has to explain how two events can be experienced as the same despite the fact that their realisation in the brain differs.

progressive research programme: notion introduced by Lakatos to indicate a paradigm that allows researchers to make new, hitherto unexpected predictions that can be tested empirically.

Protestant Reformation: movement against the Roman Catholic Church, which was important for the development of science, because it emphasised the need for education, critical thinking, hard work and worldly success.

pseudohistory of science: text that looks like a history of science, but that contains systematic errors because of a desire to present the research as more impressive and important than it was and to depict the scientist as a genius who has to battle against the lack of understanding and appreciation by the peers.

pseudoscience: branch of knowledge that pretends to be scientific but that violates the scientific method on essential aspects, such as lack of openness to testing by others and reliance on confirmation rather than falsification

psychoactive drugs: medicines prescribed for mental disorders.

psychoanalysis: name given to Freud's theory and therapy.

psychological treatment: treatment of mental health problems consisting of conversations between the patient and the therapist; initiated by Freud as an alternative to the prevailing medical and educational treatments.

psychologisation: word used with two different meanings referring to: (1) the fact that emotional ties and personal well-being become important in primary social relations, or (2) the growing impact of psychology on the way people see themselves and interact with others.

psychophysics: part of psychological research dealing with the relationship between physical stimuli and the corresponding sensation.

purposive behaviourism: version of behaviourism, defended by Tolman, which saw behaviour as goal-related (means to an end); agreed with other behaviourists that psychology should be based on observable behaviour.

qualia: qualities of conscious thoughts that give the thoughts a rich and vivid meaning, grounded in the interactions with the world.

qualifying test: test to find the best person for a task.

qualitative research methods: research methods based on understanding phenomena in their historical and socio-cultural context; are associated with the hermeneutic approach based on understanding the meaning of a situation.

quantitative imperative: a bias only to find measurable topics interesting because quantitative research methods require numerical data.

quantitative research methods: research methods based on quantifiable data; are associated with the natural-science approach based on the hypothetico-deductive model.

radical behaviourism: strong version of behaviourism, defended by Skinner, which denies the relevance of information processing in the mind and holds that all human behaviour can be understood on the basis of S-R associations.

rationalism: view according to which knowledge is obtained by means of reasoning; usually through deductive reasoning on the basis of innate knowledge.

realism: view within philosophy that human knowledge tries to reveal real things in the world; the truth of knowledge is determined by the correspondence of the knowledge with the real world.

reflex arc: notion introduced in the nineteenth century to describe the processes underlying a reflex: a signal is picked up by sensory receptors, transmitted to the spinal cord through an afferent nerve, transferred to interneurons, which activate motor neurons that send a motor command over an efferent nerve to initiate the withdrawal movement.

reliability: in test research the degree to which the outcome of a test is the same if the test is repeated under unchanged circumstances or if an equivalent test is used.

Renaissance: cultural movement from the fourteenth to the seventeenth century based on a rediscovery and imitation of the classical Greek and Roman civilisations.

scholastic method: study method in which students unquestioningly memorise and recite texts that are thought to convey unchanging truths.

science wars: notion used by the postmodernists to refer to their attacks against the special status of science and their unmasking of scientific knowledge as a social construction.

scientific method: until halfway through the twentieth century seen as a method of accumulating information by means of learning the existing knowledge and adding new knowledge on the basis of objective, value-free observation, careful measurement and experimentation; the definition became more complicated in the second half of the twentieth century (Chapter 8).

scientific revolution: name given to a series of discoveries in the seventeenth century, involving Galilei, Descartes and Newton, that enhanced the status of science in society.

self: the feeling of being an individual with private experiences, feelings and beliefs, who interacts in a coherent and purposeful way with the environment.

semi-structured interview: interview in which each interviewee gets a small set of core questions, but for the rest is encouraged to speak freely; achieved by making use of open-ended, non-directive questions.

shellshock: anxiety response on battlefield that prevents soldiers from functioning properly; was one of the first topics addressed by applied psychology.

social construction: notion used by postmodernists to indicate that scientific knowledge is not objective knowledge discovering the workings of an external reality, but a story told by a particular scientific community on the basis of their language and culture.

social Darwinism: belief in Victorian England and the USA that progress in a society could be made by allowing the strong members to flourish and the weak members to die.

social desirability: bias people have to present themselves in a manner they think will be viewed favourably by others.

social management: management and control of deviant individuals and individuals in need by official social services.

spiritualism: belief that the spirits of the dead can be contacted by mediums; flourished in English-speaking countries at the end of the nineteenth and the beginning of the twentieth century.

standardised psychological test: test of which psychologists have examined the reliability and the validity, for which they have information about the expected performance, and which are administered in a uniform way.

stigma: attribute that is deeply discrediting and that reduces the bearer to a tainted and discounted person.

strong social situation: a situation in which nearly all individuals act virtually the same, despite differences in biological make-up and differences in learning history.

structuralism: name given by Titchener to his approach to psychology, consisting of trying to discover the structure of the human mind by means of introspection.

structured interview: interview in which all interviewees receive the same set of questions.

survival of the fittest: term introduced by Herbert Spencer to describe the outcome of natural selection: only organisms that fit within the environment and can produce viable offspring survive.

The Origin of Species: book by Charles Darwin (1859) in which he presented the evolutionary theory.

thought experiment: hypothetical scenario that helps with the understanding of a philosophical argument.

tit-for-tat strategy: strategy proposed in evolutionary psychology to explain how evolutionarily motivated individuals cooperate in situations of mutual dependency and benefit.

top-down process: process by which information from a higher processing stage is fed back to previous processing stages and influences the processing at these stages; found to be a helpful (and even essential) element in many computational models.

transcranial magnetic stimulation (TMS): stimulation of a brain region by means of a coil placed on the head; allows temporary interference with the processing of a small part of the brain.

Turing machine: basic (hypothetical) machine operating on the basis of Boolean logic and able to simulate the processing of more complex machines operating according to these principles.

Turing test: test described by Alan Turing, which involves a human interacting with a machine and another human without being able to discriminate the machine from the human; machines that pass the Turing test are seen as the goal of artificial intelligence.

unconscious plagiarism: term used by Bornstein to indicate how the scientific and the hermeneutic approach in psychology have influenced each other without the proponents being aware of it.

validity: in test research the degree to which a test measures what it claims to measure; determined by correlating the test results with an external criterion.

ventricles: apertures in the middle of the brain, which for a long time were thought to contain perceptions, memories and thoughts; seat of the animal spirits.

verification: principle that up to the 1950s formed the core of the scientific method: a proposition was meaningful (scientific) if its truth could be empirically verified.

verificationism: adherence to the principle that a proposition is meaningful only if it can be verified as true or false; with respect to science states that a proposition is scientific only if it can be verified through objective, value-free observation.

vital force: animistic substance thought to be present in living matter before the chemical and biological differences between living and non-living matter were understood.

welfare state: socio-political system in which individuals insure themselves against setbacks via taxes, which are used by the state to provide welfare services.

Würzburg school: group of psychologists at the University of Würzburg who used introspection as the research method, but came to different conclusions from those of Wundt and Titchener; in particular they claimed that many thought processes were not available to introspection (imageless thoughts).

zeitgeist: word used in the history of science to indicate that the time was right for a certain discovery; the discovery did not originate from a single genius, but from a much wider development leading to the discovery.

zombie thought experiment: thought experiment proposed by Chalmers to illustrate that consciousness is more than the working of the brain or the implementation of information on a Turing machine because it involves a subjective component with qualia.

Bibliography

Abma, R. (2004) 'Madness and mental health.' In J. Jansz and P. van Drunen (eds.), *A social history of psychology*. Oxford: Blackwell, pp. 93–128.

Achterhuis, H. (1979) *De markt van welzijn en geluk [The market of well-being and happiness]*. The Netherlands: Uitgeverij Ambo.

Adair, J.G. (1984) 'The Hawthorne effect: A reconsideration of the methodological artifact', *Journal of Applied Psychology*, **69**: 334–45.

Allchin, D. (2002) 'To err and win a Nobel Prize: Paul Boyer, ATP synthase and the emergence of bioenergetics', *Journal of the History of Biology*, 35: 149–72.

Allchin, D. (2003) 'Scientific myth-conceptions', *Science Education*, 87: 329–51.

Allchin, D. (2004) 'Pseudohistory and pseudo-science', *Science & Education*, **13**: 179–95.

Allport, G.W. (1947) 'Scientific models and human morals', *Psychological Review*, **54**: 182–92.

Allport, G.W. and Odbert, H.S. (1936) 'Trait-names, a psycho-lexical study', *Psychological Monographs*, **47**(1).

Alvesson, M. (2000) 'Taking the linguistic turn in organizational research', *Journal of Applied Behavioral Science*, 36: 136–58.

Anderson, C.A. and Bushman, B.J. (2002) 'Human aggression', *Annual Review of Psychology*, 53: 27–51.

Anderson, C.A. *et al.* (2003) 'The influence of media violence on youth', *Psychological Science in the Public Interest*, **4**: 81–110.

Andrewes, D.G. (2002) *Neuropsychology: From theory to practice*. Hove: Psychology Press.

Andrews, R. (1987) *The Routledge dictionary of quotations*. London: Routledge.

Angermeyer, M.C. and Matschinger, H. (2005) 'What is a bipolar disorder? Results of a representative survey of the German population', *Psychiatrische Praxis*, **32**: 289–91.

Angermeyer, M.C., Dietrich, S., Potl, D. and Matschinger, H. (2005) 'Media consumption and desire for social distance towards people with schizophrenia', *European Psychiatry*, **20**: 246–50.

APA Presidential Task Force on Evidence-based Practice (2006) 'Evidence-based practice in psychology', *American Psychologist*, **61**: 271–85.

Appelbaum, P.S., Robbins, P.C. and Roth, L.H. (1999) 'Dimensional approach to delusions: Comparisons across types and diagnoses', *American Journal of Psychiatry*, **156**: 1938–1943.

Arboleda-Florez, J. (1998) 'Mental illness and violence: An epidemiological appraisal of the evidence', *Canadian Journal of Psychiatry – Revue Canadienne de Psychiatrie*, **43**: 989–96.

Ashworth, P. (2003) 'The origins of qualitative psychology.' In J.A. Smith (ed.), *Qualitative psychology: A practical guide to research methods*. London: Sage, pp. 4–24.

Axelrod, R. and Hamilton, W.D. (1981) 'The evolution of cooperation', *Science*, **211**: 1390–6.

Baars, B.J. (1986) *The cognitive revolution in psychology*. New York: Guilford Press.

Baars, B.J. (1997) *In the theater of consciousness: The workspace of the mind*. New York: Oxford University Press.

Bargh, J.A. and Chartrand, T. (1999) 'The unbearable automaticity of being', *American Psychologist*, 54: 462–79.

Bargh, J.A., Gollwitzer, P.M., Lee-Chai, A., Barndollar, K. and Trötschel, R. (2001) 'The automated will: Nonconscious activation and pursuit of behavioral goals', *Journal of Personality and Social Psychology*, 81: 1014–27.

Barrow, R. (2000) 'Determining stereotypical images of psychologists: the Draw A Psychologist Checklist', *College Student Journal*, 34: 123–33.

Bauer, R.M. (1984) 'Autonomic recognition of names and faces in prosopagnosia: A neuropsychological application of the guilty knowledge test', *Neuropsychologia*, 22: 457–69.

Bem, S. and Looren de Jong, H. (2006) *Theoretical issues in psychology: An introduction*. London: Sage Publications.

Benjafield, J.G. (2005) *A history of psychology*. Oxford: Oxford University Press.

Benjamin, L.T., Jr. (2000) 'The psychology laboratory at the turn of the 20th century', *American Psychologist*, 55: 318–21.

Berger, H. (1969) 'Hans Berger on the electroencephalogram of man: The fourteen original reports on the human electroencephalogram. *EEG & Clinical Neurophysiology*, Supp. 28.

Bernard, L. L. (1924) *Instinct: A study of social psychology*. New York:Henry Holt &Co.

Binet, A. (1904) 'A propos de la mesure de l'intelligence', *L'Année Psychologique*, 11: 69–82 (available on http://www.persee.fr/web/revues/home/prescript/revue/psy).

Binet, A. and Simon, T. (1907) 'Le développement de l'intelligence chez les enfants', *L'Année Psychologique*, 14: 1–94 (available on http://www.persee.fr/web/revues/home/prescript/revue/psy).

Bird-David, N. (1999) '"Animism" revisited: Personhood, environment, and relational epistemology', *Current Anthropology*, 40: S67–S91.

Birnbaum, L.C. (1955) 'Behaviorism in the 1920's', *American Quarterly*, 7: 15–30.

Blodgett, H.C. (1929) 'The effect of the introduction of reward upon the maze performance of rats'. Univ Calif Publ Psychol, 4: 113–134.

Bock, K. (2008) Editorial. *Journal of Memory and Language*, 58: 1–2.

Bohman, M. (1996) 'Predisposition to criminality: Swedish adoption studies in retrospect.' In G.R. Bock and J.A. Goode (eds.), *Genetics of criminal and antisocial behaviour*. Chichester: Wiley, pp. 99–114.

Bonta, J., Law, M. and Hanson, K. (1998) 'The prediction of criminal and violent recidivism among mentally disordered offenders: A meta-analysis', *Psychological Bulletin*, 123: 123–42.

Boomsma, D.I., Willemsen, G., Dolan, C.V., Hawkley, L.C. and Cacioppo, J.T. (2005) 'Genetic and environmental contributions to loneliness in adults: The Netherlands Twin Register study', *Behavior Genetics*, 35: 745–52.

Boring, E.G. (1923) 'Intelligence as the tests test it', *New Republic*, 6 June 1923, 35–7.

Boring, E.G. (1933) *The physical dimensions of consciousness*. New York: Appleton-Century.

Boring, E.G. (1950) *A history of experimental psychology* (2nd edn). New York: Appleton-Century-Crofts.

Bornstein, R.F. (2005) 'Reconnecting psychoanalysis to mainstream psychology: Challenges and opportunities', *Psychoanalytic Psychology*, 22: 323–40.

Bouchard, T.J. (1994) 'Genes, environment, and personality', *Science*, 264: 1700–1.

Bouton, M.E. (2007) *Learning and behavior: A comtemporary synthesis*. Sunderland, MA: Sinauer Associates.

Boyack, K.W., Klavans, R. and Börner, K. (2005) 'Mapping the backbone of science', *Scientometrics*, 64: 351–74.

Bradburn, N.M. and Berlew, D.G. (1961) 'Need for achievement and English economic growth', *Economic Development and Cultural Change*, 10: 8–20.

Breasted, J.H. (1930) *The Edwin Smith surgical papyrus*. Chicago: University of Chicago Press (2 vols).

Bridgman, P.W. (1927) *The logic of modern physics.* Chicago: University of Chicago Press.

Broadbent, D.E. (1958) *Perception and communication.* Elmsford, NY: Pergamon Press.

Broca, P. (1863) 'Sur les caractères des cranes basques', *Extrait des Bulletins de la Société d'anthropologie de Paris.* Retrieved on 10 January 2008, from books.google.com.

Bryson, B. (2003) *A short history of nearly everything.* London: Doubleday.

Buller, D.J. (2005) *Adapting minds: Evolutionary psychology and the persistent quest for human nature.* Cambridge, MA: MIT Press.

Burr, V. and Butt, T. (2000) 'Psychological distress and postmodern thought.' In F. Dwight (ed.), *Pathology and the postmodern.* London: Sage Publications.

Buss, D.M. (1989) 'Sex differences in human mate preference: Evolutionary hypotheses testing in 37 cultures', *Behavioral and Brain Sciences,* **12:** 1–49.

Buss, D.M. (2004) *Evolutionary psychology: The new science of the mind* (2nd edn). Boston, MA: Pearson Education.

Butterworth, B. (1999) *The mathematical brain.* London: Macmillan.

Cahan, E.D. and White, S.H. (1992) 'Proposals for a second psychology', *American Psychologist,* **47:** 224–35.

Campbell, D.T. (1960) 'Blind variation and selective retention in creative thought as in other knowledge processes', *Psychological Review,* **67:** 380–400.

Capgras, J. and Reboul-Lachaux, J. (1923) 'L'Illusion des "sosies" dans un délire systématisé chronique', *Bulletin de la Société de Médecine Mentale,* **11:** 6–16. Translated into English in Ellis, H.D., Whitley, J. and Luauté, J.-P. (1994) 'Delusional misidentification. The three original papers on the Capgras, Frégoli and intermetamorphosis delusions', *History of Psychiatry,* **5:** 117–46. If you read Dutch, also available in Draaisma, D. (2006) *Ontregelde geesten.* Groningen: Historische Uitgeverij.

Capron, C. and Duyme, M. (1989) 'Assessment of effects of socioeconomic status on IQ in a full cross-fostering design', *Nature,* **340:** 552–3.

Carnap, R. (1966) *Philosophical foundations of physics: An introduction to the philosophy of science.* New York: Basic Books.

Cattell, J.M. (1888) 'The psychological laboratory at Leipsic', *Mind,* **13:** 37–51 (available on http://psychclassics.yorku.ca).

Cattell, R.B. (1956) 'Validation and intensification of the Sixteen Personality Factor Questionnaire', *Journal of Clinical Psychology,* **12:** 205–14.

Cerullo, J.J. (1988) 'E.G. Boring: Reflections on a discipline builder', *The American Journal of Psychology,* **101:** 561–75.

Chalmers, A.F. (1999) *What is this thing called science?* (3rd edn). Maidenhead: Open University Press.

Chalmers, D.J. (1966) *The conscious mind: In search of a fundamental theory.* New York: Oxford University Press.

Changeux, J.P. (1997) *Neuronal man: The biology of mind,* translated by Laurence Garey. Princeton, NJ: Princeton University Press.

Chebat, J.C. and Michon, R. (2003) 'Impact of ambient odors on mall shoppers' emotions, cognition, and spending: A test of competitive causal theories', *Journal of Business Research,* **56:** 529–39.

Churchland, P. (1981) 'Eliminative materialism and the propositional attitudes', *The Journal of Philosophy,* **78:** 67–90.

Clarke, E. and Jacyna, L.S. (1987) *Nineteenth-century origins of neuroscientific concepts.* Berkeley: University of California Press.

Cohen, H.F. (1994) *The scientific revolution: A historiographical inquiry.* Chicago: University of Chicago Press.

Coles, P. (2001) 'Einstein, Eddington and the 1919 eclipse', *Historical Development of Modern Cosmology, ASP Conference Series,* **252.** Retrieved on 11 January 2008 from www.articles.adsabs. harvard.edu.

Coltheart, M. (2004) 'Are there lexicons?' *Quarterly Journal of Experimental Psychology,* **57A:** 1153–71.

Coltheart, M. (2006) 'What has functional neuro-imaging told us about the mind (so far)?', *Cortex,* **42:** 323–31.

Coltheart, M. (2007) 'The 33rd Sir Frederick Bartlett Lecture: Cognitive neuropsychiatry and delusional belief', *Quarterly Journal of Experimental Psychology*, **60**: 1041–62.

Coltheart, M., Patterson, K. and Marshall, J.C. (eds.) (1980) *Deep dyslexia*. London: Routledge & Kegan Paul.

Coon, D.J. (1992) 'Testing the limits of sense and science: American experimental psychologists combat spiritualism 1880–1920', *American Psychologist*, **47**: 143–51.

Corrigan, P.W. *et al.* (2005) 'Newspaper stories as measures of structural stigma', *Psychiatric Services*, **56**: 551–6.

Costall, A. (2006) '"Introspectionism" and the mythical origins of scientific psychology', *Consciousness and Cognition*, **15**: 634–54.

Coyne, J.C. and Palmer, S.C. (2007) 'Does anyone read the classic studies they cite? Reflections on claims that psychotherapy promotes the survival of cancer patients', *The European Health Psychology*, **9**: 46–9.

Crick, F. (1995) *The astonishing hypothesis: The scientific search for the soul*. London: Touchstone Books.

Danziger, K. (1990) *Constructing the subject: Historical origins of psychological research*. Cambridge: Cambridge University Press.

Danziger, K. (1997) *Naming the mind: How psychology found its language*. London: Sage.

Darley, J.M. and Latané, B. (1968) 'Bystander intervention in emergencies: Diffusion of responsibility', *Journal of Personality and Social Psychology*, **8**: 377–83.

Davis, S.N. (2003) 'Sex stereotypes in commercials targeted toward children: A content analysis', *Sociological Spectrum*, **23**: 407–24.

Dawkins, R. (1976 / 2006) *The selfish gene: 30th anniversary edition – with a new Introduction by the Author*. Oxford: Oxford University Press.

Dawkins, R. (1998) *Unweaving the rainbow: Science, delusion, and the appetite for wonder*. Boston: Houghton Mifflin.

De Araujo, I.E. Rolls, E.T., Velazco, M.I., Margot, C. and Cayeux, I. (2005) 'Cognitive modulation of olfactory processing', *Neuron*, **46**: 671–9.

De Graaf, P.M. and Kalmijn, M. (2006) 'Divorce motives in a period of rising divorce: Evidence from a Dutch life-history survey', *Journal of Family Issues*, **27**: 183–205.

Deary, I.J. (1994) 'Sensory discrimination and intelligence: Postmortem or resurrection?' *The American Journal of Psychology*, **107**: 95–115.

Dehaene, S., Naccache, L., Cohen, L., Le Bihan, D., Mangin, J.F., Poline, J.B. and Riviere, D. (2001) 'Cerebral mechanisms of word masking and unconscious repetition priming', *Nature Neuroscience*, **4**: 752–58.

Dehaene, S., Sergent, C. and Changeux, J.P. (2003) 'A neuronal network model linking subjective reports and objective physiological data during conscious perception', *Proceedings of the National Academy of Sciences of the United States of America*, **100**: 8520–5.

Dennett, D.C. (2003) *Freedom evolves*. New York: Penguin.

DeRubeis, R.J. (2005) 'Cognitive therapy vs. medications in the treatment of moderate to severe depression', *Archives of General Psychiatry*, **62**: 409–16.

Dewey, J. (1896) The reflex are concept in psychology, *Psychological Review*, 3: 357–70. Retrieved on 12 November 2007 from http://psychclassics.yorku.ca

Dewey, J. (1887) *Psychology*. New York: Harper & Brothers.

Diamond, M. and Sigmundson, H.K. (1997) 'Sex reassignment at birth: Long-term review and clinical implications', *Archives of Pediatrics and Adolescent Medicine*, **151**: 298–304.

Dickson, A., Knussen, C. and Flowers, P. (2008) '"That was my old life; it's almost like a past-life now": Identity crisis, loss and adjustment amongst people living with Chronic Fatigue Syndrome', *Psychology & Health*, **23**: 459–76.

Diener, E., Suh, E.M., Lucas, R.E. and Smith, H.L. (1998) 'Subjective well-being: Three decades of progress', *Psychological Bulletin*, **125**: 276–302.

Dienes, Z. (2008) *Understanding psychology as a science: An introduction to scientific and statistical inference*. Basingstoke: Palgrave Macmillan

Dijksterhuis, A., Bos, M.W., Nordgren, L.F. and van Baaren, R.B. (2006) 'On making the right choice:

The deliberation-without-attention effect', *Science,* **311**: 1005–7.

Dijksterhuis, A. and Nordgren, L.F. (2006) 'A theory of unconscious thought', *Perspectives on Psychological Science,* **1**: 95–109.

Dijksterhuis, A., Smith, P.K., van Baaren, R.B. and Wigboldus, D.H.J. (2005) 'The unconscious consumer: Effects of environment on consumer behavior', *Journal of Consumer Psychology,* **15**: 193–202.

Djordevic, J. *et al.* (2008) 'A rose by any other name: Would it smell as sweet?' *Journal of Neurophysiology,* **99**: 386–93.

Dodge, K.A. and Coie, J.D. (1987) 'Social-information-processing factors in reactive and proactive aggression in children's peer groups', *Journal of Personality and Social Psychology,* **53**: 1146–58.

Doll, R., Peto, R., Boreham, J. and Sutherland, I. (2004) 'Mortality in relation to smoking: 50 years' observations on male British doctors', *British Medical Journal,* **328**: 1519–28.

Dougherty, T.W., Turban, D.B. and Callender, J.C. (1994) 'Confirming first impression in the employment interview: A field-study of interviewer behavior', *Journal of Applied Psychology,* **79**: 659–65.

Draaisma, D. (2000) *Metaphors of memory. A history of ideas about the mind.* Cambridge: Cambridge University Press.

Driver-Linn, E. (2003) 'Where is psychology going? Structural fault lines revealed by psychologists' use of Kuhn', *American Psychologist,* **58**: 269–78.

Eagly, A.H., Ashmore, R.D., Makhijani, M.G. and Longo, L.C. (1991) 'What is beautiful is good, but...: A meta-analytic review of research on the physical attractiveness stereotype', *Psychological Bulletin,* **110**: 109–28.

Ebbinghaus, H. (1908/1973) *Psychology: An elementary textbook.* New York: Arno Press.

Edgell, B. (1947) 'The British Psychological Society', *British Journal of Psychology,* **37**: 113–32. (Reprinted in 2001: *British Journal of Psychology,* **92**: 3–22.)

Eicher, H. (1982) 'The rise of modern science and the genesis of romanticism', *Publications of the Modern Language Association of America,* **97**: 8–30.

Ellis, H.D. and Florence, M. (1990) 'Bodamer's (1947) paper on prosopagnosia', *Cognitive Neuropsychology,* **7**: 81–105.

Ellis, H.D. and Lewis, M.B. (2001) 'Capgras delusion: A window on face recognition', *Trends in Cognitive Sciences,* **5**: 149–56.

Ellis, H.D. and Young, A.W. (1990) 'Accounting for delusional misidentifications', *British Journal of Psychology,* **157**: 239–48.

Ellis, H.D., Young, A.W., Quayle, A.H. and de Pauw, K.W. (1997) 'Reduced autonomic responses to faces in Capgras delusion', *Proceedings of the Royal Society London: Biological Sciences,* **264**: 1085–92.

Endersby, J. (2007) *A guinea pig's history of biology: The plants and animals who taught us the facts of life.* London: William Heinemann.

Engel, G.L. (1977) 'The need for a new medical model: A challenge for biomedicine', *Science,* **196**: 129–36.

Evans, J.S.B.T. (2002) 'Logic and human reasoning: An assessment of the deduction paradigm', *Psychological Bulletin,* **128**: 978–96.

Eysenck, H.J. (1952/1992) 'The effects of psychotherapy: An evaluation', *Journal of Consulting Psychology,* **16**: 319–24. Reprinted in *Journal of Consulting and Clinical Psychology,* **60**: 659–63.

Eysenck, H.J. (1976) 'Learning theory model of neurosis: New approach', *Behaviour Research and Therapy,* **14**: 251–67.

Eysenck, H.J. and Eysenck, M.W. (1975) *Manual of the Eysenck Personality Questionnaire.* San Diego: Educational and Industrial Testing Service.

Eysenck, H.J., Eysenck, S.B.G. and Barrett, P. (1985) 'A revised version of the psychoticism scale', *Personality and Individual Differences,* **6**: 21–29.

Eysenck, M.W. and Keane, M.T. (2005) *Cognitive psychology: A student's handbook* (5th edn). Hove: Psychology Press.

Fausto-Sterling, A., Gowaty, P.A. and Zuk, M. (1997) 'Evolutionary psychology and Darwinian feminism', *Feminist Studies* **23**: 403–18.

Feyerabend, P.K. (1975) *Against method: Outline of an anarchistic theory of knowledge.* London: New Left Books.

Fodor, J.A. (1981) 'The mind–body problem', *Scientific American,* **244(1)**: 124–32.

Foucault, M. (1961) *Folie et déraison: Histoire de la folie à l'âge classique.* Paris: Librairie Plon. [English translation in 1965: *Madness and civilization: A history of insanity in the Age of Reason*; new translation in 2006: *History of madness*, Routledge.]

Foucault, M. (1976) *Surveiller et punir: Naissance de la prison.* Paris: Gallimard. [English translation: Foucault, M. (1979) *Discipline and punish: The birth of the prison.* New York: Vintage.]

Frankfurt, H.G. (2005) *On bullshit.* Princeton, NJ: Princeton University Press.

Freud, S. (1900/1913) *The interpretation of dreams* (English translation by A.A. Brill). New York: Macmillan (available on http://psychclassics. yorku.ca).

Fuchs, A.H. (2000) 'Contributions of American mental philosophers to psychology in the United States', *History of Psychology,* **3**: 3–19.

Fuchs, A.H. (2000) 'Teaching the introductory course in psychology circa 1900', *American Psychologist,* **55**: 492–5.

Furumoto, L. (1989) 'The new history of psychology.' In I. Cohen (ed.), *The G. Stanley Hall Lecture Series* (Vol. 9). Washington, DC: APA.

Gabbard, G.O. and Gabbard, K. (1999) *Psychiatry and the cinema* (2nd edn). Washington, DC: American Psychiatric Press.

Galef, B.G. (1998) 'Edward Thorndike: Revolutionary psychologist, ambiguous biologist', *American Psychologist,* **53**: 1128–34.

Gardner, H. (1987) *The mind's new science: A history of the cognitive revolution.* New York: Basic Books.

Geary, D.C., Vigil, J. and Byrd-Craven, J. (2004) 'Evolution of human mate choice', *The Journal of Sex Research,* **41**: 27–42.

Geen, R.G. (2001) *Human aggression* (2nd edn). Buckingham, UK: Open University Press.

Geertz, C. (2000) *Available light: Anthropological reflections on philosophical topics.* Princeton, NJ: Princeton University Press.

Geier, A.B., Rozin, P. and Doros, G. (2006) 'Unit bias: A new heuristic that helps explain the effect of portion size on food intake', *Psychological Science,* **17**: 521–5.

Gentner, D. and Grudin, J. (1985) 'The evolution of mental metaphors in psychology: A 90-year retrospective', *American Psychologist,* **40**: 181–92.

Gergen, K.J. (1973) 'Social psychology as history', *Journal of Personality and Social Psychology,* **26**: 309–20.

Gergen, K.J. (2001) 'Psychological science in a postmodern context', *American Psychologist,* **56**: 803–13.

Gerteis, L.S. (1991) Book review of 'Abolitionist, actuary, atheist: Elizur Wright and the reform impulse, by Lawrence B. Goodheart', *The Journal of American History* 77: 1360–1.

Geschorind, N. (1972) 'Language and the brain', *Scientific American,* **226**, 4: 76–83.

Giorgi, A. (1970) *Psychology as a human science.* New York: Harper & Row.

Glaser, B.G. and Strauss, A.L. (1967) *Discovery of grounded theory: Strategies for qualitative research.* New York: Aldine de Gruyter.

Gleick, J. (2003) *Isaac Newton.* New York: Pantheon Books.

Goffman, E. (1963) *Stigma: Notes on the management of spoiled identity.* Englewood Cliffs, NJ: Prentice Hall.

Goldberg, L.R. (1990) 'An alternative "description of personality": The big-five factor structure', *Journal of Personality and Social Psychology,* **59**: 1216–29.

Goodglass, H. (1983) 'Linguistic aspects of aphasia', *Trends in Neuroscience,* June: 241–3.

Goodglass, H. and Kaplan, E. (1983) *The assessment of aphasia and related disorders.* Philadelphia: Lea & Febiger.

Goodwin, C.J. (1991) 'Misportraying Pavlov's apparatus', *The American Journal of Psychology,* **104**: 135–41.

Gould, S.J. (1996) *The mismeasure of man* (2nd edn). London: W.W. Norton & Co.

Gratzer, W. (2002) *Eurekas and euphorias: The Oxford book of scientific anecdotes.* Oxford: Oxford University Press.

Greenhalgh, T. (1997) 'How to read a paper: Getting your bearings (deciding what the paper is about)', *British Medical Journal,* **315**: 243–46.

Greenwald, A.G. (1992) 'New look 3: Unconscious cognition reclaimed', *American Psychologist,* **47**: 766–79.

Greenwald, A.G., Spangenberg, E.R., Pratkanis, A.R. and Eskenazi, J. (1991) 'Double-blind tests of subliminal self-help audiotapes', *Psychological Science,* **2**: 119–22.

Griffith, C.R. (1921) 'Some neglected aspects of a history of psychology', *Psychological Monographs,* **30**: 17–29 (available on http:// psychclassics.yorku.ca).

Gross, C.G. (1998) *Brain, Vision, Memory: Tales in the history of neuroscience.* Cambridge, MA: The MIT Press.

Gross, R. (2003) *Themes, issues and debates in psychology* (2nd edn). Abingdon: Hodder Arnold.

Grove, W.M., Zald, D.H., Lebow, B.S., Snitz, E. and Nelson, C. (2000) 'Clinical versus mechanical prediction: A meta-analysis', *Psychological Assessment,* **12**: 19–30.

Gulerce, A. (2006) 'History of psychology in Turkey as a sign of diverse modernization and global psychologization.' In A.C. Brock (ed.), *Internationalizing the history of psychology.* New York: New York University Press, pp. 75–93.

Gundlach, H. (2004) 'Reine Psychologie, angewandte Psychologie und die Institutionalisierung der Psychologie [Fundamental psychology, applied psychology, and the institutionalization of psychology]', *Zeitschrift für Psychologie,* **212**: 183–99.

Haggbloom, S.J. *et al.* (2002) 'The 100 most eminent psychologists of the 20th century', *Review of General Psychology,* **6**: 139–52.

Halligan, P.W. and Marshall, J.C. (1996) *Method in madness: Case studies in cognitive neuropsychiatry.* Hove: Psychology Press.

Hamilton, W.D. (1964) 'The genetical evolution of social behavior I and II', *Journal of Theoretical Biology,* **7**: 1–52.

Haney, C. and Zimbardo, P. (1998) 'The past and future of US prison policy: Twenty-five years after the Stanford Prison Experiment', *American Psychologist,* **53**: 709–27.

Haney, C., Banks, W. and Zimbardo, P. (1973) 'Interpersonal dynamics in a simulated prison', *International Journal of Criminology and Penology,* **1**: 69–97.

Hanley, J.R., Masterson, J., Spencer, L.H. and Evans, D. (2004) 'How long do the advantages of learning to read a transparent orthography last? An investigation of the reading skills and reading impairment of Welsh children at 10years of age', *Quarterly Journal of Experimental Psychology,* **57A**: 1393–410.

Hanson, F.A. (1993) *Testing testing: Social consequences of the examined life.* Berkeley and Los Angeles: University of California Press.

Hanssen, M., Bak, M., Bijl, R., Vollebergh, W. and van Os, J. (2005) 'The incidence and outcome of subclinical psychotic experiences in the general population', *British Journal of Clinical Psychology,* **44**: 181–91.

Harris, B. (1979) 'Whatever happened to Little Albert?', *American Psychologist,* **34**: 151–60.

Hartwig, S.G. (2002) 'Surveying psychologists' public image with drawings of a "typical" psychologist', *South Pacific Journal of Psychology,* **14**: 69–75.

Hatch, J.A. (ed.) (1995) *Qualitative research in early childhood settings.* Westport, CT: Greenwood Publishing Group.

Hatfield, G. (1998) 'Kant and empirical psychology in the 18th century', *Psychological Science,* **9**: 423–8.

Haynes, R. (2003) 'From alchemy to artificial intelligence: Stereotypes of the scientist in Western literature', *Public Understanding of Science,* **12**: 243–53.

Hell, B., Trapmann, S., Weigand, S. and Schuler, H. (2007) 'The validity of admission interviews – a meta-analysis', *Psychologische Rundschau,* **58**: 93–102.

Helm-Estabrooks, N., Fitzpatrick, P.M. and Barresi, B. (1981) 'Response of an agrammatic patient to a syntax stimulation program for aphasia', *Journal of Hearing and Speech Disorders,* **46**: 422–7.

Hoffman, J.L. (1949) 'Clinical observations concerning schizophrenic patients treated by prefrontal leukotomy', *New England Journal of Medicine,* **241**: 233–6.

Hofstede, G. (2001) *Culture's consequences: Comparing values, behaviors, institutions, and organizations across nations.* Thousand Oaks, CA: Sage Publications.

Hofstede, G. (2005) *Cultures and organizations: Software of the mind* (2nd edn). London: McGraw-Hill Professional.

Hollingworth, H.L. (1922) *Judging human character.* New York: Appleton & Company.

Hollon, S.D. *et al.* (2005) 'Prevention of relapse following cognitive therapy vs medications in moderate to severe depression', *Archives of General Psychiatry,* **62**: 417–22.

Holmes, G.M. (1918) 'Disturbance of vision by cerebral lesions', *British Journal of Ophthalmology,* **2**: 353–84.

Hood, R.W. (2000) 'American psychology of religion and the "Journal for the Scientific Study of Religion"', *Journal for the Scientific Study of Religion,* **39**: 531–43.

Hosoda, M., Stone-Romero, E.F. and Coats, G. (2003) 'The effects of physical attractiveness on job-related outcomes: A meta-analysis of experimental studies', *Personnel Psychology,* **56**: 431–62.

Hulett, J.E. (1955) 'Book review of *Psychotherapy and personality change: Coordinated research studies in the client-centered approach*', by Carl R. Rogers and Rosalind F. Dymond, *American Sociological Review,* **20**: 369–70.

Hunt, H.T. (2005) 'Why psychology is/is not traditional science: The self-referential bases of psychological research and theory', *Review of General Psychology,* **9**: 358–74.

Hunter, Z.R., Brysbaert, M. and Knecht, S. (2007) 'Foveal word reading requires interhemispheric communication', *Journal of Cognitive Neuroscience,* **19**: 1373–87.

Ifrah, G. (1998) *The universal history of numbers: From prehistory to the invention of the computer.* London: The Harvill Press. (Translation of the French original (1994): *Histoire Universelle des chiffres.* Paris: Editions Robert Laffont.)

Illich, I. (1971) *Deschooling society.* London: Penguin Education (also available on http://reactor-core.org/deschooling.html).

Illich, I. (1973) *Tools for conviviality.* New York: Harper & Row (also available on http://clevercycles.com/tools_for_conviviality).

Illich, I. (1976) *Limits to medicine – Medical nemesis: The expropriation of health.* London: Marion Boyars (also available on www.soilandhealth.org).

Jackson, F. (1982) 'Epiphenomenal qualia', *Philosophical Quarterly,* **32**: 127–36.

Jackson, S. and Rees, A. (2007) 'The appalling appeal of nature: The popular influence of evolutionary psychology as a problem for sociology', *Sociology,* **41**: 917–30.

Jacob, S. *et al.* (2002) 'Paternally inherited HLA alleles are associated with women's choice of male odor', *Nature Genetics,* **30**: 175–9.

Jahoda, G. (2007) *A history of social psychology.* Cambridge: Cambridge University Press.

James, W. (1890) *The principles of psychology* (2 vols.) New York: Henry Holt (available on http://psychclassics.yorku.ca).

James, W. (1890) *The principles of psychology,* New York: Henry Holt.

James, W. (1892) 'A plea for psychology as a "natural science"', *The Philosophical Review,* **1**: 146–53.

Janda, L.H., England, K., Lovejoy, D. and Drury, K. (1998) 'Attitudes toward psychology relative to other disciplines', *Professional Psychology: Research and Practice,* **29**: 140–3.

Jansz, J. and Van Drunen, P. (eds.) (2004) *A social history of psychology.* Oxford: Blackwell.

Johnston, L. (2002) 'Behavioral mimicry and stigmatization', *Social Cognition,* **20**: 18–35.

Jones, D. and Elcock, J. (2001) *History and theories of psychology: A critical perspective.* London: Arnold.

Jones, S. (1999) *Almost like a whale: The origin of species updated.* London: Doubleday.

Jost, J.T., Glaser, J., Kruglanski, A.W. and Sulloway, F.J. (2003) 'Political conservatism as motivated social cognition', *Psychological Bulletin,* **129**: 339–75.

Kagitcibasi, C. (2002) 'A model of family change in cultural context'. In *Online Readings in Psychology and Culture.* Retrieved on December 10, 2007 from http://www.ac.wwu.edu/~culture/contents_complete.htm.

Kahneman, D. and Tversky, A. (1974) 'Judgment under uncertainty: Heuristics and biases', *Science,* **185:** 1124–31.

Kahneman, D. and Tversky, A. (1979) 'Prospect theory: Analysis of decision under risk', *Econometrica,* **47:** 263–91.

Kaplan, R.M. and Saccuzzo, D.P. (2005) *Psychological testing: Principles, applications, and issues* (6th edn). Belmont, CA: Thomson Wadsworth.

Keefe, F.J., Rumble, M.E., Scipio, C.D., Giordano, L.A. and Perri, L.M. (2004) 'Psychological aspects of persistent pain: Current state of the science', *The Journal of Pain,* **5:** 195–211.

Keil, F. C. (2003) 'Folkscience: Coarse interpretations of a complex reality', *Trends in Cognitive Sciences,* **7:** 368–73.

Kendler, K.S., Thornton, L.M., Gilman, S.E. and Kessler, R.C. (2000) 'Sexual orientation in a U.S. national sample of twin and nontwin sibling pairs', *American Journal of Psychiatry,* **157:** 1843–6.

Kessels, U., Rau, M. and Hannover, B. (2006) 'What goes well with physics? Measuring and altering the image of science', *British Journal of Educational Psychology,* **76:** 761–80.

Kessler, R.C., Berglund, P., Demler, O., Jin, R. and Walters, E.E. (2005) 'Lifetime prevalence and age-of-onset distributions of DSM-IV disorders in the national comorbidity survey replication', *Archives of General Psychiatry,* **62:** 593–602.

Kihlstrom, J.F. (2007) *Social neuroscience: The footprints of Phineas Gage.* Retrieved on 11 November, 2007 from http://socrates.berkeley.edu/~kihlstrm/SocialNeuroscience07.htm.

King, R.N. and Koehler, D.J. (2000) 'Illusory correlations in graphological inference', *Journal of Experimental Psychology: Applied,* **6:** 336–48.

Kirsch, I., Deacon, B.J., Huedo-Medina, T.B., Scoboria, A., Moore, T.J. and Johnson, B.T. (2008) 'Initial severity and antidepressant benefits: A metaanalysis of data submitted to the Food and Drug Administration', *PLoS Med 5(2): e45.* doi:10.1371/journal.pmed.0050045 Received 23 January 2007.

Kobayakawa, K. *et al.* (2007) 'Innate versus learned odour processing in the mouse olfactory bulb', *Nature,* **450:** 503–8.

Koch, S. (1961) 'Psychological science versus the science-humanism antinomy: Intimations of a significant science of man', *American Psychologist,* **16:** 629–39.

Kompier, M.A.J. (2006) 'The "Hawthorne effect" is a myth, but what keeps the story going?', *Scandinavian Journal of Word Environment & Health,* **32:** 402–12.

Kotowicz, Z. (2007) 'The strange case of Phineas Gage', *History of the Human Sciences,* **20:** 115–31.

Kreiner, D.S., Altis, N.A. and Voss, C.W. (2003) 'A test of the effect of reverse speech on priming', *Journal of Psychology,* **137:** 224–32.

Kuhn, T.S. (1962) *The structure of scientific revolutions.* Chicago: University of Chicago Press.

Kunda, Z. and Thagard, P. (1996) 'Forming impressions from stereotypes, traits, and behaviors: A parallel-constraint-satisfaction theory', *Psychological Review,* **103:** 284–308.

Kunst-Wilson, W.R. and Zajonc, R.B. (1980) 'Affective discrimination of stimuli that cannot be recognized', *Science,* **207:** 557–8.

Laing, R.D. (1960) *The divided self: An existential study in sanity and madness.* Harmondsworth: Penguin.

Lakatos, I. (1970) 'Falsification and the methodology of scientific research programs.' In I. Lakatos and A. Musgrave (eds.), *Criticism and the growth of knowledge.* New York: Cambridge University Press.

Lamme, V.A.F. (2006) 'Towards a true neural stance on consciousness', *Trends in Cognitive Sciences,* **10:** 494–501.

Langner, T.S. (1962) 'A twenty-two item screening score of psychiatric symptoms indicating impairment', *Journal of Health and Human Behavior,* **3:** 269–76.

Larsen, S.F. (1987) 'Remembering and the archaeology metaphor', *Metaphor and Symbol,* **2:** 187–99.

Leahey, T.H. (1992) 'The mythical revolutions of American psychology', *American Psychologist,* **47:** 308–18.

Leahey, T.H. (2004) *A history of psychology (6th edn.).* Upper Saddle River, NJ: Pearson Prentice Hall.

Leakey, R. and Lewin, R. (1992) *Origins reconsidered: In search of what makes us human.* London: Doubleday.

Leary, D.E. (ed.) (1995) *Metaphors in the history of psychology.* Cambridge: Cambridge University Press.

Leary, M.R. and Kowalski, R.M. (1990) 'Impression management: A literature review and two-component model', *Psychological Bulletin,* **107**: 34–47.

Lee, T.W., Mitchell, T.R. and Sablynski, C.J. (1999) 'Qualitative research in organizational and vocational psychology 1979–1999', *Journal of Vocational Behavior,* **55**: 161–87.

Lehman, A.F. and Steinwachs, D.M. (1998) 'At issue: Translating research into practice: The Schizophrenia Patient Outcomes Research Team (PORT) treatment recommendations', *Schizophrenia Bulletin,* **24**: 1–10.

Lemon, N. and Taylor, H. (1997) 'Caring in casualty: The phenomenology of nursing care.' In N. Hayes (ed.), *Doing qualitative analysis in psychology.* Hove: Psychology Press, pp. 227–43.

Lewin, K., Lippitt, R. and White, R. (1939) 'Patterns of aggressive behaviour in experimentally created "social climates"', *Journal of Social Psychology,* **10**: 271–99.

Li, W., Howard, J.D., Parrish, T.B. and Gottfried, J.A. (2008) 'Aversive learning enhances perceptual and cortical discrimination of indiscriminable odor cues', *Science,* **319**: 1842–5.

Libet, B. (1985) 'Unconscious cerebral initiative and the role of conscious will in voluntary action', *Behavioral and Brain Sciences,* **8**: 529–39.

Libet, B. (1999) 'Do we have free will?' *Journal of Consciousness Studies,* **6**: 47–55.

Lieberman, M.D. (2000) 'Intuition: A social cognitive neuroscience approach', *Psychological Bulletin,* **126**: 109–37.

Lieberman, M.D. (2007) 'Social cognitive neuroscience: A review of the core processes', *Annual Review of Psychology,* **58**: 259–89.

Lindberg, D.C. (1992) *The beginnings of Western science: The European scientific tradition in philosophical, religious, and institutional context, 600 B.C. to A.D. 1450.* Chicago: The University of Chicago Press.

Link, B.G., Phelan, J.C., Besnahan, M., Stueve, A. and Pescosolido, B.A. (1999) 'Public conceptions of mental illness: Labels, causes, dangerousness, and social distance', *American Journal of Public Health,* **89**: 1328–33.

Link, B.G., Yang, L.H., Phelan, J.C. and Collins, P.Y. (2004) 'Measuring mental illness stigma', *Schizophrenia Bulletin,* **30**: 511–41.

Liu, I., Blacker, D.L., Xu, R., Fitzmaurice, G., Lyons, M.J. and Tsuang, M.T. (2004) 'Genetic and environmental contributions to the development of alcohol dependence in male twins', *Archives of General Psychiatry,* **61**: 897–903.

Loftus, E.F. and Klinger, M.R. (1992) 'Is the unconscious smart or dumb?' *American Psychologist,* **47**: 761–5.

Lott, B. (1985) 'The potential enrichment of social personality psychology through feminist research and vice versa', *American Psychologist,* **40**: 155–64.

Lowery, B.S., Eisenberger, N.I., Hardin, C.D. and Sinclair, S. (2007) 'Long-term effects of subliminal priming on academic performance', *Basic and Applied Social Psychology,* **29**: 151–7.

Lucas, R.E. (2007) 'Adaptation and the set-point model of subjective well-being: Does happiness change after major life events?', *Current Directions in Psychological Science,* **16**: 75–9.

Luhrmann, T.M. (2007) 'Social defeat and the culture of chronicity: Or, why schizophrenia does so well over there and so badly here', *Culture, Medicine and Psychiatry,* **31**: 135–72.

Luyten, P., Blatt, S.J. and Corveleyn, J. (2006) 'Minding the gap between positivism and hermeneutics in psychoanalytic research', *Journal of the American Psychoanalytic Association,* **54**: 571–610.

Lyons, W. (2001) *Matters of the mind.* New York: Routledge.

Mackenzie, D.B. (1977) *Behaviorism and the limits of scientific method.* London: Routledge & Kegan Paul.

Mackintosh, N.J. (1998) *IQ and human intelligence.* Oxford: Oxford University Press.

Mahajan, S.K., Machhan, P.C., Sood, B.R., Kuman, S., Sharma, D.D., Mokta, J. and Pal, L.S. (2004) 'Neurocysticercosis presenting with psychosis', *Journal of the Association of Physicians in India,* **52**: 663–66.

Maiers, W. (1991) 'Critical psychology: Historical background and task.' In C.W. Tolman and

W. Maiers (eds.), *Critical psychology: Contributions to an historical science of the subject.* Cambridge: Cambridge University Press.

Malone, J.C. and Cruchon, N.M. (2001) 'Radical behaviorism and the rest of psychology: A review/précis of Skinner's *About Behaviorism*', *Behavior and Philosophy*, **29**: 31–57.

Mandler, G. (2007) *A history of modern experimental psychology.* Cambridge, MA: The MIT Press.

Manguel, A. (1996) *A history of reading.* London: HarperCollins.

Manning, R., Levine, M. and Collins, A. (2007) 'The Kitty Genovese Murder and the social psychology of helping: The parable of the 38 witnesses', *American Psychologist*, **62**: 555–62.

Marcel, A.J. (1983) 'Conscious and unconscious perception: Experiments on visual masking and word recognition', *Cognitive Psychology*, **15**: 197–237.

Marecek, J. (2003) 'Dancing through minefields: Toward a qualitative stance in psychology.' In P.M. Camic, J.E. Rhodes and L. Yardley (eds.), *Qualitative research in psychology: Expanding perspectives in methodology and design.* Washington DC: American Psychological Association, pp. 49–69.

Martin, L. (1986). '"Eskimo words for snow": A case study in the genesis and decay of an anthropological example', *American Anthropologist*, **88**: 418–23.

Maslow, A.H. (1966) *Psychology of science.* New York: Harper and Row.

Mayer, B. and Merckelbach, H. (1999) 'Unconscious processes, subliminal stimulation, and anxiety', *Clinical Psychology Review*, **19**: 571–90.

Mayer, J. (2008) *The dark side: The inside story of how the war on terror turned into a war on American ideals.* Garden City, NY: Doubleday.

Mayo, E. (1945) *The social problems of an industrial civilization.* Cambridge, MA: Harvard University Press.

McClelland, D.C. (1961) *The achieving society.* Princeton, NJ: Van Nostrand.

McCulloch, W.S. and Pitts, W.H. (1943) 'A logical calculus of the ideas immanent in nervous activity', *Bulletin of Mathematical Biophysics*, **5**: 115–33.

McDaniel, M.A., Whetzel, D.L., Schmidt, F.L. and Maurer, S.D. (1994) 'The validity of employment interviews: A comprehensive review and meta-analysis', *Journal of Applied Psychology*, **79**: 599–616.

McDuffie, T.E. (2001) 'Scientists – geeks & nerds? Dispelling teachers' stereotypes of scientists', *Science and Children*, **38**: 16–19.

McKeown, T. (1979) *The role of medicine: Dream, mirage or nemesis?* (2nd edn). Oxford: Basil Blackwell.

McNulty, J.K., Neff, L.A. and Karney, B.R. (2008) 'Beyond initial attraction: Physical attractiveness in newlywed marriage', *Journal of Family Psychology*, **22**: 135–43.

McReynolds, P. (1987) 'Lightner Witmer: Little-known founder of clinical psychology', *American Psychologist*, **42**: 849–58.

Medawar, P.B. (1969) *Induction and intuition in scientific thought.* London: Methuen. As cited in R. Rosenthal and R.L. Rosnow (2008) *Essentials of behavioral research: Methods and data analysis* (3rd edn). Boston: McGraw Hill.

Meehl, P.E. (1954) *Clinical vs. statistical prediction: A theoretical analysis and a review of the evidence.* Minneapolis: University of Minnesota Press.

Melzack, R. and Wall, P.D. (1965) 'Pain mechanisms: A new theory', *Science*, **150**: 971–9.

Messer, S.B. (2004) 'Evidence-based practice: Beyond empirically supported treatments', *Professional Psychology: Research and Practice*, **35**: 580–8.

Miles, D.R. and Carey, G. (1997) 'Genetic and environmental architecture of human aggression', *Journal of Personality and Social Psychology*, **72**: 207–17.

Milgram, S. (1963) 'Behavioral study of obedience', *Journal of Abnormal and Social Psychology* **67**: 371–8.

Milgram, S. (1974) *Obedience to authority: An experimental view.* New York: Harper & Row.

Miller, G.A. (1956) 'The magical number seven, plus or minus two', *Psychological Review*, **63**: 81–97.

Miller, G.A. (2003) 'The cognitive revolution: A historical perspective', *Trends in Cognitive Sciences*, **7**: 141–4.

Modderaar, J. (1966) 'Over de validiteit van de selectie voor bedrijven [On the validity of section for companies]', *Nederlands Tijdschrift voor de Psychologie,* **21:** 573–89.

Monahan, J. (1981) *The clinical prediction of violent behavior.* Washington, DC: Government Printing Office.

Money, T. and Ehrhardt, A. (1972) *Man and woman, boy and girl, the differentiation and dimorphism of gender identity from conception to maturity.* Baltimore, MD: Johns Hopkins University Press.

Morgan, M. (1998) 'Qualitative research: Science or pseudo-science?' *The Psychologist,* **11:** 481–3 (and Postscript on p. 485).

Morgeson, F.P., Campion, M.A., Dipboye, R.L., Hollenbeck, J.R., Murphy, K. and Schmitt, N. (2007) 'Reconsidering the use of personality tests in personnel selection contexts', *Personnel Psychology,* **60:** 683–729.

Morton, J. and Patterson, K. (1980) 'A new attempt at an interpretation, or, an attempt at a new interpretation.' In M. Coltheart *et al.* (eds.), *Deep dyslexia.* London: Routledge & Kegan Paul.

Müller, J.P. (1838) *Elements of physiology* (Translated by W. Baly). London.

Münsterberg, H. (1915) *Psychology: General and applied.* New York: D. Appleton & Co.

Myers-Scotton, C. (2006) *Multiple voices: An introduction to bilingualism.* Malden, MA: Blackwell Publishing.

Nagel, T. (1974) 'What is it like to be a bat?' *Philosophical Review,* **4:** 435–50.

Nairn, R.G. (2007) 'Media portrayals of mental illness, or is it madness? A review', *Australian Psychologist,* **42:** 138–46.

Nairn, R.G. and Coverdale, J.H. (2005) 'People never see us living well: An appraisal of the personal stories about mental illness in a prospective print media sample', *Australian and New Zealand Journal of Psychiatry,* **39:** 281–7.

Nangle, D.W., Erdley, C.A., Carpenter, E.M. and Newman, J.E. (2002) 'Social skills training as a treatment for aggressive children and adolescents: A developmental-clinical integration', *Aggression and Violent Behavior,* **7:** 169–99.

Nass, C., Moon, Y., Fogg, B.J., Reeves, B. and Dryer, D.C. (1995) 'Can computer personalities be human personalities?' *International Journal of Human–Computer Studies,* **43:** 223–39.

Neisser, U. (1967) *Cognitive psychology.* New York: Appleton-Century-Crofts.

Nicolas, S. and Ferrand, L. (1999). 'Wundt's laboratory at Leipzig in 1891', *History of Psychology,* **2:** 194–203.

Nisbett, R. and Ross, L. (1980) *Human inference: Strategies and shortcomings of social judgment.* Englewood Cliffs, NJ: Prentice-Hall.

Nisbett, R. and Wilson, T. (1977) 'Telling more than we can know: Verbal reports on mental processes', *Psychological Review,* **84:** 231–59.

Nolen-Hoeksema, S. (2000) 'The role of rumination in depressive disorders and mixed anxiety/depressive symptoms', *Journal of Abnormal Psychology,* **109:** 504–11.

O'Rahilly, S. and Farooqi, I.S. (2006) 'Genetics of obesity', *Philosophical Transaction of the Royal Society B – Biological Sciences,* **361:** 1095–105.

Ochsner, K.R. and Gross, J.J. (2005) 'The cognitive control of emotion', *Trends in Cognitive Sciences,* **9:** 242–9.

OECD (2007) 'Multiple comparisons of mean performance on the science scale', *PISA 2006: Science competencies for tomorrow's world,* **1.**

OECD (2007) 'Socio-economic indicators 1 and the relationship with performance in science', *PISA 2006,* **2.**

Ones, D.S., Viswesvaran, C. and Reiss, A.D. (1996) 'Role of social desirability in personality testing for personnel selection: The red herring', *Journal of Applied Psychology,* **81:** 660–79.

Orchowski, L.M., Spickard, B.A. and McNamara, J.R. (2006) 'Cinema and the valuing of psychotherapy: Implications for clinical practice', *Professional Psychology: Research and Practice,* **37:** 506–14.

Park, S.W. and Auchincloss, E.L. (2006) 'Psychoanalysis in textbooks of introductory psychology: A review', *Journal of the American Psychoanalytic Association,* **54:** 1361–80.

Patterson, G.R. (1982) *Coercive family process.* Eugene, OR: Castalia.

Pavot, W., Diener, E., Colvin, C.R. and Sandvik, E. (1991) 'Further validation of the satisfaction with life scale: Evidence for the cross-method convergence of well-being measures', *Journal of Personality Assessment,* 57: 149–61.

Peirce, C.S. (1877) 'The fixation of belief', *Popular Science monthly,* 12: (November), 1–15.

Peretz, I. and Zatorre, R.J. (2005) 'Brain organization for music processing', *Annual Review of Psychology,* 56: 89–114.

Peterson, C. (1997) *Psychology: A biopsychosocial approach.* (2nd edn). New York: Addison Wesley Longman.

Pomerantz, J.R. and Kubovy, M. (1986) 'Theoretical approaches in organization', in Boff, J.P. Kaufman and Thomas, J.P. (eds) *Handbook of perception and human performance.* New York, NY: Wiley.

Popper, K.R. (1970) 'Normal science and its dangers.' In I. Lakatos and A. Musgrave (eds.), *Criticism and growth of knowledge.* New York: Cambridge University Press.

Prins, R. and Bastiaanse, R. (2006) 'The early history of aphasiology: From the Egyptian surgeons (c. 1700 BC) to Broca (1861)', *Aphasiology,* 20: 762–91.

Puhl, R. and Brownell, K.D. (2001) 'Bias, discrimination, and obesity', *Obesity Research,* 9: 788–805.

Pulvermüller, F. (2005) 'Brain mechanisms linking language and action', *Nature Reviews Neuroscience,* 6: 576–82.

Raskind, W.H. (2001) 'Current understanding of the genetic basis of reading and spelling disability', *Learning Disability Quarterly,* 24: 141–57.

Rassin, E. (2008) *De hand in eigen boezem [Searching our own heart].* Inaugural lecture on the acceptance of the post of professor at the Erasmus University Rotterdam.

Redding, R.E. (2001) 'Sociopolitical diversity in psychology: The case for pluralism', *American Psychologist,* 56: 205–15.

Rehman, S.U., Nietert, P.J., Cope, D.W. and Kilpatrick, A.O. (2005) 'What to wear today? Effects of doctor's attire on the trust and confidence of patients', *The American Journal of Medicine,* 118: 1279–86.

Reid, K., Flowers, P. and Larkin, M. (2005) 'Exploring lived experience', *The Psychologist,* 18: 20–23.

Richards, G. (1996) *Putting psychology in its place: An introduction from a critical historical perspective.* London: Routledge.

Richards, G. (2002) *Putting psychology in its place: A critical historical overview* (2nd edn). London: Routledge.

Richardson, R.C. (2007) *Evolutionary psychology as maladapted psychology.* Cambridge, MA: MIT Press.

Rissmiller, D.J. and Rissmiller, J.H. (2006) 'Evolution of the antipsychiatry movement into mental health consumerism', *Psychiatric Services,* 57: 863–6.

Ritzer, G. and Goodman, D.J. (2004) *Modern sociological theory* (6th edn). Boston: McGraw Hill.

Rochberg-Halton, E. (1987) 'Why pragmatism now?' *Sociological Theory,* 5: 194–200.

Rogers, A. and Pilgrim, D. (2005) *A sociology of mental health and illness* (3rd edn). Maidenhead, UK: Open University Press.

Rogers, C.R. (1942) *Counseling and psychotherapy.* Boston, MA: Houghton Mifflin.

Rogers, C.R. and Dymond, R.F. (eds.) (1954). *Psychotherapy and personality change: Coordinated research studies in the client-centered approach.* Chicago: The University of Chicago Press.

Rosenblueth, A. and Wiener, N. (1945) 'The role of models in science', *Philosophy of Science,* 12: 316–21.

Rosenhan, D.L. (1973) 'On being sane in insane places', *Science,* 179: 250–8.

Rosenthal, R. and Rosnow, R.L. (2008) *Essentials of behavioral research: Methods and data analysis* (3rd edn). Boston: McGraw Hill.

Rutter, M. (2006) *Genes and behavior: Nature–nurture interplay explained.* Oxford: Blackwell Publishing.

Saenger, P. (1997) *Space between words: The origins of silent reading.* Stanford, CA: Stanford University Press.

Saggerson, A.L., George, D.N. and Honey, R.C. (2005) 'Imitative learning of stimulus–response and response–outcome associations in pigeons', *Journal of Experimental Psychology: Animal Behavior Processes,* 31: 289–300.

Salsburg, D. (2001) *The lady tasting tea: How statistics revolutionized science in the twentieth century.* New York: Freeman.

Sandoval, W.A. (2005) 'Understanding students' practical epistemologies and their influence on learning through inquiry', *Science Education,* 89: 634–56.

Schmidt, F.L. and Hunter, J.E. (1998) 'The validity and utility of selection methods in personnel psychology: Practical and theoretical implications of 85 years of research findings', *Psychological Bulletin*, **124**: 262–74.

Schneider, D.J. (1973) 'Implicit personality theory: Review', *Psychological Bulletin*, **79**: 294–309.

Schraw, G., Wadkins, T. and Olafson, L. (2007) 'Doing the things we do: A grounded theory of academic procrastination', *Journal of Educational Psychology*, **99**: 12–25.

Schulze, B. and Angermeyer, M.C. (2003) 'Subjective experiences of stigma. A focus group study of schizophrenic patients, their relatives and mental health professionals', *Social Science & Medicine*, **56**: 299–312.

Searle, J. (1980) 'Minds, brains, and programs', *Behavioral and Brain Sciences*, **3**: 417–57.

Seife, C. (2000) *Zero: The biography of a dangerous idea*. London: Souvenir Press.

Shallice, T. (1988) *From neuropsychology to mental structure*. Cambridge: Cambridge University Press.

Shepherd, G.M. (1991) *Foundations of the neuron doctrine*. New York: Oxford University Press.

Sie, M. and Wouters, A. (2008) 'The real challenge to free will and responsibility', *Trends in Cognitive Sciences*, **12**: 3–4.

Silverman, D. (2005) *Doing qualitative research: A practical handbook* (2nd edn). London: Sage Publications.

Simonton, D.K. (1999) 'Creativity as blind variation and selective retention: Is the creative process Darwinian?' *Psychological Inquiry*, **10**: 309–28.

Skinner, B.F. (1974) *About behaviorism*. New York: Knopf.

Smith, J.A. (1996) 'Beyond the divide between cognition and discourse: Using interpretative phenomenological analysis in health psychology', *Psychology and Health*, **11**: 261–71.

Smith, J.A. (ed.) (2008) '*Qualitative psychology: A practical guide to research methods* (2nd edn). London: Sage Publications.

Smith, M.B. (1994) 'Selfhood at risk: Postmodern perils and the perils of postmodernism', *American Psychologist*, **49**: 405–11.

Sokal, A. and Bricmont, J. (1997) *Impostures intellectuelles*. Paris: Editions Odile Jacob. Translated into English (1998, 2003) as *Intellectual impostures*. London: Profile Books Ltd.

Sokal, A.D. (1996) 'A physicist experiments with cultural studies', *Lingua Franca*, May/June, 62–64. (Also available on http://www.physics. nyu.edu/sokal.)

Sokal, A.D. (1996a) 'Transgressing the boundaries: Toward a transformative hermeneutics of quantum gravity', *Social Text*, **46/47** (spring/summer): 217–52 (also available on http://www.physics. nyu.edu/sokal/).

Sokal, A.D. (1996b) 'A physicist experiments with cultural studies', *Lingua Franca*, May/June, **62–64** (also available on http://www.physics. nyu.edu/sokal/).

Spangenberg, E.R., Sprott, D.E., Grohmann, B. and Tracy, D.L. (2006) 'Gender-congruent ambient scent influences on approach and avoidance behaviors in a retail store', *Journal of Business Research*, **59**: 1281–7.

Sperling, G. (1960) 'The information available in brief visual presentations', *Psychological Monographs*, **74**: 1–29.

Spurzheim, J.G. (1834) *Phrenology of the doctrine of the mental phenomenon* (3rd edn). Boston: Marsh, Caper and Lyon.

Stangor, C. (2006) *Research methods for the behavioral sciences*. Boston, MA: Houghton Mifflin.

Stanovich, K.E. (2004) *The robot's rebellion: Finding meaning in the age of Darwin*. Chicago: The University of Chicago Press.

Starks, H. and Trinidad, S.B. (2007) 'Choose your method: A comparison of phenomenology, discourse analysis, and grounded theory', *Qualitative Health Research*, **17**: 1372–80.

Sternberg, R.J. (1999) 'Twenty tips for teaching introductory psychology.' In B. Perlman, L.I. McCann and S.H. McFadden (eds.), *Lessons learned: Practical advice for the teaching of psychology* (Vol. 1). Washington, D.C.: American Psychological Society, pp. 99–104.

Stevens, S.S. (1935) 'The operational definition of psychological concepts', *Psychological Review*, **42**: 517–27.

Stevenson, C. and Cooper, N. (1997) 'Qualitative and quantitative research', *The Psychologist*, **4**: 159–60.

Stratton, P. (1997) 'Attributional coding of interview data: Meeting the needs of long-haul passengers.' In N. Hayes (ed.), *Doing qualitative analysis in psychology*. Hove: Psychology Press, pp. 115–42.

Stroop, J.R. (1935) 'Studies of interference in serial verbal reactions', *Journal of Experimental Psychology*, **18**: 643–662. (Reprinted 1992 in *Journal of Experimental Psychology: General*, **121**: 15–23.)

Stubbe, J.H., Posthuma, D., Boomsma, D.I. and De Geus, E.J.C. (2005) 'Heritability of life satisfaction in adults: A twin-family study', *Psychological Medicine*, **35**: 1581–88.

Sullivan, P.F., Kendler, K.S. and Neale, M.C. (2003) 'Schizophrenia as a complex trait: Evidence from a meta-analyis of twin studies', *Archives of General Psychiatry*, **60**: 1187–92.

Sullivan, P.F., Neale, M.C. and Kendler, K.S. (2000) 'Genetic epidemiology and major depression: Review and meta-analysis', *American Journal of Psychiatry*, **157**: 1552–62.

Swinkels, A. (2003) 'An effective exercise for teaching cognitive heuristics', *Teaching of Psychology*, **30**: 120–22.

Szasz, T.S. (1960) 'The myth of mental illness', *American Psychologist*, **15**: 113–18.

Taylor, F.W. (1911) *Scientific management*. New York: Harper & Brothers.

Teigen, K.H. (2002) 'One hundred years of laws in psychology', *The American Journal of Psychology*, **115**: 103–18.

Teo, T. (2005) *The critique of psychology: From Kant to postcolonial theory*. New York: Springer Science+Business Media, Inc.

Teo, T. (2007) 'Local institutionalization, discontinuity, and German textbooks of psychology, 1816–1854', *Journal of the History of the Behavioral Sciences*, **43**: 135–157.

Teo, T. (2008) 'Race and psychology.' In W.A. Darity (ed.), *International encyclopedia of the social sciences* (2nd edn). Detroit, MI: Macmillan, Vol. 7, pp. 21–4.

Thapar, A., Langley, K., Owen, M.J. and O'Donavan, M.C. (2007) 'Advances in genetic findings on attention deficit hyperactivity disorder', *Psychological Medicine*, **37**: 1681–92.

The British Psychological Society (2004) *Guidelines for minimum standards of ethical approval in psychological research*. Leicester, UK: The British Psychological Society. (Retrieved in March 2008 from www.bps.org.uk.)

The British Psychological Society (2006) *Code of ethics and conduct*. Leicester, UK: The British Psychological Society. (Retrieved in March 2008 from www.bps.org.uk.)

Thomas, R.K. (2007) 'Recurring errors among recent history of psychology textbooks', *American Journal of Psychology*, **120**: 477–95.

Thompson, D. (2008) *Counterknowledge: How we surrendered to conspiracy theories, quack medicine, bogus science and fake history*. London: Atlantic Books.

Thomson, J.A. (1922) *The outline of science: A plain story simply told*. New York: G.P. Putnam's Sons.

Thorndike, E.L. (1911) *Animal intelligence*. New York: Macmillan.

Thorndike, E.L. (1922) *An introduction to the theory of mental and social measurements*. New York: Teachers College.

Tizard, B. (1959) 'Theories of brain localization from Flourens to Lashley', *Medical History*, **3**: 132–45.

Todd, Z., Nerlich, B., McKeown, S. and Clarke, D.D. (2004) *Mixing methods in psychology: The integration of qualitative and quantitative methods in theory and practice*. Hove: Psychology Press.

Tolman, E.C. (1948) 'Cognitive maps in rats and men', *Psychological Review*, **55**: 189–209 (available on http://psychclassics.yorku.ca).

Torgersen, S. *et al.* (2000) 'A twin study of personality disorders', *Comprehensive Psychiatry*, **41**: 416–25.

Trivers, R.L. (1971) 'The evolution of reciprocal altruism,' *Quarterly Review of Biology*, **46**: 35–57.

Trivers, R.L. (1972) 'Parental investment and sexual selection.' In B. Campbell (ed.), *Sexual selection and the descent of man: 1871–1971*. Chicago: Aldine, pp. 136–79.

Tulving, E. and Thomson, D.M. (1971) 'Retrieval processes in recognition memory – Effects of associative context', *Journal of Experimental Psychology*, **87**: 116–24.

Turing, A. (1950) 'Computing machinery and intelligence', *Mind*, **59**: 434–60.

Twaddle, M. (1966) 'The Oxford and Cambridge admissions controversy of 1834', *British Journal of Educational Studies,* **14**: 45–58.

Twenge, J.M., Campbell, W.K. and Foster, C.A. (2003) 'Parenthood and marital satisfaction: A meta-analytic review', *Journal of Marriage and the Family,* **65**: 574–83.

UK ECT Review Group (2003) 'Efficacy and safety of electroconvulsive therapy in depressive disorders: A systematic review and meta-analysis', *The Lancet,* **361**: 799–808.

Uttal, W.R. (2001) *The new phrenology: The limits of localizing cognitive processes.* Cambridge, MA: MIT Press.

Van Drunen, P., Van Strien, P.J. and Haas, E. (2004) 'Work and organization.' In J. Jansz and P. Van Drunen (eds.) (2004) *A social history of psychology.* Oxford: Blackwell Publishing.

Van Goozen, S.H.M., Cohen-Kettenis, P.T., Gooren, L.J.G., Frijda, N.H. and Van de Poll, N.E. (1995) 'Gender differences in behaviour: Activating effects of cross-sex hormones', *Psychoneuroendocrinology,* **20**: 343–63.

Van Strien, P.J. and Dane, J. (2001) *Driekwart eeuw psychotechniek in Nederland: De magie van het testen* [Three-quarter century of psychotechnics in the Netherlands: The magic of testing]. Assen: Koninklijke Van Gorcum.

Van Vugt, M., De Cremer, D. and Janssen, D.P. (2007) 'Gender differences in cooperation and competition: The male-warrior hypothesis', *Psychological Science,* **18**: 19–23.

Vandenbroucke, J.P. (2008) 'Observational research, randomised trials, and two views of medical science', *PLoS Medicine, 5, e67,* doi:10.1371/journal.pmed.0050067.

Vilchez-Gonzalez, J.M. and Parales Palacios, F.J. (2006) 'Image of science in cartoons and its relationship with the image in comics', *Physics Education,* **41**: 240–9.

Von Sydow, K. (2007) 'The public image of psychologists, psychotherapists, and psychiatrists', *Psychotherapeut,* **52**: 322–33.

Walsh, E. and Fahy, T. (2002) 'Violence in society: Contribution of mental illness is low', *British Medical Journal,* **325**: 507–8.

Walsh, E. *et al.* (2004) 'Predicting violence in schizophrenia: A prospective study', *Schizophrenia Research,* **67**: 247–52.

Walter, H. (2001) *Neurophilosophy of free will.* Cambridge, MA: MIT Press.

Wampold, B.E. *et al.* (1997) 'A meta-analysis of outcome studies comparing bona fide psychotherapies: Empirically, "all must have prizes"', *Psychological Bulletin,* **122**: 203–15.

Wampold, B.E., Minami, T., Basking, T.W. and Tierney, S.C. (2002) 'A meta-(re)analysis of the effects of cognitive therapy versus "other therapies" for depression', *Journal of Affective Disorders,* **68**: 159–65.

Wampold, B.E., Minami, T., Tierney, S.C., Baskin, T.W. and Bhati, K.S. (2005) 'The placebo is powerful: Estimating placebo effects in medicine and psychotherapy for randomized clinical trials', *Journal of Clinical Psychology,* **61**: 835–54.

Ward, N. (1998) 'Artificial intelligence and other approaches to speech understanding: Reflections on methodology', *Journal of Experimental and Theoretical Artificial Intelligence,* **10**: 487–93.

Ward, S.C. (2002) *Modernizing the mind: Psychological knowledge and the remaking of society.* Westport, CT: Praeger.

Wason, P.C. (1960) 'On the failure to eliminate hypotheses in a conceptual task', *Quarterly Journal of Experimental Psychology,* **12**: 129–40.

Watson, J.B. (1907) 'Studying the mind of animals', *The World Today,* **12**: 421–6 (available on http://psychclassics.yorku.ca).

Watson, J.B. (1913) 'Psychology as the behaviorist views it', *Psychological Review,* **20**: 158–77 (available on http://psychclassics.yorku.ca).

Watson, J.B. (1925) *Behaviorism.* New York: People's Institute Publishing Company. (Reprinted in 1997 by Transaction Publishers.)

Watson, J.B. and Rayner, R. (1920) 'Conditioned emotional reactions', *Journal of Experimental Psychology,* **3**: 1–14 (available on http://psychclassics.yorku.ca).

Weber, M. (1904/1905) 'Die protestantische Ethik und der Geist des Kapitalismus' [Translated in 1905 as The protestant ethic and the spirit of capitalism]. *Archiv für Sozialwissenschaft und Sozialpolitik,* **20**: 1–54; **21**: 1–110.

Weindling, P.J. (2004) *Nazi medicine and the Nuremberg Trials: From medical war crimes to informed consent.* Basingstoke: Palgrave-Macmillan.

Weisbord, M.R. (1985) 'Participative work design: A personal odyssey', *Organizational Dynamics,* **13:** 4–20. (Table adapted from Trist, E. (1981) *The evolution of socio-technical systems – A conceptual framework and an action research program.* Toronto: Ontario Ministry of Labour.)

Wheen, F. (2004) *How mumbo-jumbo conquered the world: A short history of modern delusions.* London: Harper Perennial.

Willig, C. (2008) *Introducing qualitative research in psychology.* Maidenhead: McGraw-Hill/ Open University Press.

Wilson, C., Nairn, R., Coverdale, J. and Panapa, A. (1999) 'Mental illness depictions in prime-time drama: Identifying the discursive resources', *Australian and New Zealand Journal of Psychiatry,* **33:** 232–9.

Wilson, C., Nairn, R., Coverdale, J. and Panapa, A. (2000) 'How mental illness is portrayed in children's television: A prospective study', *British Journal of Psychiatry,* **176:** 440–3.

Wilson, E.O. (1975) *Sociobiology: The new synthesis.* Cambridge, MA: Harvard University Press.

Wilson, T.D. and Dunn, E.W. (2004) 'Self-knowledge: Its limits, value, and potential for improvement', *Annual Review of Psychology,* **55:** 493–518.

Wilson, T.D. and Dunn, E.W. (2004) 'Self-knowledge: Its limits, value, and potential for improvement', *Annual Review of Psychology,* **55:** 17.1–17.26.

Woodworth, R.S. (1931) *Contemporary schools of psychology.* New York: Ronald Press.

Woodworth, R.S. (1948) *Contemporary schools of psychology* (Revised edn). New York: The Ronald Press.

Wooldridge, A. (1994) *Measuring the mind: Education and psychology in England, c. 1860–c. 1990.* Cambridge: Cambridge University Press.

Wundt, W.M. (1896/1897) *Outlines of psychology* (English translation by C.H. Judd). Leipzig: Wilhelm Engelmann (available on http://psychclassics.yorku.ca).

Yardley, L. (2000) 'Dilemmas in qualitative health research', *Psychology and Health,* **15:** 215–28.

Yasar, S., Baker, D., Robinson-Kurpius, S., Krause, S. and Roberts, C. (2006) 'Development of a survey to assess K-12 teachers' perceptions of engineers and familiarity with teaching design, engineering, and technology', *Journal of Education,* **95:** 205–16.

Zehr, D. (2000) 'Portrayals of Wundt and Titchener in introductory psychology texts: A content analysis', *Teaching of Psychology,* **27:** 122–5.

Ziegler, J.C. and Goswami, U. (2005) 'Reading acquisition, developmental dyslexia, and skilled reading across languages: A psycholinguistic grain size theory', *Psychological Bulletin* **131:** 3–29.

Zimbardo, P.G. (2004) 'Power turns good soldiers into "bad apples".' Editorial in *The Boston Globe,* May 9.

Zubin, J. and Spring, B. (1977) 'Vulnerability: A new view of schizophrenia', *Journal of Abnormal Psychology,* **86:** 103–26.

Index

media
   depictions of psychologists 340–1
   depictions of scientists 339–40
   portrayals of mental health disorders
      481–2
medical science 65, 248, 474–5
   hierarchy of evidence 373–4
memes 224
memory 143–4, 452, 453
Mendel, G. 34–6
mental chronometry 67
mental health problems 464
   changes in treatment of 104–5, 247–56
   delusions 199–203
   depression 426–9, 470
   making public views of more realistic
      479–83
mental representations 145–7
Mesopotamia, ancient 8, 9, 19–20
Mesozoic era 4, 5, 6
meta-analysis 373–4
metaphors 452–3
methodolatry/methodologism 331–3
microscopes 176
Milgram experiments 218, 378
Miller, G. 143–4, 145, 151
mind 210
mind-brain problem 207–43
Money, T. 458–9
moral responsibility 354–5
Morton, S.G. 456–8
motivation 412–15
movement
   forces and 52–4
   free will and the initiation of 229–30

naming numbers 15–16
natural selection 61, 118, 418
nature-nurture debate 433–5
Naturwissenschaften 347
needs, creation of 473–6
Neisser, U. 144, 145
neolithic revolution 8
nerve cells 176–7
nerve impulses, speed of 66–8, 178–9
nervous system 167–81
neurology 105–6, 247
neurons 177–9
neuropsychology 181–7
neuroscience 188–99
neurotransmitters 179
New Intelligence Test (NIT) 471–2
Newton, I. 52–5, 66

noise 68, 366
nomothetic approach 379
non-invasive techniques 188–99
non-observable variables 297–8
normal science 150, 312, 316
numbers 14–19

objectivity 353–4, 396, 397
observable facts see facts
observation 56, 64–5, 68, 129, 293–4,
      366–7
   primacy of 290–1, 292
observational learning 431–2, 441
odours 424–5
olfaction 424–5
operational definitions 132–3, 298, 367
optics 66
organisation, psychology of work and
      273–81
Origin of Species, The (Darwin) 61–2
orthography 13
outcasts 104, 464

pain modulation 425–6
Paleozoic era 4, 5
paradigm shifts 150–2, 313–15
   see also scientific revolutions
paradigm war 364–5, 395–8
paradigms 150
   succession of 310–21
parental investment theory 419–20
parenting advice 473
partner selection 418–20
Pavlov, I.P. 127–8, 170, 280
Peirce, C. 318, 322–3
perception 294–7, 441
personality tests 267–71
personality traits 269–70
persons, history writing centred on 32–3
phenomenological analysis 385–8,
      389–90, 400
philosophy 20, 21
   functionalism in 222
   textbooks inspired by 79–80
philosophy of science 132–4, 292
   usefulness for psychology 403–6
phlogiston 214–15, 307
phonograms 11
phosphohistidine 297
phrenology 120–1, 174–6, 196–9
physics 68, 300
   formulation of the first laws of 52–5
physiognomy 174